International Journal on Advances in Software

2016 vol. 9 nr. 3&4

Printed from e-media with permission by:

Curran Associates, Inc.
57 Morehouse Lane
Red Hook, NY 12571

Some format issues inherent in the e-media version may also appear in this print version.

Printed by Curran Associates, Inc. (2018)

International Academy, Research, and Industry Association (IARIA)
412 Derby Way
Wilmington, DE 19810

Phone: (408) 893-6407
Fax: (408) 527-6351

petre@iaria.org

Additional copies of this publication are available from:

Curran Associates, Inc.
57 Morehouse Lane
Red Hook, NY 12571 USA
Phone: 845-758-0400
Fax: 845-758-2633
Email: curran@proceedings.com
Web: www.proceedings.com

The *International Journal on Advances in Software* is published by IARIA.
ISSN: 1942-2628
journals site: http://www.iariajournals.org
contact: petre@iaria.org

International Journal on Advances in Software
Volume 9, Number 3 & 4, 2016

Gianluca Franchino, Scuola Superiore Sant'Anna, Pisa, Italy
Naoki Fukuta, Shizuoka University, Japan
Martin Gaedke, Chemnitz University of Technology, Germany
Félix J. García Clemente, University of Murcia, Spain
José García-Fanjul, University of Oviedo, Spain
Felipe Garcia-Sanchez, Universidad Politecnica de Cartagena (UPCT), Spain
Michael Gebhart, Gebhart Quality Analysis (QA) 82, Germany
Tejas R. Gandhi, Virtua Health-Marlton, USA
Andrea Giachetti, Università degli Studi di Verona, Italy
Afzal Godil, National Institute of Standards and Technology, USA
Luis Gomes, Universidade Nova Lisboa, Portugal
Diego Gonzalez Aguilera, University of Salamanca - Avila, Spain
Pascual Gonzalez, University of Castilla-La Mancha, Spain
Björn Gottfried, University of Bremen, Germany
Victor Govindaswamy, Texas A&M University, USA
Gregor Grambow, University of Ulm, Germany
Carlos Granell, European Commission / Joint Research Centre, Italy
Christoph Grimm, University of Kaiserslautern, Austria
Michael Grottke, University of Erlangen-Nuernberg, Germany
Vic Grout, Glyndwr University, UK
Ensar Gul, Marmara University, Turkey
Richard Gunstone, Bournemouth University, UK
Zhensheng Guo, Siemens AG, Germany
Ismail Hababeh, German Jordanian University, Jordan
Shahliza Abd Halim, Lecturer in Universiti Teknologi Malaysia, Malaysia
Herman Hartmann, University of Groningen, The Netherlands
Jameleddine Hassine, King Fahd University of Petroleum & Mineral (KFUPM), Saudi Arabia
Tzung-Pei Hong, National University of Kaohsiung, Taiwan
Peizhao Hu, NICTA, Australia
Chih-Cheng Hung, Southern Polytechnic State University, USA
Edward Hung, Hong Kong Polytechnic University, Hong Kong
Noraini Ibrahim, Universiti Teknologi Malaysia, Malaysia
Anca Daniela Ionita, University "POLITEHNICA" of Bucharest, Romania
Chris Ireland, Open University, UK
Kyoko Iwasawa, Takushoku University - Tokyo, Japan
Mehrshid Javanbakht, Azad University - Tehran, Iran
Wassim Jaziri, ISIM Sfax, Tunisia
Dayang Norhayati Abang Jawawi, Universiti Teknologi Malaysia (UTM), Malaysia
Jinyuan Jia, Tongji University. Shanghai, China
Maria Joao Ferreira, Universidade Portucalense, Portugal
Ahmed Kamel, Concordia College, Moorhead, Minnesota, USA
Teemu Kanstrén, VTT Technical Research Centre of Finland, Finland
Nittaya Kerdprasop, Suranaree University of Technology, Thailand
Ayad ali Keshlaf, Newcastle University, UK
Nhien An Le Khac, University College Dublin, Ireland
Sadegh Kharazmi, RMIT University - Melbourne, Australia
Kyoung-Sook Kim, National Institute of Information and Communications Technology, Japan
Youngjae Kim, Oak Ridge National Laboratory, USA
Cornel Klein, Siemens AG, Germany
Alexander Knapp, University of Augsburg, Germany
Radek Koci, Brno University of Technology, Czech Republic
Christian Kop, University of Klagenfurt, Austria
Michal Krátký, VŠB - Technical University of Ostrava, Czech Republic

Narayanan Kulathuramaiyer, Universiti Malaysia Sarawak, Malaysia
Satoshi Kurihara, Osaka University, Japan
Eugenijus Kurilovas, Vilnius University, Lithuania
Philippe Lahire, Université de Nice Sophia-Antipolis, France
Alla Lake, Linfo Systems, LLC, USA
Fritz Laux, Reutlingen University, Germany
Luigi Lavazza, Università dell'Insubria, Italy
Fábio Luiz Leite Júnior, Universidade Estadual da Paraiba,Brazil
Alain Lelu, University of Franche-Comté / LORIA, France
Cynthia Y. Lester, Georgia Perimeter College, USA
Clement Leung, Hong Kong Baptist University, Hong Kong
Weidong Li, University of Connecticut, USA
Corrado Loglisci, University of Bari, Italy
Francesco Longo, University of Calabria, Italy
Sérgio F. Lopes, University of Minho, Portugal
Pericles Loucopoulos, Loughborough University, UK
Alen Lovrencic, University of Zagreb, Croatia
Qifeng Lu, MacroSys, LLC, USA
Xun Luo, Qualcomm Inc., USA
Shuai Ma, Beihang University, China
Stephane Maag, Telecom SudParis, France
Ricardo J. Machado, University of Minho, Portugal
Maryam Tayefeh Mahmoudi, Research Institute for ICT, Iran
Nicos Malevris, Athens University of Economics and Business, Greece
Herwig Mannaert, University of Antwerp, Belgium
José Manuel Molina López, Universidad Carlos III de Madrid, Spain
Francesco Marcelloni, University of Pisa, Italy
Eda Marchetti, Consiglio Nazionale delle Ricerche (CNR), Italy
Gerasimos Marketos, University of Piraeus, Greece
Abel Marrero, Bombardier Transportation, Germany
Adriana Martin, Universidad Nacional de la Patagonia Austral / Universidad Nacional del Comahue, Argentina
Goran Martinovic, J.J. Strossmayer University of Osijek, Croatia
Paulo Martins, University of Trás-os-Montes e Alto Douro (UTAD), Portugal
Stephan Mäs, Technical University of Dresden, Germany
Constandinos Mavromoustakis, University of Nicosia, Cyprus
Jose Merseguer, Universidad de Zaragoza, Spain
Seyedeh Leili Mirtaheri, Iran University of Science & Technology, Iran
Lars Moench, University of Hagen, Germany
Yasuhiko Morimoto, Hiroshima University, Japan
Antonio Navarro Martín, Universidad Complutense de Madrid, Spain
Filippo Neri, University of Naples, Italy
Muaz A. Niazi, Bahria University, Islamabad, Pakistan
Natalja Nikitina, KTH Royal Institute of Technology, Sweden
Roy Oberhauser, Aalen University, Germany
Pablo Oliveira Antonino, Fraunhofer IESE, Germany
Rocco Oliveto, University of Molise, Italy
Sascha Opletal, Universität Stuttgart, Germany
Flavio Oquendo, European University of Brittany/IRISA-UBS, France
Claus Pahl, Dublin City University, Ireland
Marcos Palacios, University of Oviedo, Spain
Constantin Paleologu, University Politehnica of Bucharest, Romania
Kai Pan, UNC Charlotte, USA
Yiannis Papadopoulos, University of Hull, UK

Andreas Papasalouros, University of the Aegean, Greece
Rodrigo Paredes, Universidad de Talca, Chile
Päivi Parviainen, VTT Technical Research Centre, Finland
João Pascoal Faria, Faculty of Engineering of University of Porto / INESC TEC, Portugal
Fabrizio Pastore, University of Milano - Bicocca, Italy
Kunal Patel, Ingenuity Systems, USA
Óscar Pereira, Instituto de Telecomunicacoes - University of Aveiro, Portugal
Willy Picard, Poznań University of Economics, Poland
Jose R. Pires Manso, University of Beira Interior, Portugal
Sören Pirk, Universität Konstanz, Germany
Meikel Poess, Oracle Corporation, USA
Thomas E. Potok, Oak Ridge National Laboratory, USA
Christian Prehofer, Fraunhofer-Einrichtung für Systeme der Kommunikationstechnik ESK, Germany
Ela Pustułka-Hunt, Bundesamt für Statistik, Neuchâtel, Switzerland
Mengyu Qiao, South Dakota School of Mines and Technology, USA
Kornelije Rabuzin, University of Zagreb, Croatia
J. Javier Rainer Granados, Universidad Politécnica de Madrid, Spain
Muthu Ramachandran, Leeds Metropolitan University, UK
Thurasamy Ramayah, Universiti Sains Malaysia, Malaysia
Prakash Ranganathan, University of North Dakota, USA
José Raúl Romero, University of Córdoba, Spain
Henrique Rebêlo, Federal University of Pernambuco, Brazil
Hassan Reza, UND Aerospace, USA
Elvinia Riccobene, Università degli Studi di Milano, Italy
Daniel Riesco, Universidad Nacional de San Luis, Argentina
Mathieu Roche, LIRMM / CNRS / Univ. Montpellier 2, France
José Rouillard, University of Lille, France
Siegfried Rouvrais, TELECOM Bretagne, France
Claus-Peter Rückemann, Leibniz Universität Hannover / Westfälische Wilhelms-Universität Münster / North-German Supercomputing Alliance, Germany
Djamel Sadok, Universidade Federal de Pernambuco, Brazil
Ismael Sanz, Universitat Jaume I, Spain
M. Saravanan, Ericsson India Pvt. Ltd -Tamil Nadu, India
Idrissa Sarr, University of Cheikh Anta Diop, Dakar, Senegal / University of Quebec, Canada
Patrizia Scandurra, University of Bergamo, Italy
Giuseppe Scanniello, Università degli Studi della Basilicata, Italy
Daniel Schall, Vienna University of Technology, Austria
Rainer Schmidt, Munich University of Applied Sciences, Germany
Cristina Seceleanu, Mälardalen University, Sweden
Sebastian Senge, TU Dortmund, Germany
Isabel Seruca, Universidade Portucalense - Porto, Portugal
Kewei Sha, Oklahoma City University, USA
Simeon Simoff, University of Western Sydney, Australia
Jacques Simonin, Institut Telecom / Telecom Bretagne, France
Cosmin Stoica Spahiu, University of Craiova, Romania
George Spanoudakis, City University London, UK
Cristian Stanciu, University Politehnica of Bucharest, Romania
Lena Strömbäck, SMHI, Sweden
Osamu Takaki, Japan Advanced Institute of Science and Technology, Japan
Antonio J. Tallón-Ballesteros, University of Seville, Spain
Wasif Tanveer, University of Engineering & Technology - Lahore, Pakistan
Ergin Tari, Istanbul Technical University, Turkey
Steffen Thiel, Furtwangen University of Applied Sciences, Germany

Jean-Claude Thill, Univ. of North Carolina at Charlotte, USA
Pierre Tiako, Langston University, USA
Božo Tomas, HT Mostar, Bosnia and Herzegovina
Davide Tosi, Università degli Studi dell'Insubria, Italy
Guglielmo Trentin, National Research Council, Italy
Dragos Truscan, Åbo Akademi University, Finland
Chrisa Tsinaraki, Technical University of Crete, Greece
Roland Ukor, FirstLinq Limited, UK
Torsten Ullrich, Fraunhofer Austria Research GmbH, Austria
José Valente de Oliveira, Universidade do Algarve, Portugal
Dieter Van Nuffel, University of Antwerp, Belgium
Shirshu Varma, Indian Institute of Information Technology, Allahabad, India
Konstantina Vassilopoulou, Harokopio University of Athens, Greece
Miroslav Velev, Aries Design Automation, USA
Tanja E. J. Vos, Universidad Politécnica de Valencia, Spain
Krzysztof Walczak, Poznan University of Economics, Poland
Yandong Wang, Wuhan University, China
Rainer Weinreich, Johannes Kepler University Linz, Austria
Stefan Wesarg, Fraunhofer IGD, Germany
Wojciech Wiza, Poznan University of Economics, Poland
Martin Wojtczyk, Technische Universität München, Germany
Hao Wu, School of Information Science and Engineering, Yunnan University, China
Mudasser F. Wyne, National University, USA
Zhengchuan Xu, Fudan University, P.R.China
Yiping Yao, National University of Defense Technology, Changsha, Hunan, China
Stoyan Yordanov Garbatov, Instituto de Engenharia de Sistemas e Computadores - Investigação e Desenvolvimento, INESC-ID, Portugal
Weihai Yu, University of Tromsø, Norway
Wenbing Zhao, Cleveland State University, USA
Hong Zhu, Oxford Brookes University, UK
Qiang Zhu, The University of Michigan - Dearborn, USA

International Journal on Advances in Software
Volume 9, Numbers 3 & 4, 2016

CONTENTS

Tacit and Explicit Knowledge in Software Development Projects: A Combined Model for Analysis

Hanna Dreyer
The Business School
University of Gloucestershire
Cheltenham, UK
Dreyer.Hanna@gmail.com

Martin Wynn
School of Computing and Technology
University of Gloucestershire
Cheltenham, UK
MWynn@glos.ac.uk

Abstract – **The development of new or updated software packages by software companies often involves the specification of new features and functionality required by customers, who may already be using a version of the software package. The on-going development and upgrade of such packages is the norm, and the effective management of knowledge in this process is critical to achieving successful enhancement of the package in line with customer expectations. Human interaction within the software development process becomes a key focus, and knowledge transfer an essential mechanism for delivering software to quality standards and within agreed timescales and budgetary constraints. This article focuses on the role and nature of knowledge within the context of software development, and puts forward a combined conceptual model to aid in the understanding of individual and group tacit knowledge in this business and operational environment.**

Keywords – software development; tacit knowledge; explicit knowledge; project management; knowledge management; conceptual model.

I. Introduction

Knowledge management, and more specifically the relationship between tacit and explicit knowledge, has been the focus of some recent research studies looking specifically at the software development process [1] [2]. Tacit knowledge is difficult to articulate but is, according to Polanyi [3], the root of all knowledge, which is then transformed into explicit, articulated knowledge. The process of tacit to explicit knowledge transformation is therefore a key component of software development projects. This article constructs a model that combines elements from other studies, showing how tacit knowledge is acquired and shared from both a group and an individual perspective. It thus provides a connection between existing theories of tacit and explicit knowledge in the workplace, and suggests a way in which teams can focus on this process for their mutual benefit.

McAfee [4] discussed the importance of interpretation within software projects and the dangers of misunderstandings arising from incorrect analysis. Such misconceptions can be explicit as well as tacit, but, generally speaking, in software development, the majority of knowledge is tacit. Ryan [5] states that "knowledge sharing is a key process in developing software products, and since expert knowledge is mostly tacit, the acquisition and sharing of tacit knowledge .... are significant in the software development process." When there are several parties involved in a project, with each being an expert in their field, the process and momentum of knowledge sharing and its acquisition for onward development is critical to project success. In addition, de Souza *et al.* [6] argue that the management of knowledge in a software development project is crucial for its capability to deal with the coordination and integration of several sources of knowledge, while often struggling with budgetary constraints and time pressures.

Individual and group knowledge are essential to a project. Individual knowledge within a group is the expertise one can share. Essentially, expert knowledge is mainly tacit, and needs to be shared explicitly within the group to positively influence project outcomes. Polanyi [3] has noted that "we can know more than we can tell," which makes it more difficult for experts to transfer their knowledge to other project actors. To comprehend the transfer of tacit knowledge within a project group, both individual and group knowledge need to be analysed and evaluated. The study of the main players, and the people they interact with, can identify the key knowledge bases within a group. In a software development project group, this will allow a better understanding and management of how information is shared and transferred.

This paper comprises seven sections. The relevant basic concepts that constitute the underpinning theoretical framework are discussed next, and two main research questions are stated. The research methodology is then outlined (Section III), and the main models relevant to this research are discussed and explained in Section IV. Section V then discusses how these models were applied and developed through field research and Section VI combines elements of these models into a framework for understanding the transfer of tacit knowledge from an individual and group perspective. Finally, the concluding section pulls together the main themes discussed in the paper and addresses the research questions.

II. Theoretical Framework

Knowledge helps the understanding of how something works and is, at its core, a collection of meaningful data put into context. There are two strategies to manage knowledge within a company, codification – making company knowledge available through systemizing and storing information – and personalization – centrally storing sources of knowledge within a company, to help gain access to information from experts [7]. This article mainly focuses on personalisation, and on how knowledge is passed on from one source to the next. Knowledge does not have a physical form, but rather remains an intellectual good, which can be difficult to articulate and cannot be touched. Tacit knowledge - non-articulated knowledge - is the most difficult to grasp. According to Berger and Luckmann [8], knowledge is created through social, face-to-face interaction and a shared reality. It commences with individual, expert, tacit knowledge, which can then be made into explicit knowledge. Social interaction is one of the most flourishing environments for tacit knowledge transfer. Through a direct response from the conversation partner, information can be directly put into context by the receiver and processed in order to enrich their individual knowledge. This interplay in social interactions can build group tacit knowledge, making it easier to ensure a common knowledge base.

Advocating the conversion of tacit into explicit knowledge, Nonaka and Takeuchi [9] view tacit knowledge as the root of all knowledge. A person's knowledge base greatly influences the position an actor has within a group during a project. The effectiveness the actor possesses to transform their expert, tacit, knowledge into explicit knowledge determines how central the actor is within the group, and whether the group can work effectively and efficiently. Transferring human knowledge is one of the greatest challenges in today's society because of its inaccessibility.

Being able to transfer tacit knowledge is not a matter of course - how to best conceptualize and formalise tacit knowledge remains a debate amongst researchers. Tacit knowledge is personal knowledge, which is not articulated, but is directly related to one's performance. Swan *et al.* [10] argue that "if people working in a group don't already share knowledge, don't already have plenty of contact, don't already understand what insights and information will be useful to each other, information technology is not likely to create it." Communication within a software development project is thus crucial for its success. Assessing vocalized tacit knowledge remains a field which is yet to be fully explored. Nonaka and Takeuchi [9] conceptualize knowledge as being a continuous, self-transcending process, allowing individuals as well as groups to alter one's self into a new self, whose world view and knowledge has grown. Knowledge is information put into context, where the context is crucial to make a meaningful basis. "Without context, it is just information, not knowledge" [9]. Within a software development project, raw information does not aid project success; only when put in a meaningful context and evaluated can it do so.

In a corporate context, to achieve competitive advantage, a large knowledge base is often viewed as a key asset. The interplay between individual, group and organizational knowledge allows actors to develop a common understanding. However, according to Schultze and Leidner [11] knowledge can be a double edged sword, where not enough can lead to expensive mistakes and too much to unwanted accountability. By differentiating between tangible and intangible knowledge assets, one can appreciate that there is a myriad of possible scenarios for sharing and transferring knowledge. Emails, briefs, telephone calls or formal as well as informal meetings, all come with advantages and disadvantages relating to the communication, storage, utilization and transfer of the shared knowledge. For the analysis of the roles played by different actors within a group, social network analysis [12] can be used to further understand the relationships formed between several actors. Key actors are central to the understanding of the origin of new ideas or technologies used by a group [13]. Within a software development project, a new network or group is formed in order to achieve a pre-determined goal. The interplay between the different actors is therefore critical to understanding the knowledge flow throughout the project.

The Office of Government Commerce defines a project as "a temporary organization that is needed to produce a unique and pre-defined outcome or result, at a pre-specified time, using predetermined resources" [14]. The time restrictions normally associated with all projects limits the time to understand and analyse the explicit and tacit knowledge of the people involved. The clearly defined beginning and ending of a project challenges the transfer of knowledge and the freedom to further explore and evaluate information. Having several experts in each field within a project scatters the knowledge, and highlights the need for a space to exchange and build knowledge within the group. Software development project teams are a group of experts coming together in order to achieve a pre-determined goal. The skills of each group member must complement the others in order to achieve project success. Ryan [5] argues that group member familiarity, as well as the communication frequency and volume, are "task characteristics of interdependence, cooperative goal interdependence and support for innovation;" and that these are critical in software development groups in engendering the sharing of tacit knowledge. Faith and comfort in one another is essential to ensure group members transfer personal experience and knowledge with team mates. Tacit knowledge transfer in software development is central to the success of the project [15]. Researchers may argue about how effective the transfer of knowledge may be, but most agree on the importance and impact it has on project outcomes [16].

Communication issues are one of the key causes of project failure, where meaningful knowledge exchange is impaired. Furthermore, once a project is completed, the infrastructure built around a project is usually dismantled, and there is a risk that knowledge produced through it may be degraded or lost altogether. When completing a project, the effective storage and processing of lessons learned throughout the project, as well as the produced knowledge, can act as a platform for improved knowledge exchange and overall outcomes in subsequent projects. A significant amount of knowledge in software development projects is transferred through virtual channels such as e-mails, or virtual message boards, and the flow of knowledge has greatly changed in the recent past. Much of the produced knowledge is not articulated, which can lead to misconceptions and misunderstanding. This can be exacerbated in a software development environment, because of time limitations and the need for quick responses to change requests and software bug fixing.

In this context, this research seeks to answer the following research questions (RQs):

RQ1: How can tacit and explicit knowledge be recognised and evaluated in software development projects?

RQ2: Can tacit and explicit knowledge be better harnessed through the development of a combined model for use in software development projects?

III. METHODOLOGY

This research focuses on the identification of tacit knowledge exchange within a software development project, and aims to understand the interplay between individual and group tacit knowledge. A shared understanding between the main players and stakeholders is essential for a software development project as it is essentially a group activity [17]. Using a case study approach, the research is mainly inductive and exploratory, with a strong qualitative methodology. Validating the composition of several models, the aim is to understand the tacit knowledge flow in software development projects, and specifically in key meetings. Subjectivism will form the basis of the philosophical understanding, while interpretivism will be the epistemological base.

The aim is to show the topic in a new way, albeit building on existing models and concepts. Through data collection and analysis in a specific case study of software development, a model to understand the interplay between individual and group tacit knowledge is developed. The data is largely generated through unstructured interviews, and in project meetings, where the growth of knowledge has been recorded and assessed in great detail. This demands a narrative evaluation of the generated data and is therefore subject to interpretation of the researchers [18]. Participant observation and personal reflection also take part in forming and contextualizing the data.

As knowledge is qualitative at its core, textual analysis can also aid in the understanding and interpretation of meetings. Expert knowledge is sometimes worked on between group meetings, to be made explicit and exchanged within meetings. Current models can help in evaluating exchanged knowledge within meetings. As knowledge does not have a physical form, the information generated throughout the meetings needs to be evaluated in a textual form. The data generated from the meetings has helped develop an understanding of tacit knowledge within the software development project and its relationship to individual and group tacit knowledge. Different expert groups can have a major influence in determining the flow of knowledge in a project.

The data was collected over a three month period and amounts to approximately 30 hours of meetings. The data collection was project based and focused on the key people involved in the project. In total, there were ten people working on the project (the "project team") - four core team members who were present at most of the meetings, two executives (one of which was the customer, the other the head of the HR consultancy company) and one programmer. These were the players who had most influence on the project, hence the focus of most of the data was on them. The meetings were "sit downs" - usually between project team members and two of the HR consultants and a software development consultant. During these meetings, programmers joined for certain periods, and there were conference calls with the client and the head of the HR consultancy firm.

The topics discussed in the meetings were evaluated and contextualized, in order to analyse the knowledge exchange throughout the meetings. The data was evaluated systematically, where first the meetings were transcribed, then ordered according to topic. They were then categorized according to the theories of Nonaka, Ryan and Clarke. The first round of categorization mainly focused on topics discussed during the meetings and whether there was evidence of tacit knowledge surfacing. The second-round assembled related topics and transcribed the conversations. During this process, evidence of constructive learning, group tacit knowledge, individual knowledge, tacit knowledge triggers, as well as decision making, was searched for. The transcribed meetings were then organized in relation to the previously found evidence (constructive learning, group tacit knowledge etc.). Within this categorization, the meetings were still also classified by topic. Finally, during the last round of data evaluation, recall decisions and various triggers (visual, conversational, recall, constructive learning and anticipation) were searched for and identified.

Data analysis has supported the construction and testing of a model representing individual and group tacit knowledge. Personal reflection and constant validation of the data aim at eliminating bias in the interpretation of results.

In summary, the main elements of the research method and design are:

1. Qualitative exploratory research
2. Inductive research
3. Participant observation
4. Personal reflection
5. Unstructured interviews

This approach assumes that it is feasible and sensible to cumulate findings and generalize results to create new knowledge. The data collected is based on one project where knowledge passed from one group member to the other has been evaluated. The concepts of tacit and explicit knowledge are analyzed in a primary research case study. A key assumption is that there is a "trigger" that acts as a catalyst for the recall and transfer of different knowledge elements, and this is examined in the software development project context. These triggers are then related to previous findings in the data. The exchange of tacit knowledge over time, from a qualitative perspective within one project, allows the analysis of group members using previously gained knowledge from one another and its usage within the group.

IV. Relevant Models in Existing Literature

This research focuses on knowledge exchange in software development and aims to help future researchers analyse the impact of knowledge on project outcomes. It attempts to shed light on how knowledge builds within a group which can aid project success. This is done by creating a framework to represent the knowledge flow, from both an individual and a group perspective; but its foundations are found in existing theory and related models, and this section provides an overview of these.

Companies share space and generally reinforce relationships between co-workers, which is the foundation for knowledge creation. These relationships are formed in different scenarios throughout the work day. Some of the knowledge is formed through informal channels, such as a discussion during a coffee break, or more formally through e-mails or meetings. When such exchanges occur, whether knowledge be explicit or tacit, the "Ba" concept developed by Nonaka and Teece [19] provides a useful basis for analysis.

"Ba" is conceived of as a fluid continuum where constant change and transformation results in new levels of knowledge. Although it is not tangible, its self-transcending nature allows knowledge evolution on a tacit level. Through social interaction, knowledge is externalized and can be processed by the actors involved. It is not a set of facts and figures, but rather a mental ongoing dynamic process between actors, allied to their capability to transfer knowledge in a meaningful manner. "Ba" is the space for constructive learning, transferred through mentoring, modeling and experimental inputs, which spark and build knowledge. The creation of knowledge is not a definitive end result, but more an ongoing process. Nonaka and Teece [19] differentiate between four different elements of "Ba" - originating, dialoging, systemizing and exercising.

Individual and face-to-face interactions are the basis of *originating* "Ba". Experience, emotions, feelings, and mental models are shared, hence the full range of physical senses and psycho-emotional reactions are in evidence. These include care, love, trust, and commitment, allowing tacit knowledge to be shared in the context of socialization. *Dialoguing* "Ba" concerns our collective and face-to-face interactions, which enable mental models and skills to be communicated to others. This produces articulated concepts, which can then be used by the receiver to self-reflect. A mix of specific knowledge and capability to manage the received knowledge is essential to consciously construct, rather than to originate, new knowledge. Collective and virtual interactions are often found in *systemising* "Ba". Tools and infrastructure, such as online networks, groupware, documentation and databanks, offer a visual and/or written context for the combination of existing explicit knowledge, whereby knowledge can easily be transmitted to a large number of people.

Finally, *exercising* "Ba" allows individual and virtual interaction, which is often communicated through virtual media, written manuals or simulation programs. Nonaka and Teece [19] contrast *exercising* and *dialoguing* "Ba" thus: "exercising 'Ba' synthesizes the transcendence and reflection that come in action, while dialoguing 'Ba' achieves this via thought."

The ongoing, spiraling, process of "Ba" gives co-workers the ability to comprehend and combine knowledge in order to complete the task at hand. Establishing "Ba" as the basis of a combined model provides a secure framework anchored in existing theory, within which knowledge can be classified and understood. From the "Ba" model of knowledge creation, Nonaka and Teece [19] developed the SECI concepts to further understand the way knowledge moves across and is created by organizations. SECI – *Socialization, Externalization, Combination and Internalization* – are the four pillars of knowledge exchange within an organization (Figure 1). They represent a spiral of knowledge creation, which can be repeated infinitively, enabling knowledge to be expanded horizontally as well as vertically across an organization. This links back to the earlier discussion of tacit and explicit knowledge, as the four sections of the SECI model represent different types of knowledge transfer - tacit to tacit, tacit to explicit, explicit to tacit and explicit to explicit.

Socialization is the conversion of tacit to tacit knowledge through shared experiences, normally characterized by learning by doing, rather than consideration of theoretical concepts. *Externalization* is the process of converting tacit to explicit knowledge, where a person articulates knowledge and shares it with others, in order to create a basis for new knowledge in a group. *Combination* is the process of converting explicit knowledge sets into more complex explicit knowledge. *Internalization* is the process of integrating explicit knowledge to make it one's own tacit knowledge. It is the counter part of *socialization*, and this internal knowledge base in a person can set off a new spiral of knowledge, where tacit knowledge can be converted to explicit and combined with more complex knowledge.

The SECI model suggests that in a corporate environment, knowledge can spiral horizontally (across departments and the organization as a whole) as well as vertically (up and down management hierarchies). As we are focusing mainly on tacit knowledge, *combination* will not be part of the adopted model, due to its purely explicit knowledge focus. SECI helps us view the general movements of knowledge creation and exchange within companies.

Ryan's Theoretical Model for the Acquisition and Sharing of Tacit Knowledge in Teams (TMTKT) [5] [20] is also of relevance. Through a quantitative research approach, Ryan analyses the movement of knowledge within a group and the moment of its creation. Beginning with current team tacit knowledge, constructive learning enhances individual knowledge, which can then again be shared within the team in order to build up what Ryan terms the "transactive memory", which is a combination of specialization, credibility and coordination, resulting in a new amplified team tacit knowledge. This new team knowledge then begins again, in order to elevate the knowledge within the group in a never ending spiral of knowledge generation.

When developing the TMTKT, Ryan made several assumptions. First, team tacit knowledge would reflect domain specific practical knowledge, which differentiates experts from novices. Secondly,

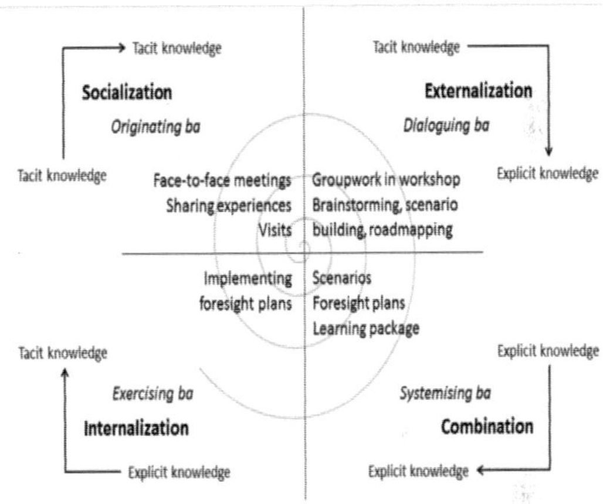

Figure 1. The Socialization, Externalization, Combination and Internalization (SECI) model [19]

the TMTKT needs to measure the tacit knowledge of the entire team, taking the weight of individual members into account. Finally, only tacit knowledge at the articulate level of abstraction can be taken into account. The model (Figure 2) comprises five main components or stages in the development of tacit knowledge:

1. Team tacit knowledge (existing)
2. Tacit knowledge is then acquired by individuals via constructive learning
3. This then becomes individual tacit knowledge
4. Tacit knowledge is then acquired through social interaction
5. Finally, the enactment of tacit knowledge into the the transactive memory takes place.

The starting point for understanding this process is to assess existing team tacit knowledge - this is their own individual tacit knowledge, but also includes any

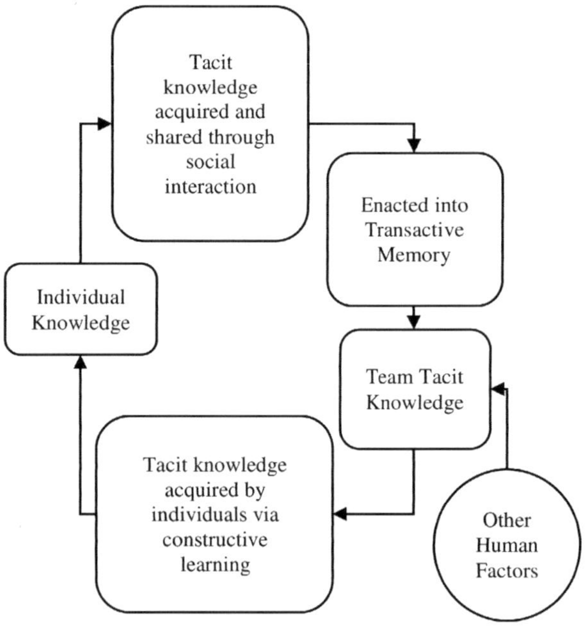

Figure 2. Theoretical Model for the Acquisition and Sharing of Tacit Knowledge in Teams (TMTKT) [5][20]

common understanding between the group members – that is, common tacit knowledge. Following group exchanges, new knowledge will be generated through constructive learning, building upon the original team tacit knowledge. The gained knowledge can then be made part of their own individual knowledge. These final two stages are a result of the social interaction, where team members gain knowledge and make it part of their transactive memory.

Clarke [21] evaluates knowledge from an individual point of view, and establishes a micro view of tacit knowledge creation. His model (Figure 3) suggests reflection on tacit knowledge can act as a trigger for the generation of new knowledge, both tacit and explicit. The process starts with the receiver being fed with knowledge – knowledge input - which is then processed, enhanced and formed into a knowledge output.

These models provide the basis for understanding the creation and general movement of knowledge in a software development project. Ryan and O'Connor [20] develops the idea of knowledge creation within a group further to specifically try to understand how knowledge is created and enhanced within teams. They provide an individual perspective of the flow of knowledge, which aids in the understanding how knowledge is processed within a person.

V. Testing and Validation Against Existing Models

During a three month period over 30 hours of meetings were recorded. The research mainly focuses on participant observation and the interaction between the project members. The conversations are analysed over this period, in order to see the development of learning over time; this aids in surfacing the range of acquired strategies which are applied in system development projects [22].

The project involved three different parties, who work on developing a cloud based human resource management software package. The developers of the software work in close contact with a human resource consultancy company, which is seeking a solution for their client. The meetings mainly consist of the developers and the human resource consultants working together to customise the software to suit the client's needs. No formal systems development methodology was used – the approach was akin to what is often termed "Rapid Application Development" based on prototyping solutions and amendments, and then acting upon user feedback to generate a new version for user review.

A total of ten actors were involved in the meetings, excluding the researcher. Each topic involved a core of six actors, where three executives took part in the decision making process, one from each company, and three employees, the head programmer and two human resource consultants. The software development executive acted in several roles during the project, performing as programmer, consultant and executive, this depending on the needs of the project.

This process involved the discussion of a range of topics, which encompassed payroll operations, recruitment, the design and content of software "pages" for the employees, a feedback option, absences, and a dashboard for the managers, as well as training for the employees. Throughout the meetings, changes were made to the software, these being at times superficial, such as choosing colour schemes, or more substantial, such as identifying internal processes where absence input did not function. The meetings relied on various channels for team communication, due to the client being in another city. Phone calls, face-to-face conversations as well as showing the software live through the internet were all used. These mediums were chosen in order to keep the client updated on the progress of the project, as well as giving input to their needs as a company. Once a week, a conference call was held with the three executives and their employees in order to discuss progress. The conference call helped

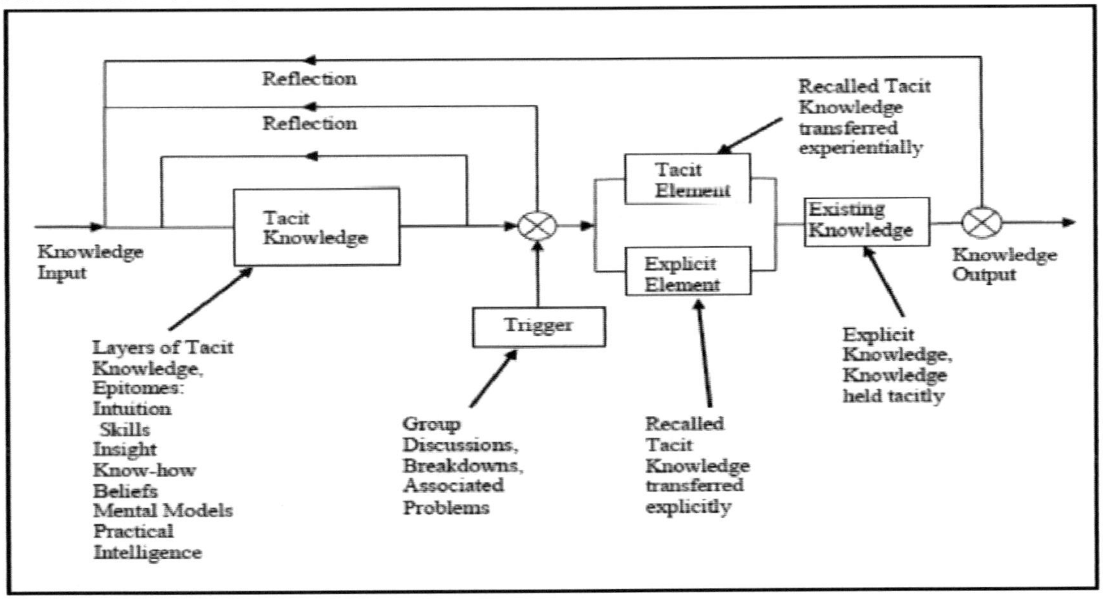

Figure 3. The Tacit Knowledge Spectrum [21]

ensure a common sharing of team tacit knowledge, allowing the different actors to then work on their individual tasks.

Knowledge regarding the different topics evolved throughout the project. The dynamic environment allowed different actors to request and exchange expert knowledge from the individuals. White and Parry [23] state that there has not been enough focus on the expert knowledge of developers, and how it affects the development of an information system. Expert knowledge from the developers and the interplay with the other teams supports White and Parry's findings. The data presented below illustrates conversations where expert knowledge is exchanged and utilized by team members. These exchanges helped validate the developed model, discussed below in Section VI.

One of the major issues that surfaced throughout the project was the complexity of the pension scheme of the end user. Integrating the correct values was vital for an accurate balance sheet and for payroll. The outsourced human resource management team of the user was not sure about certain aspects of the scheme, and needed the user human resource executive to explain in detail what was needed in order to make the software able to calculate a correct payroll. One of the outsourced HR consultants stated to the software development consultant: "Pensions is the most complicated thing. Ask the client on Monday to explain it to all of us." The HR consultant was thus suggesting the creation of a dynamic environment, where the software development company as well as the HR consultants themselves could learn about the pension scheme. On Monday, the consultant asked the client to explain their pension scheme: "I tried to explain pensions, but I could only do it poorly and I said that I only understand it when you (the client) explains it. So, could you please explain pensions to us, so that we are then hopefully all on the same page." The client went on to explain pensions, where occasional questions from the software developers as well as the HR consultants supported the comprehension of the group. By giving the client the opportunity to transfer his tacit knowledge, a "Ba" environment was created. This allowed group knowledge to emerge by the participants acquiring new knowledge and making it their own.

The analysis of these interactions provide the material for the construction of our combined model discussed below. We can see that knowledge input was given by the HR consultant through *socialization*, whereby tacit knowledge was shared through social interaction. This triggered the process of *internalization*, in which the user HR executive extracted tacit knowledge concerning pensions and transformed it into a knowledge output - *externalization*, being tacit knowledge acquired through constructive learning. This output was then received by each individual of the group, internalized and made into team tacit knowledge. At this point, the process starts anew, where unclear aspects are clarified by team members and externalized through social interaction. This process can lead the team to different areas of the discussed topic, where the input of different actors plays a vital role in shedding light on problems as well as identifying opportunities.

Another major issue that was in evidence during the project was the development of the time feature in the software. Within the time feature a calendar for sick leave, holidays or paternity was added. This was linked to the payroll since it was vital to know how much people get paid during which period. The interaction of the payroll and time in the software was very difficult to program. This part of the software was therefore explained by the programming executive, to make sure all needs of the customer were met. Here, the focus shifted to the HR consultants and the programmers. The end user was not involved in this process, since no expertise was needed and the user's main requirement was simply for it to work. The software consultant took a step aside, since this was not part of their expertise, and advised the software programmers to make sure the exchanged information was accurate. During the conversation not only were questions asked by the HR consultants, but also from the software development consultants. The programmer explained time and the time sheets, and during this discussion a knowledge exchange between the three parties created a dynamic environment, where group tacit knowledge was created.

Programmer: "We only want them to add days into the calendar where they should have been actually working – so that we can calculate the genuine days of holiday or leave. So if they are not due to work on a Monday, you don't want to count this as leave on a Monday. So it will only be inserted according to their working pattern."

Software consultant: "So the time sheet and calendar do the same thing?"

Programmer: "Yes, you choose against the service item, if the item should go into the calendar; so what will happen? - it will insert everything into the time sheet but then it will pick and choose which ones go into the calendar and which into the time sheet. So holidays will go into the calendar, but not go into the time sheet."

Software consultant: "You have a calendar in activities, which might show that a person is on holiday from x to y."

HR consultant: "But you might not want someone to know they are on maternity leave."

Software consultant: "But the time sheet is only working days, so you've got both options."

The conversation above demonstrates the process of knowledge input, *internalization*, output, group tacit knowledge as well as knowledge surfacing through a dynamic knowledge exchange. The programmer explains time sheets, which is then internalized by the software consultant, this then triggers a question, which leads to knowledge output. The programmer internalizes the question and creates a response through *socialization*. The spiral continues within the dynamic environment, and paves the way for knowledge to surface and to be used as well as internalized by the members of the team.

Throughout the analysis of the data this pattern of knowledge input, *internalization* and output was in evidence. This points to the significance of knowledge triggers to better understand the overall decision making process.

VI. Towards a Combined Conceptual Model

Building on the previous section, this section now examines how the theories of Nonaka, Ryan, and Clarke can be utilised in a new combined model which demonstrates how knowledge is created and built upon within a company at a group, as well as individual, level. The "Ba" concepts of Nonaka's SECI model provide the background framework that defines the dynamic space within which knowledge is created, although as noted above, the *combination* element is not used here as it deals exclusively with explicit knowledge (Figure 4). We will use the acronym SEI (rather than SECI) in the specific context of the combined model discussed in this section. The SEI concepts demonstrate the movement of knowledge, which can be continuously developed.

Ryan's TMTKT uses elements which overlap with Nonaka's SECI model. When combining the two an overlap in the processes can be found, although a more detailed view is provided by Ryan. When

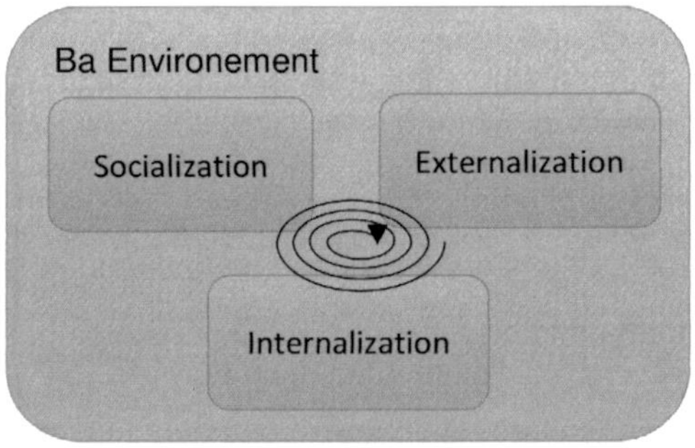

Figure 4. Three elements of SECI used in the conceptual model

analysing Nonaka's SECI, the process of internalization is explained in one step, unlike Ryan, who divides it into two steps rather than one. The *internalization* process is seen by Ryan as individual knowledge, which is then enacted into transactive memory, representing a deeper conceptualization of how people combine and internalize tacit knowledge.

According to the "Ba" concept, continuous knowledge creation is established within a dynamic environment, which supports the development of knowledge as it evolves from one stage to another. Figure 5 depicts how tacit knowledge is created, shared and internalized. Socialization indicates social interaction, where knowledge is acquired and shared through social interaction. Internalization entails making the knowledge one's own and combining it with previous knowledge, it being committed to transactive memory. Finally, externalization is knowledge acquired through constructive learning. Ryan's model focuses on tacit knowledge from a team perspective.

The last elements of the constructed model come from Clarke's Tacit Knowledge Spectrum [21]. This helps develop Nonaka's internalization process from a personal perspective. It provides a focus on one member of the team to complement Nonaka and Ryan's team perspective. Knowledge input commences the process, and different stages of knowledge intake make the knowledge individual knowledge. This focus on individual knowledge is encompassed in the internalization and enacted transactive memory stages of Nonaka's and Ryan's models, but it is treated in less detail.

Clarke's tacit knowledge spectrum commences with knowledge input, which is transformed into tacit knowledge. This tacit knowledge is then processed through reflection and at times, due to triggers such as additional information, the reflection process needs to be repeated in order to reveal new layers of tacit knowledge. The tacit and explicit elements permit additional layers of individual knowledge to be revealed, which can be through both explicit and tacit channels. Finally the new knowledge becomes part of the individual's existing knowledge. Existing knowledge can then once again be transferred into a knowledge output (Figure 3).

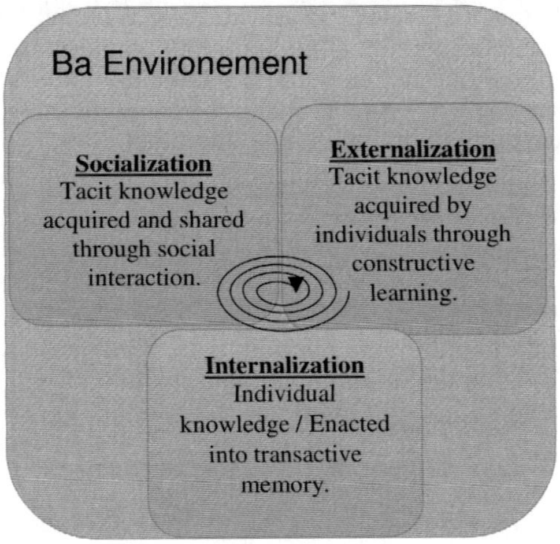

Figure 5. Combined elements of "Ba", SEI and TMTKT models.

Table I notes the main elements of the 3 approaches of Nonaka, Clarke and Ryan that are combined in the model used for case study analysis. At the macro level are Nonaka's concepts of "Ba", SEI and the spiral of knowledge. Ryan's model provides a group tacit knowledge perspective, complemented by Clarke's focus on the micro, individual knowledge generation process. The *internalization* and the *socialization* processes can involve both input and output, depending on the individual's point of knowledge acquisition – student or teacher.

TABLE I. ELEMENTS OF THE MODELS OF RYAN, CLARKE AND NONAKA USED IN THE COMBINED IGTKS MODEL

Nonaka	Ryan	Clarke
Socialization tacit to tacit	Tacit knowledge acquired and shared through social interaction.	Knowledge in- and output.
Externalization tacit to explicit	Tacit knowledge acquired by individuals through constructive learning.	Knowledge in- and output
Internalization explicit to tacit	Individual knowledge / Enacted into transactive memory.	Process of acquiring and processing tacit knowledge (reflection – trigger – tacit and/or explicit element – existing knowledge)

Nonaka's concept of "Ba" and its dynamic environment to support the exchange of knowledge provides the basis for a combined model, which we term the Individual and Group Tacit Knowledge Spiral (IGTKS). His theories also outline the different steps of the model, using *socialization* and *externalization* as knowledge in-and outputs, and the *internalization* process which represents individual knowledge. Clarke's model provides a more detailed view of the *internalization* process, which has been simplified somewhat in the combined model, concentrating on the trigger points, the reflection process and the enhancement of existing knowledge. Finally, Ryan's team tacit knowledge creates a point of "common knowledge" between the team members.

The combined model (Figure 6) aims to represent the process of continuous knowledge creation and exchange in a software development project team. The *internalization* process is an edited version of

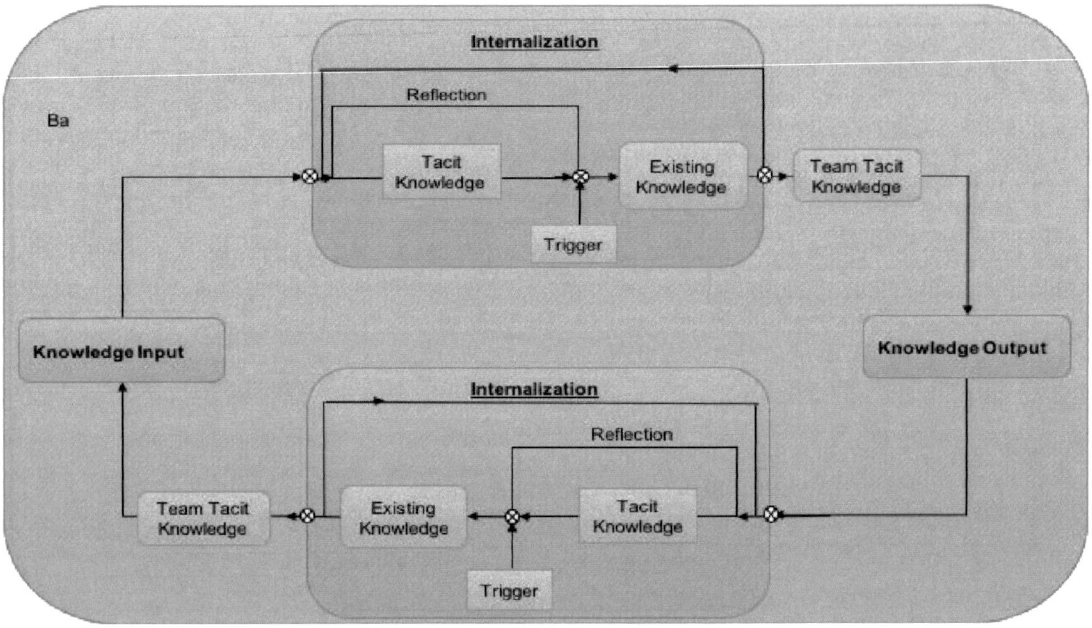

Figure 6. Individual and Group Tacit Knowledge Spiral (IGTKS)
(Triggers are represented by a circle with a cross in the middle)

Clarke's model - due to the focus on triggers it was not necessary to include the other elements of his model. The other human factors of Ryan's model were also modified, since the knowledge triggers entail the notion of personal experiences affecting tacit knowledge.

Knowledge is set in the "Ba" dynamic environment, where knowledge is freely exchanged and enhanced. The first step of the process is knowledge input, which can be knowledge exchange through social interaction or constructive learning. The knowledge input triggers the process of *internalization*.

Unlike Clarke, who only shows one trigger point, the IGTKS has three in every *internalization* process: one at the beginning, the initial trigger, which kicks off the *internalization* process; the second one is found after the development and combination of tacit knowledge which through reflection is developed to become a part of one's existing knowledge. The final trigger is at the end of the *internalization* process, where either the process is re-launched through an internal trigger or converted into team tacit knowledge. When the team arrives at the point where everyone has a common understanding of the knowledge, transferred through the initial knowledge input, then the team can react by sharing knowledge within the group via knowledge output transferred by *socialization* or constructive learning. This then again sets off the team members *internalization* process, where the knowledge put out by the team member is processed and embedded into their existing knowledge. Once this *internalization* process ends, the team has once again gained a common understanding of the exchanged knowledge and the cycle recommences. The data analysis demonstrated tacit knowledge creation and sharing through socialization, internalization and group tacit knowledge in 45 examples. Externalization was found 28 times, combination 9 and constructive learning 18 times (Figure 7).

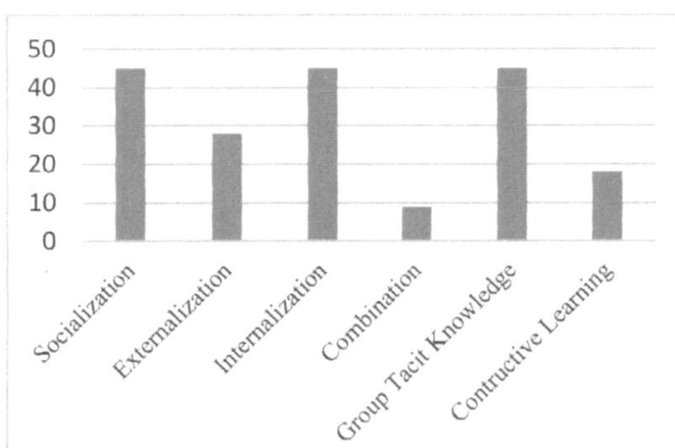

Figure 7. Number of examples of tacit knowledge sharing and creation in analysed conversations.

In addition, the trigger points showed conversations as the main factor in tacit knowledge acquisition and sharing, surfacing in 39 extracts. Visual triggers were shown to help tacit knowledge in 18 incidents, constructive learning 19, recall 7 and anticipation 2 (Figure 8).

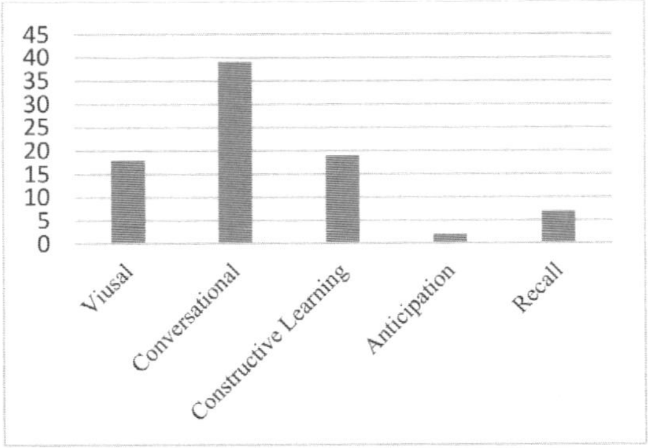

Figure 8. Number of tacit knowledge triggers identified in analysed conversations.

The IGTKS (Figure 6) can be used to model and analyze a conversation during a software development meeting, where, for example, team member A commences the meeting by asking a question about X. This question is then internalized by the other team members, B, C and D. A, B, C and D are now all aware that the topic of discussion is X, and understand the issue with it, and at this point the team has a common team tacit knowledge. However, topic X mainly concerns team member C, who therefore answers the question through knowledge output and constructive learning. Once C has explained X, the team again has a common team tacit knowledge. Now the cycle restarts, spirals, and other team members add knowledge within this dynamic knowledge environment.

Relating the model to this example, one can see how a conversation commences within the team. This then allows each individual to take the knowledge in, and make it their own tacit knowledge. During the internalization process, several triggers allow the creation of tacit knowledge. One of the triggers can be at the beginning of the internalization process - the unfiltered knowledge passed on by a project member which allows the internalization process to start. Then the knowledge is combined with previously gained knowledge; when newly received knowledge is complex, new thought processes can be triggered. Each individual then gains new tacit knowledge, which allows a new common group tacit knowledge. When the newly gained knowledge is incomplete, or when the receiver can complete or add to the knowledge, a response is triggered. This then commences the cycle to begin anew.

The aim of a meeting is to fill in gaps of knowledge within the project team, which allows teams to work together better. When the core people of a team or the expert within a field are not present, the project comes to a halt, until the knowledge is gained by the people in need of it. The model enables project teams to consider how knowledge is passed within the team. It demonstrates on a team, as well as on an individual level, the knowledge exchange process, and its limitations when key players are not present during a meeting. Utilizing knowledge from group members elevates the knowledge from each individual over time. Each member is needed to give input, and allow tacit knowledge to surface when needed. The process of absorbing knowledge, making it one's own tacit knowledge, and allowing a common base of group tacit knowledge to develop, can constitute a key influencer of project outcomes.

VII. Conclusion

Peter Drucker used to tell his students that when intelligent, moral, and rational people make decisions that appear inexplicable, it's because they see a reality different to the one seen by others [24]. This observation by one of the leading lights of modern management science underscores the importance of knowledge perception and knowledge development. With regard to software projects, McAfee [4] noted that "the coordination, managerial oversight and marshalling of resources needed to implement these systems make a change effort like no other". Yet, although software project successes and failures have been analysed within a range of analytical frameworks, few studies have focused on knowledge development.

Tacit knowledge in particular is one of the more complex and difficult aspects to analyse. Creating a well-functioning project team where knowledge can prosper within each individual is a great challenge, even more so when working within the time constraints of a software development project. Within this dynamic environment, tacit knowledge needs to flourish and evolve throughout the team, so each member can collect and harness information provided by the team to support task and overall project delivery. The comprehension of tacit knowledge processes within a software development project can help future projects enhance communication channels within the project to ensure project success. Project outcomes rely on the process of experts sharing their tacit knowledge, and building it up over the course of the project.

To return to the RQs noted in Section II, this research concludes that the combined theories of Ryan, Nonaka and Clarke can be used to establish an understanding of tacit knowledge, and provide a framework for recognizing it, in software development projects (RQ1). The analysis of meeting conversations provided the foundation for understanding the flow of knowledge within a software development project. Through the exploration of these conversations, different theories could be tested and applied, which helped to build the IGTKS model, demonstrating the knowledge interplay between different teams and people within the project. It facilitates the analysis of conversations on an individual as well as a group basis, to comprehend when an individual has received and processed information into knowledge. It seeks to demonstrate at what point the team has accepted information or knowledge as common group tacit knowledge, and in which circumstances more information or knowledge needs to be provided by other team members.

The combined model presented here can be used to further explore and evaluate knowledge flow on an individual and group level in software development projects. Unless it is rendered ineffective due to an absence of knowledge sharing, the knowledge spiral continues until common group tacit knowledge has been reached. The model allows the practitioner or researcher to pinpoint the moments where external and internal triggers launch the generation of tacit knowledge within an individual. This phenomenon requires further research into the interaction and communication of knowledge within and between project teams and their varying contexts, but this research suggests the combined model can be applied to better exploit tacit and explicit knowledge in the specific context of software development (RQ2). It supports the development of knowledge through a dynamic and open knowledge exchange environment, and suggests a way in which teams can focus on this for their mutual benefit. This can materially impact the software development process, and thus has the potential to significantly enhance the quality and subsequent functioning of the final software products.

REFERENCES

[1] H. Dreyer, M. Wynn, and R. Bown, "Tacit and Explicit Knowledge in a Software Development Project: Towards a Conceptual Framework for Analysis," The Seventh International Conference on Information, Process and Knowledge Management, Lisbon, Feb 22nd – Feb 27th, ThinkMind, ISBN: 978-1-61208-386-5; ISSN: 2308-4375; 2015.

[2] F.O. Bjørnson and T. Dingsøyr, "Knowledge management in software engineering: A systematic review of studied concepts, findings and research methods used," Information and Software Technology, Volume 50, Issue 11, October 2008, Pages 1055-1068, ISSN 0950-5849, http://dx.doi.org/10.1016/j.infsof.2008.03.006. (http://www.sciencedirect.com/science/article/pii/S0950584908000487

[3] M. Polanyi. The tacit dimension. The University of Chicago Press, 1966.

[4] A. McAfee, "When too much IT knowledge is a dangerous thing," MIT Sloane Management Review, Winter, 2003, pp. 83-89.

[5] S. Ryan. Acquiring and sharing tacit knowledge in software development teams. The University of Dublin, 2012.

[6] K. de Souza, Y. Awazu and P. Baloh, "Managing Knowledge in Global Software Development Efforts: Issues and Practices," IEEE Software, vol. 23, Issue 5, September, 2006, pp. 30 – 37.

[7] M.T. Hansen, N. Nohria and T. Tierney, "What is your strategy for managing knowledge?", Harvard Business Review 77 (2), 1999, pp. 106–116.

[8] P. Berger and T. Luckmann, The Social Construction of Reality, Anchor, New York, 1967.

[9] I. Nonaka and H. Takeuchi, The knowledge-creating company: How Japanese companies create the dynamics of innovation. Oxford: Oxford University Press, 1995.

[10] J. Swan, H. Scarbrough and J. Preston, "Knowledge management – the next fad to forget people?", Proceedings of the Seventh European Conference on Information Systems, 1999, pp. 668–678.

[11] U. Schultze and D.E. Leidner, "Studying knowledge management in information systems research: discourses and theoretical assumptions," MIS Quarterly, 26, 2002, pp. 213–242.

[12] C. Prell, Social Network Analysis: History, Theory and Methodology, 2012, London: Sage.

[13] T. W. Valente and R. Davies, "Accelerating the diffusion of innovations using opinion leaders," The Annals of the American Academy of Political and Social Science, vol. 566, 1999, pp. 55-67.

[14] Office of Government Commerce (OGC), Managing Successful Projects with PRINCE2, 2009, London: The Stationery Office/Tso

[15] T. Clancy, The Standish Group Report Chaos, 1996.

[16] Z. Erden, G. von Krogh and I. Nonaka, The quality of group tacit knowledge, 2008.

[17] G. Fischer and J. Ostwald, "Knowledge management: problems, promises, realities, and challenges", IEEE Intell. Syst., 16, 2001, pp. 60–72.

[18] T. Langford and W. Poteat, "Upon first sitting down to read Personal Knowledge: an introduction," in Intellect and Hope: Essays in the thought of Michael Polanyi, 1968, pp. 3-18.

[19] I. Nonaka and D.Teece, Managing Industrial Knowledge, 2001, London: Sage.

[20] S. Ryan and R. O'Connor, "Acquiring and Sharing Tacit Knowledge in Software Development Teams: An Empirical Study," Information and Software Technology, vol. 55, no. 9, 2013, pp. 1614 -1624.

[21] T. Clarke, The development of a tacit knowledge spectrum based on the interrelationships between tacit and explicit knowledge. 2010, Cardiff: UWIC.

[22] N. Vitalari and G. Dickson, "Problem solving for effective systems analysis: An experiential exploration," Communications of the Association for Information Systems, 26(11), 1983, pp. 948–956.

[23] G. White and G. Parry, "Knowledge acquisition in information system development: a case study of system developers in an international bank," Strategic Change, 25 (1), 2016, pp.81-95.

[24] B. Baker, "The fall of the firefly: An assessment of a failed project strategy,'Project Management Journal , 33 (3), 2002, pp. 53-57 .

International Journal on Advances in Software, vol 9 no 3 & 4, year 2016, http://www.iariajournals.org/software/

Automatic KDD Data Preparation Using Parallelism

Youssef Hmamouche*, Christian Ernst† and Alain Casali*
*LIF - CNRS UMR 6166, Aix Marseille Université, Marseille, France
Email: firstname.lastname@lif.univ-mrs.fr
†Email: chr29ernst@gmail.com

Abstract—**We present an original framework for automatic data preparation, applicable in most Knowledge Discovery and Data Mining systems. It is based on the study of some statistical features of the target database samples. For each attribute of the database used, we automatically propose an optimized approach allowing to (i) detect and eliminate outliers, and (ii) to identify the most appropriate discretization method. Concerning the former, we show that the detection of an outlier depends on if data distribution is normal or not. When attempting to discern the appropriated discretization method, what is important is the shape followed by the density function of its distribution law. For this reason, we propose an automatic choice for finding the optimized discretization method, based on a multi-criteria (Entropy, Variance, Stability) evaluation. Most of the associated processings are performed in parallel, using the capabilities of multicore computers. Conducted experiments validate our approach, both on rule detection and on time series prediction. In particulary, we show that the same discretization method is not the best when applied to all the attributes of a specific database.**

Keywords–Data Mining; Data Preparation; Outliers detection and cleaning; Discretization Methods, Task parallelization.

I. Introduction and Motivation

Data preparation in most of Knowledge and Discovery in Databases (KDD) systems has not been greatly developed in the literature. The single mining step is more often emphasized. And, when discussed, data preparation focuses most of the times on a single parameter (outlier detection and elimination, null values management, discretization method, *etc.*). Specific associated proposals only highlight on their advantages comparing themselves to others. There is no global nor automatic approach taking advantage of all of them. But the better data are prepared, the better results will be, and the faster mining algorithms will work.

In [1], we presented a global view of the whole data preparation process. Moreover, we proposed an automatization of most of the different steps of that process, based on the study of some statistical characteristics of the analysed database samples. This work was itself a continuation of the one exposed in [2]. In this latter, we proposed a simple but efficient approach to transform input data into a set of intervals (also called bins, clusters, classes, *etc.*). In a further step, we apply specific mining algorithms (correlation rules, *etc.*) on this set of bins. The very main difference with the former paper is that no automatization is performed. The parameters having an impact on data preparation have to be specified by the end-user before the data preparation process launches.

This paper in an extended version of [1]. Main improvements concern:

- A simplification and a better structuration of the presented concepts and processes;
- The use of parallelism in order to choose, when applicable, the most appropriate preparation method among different available methods;
- An expansion of our previous experiments. The ones concerning rule detection have been extended, and experimentations in order to forecast time series have been added.

The paper is organized as follows: Section II presents general aspects of data preparation. Section III and Section IV are dedicated to outlier detection and to discretization methods respectively. Each section is composed of two parts: (i) related work, and (ii) our approach. Section V discusses task parallelization possibilities. Here again, after introducing multicore programming, we present associated implementation issues concerning our work. In Section VI, we show the results of expanded experiments. Last section summarizes our contribution, and outlines some research perspectives.

II. Data Preparation

Raw input data must be prepared in any KDD system previous to the mining step. This is for two main reasons:

- If each value of each column is considered as a single item, there will be a combinatorial explosion of the search space, and thus very large response times;
- We cannot expect this task to be performed by hand because manual cleaning of data is time consuming and subject to many errors.

This step can be performed according to different method(ologie)s [3]. Nevertheless, it is generally divided into two tasks: (i) Preprocessing, and (ii) Transformation(s). When detailing hereafter these two tasks, focus is set on associated important parameters.

A. Preprocessing

Preprocessing consists in reducing the data structure by eliminating columns and rows of low significance [4].

a) Basic Column Elimination: Elimination of a column can be the result of, for example in the microelectronic industry, a sensor dysfunction, or the occurrence of a maintenance step; this implies that the sensor cannot transmit its values to the database. As a consequence, the associated column will contain many null/default values and must then be deleted from the input file. Elimination should be performed by using the Maximum Null Values ($MaxNV$) threshold. Furthermore, sometimes several sensors measure the same information, what produces identical columns in the database. In such a case, only a single column should be kept.

b) Elimination of Concentrated Data and Outliers: We first turn our attention to inconsistent values, such as "outliers" in noisy columns. Detection should be performed through another threshold (a convenient value of p when using the standardization method, see Section III-A). Found outliers are eliminated by forcing their values to Null. Another technique is to eliminate the columns that have a small standard deviation (threshold $MinStd$). Since their values are almost the same, we can assume that they do not have a significant impact on results; but their presence pollutes the search space and reduces response times. Similarly, the number of Distinct Values in each column should be bounded by the minimum ($MinDV$) and the maximum ($MaxDV$) values allowed.

B. Transformation

a) Data Normalization: This step is optional. It translates numeric values into a set of values comprised between 0 and 1. Standardizing data simplifies their classification.

b) Discretization: Discrete values deal with intervals of values, which are more concise to represent knowledge, so that they are easier to use and also more comprehensive than continuous values. Many discretization algorithms (*see* Section IV-A) have been proposed over the years for this. The number of used intervals ($NbBins$) as well as the selected discretization method among those available are here again parameters of the current step.

c) Pruning step: When the occurrence frequency of an interval is less than a given threshold ($MinSup$), then it is removed from the set of bins. If no bin remains in a column, then that column is entirely removed.

The presented thresholds/parameters are the ones we use for data preparation. In previous works, their values were fixed inside of a configuration file read by our software at setup. The main objective of this work is to automatically determine most of these variables without information loss. Focus is set in the two next sections on outlier and discretization management.

III. DETECTING OUTLIERS

An outlier is an atypical or erroneous value corresponding to a false measurement, an unwritten input, *etc.* Outlier detection is an uncontrolled problem because of values that deviate too greatly in comparison with the other data. In other words, they are associated with a significant deviation from the other observations [5]. In this section, we present some outlier detection methods associated to our approach using uni-variate data as input. We manage only uni-variate data because of the nature of our experimental data sets (*cf.* Section VI).

The following notations are used to describe outliers: X is a numeric attribute of a database relation, and is increasingly ordered. x is an arbitrary value, X_i is the ith value, N is the number of values for X, σ its standard deviation, μ its mean, and s a central tendency parameter (variance, inter-quartile range, ...). X_1 and X_N are respectively the minimum and the maximum values of X. p is a probability, and k a parameter specified by the user, or computed by the system.

A. Related Work

We discuss hereafter four of the main uni-variate outlier detection methods.

Elimination after Standardizing the Distribution: This is the most conventional cleaning method [5]. It consists in taking into account σ and μ to determine the limits beyond which aberrant values are eliminated. For an arbitrary distribution, the inequality of Bienaymé-Tchebyshev indicates that the probability that the absolute deviation between a variable and its average is greater than k is less than or equal to $\frac{1}{k^2}$:

$$P(\left|\frac{x-\mu}{\sigma}\right| \geq k) \leq \frac{1}{k^2} \tag{1}$$

The idea is that we can set a threshold probability as a function of σ and μ above which we accept values as non-outliers. For example, with $k = 4.47$, the risk of considering that x, satisfying $\left|\frac{x-\mu}{\sigma}\right| \geq k$, is an outlier, is bounded by $\frac{1}{k^2} = 0.05$.
Algebraic Method: This method, presented in [6], uses the relative distance of a point to the "center" of the distribution, defined by: $d_i = \frac{|X_i-\mu|}{\sigma}$. Outliers are detected outside of the interval $[\mu - k \times Q_1, \mu + k \times Q_3]$, where k is generally fixed to 1.5, 2 or 3. Q_1 and Q_3 are the first and the third quartiles respectively.
Box Plot: This method, attributed to Tukey [7], is based on the difference between quartiles Q_1 and Q_3. It distinguishes two categories of extreme values determined outside the lower bound (LB) and the upper bound (UB):

$$\begin{cases} LB = Q_1 - k \times (Q_3 - Q_1) \\ UB = Q_3 + k \times (Q_3 - Q_1) \end{cases} \tag{2}$$

Grubbs' Test: Grubbs' method, presented in [8], is a statistical test for lower or higher abnormal data. It uses the difference between the average and the extreme values of the sample. The test is based on the assumption that the data have a normal distribution. The statistic used is: $T = max(\frac{X_N-\mu}{\sigma}, \frac{\mu-X_1}{\sigma})$. The assumption that the tested value (X_1 or X_N) is not an outlier is rejected at significance level α if:

$$T > \frac{N-1}{\sqrt{n}}\sqrt{\frac{\beta}{n-2\beta}} \tag{3}$$

where $\beta = t_{\alpha/(2n),n-2}$ is the quartile of order $\alpha/(2n)$ of the Student distribution with $n-2$ degrees of freedom.

B. An Original Method for Outlier Detection

Most of the existing outlier detection methods assume that the distribution is normal. However, in reality, many samples have asymmetric and multimodal distributions, and the use of these methods can have a significant influence at the data mining step. In such a case, each "distribution" has to be processed using an appropriated method. The considered approach consists in eliminating outliers in each column based on the normality of data, in order to minimize the risk of eliminating normal values.

Many tests have been proposed in the literature to evaluate the normality of a distribution: Kolmogorov-Smirnov [9], Shapiro-Wilks, Anderson-Darling, Jarque-Bera [10], *etc.* If the Kolmogorov-Smirnov test gives the best results whatever the distribution of the analysed data may be, it is nevertheless much more time consuming to compute then the others. This is why we have chosen the Jarque-Bera test (noted JB hereafter), much more simpler to implement as the others, as shown below:

$$JB = \frac{n}{6}({\gamma_3}^2 + \frac{\gamma_2^2}{4}) \quad (4)$$

This test follows a law of χ^2 with two degrees of freedom, and uses the *Skewness* $\gamma 3$ and the *Kurtosis* γ_2 statistics, defined respectively as follows:

$$\gamma_3 = E[(\frac{x-\mu}{\sigma})^3] \quad (5)$$

$$\gamma_2 = E[(\frac{x-\mu}{\sigma})^4] - 3 \quad (6)$$

If the JB normality test is not significant (the variable is normally distributed), then the Grubbs' test is used at a significance level of systematically 5%, otherwise the Box Plot method is used with parameter k automatically set to 3 in order to not to be too exhaustive toward outlier detection.

Figure 1 summarizes the process we chose to detect and eliminate outliers.

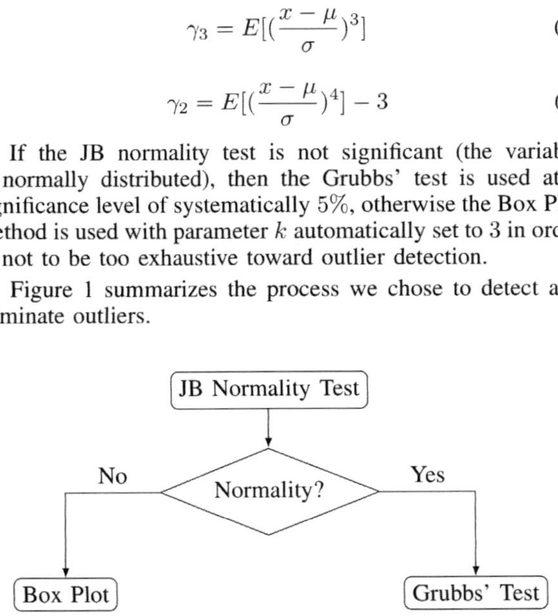

Figure 1: The outlier detection process.

Finally, the computation of $\gamma 3$ and $\gamma 2$ to evaluate the value of JB, so as other statistics needed by the Grubb's test and the Box Plot calculus, are performed in parallel in the manner shown in Listing 1 (*cf.* Section V). This in order to fasten the response times. Other statistics used in the next section are simultaneously collected here. Because the corresponding algorithm is very simple (the computation of each statistic is considered as a single task), we do not present it.

IV. Discretization Methods

Discretization of an attribute consists in finding $NbBins$ pairwise disjoint intervals that will further represent it in an efficient way. The final objective of discretization methods is to ensure that the mining part of the KDD process generates substantial results. In our approach, we only employ direct discretization methods in which $NbBins$ must be known in advance (and be the same for every column of the input data). $NbBins$ was in previous works a parameter fixed by the end-user. The literature proposes several formulas as an alternative (Rooks-Carruthers, Huntsberger, Scott, *etc.*) for computing such a number. Therefore, we switched to the Huntsberger formula, the most fitting from a theoretical point of view [11], and given by: $1 + 3.3 \times log_{10}(N)$.

A. Related Work

In this section, we only highlight the final discretization methods kept for this work. This is because the other tested methods have not revealed themselves to be as efficient as expected (such as Embedded Means Discretization), or are not a worthy alternative (such as Quantiles based Discretization) to the ones presented. In other words, the approach that we chose and which is discussed in the next sections, barely selected none of these alternative methods. Thus the methods we use are: Equal Width Discretization (EWD), Equal Frequency-Jenks Discretization (EFD-Jenks), AVerage and STandard deviation based discretization (AVST), and K-Means (KMEANS). These methods, which are unsupervised [12] and static [13], have been widely discussed in the literature: see for example [14] for EWD and AVST, [15] for EFD-Jenks, or [16] and [17] for KMEANS. For these reasons, we only summarize their main characteristics and their field of applicability in Table I.

TABLE I: SUMMARY OF THE DISCRETIZATION METHODS USED.

Method	Principle	Applicability
EWD	This simple to implement method creates intervals of equal width.	The approach cannot be applied to asymmetric or multi-modal distributions.
EFD-Jenks	Jenks' method provides classes with, if possible, the same number of values, while minimizing internal variance of intervals.	The method is effective from all statistical points of view but presents some complexity in the generation of the bins.
AVST	Bins are symmetrically centered around the mean and have a width equal to the standard deviation.	Intended only for normally distributed datasets.
KMEANS	Based on the Euclidean distance, this method determines a partition minimizing the quadratic error between the mean and the points of each interval.	Running time linear in $O(N \times NbBins \times k)$, where k in the number of iterations [?]. It is applicable to each form of distribution.

Let us underline that the upper limit fixed by the Huntsberger formula to the number of intervals to use is not always reached. It depends on the applied discretization method. Thus, EFD-Jenks and KMEANS methods generate most of the times less than $NbBins$ bins. This implies that other methods, which generate the $NbBins$ value differently for example through iteration steps, may apply if $NbBins$ can be upper bounded.

Example 1: Let us consider the numeric attribute $S_X = \{4.04, 5.13, 5.93, 6.81, 7.42, 9.26, 15.34, 17.89, 19.42, 24.40, 25.46, 26.37\}$. S_X contains 12 values, so by applying the Huntsberger's formula, if we aim to discretize this set, we have to use 4 bins.

Table II shows the bins obtained by applying all the discretization methods proposed in Table I. Figure 2 shows the number of values of S_X belonging to each bin associated to every discretization method.

As it is easy to understand, we cannot find two discretization methods producing the same set of bins. As a consequence, the distribution of the values of S_X is different depending on the method used.

B. Discretization Methods and Statistical Characteristics

When attempting to find the most appropriate discretization method for a column, what is important is not the law followed

TABLE II: SET OF BINS ASSOCIATED TO SAMPLE S_X.

Method	Bin_1	Bin_2	Bin_3	Bin_4
EWD	[4.04, 9.62[	[9.62, 15.21[	[15.21, 20.79[	[20.79, 26.37]
EFD-Jenks	[4.04; 5.94]	]5.94, 9.26]	]9.26, 19.42]	]19.42, 26.37]
AVST	[4.04; 5.53[	[5.53, 13.65[	[13.65, 21.78[	[21.78, 26.37]
KMEANS	[4.04; 6.37[	[6.37, 12.3[	[12.3, 22.95[	[22.95, 26.37]

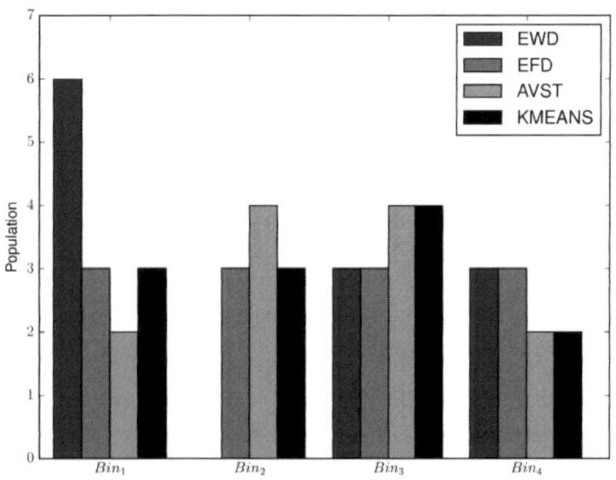

Figure 2: Population of each bin of sample S_X.

by its distribution, but the shape of its density function. This is why we first perform a descriptive analysis of the data in order to characterize, and finally to classify, each column according to normal, uniform, symmetric, antisymmetric or multimodal distributions. This is done in order to determine what discretization method(s) may apply. Concretely, we perform the following tests, which have to be carried out in the presented order:

1) We use the Kernel method introduced in [18] to characterize multimodal distributions. The method is based on estimating the density function of the sample by building a continuous function, and then calculating the number of peaks using its second derivative. This function allows us to approximate automatically the shape of the distribution. The multimodal distributions are those having a number of peaks strictly greater than 1.
2) To characterize antisymmetric and symmetric distributions in a next step, we use the skewness γ_3 (see formula (5)). The distribution is symmetric if $\gamma_3 = 0$. Practically, this rule is too exhaustive, so we relaxed it by imposing limits around 0 to set a fairly tolerant rule, which allows us to decide whether a distribution is considered antisymmetric or not. The associated method is based on a statistical test. The null hypothesis is that the distribution is symmetric. Consider the statistic: $T_{Skew} = \frac{N}{6}(\gamma_3^2)$. Under the null hypothesis, T_{Skew} follows a law of χ^2 with one degree of freedom. In this case, the distribution is antisymmetric with $\alpha = 5\%$ if $T_{Skew} > 3.8415$.
3) We use then the normalized Kurtosis, noted γ_2 (see formula (6)), to measure the peakedness of the distribution or the grouping of probability densities around the average, compared with the normal distribution. When γ_2 is close to zero, the distribution has a normalized peakedness.
A statistical test is used again to automatically decide whether the distribution has normalized peakedness or not. The null hypothesis is that the distribution has a normalized peakedness, and thus is uniform.
Consider the statistic: $T_{Kurto} = \frac{N}{6}(\frac{\gamma_2^2}{4})$. Under the null hypothesis, T_{Kurto} follows a law of χ^2 with one degree of freedom. The null hypothesis is rejected at level of significance $\alpha = 0.05$ if $T_{Kurto} > 6.6349$.
4) To characterize normal distributions, we use the Jarque-Bera test (see equation (4) and relevant comments).

These four successive tests allow us to characterize the shape of the (density function of the) distribution of every column. Combined with the main characteristics of the discretization methods presented in the last section, we get Table III. This summarizes what discretization method(s) can be invoked depending on specific column statistics.

TABLE III: APPLICABILITY OF DISCRETIZATION METHODS DEPENDING ON THE DISTRIBUTION'S SHAPE.

	Normal	Uniform	Symmetric	Antisymmetric	Multimodal
EWD	*	*	*		
EFD-Jenks	*	*	*	*	*
AVST	*				
KMEANS	*	*	*	*	*

Example 2: Continuing Example 1, the Kernel Density Estimation method [18] is used to build the density function of sample S_X (*cf.* Figure 3).

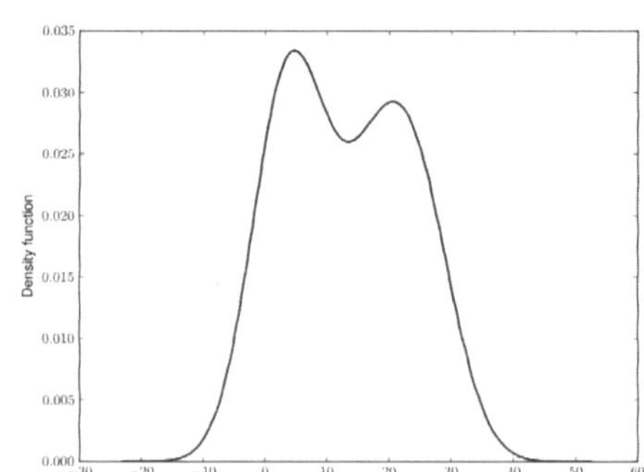

Figure 3: Density function of sample S_X using Kernel Density Estimation.

As we can see, the density function has two modes, is almost symmetric and normal. Since the density function is multimodal, we should stop at this point. But as shown in Table III, only EFD-Jenks and KMEANS produce interesting results according to our proposal. For the need of the example, let us perform the other tests. Since $\gamma_3 = -0.05$, the distribution is almost symmetric. As mentioned in (2), it depends on the threshold fixed if we consider that the distribution is symmetric or not. The distribution is not antisymmetric because $T_{Skew} = 0.005$. The distribution is not uniform since $\gamma_2 = -1.9$. As a consequence, $T_{Kurto} = 1.805$, and we have to reject the uniformity test. The Jarque-Berra test gives a p-value of 0.5191, which means that the sample is normal whatever the value set for α.

C. Multi-criteria Approach for Finding the Most Appropriate Discretization Method

Discretization must keep the initial statistical characteristics so as the homogeneity of the intervals, and reduce the size of the final data produced. Consequently, the discretization objectives are many and contradictory. For this reason, we chose a multi-criteria analysis to evaluate the available applicable methods of discretization. We use three criteria:

- The entropy H measures the uniformity of intervals. The higher the entropy, the more the discretization is adequate from the viewpoint of the number of elements in each interval:

$$H = -\sum_{i=1}^{NbBins} p_i \log_2(p_i) \qquad (7)$$

  where p_i is the number of points of interval i divided by the total number of points (N), and $NbBins$ is the number of intervals. The maximum of H is computed by discretizing the attribute into $NbBins$ intervals with the same number of elements. In this case, H reduces to $log_2(NbBins)$.

- The index of variance J, introduced in [19], measures the interclass variances proportionally to the total variance. The closer the index is to 1, the more homogeneous the discretization is:

$$J = 1 - \frac{\text{Intra-intervals variance}}{\text{Total variance}}$$

- Finally, the stability S corresponds to the maximum distance between the distribution functions before and after discretization. Let F_1 and F_2 be the attribute distribution functions before and after discretization respectively:

$$S = sup_x(|F_1(x) - F_2(x)|) \qquad (8)$$

The goal is to find solutions that present a compromise between the various performance measures. The evaluation of these methods should be done automatically, so we are in the category of *a priori* approaches, where the decision-maker intervenes just before the evaluation process step.

Aggregation methods are among the most widely used methods in multi-criteria analysis. The principle is to reduce to a unique criterion problem. In this category, the weighted sum method involves building a unique criterion function by associating a weight to each criterion [20], [21]. This method is limited by the choice of the weight, and requires comparable criteria. The method of inequality constraints is to maximize a single criterion by adding constraints to the values of the other criteria [22]. The disadvantage of this method is the choice of the thresholds of the added constraints.

Algorithm 1: MAD (Multi-criteria Analysis for Discretization)

Input: X set of numeric values to discretize, DM set of discretization methods applicable
Output: best discretization method for X

```
foreach method D ∈ DM do
  | Compute V_D;
end
return argmin(V);
```

In our case, the alternatives are the 4 methods of discretization, and we discretize automatically columns separately, so the implementation facility is important in our approach. Hence the interest in using the aggregation method by reducing it to a unique criterion problem, by choosing the method that minimizes the Euclidean distance from the target point ($H = log_2(NbBins)$, $J = 1$, $S = 0$).

Definition 1: Let D be an arbitrary discretization method. We can define V_D a measure of segmentation quality using the proposed multi-criteria analysis as follows:

$$V_D = \sqrt{(H_D - log_2(NbBins))^2 + (J_D - 1)^2 + S_D^2} \qquad (9)$$

The following proposition is the main result of this article: It indicates how we chose the most appropriate discretization method among all the available ones.

Proposition 1: Let DM be a set of discretization methods; the set, noted $\mathbb{D}$, that minimizes V_D (*see* equation(9)), $\forall D \in \{DM\}$, contains the best discretization methods.

Corollary 1: The set of most appropriate discretization methods $\mathbb{D}$ can be obtained as follows:

$$\mathbb{D} = argmin(\{V_D, \forall D \in DM\}) \qquad (10)$$

Let us underline that if $|\mathbb{D}| > 1$, then we have to choose one method among all. As a result of corollary 1, we propose the MAD (Multi-criteria Analysis for finding the best Discretization method) algorithm, see Algorithm 1.

Example 3: Continuing Example 1, Table IV shows the evaluation results for all the discretization methods at disposal. Let us underline that for the need of our example, all the values are computed for every discretization method, and not only for the ones that should have been selected after the step proposed in Section IV-B (*cf.* Table III).

TABLE IV: EVALUATION OF DISCRETIZATION METHODS.

	H	J	S	V_{DM}
EWD	1.5	0.972	0.25	0.559
EFD-Jenks	2	0.985	0.167	0.167
AVST	1.92	0.741	0.167	0.318
KMEANS	1.95	0.972	0.167	0.176

The results show that EFD-Jenks and KMEANS are the two methods that obtain the lowest values for V_D. The values got by the EWD and AVST methods are the worst: This is consistent with our optimization proposed in Table III, since the sample distribution is multimodal.

V. Parallelizing data preparation

Parallel architectures have become a standard today. As a result, applications can be distributed on several cores. Consequently, multicore applications run faster given that they require less process time to be executed, even if they may need on the other hand more memory for their data. But this latter inconvenient is minor when compared to the induced performances. We present in this section first some novel programming techniques, which allow to run easily different tasks in parallel. We show in a second step how we adapt these techniques to our work.

A. New Features in Multicore Encoding

Multicore processing is not a new concept, however only in the mid 2000s has the technology become mainstream with Intel and AMD. Moreover, since then, novel software environments that are able to take advantage simultaneously of the different existing processors have been designed (Cilk++, Open MP, TBB, *etc.*). They are based on the fact that looping functions are the key area where splitting parts of a loop across all available hardware resources increase application performance.

We focus hereafter on the relevant versions of the Microsoft .NET framework for C++ proposed since 2010. These enhance support for parallel programming by several utilities, among which the Task Parallel Library. This component entirely hides the multi-threading activity on the cores. The job of spawning and terminating threads, as well as scaling the number of threads according to the number of available cores, is done by the library itself.

The Parallel Patterns Library (PPL) is the corresponding available tool in the Visual C++ environment. The PPL operates on small units of work called Tasks. Each of them is defined by a λ calculus expression (see below). The PPL defines three kinds of facilities for parallel processing, where only templates for algorithms for parallel operations are of interest for this presentation.

Among the algorithms defined as templates for initiating parallel execution on multiple cores, we focus on the *parallel_invoke* algorithm used in the presented work (see end of Sections III-B and IV-C). It executes a set of two or more independent Tasks in parallel.

Another novelty introduced by the PPL is the use of λ expressions, now included in the C++11 language norm. These remove all need for scaffolding code, allowing a "function" to be defined in-line in another statement, as in the example provided by Listing 1. The λ element in the square brackets is called the capture specification. It relays to the compiler that a λ function is being created and that each local variable is being captured by reference (in our example). The final part is the function body.

```
// Returns the result of adding a value to itself
template <typename T> T twice(const T& t) {
        return t + t;
}
int n = 54; double d = 5.6; string s = "Hello";
// Call the function on each value concurrently
parallel_invoke(
        [&n] { n = twice(n); },
        [&d] { d = twice(d); },
        [&s] { s = twice(s); }
);
```

Listing 1: Parallel execution of 3 simple tasks

Listing 1 also shows the limits of parallelism. It is widely agreed that applications that may benefit from using more than one processor necessitate: (i) Operations that require a substantial amount of processor time, measured in seconds rather than milliseconds, and (ii), Operations that can be divided into significant units of calculation, which can be executed independently of one another. So the chosen example does not fit parallelization, but is used to illustrate the new features introduced by multicore programming techniques.

More details about parallel algorithms and the λ calculus can be found in [23], [24].

B. Application to data preparation

As a result of Table IV and of Proposition 1, we define the PoP (Parallel Optimized Preparation of data) method, see Algorithm 2.

For each attribute, after constructing Table III, each applicable discretization method is invoked and evaluated in order to keep finally the most appropriate. The content of these two tasks (three when involving the statistics computations) are executed in parallel using the *parallel_invoke* template (*cf.* previous section).
We discuss the advantages of this approach so as the got response times in the next section.

Algorithm 2: POP (Parallel Optimized Preparation of Data)

Input: X set of numeric values to discretize, DM set of discretization methods applicable
Output: Best set of bins for X

1 **Parallel_Invoke** *For each method* $D \in$ DM **do**
2 Compute γ_2, γ_3 and perform Jarque-Bera test;
3 **end**
4 **Parallel_Invoke** *For each method* $D \in$ DM **do**
5 Remove D from DM if it does not satisfy the criteria given in Table III;
6 **end**
7 **Parallel_Invoke** *For each method* $D \in$ DM **do**
8 Discretize X according to D;
9 $V_D = \sqrt{(H_D - log_2(NbBins))^2 + (J_D - 1)^2 + S_D^2}$;
10 **end**
11 $\mathbb{D} = argmin(\{V_D, \forall D \in DM\})$;
12 **return** set of bins obtained in line 8 according to $\mathbb{D}$;

VI. Experimental Analysis

The goal of this section is to validate experimentally our approach according to two point of views: (i) firstly, we apply our methodology to the extraction of correlation and of association rules; (ii) secondly, we use it to forecast time series. These two application fields correspond to the two mainstream approaches in data mining, which consist in defining and using descriptive or predictive models. What means that the presented work can help to solve a great variety of associated problems.

A. *Experimentation on rules detection*

In this section, we present some experimental results by evaluating five samples. We decided to implement it using the MineCor KDD Software [2], but it could have been with another one (R Project, Tanagra, *etc.*). Sample_1 and Sample_2 correspond to real data, representing parameter (in the sense of attribute) measurements provided by microelectronics manufacturers after completion of the manufacturing process. The ultimate goal was here to detect correlations between one particular parameter (the yield) and the other attributes. Sample_3 is a randomly generated file that contains heterogeneous values. Sample_4 and Sample_5 are common data taken from the UCI Machine Learning Repository website [25]. Table V sums up the characteristics of the samples.

TABLE V: CHARACTERISTICS OF THE DATABASES USED.

Sample	Number of columns	Number of rows	Type
Sample_1 (amtel.csv)	8	727	real
Sample_2 (stm.csv)	1281	296	real
Sample_3 (generated.csv)	11	201	generated
Sample_4 (abalone.csv)	9	4177	real
Sample_5 (auto_mpg.csv)	8	398	real

Experiments were performed on a 4 core computer (a DELL Workstation with a 2.8 GHz processor and 12 Gb RAM working under the Windows 7 64 bits OS). First, let us underline that we shall not focus in this section on performance issues. Of course, we have chosen to parallelize the underdone tasks in order to improve response times. As it is easy to understand, each of the *parallel_invoke* loops has a computational time closed to the most consuming calculus inside of each loop. Parallelism allows us to compute and then to evaluate different "possibilities" in order especially to chose the most efficient one for our purpose. This is done without waste of time, when comparing to a single "possibility" processing. Moreover, we can easily add other tasks to each parallelized loop (statistics computations, discretization methods, evaluation criteria). Some physical limits exist (currently): No more then seven tasks can be launched simultaneously within the 2010 C++ Microsoft .NET / PPL environment. But each individual described task does not require more than a few seconds to execute, even on the Sample_2 database.

Concerning outlier management, we recall that in the previous versions of our software (see [2]), we used the single standardization method with p set by the user (*cf.* Section III-A). With the new approach presented in Section III-B, we notice an improvement in the detection of true positive or false negative outliers by a factor of 2%.

Figures 4 summarize the evaluation of the methods used on each of our samples, except on Sample_2: we have chosen to only show the results for the 10 first columns.

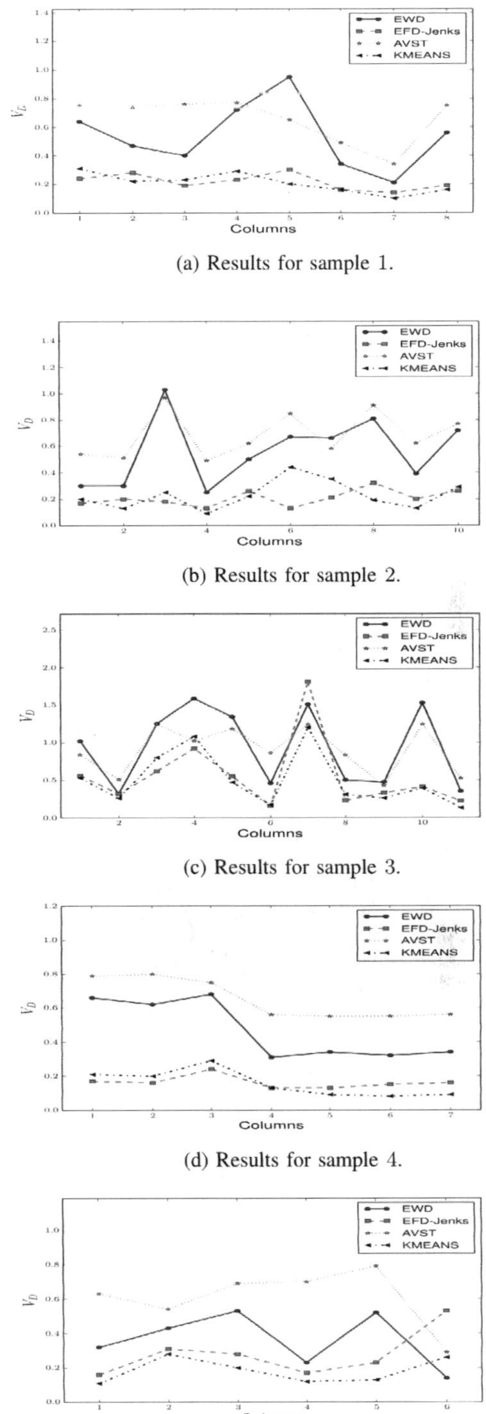

(a) Results for sample 1.

(b) Results for sample 2.

(c) Results for sample 3.

(d) Results for sample 4.

(e) Results for sample 5.

Figure 4: Discretization experimentations on the five samples.

For $Sample_1$ and $Sample_2$ attributes, which have symmetric and normal distributions, the evaluation on Figure 4a and 4b shows that the EFD-Jenks method provides generally the best results. The KMEANS method is unstable for these kinds of distributions, but sometimes provides the best discretization.

For the $Sample_3$ evaluation shown graphically in Figure 4c, the studied columns have relatively dispersed, asymmetric and multimodal distributions. "Best" discretizations are provided by EFD-Jenks and KMEANS methods. We note also that the EWD method is fast, and sometimes demonstrates good performances in comparison with the EFD-Jenks or KMEANS methods.

For $Sample_4$ and $Sample_5$ attributes, which distributions have a single mode and most of them are symmetric, the evaluation on Figures 4d and 4e shows that the KMEANS method provides generally the best results. The results given by EFD-Jenks method are closed to the ones obtained using KMEANS.

Finally, Figure 5 summarizes our approach. We have tested it over each column of each dataset. Any of the available methods is selected at least once in the dataset of the three first proposed samples (cf. Table V), which enforces our approach. As expected, EFD-Jenks is the method that is the most often kept by our software ($\simeq$ 42%). AVST and KMEANS are selected approximately a bit less than 30% each. EWD is only selected a very few times (less than 2%).

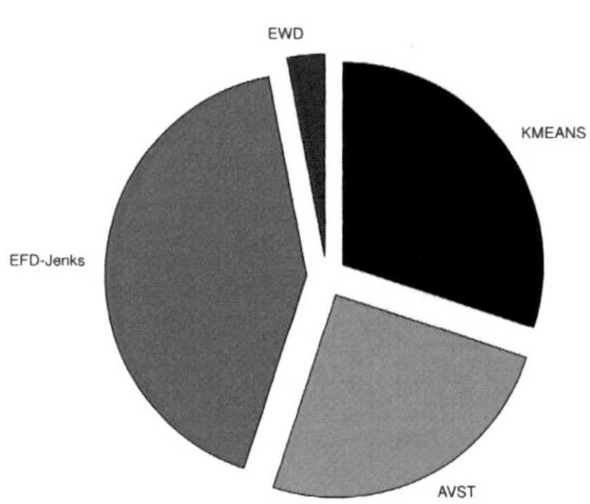

Figure 5: Global Distribution of DMs in our samples.

We focus hereafter on experiments performed in order to compare the different available discretization methods still on the three first samples. Figures 6a, 7a and 8a reference various experiments when mining Association Rules. Figures 6b, 7b and 8b correspond to experiments when mining Correlation Rules. When searching for Association Rules, the minimum confidence ($MinConf$) threshold has been arbitrarily set to 0.5. The different figures provide the number of Association or of Correlation Rules respectively, while the minimum support ($MinSup$) threshold varies. Each figure is composed of five curves. One for each of the four discretization methods presented in Table III, and one for our global method (POP). Each method is individually applied on each column of the considered database/dataset.

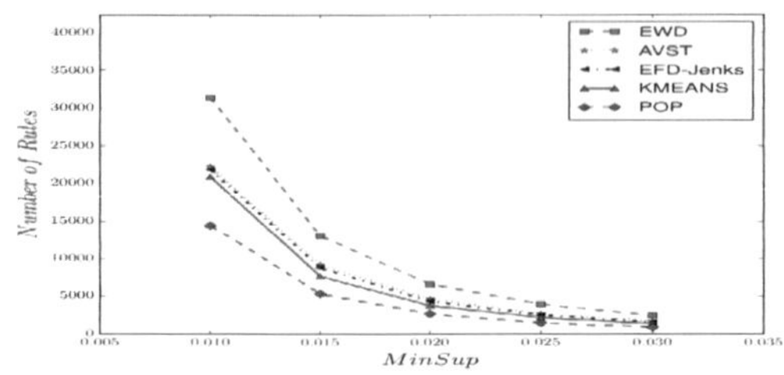

(a) Results for Apriori.

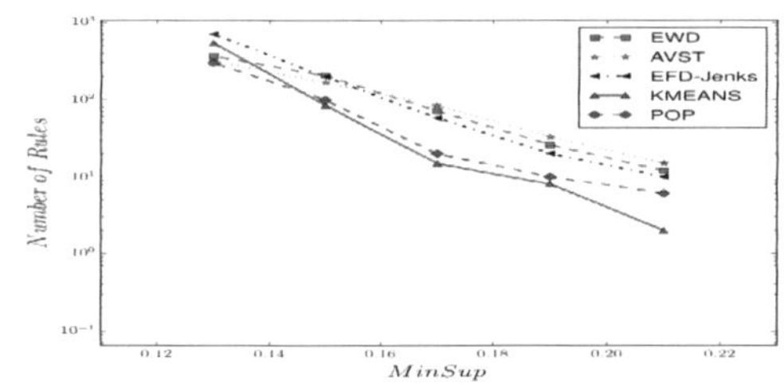

(b) Results for MineCor.

Figure 6: Execution on $Sample_1$.

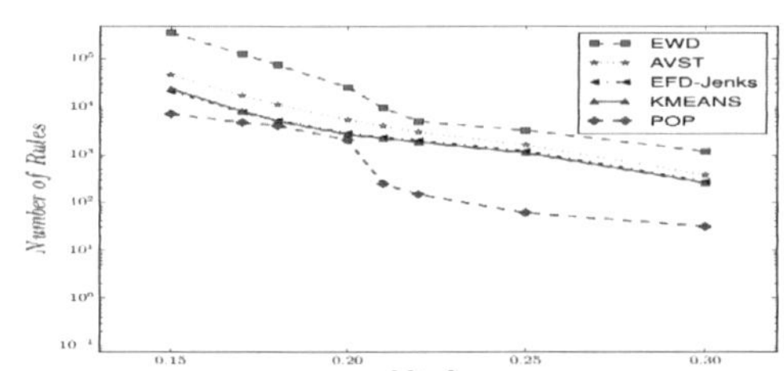

(a) Results for Apriori.

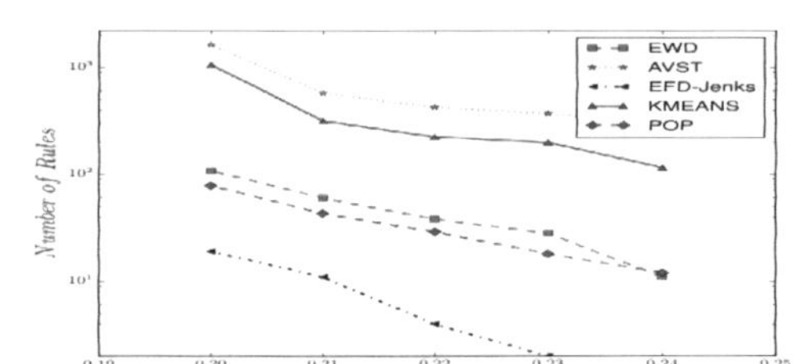

(b) Results for MineCor.

Figure 7: Execution on $Sample_2$.

Analyzing the Association Rules detection process, experiments show that POP gives the best results (few number of rules), and EWD is the worst. Using real data, the number of rules is reduced by a factor comprised between 5% and 20%. This reduction factor is even better using synthetic (generated) data and a low $MinSup$ threshold. When mining Correlation

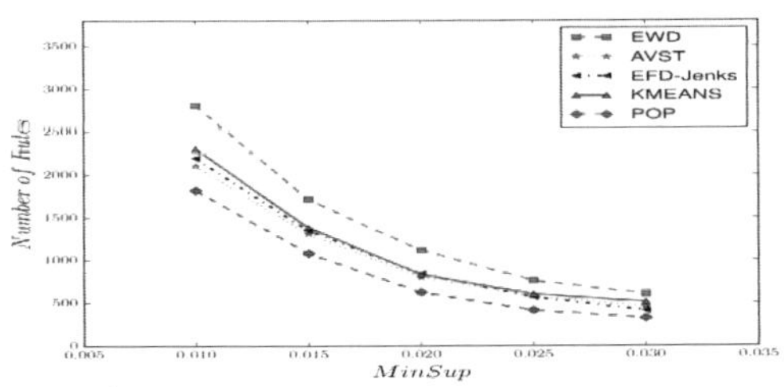

(a) Results for Apriori.

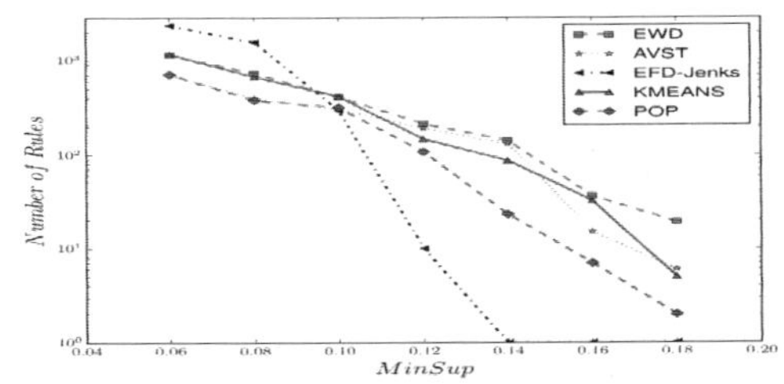

(b) Results for MineCor.

Figure 8: Execution on Sample_3.

Rules on synthetic data, the method that gives the best results with high thresholds is KMEANS, while it is POP when the support is low. This can be explained by the fact that the generated data are sparse and multimodal. When examining the results on real databases, POP gives good results. However, let us underline that the EFD-Jenks method produces unexpected results: Either we have few rules (Figures 6a and 6b), or we have a lot (Figures 7a and 7b) with a low threshold. We suppose that the high number of used bins is at the basis of this result.

B. Experimentation on time series forecasting

In this section, we present an another practical application of the proposed method. It deals with the prediction of time series on financial data. Often, in time series prediction, interest is put on significant changes, instead of small fluctuations of the evolution of the data. Beside, in the machine learning field, the learning process for real data takes a substantial amount of time in the whole prediction process. For this reason, time series segmentation is used to make data more understandable by the prediction models, and to speed up the learning process. In light of that, the proposed method can be applied in order to help in the choice of the segmentation method.

For these experiments, we use a fixed prediction model (VAR-NN [26]), and multiple time series. We study hereafter the impact of the proposed methodology on the predictions.

1) The prediction model used: The prediction model used is first briefly described. The VAR-NN (Vector Auto-Regressive Neural Network) model, presented in [26], is a prediction model derived from the classical VAR (Vector Auto-Regressive) model [27], which is expressed as follows:

Let us consider a k-dimensional set of time series y_t, each one containing exactly T observations. The $\text{VAR}(p)$ system expresses each variable of y_t as a linear function of the p previous values of itself and the p previous values of the other variables, plus an error term with a mean of zero.

$$y_t = \alpha_0 + \sum_{i=1}^{p} A_i y_{t-i} + \epsilon_t \tag{11}$$

ϵ_t is a white noise with a mean of zero, and $A_1, \ldots, A_p$ are $(k \times k)$ matrices parameters of the model. The general expression of the non linear VAR model is different from the classical model in the way that the parameters of the model values are not linear.

$$y_t = F_t(y_{t-1}, y_{t-2}, ..., y_{t-p} + x_{t-1}, x_{t-2}, ..., x_{t-p}) \tag{12}$$

We use in this experiment the VAR-NN (Vector Auto-Regressive Neural Network) model [28], with multi-layer perceptron structure, and based on the back-propagation algorithm. An example of two time series as an input of the network, with one hidden layer, is given in Figure 9.

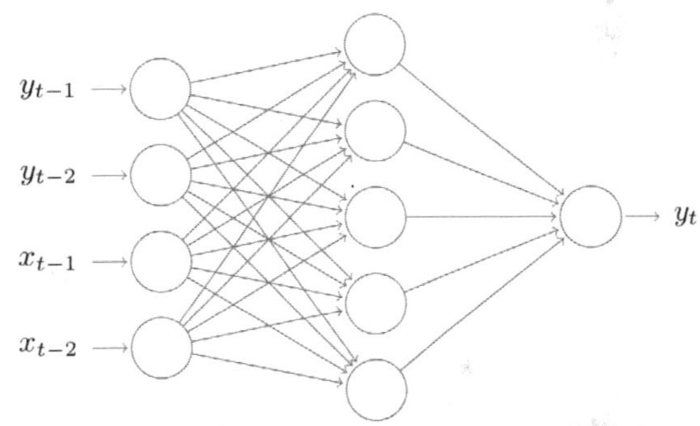

Figure 9: Illustration of a bivariate VAR-NN model with a lag parameter $p = 2$ and with one hidden layer.

2) Time series used: We use the following financial time series:

- ts_1: Financial french time series expressing the prices of 9 articles containing (Oil, Propane, Gold, euros/dollars, Butane, Cac40) and others, from what prices have been extracted between $2013/03/12$ and $2016/03/01$.
- ts_2 (w.tb3n6ms): weekly 3 and 6 months US Treasury Bill interest rates from $1958/12/12$ until $2004/08/06$, extracted from the R package **FinTS** [29].
- ts_3 (m.fac.9003): object of 168 observations giving simple excess returns of 13 stocks and the Standard and Poors 500 index over the monthly series of three-months Treasury Bill rates of the secondary market as the risk-free rate from January 1990 to December 2003, extracted from the **R** package **FinTS**.

3) Experimentations: Let p be the lag parameter of the VAR-NN model, setted in our case according to the length of the series (see Table VI), and $NbVar$ the number of the variables of the multivariate time series to predict. We use a neural network with (i) 10000 as maximum of iterations,

TABLE VI: CHARACTERISTICS OF THE TIME SERIES USED.

Time series	Number of attributes	Number of rows	Number of predictions	Lag parameter	Type
ts_1	9	1090	100	20	real
ts_2	2	2383	200	40	real
ts_3	14	168	20	9	real

TABLE VII: Detection of the best methods for both, the discretization quality and the prediction precision

Time series	Attributs	Forecasting score ($1000.MSE$)				Discretization evaluation (V_d)				best discretization	best forecaster
		ewd	efd	avst	kmeans	ewd	efd	avst	kmeans		
ts_1	**col1**	0.9	**0.4**	10.5	0.6	0.42	**0.22**	0.52	1.07	efd	efd
	col2	0.6	**0.1**	3.1	0.2	0.60	**0.18**	0.86	0.53	efd	efd
	col3	4	**2.9**	5.7	3	0.28	**0.10**	0.40	0.26	efd	efd
	col4	4.1	**3**	5.8	3.4	0.29	**0.10**	0.40	0.25	efd	efd
	col5	2.1	1.1	1.8	**0.9**	0.63	0.29	0.56	**0.28**	kmeans	kmeans
	col6	2.2	**1.1**	6.5	1.8	0.52	**0.21**	0.58	0.25	efd	efd
	col7	1.1	**0.3**	2.6	0.6	0.36	**0.18**	0.47	0.53	efd	efd
	col8	0.9	**0.5**	3	**0.5**	0.65	**0.24**	000.61	0.59	efd,kmeans	efd
	col9	3.2	**2.4**	11.6	**2.6**	0.23	0.12	000.62	**0.11**	efd	kmeans
ts_2	**col1**	**1.5**	1.7	6.5	2.8	0.48	**0.16**	0.61	0.30	efd	ewd
	col2	**1.4**	1.5	6.1	1.8	0.47	0.29	0.62	**0.22**	kmeans	ewd
ts_3	**col1**	104.5	108.4	89.9	**67**	0.53	0.23	0.52	**000.13**	kmeans	kmeans
	col2	57.7	65.5	75.1	**44.8**	0.61	0.35	0.76	**000.22**	kmeans	kmeans
	col3	93.4	**67.7**	83	76.5	0.46	**0.13**	0.57	000.16	efd	efd
	col4	127.7	120.6	131	**91.1**	0.28	0.20	0.51	**000.10**	kmeans	kmeans
	col5	91.7	**80.6**	78.9	96.6	0.33	0.28	0.52	**000.18**	kmeans	efd
	col6	113.6	122.7	**85.8**	97.2	0.48	0.26	0.58	**000.17**	kmeans	avst
	col7	105.8	**92.3**	102.6	110.2	0.53	0.22	0.56	**000.11**	kmeans	efd
	col8	84.6	**64.1**	73.8	79.5	0.58	**0.23**	0.60	**000.22**	kmeans,efd	efd
	col9	**66.9**	78.8	90.5	92.4	0.65	0.38	0.92	**000.33**	kmeans	efd
	col10	**41.3**	56	55.6	48.6	0.61	0.28	0.74	**000.15**	kmeans	ewd
	col11	**35.9**	47.6	39.1	36.1	0.69	**0.27**	0.81	000.34	efd	ewd
	col12	72.3	50.4	59.6	**42.5**	0.65	0.29	0.74	**000.21**	kmeans	kmeans
	col13	**98.7**	120	102.8	107	0.43	**0.16**	0.50	**000.15**	kmeans	ewd
	col14	**58.5**	68.4	94	105.8	0.56	0.25	0.76	**000.14**	kmeans	ewd

(ii) 4 hidden layers of size $(2/3, 1/4, 1/4, 1/4) \times k$, where $k = p \times NbVar$, is the number of inputs of the model (since we use the p previous values of $NbVar$ variables).

First, we apply the discretization methods (EWD, EFD-Jenks, AVST, KMEANS) on the time series, in order to find the best one according to formula (9). Then we select the best method for each attribute in terms of the predictions precision. And finally, we compare the results for both discretization and prediction. The learning step of the prediction model is performed on the time series without a fixed number of last values (for which we make predictions). These are setted depending on the length of the series as shown in Table VI. Experiments are made in forecasting the last values as a sliding window. Each time we make a prediction, we learn from the real one, and so on. Finally, after obtaining all the predictions, we calculate the MSE (Mean Squared Error) of the predictions. The results of finding the best methods for both, the discretization quality using the proposed multicriteria approach, and the precision of the prediction, are summarized in Table VII. We show in Figure 10 the real, discretization and predictions of one target variable among 25 possibilities. The results of the evaluations of all the attributes are summarized in Table VII.

4) Interpretation: The evaluations illustrated in Table VII show that there is a rightness of 56% between best methods of discretization and predictions. Even if the best method of discretization is not always the best predictor, it shows a good score of prediction compared with the best one. What means that the multi-criteria evaluation of the discretization methods can predict at 56% the methods that will give the best predictions, and this just basing on the statistical characteristics of the discretized series. Consequently, we demonstrate that there is an impact justified by the evaluation made on financial time series with different lengths and different variables.

VII. CONCLUSION AND FUTURE WORK

In this paper, we presented a new approach for automatic data preparation implementable in most of KDD systems. This step is generally split into two sub-steps: (i) detecting and eliminating the outliers, and (ii) applying a discretization method in order to transform any column into a set of clusters. In this article, we show that the detection of outliers depends on the knowledge of the data distribution (normal or not). As a consequence, we do not have to apply the same pruning method (Box plot *vs.* Grubb's test). Moreover, when trying to find the most appropriate discretization method, what is important is not the law followed by the column, but the shape of its density function. This is why we propose an automatic choice for finding the most appropriate discretization method based on a multi-criteria approach, according to several criteria (Entropy, Variance, Stability). Experiments tasks are performed using multicore programming. What allows us to explore different solutions, to evaluate them, and to keep the most appropriated one for the studied data set without waste of time. As main result, experimental evaluations done both on real and synthetic data, and for different mining objectives,

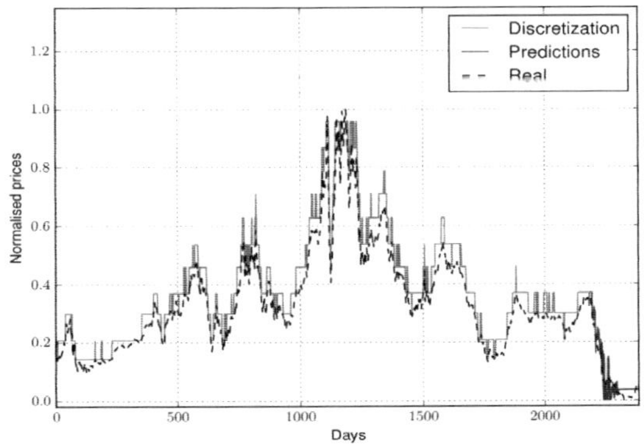

(a) Results of EWD method.

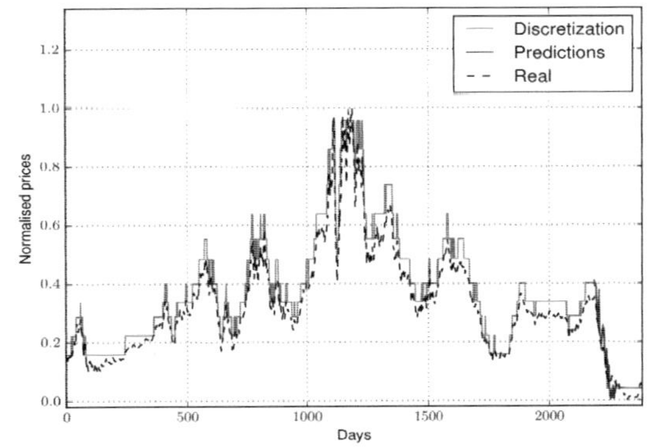

(b) Results of EFD-Jenks method.

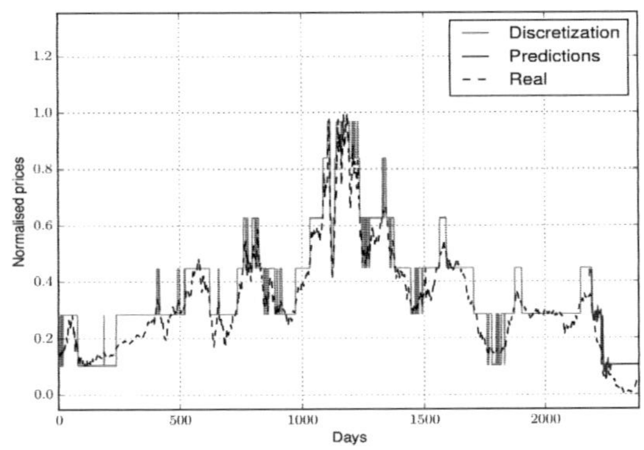

(c) Results of AVST method.

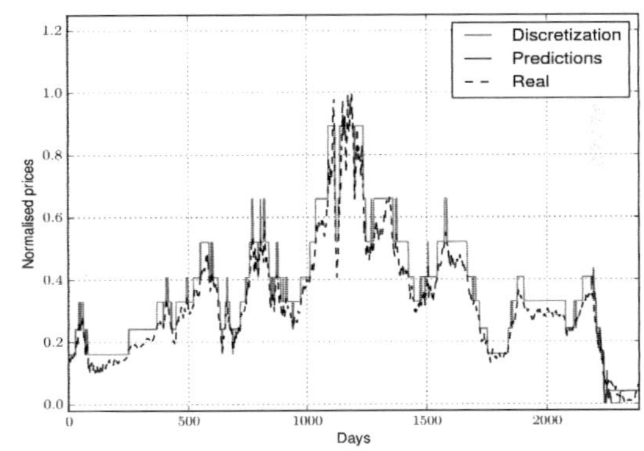

(d) Results of KMEANS method.

Figure 10: Predictions, discretized and real values for the target attribut Col2/ts_2.

validate our work, showing that it is not always the very same discretization method that is the best: Each method has its strengths and drawbacks. Moreover, experiments performed, on one hand when mining correlation rules, show a significant reduction of the number of produced rules, and, on the other hand when forecasting times series, show a significant improvement of the predictions obtained. We can conclude that our methodology produces better result in most cases.

For future works, we aim to experimentally validate the relationship between the distribution shape and the applicability of used methods, to add other discretization methods (Khiops, Chimerge, Entropy Minimization Discretization, *etc.*) to our system, and to understand why our methodology does not give always the best result in order to improve it.

References

[1] Y. Hmamouche, C. Ernst, and A. Casali, "Automatic kdd data preparation using multi-criteria features," in IMMM 2015, The Fifth International Conference on Advances in Information Mining and Management, 2015, pp. 33–38.

[2] C. Ernst and A. Casali, "Data preparation in the minecor kdd framework," in IMMM 2011, The First International Conference on Advances in Information Mining and Management, 2011, pp. 16–22.

[3] D. Pyle, Data Preparation for Data Mining. Morgan Kaufmann, 1999.

[4] O. Stepankova, P. Aubrecht, Z. Kouba, and P. Miksovsky, "Preprocessing for data mining and decision support," in Data Mining and Decision Support: Integration and Collaboration, K. A. Publishers, Ed., 2003, pp. 107–117.

[5] C. Aggarwal and P. Yu, "Outlier detection for high dimensional data," in SIGMOD Conference, S. Mehrotra and T. K. Sellis, Eds. ACM, 2001, pp. 37–46.

[6] M. Grun-Rehomme, O. Vasechko et al., "Méthodes de détection des unités atypiques: Cas des enquêtes structurelles ukrainiennes," in 42èmes Journées de Statistique, 2010.

[7] J. W. Tukey, "Exploratory data analysis. 1977," Massachusetts: Addison-Wesley, 1976.

[8] F. E. Grubbs, "Procedures for detecting outlying observations in samples," Technometrics, vol. 11, no. 1, 1969, pp. 1–21.

[9] H. W. Lilliefors, "On the kolmogorov-smirnov test for normality with mean and variance unknown," Journal of the American Statistical Association, vol. 62, no. 318, 1967, pp. 399–402.

[10] C. M. Jarque and A. K. Bera, "Efficient tests for normality, homoscedas-

ticity and serial independence of regression residuals," Economics Letters, vol. 6, no. 3, 1980, pp. 255–259.

[11] C. Cauvin, F. Escobar, and A. Serradj, Thematic Cartography, Cartography and the Impact of the Quantitative Revolution. John Wiley & Sons, 2013, vol. 2.

[12] I. Kononenko and S. J. Hong, "Attribute selection for modelling," Future Generation Computer Systems, vol. 13, no. 2, 1997, pp. 181–195.

[13] S. Kotsiantis and D. Kanellopoulos, "Discretization techniques: A recent survey," GESTS International Transactions on Computer Science and Engineering, vol. 32, no. 1, 2006, pp. 47–58.

[14] J. W. Grzymala-Busse, "Discretization based on entropy and multiple scanning," Entropy, vol. 15, no. 5, 2013, pp. 1486–1502.

[15] G. Jenks, "The data model concept in statistical mapping," in International Yearbook of Cartography, vol. 7, 1967, pp. 186–190.

[16] T. Kanungo, D. M. Mount, N. S. Netanyahu, C. D. Piatko, R. Silverman, and A. Y. Wu, "An efficient k-means clustering algorithm: Analysis and implementation," Pattern Analysis and Machine Intelligence, IEEE Transactions on, vol. 24, no. 7, 2002, pp. 881–892.

[17] A. K. Jain, "Data clustering: 50 years beyond k-means," Pattern Recognition Letters, vol. 31, no. 8, 2010, pp. 651–666.

[18] B. W. Silverman, Density estimation for statistics and data analysis. CRC press, 1986, vol. 26.

[19] C. Cauvin, F. Escobar, and A. Serradj, Cartographie thématique. 3. Méthodes quantitatives et transformations attributaires. Lavoisier, 2008.

[20] P. M. Pardalos, Y. Siskos, and C. Zopounidis, Advances in multicriteria analysis. Springer, 1995.

[21] B. Roy and P. Vincke, "Multicriteria analysis: survey and new directions," European Journal of Operational Research, vol. 8, no. 3, 1981, pp. 207–218.

[22] C. Zopounidis and P. M. Pardalos, Handbook of multicriteria analysis. Springer Science & Business Media, 2010, vol. 103.

[23] A. Casali and C. Ernst, "Extracting correlated patterns on multicore architectures," in Availability, Reliability, and Security in Information Systems and HCI - IFIP WG 8.4, 8.9, TC 5 International Cross-Domain Conference, CD-ARES 2013, Regensburg, Germany, September 2-6, 2013. Proceedings, 2013, pp. 118–133.

[24] C. Ernst, Y. Hmamouche, and A. Casali, "Pop: A parallel optimized preparation of data for data mining," in 2015 7th International Joint Conference on Knowledge Discovery, Knowledge Engineering and Knowledge Management (IC3K), vol. 1. IEEE, 2015, pp. 36–45.

[25] M. Lichman, "UCI machine learning repository," 2013. [Online]. Available: http://archive.ics.uci.edu/ml

[26] D. U. Wutsqa, S. G. Subanar, and Z. Sujuti, "Forecasting performance of var-nn and varma models," in Proceedings of the 2nd IMT-GT Regional Conference on Mathematics, 2006.

[27] D. C. Montgomery, C. L. Jennings, and M. Kulahci, Introduction to time series analysis and forecasting. John Wiley & Sons, 2015.

[28] J. Schmidhuber, "Deep learning in neural networks: An overview," Neural Networks, vol. 61, 2015, pp. 85–117.

[29] S. Graves, "The fints package," 2008. [Online]. Available: https://cran.r-project.org/web/packages/FinTS/

International Journal on Advances in Software, vol 9 no 3 & 4, year 2016, http://www.iariajournals.org/software/

Business Process Model Customisation using Domain-driven Controlled Variability Management and Rule Generation

Neel Mani, Markus Helfert

ADAPT Centre for Digital Content Technology
Dublin City University, School of Computing
Dublin, Ireland
Email: [nmani|mhelfert]@computing.dcu.ie

Claus Pahl

Free University of Bozen-Bolzano
Faculty of Computer Science
Bolzano, Italy
Email: claus.pahl@unibz.it

***Abstract*—Business process models are abstract descriptions and as such should be applicable in different situations. In order for a single process model to be reused, we need support for configuration and customisation. Often, process objects and activities are domain-specific. We use this observation and allow domain models to drive the customisation. Process variability models, known from product line modelling and manufacturing, can control this customisation by taking into account the domain models. While activities and objects have already been studied, we investigate here the constraints that govern a process execution. In order to integrate these constraints into a process model, we use a rule-based constraints language for a workflow and process model. A modelling framework will be presented as a development approach for customised rules through a feature model. Our use case is content processing, represented by an abstract ontology-based domain model in the framework and implemented by a customisation engine. The key contribution is a conceptual definition of a domain-specific rule variability language.**

Keywords–Business Process Modelling; Process Customisation; Process Constraints; Domain Model; Variability Model; Constraints Rule Language; Rule Generation.

I. INTRODUCTION

Business process models are abstract descriptions that can be applied in different situations and environments. To allow a single process model to be reused, configuration and customisation features help. Variability models, known from product line engineering, can control this customisation. While activities and objects have already been subject of customisation research, we focus on the customisation of constraints that govern a process execution here. Specifically, the emergence of business processes as a services in the cloud context (BPaaS) highlights the need to implement a reusable process resource together with a mechanism to adapt this to consumers [1].

We are primarily concerned with the utilisation of a conceptual domain model for business process management, specifically to define a domain-specific rule language for process constraints management. We present a conceptual approach in order to define a Domain Specification Rule Language (DSRL) for process constraints [2] based on a Variability Model (VM). To address the problem, we follow a feature-based approach to develop a domain-specific rule language, borrowed from product line engineering. It is beneficial to capture domain knowledge and define a solution for possibly too generic models through using a domain-specific language (DSL). A systematic DSL development approach provides the domain expert or analyst with a problem domain at a higher level of abstraction. DSLs are a favourable solution to directly represent, analyse, develop and implement domain concepts. DSLs are visual or textual languages targeted to specific problem domains, rather than general-purpose languages that aim at general software problems. With these languages or models, some behaviour inconsistencies of semantic properties can be checked by formal detection methods and tools.

Our contribution is a model development approach using of a feature model to bridge between a domain model (here in ontology form) and the domain-specific rule extension of a business process to define and implement process constraints. The feature model streamlines the constraints customisation of business processes for specific applications, bridging between domain model and rule language. The novelty lies in the use of software product line technology to customise processes.

We use digital content processing here as a domain context to illustrate the application of the proposed domain-specific technique (but we will also look at the transferability to other domains in the evaluation). We use a text-based content process involving text extraction, translation and post-editing as a sample business process. We also discuss a prototype implementation. However, note that a full integration of all model aspects is not aimed at as the focus here is on models. The objective is to outline principles of a systematic approach towards a domain-specific rule language for content processes.

The paper is organised as follows. We discuss the State-of-the-Art and Related Work in Section II. Here, we review process modelling and constraints to position the paper. In Section III, we introduce content processing from a feature-oriented DSL perspective. Section IV introduces rule language background and ideas for a domain-based rule language. We then discuss formal process models into which the rule language can be integrated. Then, we describe the implementation in Section V and evaluate the solution in Section VI.

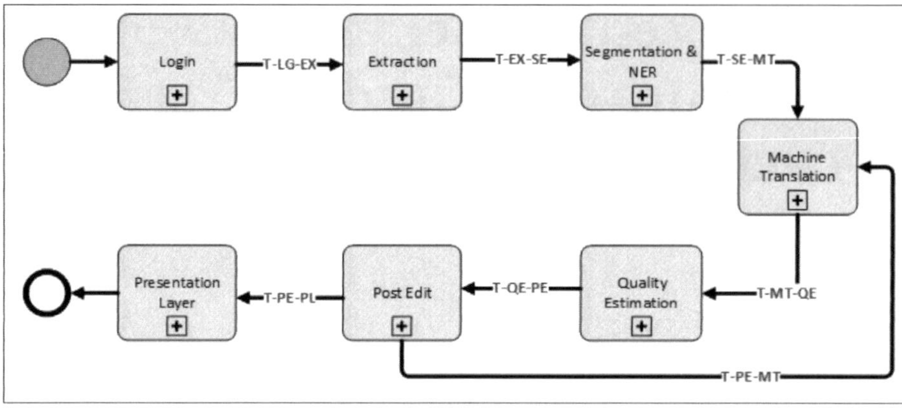

Figure 1. Sample content lifecycle process.

II. State-of-the-Art and Related Work

Current open research concerns for process management include customisation of governance and quality policies and the non-intrusive adaptation of processes to policies. Today, one-size-fits-all service process modelling and deployment techniques exist. However, their inherent structural inflexibility makes constraints difficult to manage, resulting in significant efforts and costs to adapt to individual domains needs.

A. SPL and Variability Modeling

Recently, many researchers have started applying software product line (SPL) concepts in service-oriented computing [3], [4], [5], [6]. We focus on approaches that used the SPL technique for process model configuration. For instance, [7] proposes a BPEL customization process, using a notion of a variability descriptor for modeling variability points in the process layer of service-oriented application.

There are many different approaches of process based variability in service compositions, which enable reuse and management of variability and also support Business Processes [8], [9]. Sun [9] proposes an extended version of COVAMOF; the proposed framework is based on a UML profile for variability modeling and management in web service based systems of software product families. PESOA [10] is variability mechanism represented in UML (activity diagram and state machines) and BPMN for a basic process model, which has non-functional characteristics, like maintenance of the correctness of a syntactical process. Mietzner et al. [7] propose variability descriptors that can be used to mark variability in the process layer and related artifacts of a SaaS application. The SaaS application template allows to customise processes.

B. Dynamic BPEL/BPMN Adaptation

There is related work in the field of constraints and policy definition and adaptive BPEL processes. While here a notation such as BPMN is aimed at, there is more work on WS-BPEL in our context. Work can be distinguished into two categories.

- BPEL process extensions designed to realize platform-independence: Work in [11] and [12] allows BPEL specifications to be extended with fault policies, i.e., rules that deal with erroneous situations. SRRF [13] generates BPEL processes based on defined handling policies. We do not bind domain-specific policies into business processes directly, as this would not allow to support user/domain-specific adaptation adequately.
- Platform-dependent BPEL engines: Dynamo [40] is limited in that BPEL event handlers must be statically embedded into the process prior to deployment (recovery logic is fixed and can only be customised through the event handler). It does not support customisation and adaptation. PAWS [2] extends the ActiveBPEL engine to enact a flexible process that can change behaviour dynamically, according to constraints.

Furthermore, process-centricity is a concern. Recently, business-processes-as-a-service (BPaaS) is discussed. While not addressed here as a cloud technology specifically, this perspective needs to be further complemented by an architectural style for its implementation [14]. We propose a classification of several quality and governance constraints elsewhere [15]: authorisation, accountability, workflow governance and quality. This takes the BPMN constraints extensions [16], [11] into account that suggest containment, authorisation and resource assignment as categories into account, but realises these in a less intrusive process adaptation solution.

The DSRL is a combination of rules and BPMN. Moreover, DSLR process based on BPMN and ECA rules is the main focus on the operational part of the DSRL system (i.e., to check conditions and perform actions based on an event of a BPMN process). There is no need for a general purpose language in a DSLR, though aspects are present in the process language. [17], [18], [19] discuss business process variability, though primarily from a structural customisation perspective. However, [17] also uses an ontology-based support infrastructure [20].

Several research works related to dynamic adaptation of service compositions have tended to implement variability constructs at the language level [21]. For example, VxBPEL [22] is an extension of the BPEL language allowing to capture variation points and configurations to be defined for a process in a service-centric system. SCENE [23] is also a language for composition design which, extends WS-BPEL by defining the main business logic and Event Condition Action (ECA) rules that define consequences to guide the execution of binding and rebinding self-configuration operations. Rules are used to associate a WS-BPEL workflow with the declaration of the policy to be used during (re)configuration.

C. Configuration Process Models and Templates

Recent years have resulted in a rising interest in supporting flexibility for process model activities. Most process design techniques lead to rigid processes where business policies are hard-coded into the process schema, hence reducing flexibility. Flexible process variants can be configured by using rules to a generic process template. This leads to a split the business policy and control flow. This structure can facilitate process variant configuration and retrieval [24], [25].

A multi-layered method for configuring process variants from the base layer is presented in [26]. The Provop approach [27] allows a user to manage and design to create process variants from a base process (i.e., a process template) with various options. Mohan et al. [28] discuss the automatic identification of inconsistencies resulting in the customisation of business process model and configuration procedure. The MoRE-WS tool [4] activates and deactivates features in a variability model. The changed variability model updates the composite models and its services that add and remove a fragment of WS-BPEL code at runtime. However, the tool uses services instead of direct code, but the dependency on programming and code is always associated with it. Lazovik et al. [29] developed a service-based process-independent language to express different customization options for the reference business processes.

Only a few rule language solutions consider the customization and configuration of a process model in a domain-specific environment. An exception is the work of Akhil and Wen [24] where the authors propose an template and rule for design and management of flexible process variant. Therefore, the rule template based configuration can adopt the most frequently used process. Since enterprise business processes change rapidly, the rule-based template cannot be adapted in changing situations. We need a solution that can be operated by non-technical domain experts without a semantic gap between domain expert design and development. The solution should be flexible, easy to adapt and easy to configure in terms of usability. Therefore, we have propose a domain-specific rule language, which resolves the domain constraints during the customisation process and a framework through which non-technical domain users can customise BPM with the generated set of domain-specific rules (DSRs).

D. Positioning the Approach

At the core of our solution is a process model that defines possible behaviour. This is made up of some frame of reference for the system and the corresponding attributes used to describe the possible behaviour of the process [30], [31]. The set of behaviours constitutes a process referred to as the extension of the process and individual behaviours in the extension are referred as instances. Constraints can be applied at states of the process to determine its continuing behaviour depending on the current situation. We use rules to combine a condition (constraint) with a resulting action [32], [33]. The target of our rule language (DSRL) is a standard business process notation (as in Figure 1). Rules shall thus be applied at the processing states of the process.

Our application case study is intelligent content processing. Intelligent content is digital content that allows users to create, curate and consume content in a way that satisfies dynamic and individual requirements relating to task design, context, language, and information discovery. The content is stored, exchanged and processed by a Web architecture and data will be exchanged, annotated with meta-data via web resources. Content is delivered from creators to consumers. Content follows a particular path, which contains different stages such as extraction and segmentation, name entity recognition, machine translation, quality estimation and post-editing. Each stage in the process has its own complexities governed by constraints.

We assume the content processing workflow as in Figure 1 as a sample process for the rule-based instrumentation of processes. Constraints govern this process. For instance, the quality of a machine-based text translation decides whether further post-editing is required. Generally, these constraints are domain-specific, e.g., referring to domain objects, their properties and respective activities on them.

III. Domain and Feature Model

Conceptual models (CM) are part of the analysis phase of system development, helping to understand and communicate particular domains [2]. They help to capture the requirements of the problem domain and, in ontology engineering, a CM is the basis for a formalized ontology. We utilise a conceptual domain model (in ontology form) to derive a domain-specific process rule language [34]. A domain specific language (DSL) is a programming or specification language that supports a particular application domain through appropriate notation, grammar and abstractions [35]. DSL development requires both domain knowledge and language development expertise. A prerequisite for designing DSLs is an analysis that provides structural knowledge of the application domain.

A. Feature Model

The most important result of a domain analysis is a feature model [36], [37], [38], [39]. A feature model covers both the aspects of software family members, like commonalities and variabilities, and also reflects dependencies between variable features. A feature diagram is a graphical representation of dependences between a variable feature and its components. Mandatory features are present in a concept instance if their parent is present. Optional features may be present. Alternative features are a set of features from which one is present. Groups of features are a set of features from which a subset is present if their parent is present. 'Mutex' and 'Requires' are relationships that can only exist between features. 'Requires' means that when we select a feature, the required featured must be selected too. 'Mutex' means that once we choose a feature the other feature must be excluded (mutual exclusion).

A domain-specific feature model can cover languages, transformation, tooling, and process aspects of DSLs. For feature model specification, we propose the FODA (Feature Oriented Domain Analysis) [40] method. It represents all the configurations (called instances) of a system, focusing on the features that may differ in each of the configurations [41]. We apply this concept to constraints customisation for processes. The Feature Description Language (FDL) [42] is a language to define features of a particular domain. It supports an automated normalization of feature descriptions, expansion to

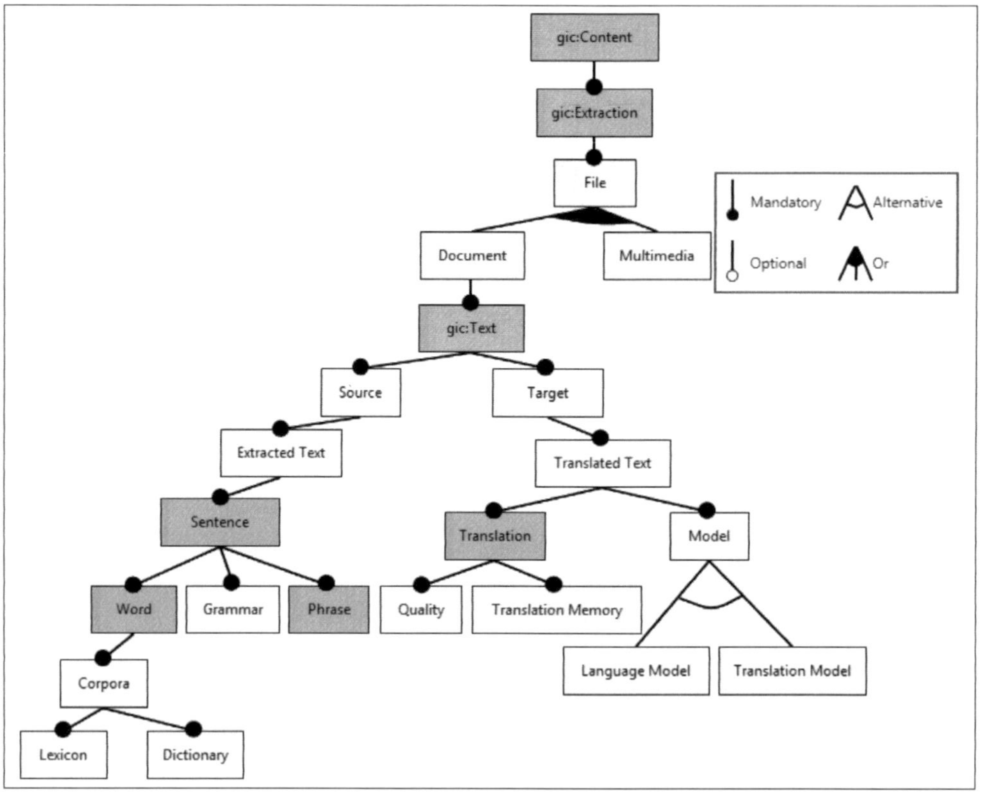

Figure 2. Feature model for intelligent content (note that the darker grey boxes will be detailed further in Figure 3).

disjunctive normal form, variability computation and constraint satisfaction. It shall be applied to the content processing use case here. The basis here is a domain ontology called GLOBIC (global intelligent content), which has been developed as part of our research centre. GLOBIC elements are prefixed by 'gic'.

Feature diagrams are a FODA graphical notation. They can be used for structuring the features of processes in specific domains. Figure 2 shows a feature diagram for the GLOBIC content extraction path, i.e., extraction as an activity that operates on content in specified formats. This is the first step in a systematic development of a domain-specific rule language (DSRL) for GLOBIC content processing use case. Here all elements are mandatory. The basic component gic:Content consists of a gic:Extraction element, a mandatory feature. A file is a mandatory component of gic:Extraction and it may either be used for Document or Multimedia elements or both. The closed triangle joining the lines for document and multimedia indicates a non-exclusive (more-of) choice between the elements. The gic:Text has two mandatory states Source and Target. Source contains ExtractedText and Target can be TranslationText. Furthermore, expanding the feature Sentence is also a mandatory component of ExtractedText. The four features Corpora, Phrase, Word and Grammar are mandatory. On the other side of gic:Text, a TranslationText is a mandatory component of Target, also containing a mandatory component Translation. A Translation has three components: TranslationMemory and Model are mandatory features, Quality could also be made an optional feature. A Model may be used as a TranslationModel or a LanguageModel or both models at same time. An instance of a feature model consists of an actual choice of atomic features matching the requirements imposed by the model. An instance corresponds to a text configuration of a gic:Text superclass.

The feature model might include for instance duplicate elements, inconsistencies or other anomalies. We can address this situation by applying consistency rules on feature diagrams. Each anomaly may indicate a different type of problem. The feature diagram algebra consists of four set of rules [41]:

- Normalization Rules – rules to simplify the feature expression by redundant feature elimination and normalize grammatical and syntactical anomalies.
- Expansion Rules – a normalized feature expression can be converted into a disjunctive normal form.
- Satisfaction Rules – the outermost operator of a disjunctive normal form is one-of. Its arguments are 'All' expressions with atomic features as arguments, resulting in a list of all possible configurations.
- Variability Rules – feature diagrams describe system variability, which can be quantified (e.g., number of possible configurations).

The feature model is important for the construction of the rule language (and thus the process customisation) here. Thus, checking internal coherence and providing a normalised format is important for its accessibility for non-technical domain experts. In our setting, the domain model provides the semantic definition for the feature-driven variability modelling.

B. Domain Model

Semantic models have been widely used in process management [43], [44]. This ranges from normal class models to capture structural properties of a domain to full ontologies to represent and reason about knowledge regarding the application domain or also the technical process domain [45], [46]. Domain-specific class diagrams are the next step from a feature model towards a DSL definition. A class is defined as a descriptor of a set of objects with common properties in terms of structure, behaviour, and relationships. A class diagram is based on a feature diagram model and helps to stabilise relationship and behaviour definitions by adding more details to the feature model. Note that there is an underlying domain ontology here, but we use the class aspects only (i.e., subsumption hierarchy only).

In the content use case, class diagrams of gic:Content and its components based on common properties are shown in Figure 3. The class diagram focuses on gic:Text, which records at top level only the presence of source and target. The respective Source and Target text strings are included in the respective classes. The two major classes are Text (Document) and Movie files (Multimedia), consisting of different type of attributes like content:string, format:string, or framerate:int. Figure 3 is the presentation of an extended part of the gic:Content model. For instance, gic:Text is classified into the two subclasses Source and Target. One file can map multiple translated texts or none. gic:Text is multi-language content (source and target content). Extracted Text is text from source content for the purposes target translation. Translated Text is a text after translation. Corpora is a set of structured texts. It may be single or multi language. gic:Sentence is a linguistic unit or combination of words with linked grammar. gic:Translation is content generated by a machine from a source language into a target language. A Grammar is set of structural rules. gic:QualityAssessment is linguistic assessment of translation in term of types of errors/defects. A Translation Memory is a linguistic database that continually captures previous translations for reuse.

Both domain and feature model feed into the process customisation activity, see Figure 4.

IV. CONSTRAINTS RULE LANGUAGE

Rule languages typically borrow their semantics from logic programming [47]. A rule is defined in the form of if-then clauses containing logical functions and operations. A rule language can enhance ontology languages, e.g., by allowing one to describe relations that cannot be described using for instance description logic (DL) underlying the definition of OWL (Ontology Web Language). We adopt Event-Condition-action (ECA) rules to express rules on content processing activities. The rules take the constituent elements of the GLOBIC model into account: content objects (e.g., text) that are processed and content processing activities (e.g., extraction or translation) that process content objects. ECA rules are then defined as follows:

- Event: on the occurrence of an event ...
- Condition: if a certain condition applies ...
- Action: then an action will be taken.

Three sample ECA rule definitions are:

- On uploading a file from user and if the filetype is valid, then progress to Extraction.
- On a specific key event and Text is inputted by the user and if text is valid, then progress Process to Segmentation.
- On a specific key event and a Web URL input is provided by user and if URL is valid, then progress to Extraction and Segmentation.

The rule model is designed for a generic process. An example shall illustrate ECA rules for 'extraction' as the activity. Different cases for extraction can be defined using feature models to derive customised versions:

- We can customise rules for specific content types (text files or multimedia content).
- We can also vary according to processing activities (extraction-only or extraction&translation).

The example below illustrates rule definitions in more concrete XML syntax. Here the rule is that a document must be post-edited before sent for QA-Rating:

```
<p1:Policy policyId="QA-Rate-policy1" priority="0">
  <p1:Objects>
    <p1:ObjectsAnyOf>
      <p1:ObjectsAllOf>
        <p1:Activity>
          <Name>QA-Rate crowd-sourced</Name>
        </p1:Activity>
      </p1:ObjectsAllOf>
    </p1:ObjectsAnyOf>
  </p1:Objects>

  <p1:ActivityStates>
    <p1:ActivityState>Validating-Pre
    </p1:ActivityState>
  </p1:ActivityStates>

  <p1:Rule priority="0"
             ruleId="constraintRule-QA-Rate">
    <p1:Conditions>
      <p1:ConditionExpression
            type="Provenance-Context">
        <p1:Para>//Document/ID</p1:Para>
        <p1:Expr>constraintRule-QA-Rate-Query
        </p1:Expr>
      </p1:ConditionExpression>
    </p1:Conditions>

    <p1:Actions>
      <p1:Pa-Violate>
        <p1:Violation>
          <Type>Functional:Protocol</Type>
        </p1:Violation>
      </p1:Pa-Violate>
    </p1:Actions>

    <p1:FaultHandler>
      <p1:Ca-Log level="5"> </p1:Ca-Log>
    </p1:FaultHandler>
  </p1:Rule>
```

In the example of a rule above, there is one constraint rule and a fault rule (the fault rule details themselves are skipped in the code). The policy (combination of rules) targets the "QA-Rate crowd-sourced" activity before it is executed. The

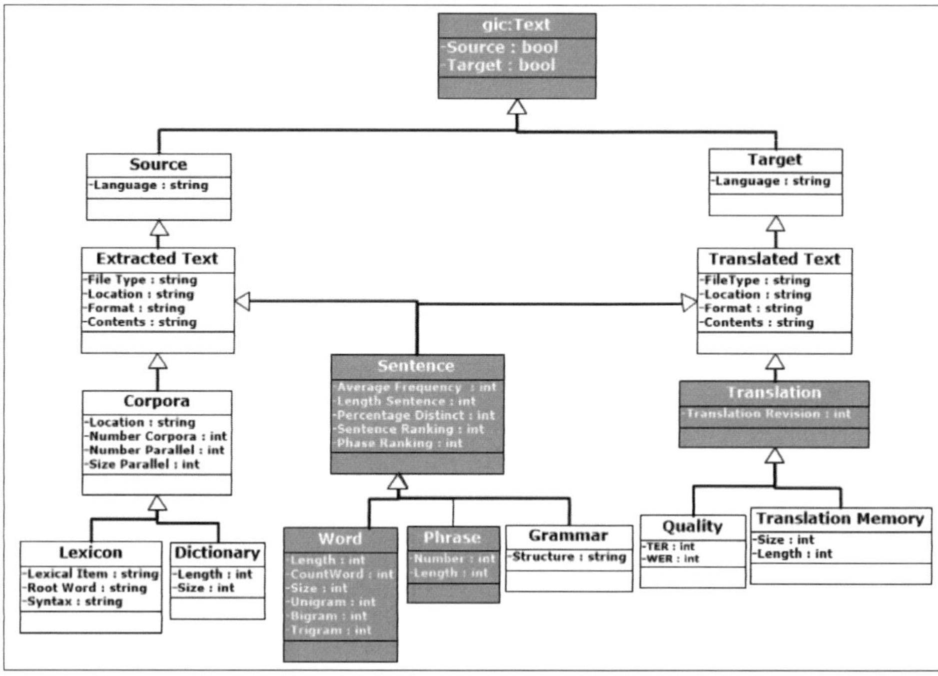

Figure 3. Domain model for intelligent content.

constraint rule has a condition on the provenance context or the document history. A parameterized query (e.g., in SPARQL – Semantic Protocol and RDF Query Language) could check if the current document (using the document ID as parameter) has NOT been post-edited. If the condition is true, then the rule results in a functional:Protocol violation. A fault rule can be defined for handling the violation. The policy will cancel the current process, if no remedy action was found in the fault rule for violation handling.

A. Rule Language Basics

We define the rule language as follows using GLOBIC concepts in the ECA-format with events, conditions and actions (to begin with, we use some sample definitions here to illustrate key concepts before providing a more complete definition later on). The core format of the rule is based on events, conditions and actions. Events are here specific to the application context, e.g., (file) upload, (text) translation or (information) extraction.

gic:Rule ::= [gic:Event] || [gic:Cond] || [gic:Action]
gic:Event::= {Upload} || {Translate} || {Extract}

While the rule syntax is simple, the important aspect is that that the syntactic elements refer to the domain model, giving it semantics and indicating variability points. Variability points are, as explained, defined in the feature model. The above three examples from the beginning of the section can be formalised using this notation. Important here is the guidance in defining rules that a domain expert gets through the domain model as a general reference framework and the feature model definition to understand and apply the variability points.

B. Rule Categories for Process Customization

To further understand the rule language, looking at pragmatics such as rule categories is useful. The rules formalised in the rule language introduced above are a syntactical construct. Semantically, we can distinguish a number of rule categories:

- Control flow rules are used for amending the control flow of a process model based on validation or case data. There are several customisation operations, like deleting, inserting, moving or replacing a task. In addition, they are moving or swapping and changing the relationship between two or more tasks.
- Resource rules depend on resource-based actions or validation of processes. They are based on conditional data or case data.
- Data rules are associated with properties or attributes of a resource related to a case.
- Authorisation rules and access control rules, i.e., the rights and roles defined for users, which is a key component in secure business processes that encourages trust for its contributing stakeholders [43].
- An authentication rule expresses the need to verify a claimed identity in an authentication process.
- Hybrid rules concern the modification of several aspects of process design. For example, they might alter the flow of control of a process as well as change the properties of a resource.

C. Control Flow Rule Examples

As an example for the rule language, a few control flow rules (first category above) shall be given for illustration.

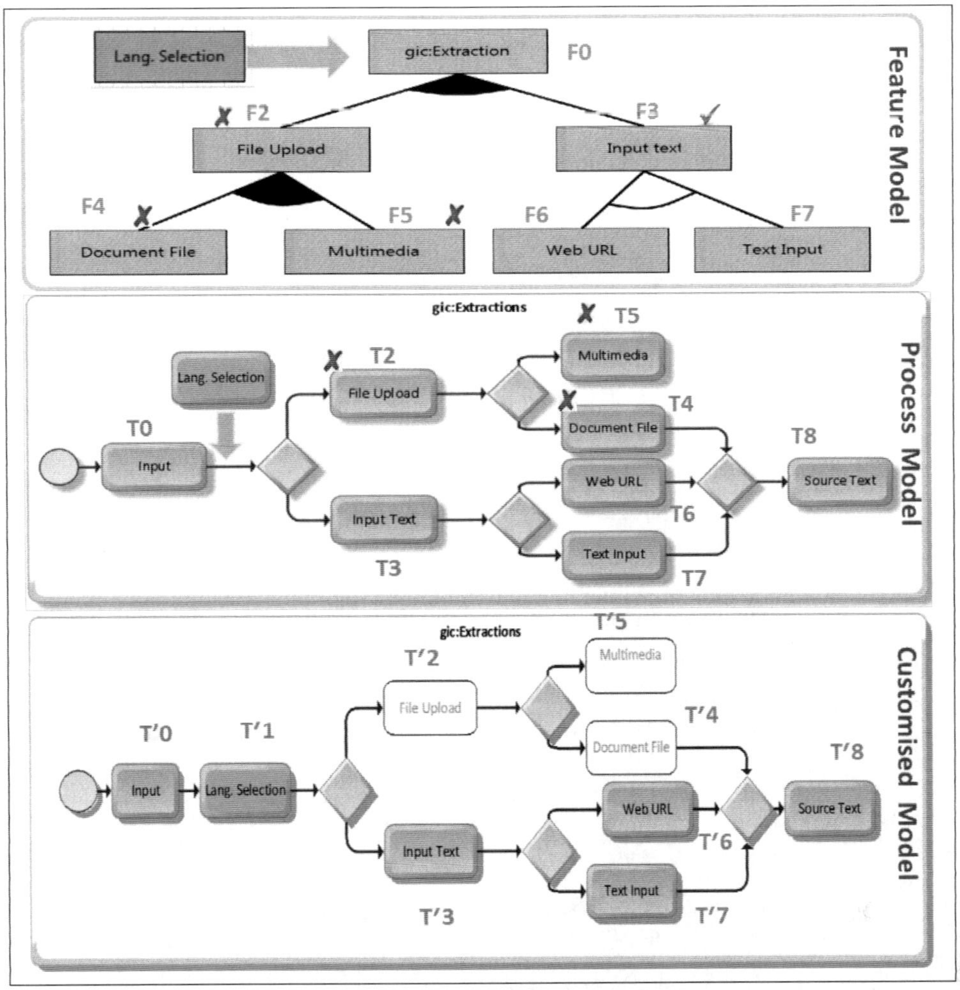

Figure 4. Content process customisation.

```
R1: T0.SourceLang==empty && T0.TargetLang=empty
        -> Insert [T1]
R2: T2.FileType == .txt||html||.xml||.doc||.pdf
        -> Delete [T3]/Deactivate [T5, T3, T6, T7]
R3: T3.TextLength < X
        -> Delete [T2, T4, T5, T6]
        -> Insert [Ttemp.LanguageDetection]
```

Rule R1, R2 and R3 are concerned with a control flow perspective. R1 inserts task T1 in a process model, when source and target language are missing at input (T0). The language selection is a mandatory input task for the Globic process chain and every sub-process has to use it in different aspects. R2 checks the validation of file, e.g., if a user or customer wants to upload a multimedia file, rather than plain text inputs. Therefore, it suggests to Delete T3 or Deactivate T5, T3, T6, T7 from the process model. Similarly, R3 deletes T2, T4, T5 and T6 from the process model, if users want to use input text instead of files, so there is no need for the file upload process. R4, R5, R6 and R7 below are resource flow-related rules and the tasks are based on data cases or validations:

```
R4: T2.FileSize < 5MB
      -> Validation [T2, NextValidation]
R5: T1.SourceLanguage==FR && T1.TargetLanguage=EN
      -> Corpora_Support(T1.SourceLanguage,
                         T1.TargetLanguage,Service)
R6: Ttemp.LanguageDetection != T1.SourceLanguage
      -> Notification (Source language and
                       file text language mismatched)
      -> BackTo([T2],R2)
R7: T6.WebURL != Valid(RegExpr)
      -> Alert(Web URL is invalid !)
      -> BackTo([T3],R4)
```

When the above set of rules is run with use case data, the corresponding rules are fired if their conditions are satisfied. Then, the actions are applied in form of configurations of variants and the process models are customised. Let us assume the sample use case data as follows:

```
fileSize<5 MB; fileType= .txt
```

Then, the rules triggered are R1, R2, R3, R4 and R5. The actions that become valid as a result of these rules are:

```
Action 1: Insert [T1]
Action 2: Delete [T3]/Deactivate [T5, T3, T6, T7]
Action 3: Insert [Ttemp.LanguageDetection]
Action 4: Validation [T2, NextValidation]
Action 5: Corpora_Support(T1.Source,T1.Target,Service)
Action 6: Notification (Exception/Validation message)
```

D. Rule Language Definition

Now we go back to the full rule definition. The Domain Specific Rule Language (DSRL) grammar is defined as follows. We start with a generic skeleton that will then be mapped to the Globic domain model.

```
<DSRL Rules> ::= <EventsList>
                 <RulesList>
                 <ProcessModelList>
<EventLists> ::= <Event> | <Event> <EventLists>
<Event>      ::= EVENT <EventName> IF <Expression> |
                 EVENT <EventName> is INTERN or EXTERN
<RulesList>  ::= <Rule> | <Rule> <RuleList>
<Rule>       ::= ON<EventName>
                 IF<Condition>DO<ActionList>
<ActionList> ::= <ActionName> |
                 <ActionName>,<ActionList>
<ProcessModelList> ::= <ProcessModel> |
                       <ProcessModel>,<ProcessModelList>
<ProcessModel> ::= PROCESSMODEL <ProcessModelName>
```

where a named process model `PROCESSMODEL` is defined by:

```
[TRANSITION_SEQUENCIAL (DISCARD|DELAY)],
[TRANSITION_PARALLEL (DISCARD|DELAY)]
[INPUTS(<InputList>)] [OUTPUTS(<OutputList>)]
```

`TRANSITION_SEQUENCIAL` and `TRANSITION_PARALLEL` are transitions of a workflow.

The description of the DSRL contains lists of events, rules and workflow states. An event can be internal or external (for rules generated as an action, it may be INTERNAL or EXTERNAL) or be generated when the expression becomes true. An event name is activated with the ON expression, which is a Boolean expression to determine the particular conditions that apply and the list of actions that have to be performed when event and condition are matched or true (preceded by DO expression). The workflow contains the state name, a certain policy to be activated in the workflow when sequential and parallel actions to perform. DISCARD allows discarding all the instructions, but the current one and DELAY allows delaying all instructions, but the current one.

```
EVENT gic:FileUpload::BOOL && gic:FileSelect::BOOL
IF    FileUpload_ON
ON    exists
        IF (gic:FileType ==True)
        DO
          ON exists
            IF (gic:FileSize <5MB)
            DO gic:Translate(File)
            ELSE Notification(File size < 5 MB)
        ELSE Notification(File format is invalid)
```

The grammar of the DSRL (in its form specific to the GLOBIC mapping, with events, conditions and actions that are domain-specific) is defined as follows:

List of Events:

```
Event_List ::=
   {gic:File->FileUpload, gic:Text->TextEnd,
    gic:Text->Parsing, gic:Text->MTStart,
    gic:Text->MTEnd, gic:Text-> QARating, ... }
Expr ::= gic:Content.Attributes
```

List of Conditions:

```
<Condition_List>::=<gic:Extraction.Condition>
   | <gic:Segmentation.Condition>
   | <gic:MachineTranslation.Condition>
   | <gic:QualityAssesment>
   | <gic:PostEdit>

<gic:Extraction.Condition> ::=    // EXTRACTION
 IF (<gic:File.FileType(X)::=FileList> )
 | IF (<gic:File.FileSize::=<Y>)
 | IF (<gic:Text.Length::=<L>)
 | IF (<Source.Language::=Language_List>)
 | IF (<Target.Language::=Language_List>)
 | IF (<MultiLanguageText(gic:Text)::=T|F>)
 | IF (<SingleLanguageDetect(gic:Text)::=T|F>)
```

where X is the file type, Y is the size of file (in MB) and L is the length of the text.

```
<gic:Segmentation.Condition)>::=  // SEGMENTATION
IF (<IsDictionaries(Source.Lang)::=T|F>)
| IF (<IsDictionaries(Target.Lang)::=T|F>)
| IF (<IsParCorpus(Source.Lang,Target.Lang)::=T|F>)
| IF (<IsParLexicon(Source.Lang,Target.Lang)::=T|F>)
| IF (<nic:Sentence.WordCount::=<WInteger>)
| IF (<IsTreeParsing(nic:Sentence)::=T|F)>)
```

where `WInteger` is the word count of the source sentence or target sentence.

```
<gic:Translation.Condition)> ::=  // TRANSLATION
 IF (<gic:Translation(Source.Lang, Target.Lang,
      gic:Text) ::= T|F>)
 | IF (<gic:Translation.Memory ::= <TM)(Mem Underfl)
 | IF (<gic:Translation.Memory ::= >TM)(Mem Overfl)
 | IF (<gic:Translation(gic:TxtSource,Source.Lang)>
        gic:Translation(gic:TxtTarget,Target.Lang)>)

<gic:Quality.Condition> ::=
 IF (<gic:Quality.TER(gic:TextTarget)::=<TERNo>)
 | IF (<gic:Quality.WER(gic:TextTarget)::=<WERNo>)
```

where `TM` is the specific memory size, `TERNo` is the Translation Error Rate number and `WERNo` is the Word Error Rate number.

Source language and target language are elements of a language list. We assume a `Language_List(L) = {L1,L2,L3,,Ln}` with `Source.Language(Ls)` ∈ `Language_List` and `Target.Language(Lt)` ∈ `Language_List`.

Actions can be state-specific constraint validations. The process can move to the next state. Acknowledgements are notifications messages to the user. The GIC process is embedded in the *Provenance* context that records Agent, Association and Activity.

List of Actions in the GIC domain:

```
ActionList ::= <Validation->Validation.Next>
               <Process->Next> ,
               <Acknowledgement>
               <Process->Provenance>

<Acknowledgement>::= <Ack_Msg>|<Ack_Msg_List>
```

```
< Ack_Msg_List> ::= <Validation.Msg_Display>
 |<System.Error>
 |<System.Delay>
 |<Process.Active>
 |<Process.Stop>
 |<Process.Abort>
 |<Process.End> (Finished)

<Process->Next> ::= <Process->gic:Text.Extraction>
 |<Process->gic:Text.GrammarCheck>
 |<Process->gic.Text.Name_Entity_Find>
 |<Process->gic:Text.Parsing>
 |<Process-> gic:Text.Segmentation>
 |<Process->gic:Translation>
 |<Process->gic:Quality Assessment>
 |<Process->PostEdit>

<Process->Provenance> ::= <prov:Agent> // PROVENANCE
                          <prov:Association>
                          <prov:Activity>

<prov:Agent> ::= <prov:InstantaneousEvent>
 |<prov:AgentInfluence>
 |<prov:Influence>
 |<prov:EntityInfluence>
 |<prov:Delegation>
 |<prov:Start>
 |<prov:End>
 |<prov:Derivation>
 |<prov:ActivityInfluence>
 |<prov:Quotation>
 |<prov:Generation>
 |<prov:Revision>

<prov:Association> ::= <prov:Role>
 | <prov:Invalidation>
 |<prov:Attribution>

<prov:Activity> ::= <prov:Entity>
 |<prov:Communication>
 |<prov:Plan>
 |<prov:Usage>
 |<prov:PrimarySource>
```

The Global Intelligent Content (GIC) semantic model is based on a abstract model and a content model. The abstract model captures the different resource types that are processed. The content model details the possible formats.

Abstract Model:

```
gic:Domain ->   gic:Resource
gic:Resource -> gic:Services |
                gic:Information Resource |
                gic:IdentifiedBy |
                gic:RefersTo |
                gic:AnnotatedBy
gic:InformationResource -> gic:Content | gic:Data
```

Content Model:

```
gic:Content -> gic:Content | cnt:Content
cnt:Content -> cnt:ContentAsBase64 |
               cnt:ContentAsText|
               cnt:ContentAsXML
cnt:ContentAsBase64-> cnt:Bytes
cnt:ContentAsText ->  cnt:Chars
cnt:ContentAsXML ->   cnt:Rest | cnt:Version |
                      cnt:LeadingMisc |
                      cnt:Standalone |
                      cnt:DeclaredEncoding |
                      cnt:dtDecl
cnt:dtDecl ->       cnt:dtDecl | cnt:DocTypeDecl
cnt:DocTypeDecl -> cnt:DocTypeName |
                   cnt:InternetSubset |
                   cnt:PublicId | cnt:SystemId
```

V. IMPLEMENTATION

While this paper focuses on the conceptual aspects such as models and languages, a prototype has been implemented. Our implementation (Figure 5) provides a platform that enables building configurable processes for content management problems and constraints running in the *Activiti* (http://activiti.org/) workflow engine. In this architecture, a cloud service layer performs data processing using the Content Service Bus (based on the *Alfresco* (https://www.alfresco.com/) content management system).

This implementation is the basis of the evaluation that looks at feasibility and transferability – see Evaluation Section VI. We introduce the business models and their implementation architecture first, before detailing the evaluation results in the next section.

A. Business Process Models

A business process model (BPM) is executed as a process in a sequential manner to validate functional and operational behaviour during the execution. Here, multiple participants work in a collaborative environment based on Activiti, Alfresco and the support services. Policy rule services define a process map of the entire application and its components (e.g., file type is valid for extraction, quality rating of translation). This process model consists of a number of content processing activities such as Extraction & Segmentation, NER, Machine Translation (MT), Quality estimation and Post-Edit.

One specific constraint, access control, shall be discussed separately. An access control policy defines the high-level set of rules according to the access control requirements. An access control model provides the access control/authorization security policy for accessing the content activities as well as security rights implemented in BPM services according to the user role. Access control mechanism enable low-level functions, which implement the access controls imposed by policies and are normally initiated by the model architecture.

Every activity has its own constraints. The flow of entire activities is performed in a sequential manner so that each activity's output becomes input to the next. The input data is processed through the content service bus (Alfresco) and the rule policy is applied to deal with constraints. The processed data is validated by the validation & verification service layer. After validation, processing progresses to the next stage of the Activiti process.

B. Architecture

The architecture of the system is based on services and standard browser thin clients. The application can be hosted on a Tomcat web server and all services could potentially be hosted on a cloud-based server. Architecturally, we separate out a service layer, see Figure 5. Reasons to architecturally separate a Service Layer from the execution engine include the introduction of loose coupling and interoperability.

The system has been developed on a 3-tier standard architecture: browser-based front-end thin clients, Tomcat Application server-based middleware, distributed database service as data service platforms. We follow the MVC (Model View

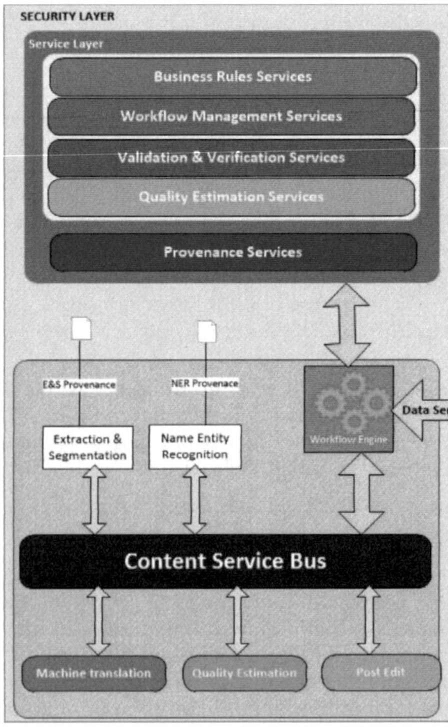

Figure 5. Prototype implementation architecture.

Controller) architecture. Multiple technologies are used to integrate each component of the content management solution:

- Common Bus/Hub: Alfresco is providing a common bus platform for all the activities.
- Application connectivity: Activiti and a cloud service layer play an important role to solve connectivity issues in the architecture.
- Data format and transformation: By using web services and other APIs, we maintain a common format for the entire application.
- Integration module: This module connects different sections of the application: Activiti, data and service bus, cloud service layer, Alfresco, and databases.

VI. EVALUATION

Explicit variability representation has benefits for the modelling stage. The feature and domain models control the variability, i.e., add dependability to the process design stage. It also allows formal reasoning about families of processes.

In this evaluation, we look at utility, transferability and feasibility. We balance this discussion by a consideration of restrictions and limitations.

A. Utility

The general utility is demonstrated empirically. The domain and feature models here specifically support domain experts.

Process and Cohort. We have worked with seven experts in the digital media and language technology space as part of our research centre. While these were largely researchers, their background was language technology and content management and all had development experience in that space, some also industrial experience. These experts were also from different universities. Despite being researchers, they act as application domain specialists in our case, being essentially language technology experts, but not business process experts. In total, seven expert have contributed to this process. However, we counted them as multipliiers as each of them had worked with other researchers, developers and users in industry.

Mechanism. The qualitative feedback, based on the expert interviews as the mechanism, confirms the need to provide a mechanism to customise business processes in a domain-specific way. We asked the participants about their opinion on the expected benefit of the approach, specifically whether this would lead to improved efficicency in the process modelling activities and whether the approach would be suitable for a non-expert in business modellling, with background in the application domain.

Results. The results of the expert interview can be summarised as follows:

- The experts confirm with majority (71%) that using the feature model, rule templates can be filled using the different feature aspects guided by the domain model without in-depth modelling expertise.
- The majority of experts (86%) in the evaluation have confirmed simplification or significant simplification in process modelling.

This confirms our hypothesis in this research laid out at the beginning.

B. Transferability

In addition, we looked at another process domain to assess the transferability of the solution [48]. Learning technology as another human-centred, domain-specific field was chosen.

Application Domain. In the learning domain, we examined learner interaction with content in a learning technology system [49], [50]. Again, the need to provide domain expert support to define constraints and rules for these processes became evident.

Observations. Here, educators act as process modellers and managers [15], specifically managing the educational content processing as an interactive process between learners, educators and content. Having been involved in the development of learning technology systems for years, tailoring these to specific courses and classes is required.

C. Feasibility Analysis

From a more technical perspective, we looked at the feasibility of implementing a production system from the existing prototype. The feasibility study (analysis of alternatives) is used to justify a project. It compares the various implementation alternatives based on their economic, technical and operational feasibility. The steps of creating a feasibility study are as follows [41]:

Determine implementation alternatives. We have discussed architectural choices in the Implementation.

Assess the economic feasibility for each alternative. The basic question is how well will the software product pay for itself? This has been looked at by performing a cost/benefit analysis. In this case, using open-source components has helped to reduce and justify the expenses for a research prototype.

Assess the technical feasibility for each alternative. The basic question is the possibility to build the software system. The set of feasible technologies is usually the intersection of the aspects implementation and integration. This has been demonstrated through the implementation with Activiti and Alfresco as core platforms that are widely used in practice.

D. Restrictions, Limitations and Constraints

The concerns below explain aspects, which impact on the specification, design, or implementation of the software system. These items may also contribute to restrict the scalability and performance of the system as well. Because of either the complexity or the cost of the implementation, the quality or delivery of the system may suffer.

Constraints that have impacted on the design of our solution are the following:

- The information and data exchanging between two activities during workflow processing.
- User management and security of overall system including alfresco CMS, workflow engine, rule engine and CNGL2 challenges.
- Validation of different systems at runtime.
- Interoperability between features and functions.
- Major constraint utilisation of translation memory and language model through services.
- Process acknowledgement or transaction information sharing between different activities of workflow.
- Error tracking and tracing during transaction.

VII. Conclusions

In presenting a variability and feature-oriented development approach for a domain-specific rule language for business process constraints, we have added adaptivity to process modelling. This benefits as follows:

- Often, business processes take domain-specific objects and activities into account in the process specification. Our aim is to make the process specification accessible to domain experts. We can provide domain experts with a set of structured variation mechanisms for the specification, processing and management of process rules as well as managing frequency changes of business processes along the variability scheme at for notations like BPMN.
- The technical contribution core is a rule generation technique for process variability and customisation. The novelty of our approach is a focus on process constraints and their rule-based management, advancing on structural variability. The result is flexible customisation of processes through constraints adaptation, rather than more intrusive process restructuring.

Cloud-based business processes-as-a-service (BPaaS) as an emerging trend signifies the need to adapt resources such as processes to different consumer needs (called customisation of multi-tenant resources in the cloud) [51]. Furthermore, self-service provisioning of resources also requires non-expert to manage this configuration. BPaaS relies on providing processes as customisable entities. Targeting constraints as the customisation point is clearly advantageous compared to customisation through restructuring. For BPaaS, if a generic service is provided to external users, the dynamic customisation of individual process instances would require the utilisation of a coordinated approach, e.g., through using a coordination model [52], [53]. Other architecture techniques can also be used to facilitate flexible and lightweight cloud-based provisioning of process instances, e.g., through containerisation [54].

We also see the need for further research that focuses on how to adapt the DSRL across different domains and how to convert conceptual models into generic domain-specific rule language, which are applicable to other domains. So far, this translation is semi-automatic, but shall be improved with a system that learns from existing rules and domain models, driven by the feature approach, to result in an automated DSRL generation.

Acknowledgment

This material is based upon works supported by the Science Foundation Ireland under Grant No. 07/CE/I1142 as part of the Centre for Global Intelligent Content (www.cngl.ie) at DCU.

References

[1] N. Mani and C. Pahl, "Controlled Variability Management for Business Process Model Constraints," International Conference on Software Engineering Advances ICSEA'2015, pp. 445-450. 2015.

[2] Ö. Tanrver and S. Bilgen, "A framework for reviewing domain specific conceptual models," CompStand & Interf, vol. 33, pp. 448-464, 2011.

[3] M. Asadi, B. Mohabbati, G. Groner, and D. Gasevic, "Development and validation of customized process models," Journal of Systems and Software, vol. 96, pp. 73-92, 2014.

[4] G. H. Alferez, V. Pelechano, R. Mazo, C. Salinesi, and D. Diaz, "Dynamic adaptation of service compositions with variability models," Journal of Systems and Software, vol. 91, pp. 24-47, 2014.

[5] J. Park, M. Moon, and K. Yeom, "Variability modeling to develop flexible service-oriented applications," Journal of Systems Science and Systems Engineering, vol. 20, pp. 193-216, 2011.

[6] M. Galster and A. Eberlein, "Identifying potential core assets in service-based systems to support the transition to service-oriented product lines," in 18th IEEE International Conference and Workshops on Engineering of Computer Based Systems (ECBS), pp. 179-186. 2011.

[7] R. Mietzner and F. Leymann, "Generation of BPEL customization processes for SaaS applications from variability descriptors," in IEEE International Conference on Services Computing, pp. 359-366. 2008.

[8] T. Nguyen, A. Colman, and J. Han, "Modeling and managing variability in process-based service compositions," in Service-Oriented Computing, Springer, pp. 404-420, 2011.

[9] C.-A. Sun, R. Rossing, M. Sinnema, P. Bulanov, and M. Aiello, "Modeling and managing the variability of Web service-based systems," Journal of Systems and Software, vol. 83, pp. 502-516, 2010.

[10] F. Puhlmann, A. Schnieders, J. Weiland, and M. Weske, "Variability mechanisms for process models," PESOA-Report TR17, pp. 10-61, 2005.

[11] M. L. Griss, J. Favaro, and M. d'Alessandro, "Integrating feature modeling with the RSEB," in International Conference on Software Reuse, 1998, pp. 76-85.

[12] D. Beuche, "Modeling and building software product lines with pure variants," in International Software Product Line Conference, Volume 2, 2012, pp. 255-255.

[13] T. Soininen and I. Niemel, "Developing a declarative rule language for applications in product configuration," in practical aspects of declarative languages, ed: Springer, 1998, pp. 305-319.

[14] S. Van Langenhove, "Towards the correctness of software behavior in uml: A model checking approach based on slicing," Ghent Univ, 2006.

[15] C. Pahl and N. Mani. "Managing Quality Constraints in Technology-managed Learning Content Processes," In: EdMedia'2014 Conference on Educational Media and Technology. 2014.

[16] K. C. Kang, S. Kim, J. Lee, K. Kim, E. Shin, and M. Huh, "FORM: A feature-oriented reuse method with domain-specific reference architectures," Annals of Software Engineering, vol. 5, pp. 143-168, 1998.

[17] M.X. Wang, K.Y. Bandara, and C. Pahl, "Process as a service distributed multi-tenant policy-based process runtime governance," IEEE International Conference on Services Computing, IEEE, 2010.

[18] Y. Huang, Z. Feng, K. He, and Y. Huang, "Ontology-based configuration for service-based business process model," In: IEEE International Conference on Services Computing, pp. 296303. 2013.

[19] N. Assy, W. Gaaloul, and B. Defude, "Mining configurable process fragments for business process design," In: Advancing the Impact of Design Science: Moving from Theory to Practice, DESRIST'2014. LNCS 8463, pp. 209224. 2014.

[20] M. Javed, Y. Abgaz and C. Pahl, "A Pattern-based Framework of Change Operators for Ontology Evolution," 4th International Workshop on Ontology Content OnToContent'09. 2009.

[21] C. Pahl, "A Pi-Calculus based framework for the composition and replacement of components," Conference on Object-Oriented Programming, Systems, Languages, and Applications OOPSLA'2001 Workshop on Specification and Verification of Component-Based Systems, 2001.

[22] M. Koning, C.-A. Sun, M. Sinnema, and P. Avgeriou, "VxBPEL: Supporting variability for Web services in BPEL," Information and Software Technology, vol. 51, pp. 258-269, 2009.

[23] M. Colombo, E. Di Nitto, and M. Mauri, "Scene: A service composition execution environment supporting dynamic changes disciplined through rules," in Service-Oriented Computing, pp. 191-202. 2006.

[24] A. Kumar and W. Yao, "Design and management of flexible process variants using templates and rules," Computers in Industry, vol. 63, pp. 112-130, 2012.

[25] D. Fang, X. Liu, I. Romdhani, P. Jamshidi, and C. Pahl, "An agility-oriented and fuzziness-embedded semantic model for collaborative cloud service search, retrieval and recommendation," Future Generation Computer Systems, Volume 56, pp. 11-26. 2016.

[26] M. Nakamura, T. Kushida, A. Bhamidipaty, and M. Chetlur, "A multi-layered architecture for process variation management," in World Conference on Services-II, SERVICES'09, pp. 71-78, 2009.

[27] A. Hallerbach, T. Bauer, and M. Reichert, "Capturing variability in business process models: the Provop approach," Jrnl of Software Maintenance and Evolution: Research and Practice 22, pp. 519-546, 2010.

[28] R. Mohan, M. A. Cohen, and J. Schiefer, "A state machine based approach for a process driven development of web-applications," in Advanced Information Systems Engineering, 2002, pp. 52-66.

[29] A. Lazovik and H. Ludwig, "Managing process customizability and customization: Model, language and process," in Web Information Systems Engineering, 2007, pp. 373-384.

[30] M. Helfert, "Business informatics: An engineering perspective on information systems." Journal of Information Technology Education 7:223-245. 2008.

[31] P. Jamshidi, M. Ghafari, A. Ahmad, and C. Pahl, "A framework for classifying and comparing architecture-centric software evolution research," European Conference on Software Maintenance and Reengineering, 2013.

[32] Y.-J. Hu, C.-L. Yeh, and W. Laun, "Challenges for rule systems on the web," Rule Interchange and Applications, 2009, pp. 4-16.

[33] A. Paschke, H. Boley, Z. Zhao, K. Teymourian, and T. Athan, "Reaction RuleML 1.0" in Rules on the Web: Research and Applications, 2012, pp. 100-119.

[34] A. van Deursen, P. Klint, and J. Visser, "Domain-specific languages: an annotated bibliography," SIGPLAN Not., vol. 35, pp. 26-36, 2000

[35] M. Mernik, J. Heering, and A. M. Sloane, "When and how to develop domain-specific languages," ACM computing surveys, 37:316-344, 2005.

[36] P.-Y. Schobbens, P. Heymans, J.-C. Trigaux, and Y. Bontemps, "Generic semantics of feature diagrams," Computer Networks, vol. 51, pp. 456-479, 2/7/ 2007.

[37] D. Benavides, S. Segura, P. Trinidad, and A. R. Corts, "FAMA: Tooling a framework for the automated analysis of feature models," VaMoS, 2007.

[38] M. Antkiewicz and K. Czarnecki, "FeaturePlugin: feature modeling plug-in for Eclipse," Workshop on Eclipse Techn, 2004, pp. 67-72.

[39] A. Classen, Q. Boucher, and P. Heymans, "A text-based approach to feature modelling: Syntax and semantics of TVL," Science of Computer Programming, vol. 76, pp. 1130-1143, 2011.

[40] K. C. Kang, S. G. Cohen, J. A. Hess, W. E. Novak, and A. S. Peterson, "Feature-oriented domain analysis (FODA) feasibility study," DTIC. 1990.

[41] A. van Deursen and P. Klint, "Domain-specific language design requires feature descriptions," Jrnl of Comp and Inf Technology, vol. 10, pp. 1-17, 2002.

[42] M. Acher, P. Collet, P. Lahire, and R. B. France, "A domain-specific language for managing feature models," in ACM Symp on Applied Computing, 2011, pp. 1333-1340.

[43] C. Pahl, "A Formal Composition and Interaction Model for a Web Component Platform," Electronic Notes in Theoretical Computer Science, Volume 66, Issue 4, Pages 67-81, Formal Methods and Component Interaction (ICALP 2002 Satellite Workshop), 2002.

[44] C. Pahl, S. Giesecke, and W. Hasselbring, "Ontology-based Modelling of Architectural Styles," Information and Software Technology, vol. 51(12), pp. 1739-1749, 2009.

[45] C. Pahl, "An ontology for software component matching," International Journal on Software Tools for Technology Transfer, vol 9(2), pp. 169-178, 2007.

[46] M.X. Wang, K.Y. Bandara, and C. Pahl, "Integrated constraint violation handling for dynamic service composition," IEEE International Conference on Services Computing, 2009, pp. 168-175.

[47] H. Boley, A. Paschke, and O. Shafiq, "RuleML 1.0: the overarching specification of web rules," Lecture Notes in Computer Science. 6403, 162-178, 2010.

[48] M. Helfert, "Challenges of business processes management in healthcare: Experience in the Irish healthcare sector." Business Process Management Journal 15, no. 6, 937-952. 2009.

[49] S. Murray, J. Ryan, and C. Pahl. "A tool-mediated cognitive apprenticeship approach for a computer engineering course," 3rd IEEE Conference on Advanced Learning Technologies, 2003.

[50] X. Lei, C. Pahl, and D. Donnellan, "An evaluation technique for content interaction in web-based teaching and learning environments," The 3rd IEEE International Conference on Advanced Learning Technologies 2003, IEEE, 2003.

[51] C. Pahl and H. Xiong, "Migration to PaaS Clouds - Migration Process and Architectural Concerns," IEEE 7th International Symposium on the Maintenance and Evolution of Service-Oriented and Cloud-Based Systems MESOCA'13. IEEE. 2013.

[52] E.-E. Doberkat, W. Franke, U. Gutenbeil, W. Hasselbring, U. Lammers, and C. Pahl, "PROSET - a Language for Prototyping with Sets," International Workshop on Rapid System Prototyping, pp. 235-248. 1992.

[53] F. Fowley, C. Pahl, and L. Zhang, "A comparison framework and review of service brokerage solutions for cloud architectures," 1st International Workshop on Cloud Service Brokerage (CSB'2013). 2013.

[54] C. Pahl, "Containerisation and the PaaS Cloud," IEEE Cloud Computing, 2(3). pp. 24-31, 2015.

Automatic Information Flow Validation for High-Assurance Systems

Kevin Müller*, Sascha Uhrig*, Flemming Nielson†, Hanne Riis Nielson†,
Ximeng Li‡†, Michael Paulitsch§ and Georg Sigl¶
*Airbus Group · Munich, Germany · Email: [Kevin.Mueller|Sascha.Uhrig]@airbus.com
†DTU Compute · Technical University of Denmark · Email: [fnie|hrni|ximl]@dtu.dk
‡Technische Universität Darmstadt · Darmstadt, Germany · Email: li@mais.informatik.tu-darmstadt.de
§Thales Austria GmbH · Vienna, Austria · Email: Michael.Paulitsch@thalesgroup.com
¶Technische Universität München · Munich, Germany · Email: sigl@tum.de

Abstract*—Nowaydays, safety-critical systems in high-assurance domains such as aviation or transportation need to consider secure operation and demonstrate its reliable operation by presenting domain-specific level of evidences. Many tools for automated code analyses and automated testing exist to ensure safe and secure operation; however, ensuring secure information flows is new in the high-assurance domains. The Decentralized Label Model (DLM) allows to partially automate, model and prove correct information flows in applications' source code. Unfortunately, the DLM targets Java applications; hence, it is not applicable for many high-assurance domains with strong real-time guarantees. Reasons are issues with the dynamic character of object-oriented programming or the in general uncertain behaviors of features like garbage collectors of the commonly necessary runtime environments. Hence, many high-assurance systems are still implemented in C. In this article, we discuss DLM in the context of such high-assurance systems. For this, we adjust the DLM to the programming language C and developed a suitable tool checker, called *Cif*. Apart from proving the correctness of information flows statically, Cif is able to illustrate the implemented information flows graphically in a dependency graph. We present this power on generic use cases appearing in almost each program. We further investigate use cases from the high-assurance domains of avionics and railway to identify commonalities regarding security. A common challenge is the development of secure gateways mediating the data transfer between security domains. To demonstrate the benefits of Cif, we applied our method to such a gateway implementation. During the DLM annotation of the use case's C source code, we identified issues in the current DLM policies, in particular, on annotating special data-dependencies. To solve these issues, we extend the data agnostic character of the traditional DLM and present our new concept on the gateway use case. Even though this paper uses examples from aviation and railway, our approach can be applied equally well to any other safety-critical or security-critical system. This paper demonstrates the power of Cif and its capability to graphically illustrate information flows, and discusses its utility on selected C code examples. It also presents extension to the DLM theory to overcome identified shortcomings.

***Index Terms*—Security; High-Assurance; Information Flow; Decentralized Label Model**

I. Introduction

Safety-critical systems in the domains of aviation, transportation systems, automotive, medical applications or industrial control have to show their correct implementation with a domain-dependent level of assurance. Due to the changing IT environments and the increased connectivity demands in the recent years, these system do not operate isolated anymore. Moreover, they are subject of attacks that require additional means to protect the security of the systems. The use cases discussed by this article are derived by the safety and security demands of the avionic and railway domains, both highly restricted and controlled domains for high-assurance systems. This article extends our previous contribution [1] on presenting how security-typed languages can improve the code quality and the automated assurance of correct implementation of C programs, with use cases from both mentioned domains. Furthermore, the paper will provide improvements to the theory of the Decentralized Label Model (DLM); being anon an example for security-typed technologies.

Aviation software [2] and hardware [3] have to follow strict development processes and require certification by national authorities. Recently, developers of avionics, the electronics on-board of aircrafts, have implemented systems following the concepts of Integrated Modular Avionics (IMA) [4] to reduce costs and increase functionality. IMA achieves a system design of safe integration and consolidation of applications with various criticality on one hardware platform. The architecture depends on the provision of separated runtime environments, so called partitions. Targeting security aspects of systems, a similar architectural approach has been developed with the concept of Multiple Independent Levels of Security (MILS) [5]. This architectural approach depends on strict separation of processing resources and information flow control. A *Separation Kernel* [6] is a special certifiable operating system that can provide both mentioned properties.

Apart from having such architectural approaches to handle the emerging safety and security requirements for high assurance systems, the developers also have to prove the correct implementation of their software applications. For safety, the aviation industry applies various forms of code analysis [7][8][9] in order to evidently ensure correct implementation of requirements. For security, in particular on secure information flows, the aviation industry only has limited means available, which are not mandatory yet.

The base for *secure* or *correct information flows* in this paper are security policies for systems that contain rules on flow restrictions from input to outputs of the system, or fine-grained, between variables in a program code. On secure information flow, the DLM [10] is a promising approach.

DLM introduces annotations into the source code. These annotations allow to model an information flow policy directly on source code level, mainly by extending the declaration of variables. This avoids additional translations between model and implementation. Tool support allows to prove the implemented information flows and the defined flow policy regarding consistency. In short, DLM extends the type system of a programming language to assure that a security policy modeled by label annotations of variables is not violated in the program flow.

Our research challenge here is to apply this model to a recurring generic use case of a gateway application. After analyzing use cases of two high assurance industries, we identified this use case as a common assurance challenge in both, the avionic and railway industry. DLM is currently available for the Java programming language [11]. Java is a relatively strongly typed language and, hence, appears at first sight as a very good choice. However, among other aspects the dynamic character of object-oriented languages such as Java introduces additional issues for the certification process [12]. Furthermore, common features such as the Java Runtime Environment introduces potentially unpredictable and harmful delays during execution. For high-criticality applications this is not acceptable as they require high availability and real-time properties like low response times. Hence, as most high-assurance systems remain to be implemented in C, our first task is the adaption of DLM to the C language. Then, we leverage the compositional nature of the MILS architecture to deliver overall security guarantees by combining the evidences of correct information flow provided by the DLM-certified application and by the underlying Separation Kernel. This combination of evidences will also help to obtain security certifications for such complex systems in the future.

In this article we will discuss the following contributions:

DLM for C language: We propose an extension of the C language in order to express and check information flow policies by code annotations; we discuss in Section IV the challenges in adapting to C rather than Java.

Real Use-Case Annotations: While DLM has been successfully developed to deal with typical applications written in Java, we investigate the extent to which embedded applications written in C present other challenges. To be concrete we study in Sections V-VI the application of the DLM to a real-world use case from the avionic and railway domains, namely a demultiplexer that is present in many high security-demanding applications, in particular in the high assurance gateway being developed as a research demonstrator.

Graphical Representation of Information Flows: To make information flow policies useful for engineers working in avionics and automotive, we consider it important to develop a useful graphical representation. To this end we develop a graphical format for presenting the information flows. This helps engineers to identify unspecified flows and to avoid information leakage due to negligent programming.

Improvements to DLM Theory: It turns out that the straight adaptation of DLM to real source code for embedded systems written in C gives rise to some overhead regarding code size increase. In order to reduce this overhead, we suggest in Section IX improvements to the DLM so as to better deal with the content-dependent nature of policies as is typical of systems making use of demultiplexers.

This article is structured as follows: Section II discusses recent research papers fitting to the topic of this paper. In Section III, we introduce the DLM as described by Myers initially. Our adaptation of DLM to the C language and the resulting tool checker *Cif* are described in Section IV. In Section V, we discuss common code snippets and their verification using *Cif*. This also includes the demonstration of the graphical information flow output of our tool. Section VI and Section VII present the security domains inside the aviation and railway industry to motivate our use case. Section VIII discusses this high assurance use case identified as challenging question of both domains. The section further connects security-typed languages with security design principles, such as MILS. In this chapter, we also assess our approach and identify shortcomings in the current DLM theory. Section IX uses the previous assessment and suggests improvements to the DLM theory. Finally, we conclude our work in Section X.

II. Related Work

Sabelfeld and Myers present in [13] an extensive survey on research of security typed languages within the last decades. The content of the entire paper provides a good overview to position the research contribution of our paper.

The DLM on which this paper is based was proposed by Myers and Liskov [10] for secure information flow in the Java language. This model features decentralized trust relation between security principals. Known applications (appearing to be of mostly academic nature) are:

- *Civitas*: a secure voting system
- *JPmail*: an email client with information-flow control
- *Fabric*, *SIF* and *Swift*: being web applications.

In this paper, we adapt DLM to the C programming language, extending its usage scope to high-assurance embedded systems adopted in real-world industry.

An alternative approach closely related to ours is the Data Flow Logic (DFL) proposed by Greve in [14]. This features a C language extension that augments source code and adds security domains to variables. Furthermore, his approach allows to formulate flow contracts between domains. These annotations describe an information flow policy, which can be analyzed by a DFL prover. DFL has been used to annotate the source code of a Xen-based Separation Kernel [15]. Whereas Greve builds largely on Mandatory Access Control, we base our approach on Decentralized Information Flow Control. The decentralized approach introduces a mutual distrust among data owners, all having an equal security level. Hence, DLM avoids the automatically given hierarchy of the approaches of mandatory access control usually relying on at least one super user.

III. Decentralized Label Model (DLM)

The DLM [10] is a language-based technology allowing to prove correct information flows within a program's source code. Section III-A introduces the fundamentals of the model. The following Section III-B focusses on the information flow control.

A. General Model

The model uses *principals* to express flow policies. By default a mutual distrust is present between all defined principals. Principals can delegate their authority to other principals and, hence, can issue a trust relation. In DLM, principals own data and can define read (confidentiality) and write (integrity) policies for other principals in order to allow access to the data. Consequently, the union of owners and readers or writers respectively defines the effective set of readers or writers of a data item. DLM offers two special principals:

1) Top Principal $*$: As owner representing the set of all principals; as reader or writer representing the empty set of principals, i.e., effectively no other principal except the involved owners of this policy
2) Bottom Principal _: As owner representing the empty set of principals; as reader or writer representing the set of all principals.

Additional information on this are described in [16]. In practice *labels*, which annotate the source code, express the DLM policies. An example is:

```
int {Alice->Bob; Alice<-_} x;
int {*->_; *<-*} y;
```

Listing 1. Declaration of a DLM-annotated Variable

This presents a label definition using curly brackets as token[1]. In this example the principal `Alice` owns the data stored in the integer variable `x` for both the confidentiality and integrity policy. The first part of the label `Alice->Bob` expresses a confidentiality policy, also called reader policy. In this example the owner Alice allows Bob to read the data. The second part of the label expresses an integrity policy, or writer policy. In this example it defines that Alice allows all other principals write access to the variable `x`. For the declaration of `y` the reader policy expresses that all principals believe that all principals can read the data and the writer policy expresses that all principals believe that no principal has modified the data. Overall, this variable has low flow restrictions.

In DLM one may also form a conjunction of principals, like `Alice&Bob->Chuck`. This confidentiality policy is equivalent to `Alice->Chuck;Bob->Chuck` and means that the beliefs of Alice and Bob have to be fulfilled [17].

[1]In the following we will use the compiler technology-based term *token* and the DLM-based term *annotation* as synonyms.

B. Information Flow Control

Using these augmentations on a piece of source code, a static checking tool is able to prove whether all beliefs expressed by labels are fulfilled. A data flow from a source to an *at least equally restricted* destination is a *correct* information flow. In contrast an invalid flow is detected if data flows from a source to a destination that is less restricted than the source. A destination is *at least as restricted* as the source if:

- the confidentiality policy keeps or increases the set of owners and/or keeps or decreases the set of readers, and
- the integrity policy keeps or decreases the set of owners and/or keeps or increases the set of writers

```
int {Alice->Bob; Alice<-_}
  x = 1;
int {Alice&Bob->*; Alice<-_}
  y = 0;

y = x;
```

Listing 2. Valid Direct Information Flow

```
int {Alice->Bob; Alice<-_}
  x = 1;
int {Alice&Bob->*; Alice<-_}
  y = 0;

if(y == 0)
  x = 0;
```

Listing 3. Invalid Implicit Information Flow

Listing 2 shows an example of a valid direct information flow from the source variable x to the destination y. Apart from these direct assignments, DLM is also able to detect invalid implicit flows. The example in Listing 3 causes an influence on variable x if the condition $y == 0$ is true. Hence, depending on the value of y the data in variable x gets modified, i.e., allowing x to observe the status of y. However, y is more restrictive than x, i.e., x is not allowed to observe the value of y. Thus, the flow in Listing 3 is invalid.

To analyse those implicit flows, DLM also examines each instruction against the current label of the Program Counter (PC). As in Java Information Flow (Jif) [18], the PC represents the current context in the program and not the actual program counter register. A statement is only valid if the PC is *no more restrictive* than the involved variables of the statement. The PC label is calculated for each program block and is re-calculated at its entrance depending on the condition the block has been entered.

IV. Decentralized Label Model (DLM) for C Language (Cif)

During our application of the DLM to the C language we run into several challenges. The following sections provides design choices and implementation details on our implementation.

A. Type Checking Tool

The first step of our work was to define C annotations in order to apply DLM to this language. An annotated C program shall act as input for the DLM checker, in the following called *C Information Flow (Cif)*. Cif analyzes the program according to the defined information flow policy. Depending on the syntax of the annotations, the resulting C code can no longer be used as input for usual C compilers, such as the *gcc*. To still be able to compile the program, three major possibilities for implementing the Cif are available:

1) a Cif checking tool that translates the annotated input source code into valid C code by removing all labels
2) a DLM extension to available compilers, such as *gcc*
3) embedding labels into compiler-transparent comments using */* label */*

We decided for Option 1. We did not consider Option 2 to avoid necessary coding efforts for modifying and maintaining a specialized C compiler. We also did not take Option 3, due to the higher error-proneness resulting from the fact that our checker, additionally, had to decide whether a comment's content is a label or a comment. If a developer does not comply with the recognition syntax for labels, the checker could interpret actual labels as comments and omit their analysis. In the worst case the checker could vacuously report correct information flow for a program without carrying out any label comparison.

For being able to analyze the C source code statically, the first step in the tool chain is to resolve all macro definitions and to include the header files into one file. Fortunately, this step can be performed by using the *gcc*, since the compiler does not perform a syntax verification during the macro replacement. The resulting file then is used as input for our Cif checking tool. If Cif does not report any information flow violation, the tool will create a C-compliant source code by removing all annotations. Additional source code verifications, e.g., by Astrée [8], or the compilation for the final binary process on this plain C source file.

B. Syntax Extension of C Language

For the format and semantics of annotations, we decided to adapt the concepts of Jif [18], the DLM implementation for Java. So, we use curly brackets as token for the labels. For variable declarations, these labels have to be placed in between the type indicator and the name of the variable (cf. Listing 1). Compared to the reference implementation of Jif, in Cif we additionally had to deal with pointers of the C language. We annotate and handle pointers the same way as usual variables, i.e., when using a pointer to reference to an array element or other values, the labels of pointer and target variable have to match accordingly to DLM. However, Cif does not monitor overflows or invalid references whose detection calls for pointer calculations. We expect that additional tools (e.g., Astrée [8]) detect such coding errors. This tool is already used successfully for checking code of avionic equipment.

In addition to the new label tokens, we extended the syntax of the C language with five further tokens:

principal *p1, ..., pn*: This token announces all used principals to the Cif.

actsFor(*p, q*): This token statically creates a trust relation that principal p is allowed to act for principal q in the entire source code.

declassify(*variable*, {*label*}): This token allows to loosen a confidentiality policy in order to relabel variables if required. Cif checks whether the new confidentiality policy is less restrictive than the present one.

endorse(*variable*, {*label*}): This token allows to loosen an integrity policy in order to relabel variables if required. Cif checks whether the new integrity policy is less restrictive than the present one.

PC_bypass({*label*}): This token allows to relabel the PC label without further checks of correct usage.

C. Function Declaration

In the C language functions can have a separate declaration called prototype. For the declaration of functions and prototypes, we also adapted the already developed concepts from Jif. In Jif a method (the representation for a function in object-oriented languages) has four labels:

1) **Begin Label** defines the side effects of the function like accesses to global variables. The begin label is the initial PC label for the function's body. From a function caller's perspective the current caller's PC label needs to be *no more restrictive* than the begin label of the called function.
2) **Parameter Labels** define for each parameter the corresponding label. From a caller's perspective these parameter labels have to match with the assigned values.
3) **Return Label** defines the label of the return value of the function. In Cif, a function returning *void* cannot have a return label. From a caller's perspective the variable that receives the returned value needs to be at least equally restrictive as the return label.
4) **End Label** defines a label for the caller's observation how the function terminates. Since C does not throw exceptions and functions return equally every time, we omitted verifications of end labels in our Cif implementation.

Listing 4 shows the syntax for defining a function prototype with label annotations in Cif.

The definition of function labels regarding their optional prototype labels needs to be at least as restrictive, i.e., Cif allows functions to be more restrictive than their prototypes. All labels are optional augmentation to the C syntax. If the developer does not insert a label, Cif will use meaningful default labels that basically define the missing label most restrictively. Additionally, we implemented a label inheritance, which allows to inherit the real label of a caller's parameter value to the begin label, return label or other parameter labels of the function. This feature is useful for the annotation of

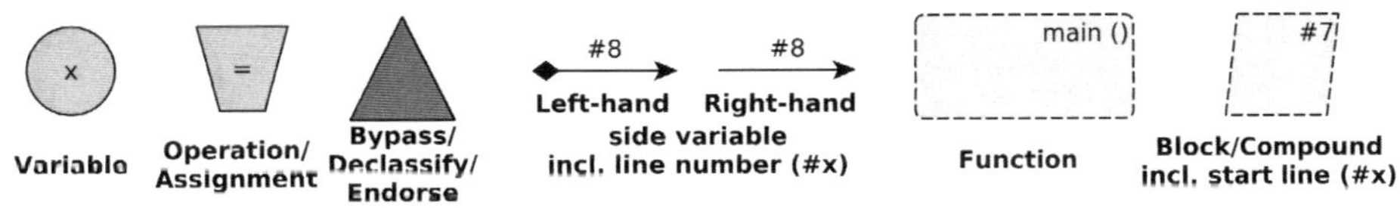

Fig. 1. Legend for Flow Graphs

```
       return label      inherited begin label   parameter label               end label
int {Alice->Bob} func {param} (int {Alice->*} param) : {Alice->*};
```

Listing 4. Definition of a function with DLM annotations in Cif.

system library functions, such as *memcpy(...)* that are used by callers with divergent parameter labels and can have side effects on global variables. At this stage Cif does not support the full inheritance of parameter labels to variable declarations inside the function's body.

D. Using System Libraries

Developers use systems libraries in their applications not only for convenience (e.g., to avoid reimplementation of common functionality) but also to perform necessary interaction with the runtime environment and the underlying operating system.

Hence, the system library provides an interface to the environment of the application, which mostly is not under the assurance control of the application's programmer. However, the code executed by library functions can heavily affect and also violate an application's information flow policy. Consequently, a system library needs to provide means for its functions to express the applied information flow policy and evidences to fully acknowledge this policy internally. In the best case, these evidences are also available by using our DLM approach. For Jif, the developers have annotated parts of the Java system library with DLM annotations that provide the major data structures and core I/O operations. Unfortunately, these annotations and its checks applied to all library functions demand many working hours and would exceed the available resource of many C development projects and, in particular, this research study. Luckily, other methods are conceivable, e.g., to gain evidences by security certification efforts of the environment. For our use case, the system software (a special Separation Kernel) was under security certification at the time of this study. Assuming the certification will be successful, we can assume its internals behave as specified. Furthermore, the research community worked on the formal specification and verification of Separation Kernels intensively, allowing us to trust the kernel if such methods have been applied [19], [20], [21]. However, we still had to create a special version of the system library's header file. This header file contains DLM-annotated prototype definitions of all functions of the Separation Kernel's system library. The Cif checker takes this file as optional input.

V. USE CASES

This section demonstrates the power of Cif by explaining usually appearing code snippets. For all examples Cif verifies the information flow modeled with the code annotations. If the information flow is valid according to the defined policy, Cif will output an unlabeled version of the C source code and a graphical representation of the flows in the source code. The format of this graphical representation is "graphml", hence, capable of further parsing and easy to import into other tools as well as documentation. Figure 1 shows the used symbols and their interpretations in these graphs. In general, the # symbol and its following number indicates the line of the command's or flow's implementation in the source code.

A. Direct Assignment

Listing 5 presents the first use case with a sequence of normal assignments.

```
principal Alice, Bob, Chuck;

void main {_->_;*<-*} ()
{
  int {Alice->Bob, Chuck} x = 0;
  int {Alice->Bob} y;
  int {Alice->*} z;

  y = x;
  z = y;
  z = x;
}
```

Listing 5. Sequence of Valid Direct Flows

In this example x is the least restrictive variable, y the second most restrictive variable and z the most restrictive variable. Thus, flows from $x \to y$, $y \to z$ and $x \to z$ are valid. Cif verifies this source code successfully and create the graphical flow representation depicted in Figure 2.

B. Indirect Assignment

Listing 6 shows an example of invalid indirect information flow. Cif reports an information flow violation, since all flows in the compound environment of the true if statement need to be at least as restrictive as the label of the decision variable

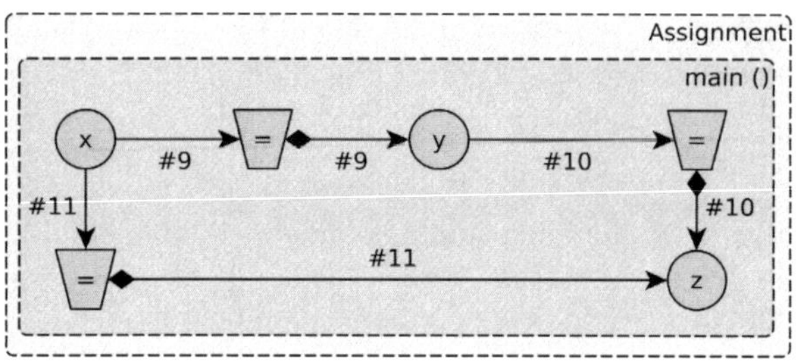

Fig. 2. Flow Graph for Listing 5

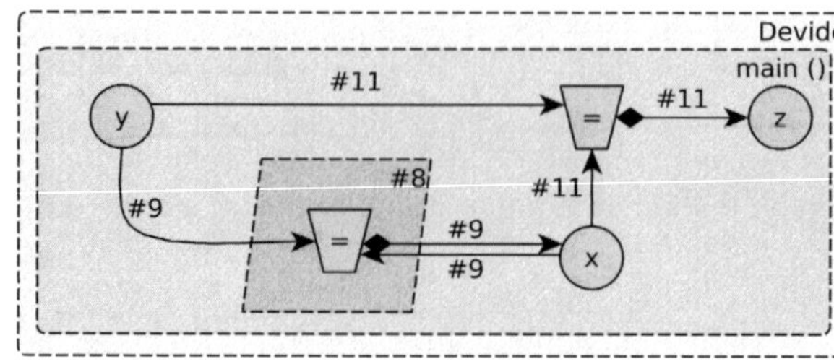

Fig. 3. Flow Graph for Listing 7

z. However, x and y are less restrictive and, hence, a flow to x is not allow. Additionally, this example shows how Cif can detect coding mistakes. It is obvious that the programmer wants to prove that y is not equal to 0 to avoid the Divide-by-Zero fault. However, the programmer puts the wrong variable in the if statement. Listing 7 corrects this coding mistake. For this source code, Cif verifies that the information flow is correct. Additionally, it generates the graphical output shown in Figure 3.

```
1  principal Alice, Bob;
2
3  void main {_->_;*<-*} ()
4  {
5    int {Alice->Bob} x, y;
6    int {Alice->*} z = 0;
7
8    if(z != 0) {
9      x = x / y;
10   }
11   z = x;
12 }
```

Listing 6. Invalid Indirect Flow

```
1  principal Alice, Bob;
2
3  void main {_->_;*<-*} ()
4  {
5    int {Alice->Bob} x, y;
6    int {Alice->*} z = 0;
7
8    if(y != 0) {
9      x = x / y;
10   }
11   z = x;
12 }
```

Listing 7. Valid Indirect Flow

Remarkable in Figure 3 is the assignment operation in line 9, represented inside the block environment of the if statement but depending on variables located outside of the block. Hence, Cif parses the code correctly. Also note, in the graphical representation z depends on input of x and y, even if the source code only assigns x to z in line 11. This relation is also depicted correctly, due to the operation in line 9 on which y influences x and, thus, also z indirectly.

Another valid indirect flow is shown in Listing 8. Interesting on this example is the proper representation of the graphical output in Figure 4. This output visualizes the influence of z on the operation in the positive if environment, even if z is not directly involved in the operation.

```
principal Alice, Bob;

void main {_->_;*<-*} ()
{
  int {Alice->Bob} x, y, z;

  if(z != 0) {
    x = x + y;
  }
}
```

Listing 8. Valid Indirect Flow

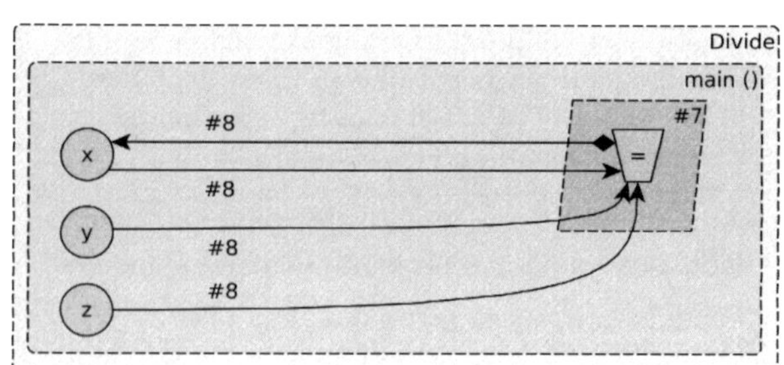

Fig. 4. Flow Graph for Listing 8

C. Function Calls

A more sophisticated example is the execution of functions. Listing 9 shows a common function call using the inheritance of DLM annotations. Line 3 declares the function. The label {a} signals the DLM interpreter to inherit the label of the declared parameter when calling the function; i.e., the label of parameter a for both, the label of parameter b and the return label. Essentially, this annotation of the function means that the data labels keep their restrictveness during the execution of the function. Line 14 and line 15 call the function twice with different parameters. The graphical representation of this flow in Figure 5 identifies the two independent function calls by the different lines of the code in which the function and operation is placed.

```
1  principal Alice, Bob;
2
3  float {a} func (int {Alice->Bob} a,
       float {a} b)
4  {
5    return a + b;
6  }
7
8  int {*->*} main {_->_} ()
9  {
10   int {Alice->Bob} y;
11   float {Alice->Bob} x;
12   float {Alice->*} z;
13
14   x = func(y,x);
15   z = func(y,0);
16
17   return 0;
18 }
```

Listing 9. Valid Function Calls

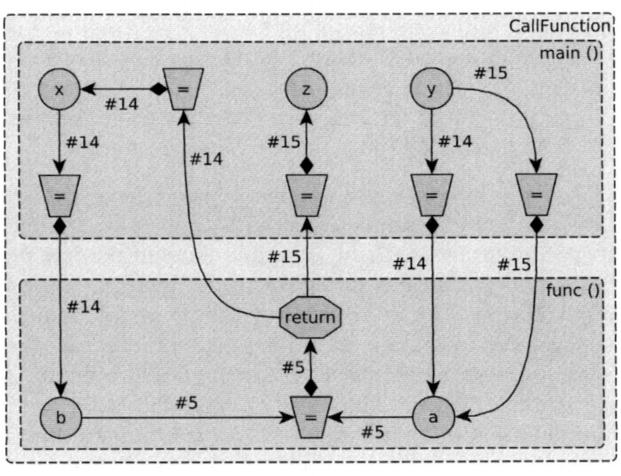

Fig. 5. Flow Graph for Listing 9

D. Declassify, Endorse and Bypassing the PC

1) Using Declassify and Endorse: Strictly adhering to the basic rules of DLM incurs the label-creeping problem [13]; the developer has to make information flow to more and more restrictive destinations. This unavoidably leads to the situation that information will be stored in the most restrictive variable and is not allowed to flow to some lower restricted destinations. Hence, sometimes developers need to manually declassify (for confidentiality) or endorse (for integrity) variables in order to make them usable for some other parts of the program. These intended breaches in the information flow policy need special care in code reviews and, hence, it is desirable that our Cif allows the identification of such sections in an analyzable way. Listing 10 provides an example using both, the endorse and declassify statement. To allow an assignment of a to b in line 9 an endorsement of the information stored in a is necessary. The destination b of this flow is less restrictive in its integrity policy than a, since `Alice` restricts `Bob` to not modify b anymore. In line 10, we perform a similar operation with the confidentiality policy. The destination c is less restrictive than b, since `Alice` believes for b that `Bob` cannot read the information, while `Bob` can read c.

The graphical output in Figure 6 depicts both statements correctly, and marks them with a special shape and color in order to attract attention to these downgrading-related elements.

```
1  principal Alice, Bob;
2
3  void main {_->_;*<-*} ()
4  {
5    int {Alice->*; Alice<-Bob} a;
6    int {Alice->*; Alice<-*}   b;
7    int {Alice->Bob; Alice<-*} c;
8
9    b = endorse(a, {Alice->*;
                     Alice<-*});
10   c = declassify(b, {Alice->Bob;
                     Alice<-*});
11 }
```

Listing 10. Endorse and Declassify

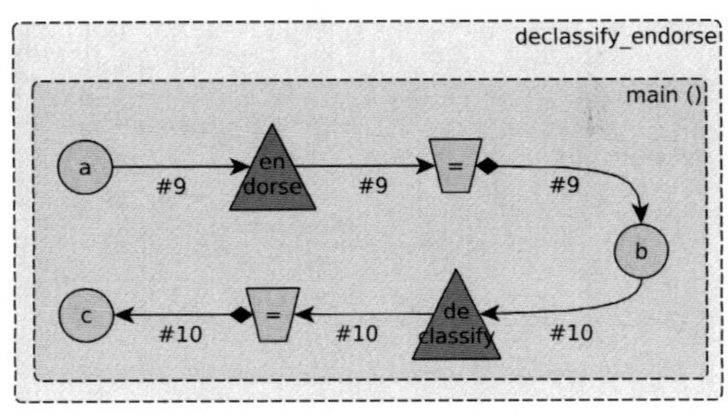

Fig. 6. Flow Graph for Listing 10

2) Bypassing the PC label: In the example of Listing 11 we use a simple login function to prove a user-provided uID and $pass$ against the stored login credentials. If the userID and the password match, a global variable $loggedIn$ is set to 1 to signal other parts of the application that the user is logged-in. The principal $System$ owns this status variable and represents the only reader of the variable. The principal $User$ owns both input variables uID and $pass$. The interesting lines of this example are lines 16–18, i.e., the conditional block that checks whether the provided credentials are correct and change the status variable $loggedIn$. Note, that this examples also presents Cif's treatment of pointers on the `strcmp` function. Due to the variables in the boolean condition of the *if* statement, the PC label inside the following block is `System->` & `User->`. However, this PC is not more restrictive than the label of *loggedIn* labeled with `System->`. Hence, Cif would report an invalid indirect information flow on this line. To finally allow this light and useful violation of the information flow requirement, the programmer needs to manually downgrade or bypass the PC label as shown in line 17. In order to identify such manual modifications of the information flow policy, Cif also adds this information in the generated graphical representation by using a red triangle indicating the warning (see Figure 7). This shall enable code reviewers to identify the critical sections of the code to perform their (manual) review on these sections intensively.

```
1   principal User, System;
2
3   int {System->*} loggedIn = 0;
4
5   int {*->*} strcmp {*->*}
        (const char {*->*} *str1,
         const char {*->*} *str2)
6   {
7     for(; *str1==*str2 && *str1; str1++,
          str2++) ;
8     return *str1 - *str2;
9   }
10
11  void checkUser {System->*}
        (const int {User->*} uID,
         const char {User->*} * const pass)
12  {
13    const int {System->*} regUID = 1;
14    const char {System->*} const
          regPass[] = "";
15
16    if(regUID == uID &&
          !strcmp(regPass, pass)) {
17      PC_bypass({System->*});
18      loggedIn = 1;
19    }
20  }
```

Listing 11. Login Function

VI. Use-Case: The Avionics Security Domains

Due to their diversity in functions and criticality on the aircraft's safety, on-board networks are divided into security domains. The ARINC standards (ARINC 664 [22] and ARINC 811 [23]) define four domains also depicted in Figure 8:

1. **Aircraft Control:** The most critical domain hosting systems that support the safe operation of the aircraft, such as cockpit displays and system for environmental or propulsion control. This domain provides information to other (lower) domains but does not depend on them.
2. **Airline Information Services:** This domain acts as security perimeter between the Aircraft Control Domain and lower domains. Among others it hosts systems for crew information or maintenance.
3. **Passenger Information and Entertainment Services:** While being the most dynamic on-board domain regarding software updates, this domain hosts systems related to the passenger's entertainment and other services such as Internet access.
4. **Passenger-owned Devices:** This domain hosts mobile systems brought on-board by the passengers. They may connect to aircraft services via an interface of the Passenger Information and Entertainment Services Domain.

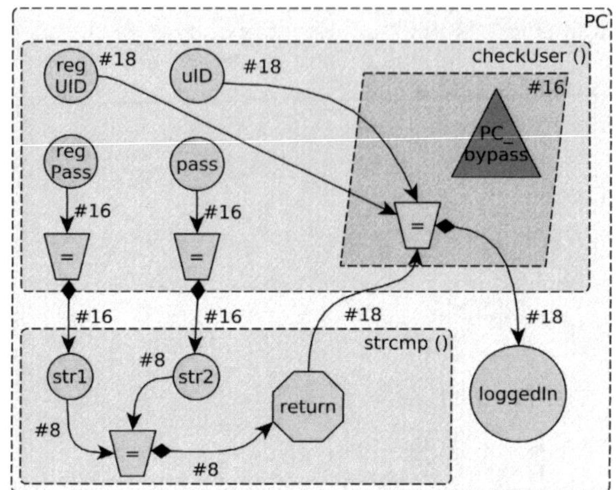

Fig. 7. Flow Graph for Listing 11

To allow information exchange between those domains, additional security perimeters have to be in place to control the data exchange. Usually, information can freely flow from higher critical domains to lower critical domains. However, information sent by lower domains and processed by higher domains need to be controlled. This channel is more and more demanded, e.g., by the use case of the maintenance interface that is usually hosted within the Airline Information Service Domain but also should be used for updating the Aircraft Control Domain. For protecting higher domains from the threat of vulnerable data a security gateway can be put in service in order to assure integrity of the higher criticality domains. This security gateway examines any data exchange and assures integrity of the communication data and consequently of the high integrity domain. Since this gateway is also a highly critical system, it requires similar design and implementation assurances regarding safety and security as the systems it protects.

VII. Use-Case: The Railway Security Domains

The railway industry needs to protect the integrity and availability of their control network, managing signals, positions of trains and driving parameters of trains. Hence, also the

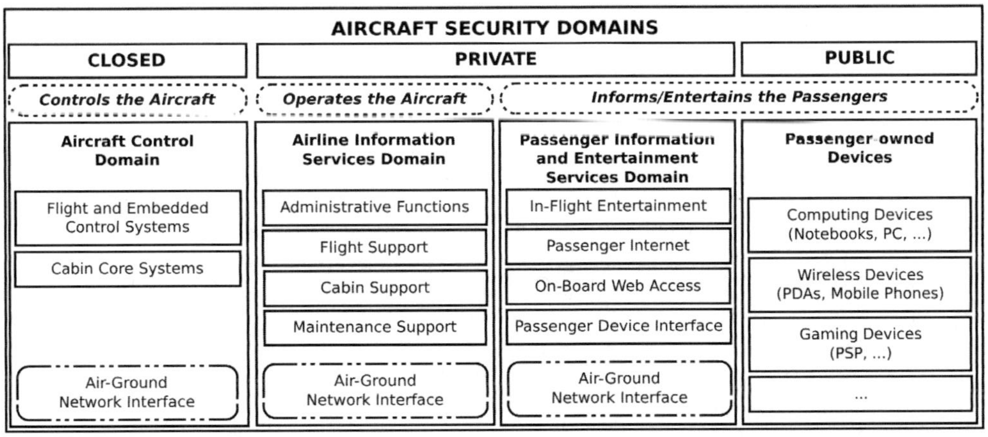

Fig. 8. Avonic Security Domains as defined by ARINC 664 [22] and ARINC 811 [23].

railway industry has categorized their systems and interfaces into security domains.

Railway control consists of several domains from control centers over interlocking systems to field elements all interacting in one way or the other with onboard systems. For interlocking, DIN VDE V 0831-104 [24] defines a typical architecture from a security zone perspective, which is depicted in Figure 9.

For interlocking, Figure 9 shows that different levels of maintenance and diagnosis are needed. Local maintenance interacts via a gateway (demilitarized zone) with control elements interlocking logic, operator computers and field elements Considering in this example the diagnosis information, the diagnosis database needs a method for data acquisition without adding risks of propagating data into the interlocking zone. To implement this, a simple diode-based approach is deemed sufficient. Remote diagnosis is more complicated with access to diagnosis as well as the interlocking zone, but again using gateways to access control elements (interlocking, operator, and field element computers).

This example of accessing interlocking for diagnosis and maintenance purposes reflects the potential need for security gateways. In case of operation centers where many interlockings are controlled and monitored remotely, similar security measure are to be taken if connected via open networks. Similarly if within different interlockings communication runs over open networks, encryption and potentially also gateway approaches may be needed.

In current and future signalling, control and train protection systems such as European Train Control System (ETCS) level 2 or higher security aspects need to consider aspects of wireless communication and – similarly to approaches described above – need to protect different system components and systems.

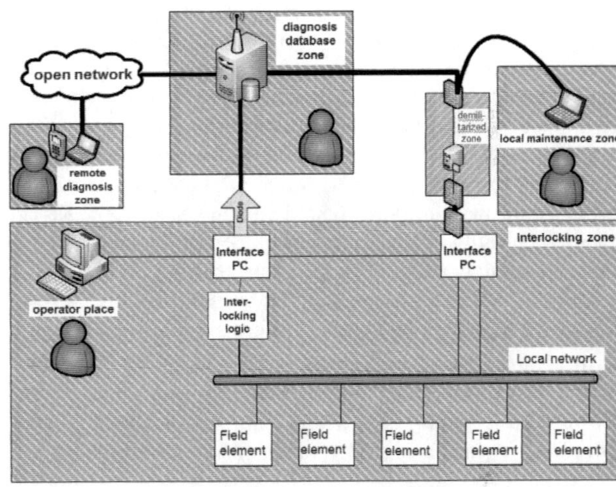

Fig. 9. Railway Security Zones [24]

VIII. The MILS Gateway

The avionic and railway use case share one major commonality regarding security. Both industries elaborated security classifications for their systems; depending on the criticality and users systems are categorized into security domains. However, systems of these security domains mostly cannot operate independent but often demand data from systems of other domains. For example, services of the avionic Passenger Information and Entertainment Services domain need data from systems of the Aircraft Control domain, such as the altitude and position of the aircraft for enabling or disabling the on-board WiFi network due to regulations by governmental authorities. In railway an example for data exchange is the external adjustment of the maximum allowed train speed, triggered by the train network operator. To still protect a domain against invalid accesses or malicious data, control instances such as Secure Network Gateways are deployed. These gateways mediate and control the data exchange on the domain borders and filter the data according to a defined information flow policy.

In previous work we have introduced a Secure Network Gateway [25] based on the MILS approach.

The MILS architecture, originally introduced in [26] and further refined in [5], is based on the concept of spatial and temporal separation connected with controlled information flow. These properties are provided by a special operating system called a Separation Kernel. MILS systems enable one to run applications of different criticality integrated together on one hardware platform.

Leveraging these properties the gateway is decomposed into several subfunctions that operate together in order to achieve the gateway functionality. Figure 10a shows the partitioned system architecture. The benefit of the decomposition is the ability to define local security policies for the different gateway components. The system components themselves run isolated among each other within the provided environments of a Separation Kernel. Using a Separation Kernel as a foundational operating system guarantees non-interference between the identified gateway subfunctions except when an interaction is granted. Hence, the Separation Kernel provides a coarse information flow control in order to prove which component is allowed to communicate to which other component. However, within the partition's boundaries the Separation Kernel cannot control the correct implementation of the defined local information flow policy. This paper presents a new concept of connecting MILS with the DLM in order to fill this gap and to provide system-wide evidence of correct information flows.

In comparison to our unidirectional gateway of [25] comprising just two partitions to perform information flow control on very basic protocols only, our improved gateway is composed of four major logical components (cf. also Figure 10a):

1) The Receiver Components
2) Filter Component(s)*
3) The Transmitter Components
4) Health Monitoring and Audit Component*

* (not depicted in Figure 10a)

Figure 10b extracts the internal architecture of the Receiver Component being a part of our gateway system. The task of this component is to receive network packets from a physical network adapter, to decide whether the packet contains TCP or UDP data, and to parse and process the protocols accordingly. Hence, this component is composed of three subfunctions hosted in three partitions[2] of the Separation Kernel:

1) **DeMux:** Receiving network packets from the physical network adapter, and analyzing and processing the data traffic on lower network protocol levels (i.e., Ethernet/-MAC and IPv4[3])
2) **TCP_Decoder:** Analysing and processing of identified TCP packets
3) **UDP_Decoder:** Analysing and processing of identified UDP packets

The advantage of this encapsulation of subfunctionality into three partitions is the limitation of possible attack impacts and fault propagation. Generally, implementations of TCP stacks are considered more vulnerable to attacks than UDP stacks, due to the increased functionality of the TCP protocol compared to the UDP protocol. Hence, the TCP stack implemented in the TCP_Decoder can be assumed as more vulnerable. A possible attack vector to a gateway application is to attack the TCP stack in order to circumvent or to perform denial-of-service on the gateway. If all three subfunctions run inside one partition, the entire Receiver Component would be affected by a successful attack on the TCP stack. However, in this distributed implementation using the separation property of the Separation Kernel only the TCP_Decoder would be affected by a successful attack. A propagation of the attack impact (or fault) to the UDP_Decoder or DeMux is limited due to the security properties of the Separation Kernel.

Further developing the gateway example, the strength of using DLM is to assure a correct implementation of the demultiplexer running in the DeMux partition. Considering the C code in Listing 12 the essential part of the demultiplexer requires the following actions:

- Line 2 and line 3 define the prototypes of the functions that send the data to the subsequent partitions using either channel *TCP data* or channel *UDP data* of Figure 10b.
- Line 5 defines the structure of the configuration array containing an integer value and a function-pointer to one of the previously defined functions.
- The code snippet following line 11 configures the demultiplexer by adding tuples for the TCP and UDP handlers to the array. The integer complies with the RFC of the IPv4 identifying the protocol on the transport layer.
- Line 29 implements the selection of the correct handler by iterating to the correct element of the configuration array and comparing the type field of the input packet with the protocol value of the configuration tuples. Note that the loop does not contain any further instructions due to the final ';'.
- The appropriate function is finally called by line 32.

A. DLM Applied to the Gateway Use Case

We consider again the use case presented in Figure 10b. In order to use DLM for the DeMux of the Receiver Component an annotation of Listing 12 is needed. Listing 13 shows this annotated version. The graphical representation is depicted in Figure 11.

- Line 1 announces all used principals of this code segment to the Cif checker.
- In line 3 and line 4 we label the begin label and the data parameter of the two prototype declarations with labels

[2]A *partition* is a runtime container in a Separation Kernel that guarantees non-interfered execution. A *communication channel* is an a priori defined means of interaction between a source partition and one or more destination partitions.

[3]For the following we assume our network implements Ethernet and IPv4, only.

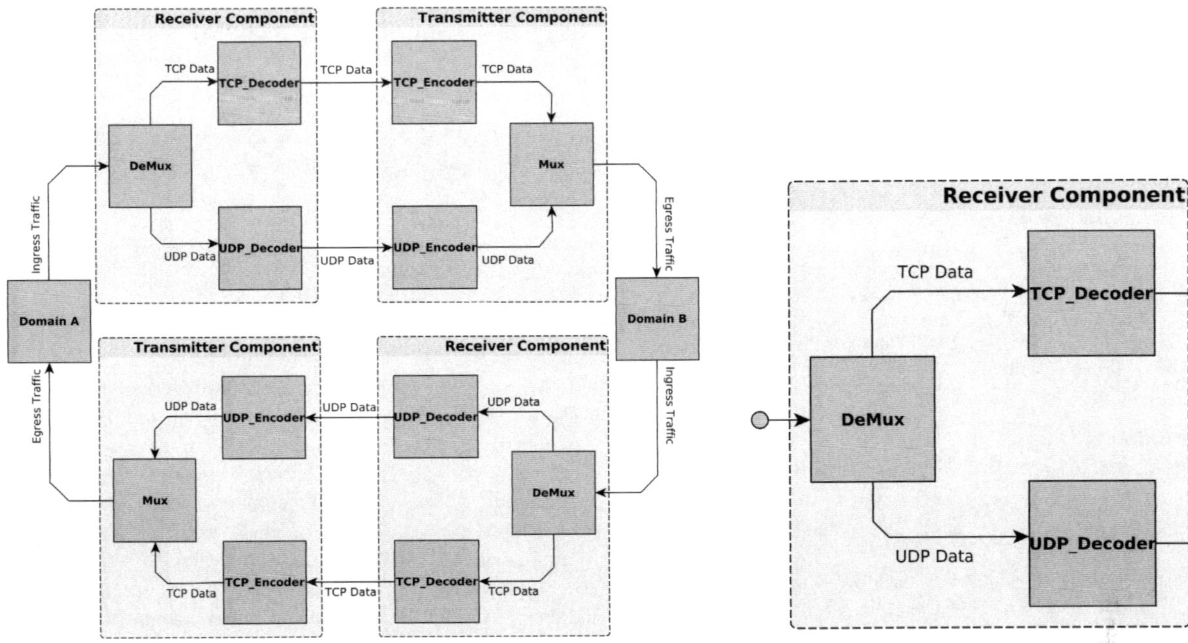

(a) Global system architecture

(b) The Receiver Component is a function composed of three partitions.

Fig. 10. MILS Gateway Architecture. Blue boxes indicate partitions.
The Separation Kernel assures partition boundaries and communication channels (arrowed lines).

that either principal TCP or principal UDP owns the data starting with the time the function is called.

- The definition of the input buffer in line 13 receives also a label. For the confidentiality policy the data is owned by the *Ethernet*, since data will be received from the network and we assume it is an Ethernet packet. This owner *Ethernet* allows both *TCP* and *UDP* to read its data. The integrity policy of line 13 is a bit different. The top principal can act for all principals and, hence, the data is owned by all principals. However, all principals assume that only Ethernet has modified the data. This assumption is correct, since data is received from the network.
- The main function of our program (line 15) now contains a begin label. This label grants the function to have a side effect on the global INPUT variable (i.e., the input buffer).
- Due to our language extension we had to replace the more elegant *for* loop (cf. line 29 in Listing 12) by a *switch-case* block (cf. line 17)). Within each case branch, we have to relabel the data stored in INPUT in order to match the prototype labels of line 3 or line 4 accordingly. The first step of this relabeling is a normal information flow by adding *TCP* (or *UDP*) as owner to the confidentiality policy and integrity policy (cf. line 20 and line 28). This step is performed compliantly to the DLM defined in Section III-B. Then, we *bypass* the PC label in order to change to the new environment and to match the begin label of the associated decoder function (cf. line 21 and line 29). As a second relabeling step, we still need to remove the principal *Ethernet* from the confidentiality and integrity policies. Removing this principal does not comply with the allowed information flow of DLM, since both resulting policies are less restrictive than the source policies. Hence, we have to declassify (for the confidentiality policy) and endorse (for the integrity policy) by using the statements of line 22 and line 30.
- Finally we can call the sending functions in line 23 and line 31 accordingly.

```
1  principal Ethernet, UDP, TCP;
2
3  TCP_SendDecode {TCP->*; TCP<-*} (void {TCP
       ->*; TCP<-*} *data);
4  UDP_SendDecode {UDP->*; UDP<-*} (void {UDP
       ->*; UDP<-*} *data);
5
6  static union {
7    struct {
8      /* [...] further fields of protocols
         */
9      char protocol;
10     /* [...] further fields of protocols
         */
11   } u;
12   char buf[0xffff];
13 } {Ethernet->TCP, UDP; *<-Ethernet} INPUT;
14
15 int main {Ethernet->TCP, UDP; *<-Ethernet}
```

```
/* DECLARATION */
TCP_SendDecode(void *data);
UDP_SendDecode(void *data);

typedef struct {
  char protocol;
  void (*func)(void* data);
} DeMux;

/* CONFIGURATION */
static DeMux handler[] = {
  { 0x06, &TCP_SendDecode }, // 0x06
      indicates TCP in IPv4
  { 0x11, &UDP_SendDecode }, // 0x11
      indicates UDP in IPv4
  { 0x00, 0 }         // final entry
};

union { struct {
    /* [...] further fields of protocols
       */
    char protocol;
    /* [...] further fields of protocols
       */
  } u;
  char buf[0xffff];
} INPUT;

int main() {
  /* [...] load data from network into
      INPUT */
/* PROCESSING */
  DeMux* itr = 0;
  for(itr = handler; itr->protocol != 0 &&
    itr->protocol != INPUT.u.protocol; itr
      ++) ;
  if(itr->func != 0)
    (*itr->func)(INPUT);
  else
    Error();
}
```

Listing 12. Demultiplexer of the Receiver Component

```
      () {
16  /* [...] load data from network into
       INPUT */
17  switch(INPUT.u.protocol) {
18    case 0x06: /* 0x06 in IPv4 indicates
          TCP */
19    {
20      void {Ethernet & TCP->*; TCP<-
          Ethernet} *ptr = INPUT.buf;
21      PC_bypass({TCP->*; TCP<-*});
22      void {TCP->*; TCP<-*} *tcp = endorse
          (declassify(ptr, {TCP->*; TCP<-
          Ethernet}), {TCP->*; TCP<-*});
23      TCP_SendDecode(tcp);
24      break;
25    }
26    case 0x11: /* 0x11 in IPv4 indicates
          UDP */
27    {
28      void {Ethernet & UDP->*; UDP<-
          Ethernet} *ptr = INPUT.buf;
29      PC_bypass({UDP->*; UDP<-*});
30      void {UDP->*; UDP<-*} *udp = endorse
          (declassify(ptr, {UDP->*; UDP<-
          Ethernet}), {UDP->*; UDP<-*});
31      UDP_SendDecode(udp);
32      break;
33    }
34    default:
35    {
36      Error();
37    }
38  }
39 }
```

Listing 13. Annotated Receiver Component

Clearly, Figure 11 indicated six warnings inside the source code by the red triangle. The bypass of the PC label in line line:cif-tcp-bypass and line line:cif-udp-bypass reason two of these warnings. The remaining four warnings are due to the endorse and declassification (two each) of the DLM information flow policy in order to allow the assignments in line 22 and line 30. As DLM provides information flow assurance, code reviewers just need to concentrate on these indicated sections of the code to perform manual validation. The remaining source code is validated thanks to the DLM

Using the presented technology we also annotate other critical gateway components hosted in other partitions of the MILS system. The *Cif* tool is able to process all needed C language features of our implementation, e.g., loops, decision branches, switch-case blocks, function calls, pointer arithmetics, and also function pointers as long as their DLM policy is homogeneous (cf. Section IX). Since the tool does not report information flow violations of the local defined policies, we gain additional evidence of the correct implementation of the gateway's components. Together with the defined MILS information flow policy ensured by the Separation Kernel we can assure a correct implementation of the system-wide information flow. Currently, we have still had to map both evidences manually for developing the prove of concept. Future planning of our implementation involves to automatically combine both steps.

IX. Enhancing the Decentralized Label Model

A. *Assessment of DLM applied to the Gateway Use Case*

The application of DLM to the gateway use case identified some advantages and disadvantages. The **advantages** are on easing the assurance process and on the improved identification of code flaws, being more detailed:

Automatic Proof of Correct Information Flows: The presented source code in Listing 13 complies with a formally proven information flow model, the DLM. The proof of this properties of complient information flows could be achieved automatically with tool support. Hence, it can be considered as highly assured that the present information flows are correct. The graphical representatio clearly identifies code sections that endorsing or declassifying the modeled information flow policy. This allows to reduce

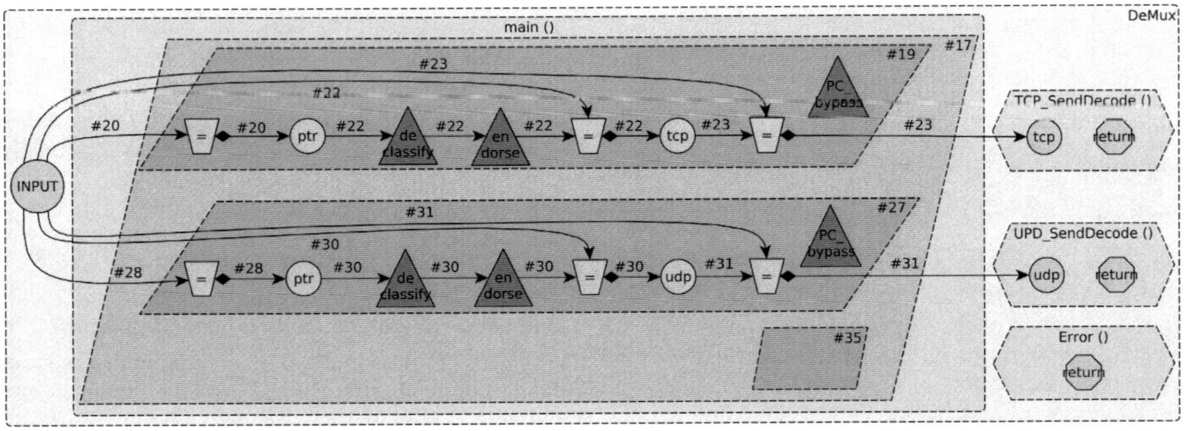

Fig. 11. DLM Information Flows in the Demultiplexer of the MILS Gateway implemented by Listing 13.

efforts for code reviews, as the reviewers can focus on these parts of the code. In contrast, all the code in Listing 12 requires detailed and manual code review in order to provide the same level of assurances.

Increased Robustness against Coding Flaws: Compared to Listing 12, the DLM-inducted code snippet of Listing 13 is more robust against coding flaws. Imagine a distracted programmer swaps the two function pointers in the configuration array of Listing 12. This modification will result in a probably hardly debugable runtime error, since UDP traffic will now be sent to the TCP_Decoder and the other way around. In contrast, if swapping the function calls of line 23 and line 31 of Listing 13 the Cif checker will raise an information flow breach due to the invalid labels of the function call and the labels of the parameter. Hence, this DLM allows detection of possible runtime errors before compilation.

Contrary, the following **disadvantages** have been identified:

Larger Code Size: Comparing both demultiplexer implementations of Listing 12 and Listing 13 it is obvious that the DLM-inducted version increases the code size due to the different employed programming styles. In the former, we use a table-based programming technique (see the *for* loop) whereas in the latter we use a code-based programming technique (see the *switch* statement). Another reasons for the bigger foot print is the relabeling directives within the *case* blocks. This relabeling introduces new variables and statements that are only required for inducting DLM. From a program control flow perspective, those statements are useless and (hopefully) detected and removed by the compiler during optimization.

Reduced Readability: The label annotations of DLM itself form another disadvantage. Their introduction may reduce readability of the code due to the unusuality of their use. However, using DLM increases the level of automation in providing assurance, and thus, the need of manual code review. The best case avoids manual code reading entirely.

Considering the identified disadvantages, we elaborate on a solution to reduce the code size by extending DLM to allow expressing DLM policies on the table-based programming technique of Listing 12.

B. Extensions to the DLM

Based on [27], [28] we will now describe a possible extension of Cif intended to overcome the shortcoming. Listing 14 displays the resulting code. It should be clear that it is rather close to that of Listing 12; a similar version could be developed for Listing 13.

```
/* DECLARATION */
principal Ethernet, UDP, TCP;

policy GatewayHandler
= (self.protocol==0x06 =>
self.func=={TCP->*; TCP<-*} (void {TCP->*; TCP<-*} *))
&& (self.protocol==0x11 =>
self.func=={UDP->*; UDP<-*} (void {UDP->*; UDP<-*} *));

policy Gateway
= (self.protocol==0x06 => self=={TCP->*; TCP<-*})
&& (self.protocol==0x11 => self=={UDP->*; UDP<-*});

TCP_SendDecode {TCP->*; TCP<-*} (void {TCP ->*; TCP<-*} *data);
UDP_SendDecode {UDP->*; UDP<-*} (void {UDP ->*; UDP<-*} *data);

typedef struct {
  char protocol;
  void (*func)(void* data);
} {GatewayHandler} DeMux;
```

```
21
22  /* CONFIGURATION */
23  static DeMux {GatewayHandler} handler[] = {
24    { 0x06, &TCP_SendDecode },
25    { 0x11, &UDP_SendDecode },
26    { 0x00, 0}
27  };
28
29  union {
30    struct {
31      /* [...] further protocol fields */
32      char protocol;
33      /* [...] further protocol fields */
34    } u;
35    char buf[0xffff];
36  } {Gateway} INPUT;
37
38  int main() {
39    /* [...] load data from network into INPUT */
40    /* and if necessary declassify to give it the right type */
41
42    /* PROCESSING */
43    DeMux* itr = 0;
44    for(itr = handler; itr->protocol != 0x00 && itr->protocol != INPUT.u.protocol; itr++) ;
45    if (itr->protocol != 0)
46      (*itr->func)(INPUT);
47    else
48      /* Neither a TCP nor UDP packet --> ERROR */
49  }
```

Listing 14. Annotated Receiver Component in Enhanced DLM

The basic idea is to extend DLM with policies that depend on the actual values of data. Consider the Gateway policy defined in line 10 onwards. The intention is that the entire field should obey the policy `{TCP->*; TCP<-*}` in case the protocol component (INPUT.u.protocol) equals 0x06; it should obey the policy `{UDP->*; UDP<-*}` in case the protocol component equals 0x11; and if the protocol component has a value different from 0x06 and 0x11 no requirements are imposed on the entire field.

The general form of the syntax used is to let policies be constructed according to the following grammar:

```
   policy    ::= field==DLMpolicy
               | policy && policy
               | policy || policy
               | condition => policy
               | condition && policy | ···
 condition   ::= field==value
               | condition && condition | ···
     field   :=  self | field.component
 DLMpolicy   :=  as previously used but extended to
                 function types
```

Here => denotes implication, `&&` denotes conjunction, and `||` denotes disjunction. The identifier `self` is a reserved token for the data structure in question and *component* lists possible components.

To make use of such extended policies one needs to track not only the DLM policies and the types pertaining the data but also to track the information about the values of data that can be learnt from the various tests, branches and switches being performed in the program. The development in [27][28] achieves this by combining a Hoare logic for tracking the information about the values of data with the DLM policies and allows us to validate the code snippet in Listing 14.

This suffices for solving two shortcomings discussed above. First, it reduces the need to use declassification and PC_bypass for adhering to the policy thereby reducing the need for detailed code inspection. Second, it permits a more permissive programming style that facilitates the adoption of our method by programmers.

From an engineering point of view, the ease of use of conditional policies are likely to depend on the style in which the conditional policies are expressed. The development in [27] considers policies that in our notation would be written in the form of policies in Disjuntive Normal Form (using `||` at top-level and `&&` at lower levels), whereas the development in [28] considers policies that in our notation would be written in the form of policies in Implication Normal Form (using `&&` at top-level and `=>` at lower levels). The pilot implementation in [29], [30] seems to suggest that forcing policies to be in Implication Normal Form might be more intuitive and this is likely the way we will be extending Cif.

From an expressiveness point of view, it does not matter whether one uses Disjunctive Normal Form or Implication Normal Form. For example, we might consider to change the Gateway policy to the more demanding policy

```
policy Gateway
= (self.u.protocol==0x06 && self=={TCP->*; TCP<-*})
|| (self.u.protocol==0x11 && self=={UDP->*; UDP<-*})
```

expressing that there are no other permitted possibilities for the protocol component than to be either 0x06 or 0x11. This is desirable for the code snippet illustrated because line 48 would then not be reachable; however, it may be harder to ensure that the INPUT received from the network adheres to this policy. While the Disjunctive Normal Form expresses this, we could obtain the same result in Implication Normal Form by writing

```
policy Gateway
= (self.u.protocol==0x06 => self=={TCP->*; TCP<-*})
&& (self.u.protocol==0x11 => self=={UDP->*; UDP<-*})
&& (self.u.protocol!=0x06 && self.u.protocol!=0x11 => self=={Z->Z;Z<-Z})
```

where Z is an otherwise unused principal and hence the policy $= Z \to Z; Z \leftarrow Z$ is unattainable.

A final problem that would need to be overcome is how to interface the checking of conditions to the programmer. In the pilot implementation reported in [29][30] it is demanded that the programmer provides invariants for all while loops (since in general this is undecidable).

We are therefore experimenting with ways of using the results of the powerful static analyser Astree to provide the required invariants and possibly to use the abstract properties of Astree in expressing the policies. Current results [31] suggest that this approach to be very promising, which would make it a strong candidate for inclusion into Cif.

X. Conclusion

In this article, we presented C Information Flow (Cif), a static verification tool to check information flows modeled directly in C source code. Cif is an implementation of the Decentralized Label Model (DLM) [10] for the programming language C. To the best of our knowledge, we applied DLM to the C language for the first time. During the application of DLM to C, we tried to stick to the reference implementation of Java/Jif. However, we had to solve some language-specific issues, such as pointer arithmetic or the absence of exceptions. Additionally, we added the possibility of defining annotations to function prototypes only, in case a library's source code is not available for public access. Then, we also introduced rules for differing annotations of function prototypes compared to function implementations.

In various code snippets, we discussed information flows as they appear commonly in C implementations. Cif is able to verify all of these examples successfully. In case of valid information flows through the entire source code, Cif generates a graphical representation of the occurring flows and dependencies — a distinguishing feature not possessed by Jif. This graphical representation covers direct assignments of variables, logical and arithmetic operations, indirect dependencies due to decision branches and function calls. Cif allows the programmer to make declassifications and endorsements as in DLM, and additionally marks the places where flow policies are loosened with declassifications and endorsements in the graphical representation. Since DLM-annotated source code shall reduce the efforts of manual code reviews, these graphical indications allow to identify critical parts of the source code. Such parts usually require then special investigation during code reviews.

Further on, we presented how the security-typed language system [13] of the DLM can be connected to Multiple Independent Levels of Security (MILS) systems. MILS [26] is a system architecture to build high-assurance systems [5]. Various industrial domains require such high-assurance systems to fulfill special safety and security demands. MILS bases on the properties of separation and controlled information flow, both provided by a special kind of operating system, called a Separation Kernel. Such kernels provide separated runtime environments to host applications and to assure a configurable information flow policy among those environments. However, the Separation Kernel is not able to control the internals of these runtime environments. Security typed languages such as the DLM can fill this gap.

In our use case, we target the example of a gateway application. In our study, we have identified this use case as a common implementation challenge for high assurance systems from the avionics and railway industry; however, our approach is not limited to those two industries but is also conceivable for other industries such as smart meters or automotive. This gateway supervises the information exchange between security domains, either on-board aircraft or between a train and its railway operational control network. Architecturally, the gateway follows the design principles of MILS. To control the system's information flows we connected the coarse information flows assured by the Separation Kernel with the application-dependent information flows, expressed by DLM-annotated C source code of the gateway's implementation. Compared to other security-typed languages for C, e.g., as proposed by Greve [14] using a mandatory access control-based approach, we used a decentralized approach for assuring correct information flow. This has the advantage of revealing subtler unwwanted dependencies in code, and explicating the mutual distrust between different software components. The latter also provides more flexibility in modeling the information flow policy.

We applied DLM annotations to a typical security function for high assurance systems: a demultiplexer which is part of the MILS-based gateway application. Using our developed Cif, we are able to ensure secure information flows within the gateway's components according to the defined information flow policy. Particularly, the visualization of indirect flows, e.g., Listing 7 or Listing 8, and function calls, e.g., Listing 9, were very useful during the evaluation of the use case. Additionally, this activity showed that Cif is able to cover larger projects, too. Connecting DLM proofs with the information flow assurance of the Separation Kernel provides system-wide evidences of correct implementation, e.g., as required by high Evaluation Assurance Levels of Common Criteria certifications. However, to annotate source code using the current model of DLM implemented by our Cif required to change parts of the source code. Using the presented technology we annotated further critical parts of our gateway to prove their correct implementation.

Additionally, we evaluated the benefits and drawbacks of applying DLM to C. While the benefits are clearly in the automation of gaining assurances of correct code and the reduction of manual code review, the drawbacks are the usability and increased code's footprint. Both disadvantages are critical for the future developer's acceptance of our approach and will finally decide on whether this DLM assurance can be successful in a wider field of application. To improve usability, we proposed an enhancement to the DLM, theoretically rooted in

[27], that removes the need of the presented code modification. We implemented a proof-of-concept checker [29] in parallel to Cif, to assure correct information flows within this new DLM-aware theory. Compared with Cif, this prototype checker does not support rich language features or the generation of graphical representations at the current stage.

As future work, we will evaluate on merging the features of Cif with the extended assurance of this prototyped implementation.

ACKNOWLEDGMENT

This work was supported by the ARTEMiS Project SeSaMo, the European Union's 7th Framework Programme project EURO-MILS (ID: ICT-318353), the German BMBF project SiBASE (ID: 01IS13020) and the project EMC2 (grant agreement No 621429, Austrian Research Promotion Agency (FFG) project No 84256,8 and German BMBF project ID 01IS14002). We also thank Kawthar Balti, Tomasz Maciazek and Andre Ryll for their input.

REFERENCES

[1] K. Müller, S. Uhrig, M. Paulitsch, and S. Uhrig, "Cif: A Static Decentralized Label Model (DLM) Analyzer to Assure Correct Information Flow in C," in *Proc. of the* 10th *International Conference on Software Engineering Advances (ICSEA 2015)*. Barcelona, Spain: IARIA, Nov. 2015, pp. 369–375. [Online]. Available: http://www.thinkmind.org/index.php?view=article&articleid=icsea_2015_14_20_10272

[2] EUROCAE/RTCA, "ED-12C/DO-178C: Software Considerations in Airborne Systems and Equipment Certification," European Organisation for Civil Aviation Equipment / Radio Technical Commission for Aeronautics, Tech. Rep., 2012.

[3] ——, "ED-80/DO-254, Design Assurance Guidance for Airborne Electronic Hardware," European Organisation for Civil Aviation Equipment / Radio Technical Commission for Aeronautics, Tech. Rep., 2000.

[4] H. Butz, "The Airbus Approach to Open Integrated Modular Avionics (IMA): Technology, Methods, Processes and Future Road Map," Hamburg, Germany, March 2007.

[5] J. Rushby, "Separation and Integration in MILS (The MILS Constitution)," SRI International, Tech. Rep. SRI-CSL-08-XX, Feb. 2008.

[6] J. Alves-Foss, W. S. Harrison, P. W. Oman, and C. Taylor, "The MILS Architecture for High-Assurance Embedded Systems," Tech. Rep., 2006.

[7] K. J. Hayhurst, D. S. Veerhusen, J. J. Chilenski, and L. K. Rierson, "A Practical Tutorial on Modified Condition/Decision Coverage," NASA, Tech. Rep. May, 2001. [Online]. Available: http://shemesh.larc.nasa.gov/fm/papers/Hayhurst-2001-tm210876-MCDC.pdfhttp://dl.acm.org/citation.cfm?id=886632

[8] D. Kästner, S. Wilhelm, S. Nenova, P. Cousot, R. Cousot, J. Feret, A. Miné, X. Rival, L. Mauborgne, A. Angewandte, I. Gmbh, S. Park, and D. Saarbrücken, "Astrée: Proving the Absence of Runtime Errors," in *Proc. of the Embedded Real Time Software and Systems (ERTS2'10)*, Toulouse, France, 2010, pp. 1–9.

[9] J. C. King, "Symbolic Execution and Program Testing," *Communications of the ACM*, vol. 19, no. 7, pp. 385–394, Jul. 1976. [Online]. Available: http://dl.acm.org/citation.cfm?id=360248.360252

[10] A. C. Myers and B. Liskov, "A Decentralized Model for Information Flow Control," in *Proc. of the* 16th *ACM symposium on Operating systems principles (SOSP'97)*, no. October. Saint-Malo, France: ACM, 1997, pp. 129–142. [Online]. Available: http://www.pmg.lcs.mit.edu/papers/iflow-sosp97.pdf

[11] A. C. Myers, "JFlow: Practical Mostly-Static Information Flow Control," in *Proc. of the* 26th *ACM Symposium on Principles of Programming Languages (POPL'99)*, no. January. San Antonio, Texas, USA: ACM, Jan. 1999. [Online]. Available: http://www.cs.cornell.edu/andru/papers/popl99/popl99.pdf

[12] EASA, "Notification of a Proposal to Issue a Certification Memorandum: Software Aspects of Certification," EASA, Tech. Rep., Feb. 2011.

[13] A. Sabelfeld and A. C. Myers, "Language-Based Information-Flow Security," *IEEE Journal on Selected Areas in Communications*, vol. 21, Jan. 2003.

[14] D. Greve, "Data Flow Logic: Analyzing Information Flow Properties of C Programs," in *Proc. of the* 5th *Layered Assurance Workshop (LAW'11)*. Orlando, Florida, USA: Rockwell Collins, Research sponsored by Space and Naval Warfare Systems Command Contract N65236-08-D-6805, Dec. 2011. [Online]. Available: http://fm.csl.sri.com/LAW/2011/law2011-paper-greve.pdf

[15] D. Greve and S. Vanderleest, "Data Flow Analysis of a Xen-based Separation Kernel," in *Proc. of the* 7th *Layered Assurance Workshop (LAW'13)*, no. December. New Orleans, Louisiana, USA: Rockwell Collins, Research sponsored by Space and Naval Warfare Systems Command Contract N66001-12-C-5221, Dec. 2013. [Online]. Available: http://www.acsac.org/2013/workshops/law/files/LAW-2013-Greve.pdf

[16] S. Chong and A. C. Myers, "Decentralized Robustness," in *Proc. of the* 19th *IEEE Computer Security Foundations Workshop (CSFW'06)*. Washington, D.C, USA: IEEE, Jul. 2006, pp. 242–253. [Online]. Available: http://dl.acm.org/citation.cfm?id=1155681

[17] L. Zheng and A. C. Myers, "End-to-End Availability Policies and Noninterference," in *Proc. of the* 18th *IEEE Computer Security Foundations Workshop (CSFW'05)*. IEEE, Jun. 2005, pp. 272–286. [Online]. Available: http://www.cs.cornell.edu/andru/papers/avail.pdf

[18] S. Chong, A. C. Myers, K. Vikram, and L. Zheng, *Jif Reference Manual*, http://www.cs.cornell.edu/jif/doc/jif-3.3.0/manual.html, Feb 2009, jif Version: 3.3.1.

[19] T. Murray, D. Matichuk, M. Brassil, P. Gammie, T. Bourke, S. Seefried, C. Lewis, X. Gao, and G. Klein, "seL4: From general purpose to a proof of information flow enforcement," in *Proc. of the IEEE Symposium on Security and Privacy (SP) 2013*, May 2013, pp. 415–429.

[20] F. Verbeek, J. Schmaltz, S. Tverdyshev, O. Havle, H. Blasum, B. Langenstein, W. Stephan, A. Feliachi, Y. Nemouchi, and B. Wolff, "Formal Specification of a Generic Separation Kernel," Apr. 2014. [Online]. Available: http://dx.doi.org/10.5281/zenodo.47299

[21] H. Blasum, O. Havle, S. Tverdyshev, B. Langenstein, W. Stephan, Feliachi, A. Y. Nemouch, B. Wolff, C. Proch, F. Verbeek, and J. Schmaltz, "EURO-MILS: Used Formal Methods," 2015. [Online]. Available: http://www.euromils.eu/downloads/Deliverables/Y2/2015-EM-UsedFormalMethods-WhitePaper-October2015.pdf

[22] Aeronautical Radio Incorporated (ARINC), "Aircraft Data Network Part 5: Network Domain Characteristics and Interconnection," Apr. 2005.

[23] ——, "ARINC 811: Commercial Aircraft Information Security Concepts of Operation and Process Framework," 2005.

[24] Deutsche Kommission Elektrotechnik Elektronik Informationstechnik im DIN und VDE, "Electric signalling systems for railways - Part 104: IT Security Guideline based on IEC 62443," Sep. 2014.

[25] K. Müller, M. Paulitsch, S. Tverdyshev, and H. Blasum, "MILS-Related Information Flow Control in the Avionic Domain: A View on Security-Enhancing Software Architectures," in *Proc. of the* 42nd *International Conference on Dependable Systems and Networks Workshops (DSN-W)*, Jun. 2012. [Online]. Available: http://ieeexplore.ieee.org/xpl/articleDetails.jsp?arnumber=6264665

[26] J. Rushby, "Design and Verification of Secure Systems," in *Proc. of the* 8th *ACM Symposium on Operating Systems Principles*. Pacific Grove, California, USA: ACM, Dec. 1981.

[27] H. R. Nielson, F. Nielson, and X. Li, "Hoare Logic for Disjunctive Information Flow," in *Programming Languages with Applications to Biology and Security - Essays Dedicated to Pierpaolo Degano on the Occasion of His 65th Birthday*, ser. Lecture Notes in Computer Science, vol. 9465. Springer, 2015, pp. 47–65.

[28] H. R. Nielson and F. Nielson, "Content Dependent Information Flow Control," in *J.Log. Algebraic Methods Program*, 2016. [Online]. Available: http://dx.doi.org/10.1016/j.jlamp.2016.09.005

[29] T. Maciazek, "Content-Based Information Flow Verification for C," MSc thesis, Technical University of Denmark, 2015.

[30] T. Maciazek, H. R. Nielson, and F. Nielson, "Content-Dependent Security Policies in Avionics," in *Proc. of* 2nd *International Workshop on MILS: Architecture and Assurance for Secure Systems, 2016*, 2016. [Online]. Available: http://mils-workshop.euromils.eu/downloads/hipeac_literature_2016/07-Article.pdf

[31] P. Vasilikos, "Static Analysis for Content Dependent Information Flow Control," MSc thesis, Technical University of Denmark, 2016.

An Ontological Perspective on the Digital Gamification of Software Engineering Concepts

Roy Oberhauser
Computer Science Dept.
Aalen University
Aalen, Germany
roy.oberhauser@hs-aalen.de

Abstract - **Software engineering (SE), because of its abstract nature, faces awareness, perception, and public image challenges that affect its ability to attract sufficient secondary school (high school) age students to its higher education programs. This paper presents an edutainment approach called Software Engineering for Secondary Education (SWE4SE), which combines short informational videos and a variety of simple digital games to convey certain SE concepts in an entertaining way without necessitating or intending any skill development such as programming. Our realization mapped various SE concepts to seven digital games and these are described using the Software Engineering Body of Knowledge (SWEBOK) and game elements ontologies. We also investigated the maturity of ontologies for concepts in this area to determine the feasibility for a methodological mapping of SE concepts to game element and game logic to further automation. Results of SWE4SE with secondary students showed a significant improvement in the perception, attractiveness, and understanding of SE can be achieved within just an hour of play, suggesting such an edutainment approach is economical, effective, and efficient for reaching and presenting SE within secondary school classrooms. Our ontological investigation showed significant gaps towards formalizing or automating the approach.**

Keywords - software engineering education; software engineering games; educational computer games; digital game-based learning; digital games; ontologies.

I. INTRODUCTION

This paper is an extended version of a paper presented at the Tenth International Conference on Software Engineering Advances (ICSEA 2015) [1].

As digitalization sweeps through society, the demand for software engineers appears insatiable. As attractive as a software development career may appear in the media or press, computer science (CS) faculties and the software engineering (SE) discipline in particular appear to be steadily challenged in attracting and supplying sufficient students to fulfill the job market demand.

To each higher education institution and country, it may appear to be only a local or regional problem, yet the challenge may indeed be more common and broader in nature. Statistics for SE are not as readily available as those for CS. Since SE can be viewed as being a subset of CS, and not all CS faculties offer a separate SE degree or concentration (but may include applicable SE courses and electives in their curriculum), we focus on available statistics for CS majors and assume they correlate to SE in this paper. For example, in the United States in 2005, after a boom beginning around 2000, a 60% decrease over 4 years in the number of freshmen specifying CS as a major was observed [2]. And US bachelor degrees in CS in 2011 were roughly equivalent to that seen in 1986 both in total number (~42,000) and as a percentage of 23 year olds (~1%) [3]. As another example, Germany also observed a negative trend from a record number of CS students in 2000, and one 2009 news article [4] blamed the negative image of CS among the young generation. While the number of starting CS undergrads in Germany has since increased, roughly 33,000 software developer positions in Germany remain unfilled in 2014 [5]. In addition, the demographic effects forecast for various industrial countries imply a decreasing younger population, reducing the overall supply and thus increasing the competition between disciplines to attract students and eventually qualified workers. Thus, it remains a worldwide issue to attract young women and men to study SE.

Concerning SE's image, according to D. Parnas [6] there is apparently confusion in higher education institutions as to the difference between CS and SE, and we assert this affects secondary education as well. The CS equivalent term in Germany, *informatics*, is much more publically known and marketed as a discipline or field of study than is SE. Thus, SE programs struggle in the overall competition between disciplines to attract secondary students for this critical area to society, since SE must first raise awareness about its field.

The concepts inherent in SE are exemplified in the SWEBOK [7]. The objectives of the SWEBOK include promoting a consistent view of SE, clarifying the bounds of and characterizing the contents of SE with respect to other disciplines, and providing a topical access to the SE Body of Knowledge. Knowledge areas (KAs) have a common structure, including a subclassification of topics, topic descriptions with references. The KAs with the abbreviations used in this paper are shown in Table I and Related Disciplines and shown in Table II. These KAs tend themselves to be abstract and to deal with abstractions. Thus, they are difficult to convey, especially to secondary school students who have not significantly dealt with such abstractions, and cannot thus practically imagine what they mean. Furthermore, secondary school teachers and institutions are challenged in teaching CS, and have likely themselves not been introduced to SE.

Learning is a fundamental motivation for all game-playing, as game designer C. Crawford [8] once stated. Computer games involving the learning of some knowledge area are called educational computer games [9]. Both persuasive games [10] and serious games [11][12] have been used with the intent to change behavior or attitudes in various areas. With respect to engagement and learning, a study by [13] identifying 7392 papers that included 129 with empirical evidence found that the most frequently reported outcome and impact of playing games were affective and motivational as well as knowledge acquisition or content understanding. Thus, a gamification and edutainment fun approach targeting secondary school students appears promising for addressing both the aforementioned SE attractiveness and learning about SE concepts and the SE discipline in general.

TABLE I. SWEBOK KNOWLEDGE AREAS (KA)

Knowledge Area	Abbreviation
Software requirements	SR
Software design	SD
Software construction	SC
Software testing	ST
Software maintenance	SM
Software configuration management	CM
Software engineering management	EM
Software engineering process	EP
Software engineering models and methods	MM
Software quality	SQ
Software engineering professional practice	PP
Software engineering economics	EE
Computing foundations	CF
Mathematical foundations	MF
Engineering foundations	EF

TABLE II. SWEBOK RELATED DISCIPLINES

Related Discipline	Abbreviation
Computer engineering	CE
Systems engineering	SY
Project management	PM
Quality management	QM
General management	GM

This paper, extending [1] with further details and incorporating an ontological perspective, contributes an SE edutainment approach we call SWE4SE for gamifying and conveying SE concepts to high school students. It describes SWE4SE principles, example mappings of SWEBOK concepts onto digital game (DG) elements, its realization, and evaluates its viability with an empirical study. It also investigates the feasibility of a methodological mapping of SE concepts to game element and game logic. Towards supporting efficient production of DGs for SE, we sought a viable method or platform for finding and using DGs for SE, or at least some support for (semi-)automatic mapping of SE concepts to DGs exists. Research questions investigated included: Is there clarity in the SE research or educational community as to which SE concepts can be effectively conveyed using which DG genre and game element types? Is this area mature, or is it subject to trial-and-error approaches? What sources of information or ontologies exist for this type of information? Where information is available, is this knowledge described more abstractly or formally to further reuse (e.g., for different DG genres or via standardized ontology formats)?

The paper is structured as follows: Section II provides background material about DGs and reviews literature on the application of digital game-based learning (DGBL) in SE education (SEE). Section III describes related work and Section IV the SWE4SE concept, followed by its realization. Section VI details the evaluation, and this is followed by a discussion. Section VIII provides a conclusion and describes future work.

II. BACKGROUND

This section provides background material about DG and reviews literature on the application of digital game-based learning (DGBL) in SE education (SEE).

A. DG Genres

According to [9], video game genres include Abstract, Adaptation, Adventure, Artificial Life, Board Games, Capturing, Card Games, Catching, Chase, Collecting, Combat, Demo, Diagnostic, Dodging, Driving, Educational, Escape, Fighting, Flying, Gambling, Interactive Movie, Management Simulation, Maze, Obstacle Course, Pencil-and-Paper Games, Pinball, Platform (levels and locomotion, e.g. Donkey Kong), Programming Games, Puzzle, Quiz, Racing, Role-Playing, Rhythm and Dance, Shoot 'Em Up, Simulation, Sports, Strategy, Table-Top Games, Target, Text Adventure, Training Simulation, and Utility.

B. Digital Game-based Learning (DGBL)

As argued in [14], DGBL research has largely shown that it is now accepted that DG can be an effective learning tool . However, further research is needed to explain why DGBL is effective and engaging, and "practical guidance for how (when, with whom, and under what conditions) games can be integrated into the learning process to maximize their learning potential." We lack research-supported guidance as to how and why DGBL is effective and how to actually implement DGBL. Conversely, [15] did not find strong evidence that games lead to more effective learning.

C. Motivational Aspects to Gaming

[15] found that users liked game-based learning and found it motivating and enjoyable. According to the Fogg Behavior Model [16], the motivation and the ability to perform must converge at the same moment for a behavior to occur. In the context of motivation in gaming, for the user to remain interested in the game positive feedback from game mechanics should continuously trigger a user to perform specific actions that the user has the ability to invoke. As such, any DGs targeted for secondary education students should appropriate for their knowledge and ability.

D. Game Ontology and Description

The goal of the Game Ontology Project (GOP) [17][18][19] is an ontology framework for describing, analyzing, and studying the design space of games with the focus on gameplay. Its top-level concepts are Goals, Interfaces, Rules, Entity Manipulation, and Entities, whereby Entities are not further developed. GOP borrows concepts and methods from prototype theory [20] as well as grounded theory [21]. In contrast to gaming patterns [22], it provides the ability to identify and describe key structural elements rather than focusing on well-known solutions to recurring game design problems that have been codified as patterns. GOP concepts will be used to describe the realization of various games; however, it lacks the specification of genre and game logic. Other work on game ontologies includes [23], who investigated using Resource Description Framework (RDF) and Web Ontology Language (OWL) models to represent the knowledge within a role-playing DG.

[24] proposed the Video Game Description Language (VGDL) to be able to classify and describe the game logic, features, and mechanics of a game for the purposes of human and software agent understanding, as well as for automatic game generation from such a description. They focused on arcade games.

E. Literature Review of DGs Applied to SE

Rather than using the SWEBOK KAs, [13] used and extended the ISO/IEC 12207 to classify the SE process areas that were gamified in certain studies. Most of them focus on SD, and to a lesser extent SR, PM, and other support areas. Gamification elements employed by the primary studies were primarily points (14), badges (7), rankings (4), social reputation (4), voting (3), levels (2), visual metaphor (2), and otherwise quests, dashboard, betting, and awards.

Not all of the aforementioned studies explicitly differentiate on the axis of digital game (DG) from other serious game types, nor differentiate serious vs. fun games. Also, we noted that sometimes games were classified as pertaining to project management, but the work did not specifically focus on software project management.

Table III provides a summary of certain DG (based primarily on [13][25][26]) listing its genre with our own interpretation of the SWEBOK KA or SE-related concepts conveyed by various SE DG, extended with additional games. Our interpretation of the KA involved in certain games in [25] and [26] differ. If a paper provided no screenshot and no further evidence was found, then it is assumed not necessarily to be a digital game and was not included. If the game is not specifically focused on SE, then it was excluded. Note that while the [13] study appears to broadly cover SE gamification, for our purposes only 3 of the 29 cited primary papers, namely Trogon, HALO, and iThink, actually deal with digital games (have screenshots) that are focused on topics linked somewhat with SE.

[15] found that most common game genres in research were simulations (43), action games (14), puzzles (11), role-playing (8), strategy (6), and adventure (5). Only 1 of the 129 papers (that of Papastergiou) addressed a computing subject directly and only 3 of the 43 simulation game types were focused on entertainment as an intention, the rest were learning or serious games. This indicates that the simulation genre is most widespread in game research but entertainment is an uncommon intention for this genre. This correlates with our findings in Table III that simulation is a popular SE game genre in literature, and the likely intention of these games is primarily learning and not entertainment.

TABLE III. SELECTED EXAMPLES OF DIGITAL GAMES AND THE SE CONCEPTS THEY ATTEMPT TO CONVEY

Digital Game	Reference	Genre	SE Concepts Conveyed
Serious-AV (AVuSG)	Shabanah [27]	Simulation	CF
SimjavaSP	Shaw & Dermoudy [28]	Simulation	EM; PM
The Incredible Manager	Barros et al. [29]	Simulation	EM; PM
SimVBSE	Jain & Boehm [30]	Simulation	EM; PM
SimSoft	Caulfield et al. [31]	Simulation	EM; PM
Therefore iManage	Collofello [32]	Simulation	EM; EP; PM; EP
SESAM (Software Engineering Simulation by Animated Models)	Drappa & Ludewig [33]	Simulation	EM; EP; PM; EP
SimSE	Navarro & van der Hoek [34]	Simulation	EM; PM; EP; SR; EP; EM; PM
DesigMPS	Chaves et al. [35]	Simulation	EP
MO-SEProcess (SimSE in Second Life)	Wang & Zhu [36]	Simulation & Virtual Reality	EP; EM; PM
Trogon	Ašeriškis & Damaševičius [37]	Collaborative Simulation	PM
Pex4Fun	Xie et al. [38]	Social interactive coding	SC
-	Knauss et al. [39]	Simulation	SR
-	Hainey et al. [40]	Collaborative, Avatar	SR
iThink	Fernandes [41]	Simulation	SR
CIRCE, Production Cell, SummerSun, Quality Certification	Sharp & Hall [42]	Simulation	SR; SD; SC; SQ
HALO	Bell et al. [43]	Social quest	SD, ST

Unlisted are the plethora of software programming educational games or tools focused on teaching programming to kids, such as CodeCombat, CodeMonkey, CodinGame, Swift Playgrounds, Scratch, Alice, etc. However, our intent is not to teach a skill such as programming but to create an understanding and awareness about a SE topic. One reason for this is that we consider learning a skill (rather than learning about a skill) as requiring significantly more time investment for a DG user. Furthermore, programming overlaps with CS and does not help us to differentiate SE from CS.

Table III also shows that the most common KAs (10 of the 16) games listed are EM, PM, or EP and that a broader coverage of the 15 SWEBOK KAs with DGs is not apparent, be it any single game nor across multiple games.

F. SE Ontology Concepts

[44] and [45] provide an overview of the usage of various ontologies in SE.

Work on SWEBOK ontologies in particular include [46], which performed an almost literal transcription, identifying over 4000 concepts, 400 relationships, 1200 facts, and 15 principles. While other work has also been done on a SWEBOK ontology, we were unable to access a any substantial SWEBOK ontology.

As far as utilizing the SWEBOK for SE education, [47] discusses modeling such an ontology.

III. Related Work

Beyond the related work in Section II, studies concerning the perception and attractiveness among secondary students of choosing CS as a college major, the study by [48] of 836 High School students from 9 schools in 2 US states concluded that the vast majority of High School students had no idea what CS is or what CS majors learn. This conclusion can most likely be transposed to the lesser known discipline of SE. The number one positive influence towards a major in CS for males was interest in computer games and for females, gaming was third. Among females, the primary positive motivator was the desire to use CS in another field, while this factor was third for males.

Serious games [12] have an explicit educational focus and tend to simulate real-world situations with intended audiences beyond secondary education. With regard to the use of gaming within the SE education field, [25] performed a literature search of games-based learning in SE and "found a significant dearth of empirical research to support this approach." They examine issues in teaching the abstract and complex domain of requirements collection and analysis and, more generally, SE. A systematic survey on SE games by [26] analyzed 36 papers, all of which had targeted primarily undergraduate or graduates. A more recent study [13] carried out a systematic mapping to characterize the state of SE gamification, analyzing 29 primary studies from 2011-2014. It concluded that the and the application of gamification in SE is still in an initial stage, research in this area is quite preliminary, there is little sound evidence of its impact, and scarce empirical evidence.

Approaches for creating DGs include SimSYS [49], a model-driven engineering (MDE) based approach that integrates traditional entertainment game design elements, pedagogical content, and software engineering methodologies. Starting with informal models, it organizes games by acts, scenes, screens, and challenges and, using IBM Rhapsody, generates formal UML executable state chart models and XML for the SimSYS gameplay engine. However, this work does not describe which SE concepts map well to which game genres or game elements, nor does it attempt to utilize ontologies. [27] details game specifications, game genres, and game design, but is focused on the relatively narrow area of algorithm learning and visualization.

We were unable to find work related to the combination of SE or SWEBOK and DG ontologies or any more concrete method or mapping of SE concepts to game elements or game logic.

SWE4SE is targeted not towards higher education, but rather secondary school students with an explicit non-serious game approach. In secondary education, whereas initiatives for teaching programming are more common, conveying SE concepts in general and gamifying SE as a non-serious games has not hitherto been extensively studied, nor has the educational value of explicitly "non-serious" (or fun) games for this population stratum. While we study a secondary education population as does [48], our results go further in showing that an edutainment approach can improve the perception and attractiveness of SE. Compared to other learning game approaches, it explicitly makes the tradeoff to value entertainment more and education less in order to retain student engagement and enjoyment. It also explicitly includes short informational and entertaining video sequences to enhance the experience beyond gaming alone. Furthermore, it attempts to explicitly describe the mapping of SE concepts to various DGs and game elements.

IV. SWE4SE Concept

SWE4SE consists of a hybrid mix of short informational and entertaining videos and a variety of relatively simple digital games. Our solution is necessarily based on certain assumptions and constraints. For instance, we assumed that the players may not only be playing in a compulsory classroom setting, but may play voluntarily on their own time, meaning that they could choose to stop playing if it becomes boring or frustrating and discard the game for some more interesting game. Thus, the edutainment is considered to be "competing" with available pure entertainment options. However, we expect that the game may be promoted to secondary school teachers where they would introduce students to the game, meaning that our concept must not necessarily compete solely with commercial products and other entertainment. We also assumed that the motivational factors for students in the SWE4SE are curiosity, exploration, discovering different games, and finding fun areas.

Based on the motivational aspect of gaming discussed in Section II, since our target behavior is interest in the subject matter of SE, for our target audience of secondary students lacking SE knowledge a typical SE DG that requires pre-knowledge of SE concepts will not motivate since they are lacking the skills to achieve the target behavior. This implies a SEE DG for our target audience should avoid the direct use of SE concepts in order to play the game.

A. Design Principles

Web-browser Principle (P:Web): To broadly reach the target audience (secondary students ages 12-18), we chose to focus our initial design and implementation on a web-based game solution and avoid the installation of components on game or various OS platforms. This constrains the available game options, but increases the reachable population.

Engagement / Enjoyment Principle (P:En): We want to keep the students engaged and to emotionally enjoy the experience. To reduce the likelihood of a player discontinuing due to lack of fun, we chose to value and prioritize the fun aspect more than pushing the learning of SE educational concepts. We are thus aware of the fact that less of the SE material may be conveyed and retained, but by retaining engagement over a longer timeframe, further possibilities for SE concept conveyance result.

Game Reuse Principle (P:GR): Leverage known games and game concepts (repurposing) when possible, such as those in [50]. Players may thus already know the basics of how the original game works - reducing the time to become proficient, and they may find the new twist involving SE concepts interesting. Also, more time and cognitive capacity may be available for the mapping of SE concepts to the game elements when compared with completely unfamiliar games.

Simple Game Principle (P:SG): Utilize relatively simple games when not utilizing already known games (cp. *P:GR*). This reduces the overall effort required to acquire game proficiency and to acquire the SE concepts.

SE Concept Reinforcement via Game Action Principle (P:GA): during the games, immediate feedback messages that reinforce game associations to SE concepts are given, e.g., "Correct, the quality was OK" or "Oops, the component was released with quality defects" for a software quality control (SQC) game. This makes it more transparent how choices and actions are reflected in SE concepts.

Lower Bloom's Taxonomy Focus (P:BT): due to the limited time and attention for conveying SE concepts in the secondary school environment, the DGBL SE content and questions focus primarily on the lower levels of the cognitive domain: remembering (in the revised Bloom taxonomy [51]) or knowledge and comprehension (in the original Bloom taxonomy [52]). Note that the older 2004 version of the SWEBOK utilized the Bloom taxonomy to classify its knowledge content for educational purposes.

The aforementioned solution design principles are summarized in Table IV.

TABLE IV. SUMMARY OF SOLUTION DESIGN PRINCIPLES

Principle	Abbrev.
Web-browser Principle	P:Web
Engagement / Enjoyment Principle	P:En
Game Reuse Principle	P:GR
Simple Game Principle	P:SG
SE Concept Reinforcement via Game Action Principle	P:GA
Lower Bloom's Taxonomy Focus	P:BT

B. Edutainment Elements and SE Concept Mappings

We believe that certain aspects of SE cannot be conveyed well solely with games and should thus be supplemented.

Text components: a brief amount of onscreen text was used to introduce the topic area, relevant SE concepts, and the game objective and major game elements. Such a short text that can be clicked away does not overly interfere with the experience, and can be read or skimmed rather quickly. Using these, later bonus-level text questions can reference some prior text or video as a way to verify comprehension.

Video components: a short 5-minute informational video described how prevalent code is, society's dependence on software, and how important software development and software engineers are. The ability to include relevant videos, and the ability for users to explore and discover such videos, adds to the "adventure".

Game components: Various concepts from the SWEBOK were chosen, with the selection subjectively constrained by our project resources, technical and game engine constraints, and how well a concept might map to a game concept. The selection, mapping, and prioritization of what to realize was subjectively reflected and decided on as a team, as summarized in Table V and detailed in Section V.

TABLE V. SE CONCEPT TO GAME MAPPING

SE Concept	SWEBOK KA	SWE4SE Game Variant	Analogous Common Game
Processes	EP, SC	ProcMan	Pac-Man
Quality control	SQ	Q-Check	Pinball
Requirements	SR	ReqAbdeck	Tower Defense
Testing	ST, SD	Angry Nerds	Angry birds
Construction	SC	Reverse Angry Nerds	Angry birds
Defect remediation	SM, CF	Bug Invaders	Space invaders
Project management	EM, PM	Path Management	Maze

The mapping should be interpreted as exploratory and not prescriptive; our intention here is rather to demonstrate the possibilities for conveying SE concepts such an edutainment approach provides.

V. SWE4SE REALIZATION

To develop the web-based games, Scirra Construct 2 was used, an HTML5 and JavaScript 2D game visual editor with a behavior-based logic system. Layouts and Event sheets were used, and each game object type is given properties with certain states and behavior. Sounds and music were integrated. The web browser requires HTML5 and Javascript support. Text components were initially German because we did not want language barriers for secondary students to affect our evaluation results, but the game text could be readily internationalized.

In the following description of each game, the entire upper levels of the SWEBOK ontology of the KA are also provided so that the actual SE concepts conveyed can be considered in context relative to other topics that were not conveyed. Since there was significant overlap in the GOP ontological game concepts used among the various games, these are presented at the end of the section.

A. Conveying SE Concepts in the Various Games

For each game, we describe how the analogous common games and their game concepts were mapped to corresponding SE concepts.

1) ***ProcMan**:* this game is analogous to the well-known Pac-Man game (see Figure 1), which has the highest brand awareness of U.S. consumers (94%) of any video game character [53].

a) Game Play: As in Pac-Man, the player controls the ProcMan traveling within a maze. Points are scored by eating the yellow pac-dots and bonus points are given if the cherries are eaten while shown just below the center. Starting with three lives, if during play one of the four chasing ghosts manages to touch the ProcMan a life is lost.

In our variant there is a twist that, whereas in PacMan one got points by traveling everywhere in the maze in any order, the goal here for the player is to follow a given SE process sequence by having ProcMan consume the distributed initial letter standing for each phase in the expected order while also avoiding the enemy ghosts.

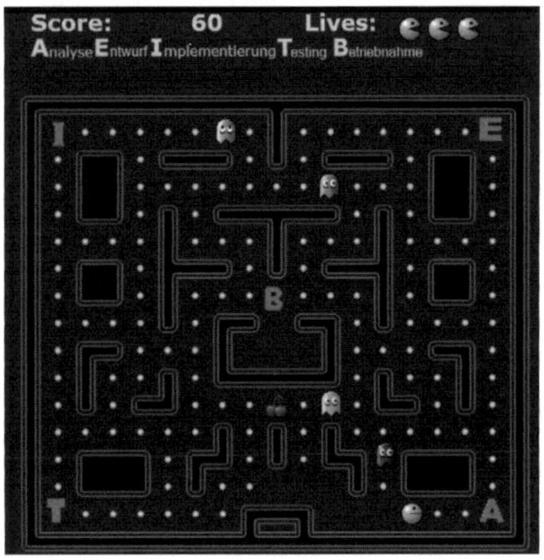

Figure 1. ProcMan game conveys SE processes (screenshot).

b) SE Concept: SE Processes. To convey an engineering process, we chose to introduce the activities common to almost any SE process. Based on the sequential waterfall process, these were Analysis, Design, Implementation, Testing, and Operations (ADITO, or equivalently AEITB in German). We also provided a test-driven development (TDD) variant where the Testing occurs before Implementation (ADTIO).

c) SE Ontology Elements: within the EP KA, the SE concepts of Software Life Cycle Models and Software Process Adaptation are conveyed (see Figure 2).

- Software Engineering Process
  - Software Process Definition
    - Software Process Management
    - Software Process Infrastructure
  - Software Life Cycles
    - Categories of Software Processes
    - **Software Life Cycle Models**
    - **Software Process Adaptation**
    - Practical Considerations
  - Software Process Assessment and Improvement
    - Software Process Assessment Models
    - Software Process Assessment Methods
    - Software Process Improvement Models
    - Continuous and Staged Software Process Ratings
  - Software Measurement
    - Software Process and Product Measurement
    - Quality of Measurement Results
    - Software Information Models
    - Software Process Measurement Techniques
  - Software Engineering Process Tools

Figure 2. SWEBOK EP KA concepts (in bold) conveyed by ProcMan.

Within the SC KA, the SE concept of Test-First Programming is conveyed (see Figure 3).

- Software Construction
  - Software Construction Fundamentals
    - Minimizing Complexity
    - Anticipating Change
    - Constructing for Verification
    - Reuse
    - Standards in Construction
  - Managing Construction
    - Construction in Life Cycle Models
    - Construction Planning
    - Construction Measurement
  - Practical Considerations
    - Construction Design
    - Construction Languages
    - Coding
    - Construction Testing
    - Construction for Reuse
    - Construction with Reuse
    - Construction Quality
    - Integration
  - Construction Technologies
    - API Design and Use
    - Object-Oriented Runtime Issues
    - Parameterization and Generics
    - Assertions, Design by Contract, and Defensive Programming
    - Error Handling, Exception Handling, and Fault Tolerance
    - Executable Models
    - State-Based and Table-Driven Construction Techniques
    - Runtime Configuration and Internationalization
    - Grammar-Based Input Processing
    - Concurrency Primitives
    - Middleware
    - Construction Methods for Distributed Software
    - Constructing Heterogeneous Systems
    - Performance Analysis and Tuning
    - Platform Standards
    - **Test-First Programming**
  - Software Construction Tools
    - Development Environments
    - GUI Builders
    - Unit Testing Tools
    - Profiling, Performance Analysis, and Slicing Tools

Figure 3. SWEBOK SC KA concepts (in bold) conveyed by ProcMan.

*2) **Q-Check**:* this game is loosely analogous to pinball (see Figure 4).

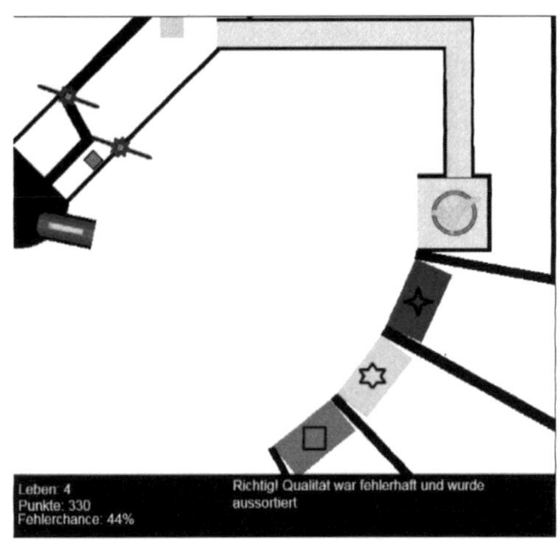

Figure 4. Q-Check game conveys SE quality control (screenshot).

a) Game Play: Software components (SoCos) portrayed as colored shapes spin and drop into a funnel, while a cannon (blue on the left) automatically shoots them individually after a certain time transpires (indicated via a decreasing green bar on the cannon). The player's goal is to select the process (tunnel on the right) that matches the SoCo type currently in the cannon based on both color and shape, or reject it for rework (yellow) if it is defective, improving the future error rate.

b) SE Concept: Software quality control (SQC). Quality expectations differ based on the type of software component being inspected (e.g., GUI, database, business logic). Quality awareness and attention to detail matter, and the appropriate quality process, tools, and testing procedures must be chosen dependent on the assessed object.

c) SE Ontology Elements: within the SQ KA, the SE concept of Software Quality Management Processes is conveyed as shown in Figure 5.

Figure 5. SWEBOK concepts (in bold) conveyed by Q-Check.

3) ***ReqAbdeck:*** ("Abdeckung" in German means "coverage") this game is analogous to the popular game Tower Defense (see Figure 6).

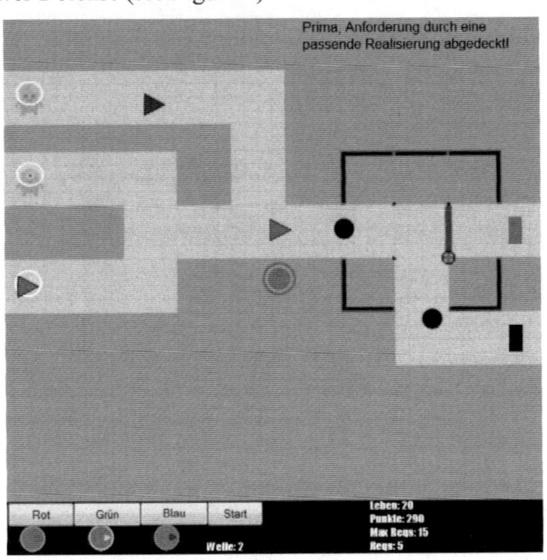

Figure 6. ReqAbdeck conveys SE requirement coverage (screenshot).

a) Game Play: waves of "reqs" (requirements as colored triangles) flow from left to right, and towers in various colors that cover (fire) only at their requirement color must be dragged to the appropriate vicinity before the "reqs" reach the gate. The towers disappear after a short time indicated on their border. Thus, one is not covering critical requirements in time with the matching implementation, ignoring or forgetting a requirement, or not dropping via a gate those requirements without business value (denoted by black circles). One example action message here is "Great, requirement was covered by a suitable realization.

b) SE Concept: Software requirements. ReqAbdeck concerns itself with the SE concept of requirements coverage, for instance not overlooking a requirement, determining which requirements to fulfill how and when (different requirement types need different specialized competencies), which requirements to jettison (e.g., due to insufficient business value).

c) SE Ontology Elements: within the SR KA, the SE concepts of Requirements Process Quality and Improvement and Requirements Classification are conveyed as shown in Figure 7.

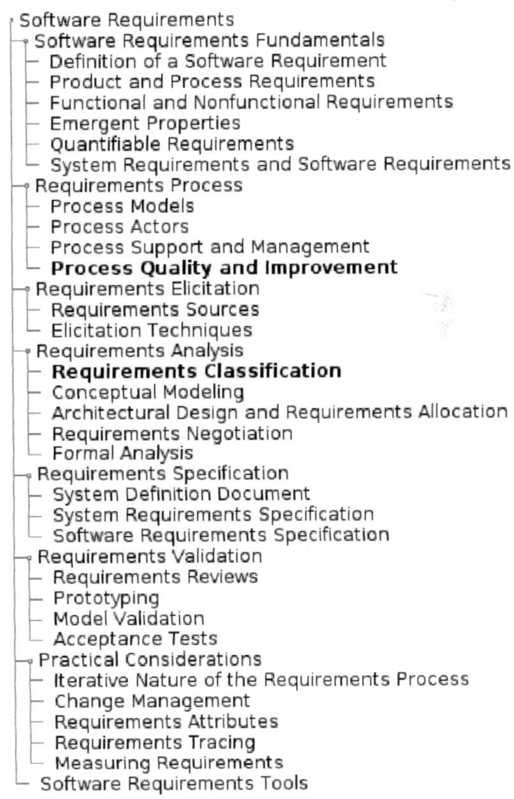

Figure 7. SWEBOK concepts (in bold) conveyed by ReqAbdeck.

4) ***Angry Nerds:*** this game is loosely analogous to the popular game Angry Birds (see Figure 8).

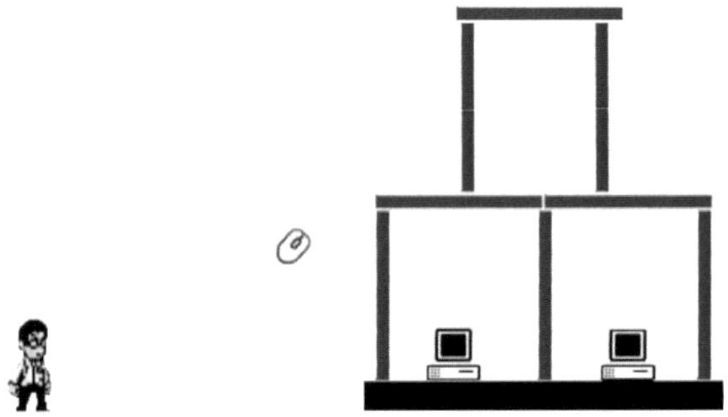

Figure 8. AngryNerds conveys SE testing (screenshot).

a) Game Play: we chose to depict hardware-like testing here of children's blocks, since it was not obvious to us how to quickly convey code-based testing in an obvious manner without necessitating extra explanations about programming. The player's goal in this case is to test a given construct of slabs surrounding PCs by determining where and how hard to throw a mouse at it to knock it completely over. They realize that multiple tests are necessary to discover its weaknesses.

b) SE Concept: Software testing. The SE focus of this game is to convey the objectives of testing (finding deficiencies and building confidence in one's construct) determining where to test to find deficiencies in some software construct.

c) SE Ontology Elements: within the ST KA, the SE concept of Objectives of Testing is conveyed as shown in Figure 9.

- Software Testing
  - Software Testing Fundamentals
    - Testing-Related Terminology
    - Key Issues
    - Relationship of Testing to Other Activities
  - Test Levels
    - The Target of the Test
    - **Objectives of Testing**
  - Test Techniques
    - Based on the Software Engineer's Intuition and Experience
    - Input Domain-Based Techniques
    - Code-Based Techniques
    - Fault-Based Techniques
    - Usage-Based Techniques
    - Model-Based Testing Techniques
    - Techniques Based on the Nature of the Application
    - Selecting and Combining Techniques
  - Test-Related Measures
    - Evaluation of the Program Under Test
    - Evaluation of the Tests Performed
  - Test Process
    - Practical Considerations
    - Test Activities
  - Software Testing Tools
    - Testing Tool Support
    - Categories of Tools

Figure 9. SWEBOK ST concepts (in bold) conveyed by Angry Nerds.

Within the KA SD, the SE concept of Quality Analysis and Evaluation Techniques is conveyed as shown in Figure 10.

- Software Design
  - Software Design Fundamentals
    - General Design Concepts
    - Context of Software Design
    - Software Design Process
    - Software Design Principles
  - Key Issues in Software Design
    - Concurrency
    - Control and Handling of Events
    - Data Persistence
    - Distribution of Components
    - Error and Exception Handling and Fault Tolerance
    - Interaction and Presentation
    - Security
  - Software Structure and Architecture
    - Architectural Structures and Viewpoints
    - Architectural Styles
    - Design Patterns
    - Architecture Design Decisions
    - Families of Programs and Frameworks
  - User Interface Design
    - General User Interface Design Principles
    - User Interface Design Issues
    - The Design of User Interaction Modalities
    - The Design of Information Presentation
    - User Interface Design Process
    - Localization and Internationalization
    - Metaphors and Conceptual Models
  - Software Design Quality Analysis and Evaluation
    - Quality Attributes
    - **Quality Analysis and Evaluation Techniques**
    - Measures
  - Software Design Notations
    - Structural Descriptions (Static View)
    - Behavioral Descriptions (Dynamic View)
  - Software Design Strategies and Methods
    - General Strategies
    - Function-Oriented (Structured) Design
    - Object-Oriented Design
    - Data Structure-Centered Design
    - Component-Based Design (CBD)
    - Other Methods
  - Software Design Tools

Figure 10. SWEBOK SD concepts (in bold) conveyed by Angry Nerds.

5) ***Reverse Angry Nerds****:* this game actually becomes available in the bonus level of the previous game, but the gameplay is different, in that it reverses the role as shown in Figure 11.

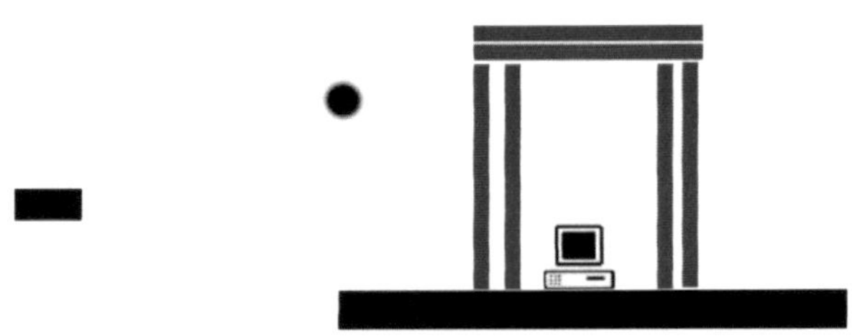

Figure 11. Reverse AngryNerds game conveys SE construction (screenshot).

a) Game Play: the player must now try to build a resilient construct by dragging and placing slabs in such a way that it withstands the automated testing (that being a cannonball shot at the construct).

b) SE Concept: Software construction. The point of this exercise is to construct something (analogous to software) such that it exhibits resiliency.

c) SE Ontology Elements: within the ST KA, the SE concept of Construction Design is conveyed as shown in Figure 12.

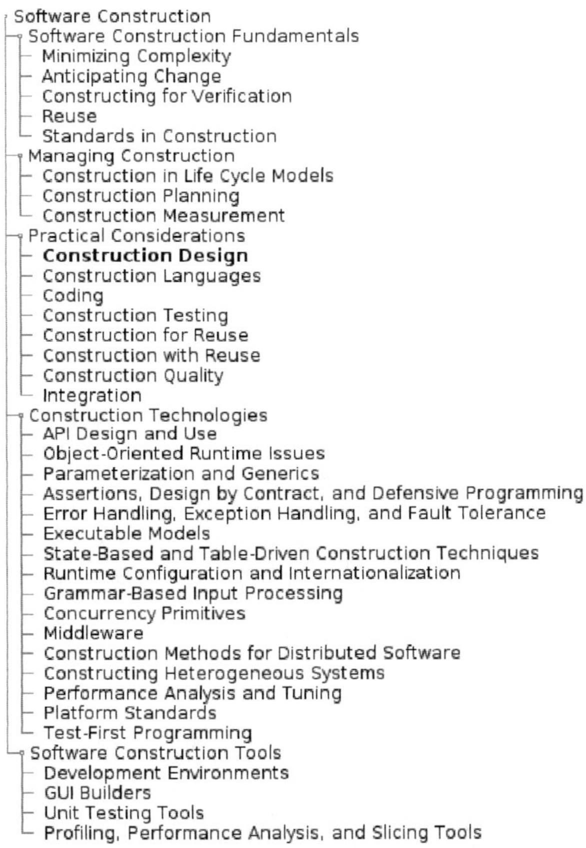

Figure 12. SWEBOK concepts (in bold) conveyed by Angry Nerds.

6) ***Bug Invaders****:* this game is analogous to space invaders, see Figure 13.

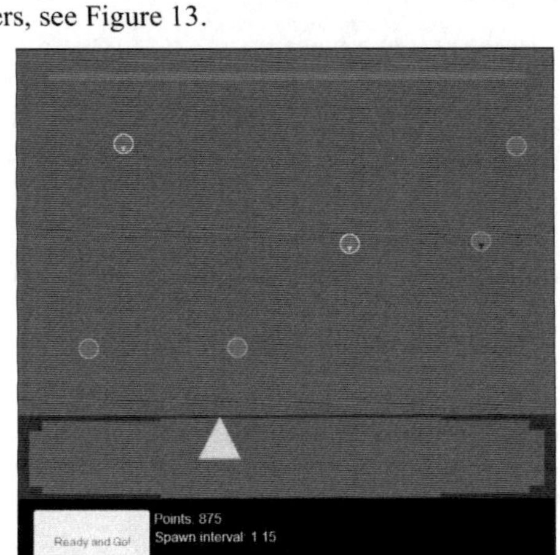

Figure 13. Bug Invaders convey SE defect remediation (screenshot).

a) Game Play: a matching remediation technique (maps to ammunition color in the lower shooter) and firing accuracy (maps to exact causal code location) are needed to destroy exactly that specific bug type that drops down quickly before it creates project damage.

b) SE Concept: Software defect remediation. The SE focus of this game is to convey that different defect types require different remediation techniques and countermeasures applied accurately.

c) SE Ontology Elements: within the KA SM, the SE concept of Maintenance Activities is conveyed as shown in Figure 14.

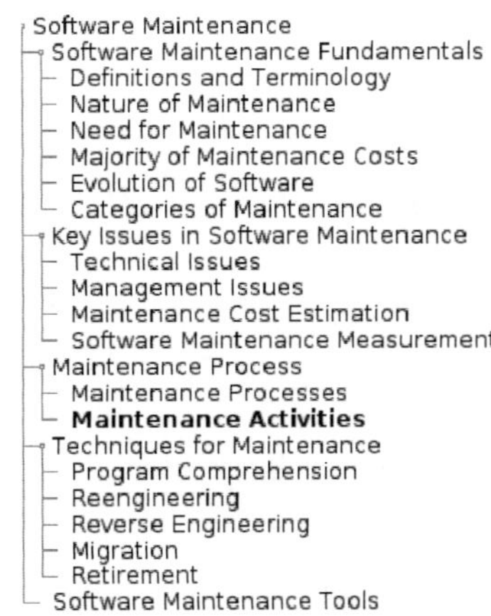

Figure 14. SWEBOK SM concepts (in bold) conveyed by Bug Invaders.

Within the CF KA, the SE concepts of Types of Errors and Debugging Techniques are conveyed as shown in Figure 16.

7) ***Path Management****:* this game is analogous to a maze, see Figure 15.

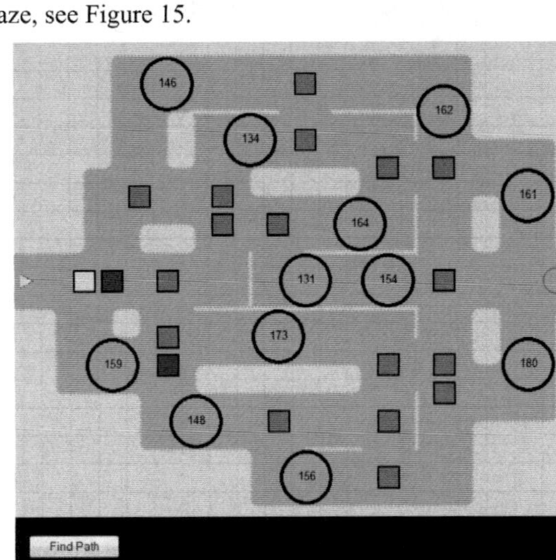

Figure 15. Path Management conveys SE project management (screenshot).

- Computing Foundations
  - Problem Solving Techniques
    - Definition of Problem Solving
    - Formulating the Real Problem
    - Analyze the Problem
    - Design a Solution Search Strategy
    - Problem Solving Using Programs
  - Abstraction
    - Levels of Abstraction
    - Encapsulation
    - Hierarchy
    - Alternate Abstractions
  - Programming Fundamentals
    - The Programming Process
    - Programming Paradigms
  - Programming Language Basics
    - Programming Language Overview
    - Syntax and Semantics of Programming Languages
    - Low-Level Programming Languages
    - High-Level Programming Languages
    - Declarative v+ Imperative Programming Languages
  - Debugging Tools and Techniques
    - **Types of Errors**
    - **Debugging Techniques**
    - Debugging Tools
  - Data Structure and Representation
    - Data Structure Overview
    - Types of Data Structure
    - Operations on Data Structures
  - Algorithms and Complexity
    - Overview of Algorithms
    - Attributes of Algorithms
    - Algorithmic Analysis
    - Algorithmic Design Strategies
    - Algorithmic Analysis Strategies
  - Basic Concept of a System
    - Emergent System Properties
    - Systems Engineering
    - Overview of a Computer System
  - Computer Organization
    - Computer Organization Overview
    - Digital Systems
    - Digital Logic
    - Computer Expression of Data
    - The Central Processing Unit (CPU)
    - Memory System Organization
    - Input and Output (I/O)
  - Compiler Basics
    - Compiler/Interpreter Overview
    - Interpretation and Compilation
    - The Compilation Process
  - Operating Systems Basics
    - Operating Systems Overview
    - Tasks of an Operating System
    - Operating System Abstractions
    - Operating Systems Classification
  - Database Basics and Data Management
    - Entity and Schema
    - Database Management Systems (DBMS)
    - Database Query Language
    - Tasks of DBMS Packages
    - Data Management
    - Data Mining
  - Network Communication Basics
    - Types of Network
    - Basic Network Components
    - Networking Protocols and Standards
    - The Internet
    - Internet of Things
    - Virtual Private Network (VPN)
  - Parallel and Distributed Computing
    - Parallel and Distributed Computing Overview
    - Difference between Parallel and Distributed Computing
    - Parallel and Distributed Computing Models
    - Main Issues in Distributed Computing
  - Basic User Human Factors
    - Input and Output
    - Error Messages
    - Software Robustness
  - Basic Developer Human Factors
    - Structure
    - Comments
  - Secure Software Development and Maintenance
    - Software Requirements Security
    - Software Design Security
    - Software Construction Security
    - Software Testing Security
    - Build Security into Software Engineering Process
    - Software Security Guidelines

Figure 16. SWEBOK CF concepts (in bold) conveyed by Bug Invaders.

*a) Game Play:.*a player must manage a starting budget in points efficiently. From the project start (green triangle) a path selection is made to take it to the end (red circle). Red blocks depict possible steps, blue steps the currently available choices, and green the current position. Each step costs 100 points, while randomly generated problems (black circles) add to the planned costs.

b) SE Concept: software project management. The SE concept conveyed is that multiple choices towards optimizing project costs exist, and the process is planned and resources allocated considering various risks. With appropriate planning, the project goal can be reached with the allotted resources, despite unexpected problems (risk transition) that must be overcome but nevertheless result in unplanned additional resource costs.

c) SE Ontology Elements: within the KA of EM, the concepts of Process Planning;, Effort, Schedule, and Cost Estimation; Resource Allocation; and Risk Management are conveyed, see Figure 17.

- Software Engineering Management
  - Initiation and Scope Definition
    - Determination and Negotiation of Requirements
    - Feasibility Analysis
    - Process for the Review and Revision of Requirements
  - Software Project Planning
    - **Process Planning**
    - Determine Deliverables
    - **Effort, Schedule, and Cost Estimation**
    - **Resource Allocation**
    - **Risk Management**
    - Quality Management
    - Plan Management
  - Software Project Enactment
    - Implementation of Plans
    - Software Acquisition and Supplier Contract Management
    - Implementation of Measurement Process
    - Monitor Process
    - Control Process
    - Reporting
  - Review and Evaluation
    - Determining Satisfaction of Requirements
    - Reviewing and Evaluating Performance
  - Closure
    - Determining Closure
    - Closure Activities
  - Software Engineering Measurement
    - Establish and Sustain Measurement Commitment
    - Plan the Measurement Process
    - Perform the Measurement Process
    - Evaluate Measurement
  - Software Engineering Management Tools

Figure 17. SWEBOK concepts (in bold) conveyed by Path Management.

B. Realization of the Game World SE Exploration Concept

To tie the various DGs together, the realization includes a SE universe to navigate to and discover various SE planets. Figure 18 shows the spaceship navigating in two dimensions. A shield level, reduced when colliding with asteroids, is shown as a colored line next to the ship. The game ends when the shields are lost or on collision with the sun. The bottom right of the screen shows a navigation map with the location of all planets (red first, green when visited, and violet for the home planet, and the spaceship as an arrow.

When arriving at a planet (Figure 19), a short text about SE concepts that relates to the game is shown, which when understood, can later be used to answer bonus questions at a gate. The portal to the game is shown on the left. The brown gate and fence shows a darkened advanced level area only accessible by successfully passing a gate requiring that SE challenge questions be answered correctly. This then enables passage and undarkens the upper bonus region top.

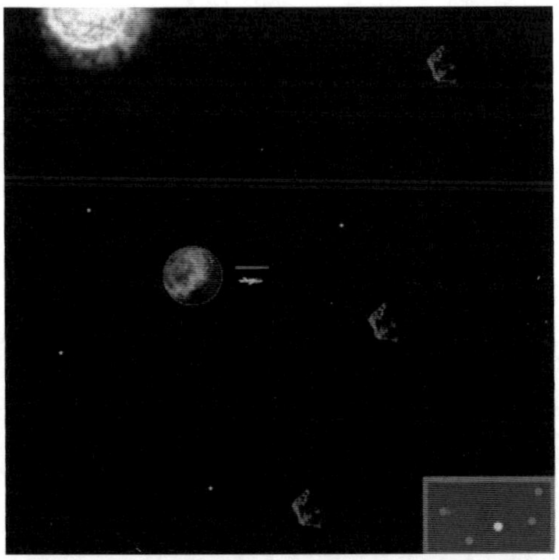

Figure 18. Spaceship navigating the SE universe (screenshot).

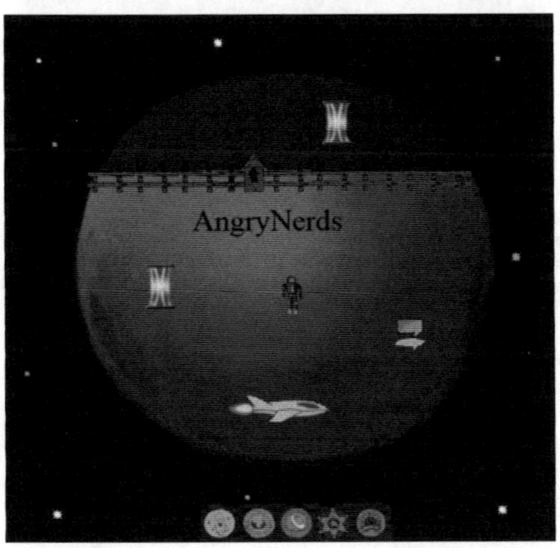

Figure 19. Example of a uniquely named SE game planet (screenshot).

On the home planet, a TV tower shows the video.

The realization is economical in that it can be widely distributed (*P:Web*) without client installation costs or large cloud server investments (it runs locally in the browser).

C. Game Ontology

Instantiated GOP game ontology concepts are marked with italics in Figure 20, with constraints or notes provided in parentheses. Additional unutilized GOP leaf nodes are not depicted due to space limitations.

- GOP
  - Interface
    - Input
      - Input Devices
        - *Keyboard*
        - *Mouse*
    - Input Method
      - Locus of Manipulation
        - *Single Entity Manipulation*
      - Manipulation Method
        - Indirect Manipulation
          - *Point and Click Interface*
    - Presentation
      - Presentation Hardware
        - Visual Display Hardware
          - *Video Monitor*
      - Cardinality Of Gameworld
        - *2-Dimensional Gameworld*
      - Presentation Software
        - Sensory Output
          - Visual Output
            - Head Up Display
              - *Lives Indicator* (except PathManagement)
              - *Points Indicator*
              - *Health Indicator*
              - *Map Display* (Universe)
              - *Next Piece Indicator* (Q-Check)
          - *Aural Output* (music)
        - Point of View
          - *Second-person Point of View*
        - Feedback
          - *Confirmation* (messages, badges)
  - Entity Manipulation
    - *To Move*
    - *To Remove* (except Path Management, Reverse AngryNerds, Universe)
    - *To Rotate* (ReqAbdeck, Universe, Q-Check)
    - *To Collide* (ProcMan, Universe)
    - *To Select*
    - Compound Action
      - *To Shoot* (AngryNerds)
      - *To Manage Resources* (Reverse AngryNerds)
  - Rules
    - Gameworld Rules
      - Pseudo-Physical Rules
        - *Solidity* (AngryNerds, Reverse AngryNerds)
        - *Gravity* (AngryNerds, Reverse AngryNerds, Universe)
    - Gameplay Rules
      - Cardinality of Gameplay
        - *0D Gameplay* (Q-Check, AngryNerds, Reverse AngryNerds)
        - *1D Gameplay* (Bug Invaders)
        - *2D Gameplay* (ProcMan, ReqAbdeck, Universe)
      - *Lives*
      - *Randomness*
      - Game Ends
        - *Resource Exhaustion* (if lives lost)
        - *Gameworld Exhaustion* (some max. time)
        - *No Game End* (Universe)
      - Segmentation of Gameplay
        - Spatial Segmentation
          - *Level* (advanced planet areas)
        - Challenge Segmentation
          - *Wave* (ReqAbdeck, Bug Invaders)
          - *Puzzle* (PathManagement)
          - *Bonus Stage*
        - Temporal Segmentation
          - *Temporal Resource* (time limits)
      - Rules Synergies
        - *Complete Information* (except PathManagement)
        - *Dynamic Difficulty Adjustment* (Q-Check, ReqAbdeck, Bug Invaders)
      - *Spawnpoint*
  - Goals
    - Game Goals
      - *Required Goals*
    - Goal Metrics
      - *Score*

Figure 20. GOP concepts (in italics) utilized by SWE4SE.

D. Realization via Game Framework

Construct 2 was used to realize the games. Generally, the browser must support HTML5 and Javascript and popups must be activated. Scirra Ltd. recommends Mozilla Firefox, Google Chrome, or Opera. Internet Explorer 9+ can be used from Windows Vista on, Windows XP cannot used IE. We had problems with sound using IE (11 was tested).

VI. SWE4SE Evaluation

The convenience sampling technique [54], common in educational settings, was selected to evaluate our SE edutainment approach due to various constraints otherwise inhibiting direct access to a larger random population sample of the target population stratum. These constraints include logistical and marketing effort and budget, privacy issues, and acquiring parental consent for school age children.

A. Evaluation Setting

Two teachers at two different public university preparatory (secondary) schools in different cities in the local German region gave us access for 90 minutes to 20 total students that attend their informatics interest groups. *Setting A* using an alpha version of the software tested with a group of 8 males, and a later *setting B* using a beta version in a different city with 6 females and 6 males students. Figure 21 shows the age and gender distribution, and Figure 22 indicates their current game usage frequency.

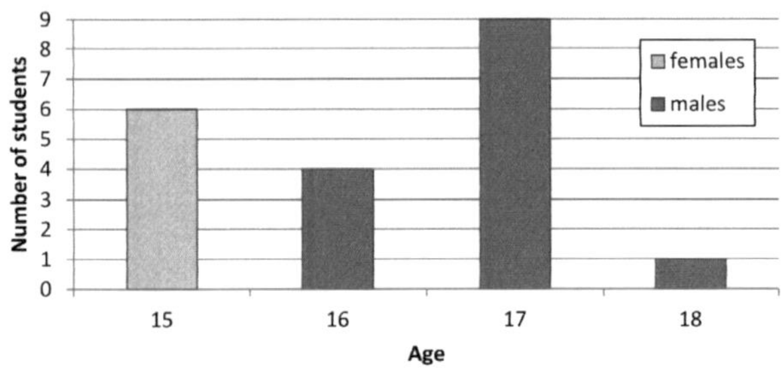

Figure 21. Student age and gender distribution.

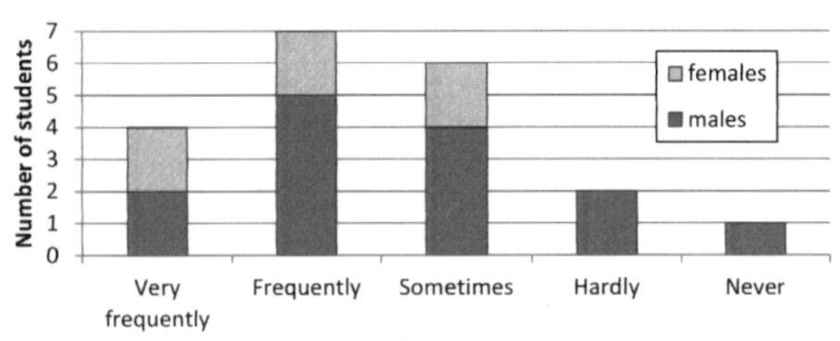

Figure 22. Prior game usage frequency distribution.

B. Evaluation Method

While we considered utilizing the GEQ [55], it appeared more appropriate for more immersive games rather than our game genres. Due to factors such as the player ages, the limited time they had for playing multiple different short games (7 games in one hour), and the limited time, attention, and incentives for filling out pre- and post-questionnaires (10 minutes respectively), only a few questions about their state before and after with regard to negative or positive affect were included. They were asked but not compelled to answer all questions, so some fields were left blank by some students, which could be interpreted to mean they did not understand the question, or did not know how to answer, or did not care to answer the question. Blank answers were thus omitted.

The empirical evaluation consisted of 90-minute sessions held in two different settings A and B. The first 5 minutes consisted of a short introduction as to the purpose of our visit and what to expect, involving no teaching. Students were then given 10 minutes to fill out anonymous printed questionnaires in German that provided us with initial basic data. When all were done, they began their one-hour edutainment experience. In the 10 minutes directly thereafter, monitors were turned off and they completed the second part of their questionnaire, which focused on their experience and understanding, after which we held a 5-minute group feedback session.

C. Evaluation Results

We observed that all students were engaged with SWE4SE for the entire hour and appeared to enjoy the experience *(P:En),* and occasionally interacted excitedly with fellow students. Table VI provides our analysis of the questionnaire results. Unless otherwise indicated, averages were based on a scale of 1 to 5 (1 being very good, 5 bad):

TABLE VI. User Experience

Factor	Rating	Relates to
Overall experience	2.1	*P:En*
Game enjoyment	2.0	*P:En*
Helpful conveying several SE concepts via different games	Yes (16) No (1)	*P:SG, P:GR*
Success rate recalling the SE concepts associated with each named game[a]	62%	*P:GA* Text Components
Watched the video attentively	Yes (20)	
Video and its quality	Good (20)	
Video length of 5 minutes	Keep (19) Lengthen (1)	

a. Open answers. The game names in the questions could serve as a hint, but these did not include the complete and explicit SE concept nor was the game accessible.

Table VII shows the change in perception, attractiveness, and understanding of SE after the experience.

TABLE VII. Change in SE Perceptions

Change in responses	Before	After	Improvement
Importance of SE for society[a]	1.7	1.2	33%
Attractiveness of SE as a personal career path[b]	3.3	2.7	16%
Ability to define what SE is[c]	2.9	2.3	20%

a. Scale of 1 to 3 (1=very important, 3=not important); 2 wrote "don't know" in the prequestionnaire.
b. Scale of 1 to 5 (1=very attractive, 5=not attractive)
c. Answer graded (1 excellent, 2 very good, 3 satisfactory, 4 sufficient) for B group only.

As to interpreting the results, a convenience sample can obviously contain a number of biases, including under- or overrepresentation. Our supervision of the evaluation process and physically observing that the software was actually used for an hour by each of the students separately, and that each questionnaire was individually filled out, removed certain other kinds of threats to validity.

VII. Discussion

We now discuss our evaluation results and findings.

A. Evaluation

Our evaluation showed that the SWE4SE approach can be effective: because students in this age group had previous familiarity with gaming, they had no difficulty rapidly discovering and playing the games intuitively without training or help, they understood the intended mapping of SE concepts onto game elements, and the perception, attractiveness, and understanding of SE improved significantly without discernable gender differences. It was efficient in achieving these effects in the relatively short span of an hour of usage. An edutainment approach with short videos, short text components, and a variety of simple games appears promising for effectively and efficiently improving the awareness about and image SE, at least for our target population stratum.

B. Ontologies and Methods supporting DGBL in SE

In our investigation of which types of SE concepts lend themselves to being conveyed with which game genres, elements, and gameplay or logic we noticed various difficulties with regard to achieving clarity or more formalization as to a method for mapping SE educational concepts to game genres or elements. This was due to a number of reasons, such as a lack of additional information to more precisely categorize the concepts from various viewpoints, and lack of accessibility of standardized ontologies in standard formats.

For instance, while we were able to categorize the SWEBOK knowledge being conveyed at a relatively coarse granularity in its taxonomy, we found it to be missing additional ontological relations or properties. For one, Bloom's taxonomy has now been removed from the SWEBOK, making it more difficult to automatically or quickly assess the type of knowledge. E.g., if we are only interested in the remembering level of knowledge we cannot easily cull this from the rest.

From the DG standpoint, we were able to describe the various low-level game elements with the GOP. However, we lacked the ability to describe the gameplay logic. For instance, does the game involve sequencing, or differentiating objects, constructing, destroying, analysis, or planning?

A method for mapping we could conceive of would be that any SE concept of the type *process* could perhaps be mapped to a DG that involves sequencing, or SE concept of the type *analysis* could utilize a DG that involves differentiation.

C. State of DGBL in SE

Our literature review of DG in SE did not find a broad coverage of KAs. For the purpose of conveying SE concepts specifically in the secondary education this may not be necessary, but it does perhaps indicate that DG have concentrated in certain more obvious areas and that other SE areas for applying DGs have perhaps not been sufficiently explored.

Other than programming games, there appears to be little commercial interest or incentive to provide professional DG to the SE educational community. It is our opinion that DGBL for SE is currently in a relatively immature state, that developed DGs are typically analogous to islands in an uncharted sea and not readily discoverable, accessible, and reusable. We thus suggest that the SE community develop a common SE DG platform that would provide convenient access to such DGs, broadening their discovery and reuse, supporting their open source evolution, and providing feedback. If the community had a categorization utilizing the SWEBOK or similar SE ontology and linked available DGs that address these, then DGBL reuse could be furthered for conveying SE concepts.

VIII. Conclusion and Future Work

We described SWE4SE, an edutainment approach for gamifying and conveying software engineering concepts to secondary school students. Various principles used of the edutainment approach were elucidated, and it was shown from an ontological perspective how various SE concepts could be mapped and realized with various digital game concepts and elements.

As an indicator of the economic realizability of SWE4SE, our DG realization was done by two students in a 10 credit project in one semester, equivalent to approximately 600 hours workload.

The evaluation showed that an edutainment approach, combining short videos and text elements, and a variety of simple digital games, can be promising for improving SE awareness in our target population stratum. Since this target age group is already familiar with gaming and utilizes gaming relatively frequently, the approach appears reasonable for reaching a larger populace. A challenge remains in making secondary students aware of the availability the edutainment and motivating them to utilize it on a direct or individual basis. While social networks appear feasible for raising awareness, in the face of the abundance of entertainment and game options available, we believe that the most promising approach will likely be informational publicity campaigns towards informatics teachers in secondary schools where groups (i.e., interest groups or classrooms) utilize the software together in a structured setting.

As to further development, refinement, and evolution of such an SWE4SE or similar game development approach, we believe ontologies to be promising for more formally conveying knowledge concepts for the SE domain and for describing various game concepts. However, our investigation determined that a severe gap and immaturity exists in this area that prevents the (semi-)automated inclusion and mapping of SE concepts to game objects or gameplay logic (e.g., via game description languages). This area should thus be further investigated, developed, and formalized to more effectively support DGBL and DG reuse and know-how for SEE and move this area from a trail-and-error experimental craft to more professional engineering.

Future work includes investigating the integration both game and SE domain ontologies into game engines and description languages, a longitudinal study on motivational effect retention and other interfering or conflicting influences, and integrated game and web analytics to provide further insights into game playing behavior.

ACKNOWLEDGMENT

The author thanks Carsten Lecon, Christian Wilhelm, Flamur Kastrati, and Lisa Philipp for their assistance with the concepts, realization, and graphics.

REFERENCES

[1] R. Oberhauser, "Gamifying and Conveying Software Engineering Concepts for Secondary Education: An Edutainment Approach," In: Proc. of the Tenth International Conf. on Software Engineering Advances (ICSEA 2015). IARIA XPS Press, 2015. pp. 432-437, ISBN: 978-1-61208-367-4.

[2] J. Vegso, "Interest in CS as a Major Drops Among Incoming Freshmen," Computing Research News, vol. 17, no.3, 2005.

[3] B. Schmidt, "How are college majors changing?" [Online]. Available from: http://benschmidt.org/Degrees/

[4] U. Hanselmann, "Die große Kraft," Engl: "The major force," Die Zeit, No. 22, 2009. [Online]. Available from: http://www.zeit.de/2009/22/C-Faecherportraet-Informatik/komplettansicht.

[5] Bitkom, "In Deutschland fehlen 41.000 IT-Experten," 2014. [Online]. Available from: https://www.bitkom.org/Presse/Presseinformation/Pressemitteilung_1704.html.

[6] D. Parnas, "Software engineering programs are not computer science programs," IEEE Software, 16(6), 1999, pp. 19-30.

[7] P. Bourque and R. Fairley, "Guide to the Software Engineering Body of Knowledge (SWEBOK (R)): Version 3.0," IEEE Computer Society Press, 2014.

[8] C. Crawford, The art of computer game design. McGraw-Hill/Osborne Media, 1984.

[9] M. Wolf, The medium of the video game. University of Texas Press, 2002.

[10] I. Bogost, Persuasive games: The expressive power of videogames. The MIT Press, 2007.

[11] D.R. Michael and S.L. Chen, , Serious games: Games that educate, train, and inform. Muska & Lipman/Premier-Trade. 2005.

[12] C. Abt, "Serious Games," The Viking Press, 1970.

[13] O. Pedreira, F. García, N. Brisaboa, and M. Piattini,. "Gamification in software engineering–A systematic mapping," Information and Software Technology, 57, 2015, pp.157-168.

[14] Van Eck, R., 2006. Digital game-based learning: It's not just the digital natives who are restless. EDUCAUSE review, 41(2), p.16.

[15] T. M. Connolly, E. A. Boyle, E. MacArthur T. Hainey, J. M. Boyle, "A systematic literature review of empirical evidence on computer games and serious games," Computers & Education, 59, Elsevier Ltd., 2012, pp. 661–686.

[16] B. J. Fogg, "A behavior model for persuasive design," In Proceedings of the 4th international Conference on Persuasive Technology, ACM, 2009. pp. 40-46.

[17] The Game Ontology Project. [Online]. Available from: http://www.gameontology.com

[18] J. P. Zagal and A. Bruckman, "The game ontology project: supporting learning while contributing authentically to game studies," in Proc. 8th International conference for the learning sciences (ICLS '08), Vol. 2, International Society of the Learning Sciences, 2008, pp. 499-506.

[19] J.P. Zagal, Ludoliteracy: Defining, Understanding, and Supporting Games Education. ETC Press, 2011.

[20] G. Lakoff, Women, Fire, and Dangerous Things: What Categories Reveal About the Mind. The University of Chicago Press, Chicago, 1987.

[21] B. Glaser and A. Strauss, The Discovery of Grounded Theory: Strategies for Qualitative Research. Aldine, Chicago, 1967.

[22] D. Ašeriškis and R. Damaševičius, "Gamification Patterns for Gamification Applications," in Proc. of the 6th international conference on Intelligent Human Computer Interaction (IHCI 2014), Procedia Computer Science, Vol. 39, 2014, pp.83-90.

[23] J. T. Chan and W. Y. Yuen, "Digital Game Ontology: Semantic Web Approach on Enhancing Game Studies," In Proceedings of 2008 IEEE 9th International Conference on Computer-Aided Industrial Design & Conceptual Design, Vol. 1, 2008.

[24] M. Ebner et al., "Towards a video game description language," In: Artificial and Computational Intelligence in Games, Dagstuhl Follow-ups, 6. Dagstuhl Publishing, Wadern, 2013, pp. 85-100, ISBN 9783939897620.

[25] T. Connolly, M. Stansfield, and T. Hainey, "An application of games-based learning within software engineering," British Journal of Educational Technology, 38(3), 2007, pp. 416-428.

[26] C. Caulfield, J. Xia, D. Veal, and S. Maj, "A systematic survey of games used for software engineering education," Modern Applied Science, 5(6), 2011, pp. 28-43.

[27] S. Shabanah, "Computer Games for Algorithm Learning," In Handbook of Research on Improving Learning and Motivation through Educational Games: Multidisciplinary Approaches, ed. Patrick Felicia, 2011, pp. 1036-1063.

[28] K. Shaw and J. Dermoudy, "Engendering an Empathy for Software Engineering," In Proceedings of the 7th Australasian conference on Computing education-Volume 42. Australian Computer Society, Inc., 2005, pp. 135-144.

[29] M. d. O. Barros, A. R. Dantas, G. O. Veronese, and C. M. L. Werner, "Model-Driven Game Development: Experience and Model Enhancements in Software Project Management Education," in Software Process: Improvement and Practice. 11(4), 2006, pp. 411–421, doi:10.1002/spip.279.

[30] A. Jain and B. Boehm, "SimVBSE: Developing a Game for Value-Based Software Engineering," In Proceedings of the 19th Conference on Software Engineering Education & Training (CSEET'06), IEEE, 2006, pp. 103-114, doi:10.1109/cseet.2006.31.

[31] C. W. Caulfield, D. Veal, and S. P. Maj, "Teaching software engineering management–issues and perspectives," International Journal of Computer Science and Network Security, 11(7), 2011, pp.50-54.

[32] J. S. Collofello, "University/industry collaboration in developing a simulation-based software project management training course," IEEE Transactions on Education, 43(4), IEEE, 2000, pp.389-393.

[33] A. Drappa and J. Ludewig, "Simulation in software engineering training," in Proceedings of the 22nd International Conference on Software Engineering, 2000, pp. 199–208.

[34] E. O., Navarro and A. van der Hoek, "Multi-Site Evaluation of SimSE," Proceedings of The 40th ACM Technical Symposium on Computer Science Education, (SIGCSE '09). ACM, 2009, pp. 326-330, doi:10.1145/1508865.1508981.

[35] R. O. Chaves et al., "Experimental evaluation of a serious game for teaching software process modeling," IEEE Transactions on Education, 58(4), 2015, pp.289-296.

[36] T. Wang and Q. Zhu, "A Software Engineering Education Game in a 3-D Online Virtual Environment," Proceedings of The First International Workshop on Education Technology

and Computer Science, Vol. 2. IEEE, 2009. pp. 708-710, doi:10.1109/ETCS.2009.418.

[37] D. Ašeriškis and R. Damaševičius, "Gamification of a project management system," in Proc. of Int. Conf. on Advances in Computer-Human Interactions (ACHI2014), 2014, pp. 200-207.

[38] T. Xie, N. Tillmann, and J. De Halleux, "Educational software engineering: Where software engineering, education, and gaming meet," In Proceedings of the 3rd International Workshop on Games and Software Engineering: Engineering Computer Games to Enable Positive, Progressive Change. IEEE Press, 2013, pp. 36-39.

[39] E. Knauss, K. Schneider, K., and K. Stapel, "A Game for Taking Requirements Engineering More Seriously," Proceedings of The Third International Workshop on Multimedia and Enjoyable Requirements Engineering - Beyond Mere Descriptions and with More Fun and Games. IEEE, 2008, pp. 22-26, doi:10.1109/MERE.2008.1.

[40] T. Hainey, T. J. Connelly, M. Stansfield, and E. A. Boyle, "Evaluation of a Game to Teach Requirements Collection and Analysis in Software Engineering at Tertiary Education Level," Computers & Education, 56(1), 2010, pp. 21–35, doi: 10.1016/j.compedu.2010.09.0.

[41] J. Fernandes et al., "iThink: A Game-Based Approach Towards Improving Collaboration and Participation in Requirement Elicitation," in Proc. of the 4th International Conference on Games and Virtual Worlds for Serious Applications (VS-GAMES'12). Procedia Computer Science, vol. 15, 2012, pp. 66-77, doi:10.1016/j.procs.2012.10.059.

[42] H. Sharp and P. Hall, "An Interactive Multimedia Software House Simulation for Postgraduate Software Engineers," in Proceedings of the 22nd International Conference on Software Engineering. ACM, 2000, pp. 688-691.

[43] J. Bell, S. Sheth, S., and G. Kaiser, "Secret ninja testing with HALO software engineering," In Proceedings of the 4th international workshop on social software engineering. ACM, 2011, pp. 43-47.

[44] C. Calero, F. Ruiz, and M. Piattini, M. (eds.), Ontologies for software engineering and software technology. Springer Science & Business Media, 2006.

[45] M. P. S. Bhatia, A. Kumar, and R. Beniwal, "Ontologies for Software Engineering: Past, Present and Future," Indian Journal of Science and Technology, 9(9), 2016, pp. 1-16.

[46] O. Mendes and A. Abran, "Issues in the development of an ontology for an emerging engineering discipline," In Proceedings of the 17th International Conference on Software Engineering and Knowledge Engineering (SEKE'2005), 2005, pp. 139-144.

[47] C. Wille, R. R. Dumke, A. Abran, and J. M. Desharnais, "E-learning infrastructure for software engineering education: Steps in ontology modeling for SWEBOK," In IASTED International Conf. on Software Engineering, 2004, pp. 520-525.

[48] L. Carter, "Why students with an apparent aptitude for computer science don't choose to major in computer science," SIGCSE Bulletin, ACM, vol. 38, no. 1, Mar. 2006, pp. 27-31.

[49] K. M. Cooper and C. S. Longstreet, "Model-driven Engineering of Serious Educational Games: Integrating Learning Objectives for Subject Specific Topics and Transferable Skills," In Computer Games and Software Engineering (1st ed.), K. M. Cooper and W. Scacchi, Eds. Chapman & Hall/CRC, 2015, pp. 59-90.

[50] S. Kent, The Ultimate History of Video Games. Three Rivers Press, 2001.

[51] Anderson, L., Krathwohl, David R, & Bloom, Benjamin S. (2001). A taxonomy for learning, teaching, and assessing : A revision of Bloom's taxonomy of educational objectives. New York: Longman.

[52] Bloom, B. S.; Engelhart, M. D.; Furst, E. J.; Hill, W. H.; Krathwohl, D. R. (1956). Taxonomy of educational objectives: The classification of educational goals. Handbook I: Cognitive domain. New York: David McKay Company.

[53] Davie Brown Entertainment, "Davie Brown Celebrity Index: Mario, Pac-Man Most Appealing Video Game Characters Among Consumers". PR Newswire, 2008. [Online]. Available from: http://www.prnewswire.com/news-releases/davie-brown-celebrity-index-mario-pac-man-most-appealing-video-game-characters-among-consumers-57256317.html

[54] L. Given (Ed.), The Sage encyclopedia of qualitative research methods. Sage Publications, 2008.

[55] W. IJsselsteijn, K. Poels, and Y. De Kort, "The Game Experience Questionnaire: Development of a self-report measure to assess player experiences of digital games," TU Eindhoven, Eindhoven, The Netherlands, 2008.

Requirements Engineering in Model Transformation Development: A Technique Suitability Framework for Model Transformation Applications

Sobhan Yassipour Tehrani, Kevin Lano
Department of Informatics, King's College London, London WC2R 2LS, U.K.
E-mail: {sobhan.yassipour_tehrani, kevin.lano}@kcl.ac.uk

***Abstract*—Model transformations (MTs) are central to model-driven engineering (MDE). They can be used for a range of purposes, including to improve the quality of models, to refactor models, to migrate or translate models from one representation to another, and to generate code or other artifacts from models. At present, the development of model transformation is mainly focused on the specification and implementation phases, whereas there is a lack of support in other phases including: requirements, analysis, design and testing. Furthermore, there is a lack of cohesive support for transformations including: notations, methods and tools within all phases during the development process, which makes the maintenance and understandability of the transformation code problematic. One of the main hindrances for not using a systematic Requirements Engineering (RE) process, the initial phase of the software development life-cycle where software's specifications are declared, before starting the development, could be the false assumption that it is a waste of time/cost and would delay implementation. The goal of this paper is to evaluate model transformation technology from a requirements engineering process point of view. Moreover, we identify criteria for selecting appropriate requirements engineering techniques, and we propose a framework for this selection process.**

***Index Terms*—model transformations; requirements engineering; requirements engineering framework; model transformation case study; RE technique framework**

I. INTRODUCTION

Requirements engineering (RE) has been a relatively neglected aspect of model transformation (MT) development because the emphasis in transformation development has been upon specifications and implementations. The failure to explicitly identify requirements may result in developed transformations, which do not satisfy the needs of the users of the transformation. Problems may arise because implicitly-assumed requirements have not been explicitly stated; for instance, that a migration or refactoring transformation should preserve the semantics of its source model in the target model, or that a transformation is only required to operate on a restricted range of input models. Without thorough requirements elicitation, important requirements may be omitted from consideration, resulting in a developed transformation, which fails to achieve its intended purpose.

In [1] we reviewed the current practice of RE for MT and identified a framework for an improved RE process. In this paper we extend [1] with more details of the framework, and we give extracts from a large-scale application of the framework to a C code generator.

We use the 4-phase RE process model proposed by Sommerville [2] and adapt it according to our specific needs. This process model is widely accepted by researchers and professional experts. The model defines the following as the most important phases of RE, which should be applied: domain analysis and requirements elicitation, evaluation and negotiation, specification and documentation, validation and verification.

In Section II we describe related work. Section III gives a background on requirements engineering for model transformations as well as transformation semantics and its nature. We also identify how formalised requirements can be validated and can be used to guide the selection of design patterns for the development of the transformation. In Section IV we examine RE techniques and identify how these can be applied to MT development. In Section V we present a framework for an RE process and RE technique selection for MT. In Section VI we give a case study to evaluate the application of our framework.

II. RELATED WORK

The increasing complexity and size of today's software systems has resulted in raising the complexity and size of model transformations. Although there have been different transformation tools and languages, most of them are focused on the specification and implementation phases. According to [3], most of the transformation languages proposed by Model Driven Engineering (MDE), a software development methodology, are only focused towards the implementation phase and are not integrated in a unified engineering process. It could be said that at the moment, the transformation process is performed in an ad-hoc manner; defining the problem and then directly beginning the implementation process. At present, the development of model transformation is mainly focused on the specification and implementation phases, whereas there is a lack of support in other phases including: requirements, analysis, design and testing. Furthermore, there is a lack of cohesive support for transformations including: notations, methods and tools within all phases during the development process, which makes the maintenance and understandability of the transformation code problematic [3].

As Selic [4] argues, "we are far from making the writing of model transformations an established and repeatable technical task". The software engineering of model transformations has only recently been considered in a systematic way, and most of this work [5][6] is focussed upon design and verification rather than upon requirements engineering. The work on requirements engineering in *trans*ML is focused upon functional requirements, and the use of abstract syntax rules to express them. Here, we consider a full range of functional and non-functional requirements and we use concrete syntax rules for the initial expression of functional requirements.

In order to trace the requirements into subsequent steps, *trans*ML defines a modelling language, which represents the requirements in the form of Systems Modeling Language (SysML) [7] diagrams. This allows the transformer(s) to link requirements of a model transformation to its corresponding analysis and design models, code and other artifacts. Having a connection amongst different artifacts in the model transformation development process enables the transformer(s) to check the correctness and completeness of all requirements [8].

We have carried out a survey and interview study of RE for MT in industrial cases [9]. This study showed that RE techniques are not used in a systematic way in current industrial MT practice. In this paper, we describe a requirements engineering process for transformations based on adaptions of the standard RE process model, and upon adaptions of RE techniques for transformations.

III. Requirements for Model Transformations

Requirements for a software product are generally divided into two main categories: functional requirements, which identify what functional capabilities the system should provide, and non-functional requirements, which identify quality characteristics expected from the developed system and restrictions upon the development process itself.

The functional requirements of a model transformation $\tau{:}S \rightarrow T$, which maps models of a source language S to a target language T are defined in terms of the effect of τ on model m of S, and the relationship of the resulting model n of T to m. It is a characteristic of model transformations that such functional requirements are usually decomposed into a set of mapping requirements for different cases of structures and elements within S. In addition, assumptions about the input model should be identified as part of the functional requirements.

It can be observed in many published examples of model transformations that the initial descriptions of their intended functional behaviour is in terms of a concrete syntax for the source and target languages, which they operate upon. For instance in [10], the three key effects of the transformation are expressed in terms of rewritings of Unified Modeling Language (UML) class diagrams. In [11], the transformation effects are expressed by parallel rewritings of Petri Nets and statecharts. In general, specification of the intended functionality of the transformation in terms of concrete syntax rules is more natural and comprehensible for the stakeholders than is specification in terms of abstract syntax. However, this form of description has the disadvantage that it may be imprecise; there may be significant details of models, which have no representation in the concrete syntax, or there may be ambiguities in the concrete syntax representation. Therefore, conversion of the concrete syntax rules into precise abstract syntax rules is a necessary step as part of the formalisation of the requirements.

Requirements may be functional or non-functional (e.g., concerned with the size of generated models, transformation efficiency or confluence). Another distinction, which is useful for transformations is between local and global requirements:

- Local requirements are concerned with localised parts of one or more models. Mapping requirements define when and how a part of one model should be mapped onto a part of another. Rewriting requirements dictate when and how a part of a model should be refactored/transformed in-place.
- Global requirements identify properties of an entire model. For example that some global measure of complexity or redundancy is decreased by a refactoring transformation. Invariants, assumptions and postconditions of a transformation usually apply at the entire model level.

Figure 1 shows a taxonomy of functional requirements for model transformations based on our experience of transformation requirements.

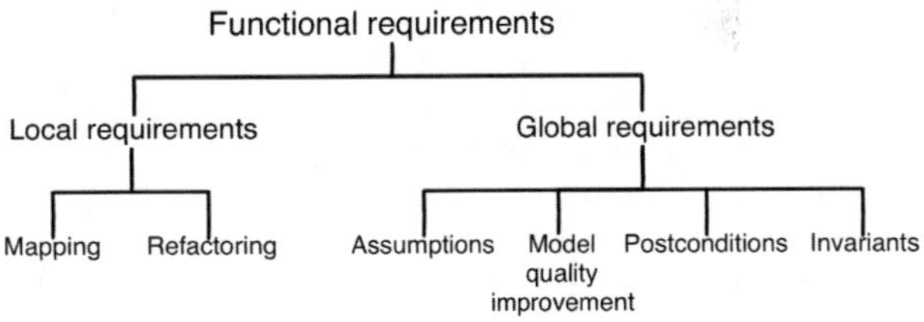

Figure 1. A taxonomy of functional requirements

We have also created a taxonomy of the non-functional requirements that one has to consider during the RE process. Figure 2 shows a general decomposition of non-functional requirements for model transformations. The quality of service categories correspond closely to the software quality characteristics identified by the IEC 25010 software quality standard [12].

Non-functional requirements for model transformations could be further detailed. For instance, regarding the performance requirements, boundaries (upper/lower) could be set on execution time, memory usage for models of a given size, and the maximum capability of the transformation (the largest model it can process within a given time). Restrictions can also be placed upon the rate of growth of execution time with input model size (for example, that this should be linear). Taxonomizing the requirements according to their type not only would make it clearer to understand what the requirements refer to, but also by having this type of distinction among them will allow for a more semantic characterization of requirements.

Maturity and fault tolerance are a subset of reliability requirements for a transformation. Depending on its history and to the extent to which a transformation has been used, maturity requirements could be measured. Fault tolerance requirements

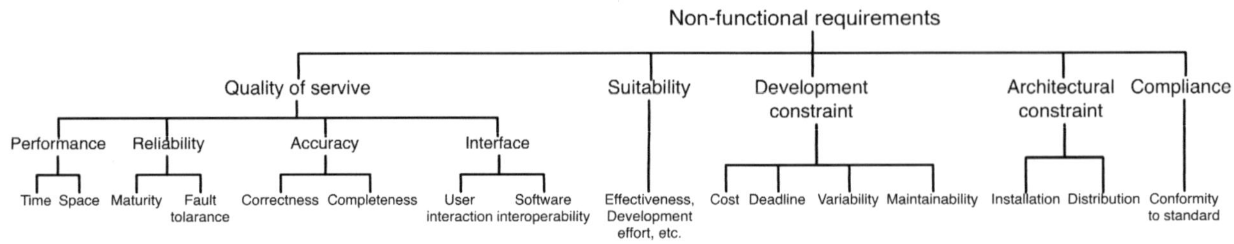

Figure 2. A taxonomy of non-functional requirements for MT

can be quantified in terms of the proportion of execution errors, which are successfully caught by an exception handling mechanism, and in terms of the ability of the transformation to detect and reject invalid input models.

As depicted in the above figure, the accuracy characteristic includes two sub-characteristics: correctness and completeness. Correctness requirements can be further divided into the following forms [13]:

- *Syntactic correctness*: a transformation τ is syntactically correct when a valid input model *m* from source language *S* is transformed to target language *T*, then (if τ terminates) it produces a valid result, in terms of conformation to the *T*'s language constraints.
- *Termination*: a transformation τ will always terminate if applied to a valid *S* model.
- *Confluence*: all result models produced by transformation τ from a single source model are isomorphic.
- *Model-level semantic preservation*: a transformation τ is preserved model-level semantically, if *m* and *n* have equivalent semantics under semantics-assigning maps Sem_S on models of S and Sem_T on models of T.
- *Invariance*: some properties *Inv* should be preserved as true during the entire execution of transformation τ [13].

An additional accuracy property that can be considered is the existence of invertibility in a transformation $\sigma : T \rightarrow S$, which inverts the effect of τ. Given a model *n* derived from *m* by τ, σ applied to *n* produces a model m' of *S* isomorphic to *m*. A related property is change propagation, which means that small changes to a source model can be propagated to the target model without re-executing the transformation on the entire source model. A further property of verifiability is important for transformations, which is part of a business-critical or safety-critical process. This property identifies how effectively a transformation can be verified. Size, complexity, abstraction level and modularity are contributory factors to this property. The traceability property is the requirement that an explicit trace between mapped target model elements and their corresponding source model elements should be maintained by the transformation, and be available at its termination. Under interface are requirements categories of User interaction (subdivided into usability and convenience) and software interoperability. Usability requirements can be decomposed into aspects, such as understandability, learnability and attractiveness [14]. Software interoperability can be decomposed into interoperability capabilities of the system with each intended environment and software system, with which it is expected to operate.

Based on [14], we define suitability as the capability of a transformation approach to provide an appropriate means to express the functionality of a transformation problem at an appropriate level of abstraction, and to solve the transformation problem effectively and with acceptable use of resources (developer time, computational resources, etc.). In [10] we identified the following subcharacteristics for the suitability quality characteristic of model transformation specifications: abstraction level, size, complexity, effectiveness and development effort.

Requirements of single transformations can be documented using the SysML notation adopted in [3], but with a wider range of requirement types represented. Use case diagrams can be used to describe the requirements of a system of transformations. Each use case represents an individual transformation, which may be available as a service for external users, or which may be used internally within the system as a subtransformation of other transformations.

We have investigated a specific functional requirements taxonomy according to the characteristic of model transformations (Table I). All types of functional requirements for model transformations including: mapping, assumptions and post-conditions requirements could be formalized as predicates or diagrams at the concrete and abstract syntax levels. Concrete syntax is often used at the early stages (RE stages) in the development cycle in order to validate the requirements by stakeholders since the concrete syntax level is more convenient, whereas abstract syntax rule, is often used in the implementation phase for developers. However, there should be a direct correspondence between the concrete syntax elements in the informal/semi-formal expression of the requirements, and the abstract syntax elements in the formalised versions.

IV. Application of RE in MT

In model transformation, requirements and specifications are very similar and sometimes are considered as the same element. Requirements determine what is needed and what needs to be achieved while taking into account the different

TABLE I. TRANSFORMATION REQUIREMENTS CATALOGUE

	Refactoring	Refinement	Migration
Local Functional	Rewrites/ Refactorings	Mappings	Mappings
Local Non-functional	Completeness (all cases considered)	Completeness (all source entities, features considered)	Completeness (all source entities, features considered)
Global Functional	Improvement in quality measure(s), Invariance of language constraints, Assumptions, Postconditions	Invariance, Assumptions, Postconditions	Invariance, Assumptions, Postconditions
Global Non-functional	Termination, Efficiency, Modularity, Model-level semantic preservation, Confluence, Fault tolerance, Security	Termination, Efficiency, Modularity, Traceability, Confluence, Fault tolerance, Security	Termination, Efficiency, Modularity, Traceability, Confluence, Fault tolerance

stakeholders, whereas specifications define precisely what is to be developed.

Requirements engineering for model transformations involves specialised techniques and approaches because transformations (i) have highly complex behaviour, involving non-deterministic application of rules and inspection/ construction of complex model data, (ii) are often high-integrity and business-critical systems with strong requirements for reliability and correctness.

Transformations do not usually involve much user interaction, but may have security requirements if they process secure data. Correctness requirements, which are specific to transformations, due to their characteristic execution as a series of rewrite rule applications, with the order of these applications not algorithmically determined, are: (i) confluence (that the output models produced by the transformation are equivalent, regardless of the rule application orders), (ii) termination (regardless of the execution order), (iii) to achieve specified properties of the target model, regardless of the execution order, which is referred to as semantic correctness [9].

The source and target languages of a transformation may be precisely specified by metamodels, whereas the requirements for its processing may initially be quite unclear. For a migration transformation, analysis will be needed to identify how elements of the source language should be mapped to elements of the target. There may not be a clear relationship between parts of these languages, there may be ambiguities and choices in mapping, and there may be necessary assumptions on the input models for a given mapping strategy to be well-defined. The requirements engineer should identify how each entity type and feature of the source language should be migrated.

For refactorings, the additional complications arising from update-in-place processing need to be considered and the application of one rule to a model may enable further rule applications, which were not originally enabled. The requirements engineer should identify all the distinct situations, which need to be processed by the transformation such as arrangements of model elements and their inter-relationships and significant feature values.

A. Application of RE Techniques for MT

A large number of requirements elicitation techniques have been devised. Through the analysis of surveys and case studies, we have identified the following adaption of RE techniques for MT.

The following techniques are the most suitable RE techniques to use during the requirements elicitation stage, which have been adapted according to the nature of model transformation technology.

Structured interviews: in this technique the requirements engineer asks stakeholders specific prepared questions about the domain and the system. The requirements engineer needs to define appropriate questions, which help to identify issues of scope and product (output model) requirements, similar to that of unstructured interviews. This technique is relevant to all forms of transformation problems. We have defined a catalogue of MT requirements for refactorings, refinements and migrations, as an aid for structured interviews, and as a checklist to ensure that all forms of requirements appropriate for the transformation are considered.

Rapid prototyping: in this technique a stakeholder is asked to comment on a prototype solution. This technique is relevant for all forms of transformation, where the transformation can be effectively prototyped. Rules could be expressed in a concrete grammar form and reviewed by stakeholders, along with visualisations of input and output models. This approach fits well with an Agile development process for transformations.

Scenario analysis: in this approach the requirements engineer formulates detailed scenarios/use cases of the system for discussion with the stakeholders. This is highly relevant for MT requirements elicitation. Scenarios can be defined for different required cases of transformation processing. The scenarios can be used as the basis of requirements formalisation. This technique is proposed for transformations in [3]. A risk with scenario analysis is that this may fail to be complete and may not cover all cases of expected transformation processing. It is more suited to the identification of local rather than global requirements.

Regarding the requirements evaluation and negotiation stage, prototyping techniques are useful for evaluating requirements, and for identifying deficiencies and areas where the intended behaviour is not yet understood. A goal-oriented analysis technique such as Knowledge Acquisition in automated specification (KAOS) or SysML can be used to decompose requirements into sub-goals. A formal modelling notation such as Object Constraint Language (OCL) or state machines/state charts can be used to expose the implications of requirements. For transformations, state machines may be useful to identify implicit orderings or conflicts of rules, which arise because the effect of one rule may enable or disable the occurrence of another. Requirements have to be prioritized according to

TABLE II. REQUIREMENTS PRIORITY FOR DIFFERENT TRANSFORMATIONS

Category	Primary requirement	Secondary requirement
Refactoring	Model quality improvement Model-level semantic preservation Syntactic correctness Termination	Invariance Confluence
Migration	Syntactic correctness Model-level semantic preservation Termination	Invertibility Confluence Traceability
Refinement	Syntactic correctness Model-level semantic preservation Confluence Termination	Traceability

their importance and the type of transformation. For instance, in a refinement transformation, the semantics of the source and target model have to be equivalent as the primary requirement and to have a traceability feature as a secondary requirement. Also, there should be no conflict among the requirements. For instance, there is often a conflict between the time, quality and budget of a project. The quality of the target model should be satisfactory with respect to the performance (time, cost and space) of the transformation. Several RE techniques exist, which could be applicable to MT during the requirements specification phase in which business goals are represented in terms of functional and non-functional requirements. In Table II, requirements have been categorised according to the type of the transformation.

Techniques for requirements specification and documentation stage include: UML and OCL, structured natural language, and formal modelling languages. At the initial stages of requirements elicitation and analysis, the intended effect of a transformation is often expressed by sketches or diagrams using the concrete grammar of the source and target languages concerned (if such grammars exist), or by node and line graphs if there is no concrete grammar. A benefit of concrete grammar rules is that they are directly understandable by stakeholders with knowledge of the source and target language notations. They are also independent of specific MT languages or technologies. Concrete grammar diagrams can be made more precise during requirements formalisation, or refined into abstract grammar rules. An informal mapping/refactoring requirement of the form of

> *"For each instance e of entity type E, that satisfies condition Cond, establish Pred "*

can be formalised as a use case postcondition such as:

E::

$Cond' \Rightarrow Pred'$

where *Cond′* formalises Cond, and *Pred′* formalises Pred.

For requirements verification and validation stage, the formalised rules can be checked for internal correctness properties such as definedness and determinacy, which should hold for meaningful rules. A prototype implementation can be generated, and its behaviour on a range of input models covering all of the scenarios considered during requirements elicitation can be checked. When a precise expression of the functional and non-functional requirements has been defined, it can be validated with the stakeholders to confirm that it does indeed accurately express the stakeholders intentions and needs for the system. The formalised requirements of a transformation τ: $S \rightarrow T$ can also be verified to check that they are consistent; the functional requirements must be mutually consistent. The assumptions and invariant of τ, and the language constraints of S must be jointly consistent. The invariant and postconditions of τ, and the language constraints of T must be jointly consistent. Each mapping rule Left-Hand Side (LHS) must be consistent with the invariant, as must each mapping rule Right-Hand Side (RHS).

These consistency properties can be checked using tools such as Z3 or Alloy, given suitable encodings [15], [16]. Model-level semantics preservation requirements can in some cases be characterised by additional invariant properties, which the transformation should maintain. For each functional and non-functional requirement, justification should be given as to why the formalised specification satisfies these requirements. For example, to justify termination, some variant quantity Q: Integer could be identified, which is always non-negative and which is strictly decreased by each application of a mapping rule [13]. Formalised requirements in temporal logic could then be checked for particular implementations using model-checking techniques, as in [17].

V. RE Technique Framework for MT

There are several methods and techniques proposed by the requirements engineering community, however selecting an appropriate set of requirements engineering techniques for a project is a challenging issue. Most of these methods and techniques were designed for a specific purpose and none cover the entire RE process. Researchers have classified RE techniques and categorised them according to their characteristics. For instance, Hickey *et al.* [18] proposed a selection model of elicitation techniques, Maiden *et al.* [19] came up with a framework for requirements acquisition methods and techniques. However, lack of support for selecting the most appropriate set of techniques for a software project has made requirements engineering one of the most complex parts of software engineering process. At the moment, RE techniques are selected mainly based on personal preference rather than characteristics and specifications of a project. In the following sections, we analyse the attributes of requirements engineering techniques and organizations in which the project is delivered and the actual type of project, in order to select a suitable set of RE techniques for specific projects.

A. RE Attribute Analysis

In general, a project is assigned to an organization in order to be developed. Usually the software developing organization is selected according to the type of project. Classification of RE techniques have a direct relation with the type of the proposed project, the organization and the internal attributes of a specific technique. In this section, we analyse the attributes of techniques, the project and the organization in order to identify the most well-suited set of techniques for a particular type of project.

1) Technique Attribute: As mentioned earlier, multiple techniques exist in requirements engineering. Each technique has some attributes that could be used in choosing RE techniques. Identifying the technique attributes could be very useful as they allow us to compare different techniques. We have identified 33 attributes from which 23 were defined by [20]. These attributes are categorized according to the RE phase (*Kotonya* and *Sommerville* model) that they belong to. These attributes are selected based on characteristics of RE techniques as well as other researchers' criteria and frameworks [19], [21], [2]. For instance, some RE techniques are well-suited for identifying non-functional requirements. Therefore if non-functional requirements in a particular project have high priority then the attribute of *ability to help identify non-functional requirements* is important and applying the appropriate RE technique to find non-functional requirements would be necessary (such as the NFR framework). In Table III we have adapted the attributes of [20] to make them specific for MT.

2) Transformation Project Attribute: A transformation project's attribute is also an important factor in order to select RE techniques. Each project has a set of attributes and the priority of its attributes may vary based on the characteristics of a project. For instance, the category of a project that it belongs to is an attribute, therefore RE techniques for a category of safety-critical system may vary from a non-critical system. In this research, we have identified nine attributes, which shall be analysed in more detail relevant to a project. In Table IV, we have explained the selected transformation attributes in more detail.

3) Organization Attribute: Every software developing organization applies the RE process in a different manner. This difference is caused by the behaviour of developers and stakeholders involved in the project. This behaviour is influenced by different factors of the organization such as: size, culture, policy and complexity. These factors have a direct effect on the way the RE process is performed. For instance, in a small organization, new technologies and expensive RE techniques may not be the first choice due to the high cost of it, whereas in a large and complex organization more flexible and disciplined techniques are required to do RE tasks. Although there is no limit to the attributes of an organization we have identified the following:

- Ability to support customer/client involvement
- Ability to classify requirements based on different stakeholders
- Ability to predict and manage sudden requirements modifications by stakeholders
- Ability to assure stakeholders about their confidentiality and privacy.

B. Technique Framework

Our overall procedure for selecting RE techniques for a MT project involves:

- The set all suitable RE techniques (e.g. interview, prototype) in each category (i.e. elicitation, negotiation, specification, verification) is identified.
- For each requirement identified within the project, each RE technique $\mathtt{t}$ is assigned a value $\mathtt{RA}(t)$ (for Requirement Attribute) representing the suitability of applying $\mathtt{t}$ to fulfil this requirement, based on the technique's attributes. Tables (III, V, VI, VII, VIII) give examples of these adapted attribute measures.
- For each requirement identified within the project, each RE technique $\mathtt{t}$ is assigned a value $\mathtt{PD}(\mathtt{t})$ (for Project Description) representing the suitability of applying $\mathtt{t}$ to fulfil this requirement, based on the project's descriptions.
- Evaluating the degree $\mathtt{E}$ (for Experience) of experience/-expertise regarding the RE technique $\mathtt{t}$ available in the development team. $\mathtt{E}(\mathtt{t})$ represents the level of experience and practical and theoretical knowledge of the developer regarding $\mathtt{t}$.
- Using $\mathtt{S}(\mathtt{t})$, the overall suitability score of a particular RE technique ($\mathtt{t} \in \mathtt{T}$) can be calculated, and hence it would be possible to define a ranking of techniques $\mathtt{t}$ based on their suitability scores $\mathtt{S}(\mathtt{t})$ for use in the project. $\mathtt{S}(\mathtt{t})$ is defined as:

  $$\mathtt{S}(\mathtt{t}) = \mathtt{RA}(\mathtt{t}) \times \mathtt{PD}(\mathtt{t}) \times \mathtt{E}(\mathtt{t})$$

  See the Appendix for more details.

In the following sections, we will discuss the techniques and their attributes in more detail, we will consider only those types of RE techniques that are most relevant to MT development (according to our survey of industrial cases, and from expert experience).

VI. Evaluation

In this section of the paper, we will evaluate the framework by applying it to a real industrial case study. This case study concerns the development of a code generator for the UML-Rigorous Systems Design Support (UML-RSDS) [22] dialect of UML. UML-RSDS is a model transformation tool, which is able to manufacture software systems in an automated manner which takes as input a text representation of a class diagram and use cases conforming to the UML-RSDS design metamodels, and produces as output text files in valid ANSI C, as defined in the current ANSI standard. Given a valid UML-RSDS model, the translator should produce a C application with the same semantics. The target code should be structured in the standard C style with header and code files and standard C libraries may be used. The produced code should be of comparable efficiency to hand-written code. The code generation process should not take longer than 1 minute for class diagrams with fewer than 100 classes.

The identified stakeholders included: (i) the UML-RSDS development team; (ii) users of UML-RSDS who require C

TABLE III. RE TECHNIQUE ATTRIBUTES AND CLASSIFICATIONS [20]

ID	*Categories*	*Attributes of techniques*
1		Ability to elicit MT requirements
2		Ability to facilitate communication
3		Ability to help understand social issues
4		Ability to help getting domain knowledge
5	Elicitation	Ability to help getting implicit knowledge
6		Ability to help identifying MT stakeholders
7		Ability to help identifying non-functional requirements
8		Ability to help identifying viewpoints
9		Ability to help model and understand requirements
10		Ability to analyse and model requirements with relevant MT notations
11		Ability to help analyse non-functional requirements
12	Evaluation & Negotiation	Ability to facilitate negotiation with customers
13		Ability to help prioritizing requirements according to stakeholders need
14		Ability to help prioritizing requirements according to the transformation
15		Ability to help identify accessibility of the transformation
16		Ability to help model interface requirements
17		Ability to help re-usability of MT requirements
18		Ability to represent MT requirements
19		Ability to help requirements verification
20		Completeness of the semantics of the notation
21	Specification & Documentation	Ability to help write precise requirements using MT notation
22		Ability to help write complete requirements
23		Ability to help with requirements management
24		Ability to help design highly modular systems
25		Implementability of the notation used
26		Ability to help identify ambiguous requirements
27	Validation & Verification	Ability to help identify inconsistency and conflict
28		Ability to help identify incomplete requirements
29		Ability to support MT language
30		Maturity of supporting tool
31	Other aspects	Learning curve (Introduction cost)
32		Application cost
33		Complexity of technique

code for embedded or limited resource systems; (iii) end-users of such systems. Direct access was only possible to stakeholders (i). Access to other stakeholders was substituted by research into the needs of such stakeholders. According to our RE technique framework, an initial phase of requirements elicitation for this system used document mining (research into the ANSI C language and existing UML to C translators) and a semi-structured interview with the principal stakeholder. This produced an initial set of requirements, with priorities.

The translator has the high-level functional (F) requirement:

F1: Translate UML-RSDS designs (class diagrams, OCL, activities and use cases) into ANSI C code.

The functional requirement was decomposed into five high-priority subgoals, each of which is the responsibility of a separate subtransformation including:

- F1.1: Translation of types
- F1.2: Translation of class diagrams
- F1.3: Translation of OCL expressions
- F1.4: Translation of activities
- F1.5: Translation of use cases

Each translation in this list is dependent upon all of the preceding translations. In addition, the translation of operations of classes depends upon the translation of expressions and activities. The development was therefore organised into five iterations, one for each translator part, and each iteration was given a maximum duration of one month. Other high-priority requirements identified for the translator were the following functional and non-functional (NF) system (product) requirements:

- NF1: Termination: given correct input
- F2: Syntactic correctness: given correct input, a valid C program will be produced
- F3: Model-level semantic preservation: the semantics of the source and target models are equivalent
- F4: Traceability: a record should be maintained of the correspondence between source and target elements

Medium-level priority requirements were:

- F5: Bidirectionality between source and target
- NF2: Efficiency: input models with 100 classes and 100 attributes should be processed within 30 seconds
- NF3: Modularity of the transformation

Low-priority requirements were:

- F6: Confluence
- NF4: Flexibility: ability to choose different C interpretations for UML elements

TABLE IV. TRANSFORMATION PROJECT ATTRIBUTE MEASURES

Transformation attributes	***Value***
Transformation size	*Very Big*: when the number of transformation rules are more than 300 *Big:* when the number of transformation rules are between 150 and 300 *Medium:* when the number of transformation rules are between 100 and 150 *Small:* when the number of transformation rules are between 50 and 100 *Very Small:* when the number of transformation rules are less than 50
Transformation complexity	*Very High:* transformation correctness, completeness and effectiveness are very complicated *High:* transformation correctness, completeness and effectiveness are complicated *Medium:* transformation correctness, completeness and effectiveness are medium level *Small:* transformation correctness, completeness and effectiveness are clear *Very small:* transformation correctness, completeness and effectiveness are easy to achieve
Transformation requirements volatility	*Very High:* transformation requirements keep changing throughout the entire development (more than 50% change of requirements) *High:* transformation requirements keep changing throughout the entire development (25%-50% change of requirements) *Medium:* Some of the requirements change during the development (10%-25% change of requirements) *Low:* A few requirements might change during the development (5%-10% change of requirements) *Very Low:* Change of requirements is unlikely to happen
Developer-customer relationship	*Very High:* there is a very good and constant interaction amongst the developers and the customer *High:* there is a good and constant interaction amongst the developers and the customer *Medium:* there are some contacts between the developers and customers when it is necessary *Low:* there are few meetings between the two parties only when it is essential *Very Low:* there is no contact between the customer and developers throughout the development
Transformation safety	*Very High:* there is a very high likelihood that the transformation will have safety consequences *High:* there is a high likelihood that the transformation will have safety consequences *Medium:* there is moderate likelihood that the transformation will have safety consequences *Low:* there is low possibility that the transformation could cause any danger *Very Low:* the transformation has no possibility of causing any danger
Transformation quality criteria	*Very High:* the transformation has a very high level of functionality, reliability and usability requirements *High:* the transformation has a high of functionality, reliability and usability requirements *Medium:* the transformation has a medium level of functionality, and usability requirements *Low:* there are low reliability, etc requirements *Very Low:* there are very low levels of reliability, etc requirements
Time constraint	*Very High:* the transformation has a very high level of efficiency, timing requirements *High:* the transformation has a high level of timing and efficiency requirements *Medium:* the transformation has a medium level of timing and efficiency requirements *Low:* there are low timing requirements *Very Low:* the transformation has no timing requirements
Cost constraint	*Very High:* the budget is very tight *High:* the budget is tight *Medium:* the transformation has a limited budget *Low:* the transformation has the budget to cover different aspects and unforeseen circumstances *Very Low:* the budgets are flexible
Understanding of domain	*Very High:* developers have a good background knowledge and previous experience regarding the domain *High:* there is a good amount of knowledge and experience regarding the domain *Medium:* there are some background knowledge and experience regarding the domain *Low:* the amount of experience and knowledge regarding the domain is low *Very Low:* there are no experience or knowledge about the domain

TABLE V. REQUIREMENTS ELICITATION TECHNIQUES EVALUATION

Attribute	*Interview*	*Question-naire*	*Document Mining*	*Brainstor-ming*	*Proto-types*	*Scenarios*	*Ethno Methodology*
Eliciting MT requirements	1	0.8	1	0.8	1	1	0.8
Facilitating communication	1	1	0	0.8	0.8	1	0.6
Understanding social issues	0.8	1	0.8	0.4	0.2	0.6	0.8
Getting domain knowledge	0.6	0.6	1	1	0.4	0.4	1
Getting implicit knowledge	0.2	0.2	0.2	0.2	0.2	0.2	1
identifying MT stakeholders	1	0.8	0.2	1	0	0.4	0.6
Identifying non-functional requirements	1	0.6	0.8	1	0.2	0.2	0.4
Identifying viewpoints	0.8	0.6	0.4	0.8	0	0.8	0.4

TABLE VI. REQUIREMENTS NEGOTIATION TECHNIQUES EVALUATION

Attribute	*Proto-types*	*Scen-arios*	*UML*	*Goal-oriented Analysis*	*Functional Decom-position*
Modelling MT requirements	0.8	1	1	0.8	0.6
Analysing requirements with relevant MT notations	0.6	1	0.8	0.8	0.8
Analysing non-functional requirements	0.2	0.2	0	0.6	0.2
Facilitate negotiation with stakeholders	0.8	0.6	0.8	0.8	0.4
Prioritizing requirements based on stakeholders	0.2	0.4	0	0.4	0.2
Identifying accessibility of the transformation	0.8	0.8	0.6	0.6	0.2
Modeling interface requirements	0.6	1	1	0.4	0.2
Re-usability of MT requirements	0	0	1	0.2	0

It was identified that a suitable overall architecture for the transformation was a sequential decomposition of a model-to-model transformation *design2C*, and a model-to-text transformation *genCtext*. Decomposing the code generator into two sub-transformations improves its modularity, and simplifies the constraints, which would otherwise need to combine language translation and text production. Figure 3 shows the resulting transformation architecture.

After a further interview, the application of model-based testing and bx to achieve F3 was identified as an important area of work. Tests for the synthesised C code should, ideally, be automatically generated based on the source UML model. The bx property can be utilised for testing semantic equivalence by transforming UML to C, applying the reverse transformation, and comparing to identify if the two UML models are isomorphic.

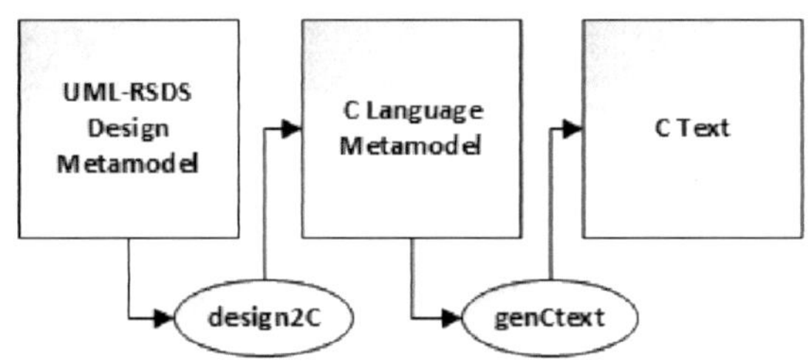

Figure 3. C code generator architecture

Evaluating four RE techniques according to the technique attribute measures `RA(t)` gives the following results for the UML to C case study for the elicitation stage (Table IX).

The framework interestingly reveals that there is no particular technique that helps strongly in prioritising requirements. A further technique appropriate for this project need should be selected. Evaluating a further three elicitation techniques gives Table X.

The overall ranking of techniques according to technique attributes is therefore: (i) *Questionnaire*; (ii) *Brainstorming*; (iii) *Mining*; (iv) *Interviews*.

Furthermore, we need to weight the techniques by a factor `PD(t)` representing the suitability of the technique in the context of the particular project environment. For example, techniques that depend on close customer collaboration are not favoured if the project customer relationship is low. In addition, a factor `E(t)` representing the experience in the technique in the development team or organisation is included. If, instead of rejecting a technique such as brainstorming because of lack of experience in it, in favour of introducing the technique, then the learning curve and cost of introduction need to be considered.. According to [23], this is relatively small for brainstorming. Table XI shows the overall evaluation for elicitation techniques for the case study.

Table XII shows the evaluation of techniques for the eval-

TABLE VII. REQUIREMENTS SPECIFICATION TECHNIQUES EVALUATION

Attribute	*SysML*	*KAOS*	*Structured language template*	*SADT*	*Evolutionary Prototypes*	*UML*
Representing MT requirements	0.8	0.8	0.8	0.6	0.8	1
Requirements verification	1	1	0	0.4	0.8	0.8
Semantics completeness	0.8	1	0.4	0.6	0.2	0.8
Representing requirements using MT notations	0.6	0.4	0.4	0.4	0.2	1
Writing complete requirements	0.8	0.8	0.6	0.6	0.4	0.8
Requirements management	0.8	0.4	0.6	1	0	0.8
Designing highly modular systems	0.8	0.6	0	0	0	0.8
Implementability of the notation(s)	1	1	0	0	0.8	0.8

TABLE VIII. REQUIREMENTS VALIDATION TECHNIQUES EVALUATION

Attribute	*Inspection*	*Desk-Checks*	*Rapid Prototyping*	*Checklist*
Identifying ambiguous requirements	0.4	0	0.4	0
Identifying inconsistency and conflict	0.4	1	0.8	1
Identifying incomplete requirements	0.8	0.8	0.8	0.8

TABLE IX. ELICITATION TECHNIQUE EVALUATION FOR UML TO C CASE (1)

Attribute	*Brainstorming*	*Interviews*	*Mining*	*Scenarios*
Elicit domain knowledge	1	0.6	1	0.4
Identify non-functional requirements	1	1	0.8	0.2
Requirements prioritisation	0	0	0	0.4
Totals RA(t):	2	1.6	1.8	1

TABLE X. ELICITATION TECHNIQUE EVALUATION FOR UML TO C CASE (2)

Attribute	*Questionnaire*	*Prototypes*	*Observation*
Elicit domain knowledge	0.6	0.4	1
Identify non-functional requirements	0.6	0.2	0.4
Requirements prioritisation	1	0.2	0
Totals RA(t):	2.2	0.8	1.4

TABLE XI. ELICITATION TECHNIQUE SELECTION FOR UML TO C CASE

Measure	*Brainstorming*	*Interviews*	*Mining*	*Scenarios*
RA(t)	2	1.6	1.8	1
PD(t)	X	0.66	0.68	0.66
E(t)	0	1	0.6	1
Totals S(t):	0	1.056	0.734	0.66

uation and negotiation stage.

Specific to MT is the ability to represent local and global functional requirements. The overall ranking of techniques is then: (i) UML; (ii) Prototypes; (iii) Scenarios. As with elicitation, factors PD(t) and E(t) need also to be considered to give an overall selection.

The most appropriate specification and documentation techniques are shown in Table XIII. The overall ranking for techniques is: (i) SysML; (ii) UML; (iii) Natural language. Figure 4 shows part of the requirements refinement and goal decomposition using SysML.

Validation and verification techniques are shown in Table XIV. The overall ranking for techniques is: (i) SysML; (ii) UML; (iii) Prototypes.

In the following subsections we present the application of the selected RE techniques on the case study.

A. F1.1: Type Translation

This iteration was divided into three phases: detailed requirements analysis; specification; testing. Detailed requirements elicitation used structured interviews to identify (i) the source language; (ii) the mapping requirements; (iii) the target language; (iv) other functional and non-functional requirements for this sub-transformation. Scenarios and test cases were prepared.

Using goal decomposition, the requirements were decomposed into specific mapping requirements, these are the local functional requirements F1.1.1 to F1.1.4 in Figure 4. Table XV shows the informal scenarios for these local mapping requirements, based on the concrete metaclasses of Type and the different cases of instances of these metaclasses. The schematic concrete grammar is shown for the C elements representing the UML concepts. As a result of requirements evaluation and negotiation with the principal stakeholder, using exploratory prototyping, it was determined that all these local requirements are of high priority except for the mapping F1.1.2 of enumerations (medium priority). The justification for this is that enumerations are not an essential UML language element. Bidirectionality was considered a high priority for this sub-transformation. It was identified that to meet this requirement, all source model Property elements must have a defined type, and specifically that elements representing many-valued association ends must have some CollectionType representing

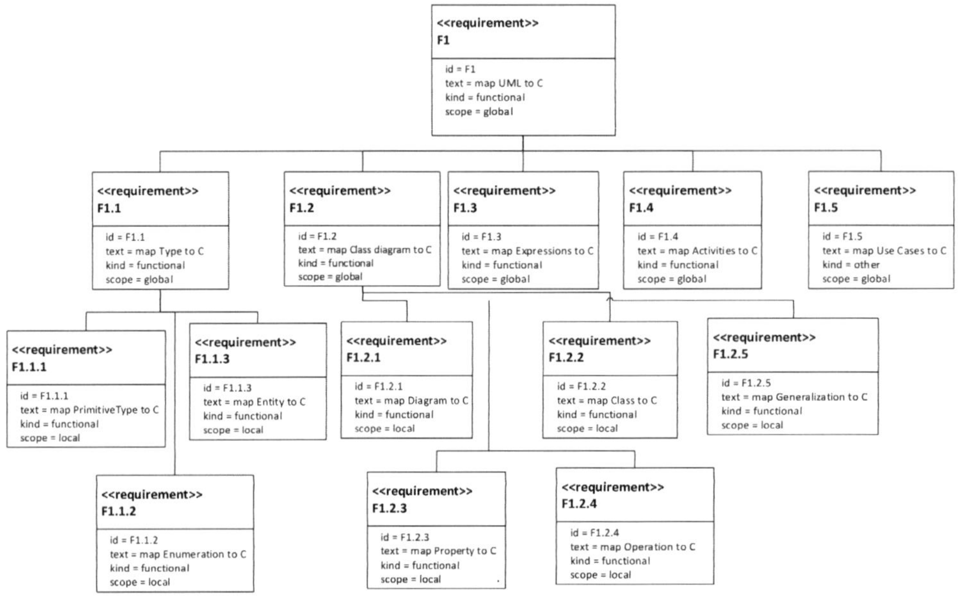

Figure 4. Functional requirements decomposition in SysML

TABLE XII. EVALUATION/NEGOTIATION TECHNIQUE EVALUATION FOR UML TO C CASE

Attribute	*Prototypes*	*State machines*	*UML*	*Scenarios*
Represent MT requirements	0.8	0.4	1	1
Identify incomplete requirements	0.8	0	0.4	0.2
Identify ambiguous requirements	0.4	0.6	0.6	0.4
Facilitate negotiation	0.8	0.4	0.8	0.4
Totals RA(t):	2.8	1.4	2.8	2

TABLE XIII. SPECIFICATION/DOCUMENTATION TECHNIQUE EVALUATION FOR UML TO C CASE

Attribute	*Natural language*	*UML*	*SysML*
Write unambiguous and precise specication	0.6	0.8	1
Write complete requirements	0.6	0.8	0.8
Modularity	0	0.8	0.8
Totals RA(t):	1.2	2.4	2.6

TABLE XIV. VALIDATION AND VERIFICATION TECHNIQUE EVALUATION FOR UML TO C CASE

Attribute	*Prototypes*	*Scenarios*	*UML*	*SysML*
Implementability/ executability	0.8	0.4	0.8	1
Requirements verification	0.8	0.6	0.8	1
Notation	0.2	0.6	1	0.6
Totals RA(t):	1.8	1.6	2.6	2.6

TABLE XV. INFORMAL SCENARIOS FOR TYPES2C

Scenario	*UML element*	*C representation e'*
F1.1.1.1	*String type*	*char**
F1.1.1.2	*int, long, double types,*	*same-named C types*
F1.1.1.3	*boolean type*	*unsigned char*
F1.1.2	*Enumeration type*	*C enum*
F1.1.3	*Entity type E*	*struct E* type*
F1.1.4.1	*Set(E) type*	*struct E** (array of E, without duplicates)*
F1.1.4.2	*Sequence(E) type*	*struct E** (array of E, possibly with duplicates)*

their actual type. A limitation of the proposed mapping is that mapping collections of primitive values (integers, doubles, booleans) to C is not possible, because there is no means to identify the end of the collection in C (NULL is used as the terminator for collections of objects and collections of strings).

B. F1.2: Translation of Class Diagram

This iteration also used a three-phase approach, to define a subtransformation classdiagram2C. The class diagram elements *Property, Operation, Entity, Generalization* were identified as the input language. Exploratory prototyping was used for requirements elicitation and evaluation. During re-

TABLE XVI. INFORMAL SCENARIOS FOR THE MAPPING OF UML CLASS DIAGRAMS TO C

Scenario	*UML element e*	*C representation e'*
F1.2.1	Class diagram D	C program with D's name
F1.2.2	Class E	struct E {...}, Global variable struct E** e_instances; Global variable int e_size; struct E* createE() operation struct E** newEList() operation
F1.2.3.1	Property p : T (not principal identity attribute)	Member T' p; of the struct for p's owner, where T' represents T Operations T' getE_p(E' self) and setE_p(E' self, T' px)
F1.2.3.2	Principal identity attribute p : String of class E	Operation struct E* getEByPK(char* v) Key member char* p; of the struct for E
F1.2.4	Operation op(p : P) : T of E	C operation T' op(E' self, P' p) with scope = entity
F1.2.5	Inheritance of A by B	Member struct A* super; of struct B

quirements evaluation and negotiation it was agreed that the metafeatures *isStatic, isReadOnly, isDerived, isCached* would not be represented in C, nor would *addOnly, aggregation, constraint* or *linkedClass*. This means that aggregations, association classes and static/constant features are not specifically represented in C. Interfaces are not represented. Only single inheritance is represented.

The scenarios of the local mapping requirements for class diagram elements are shown in Table XVI.

C. F1.3: Translation of OCL Expressions

In this iteration, the detailed requirements for mapping OCL expressions to C are identified, then this subtransformation, expressions2C, is specified and tested. There are many cases to consider in the mapping requirements, so we divided these into four subgroups: (i) mapping of basic expressions; (ii) mapping of logical expressions; (iii) mapping of comparitor, numeric and string expressions; (iv) mapping of collection expressions. These were considered the natural groupings of operations and operators, and these follow in part the metaclass organisation of UML expressions.

1) Basic Expressions: The basic expressions of OCL generally map directly to corresponding C basic expressions. Table XVII shows the mapping for these. These mapping requirements are grouped together as requirement F1.3.1.

2) Logical Expressions: Table XVIII shows the mapping of logical expressions and operators to C. These mappings are grouped together as requirement F1.3.2.

3) Comparitor, Numeric and String Expressions: Table XIX lists the comparitor operators and their mappings to C. These mappings are grouped as requirement 1.3.3. Numeric operators for integers and real numbers are shown in Table XX. The types int, double and long are not guaranteed to have particular sizes in C. All operators take double values as arguments except mod and Integer.subrange, which have int parameters.

TABLE XVII. MAPPING SCENARIOS FOR BASIC EXPRESSIONS

OCL expression e	***C representation e'***
self	*self* as an operation parameter
Variable *v* or *v[ind]*	v *v[ind - 1]*
Data feature *f* with no objectRef	*self* → *f*
Data feature *f* of instance *ex*	*ex'* → *f*
Operation call *op(e1,...,en)* or *obj.op(e1,...,en)*	op(self, e1', ..., en') op(obj', e1', ..., en')
Attribute *f* of collection *exs*	get*AllE_f (exs')* (duplicate values preserved)
Single-valued role r : F of collection exs	*getAllE_r(exs')* defined by *(struct* F **) *collectE(exs', getE_r)*
col [ind] ordered collection col	(col')[ind-1]
E[v] *v* single-valued	getEByPK(v')
E[*vs*] *vs* collection-valued	getEByPKs(vs')
E.allInstances	*e_instances*
value of enumerated type, numeric or string value	*value*
boolean true, false	TRUE, FALSE

TABLE XVIII. MAPPING SCENARIOS FOR LOGICAL EXPRESSIONS

OCL expression e	***C representation e'***
A =>B	!A' || B'
A & B	A' && B'
A or B	A' || B'
not(A)	!A'
E->exists(P)	existsE(e_instances,fP) fP evaluates P
e->exists(P)	existsE(e',fP)
E->exists1(P)	exists1E(e_instances,fP) fP evaluates P
e->exists1(P)	exists1E(e',fP)
E->forAll(P)	forAllE(e instances,fP) fP evaluates P
e->forAll(P)	forAllE(e',fP)

Other math operators directly available in C are: log10, tanh, cosh, sinh, asin, acos, atan. These are double-valued functions of double-valued arguments. cbrt is missing and needs to be implemented as pow(x, 1.0/3).

4) Collection Expressions: Table XXII shows the values and operators that apply to sets and sequences, and their C translations. Some operators (unionAll, intersectAll, symmetricDifference, subcollections) were considered a low priority, because these are infrequently used, and were not translated. The requirements are grouped as F1.3.6. After evaluation and negotiation, it was decided that full implementation of *delete* should be deferred, because of the complex semantics of data deletion in C. In addition, prototyping revealed that compiler differences made the use of qsort impractical, and instead a custom sorting algorithm, *treesort*, was implemented. This has the signature (*void*** *treesort(void* col[], int (*comp)(void*, void*)*) and the translation of *x→sort()* is then: (rt) treesort((void**) x', comp) for the appropriate result type *rt* and comparitor function *comp*. Table XXI shows the translation of select and collect operators. These mappings are grouped as requirement F1.3.7.

TABLE XIX. MAPPING SCENARIOS FOR COMPARITOR EXPRESSIONS

OCL expression e	*C representation e'*
x : E E entity type	isIn((void∗ x', (void ∗∗) e instances)
x : s s collection	isIn((*void*∗) x', (void ∗∗) s')
s->includes(x) s collection	Same as x : s
x / : E E entity type	!isIn((void∗) x', (void ∗∗) e instances)
x / : s s collection	!isIn((void∗) x', (void ∗∗) s')
s->excludes(x) s collection	Same as x / : s
x = y	x'== y'
Numerics, Booleans	
Strings	strcmp(x', y') == 0
Objects	x'== y'
Sets	equalsSet((void ∗∗) x', (void ∗∗) y')
Sequences	equalsSequence((void ∗∗) x', (void ∗∗) y')
x <y	x'<y'
Numerics	
Strings	strcmp(x', y') <0
Similarly for >, <=, >=, /=	>, <=, >=, ! =
s <: t s, t collections	containsAll ((void ∗∗) t', (void ∗∗) s')
t->includesAll(s)	Same as s <: t
t->excludesAll(s)	disjoint((void∗∗) t', (void∗∗) s')

TABLE XX. MAPPING SCENARIOS FOR NUMERIC EXPRESSIONS

OCL expression e	*Representation in C*
-x	-x'
x + y	x' + y'
numbers	
x - y	x' - y'
x* y	x' * y'
x / y	x' / y'
x mod y	x' % y'
x.sqr	(x' * x')
x.sqrt	sqrt(x')
x.floor	oclFloor(x') defined as: ((int) floor(x'))
x.round	oclRound(x')
x.ceil	oclCeil(x') defined as: ((int) ceil(x'))
x.abs	fabs(x')
x.exp	exp(x')
x.log	log(x')
x.pow(y)	pow(x',y')
x.sin, x.cos, x.tan	sin(x'), cos(x'), tan(x')
Integer.subrange(st,en)	intSubrange(st',en')

Unlike the types and class diagram mappings, a recursive descent style of specification is needed for the expressions mapping (and for activities). This is because the subordinate parts of an expression are themselves expressions. Thus it is not possible in general to map all the subordinate parts of an expression by prior rules: even for basic expressions, the parameters may be general expressions. In contrast, the element types of collection types cannot themselves be collection types or involve subparts that are collection types, so it is possible to map all element types before considering collection types. A recursive descent style of mapping specification uses operations of each source entity type to map instances of that type, invoking mapping operations recursively to map subparts of the instances.

TABLE XXI. SCENARIOS FOR THE MAPPING OF SELECTION AND COLLECTION EXPRESSIONS

UML expression e	C translation e'
s->select(P)	selectE(s', fP) fP evaluates P
s->select(x | P)	as above
s->reject(P)	rejectE(s', fP)
s->reject(x | P)	as above
s->collect(e)	(et'∗) collectE(s', fe)
e of type et	fe evaluates e'
s->collect(x | e)	as above
s->selectMaximals(e)	-
s->selectMinimals(e)	-

D. Activities Translation

In this iteration, UML-RSDS activities are mapped to C statements by a subtransformation statements2C. UML-RSDS statements correspond closely to those of C. Table XXIII shows the main cases of the mapping of UML activities to C statements.

E. Use case Translation

In this iteration, the mapping usecases2C of use cases is specified and implemented. A large part of this iteration was also taken up with integration testing of the complete transformation.

F1.5.1: A use case uc is mapped to a C operation with *application* scope, and with parameters corresponding to those of uc. Its code is given by the C translation of the activity classifierBehaviour of uc.

F1.5.2: Included use cases are also mapped to operations, and invoked from the including use case.

F1.5.3: Operation activities are mapped to C code for the corresponding COperation.

F1.5.1 is formalised as:

```
UseCase::
COperation->exists( cop | cop.name = name &
cop.scope = "application" &
cop.isQuery = false &
cop.code = classifierBehaviour.mapStatement() &
cop.parameters = parameters.mapExpression() &
cop.returnType = CType[returnType.typeId] )
```

Similarly for the activities of UML operations.

This case study is the largest transformation, which has been developed using UML-RSDS, in terms of the number of rules (over 150 rules/operations in 5 subtransformations). By using a systematic requirements engineering and agile development approach, we were able to effectively modularise the transformation and to organise its structure and manage its

TABLE XXII. SCENARIOS FOR THE TRANSLATION OF COLLECTION OPERATORS

Expression e	*C translation e'*
Set{}	newEList()
Sequence{}	newEList()
Set{x1, x2, ... , xn}	insertE(... insertE(newEList(), x1'), ..., xn')
Sequence{x1, x2, ..., xn}	appendE(... appendE(newEList(), x1'), ..., xn')
s->size()	length((void**) s')
s->including(x)	insertE(s',x') or appendE(s',x')
s->excluding(x)	removeE(s',x')
s - t	removeAllE(s',t')
s->prepend(x)	-
s->append(x)	appendE(s',x')
s->count(x)	count((void*) x', (void**) s')
s->indexOf(x)	indexOf((void*) x', (void**) s')
$x \vee y$	unionE(x',y')
$x \wedge y$	intersectionE(x',y')
$x \frown y$	concatenateE(x',y)
x->union(y)	unionE(x',y')
x->intersection(y)	intersectionE(x', y')
x->unionAll(e)	-
x->intersectAll(e)	-
x->symmetricDifference(y)	-
x->any()	x'[0]
x->subcollections()	-
x->reverse()	reverseE(x')
x->front()	subrangeE(x',1,length((void**) x')-1)
x->tail()	subrangeE(x',2,length((void**) x'))
x->first()	x'[0]
x->last()	x'[length((void**) x')-1]
x->sort()	qsort((void**) x', length((void**) x'), sizeof(struct E*), compareToE)
x->sortedBy(e)	qsort((void**) x', length((void**) x'), sizeof(struct E*), compare) compare defines e-order
x->sum()	sumString(x'), sumint(x'), sumlong(x'), sumdouble(x')
x->prd()	prdint(x'), prdlong(x'), prddouble(x')
Integer.Sum(a,b,x,e)	sumInt(a',b',fe), sumDouble(a',b',fe) fe computes e'(x')
Integer.Prd(a,b,x,e)	prdInt(a',b',fe), prdDouble(a',b',fe)
x->max()	maxInt(x'), maxLong(x'), maxDouble(x'), maxString(x')
x->min()	minInt(x'), minLong(x'), minDouble(x'), minString(x')
x->asSet()	asSetE(x')
x->asSequence()	x'
s->isUnique(e)	isUniqueE(s',fe)
x->isDeleted()	killE(x')

requirements. Despite the complexity of the transformation, it was possible to use patterns to enforce bx and other properties, and to effectively prove these properties.

VII. Conclusion and Future Work

We have identified ways in which requirements engineering can be applied systematically to model transformations. Comprehensive catalogues of functional and non-functional requirements categories for model transformations have been defined. We have examined a case study, which is typical of the current state of the art in transformation development, and identified how formal treatment of functional and non-functional requirements can benefit such developments. In this paper we have identified the need for a systematic requirements engineering process for model transformations. We have proposed such a process, and identified RE techniques that can be used in this process. Moreover, we have identified a requirements engineering process for model transformations, and requirements engineering techniques that can be used in this process. The process can be used to develop specifications in a range of declarative and hybrid MT languages. We have evaluated the process and techniques on a real industrial case study, UML to C translation, with positive results.

In future work, we will construct tool support for recording and tracing transformation requirements, which will help to ensure that developers systematically consider all necessary requirements and that these are all formalised, validated and verified correctly. We are currently carrying out research into improving the requirements engineering process in model transformation. We will investigate formal languages to express the requirements, as formalised rules can be checked for internal correctness properties, such as definedness and determinacy, which should hold for meaningful rules. Temporal logic can be used to define the specialised characteristics of particular transformation and to define transformation requirements in a formal but language-independent manner languages as model transformation systems necessarily involve a notion of time. Finally, we will be evaluating large case studies in order to compare results with and without RE process.

TABLE XXIII. SCENARIOS FOR MAPPING OF STATEMENTS TO C

Requirement	*UML activity st*	*C statement st'*
F1.4.1	Creation statement x : T defaultT' is default value of T'	T' x = defaultT';
F1.4.2	Assign statement v := e	v' = e';
F1.4.3	Sequence statement st1 ; ... ; stn	st1' ... stn'
F1.4.4	Conditional statement if e then st1 else st2	if e' {st1'} else {st2'}
F1.4.5	Return statement return e	return e';
F1.4.6	Break statement break	break;
F1.4.7	Bounded loop for (x : e) do st on object collection e of entity element type E	int i = 0; for (; i <length((void**) e'); i++) { struct E* x = e'[i]; st' } New index variable i
F1.4.8	Unbounded loop while e do st	while (e') { st' }
F1.4.9	Operation call ex.op(pars)	op(ex',pars')

Appendix

The procedure for selecting RE techniques for a MT project in more detail involves:

1) The set T of all suitable RE techniques (e.g. interview, prototype) in each category (i.e. elicitation, negotiation, specification, verification) is identified.
2) For each requirement identified within the project, each RE technique $t \in T$ is assigned a value $RA(t)$ (for

Requirement Attribute) representing the suitability of applying t to fulfil this requirement, based on the requirement's attributes. The function $\mathtt{RA} : \mathtt{T} \longmapsto [0, 1]$ is defined as:

$$\mathtt{RA}(t) = \frac{\sum_{a_x \in \mathtt{A}} \mathtt{I}(a_x) \times \mathtt{V}(a_x, \mathtt{t})}{|\mathtt{A}|}$$

where:

- The set of all technique attributes (e.g. facilitating communication, identifying MT stakeholders) is A (Table III). For instance, A = {Eliciting MT requirements, facilitating communication, ..., identifying incomplete requirements}.
- $\mathtt{I}(a_x)$ which is in $[0, 1]$, represents the importance of an attribute $a_x \in \mathtt{A}$ for a specific requirement of the project. A low $\mathtt{I}(a_x)$ value for an attribute $a_x \in \mathtt{A}$ means a_x is not important for the requirement of the MT project and a high value represents high importance. The assignment of $\mathtt{I}(a_x)$ to each $a_x \in \mathtt{A}$ is done by MT developers.
- $\mathtt{V}(a_x, t)$ is a function $\mathtt{V} : \mathtt{T} \times \mathtt{A} \longmapsto [0, 1]$ which given a technique attribute and an RE technique, assigns a $[0, 1]$ value. These values are based on the technique attribute measures of [23] as well as others that are identified in this research. Tables (V, VI, VII, VIII) give examples of these adapted attribute measures.

3) For each requirement identified within the project, each RE technique $\mathtt{t} \in \mathtt{T}$ is assigned a value $\mathtt{PD}(\mathtt{t})$ (for Project Description) representing the suitability of applying t to fulfil this requirement, based on the project's descriptions. The function $\mathtt{PD} : \mathtt{T} \longmapsto [0, 1]$ is defined as:

$$\mathtt{PD}(\mathtt{t}) = \prod_{\mathtt{d}_x \in \mathtt{D}} \begin{cases} 1 - \mathtt{W}(\mathtt{d}_x) & \text{if } \mathtt{d}_x \in \mathtt{ID_t} \\ \mathtt{W}(\mathtt{d}_x) & \text{otherwise} \end{cases}$$

where:

- The set of all project descriptors (e.g. size, complexity) is D. For instance, in this thesis, we are considering D = {size, complexity, volatility, relationship, safety, quality, time, cost, domain understanding}.
- $\mathtt{W}(d_x)$ is a function $\mathtt{W} : \mathtt{D} \longmapsto [0, 1]$ which represents the magnitude of a specific descriptor in the project. For example, for d = cost, a high value represents that the budget of the project is tight, while a low value indicates that the budget is flexible. Then for d = size, a high value means that the project involves a large number of transformation rules while a low value indicates a small number of rules involved.
- $\mathtt{ID_t} \subseteq \mathtt{D}$ is a set containing all descriptors with inverse impact for a specific RE technique t. More specifically, for each $\mathtt{d} \in \mathtt{ID_t}$, the higher the value of $\mathtt{W}(d_x)$ the more negative the impact of applying t in that project. An example of such a descriptor for technique "interview" is time, where the higher the value of W(time) in a specific project, the more negative the effectiveness of interviewing as a technique to fulfil a requirement in this project.

4) Evaluating the degree E (for Experience) of experience/-expertise regarding the RE technique t available in the development team. $\mathtt{E} : \mathtt{T} \longmapsto [0, 1]$ is a function where $\mathtt{E}(\mathtt{t})$ represents the level of experience and practical and theoretical knowledge of the developer regarding t.
5) Using $\mathtt{S}(\mathtt{t})$, the overall suitability score of a particular RE technique ($\mathtt{t} \in \mathtt{T}$) can be calculated, and hence it would be possible to define a ranking of techniques t based on their suitability scores $\mathtt{S}(\mathtt{t})$ for use in the project. $\mathtt{S}(\mathtt{t})$ is defined in terms of the requirement attribute score $\mathtt{RA}(\mathtt{t})$, the project description score $\mathtt{PD}(\mathtt{t})$, and the experience score $\mathtt{E}(\mathtt{t})$ of RE technique t as follows:

$$\mathtt{S}(\mathtt{t}) = \mathtt{RA}(\mathtt{t}) \times \mathtt{PD}(\mathtt{t}) \times \mathtt{E}(\mathtt{t})$$

REFERENCES

[1] S. Yassipour Tehrani and K. Lano, "Model transformation applications from requirements engineering perspective," in The 10th International Conference on Software Engineering Advances, 2015.

[2] I. Sommerville and G. Kotonya, Requirements engineering: processes and techniques. John Wiley & Sons, Inc., 1998.

[3] E. Guerra, J. De Lara, D. S. Kolovos, R. F. Paige, and O. M. dos Santos, "transml: A family of languages to model model transformations," in Model Driven Engineering Languages and Systems. Springer, 2010, pp. 106–120.

[4] B. Selic, "What will it take? a view on adoption of model-based methods in practice," Software & Systems Modeling, vol. 11, no. 4, 2012, pp. 513–526.

[5] K. Lano and S. Kolahdouz-Rahimi, "Model-driven development of model transformations," in Theory and practice of model transformations. Springer, 2011, pp. 47–61.

[6] K. Lano and S. Rahimi, "Constraint-based specification of model transformations," Journal of Systems and Software, vol. 86, no. 2, 2013, pp. 412–436.

[7] S. Friedenthal, A. Moore, and R. Steiner, A practical guide to SysML: the systems modeling language. Morgan Kaufmann, 2014.

[8] T. Yue, L. C. Briand, and Y. Labiche, "A systematic review of transformation approaches between user requirements and analysis models," Requirements Engineering, vol. 16, no. 2, 2011, pp. 75–99.

[9] S. Y. Tehrani, S. Zschaler, and K. Lano, "Requirements engineering in model-transformation development: An interview-based study," in International Conference on Theory and Practice of Model Transformations. Springer, 2016, pp. 123–137.

[10] S. Kolahdouz-Rahimi, K. Lano, S. Pillay, J. Troya, and P. Van Gorp, "Evaluation of model transformation approaches for model refactoring," Science of Computer Programming, vol. 85, 2014, pp. 5–40.

[11] P. Van Gorp and L. M. Rose, "The petri-nets to statecharts transformation case," arXiv preprint arXiv:1312.0342, 2013.

[12] I. Iso, "Iec 25010: 2011,," Systems and Software EngineeringSystems and Software Quality Requirements and Evaluation (SQuaRE)System and Software Quality Models, 2011.

[13] K. Lano, S. Kolahdouz-Rahimi, and T. Clark, "Comparing verification techniques for model transformations," in Proceedings of the Workshop on Model-Driven Engineering, Verification and Validation. ACM, 2012, pp. 23–28.

[14] I. O. F. S. E. Commission et al., "Software engineering–product quality–part 1: Quality model," ISO/IEC, vol. 9126, 2001, p. 2001.

[15] K. Anastasakis, B. Bordbar, and J. M. Küster, "Analysis of model transformations via alloy," in Proceedings of the 4th MoDeVVa workshop Model-Driven Engineering, Verification and Validation, 2007, pp. 47–56.

[16] L. de Moura and N. Bjørner, "Z3–a tutorial," 2006.

[17] S. Yassipour Tehrani and K. Lano, "Temporal logic specification and analysis for model transformations," in Verification of Model Transformations, VOLT 2015, 2015.

[18] A. M. Hickey and A. M. Davis, "Requirements elicitation and elicitation technique selection: model for two knowledge-intensive software development processes," in System Sciences, 2003. Proceedings of the 36th Annual Hawaii International Conference on. IEEE, 2003, pp. 10–pp.

[19] N. Maiden and G. Rugg, "Acre: selecting methods for requirements acquisition," Software Engineering Journal, vol. 11, no. 3, 1996, pp. 183–192.

[20] L. Jiang, A. Eberlein, B. H. Far, and M. Mousavi, "A methodology for the selection of requirements engineering techniques," Software & Systems Modeling, vol. 7, no. 3, 2008, pp. 303–328.

[21] L. Macaulay, "Requirements for requirements engineering techniques," in Requirements Engineering, 1996., Proceedings of the Second International Conference on. IEEE, 1996, pp. 157–164.

[22] K. Lano, "The uml-rsds manual," 2014.

[23] L. Jiang, A framework for the requirements engineering process development. University of Calgary, 2005.

A Computational Model of Place on the Linked Data Web

Alia I Abdelmoty, Khalid O. Al-Muzaini

School of Computer Science & Informatics, Cardiff University, Wales, UK
Email: {A.I.Abdelmoty, Almuzainiko}@cs.cf.ac.uk

***Abstract*—The Linked Data Web (LDW) is an evolution of the traditional Web from a global information space of linked documents to one where both documents and data are linked. A significant amount of geographic information about places is currently being published on this LDW. These are used to qualify the location of other types of datasets. This paper examines the limitations in the nature of location representation in some typical examples of these Resource Description Framework (RDF) resources, primarily resulting from the simplified geometric representation of location and the incomplete and random use of spatial relationships to link place information. The paper proposes a qualitative model of place location that enforces an ordered representation of relative spatial relationships between places. This work further explores how semantic properties of place can be included to derive meaningful location expressions. The model facilitates the application of qualitative spatial reasoning on places to extract a potentially large percentage of implicit links between place resources, thus allowing place information to be linked and to be explored more fully and more consistently than what is currently possible. The paper describes the model and presents experimental results demonstrating the effectiveness of the model on realistic examples of geospatial RDF resources.**

***Keywords*–qualitative place models; spatial reasoning; geospatial web.**

I. Introduction

One of the 'Linked Data Principles' is to include links to connect the data to allow the discovery of related things. However, identifying links between data items remains a considerable challenge that needs to be addressed [1], [2], [3]. A key research task in this respect is identity resolution, i.e., to recognise when two things denoted by two URIs are the same and when they are not. Automatic linking can easily create inadequate links, and manual linking is often too time consuming [4]. Geo-referencing data on the LDW can address this problem [5], whereby links can be inferred between data items by tracing their spatial (and temporal) footprints. For example, the BBC uses RDF place gazetteers as an anchor to relate information on weather, travel and local news [6].

Yet, for geospatial linked data to serve its purpose, links within and amongst the geographic RDF resources need themselves to be resolved. That is to allow place resources to be uniquely identified and thus a place description in one dataset can be matched to another describing the same place in a different dataset. A scheme that allows such links between place resources to be discovered would be a valuable step towards the realisation of the LDW as a whole.

In this paper, location is used as a key identifier for place resources and the question to be addressed is how location can be used to define a *linked* place model that is sufficient to enable place resources to be uniquely identified on the LDW. Several challenges need to be addressed, namely, 1) location representation of RDF place resources is simple; defined as point coordinates in some resources, detailed; defined with extended geometries in others, and sometimes missing all together, 2) coordinates of locations may not match exactly across data sources, where volunteered data mapped by individuals is mashed up with authoritative map datasets, 3) non-standardised vocabularies for expressing relative location is used in most datasets, e.g., in DBpedia, properties such as *dbp:location*, *dbp-ont:region* and *dbp-ont:principalarea* are used to indicate that the subject place lies inside the object place.

Towards addressing this problem, a linked place model is proposed that uses qualitative spatial relationships to describe unique place location profiles, as presented in [1]. The profiles don't rely on the provision of exact geometries and hence can be used homogeneously with different types of place resources. They can be expressed as RDF statements and can thus be integrated directly with the resource descriptions. The rationale behind the choice of links to be modelled is primarily twofold: to allow for a sensible unique description of place location and to support qualitative spatial reasoning over place resources.

The model is further adapted to consider semantic aspects of place location definition. In particular, the notion of salience of place is used to scope the type of relationships used in the location expressions in the defined place profiles. It is shown how the proposed representation scheme is flexible to allow for the encoding of relevant location expressions, whilst also retaining the power of spatial reasoning within the framework proposed.

The value of the linked place model is illustrated by measuring its ability to make the underlying RDF graph of geographic place resources browsable. Samples of realistic geographic linked datasets are used in the experiments presented and results demonstrate significant potential value of the methods proposed.

The paper is structured as follows. An overview of related work on the representation and manipulation of place resources on the LDW is given in section II, In section III the proposed relative location model, as well its adaptation to include semantic aspects of place definition, are described. In section IV, application of the models proposed is evaluated on two different realistic datasets. Conclusions and an overview of future work is given in section VI.

II. Related Work

Here related work on the topics of representing place resources and reasoning with them on the LDW are reviewed.

A. Representing RDF place Resources on the LDW

Sources of geographic data on the LDW are either volunteered (crowdsourced) resources, henceforth denoted Volunteered Geographic Information (VGI), created by individuals with only informal procedures for validating the content, or authoritative resources produced by mapping organizations, henceforth denoted Authoritative Geographic Information (AGI). Example of VGIs are DBpedia (dbpedia.org), GeoNames (geonames.org), and OpenSreetMaps (linkedgeodata.org) [7] and examples of AGIs are the Ordnance Survey linked data [8] and the Spanish linked data [9]. Data collected from users on the Social Web, e.g., on Twitter and Foursquare, can also be considered as VGIs [10].

The volume of VGI resources is increasing steadily, providing a wealth of information on geographic places and creating detailed maps of the world. DBpedia contains hundreds of thousands of place entities, whose locations are represented as point geometry. GeoNames is a gazetteer that collects both spatial and thematic information for various place names around the world. In both datasets, place location is represented by a single point coordinates. While DBpedia does not enforce any constraints on the definition of place location (e.g., coordinates may be missing in place resources), reference to some relative spatial relationships, and in particular to represent containment within a geographic region, is normally maintained. A detailed analysis of the spatial data content of DBpedia can be found in [11], [12]. GeoNames places are also interlinked with each other by defining associated parent places.

In [13], the LinkedGeoData effort is described where OpenStreetMap (OSM) data is transformed into RDF and made available on the Web. OSM data is represented with a relatively simple data model that captures the underlying geometry of the features. It comprises three basic types, nodes (representing points on Earth and have longitude and latitude values), ways (ordered sequences of nodes that form a polyline or a polygon) and relations (groupings of multiple nodes and/or ways). Furthermore, [14] presented methods to determine links between map features in OSM and equivalent instances documented in DBpedia, as well as between OSM and Geonames. Their matching is based on a combination of the Jaro-Winkler string distance between the text of the respective place names and the geographic distance between the entities. Example of other work on linking geodata on the Semantic Web is [15], which employs the Hausdorff distance to establish similarity between spatially extensive linear or polygonal features.

In contrast to VGI resources that manages geographic resource as points (represented by a coordinate of latitude and longitude), AGI resources deal with more complex geometries as well, such as line strings. AGIs tend to utilise well-defined standards and ontologies for representing geographic features and geometries. Ordnance Survey linked data also demonstrates the use of qualitative spatial relations to describe spatial relationships in its datasets. Two ontologies, the Geometry Ontology and the Spatial Relations Ontology, are used to provide geospatial vocabulary. These ontologies describe abstract geometries and topological relations (equivalent to RCC8 [16]) respectively.

In summary, the spatial representation of place resources in VGI datasets is generally limited to point representation, and is managed within simple ontologies that encode non-spatial semantics and in some cases limited spatial relationships. On the other hand, place data provided as AGI tend to present more structured and detailed spatial representations, but is also limited to specific types and scales of representation. Use of some qualitative spatial relationships has been demonstrated for capturing the spatial structure in some example datasets. The model proposed in this paper offers a systematic and homogenous representation of place location that can be consistently applied to VGIs or AGIs and demonstrates the value of heterogenous qualitative spatial relations in representing place information on the LDW.

B. Manipulating and Querying RDF place resources on the LDW

Recently, much work has been done on extending RDF for representing geospatial information through defining and utilising appropriate vocabularies encoded in ontologies to represent space and time. The work capitalises on specification of standards, defined by the Open Geospatial Consortium (OGC)(opengeospatial.org), for modeling core concepts related to geospatial data. Prominent examples are the geographic query language for RDF (GeoSPARQL), an OGC standard [17] and stRDF/stSPARQL (st stands for spatiotemporal) [18]. Both proposals provide vocabulary (classes, properties, and functions) that can be used in RDF graphs and SPARQL queries to represent and query geospatial data, for example *geo:SpatialObject*, which has as instances everything that can have a spatial representation and *geo:Geometry* as the superclass of all geometry classes. In addition, geometric functions and topological functions are offered for performing computations, such as *geof:distance* and for asserting topological relations between spatial objects, e.g., *dbpedia:Cardiff geo:sfWithin dbpedia:Wales*.

Qualitative spatial representation and reasoning (QSRR) are established areas of research [19], [20], whose results have influenced the definition of models of spatial relationships in international standards, e.g., the OGC models, and commercial spatial database systems (for example, in the Oracle DB system). $RCC8$, a QSRR model, has been recently adopted by GeoSPARQL [17], and there is an ever increasing interest in coupling QSR techniques with Linked Geospatial Data that are constantly being made available [18]. On the other hand, Semantic Web reasoning engines have been extended to support qualitative spatial relations, e.g., Racerpro [21] and PelletSpatial [22]. Scalability of the spatial reasoning is recognised and reported challenge. Scalable implementations of constraint network algorithms for qualitative and quantitative spatial constraints are needed, as RDF stores supporting Linked Geospatial Data are expected to scale to billions of triples [18]. Lately, promising results have been reported by [23], who proposed an approach for removing redundancy in RCC8 networks and by [24], who examined graph-partitioning techniques as a method for coping with large networks; in both cases leading to more effective application of spatial reasoning mechanisms. Finally, qualitative methods were used to complement existing quantitative methods for representing the geometry of spatial locations. In [25], heterogenous reasoning methods are proposed that combine calls between a spatial database system and a spatial reasoning engine implemented in *OWL2 RL* to check the consistency of place ontologies.

In [26], Younis et al described query plans that make use of a combination of qualitative spatial relationships associated with place resources in DBpedia and detailed representations of geometry maintained in a spatially indexed database for answering complex queries. In both cases, qualitative reasoning was limited by the fragmented and scarce availability of spatial relationships to work on. The qualitative scheme of representation of place location proposed in this paper addresses this issue and provides a novel method for defining spatial relationships that is designed to support and facilitate the effective use of qualitative spatial reasoning on the LDW.

III. A Linked Place Model for the Linked Data Web

A Relative Location model (*RelLoc*) is proposed here to capture a qualitative representation of the spatial structure of place location. Two types of spatial relations are used as follows.

1) Containment relationships, to record that a parent place directly contains a child place; i.e., one step hierarchy. For example, for three places representing a district, a city and a country, the model will explicitly record the relationships: inside(district, city) and inside(city, country), but not inside(district, country).
2) Direction-proximity relationships, to record for every place the relative direction location of its nearest neighbour places. The direction frame of reference can be selected as appropriate. For example, for a 4-cardinal direction frame of reference, a place will record its relative direction relation with its nearest neighbour in four directions.

For a given set of places Pl, let $DirPr$ be the set of all direction-proximity relations between instances of places in Pl as defined above, and let Con be the set of containment relations between instances of places in Pl as defined above. Then, $RelLoc(Pl)$ is defined as a tuple $RelLoc(Pl) := (Pl, D, C)$, where: $D \in DirPr$ and $C \in Con$. $R_{nn}(x, y)$ is used to denote that x is the nearest neighbour from the direction R to object y. For example, $N_{nn}(pl_1, pl_2)$ indicates that pl_1 is the nearest neighbour from the north direction to pl_2, etc.

To illustrate the model, consider the scene in Figure 1 that consists of a set of places, a to f, with a 4-cardinal direction frame of reference overlaid for some places in the scenes. A representative point is used to define the place location. It is further known that places represented as points a, b, c, e are inside d and places d, f are inside g. The full set of relationships used to model the scene are given in the table in Figure 1(b). Note that in some cases, no relation can be found, e.g., there are no neighbours for object c from the west direction in Figure 1(a).

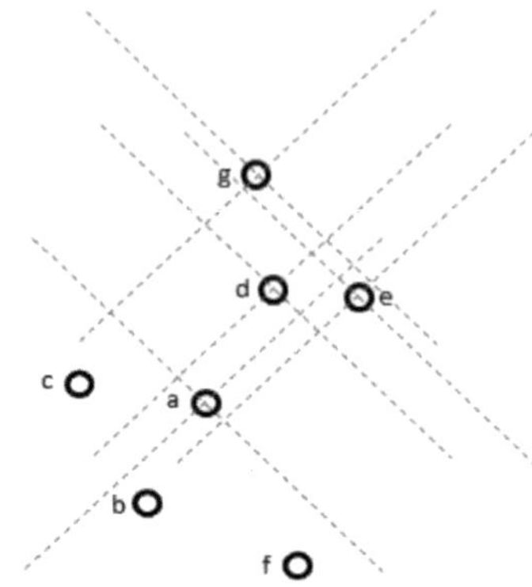

(a)

Set of spatial relations to model relative location
$N_{nn}(d, a)$, $S_{nn}(b, a)$, $W_{nn}(c, a)$, $E_{nn}(e, a)$
$N_{nn}(g, d)$, $S_{nn}(a, d)$, $W_{nn}(c, d)$, $E_{nn}(e, d)$
$N_{nn}(g, c)$, $S_{nn}(b, c)$, $E_{nn}(a, c)$
$N_{nn}(a, b)$, $E_{nn}(f, b)$
$N_{nn}(a, f)$, $W_{nn}(b, f)$
$N_{nn}(g, e)$, $S_{nn}(b, e)$, $W_{nn}(d, e)$
$S_{nn}(d, g)$
$in(a, d)$, $in(b, d)$, $in(c, d)$, $in(e, d)$,
$in(d, g)$, $in(f, g)$

(b)

Figure 1. (a) An example map scene with a set of places represented as points.(b) Set of direction, proximity and containment relations chosen to representative relative location in the proposed model.

TABLE I. COMPOSITION TABLE FOR 4-CARDINAL DIRECTION RELATIONSHIPS.

	N	E	S	W
N	N	$N \vee E$	All	$N \vee W$
E	$N \vee E$	E	$S \vee E$	All
S	All	$S \vee E$	S	$S \vee W$
W	$W \vee N$	All	$W \vee S$	W

A. Spatial Reasoning with the Relative Location Model

We can reason over the relative location model to infer more of the implicit spatial structure of place location. Qualitative spatial reasoning (QSR) tools can be utilised to propagate the defined relationships and derive new ones between places in the scene. QSR takes advantage of the transitive nature of the partial or total ordering of the quantity space in order to infer new information from the raw information presented. In particular, the transitive nature of some spatial relationships can be used to directly infer spatial hierarchies, for example, containment and cardinal direction relations. The scope of the model is deliberately focussed on general containment relationships and ignores other possible topological relations, such as overlap or touch. Hence, building containment hierarchies is straightforward using the transitivity rules: $inside(a, b) \wedge inside(b, c) \rightarrow inside(a, c)$ and $contains(a, b) \wedge contains(b, c) \rightarrow contains(a, c)$.

In the case of direction relationships, more detailed spatial reasoning can be applied using composition tables. Table I shows the composition table for a 4-cardinal direction frame of reference between point representations of spatial objects. In considering the entries of the composition tables, some of those entries provide definite conclusions of the composition operation, i.e., the composition result is only one relationship (emboldened in the table), other entries are indefinite and result in a disjunctive set of possible relationships, e.g., the composition: $N(a, b) \wedge E(b, c) \rightarrow N(a, c) \vee E(a, c)$.

Spatial reasoning can be applied on the linked place model

TABLE II. RESULT OF REASONING WITH CARDINAL RELATIONS FOR THE PLACE MODEL IN FIGURE 1.

	a	b	c	d	e	f	g
a	-	**N**	**E**	**S**	*W*	**N**	*S*
b	**S**	-	**S**	*S*	**S**	**W**	*S*
c	**W**	*W*	-	**W**	*W*	$N \vee W$	$S \vee W$
d	**N**	*N*	*E*	-	**W**	*N*	**S**
e	**E**	*N*	*E*	**E**	-	*N*	*S*
f	*S*	**E**	$S \vee E$	*S*	*S*	-	*S*
g	*N*	*N*	**N**	**N**	**N**	*N*	-

using different strategies. The most straightforward is through deriving the algebraic closure, i.e., completing the scene by deriving all possible missing relationships between objects. Path-consistency algorithms for deriving the algebraic closure has been been implemented in various tools, e.g., in the SparQ spatial reasoning engine [27]. Table II shows the result of this operation for the example scene in Figure 1. Explicit relations are shown in bold and the remaining relation are inferred by spatial reasoning. As can be seen in the table, using the 19 relationships defined for the model in Figure 1(b), reasoning was able to derive a further 19 definite relationships, completing over 90% of the possible relations in the scene.

B. Applying the Relative Location Place Model on the LDW

The underlying structure of any expression in RDF is a collection of triples, each consisting of a subject, a predicate and an object. A set of such triples is called an RDF graph, in which each triple is represented as a node-arc-node link and each triple represents a statement of a relationship between the subjects and objects, denoted by the nodes, that it links. The meaning of an RDF graph is the conjunction (logical AND) of the statements corresponding to all the triples it contains.

The *RelLoc* place model can be interpreted as a simple connected graph with nodes representing place resources and edges representing the spatial relationships between places. Thus a realisation of the place model for a specific RDF document of place resources is a subgraph of the RDF graph of the document. The *RelLoc* RDF graph is completely defined if RDF statements are used to represent all spatial relationships defined in the model, e.g., for the scene in Figure 1, 25 RDF statements are needed to encode the cardinal (19) and containment (6) relationships in the table in Figure 1(b).

Let Pl be a finite set of place class resources defined in an RDF data store and $DirPr(Pl)$ defines cardinal direction relations between members of Pl and $Con(Pl)$ describes the containment relations between members of Pl as defined by the relative location model above.

A *RelLoc* subgraph $\mathbb{G}_{\mathbb{L}} = (V_{\mathbb{L}}, E_{\mathbb{L}})$ is a simple connected graph that models Pl, where: $V_{\mathbb{L}} = Pl$ is the set of nodes, $E_{\mathbb{L}} = \{DirPr(Pl) \cup Con(Pl)\}$ is the set of edges labelled with the corresponding direction and containment relationships.

Note that there exists a subgraph of $\mathbb{G}_{\mathbb{L}}$ for every place $pl \in Pl$, which represents the subset of direction-proximity and containment relationships that completely define the relative location of pl. Thus, a *location profile* for a particular place $pl \in Pl$ can be defined as $\mathbb{L}_{pl} = \{(DirPr_{pl}, Con_{pl}\}$. $\mathbb{L}_{pl}$ is the restriction of $\mathbb{L}$ to pl, where $DirPr_{pl}$ and Con_{pl} defines direction proximity and containment relations respectively between pl and other places in Pl, as specified by our model.

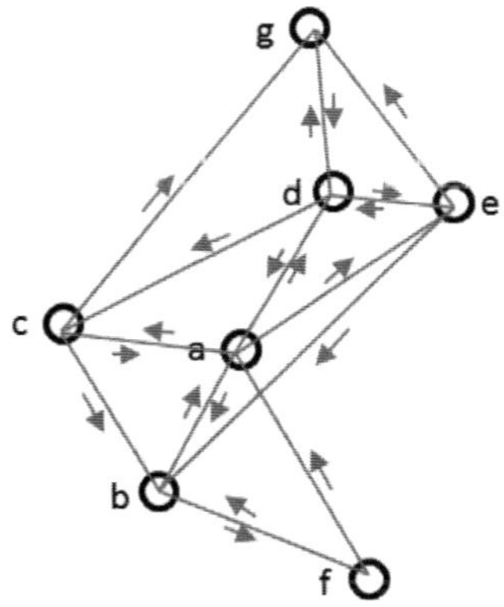

(a)

	a	b	c	d	e	f	g
a	-	1	1	1	1	0	0
b	1	-	0	0	0	1	0
c	1	1	-	0	0	0	1
d	1	0	1	-	1	0	1
e	0	1	0	1	-	0	1
f	1	1	0	0	0	-	0
g	0	0	0	1	0	0	-

(b)

	a	b	c	d	e	f	g
a	-	N	E	S	0	N	0
b	S	-	S	0	S	W	0
c	W	0	-	W	0	0	0
d	N	0	0	-	W	0	N
e	E	0	0	E	-	0	0
f	0	E	0	0	0	-	0
g	0	0	N	N	N	0	-

(c)

Figure 2. (a) A graph representing the sample map scene from Figure 1. (b) Adjacency matrix for the location graph representing nearest neighbour relationships. (c) Adjacency-orientation matrix representing nearest neighbour and direction relationships.

For example the location profile for place a in Figure 1 is the set of statements describing the relations: $N(d, a), S(b, a), W(c, a), E(e, a), in(a, d)$.

The *RelLoc* graph can be represented by a matrix to register the adjacency relationship between the place and its nearest neighbours. The scene in Figure 1 is shown as a graph with nodes and edges in Figure 2(a) and its corresponding adjacency matrix is shown in (b). The fact that two places are neighbours is represented by a value (1) in the matrix and by a value (0) otherwise. Values of (1) in the matrix can be replaced by the relative orientation relationship between the corresponding places as shown in Figure 2(c) and the resulting structure is denoted *Adjacency-Orientation Matrix*.

C. A Semantic Place Model

So far, the *RelLoc* place model considers distance and direction relationships as the primary factors for specifying place location. The importance of a place or its *salience* is another factor that is useful to consider. Salience of a place can be described from a personal or from an absolute point of view.

On a personal level, many factors can influence the importance of place to an individual [28], including, a) place dependence; how far the place satisfies the individuals behavioural goals as compared to other alternatives (e.g., [29], [30]), b) place affect; reflecting the emotional or affective bond between an individual and a place (e.g., [30], [31]), and c) place social bonding; reflecting the importance of social relationships and the context within which they occur. The specific settings of the place share the meanings attributed to them by the individuals social environment (e.g., [32], [30]).

On an absolute level, salience of a place can be defined irrelevant of attachment to specific individuals. For example, Hall, Smart and Jones [33] considered salience as a factor in defining the place location when devising methods for automatic caption generation for images (or photographs). In their work, the equation that determines the set of relative places to choose from in a particular image caption is a combination of an equal number of "ways" (highways, roads, paths, $\cdots$) and other places, ordered by their relative salience. A salience value is, in turn, a measure of how close the location of a place is to the image (i.e., its distance from the image), and its popularity (i.e., how well-known the place is). The later factor can be derived automatically from the Web, for example, from the counts of place mentions on Flickr, Wikipedia and web pages [34].

Our basic *RelLoc* place model can be adapted to handle different possible semantics of place, such as, place type, activities carried out in a place or place salience. The adapted model will, henceforth, be denoted Semantic Relative Location model, or *SemRelLoc*.

Hence, in *SemRelLoc*, a layer of salient places is first extracted from the base map layer and this acts as the anchor for place location definition. Thus, the algorithm for defining the relative location model is applied between, a) all places on the salient feature layer, and b) every place in the remaining set of places in the base map layer and the salient place layer only.

Consider the example schematic maps in Figure 3. In Figure 3(a), places on the map are not distinguished by any specific property and relationships between them are defined using *RelLoc*. In (b), a salient place layer is filtered out and used as a basis for the *SemRelLoc* model. The selection of places in this layer can be chosen to serve the application in context, for example, as a selection of particular place types, or specific place instances with high popularity, or even those of relevance to a particular individual. Note that in (b) spatial relationships are defined only with reference to the salient place instances and no relationships are defined amongst the remaining places on the base map layer, as will be described below.

Let $SalientPl$ be a finite set of place resources defined as a subset of all places Pl in an RDF data store, and $\overline{SalientPl}$ be the rest of places remaining on the base layer (i.e., $\{Pl \backslash SalientPl\}$.

A semantic relative location *SemRelLoc* subgraph $\mathbb{G}_{\mathbb{L}} = (V_{\mathbb{L}}, E_{\mathbb{L}})$ is a simple connected graph that models Pl, where: $V_{\mathbb{L}} = SalientPl$ is the set of nodes, $E_{\mathbb{L}} =$

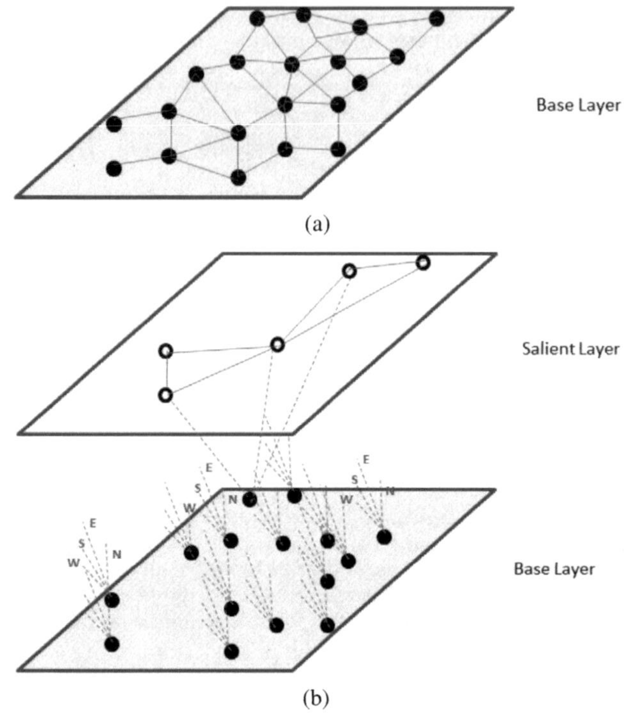

Figure 3. (a) Schematic of sample base map layer. (b) Salient place layer filtered out.

$\{DirPr(SalientPl) \cup DirPr(\overline{SalientPl}) \cup Con(Pl)\}$ is the set of edges labelled with the corresponding direction and containment relationships. $\{DirPr(SalientPl)$ is the set of direction-proximity relationships between places on the salient feature layer. $DirPr(\overline{SalientPl})$ is the set of direction-proximity relationships between the rest of places on the base layer with places on the salient layer. Hence, no inter-relationships are defined between places on the base layer itself.

Note that there exists a subgraph of $\mathbb{G}_{\mathbb{L}}$ for every place $pl \in Pl$, which represents the subset of direction-proximity and containment relationships that completely define the relative location of pl. Thus, a *Semantic location profile* for a particular place $pl \in Pl$ can be defined as follows.

$$\mathbb{L}_{pl} = \left\{ \begin{array}{ll} \{DirPr_{Salientpl}, Con_{pl}\} & ,\text{if } pl \in SalientPl \\ \{DirPr_{\overline{SalientPl}}, Con_{pl}\} & ,\forall pl \in \overline{SalientPl} \end{array} \right\}$$

Figure 4(a) shows a section of the Cardiff Bay area in Cardiff, Wales. A set of places are shown around the place: 'Cardiff Ice Rink'. Figure 4(a) shows the set of places chosen to describe the location with the original *RelLoc* model, while in 4(b) the set of some selected salient features (hotels, museums, railway stations, etc.) around the place are shown. These are used to describe the location with *SemRelLoc*. Table III lists the set of location expressions defined by both models. While both are topologically correct, the location expressions of the *SemRelLoc* model can be considered more meaningful and useful for general contexts.

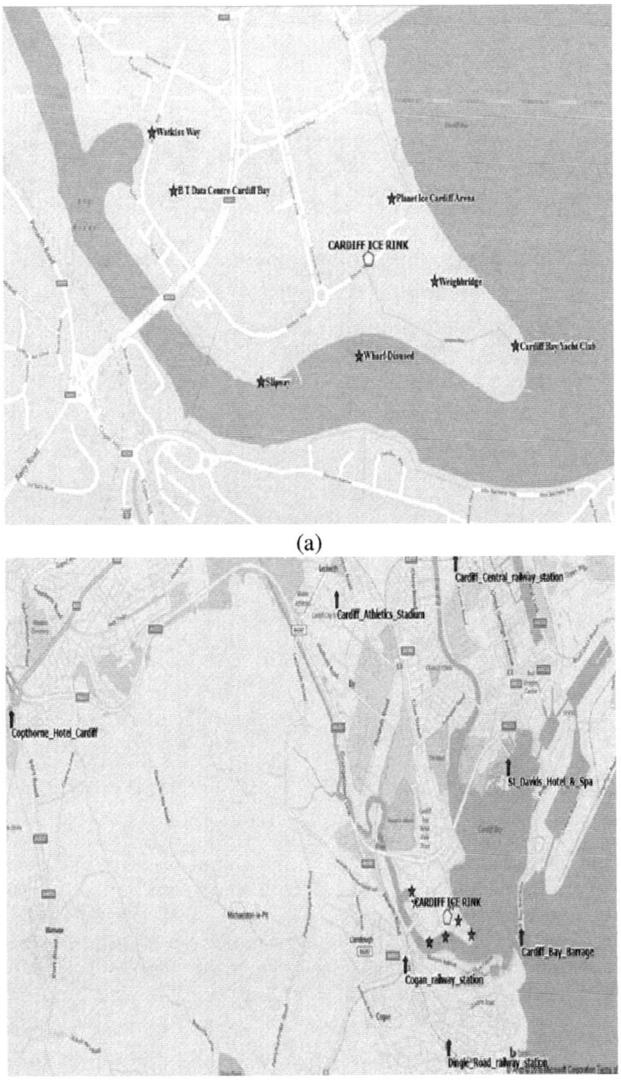

Figure 4. Sample map scene with places defining the location of "Cardiff Ice Rink": a) with *RelLoc* model, and b) with *SemRelLoc*.

TABLE III. Location expressions defining the place "Cardiff Ice Rink" in both the *RelLoc* and *SemRelLoc* models

RelLoc Model
Wharf Disused **N** Cardiff Ice Rink
Slipway **NE** Cardiff Ice Rink
BT Data Centre Cardiff Bay **E** Cardiff Ice Rink
Watkiss Way **SE** Cardiff Ice Rink
Planet Ice Cardiff Arena **SW** Cardiff Ice Rink
Weighbridge **W** Cardiff Ice Rink
Cardiff Bay Yacht Club **NW** Cardiff Ice Rink
SemRelLoc Model
Dingle Road railway station **N** Cardiff Ice Rink
Cogan railway station **NE** Cardiff Ice Rink
Copthorne Hotel Cardiff **E** Cardiff Ice Rink
Cardiff Athletics Stadium **SE** Cardiff Ice Rink
Cardiff Central railway station **S** Cardiff Ice Rink
St Davids Hotel and Spa **SW** Cardiff Ice Rink
Cardiff Bay Barrage **W** Cardiff Ice Rink

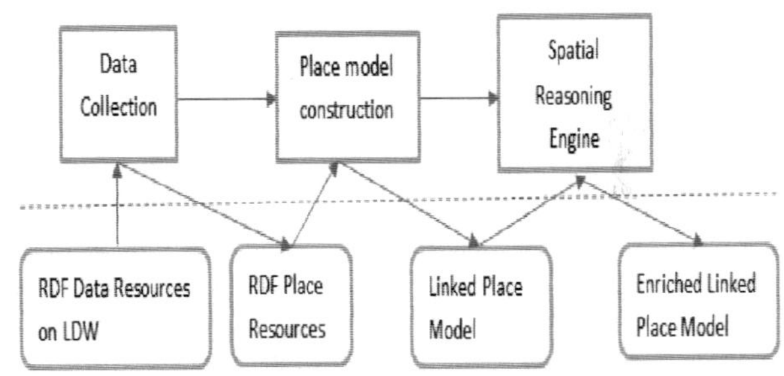

Figure 5. Components of the developed system to implement the linked place model.

$SemRelLoc$ offers two potential advantages over $RelLoc$; a) more meaningful place location expressions, using selected relevant place instances, and b) potentially a more economical data model to manage and reason with. The number of pre-defined relationships remains constant, as every place will have a set of statements defining its proximity and direction relationships. However, spatial reasoning with the semantic location graph can be more efficient with the reduction of the variety of modelled edges between places. In the following section, the effectiveness of spatial reasoning with $SemRelLoc$ will be compared against the basic $RelLoc$ model.

IV. Application and Evaluation

The main goals of the Linked Place model is to provide a representation of place location on the LDW that allows for place information to be linked effectively and consistently. The effectiveness of the proposed model can be evaluated with respect to two main aspects; whether it provides a sound definition of place location, that is to test the correctness of the place location profiles, and whether it provides a complete definition of place location, that is whether a *complete* relative location graph can be derived using the individual place location profiles.

The soundness of the location profiles is assumed as it essentially relies on the validity of the computation of the spatial relationships. Issues related to the complexity of this process are discussed in the next section.

Here, we evaluate the completeness aspect of the model. An individual place location profile defined using the model represents a finite set of spatial relationships between a place and its nearest neighbours and direct parent. Completeness of the model can be defined as the degree to which these individual profiles can be used to derive implicit links between places not defined by the model. The model is entirely complete if a full set of links between places can be derived using automatic spatial reasoning, i.e., the model can produce a complete graph, where there is a defined spatial relationship between every place in the dataset and every other place.

A system was developed that implements the Linked Place model and further builds an enriched model using spatial reasoning for evaluation purposes as shown in Figure 5.

```
prefix d: <http://dbpedia.org/ontology/>
prefix :<http://dbpedia.org/resource/>
prefix prop: <http://dbpedia.org/property/>
prefix geo: <http://www.w3.org/2003/01/geo/wgs84_pos#>

select ?place  (MAX(?lat) as ?lat)(MAX(?long) as ?long)
where{
?place ?ontology ?resource.
?place a d:Place.
?place geo:lat ?lat.
?place geo:long ?long.
filter ( ?resource = :Wales or ?resource = "Wales"@en )
}
group by ?place
order by ?place
```

Figure 6. SparQL query used to extract place data from DBpedia.

TABLE IV. RESULTS OF REASONING APPLIED ON THE DBPEDIA DATASET.

Defined	Definite	2-Relations	3-Relations	Others
2751	50340	63148	28	136
2.36%	43.24%	54.22%	0.02%	0.12%

A. *Evaluation of the Relative Location Place Model*

Two datasets were used in this experiment, DBPedia and the Ordnance Survey open data [8]. These were chosen as they exhibit different representations of place resources on the LDW and are typical of VGIs and AGIs respectively. A description of the datasets used is presented below, along with the results of the application of spatial reasoning over the constructed linked place models.

DBpedia DataSet

A sample dataset containing all Places in Wales, UK, has been downloaded from DBpedia using the SPARQL query in Figure 6.

A total of 489 places were used, for which a relative location graph of 2751 direction-proximity relations was constructed. Completing the graph resulted in 116403 total number of relations, out of which 50340 relations are definite (defining only one possible relationship).

Note that of the indefinite relationships some are a disjunction of 2 relations, e.g., $\{N, NW\}$ or $\{E, SE\}$ and some are a disjunction of 3 relations, e.g., $\{N, NE, NW\}$ or $\{NE, E, SE\}$. In both cases, relations can be generalised to a "coarser" direction relation, for example, $\{NE, E, SE\}$ can be generalised to general $East$ relationship. These results are considered useful and thus are filtered out in the presentation. The remaining results are disjunctions of unrelated directions, e.g., $\{N, NE, E\}$, and are thus considered to be ambiguous. A summary of the results is shown in Table IV. Using the Linked Place model we are able to describe nearly half the possible relations precisely (45.6%), as well as almost all of the rest of the scene (54.22%) with some useful generalised direction relations.

Ordnance Survey DataSet

The Boundary-line RDF dataset for Wales was downloaded from the Ordnance Survey open data web site [8]. The data gives a range of local government administrative and electoral boundaries.

Figure 7 shows the relative location graph constructed for the Unitary Authority dataset for Wales. Dashed edges are used to indicate that relationships (and inverses) are defined both ways between the respective nodes, but only one relation is used to label the edge in the Linked Place model. The set contains 22 regions, for which 73 direction-proximity relations were computed. Reasoning applied on this set of relations produces the results shown in Table V.

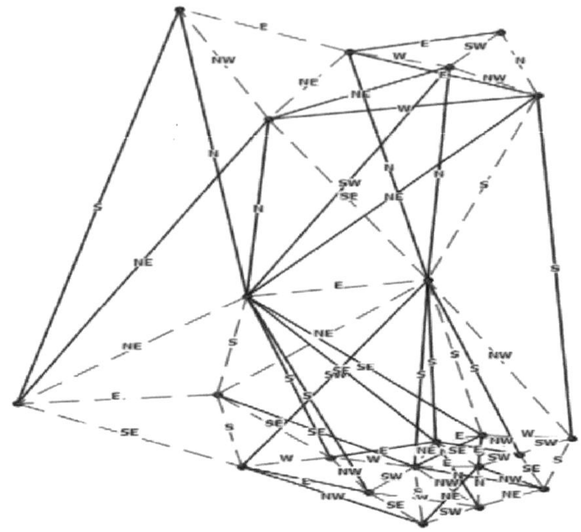

Figure 7. (a) Linked Place Graph for the Unitary Authorities in Wales from the Ordnance Survey dataset.

TABLE V. RESULTS OF REASONING APPLIED ON THE ORDNANCE SURVEY DATASET.

Defined	Definite	2-Relations	3-Relations	Others
73	94	64	0	0
31.6%	40.69%	27.7%	0	0

We can use the above results to describe the effectiveness of the linked place model in terms of the information content it was able to deduce using the ratio of the number of defined relations to the number of deduced relations. A summary is presented in Table VI.

B. *Evaluation of the Semantic Place Model*

The value of the $SemRelLoc$ model is primarily in its ability to deliver flexible and meaningful place location expressions. Here, we also evaluate its effectiveness with respect to spatial reasoning. An experiment is carried out with a sample point of interest dataset obtained from the Ordnance Survey, that records information on places and place types in the city of Cardiff, Wales, UK. A set of approximately 300 places were chosen in 5 unitary authorities in South Wales; (Cardiff, Newport, Caerphilly, Vale of Glamorgan and

TABLE VI. SUMMARY OF THE EXPERIMENT RESULTS.

	$\frac{Defined}{Definite}$	$\frac{Defined}{Useful}$
$DBpedia$	0.054	0.024
OS	0.78	0.32

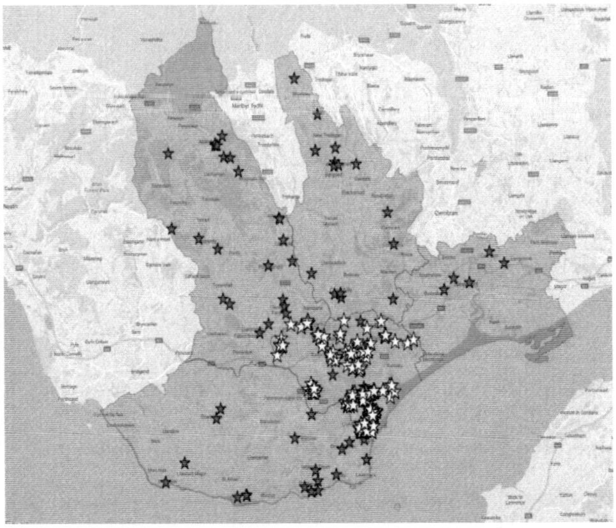

Figure 8. A map scene with a sample set of point of interest places in South Wales, UK. Red/dark stars represent salient features and white stars are all other places.

TABLE VII. RESULTS OF REASONING APPLIED ON THE SALIENT FEATURE LAYER ONLY.

Defined	Definite	2-Relations	3-Relations
538	3261	2515	2
8.52%	51.63%	39.81%	0.031%

Rhondda). Salient features were chosen on the basis of popular place types, including hotels, museums, hospitals, castles and railway stations. A map of the area chosen is shown in Figure 8 with the salient (red/dark) and other places (white) highlighted.

Table VII shows the result of applying spatial reasoning on the complete graph on the salient feature layer only. A total of 108 places were used, for which a relative location graph of 538 direction-proximity relations was defined. Completing the graph resulted in 5778 total number of relations, out of which 3261 (56%) relations are definite (defining only one possible relationship) and a further 2515 (44%) are useful 2-relations. Thus, using $RelLoc$ on the salient feature layer, and defining only 8% of relations, we were able to derive almost all of the scene with useful location expressions.

With the $SemRelLoc$ model, no relations have to be pre-defined between the base layer places. Every place on the base layer is instead linked to places on the salient feature layer. Thus, for the complete map of places in Figure 8, a further 181 other places were added to the scene and a total of 1331 pre-defined proximity direction relations are defined by the model. Completing the graph resulted in 29403, out of which 12939 (44%) relations are definite and a further 15454 (53%) are useful 2-relations. Thus, using $SemRelLoc$ model, and defining only 5% of possible relationships between places in the map scene, we were able to complete the whole graph and derive over 96% of all possible relationships between all places.

The result demonstrates that the application of spatial

TABLE VIII. RESULTS OF REASONING APPLIED ON THE WHOLE MAP SCENE with $SemRelLoc$.

Defined	Definite	2-Relations	3 Relations or more
1331	12939	15454	1010
4.52%	44%	52.56%	3.44%

reasoning on the adapted semantic model is as effective as in the case of the basic model. Further research can now be directed at the scalability of the framework with respect to both representation and reasoning on the Linked Data Web.

C. Discussion

The proposed approach to place representation and reasoning can be adopted on the LDW in different scenarios as follows.

- The spatial integrity of the linked web resources can be checked. Here, spatial reasoning can be applied on the whole resource to determine which predicates are contradictory [25]. Scalability of the reasoning engine can be an issue and methods for managing large resources need to be considered [18].
- Enriching linked web resources by the basic relative location model allows uniform and complete representation of place across resources, which in turn supports effective retrieval of place information.
- Using the reasoner to build a parallel, complementary resource of the complete set of possible spatial information that can be inferred from the basic relative location model, as was done in the experiments above. The inferred resource will need to be updated regularly to reflect the current state of the original resource and scalability of the reasoning method will also be an issue that needs to be addressed.
- Spatial reasoning can be applied 'on the fly' to support a defined set of query plans on the basic relative location structure. A possible framework to implement this scenario is given in Figure 9. Possible query plans that can be supported by this framework includes finding relationships directly supported by the model (namely, containment, nearest neighbour and direction queries) as well as those derived by spatial inference using spatial reasoning. Detailed specification of these queries are the subject of future research.

V. CONCLUSIONS

Data on geographic places are considered to be very useful on the LDW. Individuals and organisations are volunteering data to build global base maps enriched with different types of traditional and non-traditional semantics reflecting people's views of geographic space and place. In addition, geographic references to place can be used to link different types of datasets, thus enhancing the utility of these datasets on the LDW. This work explores the challenges introduced when representing place data using the simple model of RDF, with different geometries to represent location and different non-standardised vocabularies to represent spatial relationships between locations.

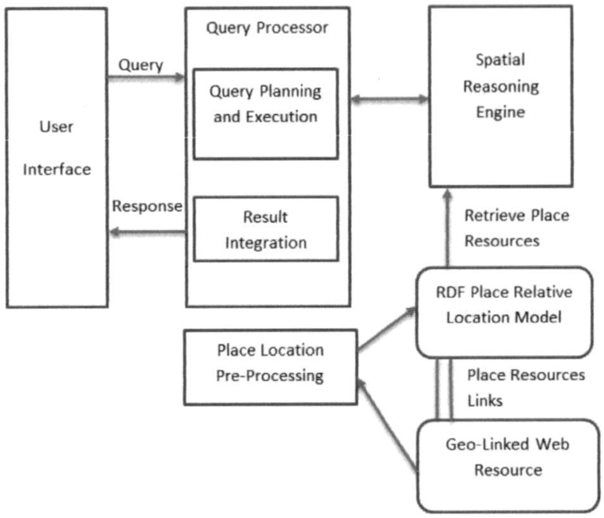

Figure 9. A framework for the implementation of the proposed approach.

A linked place model is proposed that injects certain types of spatial semantics into the RDF graph underlying the place data. Specific types of spatial relationships between place nodes are added to the graph to allow the creation of individual place location profiles that fully describe the relative spatial location of a place. It is further shown how the enriched relative location graph can allow spatial reasoning to be applied to derive implicit spatial links to produce even more richer place descriptions. Salience of place is introduced as a means of scoping out relevant and meaningful place location expressions. The representation scheme is adapted to allow for the flexible choice of place instances to be used in the model.

The results obtained from the evaluation experiments demonstrate possible significant value in the proposed model. Further work need to be done to explore the potential utility of the proposal. Some of the interesting issues that we aim to explore in the future are described below.

- Simple methods and assumptions were used to compute the direction relationships between places. Further study need to be carried out to evaluate whether more involved representations are useful [35].
- Applications of spatial reasoning need to be considered further. Describing the complete graph is not a practical (nor a useful) option. Can spatial reasoning be selectively applied, for example, as part of query processing on the location graph?
- The application of the approach on other types of data sets on the LDW as individual as well as combined resources.

APPENDIX

Follows is a sample set of relationships defining the location of "Techniquest": an educational charity in The Cardiff Bay area, Wales, UK, resulting from the application of spatial reasoning on the salient features in the map in Figure 8.

```
(Techniquest (sw) Bastion_Road)
(Techniquest (sw) Barry_Power_Station)
(Techniquest (sw) Barry_Docks_railway_station)
(Techniquest (sw) Barry_Island_railway_station)
(Techniquest (sw) Barry_Dock_Lifeboat_Station)
(Techniquest (sw w) Cowbridge_railway_station)
(Techniquest (sw w) Llantwit_Major_Roman_Villa)
(Techniquest (sw) Barry_railway_station)
(Techniquest (sw w) Aberthaw_power_stations)
(Techniquest (sw w) Aberthaw_High_Level_railway_station)
(Techniquest (sw w) Aberthaw_Low_Level_railway_station)
(Techniquest (ne) Celtic_Manor_Resort)
(Techniquest (ne) Kingsway_Shopping_Centre)
(Techniquest (ne) Allt-yr-yn)
(Techniquest (ne) Caerleon_railway_station)
(Techniquest (n nw) Caerphilly_Castle)
(Techniquest (n nw) Argoed_railway_station)
(Techniquest (n nw) Brithdir_railway_station)
(Techniquest (n nw) Aberbargoed_Hospital)
(Techniquest (n nw) Aber_Bargoed_railway_station)
(Techniquest (n ne) Crosskeys_railway_station)
(Techniquest (sw w) Atlantic_College_Lifeboat_Station)
(Techniquest (nw) Coed_Ely_railway_station)
(Techniquest (n nw) Bargoed_railway_station)
(Techniquest (n nw) Cefn_Eglwysilan)
(Techniquest (nw) Church_Village)
(Techniquest (nw) Church_Village_Halt_railway_station)
(Techniquest (nw) Sardis_Road)
(Techniquest (nw) Cross_Inn_railway_station)
(Techniquest (nw) Aberdare_Low_Level_railway_station)
(Techniquest (nw) Aberdare_railway_station)
(Techniquest (nw) Coed-Ely)
(Techniquest (n nw) Cilfynydd)
(Techniquest (n nw) Abercynon_railway_station)
(Techniquest (n nw) Abertysswg_railway_station)
(Techniquest (n nw) Darran_and_Deri_railway_station)
(Techniquest (nw) Dinas_Rhondda_railway_station)
(Techniquest (n nw) Abercynon_North_railway_station)
(Techniquest (n nw) Bute_Town)
(Techniquest (nw) Mynydd_William_Meyrick)
(Techniquest (nw) Clydach_Vale)
(Techniquest (nw) Lluest-wen_Reservoir)
(Techniquest (n nw) Abercwmboi_Halt_railway_station)
(Techniquest (n nw) Abernant_railway_station)
(Techniquest (nw) Athletic_Ground_Aberdare)
(Techniquest (nw) Aberaman_railway_station)
(Techniquest (n nw) Cwmbach_railway_station)
(Techniquest (nw) Beddau_Halt_railway_station)
(Techniquest (n) Abercarn_railway_station)
(Techniquest (s) Alberta_Place_Halt_railway_station)
(Techniquest (w) St_Fagans_National_History_Museum)
(Techniquest (sw) Dinas_Powys_railway_station)
(Techniquest (e) Pierhead_Building)
(Techniquest (e) Mermaid_Quay)
(Techniquest (n nw) Caerphilly_railway_station)
(Techniquest (n ne) Ruperra_Castle)
(Techniquest (n nw) Birchgrove_railway_station)
(Techniquest (n nw) National_Museum_Cardiff)
(Techniquest (ne) Bassaleg_Junction_railway_station)
(Techniquest (ne) RAF_Pengam_Moors)
(Techniquest (n) Childrens_Hospital_for_Wales)
(Techniquest (w) Aberthin_Platform_railway_station)
(Techniquest (n nw) Abertridwr_railway_station)
(Techniquest (n) Cefn_Onn_Halt_railway_station)
(Techniquest (nw) Creigiau_railway_station)
(Techniquest (nw) Efail_Isaf_railway_station)
(Techniquest (n nw) Aber_railway_station)
(Techniquest (nw) Castell_Coch)
(Techniquest (nw) Whitchurch_Hospital)
(Techniquest (n nw) Hilton_Cardiff)
(Techniquest (w) St_Fagans_Castle)
(Techniquest (sw) Eastbrook_railway_station)
(Techniquest (w) Cardiff_International_Sports_Stadium)
(Techniquest (s) Cardiff_Bay_Barrage)
(Techniquest (sw w) Dyffryn_Gardens)
(Techniquest (n) University_Hospital_of_Wales)
```

REFERENCES

[1] A. Abdelmoty and K. Al-Muzaini, "Reasoning with place information on the linked data web," in *The Second International Conference on Big Data, Small Data, Linked Data and Open Data- ALLDATA 2016*, V. Gudivada, D. Roman, M. di Buono, and M. Monteleone, Eds., 2016, pp. 48–53.

[2] T. Berners-Lee. Linked data. http://www.w3.org/DesignIssues/LinkedData.html. Accessed: 2016-11-30.

[3] C. Bizer, T. Heath, and T. Berners-Lee, "Linked data - the story so far," *International Journal on Semantic Web and Information Systems*, vol. 5, no. 3, pp. 1–22, 2009.

[4] J. Goodwin, C. Dolbear, and G. Hart, "Geographical linked data: The administrative geography of great britain on the semantic web," *Transactions in GIS*, vol. 12, pp. 19–30, 2008.

[5] G. Hart and C. Dolbear, *Linked Data: A Geographic Perspective*. CRC Books, 2013.

[6] C. Henden, P. Rissen, and S. Angeletou. Linked geospatial data, and the bbc. http://www.w3.org/2014/03/lgd/papers/lgd14_submission_28. Accessed: 2016-11-30.

[7] M. Hackley, "How good is volunteered geographical information? a comparative study of openstreetmap and ordnance survey datasets," *Environment and Planning B*, vol. 37, no. 4, pp. 682–703, 2010.

[8] Ordnance survey linked data platform. http://data.ordnancesurvey.co.uk/. Accessed: 2016-11-30.

[9] Geolinkeddata.es. http://linkeddata.es/. Accessed: 2016-11-30.

[10] S. Mohamed and A. Abdelmoty, "Uncovering user profiles in location based social networks," in *The Eighth International Conference on Advanced Geographic Information Systems, GEOProcessing 2016*, C.-P. Rckemann and Y. Doytsher, Eds., 2016, p. 1421.

[11] E. Younis, "Hybrid geo-spatial query processing on the semantic web," Ph.D. dissertation, Cardiff University, Cardiff Univeristy, 2013.

[12] E. M. Younis, C. Jones, V. Tanasescu, and A. Abdelmoty, "Hybrid geo-query methods on the semantic web with a spatially enhanced index of dbpedia," in *7th International Conference on Geographic Information Science, GIScience, 2012*, N. Xiao, M.-P. Kwan, M. Goodchild, and S. Shekhar, Eds., vol. LNCS 7478, 2012, pp. 340–353.

[13] S. Auer, J. Lehmann, and S. Hellmann, "Linkedgeodata- adding a spatial dimension to the web of data," in *Proc. of 7th International Semantic Web Conference (ISWC)*, vol. LNCS 5823. Springer, 2009, pp. 731–746.

[14] C. Stadler, J. Lehmann, K. Hffner, and S. Auer, "Linkedgeodata: A core for a web of spatial open data," *Semantic Web Journal*, vol. 3, no. 4, pp. 333–354, 2012.

[15] J. Salas and A. Harth, "Finding spatial equivalences accross multiple rdf datasets," in *Terra Cognita Workshop,co-located with ISWC*, R. Grtter, D. Kolas, M. Koubarakis, and D. Pfoser, Eds., 2011, pp. 114–126.

[16] A. Cohn, B. Bennett, J. Gooday, and N. Gotts, "Qualitative spatial representation and reasoning with the region connection calculus," *Geoinformatica*, vol. 1, pp. 1–44, 1997.

[17] Geosparql - a geographic query language for rdf data. http://www.opengeospatial.org/standards/geosparql. Accessed: 2016-11-30.

[18] M. Koubarakis, M. Karpathiotakis, K. Kyzirakos, C. Nikolaou, and M. Sioutis, "Data Models and Query Languages for Linked Geospatial Data," in *Reasoning Web. Semantic Technologies for Advanced Query Answering,Invited tutorial at the 8th Reasoning Web Summer School 2012 (RW 2012)*, T. Eiter and T. Krennwallner, Eds., vol. LNCS 7487. Springer, 2012, pp. 290–328.

[19] A. G. Cohn and J. Renz, *Qualitative Spatial Representation and Reasoning*, ser. Handbook of Knowledge Representation. Elsevier, 2008, pp. 551–596.

[20] B. Gottfried, "Reasoning about intervals in two dimensions," in *IEEE Int. Conf. on Systems, Man and Cybernetics*, W. e. a. Thissen, Ed., 2004, pp. 5324–5332.

[21] What is racerpro. http://www1.racer-systems.com/products/racerpro/index.phtml. Accessed: 2016-11-30.

[22] M. Stocker and E. Sirin, "Pelletspatial: A hybrid rcc-8 and rdf/owl reasoning and query engine," in *6th Intern. Workshop on OWL: Experiences and Directions (OWLED2009)*. Springer-Verlag, 2009, pp. 2–31.

[23] M. Sioutis, S. Li, and J.-F. Condotta, "On redundancy in linked geospatial data," in *2nd Workshop on Linked Data Quality (LDQ)*, ser. CEUR Workshop Proceedings, A. Rula, A. Zaveri, M. Knuth, and D. Kontokostas, Eds., no. 1376, 2015. [Online]. Available: http://ceur-ws.org/Vol-1376/#paper-05

[24] C. Nikolaou and M. Koubarakis, "Fast consistency checking of very large real-world rcc-8 constraint networks using graph partitioning," in *Proceedings of the 28th AAAI Conference on Artificial Intelligence*, 2014, pp. 2724–2730.

[25] A. Abdelmoty, P. Smart, and B. El-Geresy, "Spatial reasoning with place information on the semantic web," *International Journal on Artificial Intelligence Tools*, vol. 23, no. 5, p. 1450011, 2014.

[26] E. Younis, C. Jones, V. Tanasescu, and A. Abdelmoty, "Hybrid geo-spatial query methods on the semantic web with a spatially-enhanced index of dbpedia," in *Geographic Information Science*, ser. Lecture Notes in Computer Science, N. Xiao, M.-P. Kwan, M. Goodchild, and S. Shekhar, Eds., vol. 7478. Springer Berlin Heidelberg, 2012, pp. 340–353.

[27] D. Wolter and J. Wallgrn, "Qualitative spatial reasoning for applications: New challenges and the sparq toolbox," in *Qualitative Spatio-Temporal Representation and Reasoning: Trends and Future Directions*, S. Hazarika, Ed., 2012, pp. 336–362.

[28] G. Kyle, A. Graefe, and M. R., "Testing the dimensionality of place attachment in recreational settings," *Environment and Behavior*, vol. 37, no. 2, pp. 153–177, 2005.

[29] G. Brown and C. Raymond, "The relationship between place attachment and landscape values toward mapping place attachment," *Applied Geography*, vol. 27, no. 1, pp. 89–111, 2007.

[30] G. Kyle, K. Bricker, A. Graefe, and T. Wickham, "An examination of recreationists relationships with activities and settings." *Leisure Sciences*, vol. 26, no. 2, pp. 123–142, 2004.

[31] B. Jorgensen and R. Stedman, "Sense of place as an attitude: Lakeshore owners attitudes toward their properties." *Journal of Environmental Psychology*, vol. 21, pp. 233–248, 2001.

[32] H. Gu and C. Ryan, "Place attachment, identity and community impacts of tourism the case of a beijing hutong." *Tourism Management*, vol. 29, no. 4, pp. 637–647, 2008.

[33] M. Hall, P. Smart, and C. Jones, "Interpreting spatial language in image captions," *Cognitive Processing*, vol. 12, no. 1, pp. 67–94, 2011.

[34] M. Hall, "Modelling and reasoning with quantitative representations of vague spatial language used in photographic image captions," Ph.D. dissertation, Cardiff University, Cardiff Univeristy, 2011.

[35] X. Yao and J.-C. Thill, "How far is too far? a statistical approach to context-contingent proximity modeling," *Transactions in GIS*, vol. 9, no. 2, pp. 157–178, 2005.

A Model-Driven Engineering Approach to Software Tool Interoperability based on Linked Data

Jad El-khoury, Didem Gurdur
Department of Machine Design
KTH Royal Institute of Technology
Stockholm, Sweden
email:{jad, dgurdur}@kth.se

Mattias Nyberg
Scania CV AB
Södertälje, Sweden
email: mattias.nyberg@scania.com

***Abstract*—Product development environments need to shift from the current document-based, towards an information-based focus, in which the information from the various engineering software tools is well integrated and made digitally accessible throughout the development lifecycle. To meet this need, a Linked Data approach to software tool interoperability is being adopted, specifically through the Open Services for Lifecycle Collaboration (OSLC) interoperability standard. In this paper, we present a model-driven engineering approach to toolchain development that targets the specific challenges faced when adopting the technologies, standards and paradigm expected of Linked Data and the OSLC standard. We propose an integrated set of modelling views that supports the early specification phases of toolchain development, as well as its detailed design and implementation phases. An open-source modelling tool was developed to realize the proposed modelling views. The tool includes a code generator that synthesizes a toolchain model into almost-complete OSLC-compliant code. The study is based on a case study of developing a federated OSLC-based toolchain for the development environment at the truck manufacturer Scania AB.**

Keywords-Linked data modelling; OSLC; resource shapes; tool integration; tool interoperability, information modelling.

I. Introduction

This article is an extended version of [1], in which we expand the earlier focus on the specification phase, to present a more complete development approach to software tool interoperability. The new approach includes a tighter incorporation of the later phases of design and implementation of tool interfaces. Based on additional work on the case study, further refinements of the proposed models and supporting tools are also reflected in this article.

The heterogeneity and complexity of modern industrial products requires the use of many engineering software tools, needed by the different engineering disciplines (such as mechanical, electrical, embedded systems and software engineering), and throughout the entire development life cycle (requirements analysis, design, verification and validation, etc.). Each engineering tool handles product information that focuses on specific aspects of the product, yet such information may well be related or dependent on information handled by other tools in the development environment [2]. It is also the case that a tool normally manages its product information internally as artefacts stored on a file system or a database using a tool-specific format or schema. Therefore, unless interoperability mechanisms are developed to connect information across the engineering tools, isolated "islands of information" may result within the overall development environment. This in turn leads to an increased risk of inconsistencies, given the natural distribution of information across the many tools and data sources involved.

As an example from the automotive industry, the functional safety standard ISO 26262:2011 [3] mandates that requirements and design components are to be developed at several levels of abstraction; and that clear trace links exist between requirements from the different levels, as well as between requirements and system components. Such a demand on traceability implies that these development artifacts are readily and consistently accessible, even if they reside across different development tools. Naturally, the current industry practice, in which development artefacts are handled as text-based documentation, renders such traceability ineffective – if not impossible. The ongoing trend of adopting the Model-Driven Engineering (MDE) approach to product development is a step in the right direction, by moving away from text-based artefacts, towards models that are digitally accessible. This leads to an improvement in the quality and efficient access to product and process information. However, while MDE is more accepted in the academic research community, its complete adoption in an industrial context remains somewhat limited, where MDE is typically constrained to a subset of the development lifecycle [22]. Moreover, even where MDE is adopted, mechanisms are still needed to connect the artefacts being created by the various engineering tools, in order to comply with the standard.

In summary, current development practices need a faster shift from the localized document-based handling of artefacts, towards an **Information-based Development Environment (IDE)**, where the information from all development artefacts is made accessible, consistent and correct throughout the development phases, disciplines and tools.

One can avoid the need to integrate the information islands, by adopting a single platform (such as PTC Integrity [4] or MSR-Backbone [5]) through which product data is centrally managed. However, large organizations have specific development needs and approaches (processes, tools, workflow, in-house tools, etc.), which lead to a wide landscape of organization-specific and customized development environments. Moreover, this landscape needs to evolve organically over time, in order to adjust to future unpredictable needs of the industry. Contemporary platforms, however, offer limited customization capabilities to tailor for the organization-specific needs, requiring instead the organization to adjust itself to suite the platform. So, while they might be suitable at a smaller scale, such centralized platforms cannot scale to handle the complete heterogeneous set of data sources normally found in a large organization.

A more promising integration approach is to acknowledge the existence of distributed and independent data sources within the environment. To this end, OASIS OSLC [6] is an emerging interoperability open standard (see Section II for further details) that adopts the architecture of the Internet and its standard web technologies to integrate information from the different engineering tools - without relying on a centralized integration platform. This leads to low coupling between tools, by reducing the need for one tool to understand the deep data of another. Moreover – like the web – the approach is technology-agnostic, where tools can differ in the technologies they use to internally handle their data. That is, both the data as well as the technology is decentralized. Such an approach lends itself well to the distributed and organic nature of the IDE being desired - a Federated IDE (F-IDE), where the information from all development artefacts – across the different engineering tools – is made accessible, consistent and correct throughout the development phases, disciplines and tools.

In this paper, we advocate the use of OSLC and the Linked Data principles as a basis for such an F-IDE. Yet, when developing such a federated OSLC-based F-IDE for parts of the development environment at the truck manufacturer Scania AB, certain challenges were encountered that needed to be addressed. Put generally, there is an increased risk that one loses control over the overall product data structure that is now distributed and interrelated across the many tools. This risk is particularly aggravated if one needs to maintain changes in the F-IDE over time.

We here propose a model-driven engineering approach to F-IDE development that tries to deal with this risk. That is, how can a distributed architecture – as promoted by the Linked Data approach – be realized, while maintaining a somewhat centralized understanding and management of the overall information model handled within the F-IDE?

In the next section, we will first give some background information on Linked Data and the OASIS OSLC standard. We then present the case study that has driven and validated this work in Section III. Section IV then elaborates on the challenges experienced during our case study, before detailing the modelling approach taken to solve these challenges in Section V. Details on the modelling views, as well as their realisation in an open-source tool, are presented. Reflections on applying the modelling approach on the case study are then discussed in Section VI, followed by a discussion of related work. The article is then concluded in Section VIII.

II. LINKED DATA AND THE OASIS OSLC STANDARD

Linked Data is an approach for publishing structured data on the web, such that data from different sources can be connected, resulting in more meaningful and useful information. Linked Data builds upon standard web technologies such as HTTP, URI and the RDF family of standards. The reader is referred to [7] for Tim Berners-Lee's four principles of Linked Data.

OASIS OSLC is a standard that targets the integration of heterogeneous software tools, with a focus on the linking of data from independent sources. It builds upon the Linked Data principles, and its accompanying standards, by defining common mechanisms and patterns to access, manipulate and query resources managed by the different tools in the toolchain. In particular, OASIS OSLC is based on the W3C Linked Data Platform (LDP) [8], and it follows the Representational State Transfer (REST) architectural pattern.

This Linked Data approach to tool interoperability promotes a distributed architecture, in which each tool autonomously manages its own product data, while providing – at its interface - RESTful services through which other tools can interconnect. Figure 1 illustrates a typical architecture of an OSLC tool interface, and its relation to the tool it is interfacing. With data exposed as RESTful services, such an interface is necessarily an "OSLC Server", with the connecting tool defined as an "OSLC Client". Following the REST architectural pattern, an OSLC server allows for the manipulation of artefacts – once accessed through the services - using the standard HTTP methods C.R.U.D. to Create, Read, Update and Delete. In OSLC, tool artefacts are represented as RDF resources, which can be represented using RDF/XML, JSON, or Turtle. A tool interface can be provided natively by the tool vendor, or through a third-party as an additional adaptor. In either case, a mapping between the internal data and the exposed RDF resources needs to be done. Such mapping needs to deal with the differences in the technologies used. In addition, a mapping between the internal and external vocabulary is needed, since the vocabulary of the resources being exposed is not necessarily the same as the internal schema used to manage the data.

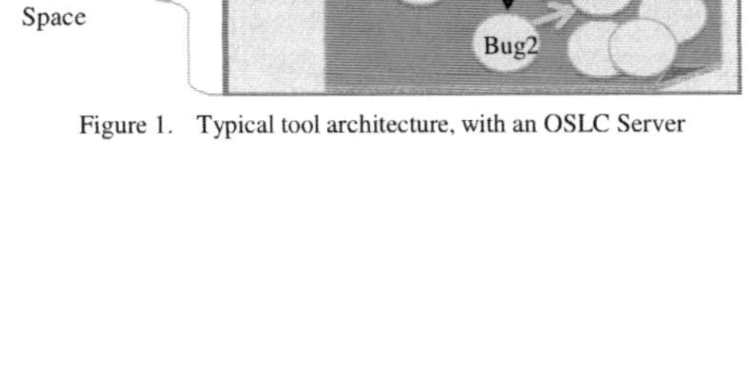

Figure 1. Typical tool architecture, with an OSLC Server

III. Case Study Description

Typical of many industrial organizations, the development environment at the truck manufacturer Scania consists of standard engineering tools, such as issue-tracking and computer-aided design (CAD) tools; as well as a range of proprietary tools that cater for specific needs in the organization. Moreover, much product information is managed as generic content in office productivity tools, such as Microsoft Word and Excel.

To comply with the ISO 26262 standard, the current development environment needs to improve in its management of vehicle architectures and requirement specifications, in order to provide the expected traceability between them. This in turn necessitates a better integration of the tools handling the architecture and requirements artefacts to allow for such traceability. To this end, five proprietary tools and data sources were to be integrated using OSLC:

1. *Code Repository* – A tool that defines the vehicle software architecture through parsers that analyze all software code to reconstruct the architecture, defining entities such as software components and their communication channels [9]. The analyzed software code resides in a typical version-control system. When defining the architecture, the tool references artefacts – defined in other external tools - dealing with communication and the hardware architecture.
2. *Communication Specifier* – A tool that centrally defines the communication network and the messages sent between components of all vehicle architectures.
3. *ModArc* – A CAD tool that defines the electrical components, including all hardware entities and their interfaces such as communication ports.
4. *Diagnostics Tool* - A tool that specifies the diagnostics functionality of all vehicle architectures, including communication messages of relevance to the diagnostics functionality.
5. *Requirements Specifier* - A proprietary tool that allows for the semi-formal specification of system requirements [10]. Requirements are specified at different levels of abstraction. By anchoring the specifications on different parts of the system architecture, the tool helps the developer define correct requirements that can only reference appropriate product artefacts within the system architecture.

As a first step, it was necessary to analyze the data that needed to be communicated between the tools. This was captured using a Class Diagram (Figure 2), as is the current state-of-practice at Scania for specifying a data model. For the purpose of this paper, it is not necessary to have full understanding of the data artefacts. It is worth highlighting that color-codes were initially used to define which tool managed which data artefact. Yet, this appeared to be a non-trivial task since an artefact might be used in multiple tools, with no clear agreement on the originating source tool. For example, a *Signal* can be found in both the *Code Repository* as well as the *Communication Specifier* tool. Given that there exists no data integration between the two tools to keep the artefact synchronized, different developers may have a different perspective over which of the two tools holds the source and correct *Signal* information, from which the other tool needs to be – manually – updated.

In addition, it is important to note that the model focuses on the data to be communicated between the tools, and not necessarily all data available internally within each tool.

IV. Identified Needs and Shortcomings

In this paper, we focus on the initial development stages of specifying and architecting the desired OSLC-based F-IDE, as well as its design and implementation. The latter verification and validation phases are not yet covered in the case study, yet there is naturally recognition of the need to support them in the near future. Based on the case study, we here elaborate on the needs and shortcomings experienced by the toolchain architects and developers during these stages:

Information specification – There is a need to specify an information model that defines the types of artefacts or resources to be communicated between the tools across the toolchain. For pragmatic reasons, a UML class diagram was initially adopted by the Scania toolchain architects to define the entities being communicated and their relationships. Clearly, the created model does not comply with the semantics of the class diagram, since the entities being modelled are not objects in the object-oriented paradigm, but resources according to the Resource Description Framework (RDF) graph data model. Since the information model is to be maintained over time, and is intended for communication among developers, using a class diagram - while implying another set of semantics – may lead to misunderstandings. A specification that is semantically compatible with the intended implementation technology (of Linked Data, and specifically the OSLC standard) is necessary. However, the initial experience from using the class diagram helped identify the necessary requirements on any appropriate solution. First, graphical models are essential to facilitate the communication of the models among the different stakeholders. It is also beneficial to – wherever possible - borrow or reuse graphical representations from common modelling frameworks (such as UML) in order to reduce the threshold of learning a new specification language. For example, adopting a hollow triangle shape to represent class inheritance (as defined in UML) would be recommended in RDF modelling as well.

Domain ownership – It is necessary to structure the information model specification into domains (such as requirements engineering, software, testing, etc.). Domains can be generic in nature. Alternatively, such domain grouping can reflect the organization units that are responsible to manage specific parts of the information model. For example, the testing department may be responsible to define and maintain the testing-related resources, while the requirements department manages the definition of the requirements resources. This is particularly relevant in an organization where different departments are responsible for their own tools and processes, and where it no longer becomes feasible to expect the information model to be centrally defined. Dependencies between the responsible departments can then be easily identified through the dependencies in the information models.

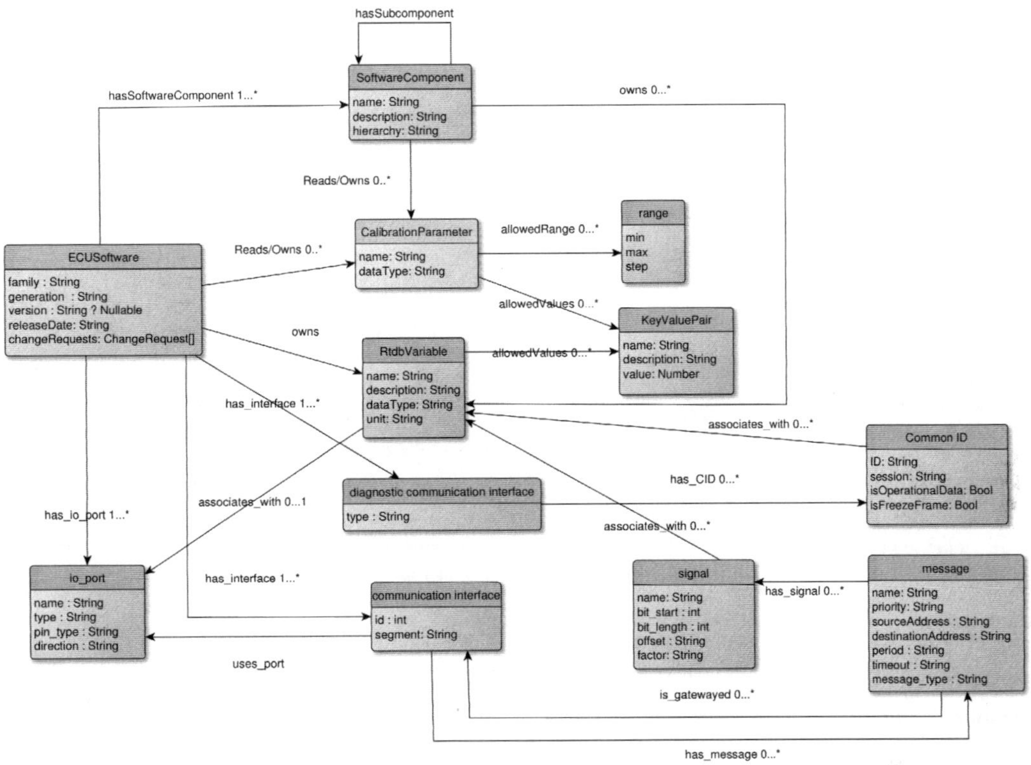

Figure 2. A UML class diagram of the resources shared in the desired F-IDE.

Tool ownership – Orthogonal to domain ownership, it is also necessary to clearly identify the data source (or authoring tool) that is expected to manage each defined resource being shared in the F-IDE. That is, while representations of a resource may be freely shared between the tools, changes or creations of such a resource can only occur via its owning tool. Assuming a Linked Data approach also implies that a resource is owned by a single source, to which other resources link. In practice, it is not uncommon for data to be duplicated in multiple sources, and hence mechanisms to synchronize data between tools are needed. For example, resources of type *Communication Interface* may be used in both *Communication Specifier* and *ModArc*, with no explicit decision on which of the tools defines it. To simplify the case study, we chose to ignore the *ModArc* source, but in reality, one needs to synchronize between the two sources, as long as it is not possible to make one of them redundant.

That is, in architecting an F-IDE, there is a need to support the data specification using Linked Data semantics, while covering the two ownership aspects of tools (ownership from the tool deployment perspective) and domains (ownership from the organizational perspective).

Avoid mega-meta-modelling – Information specifications originate from various development phases and/or development units in the organization. The resulting information models may well overlap, and would hence need to be harmonized. Hence, there is a need to harmonize the information models – while avoiding a central information model. Earlier attempts at information modeling normally resulted in large models that can easily become harder to maintain over time. The research project CESAR presents in [11] a typical interoperability approach in which such a large common meta-model is proposed. It is anticipated that the Linked Data approach would reduce the need to have such a single centralized mega information model. The correct handling of information through Domain and Tool Ownership (see above) ought to also help in that direction.

Development support – Similar to the challenge faced in general software development, there is a need to maintain the information specification and desired architecture harmonious with the eventual design and implementation of the F-IDE and its components. The current use of a class diagram works well as an initial specification, and for documentation purposes. However, there is no mechanism in place to ensure the model is updated relative to changes later performed during the development. Especially when adopting an agile development approach, the specification and architecture are expected to change over time, and hence the implementations of individual adaptors need to capture such eventual changes. Likewise, feedback from the design and implementation phases may lead to necessary changes in the specification and architecture.

Appropriate tool support is needed to make the specification models an integral part of development. This can take the form of a Software Development Kit (SDK), code generators, graphical models, analysis tools, etc. Such tool support should also help lower the threshold of learning as well as adopting OSLC, since implementing OSLC-compliant tools entails competence in a number of additional technologies such as RESTful web services and the family of RDF standards.

V. Modelling Support

We take an MDE approach to F-IDE development, in which we define a graphical modelling language that supports the toolchain architects and developers with the needs identified in the previous section.

The language is designed to act as a digital representation of the OASIS OSLC standard. This ensures that any defined toolchain complies with the standard. Such a graphical representation also helps lower the threshold of learning as well as implementing OSLC-compliant toolchains.

The language is structured into a set of views, in which each view focuses on a specific need, stakeholder and or aspect of development. The analysis of the needs from Section IV leads to the following three views:

• **Domain Specification View** – for the specification of the information to be shared across the F-IDE, with support for the organizational needs.

• **Resource Allocation View** – for the specification of information distribution and ownership across the F-IDE architecture.

• **Adaptor Design View** – for the detailed design and implementation of the tool interfaces of the F-IDE.

The next subsection presents further details of the OSLC standard, which then leads to its reflection by the proposed meta-model. Based on this OSLC meta-model, three views are then derived in Section V.B. The proposed graphical notation of each view is presented through examples from the use case of Section III. Finally, Section V.C details the open-source modelling tool developed to realize the proposed approach.

A. *The Meta-model*

The OASIS OSLC standard consists of a Core Specification and a set of Domain Specifications. The OSLC Core Specification [12] defines the set of resource services that can be offered by a tool. Figure 3 illustrates the structure of an OSLC interface and its services. A Service Provider is the central organizing entity of a tool, under which artefacts are managed. Typical examples of a Service Provider are project, module, product, etc. It is within the context of such an organizing concept that artefacts are managed (created, navigated, changed, etc.). For a given Service Provider, OSLC allows for the definition of two Services (Creation Factory & Query Capability) that provide other tools with the possibility to create and query artefacts respectively. In addition, OSLC defines Delegated UI (Selection and Creation) services that allow other tools to delegate the user interaction with an external artefact to the Service Provider under which the artefact is managed. The structure of Figure 3 allows for the discoverability of the services provided by each Service Provider, starting with a Service Provider Catalog, which acts as a catalog listing all available Service Providers exposed by a tool.

OASIS OSLC also defines Domain Specifications, which include domain vocabularies (or information models) for specific lifecycle domains. For example, the Quality Management Specification [13] defines resources and properties related to the verification phase of development such as test plans, test cases, and test results. The standardized Domain Specifications are minimalistic, focusing on the most common concepts within a particular domain, while allowing different implementations to extend this common basis.

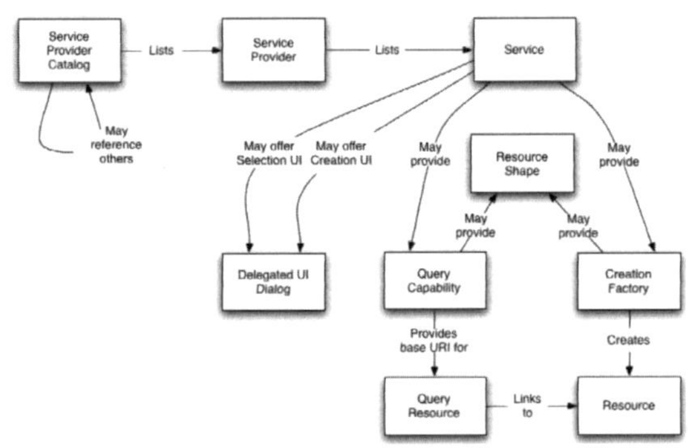

Figure 3. OSLC Core Specification concepts and relationships [12]

Using EMF [18], we define the meta-model that reflects the structure and concepts of the OASIS OSLC standard, as illustrated in Figure 4. A *Toolchain* consists of (1) a set of *AdaptorInterfaces* and (2) a set of *DomainSpecifications* (for legacy reasons grouped under a Specification element):

• An *AdaptorInterface* represents a tool's OSLC interface, and reflects the Core standard structure as illustrated in Figure 3.

• A *DomainSpecification* reflects how an OSLC Domain Specification defines vocabularies. It models the resources types, their properties and relationships, based on the Linked Data constraint language of Resource Shapes [14]. Resource Shapes is a mechanism to define the constraints on RDF resources, whereby a Resource Shape defines the properties that are allowed and/or required of a type of resource; as well as each property's cardinality, range, etc.

B. *The Modelling Views*

Based on the OSLC meta-model, we define the following three views:

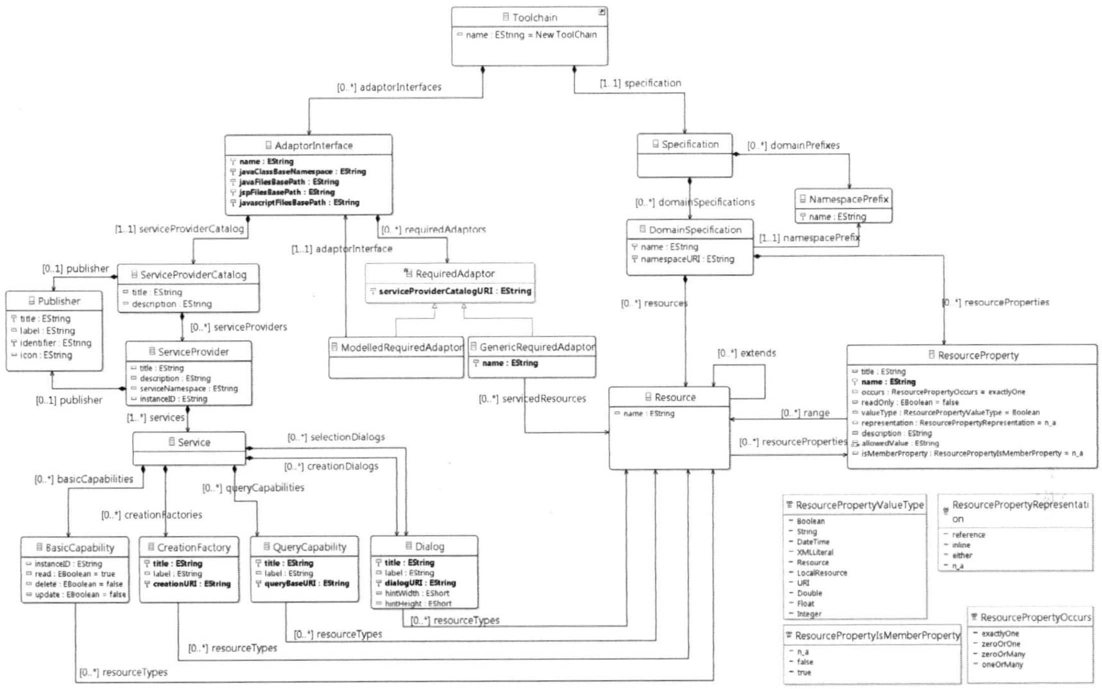

Figure 4. The underlying meta-model of the OASIS OSLC standard, reflecting the Core and Domain Specifications.

Domain Specification View From this perspective, the toolchain architect defines an information model that details the types of resources, their properties and relationships, using mechanisms compliant with the OSLC Core Specification [12] and the Resource Shape constraint language [14]. Figure 5 exemplifies the proposed graphical notation of the Domain Specification view for the resources needed in our case study.

The top-level container, *DomainSpecification*, groups related *Resources* and *Resource Properties*. Such grouping can be associated with a common topic (such as requirements or test management), or reflects the structure of the organization managing the F-IDE. This view ought to support standard specifications, such as Friend of a Friend (FOAF) [15] and RDF Schema (RDFS) [16], as well as proprietary ones. In Figure 5, three Domain Specifications are defined: *Software*, *Communication* and *Variability*, together with a subset of the standard domains of Dublin Core and RDF.

As required by the OSLC Core, a specification of a *Resource* type must provide a *name* and a *Type URI*. The *Resource* type can then also be associated with its allowed and/or required properties. These properties could belong to the same or any other *DomainSpecification*. A *Resource Property* is in turn defined by specifying its cardinality, optionality, value-type, allowed-values, etc. Figure 6 illustrates an example property specification highlighting the available constraints that can be defined. A *Literal Property* is one whose value-type is set to one of the predefined literal types (such as string or integer); while a *Reference Property* is one whose value-type is set to either "resource" or "local resource". In the latter case, the *range* property can then be used to suggest the set of resource types the *Property* can refer to.

In RDF, *Resource Properties* are defined independently, and may well be associated with multiple *Resource* types (Unlike, for example UML Classes, where a class attribute is defined within the context of a single class). For this reason, *Resource Properties* are graphically represented as first-class elements in the diagram. So, borrowing from the typical notation used to represent RDF graphs, *Resource* types are represented as ellipses, while *Properties* are represented as rectangles (A *Reference Property* is represented with an ellipse within the rectangle.).

The association between a *Resource* type and its corresponding *Properties* is represented by arrows for *Reference Properties*, while *Literal Properties* are listed graphically within the *Resource* ellipse. Such a representation renders the diagram almost similar – visually - to the UML class diagram of Figure 2. This makes the diagram intuitive and familiar for the modeler, yet with the more appropriate Linked Data semantics behind the view.

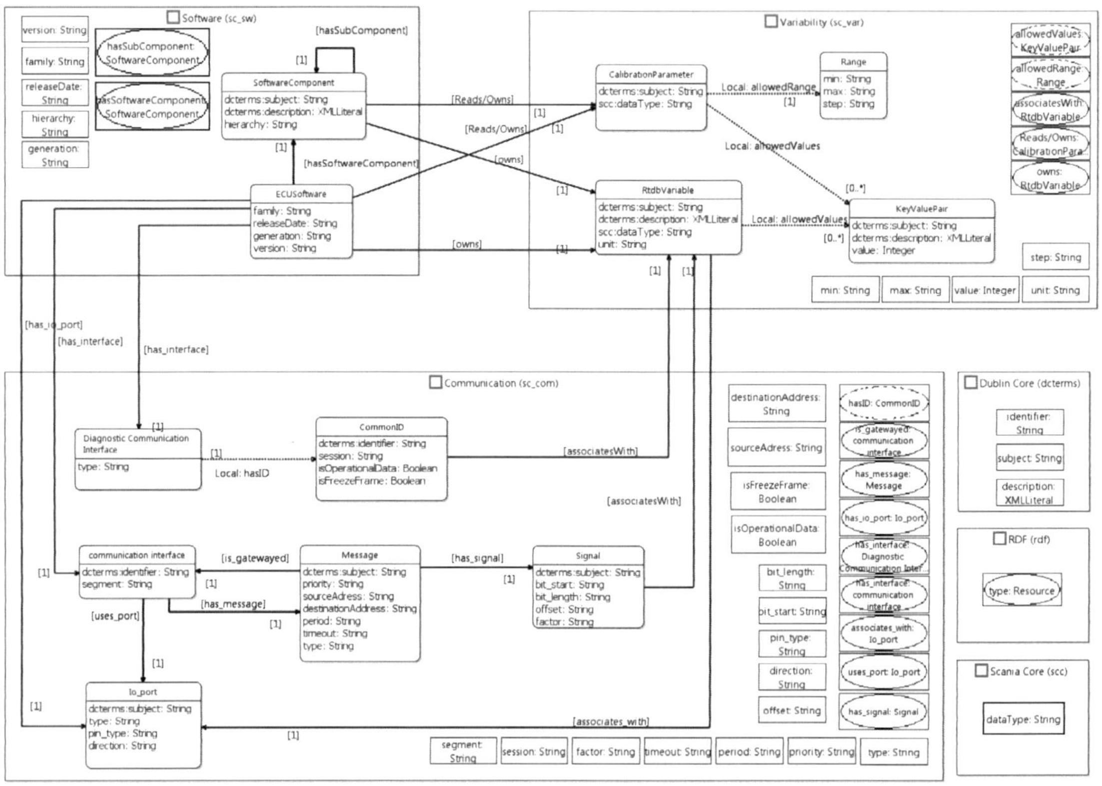

Figure 5. Domain Specification View

While the possibility to represent *Properties* as first-class elements was appreciated, it was experienced that they (The squares in Figure 5) cluttered the overall model, and did not make efficient usage of the available modeling space. An alternative representation is available, in which *Property* definitions are collected within a single sub-container, confined within its containing *DomainSpecification*. Figure 7 presents this alternative diagram for a subset of the domain specification of Figure 5, focusing on the *Communication* Domain Specification. Such a notation still ensures that *Properties* are defined independently of *Resources*, while making the graphical entities more manageable for the modeler.

Moreover, typical RDF graphs notations represent all associations between resources and properties by arrows, irrespective of whether they are Literal or Reference Properties. If desired, such a representation can be chosen as well. Figure 8 presents this alternative for a subset of the domain specification of Figure 5, focusing on the *Software* Domain Specification. Such a representation is intuitive for a small specification. However, it is experienced that for large specifications, the many associations between *Resources* and their associated *Literal Properties* cluttered the diagram. Furthermore, common *Literal Properties*, such as *dcterms:subject*, can be associated to many resources across many domains, leading to many cross-domain arrows that further clutter the diagram.

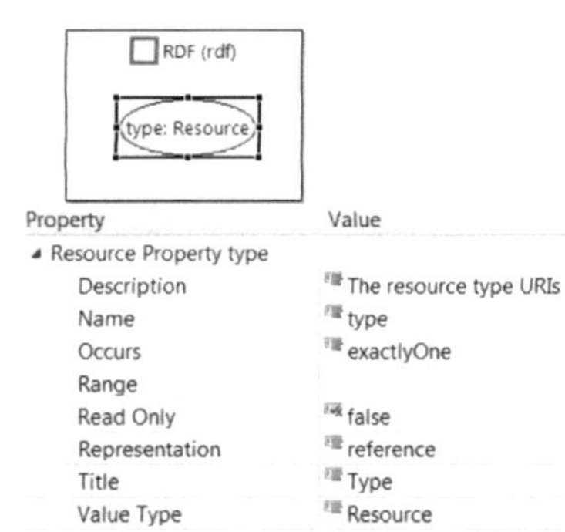

Figure 6. The specification of the rdf:type predicate, in the Domain Specification View [1]

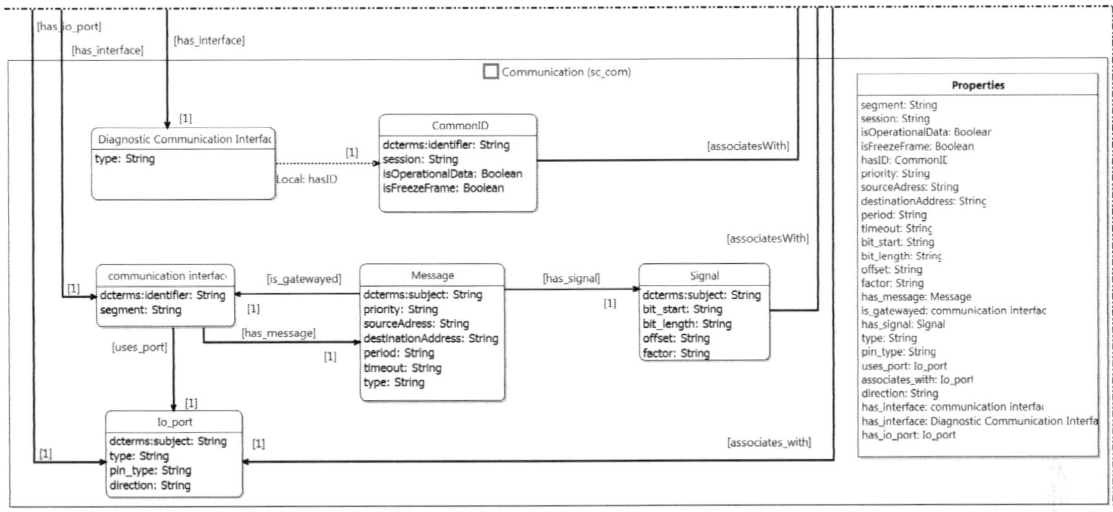

Figure 7. An alternative Domain Specification View, with Property definitions collected within a single sub-container.

The three alternative representations of *Resource Properties* and their associations with *Resources* are made available through filtering mechanisms to suite the preferences of the modeler. It is important to recall that these alternatives are semantically similar, and are based on the same meta-model of Figure 4.

Resource Allocation View provides the overall architecture of the F-IDE, where the toolchain architect allocates resources to data sources. It gives the architect an overview of where the resources are available in the F-IDE, and where they are consumed. For each data source, the architect defines the set of *Resources* it exposes; as well as those it consumes. These *Resources* are graphically represented as *"provided"* and *"required"* ports on the edge of the *AdaptorInterface* element, as illustrated in Figure 9 for our case study. For example, the *Communication Specifier* interface exposes the *Message* resource, which is then consumed by the *Requirements Specifier*.

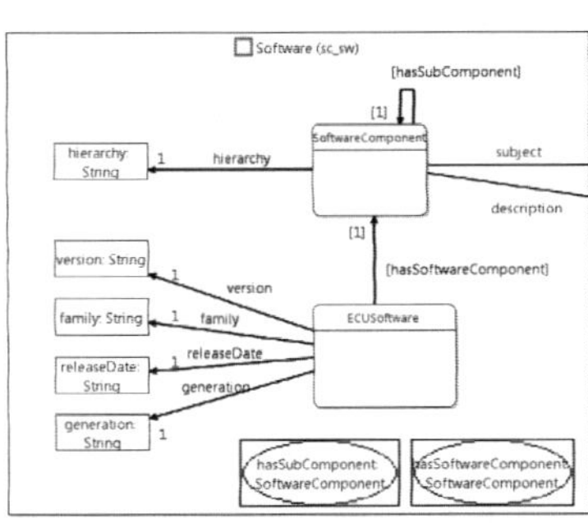

Figure 8. An alternative Domain Specification View, representing all associations between resources and properties by arrows.

In the *Resource Allocation* view, the interaction between a provider and consumer of a given resource is presented as a solid edge between the corresponding ports. In addition, any dependencies between resources that are managed by two different data sources are also represented in this model – as a dotted edge. For example, the resource *ECUSoftware*, managed by the *Code Repository*, has a property *has_io_port* that is a reference to resource *IO_port* (which is in turn managed through the data source *Modarc*). Hence, for a consumer of *ECUSoftware*, it is beneficial to identify the indirect dependency on the *Modarc* tool, since any consumption of an *ECUSoftware* resource, is likely to lead to the need to communicate with *Modarc* in order to obtain further information about the property *has_io_port*.

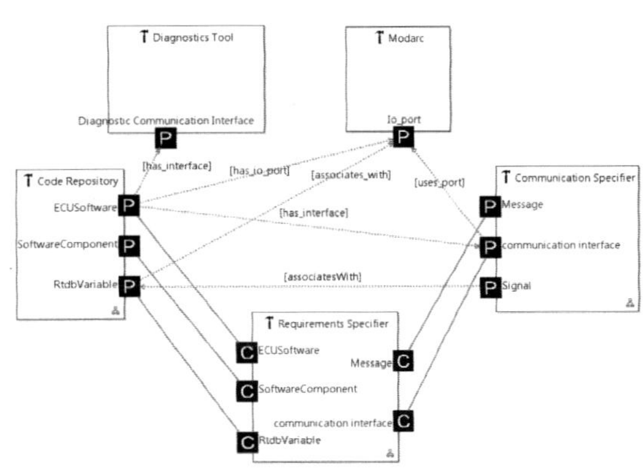

Figure 9. Resource Allocation View

Adaptor Design View is where the toolchain architect (or the tool interface developer) designs the internal details of the tool interface – according to the OSLC standard. This can be performed for any of the *Tool* entities in the *Resource Allocation* view. The *Adaptor Design* view is a realization of the OSLC interface structure of Figure 3. Sufficient information is captured in this view, so that an almost complete interface code, which is compliant with the OSLC4J software development kit (SDK) can be generated, based on the Lyo code generator [17] (See next subsection for further details.).

An example of the proposed notation from our case study is presented in Figure 10, in which the *Core Repository* provides query capabilities and creation factories on all three resources. The *Adaptor Design* view also models its consumed resources (In Figure 10, no consumed resources are defined.). Note that the provided and required resources - as defined in this view - remain synchronized with those at the interface of the *Tool* entity in the *Resource Allocation* view.

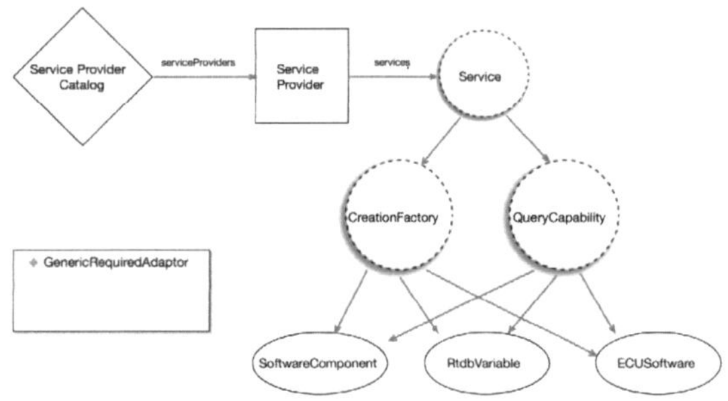

Figure 10. Adaptor Design View [1]

There is no particular ordering of the above views, and in practice, the three views can be developed in parallel. Consistency between the views is maintained since they all refer to the same model. For example, if the toolchain architect removes a resource from the *Adaptor Design* view, the same resource is also removed from the *Resource Allocation* view.

C. Architecture of Modelling Tool

An open-source Eclipse-based modelling tool was developed to realize the proposed approach, whose main components are presented in Figure 11. Central in the architecture is the *Toolchain Meta-model* component that realizes the meta-model of Figure 4, based on the Eclipse Modeling Framework (EMF) [18]. The *Graphical Modelling Editor* then allows the end-user to graphically design a toolchain based on the three views presented in Section V.B. (The figures presented in that section are snapshots of the graphical editor.) A toolchain design model is ultimately an instance of the toolchain meta-model. This model can then be inputted into the *Lyo Code Generator* [17] to generate almost-complete code for each of the tool interfaces in the toolchain.

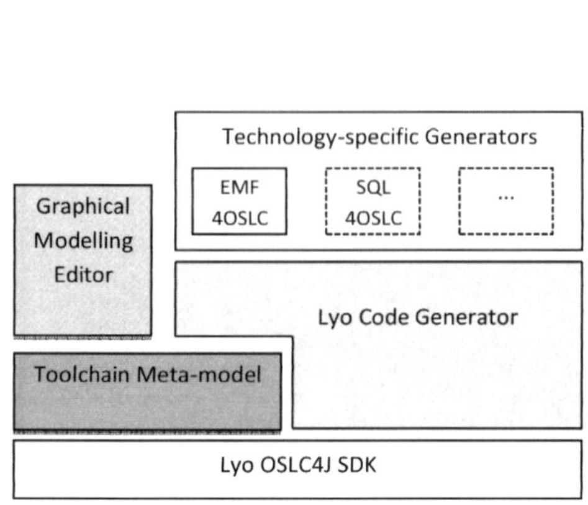

Figure 11. The layered architecture of the modelling tool, building upon the Lyo OSLC4J SDK, to provide a model-based development approach.

The *Lyo code generator* runs as a separate Eclipse project, and assumes a minimal set of plug-in dependencies. It is based on Acceleo [19], which implements the OMG MOF Model-to-Text Language (MTL) standard [20]. The code generator is designed to be independent of the *Graphical Modelling Editor*, and hence its input tool meta-model instance can be potentially created by any other EMF mechanism. This facilitates the extension of the generator with additional components as later described in this section.

The code generator builds upon the OSLC4J Software Development Kit (SDK) from the Lyo [21] project. While the OSLC4J SDK targets the implementation phase of adaptor implementation, our tool complements it with a model-based development approach, which allows one to work at a higher level of abstraction, with models used to specify the adaptor design, without needing to deal with all the technical details of the OSLC standard (such as Linked Data, RDF, etc.).

The generator produces OSLC4J-compliant Java code. Once generated, the java code has no dependencies to either the code generator, or the input toolchain model. The generated code can be further developed – as any OSLC4J adaptor – with no further connections to the generator.

Moreover, it is possible to modify the toolchain model and re-generate its code, without the loss of any code manually introduced between generations. For example, a JAX-RS class method may need to perform some additional business logic before - or after - the default handling of the designated web service. The generator ensures that such manual code remains intact after subsequent changes in the model and code generations. This promotes the incremental development of the toolchain, where the specification model and implementation can be gradually developed.

Upon generation, an adaptor is – almost – complete and ready-to-run, and needs not be modified nor complemented with additional manual code. Only a set of methods that communicate with the source tool to access its internal data need to be implemented (the dotted arrows in Figure 1). This communication is reduced to a simple set of methods to (a) get (b) create (c) search and (d) query each serviced resource. This manual code is packaged into a single class, with skeletons of the required methods generated. It remains the task of the developer to manual code these methods.

However, for specific tool technologies, a full adaptor implementation can be generated. For example, targeting EMF-based modelling tools in general, an additional *EMF4OSLC* component was developed [22] to complement the code generator with the automatic generation of the necessary code to access and manipulate the data in the backend tool. This leads to the complete generation of the adaptor. *EMF4OSLC* moreover generates the actual interface specification model based on a predefined mapping between EMF and OSLC. Similarly, an additional component – *EMF4SQL* – is being developed to handle SQL-based tools. It is anticipated that much code reuse can be gained between *EMF4OSLC* and *EMF4SQL*, while ensuring that both components build on top of the Lyo code generator.

The modelling tool and supporting documentation are available as open-source under the Eclipse Lyo [21] project.

VI. Discussion

Compared to the original approach practiced by Scania engineers of using a UML class diagram (see Figure 2) to represent the F-IDE resources, the proposed model may seem to add a level of complexity by distributing the model information into three views. However, upon further investigation, it becomes clear that the class diagram was actually used to superimpose information for both the *Domain Specification* and *Resource Allocation* views into the same diagram. For example, classes were initially color-coded to classify them according to their owning tool. However, the semantics and intentions behind this classification soon become ambiguous, since the distinction between tool and domain ownership is not identified explicitly. In the original approach, different viewers of the same model could hence draw different conclusions when analyzing the model, depending on their implicit understanding of the color codes.

Through a multi-view modelling approach, and by describing the information model from the two orthogonal views of managing domains and managing tools, the information model is no longer expected to be developed in a top-down and centralized manner. Instead, a more distributed process is envisaged, in which resources are defined within a specific domain and/or tool. Only when necessary, such sub-models can then be integrated, avoiding the need to manage a single centralized information model. Moreover, these two orthogonal views of the F-IDE allow the toolchain architect to identify dependencies within the F-IDE, from both the organizational as well as the deployment perspective:

• In the *Resource Allocation View* of the model, the toolchain architect can obtain an overview of the coupling/cohesion of the tools of the F-IDE. One could directly identify the direct producer/consumer relations, as well as the indirect dependencies, as detailed in Section V.B.

• In the *Domain Specification view*, the toolchain architect views the dependencies between the different domains (irrespective of how the resources are deployed across tools). Such dependencies reveal the relationship between the organizational entities involved in maintaining the overall information model. This explicit modelling of domain ownership helps lift important organizational decisions, which otherwise remain implicit.

Semantically, the usage of a class diagram is not compatible with the open-world view of Linked Data. Instead, a dedicated domain-specific language (DSL) that follows the expected semantics can be better used uniformly across the whole organization. We here illustrate two examples where our DSL helped communicate the correct semantics, which were previously misinterpreted or not used:

• A *Resource Property* is a first-class element that ought to be defined independently of *Resource* definitions within a *Domain Specification*. A *Property* can then be associated with multiple *Resource* types, which in turn can belong to the same or any other *Domain Specification*. For example, the *allowedValues* property (with range *KeyValuePair*) is defined within the *Variability* domain, and its definition ought not to be dependent on any particular usage within any *Resource*. This same *Property* is then being associated to the *CalibrationParameter* & *RtdbVariable* resources. Previously, two separate *Properties* were unnecessarily defined within the context of each *Resource*, which is not appropriate when adopting Linked Data and its RDF data model.

• Certain *Resources* can only exist within the context of another parent Resource, and hence ought not to have their own URI. For example, *Range* is defined as a simple structure of three properties (*min*, *max* and *step*). The *CalibrationParameter* resource contains the *allowedRange* property whose *value-types* is set to *Local Resource*, indicating that property value is a resource that is only available inside the *CalibrationParameter* instance. Our DSL helped communicate the capability of defining *Local Resources*. A class diagram does not provide a corresponding concept that can be correctly used to convey the same semantics.

Adopting a class diagram may have been satisfactory at the early stages of development, where focus was on the information specification. However, it became apparent that the diagram is not sufficient in supporting the later phases of development, when the tool interfaces need to be designed and implemented. Furthermore, no complements to the UML class diagram can provide all necessary information according to the OSLC standard. Instead, the third *Adaptor Design View* serves this need satisfactorily. In addition, by sharing a common meta-model with the other two views, it is ensured that the detailed designs remain consistent with the specification and architecture of the F-IDE. Furthermore, given that the complete model (with its three views) can lead to the generation of working code, the model's completeness and correctness is confirmed.

While the need for a dedicated DSL is convincing, the proposed notations are not necessarily final, and there remains room for improvements. The alternative representations of the *Domain Specification View* (discussed in Section V.B) highlight some of the refinements that need to be dealt with.

VII. RELATED WORK

There exists a large body of research that in various ways touches upon information modeling and tool integration. (See for example [2] and [23]). Our work - and the related work of this section - is delimited to the Linked Data paradigm, and its graphical modelling.

The most relevant work found in this area is the Ontology Definition Metamodel (ODM) [24]. ODM is an OMG specification that defines a family of Meta-Object Facility (MOF) metamodels for the modelling of ontologies. ODM also specifies a UML Profile for RDFS [16] and the Web Ontology Language (OWL) [25], which can be realized by UML-based tools, such as Enterprise Architect's ODM diagrams [26]. However, as argued in [14], OWL and RDFS are not suitable candidates to specify and validate constraints, given that they are designed for another purpose - namely for reasoning engines that can infer new knowledge. The work in this paper builds upon the Resource Shape constraint language suggested in [14], by providing a graphical model to specify such constraints on RDF resources. The constraint language is part of the OSLC standard, making for its easy adoption within our work. On the other hand, SHACL [27] is an evolving W3C working draft for a very similar constraint language, which can also be supported in the future.

Earlier work by the authors has also resulted in a modelling approach to toolchain development [28]. In this earlier work, even though the information was modelled targeting an OSLC implementation, the models were directly embedded in the specific tool adaptors, and no overall information model is readily available. The models did not support the tool and domain ownership perspectives identified in this paper.

In general, there are inspiring works done for defining a visual language for the representation of ontologies. Even if ontologies are not directly suitable for the specification of constraints, such languages can be used as inspiration for the graphical notation presented in this paper. One example is the Visual Notation for OWL Ontologies (VOWL) [29] that is based on only a handful of graphical primitives forming the alphabet of the visual language. In this visual notation, classes are represented as circles that are connected by lines and arrowheads representing the property relations. Property labels and datatypes are shown as rectangles. Information on individuals and data values is displayed either in the visualization itself or in another part of the user interface. VOWL also uses a color scheme complementing the graphical primitives. It defines colors for the visual elements to allow for an easy distinction of different types of classes and properties. In addition to the shapes and colors, VOWL also introduces dashed lines, dashed borders and double borders for visualizing class, relation or data properties.

OWLGrEd [30] is another graphical OWL editor that extends the UML class diagram to allow for OWL visualization. The work argues that the most important feature for achieving readable graphical OWL notation is the maximum compactness. The UML class diagram is used to present the core features of OWL ontologies. To overcome the difference between UML's closed-world assumption and OWL's open-world assumption, the authors changed the semantics of the UML notation and added new symbols. OWLGrEd introduces a colored background frame for the relatively autonomous sub-parts of the ontology. Furthermore, the editor contains a number of additional services to ease ontology development and exploration, such as different layout algorithms for automatic ontology visualization, search facilities, zooming, and graphical refactoring. Finally, GrOWL [31] is a visual language that attempts to accurately visualize the underlying description logic semantics of OWL ontologies, without exposing the complex OWL syntax.

Lanzenberger et al. [32] summarize the results of their literature study on tools for visualizing ontologies as: "*A huge amount of tools exist for visualizing ontologies, however, there are just a few for assisting with viewing multiple ontologies as needed for ontology alignment. ... Finally, in order to support an overview and detail approach appropriately, multiple views or distortion techniques are needed.*" We identified the need to support multiple views in this study, in order to support the different stakeholders of the same language.

VIII. CONCLUSION

In this paper, an MDE approach to F-IDE development based on Linked Data and the OSLC standard is presented. The proposed set of modelling views supports the toolchain architect with the early phases of toolchain development, with a particular focus on the specification of the information model and its distribution across the tools of the toolchain. Additionally, such views are tightly integrated with a design view supporting the detailed design of the tool interfaces. The modelling views are designed to be a digital representation of the OASIS OSLC standard. This ensures that any defined toolchain complies with the standard. It also helps lower the threshold of learning as well as implementing OSLC-compliant toolchains.

An open-source modelling tool was developed to realize the proposed modelling views. The tool includes an integrated code generator that can synthesis the specification and design models into a running implementation. This allows one to work at a higher level of abstraction, without needing to deal with all the technical details of the OSLC standard (such as Linked Data, RDF, etc.). The Eclipse-based modelling tool and supporting documentation are available as open-source under the Eclipse Lyo project.

It is envisaged that the modelling support will be extended to cover the complete development lifecycle, specifically supporting the requirements analysis phase, as well as automated testing. The current focus on data integration needs to be also extended to cover other aspects of integration, in particular control integration [33].

REFERENCES

[1] J. El-Khoury, D. Gürdür, F. Loiret, M. Törngren, D. Zhang, and M. Nyberg, "Modelling Support for a Linked Data Approach to Tool Interoperability," The Second International

Conference on Big Data, Small Data, Linked Data and Open Data, ALLDATA 2016, pp. 42-47.

[2] M. Törngren, A. Qamar, M. Biehl, F. Loiret, and J. El-khoury, "Integrating viewpoints in the development of mechatronic products," Mechatronics (Oxford), vol. 24, nr. 7, 2014, pp. 745-762.

[3] Road vehicles - functional safety, ISO standard 26262:2011, 2011.

[4] (2016, Nov.) PTC Integrity. [Online]. Available: http://www.ptc.com/application-lifecycle-management/integrity/

[5] B. Weichel and M. Herrmann, "A backbone in automotive software development based on XML and ASAM/MSR," SAE Technical Papers, 2004, doi:10.4271/2004-01-0295.

[6] (2016, Nov.) OASIS OSLC. [Online]. Available: http://www.oasis-oslc.org/

[7] T. Berners-Lee. (2016, Nov.) Linked data design issues. [Online]. Available: http://www.w3.org/DesignIssues/LinkedData.html

[8] Linked Data Platform 1.0, W3C Recommendation, 2015.

[9] X. Zhang, M. Persson, M. Nyberg, B. Mokhtari, A. Einarson, H. Linder, J. Westman, D. Chen, and M. Törngren, "Experience on Applying Software Architecture Recovery to Automotive Embedded Systems," IEEE Conference on Software Maintenance, Reengineering, and Reverse Engineering, CSMR-WCRE 2014, pp. 379-382.

[10] J. Westman, M. Nyberg, and O. Thyden, "CPS Specifier - A Specification Tool for Safety-Critical Cyber-Physical Systems," Sixth Workshop on Design, Modeling and Evaluation of Cyber Physical Systems, CyPhy'16, 2016

[11] A. Rossignol, "The reference technology platform" in CESAR - Cost-efficient methods and processes for safety-relevant embedded systems, A. Rajan and T. Wahl, Eds. Dordrecht: Springer, pp. 213-236, 2012.

[12] OSLC Core Specification, OSLC standard v2.0, 2013.

[13] OSLC Quality Management Specification, OSLC standard v2.0, 2011.

[14] A. G. Ryman, A. Le Hors, and S. Speicher, "OSLC resource shape: A language for defining constraints on linked data," CEUR Workshop Proceedings, Vol.996, 2013.

[15] (2016, Nov.) FOAF Vocabulary Specification. [Online]. Available: http://xmlns.com/foaf/spec/

[16] RDF Schema 1.1, W3C Recommendation, 2014.

[17] J. El-Khoury, "Lyo Code Generator: A Model-based Code Generator for the Development of OSLC-compliant Tool Interfaces," SoftwareX, 2016.

[18] (2016, Nov.) Eclipse EMF. [Online]. Available: https://eclipse.org/modeling/emf/

[19] (2016, Nov.) Eclipse Acceleo. [Online]. Available: https://www.eclipse.org/acceleo/

[20] MOF Model to Text Transformation Language (MOFM2T), 1.0, OMG standard, document number: formal/2008-01-16, 2008.

[21] (2016, Nov.) Eclipse Lyo. [Online]. Available: https://www.eclipse.org/lyo/

[22] J. El-Khoury, C. Ekelin, and C. Ekholm, "Supporting the Linked Data Approach to Maintain Coherence Across Rich EMF Models," Modelling Foundations and Applications: 12th European Conference, ECMFA 2016, pp. 36-47.

[23] R. Basole, A. Qamar, H. Park, C. Paredis, and L. Mcginnis, "Visual analytics for early-phase complex engineered system design support," IEEE Computer Graphics and Applications, vol. 35, nr. 2, 2015, pp. 41-51.

[24] Ontology Definition Metamodel, OMG standard, document number: formal/2014-09-02, 2014.

[25] OWL 2 Web Ontology Language, W3C Recommendation, 2012.

[26] (2016, Nov.) Enterprise Architect ODM MDG Technology. [Online]. Available: http://www.sparxsystems.com/enterprise_architect_user_guide/9.3/domain_based_models/mdg_technology_for_odm.html

[27] Shapes Constraint Language (SHACL), W3C Working Draft, 2016.

[28] M. Biehl, J. El-khoury, F. Loiret, and M. Törngren, "On the modeling and generation of service-oriented tool chains," Software & Systems Modeling, vol. 13, nr 2, 2014, pp. 461-480.

[29] S. Lohmann, S. Negru, F. Haag, and T. Ertl, "Visualizing Ontologies with VOWL," Semantic Web, vol 7, nr 4, 2016, pp. 399-419.

[30] J. Bārzdiņš, G. Bārzdiņš, K. Čerāns, R. Liepiņš, and A. Sproģis, "UML style graphical notation and editor for OWL 2," International Conference on Business Informatics Research, Springer Berlin, 2010.

[31] S. Krivov, F. Villa, R. Williams, and X. Wu, "On visualization of OWL ontologies," Semantic Web, Springer US, 2007, pp 205-221.

[32] M. Lanzenberger, J. Sampson and M. Rester, "Visualization in Ontology Tools," International Conference on Complex, Intelligent and Software Intensive Systems, 2009, pp. 705-711.

[33] A. I. Wasserman, "Tool integration in software engineering environments," the international workshop on environments on Software engineering environments, 1990, pp. 137-149.

Unsupervised curves clustering by minimizing entropy: implementation and application to air traffic

Florence Nicol
Université Fédérale de Toulouse
Ecole Nationale de l'Aviation Civile
F-31055 Toulouse FRANCE
Email: florence.nicol@enac.fr

Stéphane Puechmorel
Université Fédérale de Toulouse
Ecole Nationale de l'Aviation Civile
F-31055 Toulouse FRANCE
Email: stephane.puechmorel@enac.fr

Abstract—**In many applications such as Air Traffic Management (ATM), clustering trajectories in groups of similar curves is of crucial importance. When data considered are functional in nature, like curves, dedicated algorithms exist, mostly based on truncated expansion on Hilbert basis. When additional constraints are put on the curves, as like in applications related to air traffic where operational considerations are to be taken into account, usual procedures are no longer applicable. A new approach based on entropy minimization and Lie group modeling is presented here and its implementation is discussed in detail, especially the computation of the curve system density and the entropy minimization by a gradient descent algorithm. This algorithm yields an efficient unsupervised algorithm suitable for automated traffic analysis. It outputs cluster centroids with low curvature, making it a valuable tool in airspace design applications or route planning.**

Keywords–curve clustering; probability distribution estimation; functional statistics; minimum entropy; Lie group modeling; air traffic management.

I. INTRODUCTION

Clustering aircraft trajectories is an important problem in Air Traffic Management (ATM). It is a central question in the design of procedures at take-off and landing, the so called sid-star (Standard Instrument Departure and Standard Terminal Arrival Routes). In such a case, one wants to minimize the noise and pollutants exposure of nearby residents while ensuring runway efficiency in terms of the number of aircraft managed per time unit.

The same question arises with cruising aircraft, this time the mean flight path in each cluster being used to optimally design the airspace elements (sectors and airways). This information is also crucial in the context of future air traffic management systems where reference trajectories will be negotiated in advance so as to reduce congestion. A special instance of this problem is the automatic generation of safe and efficient trajectories, but in such a way that the resulting flight paths are still manageable by human operators. Clustering is a key component for such tools: major traffic flows must be organized in such a way that the overall pattern is not too far from the current organization, with aircraft flying along airways. The classification algorithm has thus not only to cluster similar trajectories but at the same time makes them as close as possible to operational trajectories. In particular, straightness of the flight segments must be enforced, along with a global structure close to a graph with nodes corresponding to merging/splitting points and edges the airways. Moreover, the clustering procedure has to deal with trajectories that are very similar in shape but are oriented in opposite directions. These flight paths should be sufficiently separate in order to prevent hazardous encounters. Using the approach developed in [1], a Lie group modeling is proposed to take into account the direction and the position of the aircraft trajectories. The main computational complexity of such a clustering algorithm focuses on the computation of the curve system density. This computational cost can be reduced by choosing appropriate kernel functions.

This paper is organized as follows. First, previous related works is presented. Next, in Section III, the notion of spatial curve density and the related entropy are introduced for dealing with curve systems. Then, the modeling of trajectories with a Lie group approach and the statistical estimation of Lie group densities are presented. In Section IV, the unsupervised entropy clustering approach developed in [2] is extended to the new setting of Lie group modeling. In Section V, a discussion on fast implementation and algorithms presented in [1] is detailed. Finally, results on synthetic examples and real trajectory data are given and a conclusion is drawn.

II. PREVIOUS RELATED WORK

Several well established algorithms may be used for performing clustering on a set of trajectories, although only a few of them were eventually applied to air traffic analysis. The spectral approach relies on trajectories modeling as vectors of samples in a high dimensional space, and uses random projections as means of reducing the dimensionality. The huge computational cost of the required singular values decomposition is thus alleviated, allowing use on real recorded traffic over several months. It was applied in a study conducted by the Mitre corporation on behalf of the Federal Aviation Authority (FAA) [3]. The most important limitation of this approach is that the shape of the trajectories is not taken into account when applying the clustering procedure unless a resampling procedure based on arclength is applied: changing the time parametrization of the flight paths will induce a change in the classification. Furthermore, there is no means to put a constraint on the mean trajectory produced in each cluster: curvature may be quite arbitrary even if samples individually comply with flight dynamics.

Another approach is taken in [4], with an explicit use of an underlying graph structure. It is well adapted to road traffic as vehicles are bound to follow predetermined segments. A spatial segment density is computed then used to gather trajectories sharing common parts. For air traffic applications, it may be of interest for investigating present situations, using the airways and beacons as a structure graph, but will misclassify aircraft following direct routes which is quite a common situation, and is unable to work on an unknown airspace organization. This point is very important in applications since trajectory datamining tools are mainly used in airspace redesign. A similar approach is taken in [5] with a different measure of similarity. It has to be noted that many graph-based algorithms are derived from the original work presented in [6], and exhibit the aforementioned drawbacks for air traffic analysis applications.

An interesting vector fieldbased algorithm is presented in [7]. A salient feature is the ability to distinguish between close trajectories with opposite orientations. Nevertheless, putting constraints on the geometry of the mean path in a cluster is quite awkward, making the method unsuitable for our application.

Due to the functional nature of trajectories, that are basically mappings defined on a time interval, it seems more appropriate to resort to techniques based on times series as surveyed in [8], [9], or functional data statistics, with standard references [10], [11]. In both approaches, a distance between pairs of trajectories or, in a weaker form, a measure of similarity must be available. The algorithms of the first category are based on sequences, possibly in conjunction with dynamic time warping [12], while in functional data analysis, samples are assumed to come from an unknown underlying function belonging to a given Hilbert space. However, it has to be noticed that apart from this last assumption, both approaches yield similar end algorithms, since functional data revert for implementation to usual finite dimensional vectors of expansion coefficients on a suitable truncated basis. For the same reason, model-based clustering may be used in the context of functional data even if no notion of probability density exists in the original infinite dimensional Hilbert space as mentioned in [13]. A nice example of a model-based approach working on functional data is funHDDC [14].

III. DEALING WITH CURVE SYSTEMS: A PARADIGM CHANGE

When working with aircraft trajectories, some specific characteristics must be taken into account. First of all, flight paths consist mainly of straight segments connected by arcs of circles, with transitions that may be assumed smooth up to at least the second derivative. This last property comes from the fact that pilot's actions result in changes on aerodynamic forces and torques and a straightforward application of the equations of motion. When dealing with sampled trajectories, this induces a huge level of redundancy within the data, the relevant information being concentrated around the transitions. Second, flight paths must be modeled as functions from a time interval $[a, b]$ to $\mathbb{R}^3$ which is not the usual setting for functional data statistics: most of the work is dedicated to real valued mappings and not vector ones. A simple approach will be to assume independence between coordinates, so that the problem falls within the standard case. However, even with this simplifying hypothesis, vertical dimension must be treated in a special way as both the separation norms and the aircraft maneuverability are different from those in the horizontal plane.

Finally, being able to cope with the initial requirement of compliance with the current airspace structure in airways is not addressed by general algorithms. In the present work, a new kind of functional unsupervised classifier is introduced, that has in common with graph-based algorithms an estimation of traffic density but works in a continuous setting. For operational applications, a major benefit is the automatic building of a route-like structure that may be used to infer new airspace designs. Furthermore, smoothness of the mean cluster trajectory, especially low curvature, is guaranteed by design. Such a feature is unique among existing clustering procedures. Finally, our Lie group approach makes easy the separation between neighboring flows oriented in opposite directions. Once again, it is mandatory in air traffic analysis where such a situation is common.

A. *The entropy of a system of curves*

Considering trajectories as mappings $\gamma\colon [t_0, t_1] \to \mathbb{R}^3$ induces a notion of spatial density as presented in [15]. Assuming that after a suitable registration process all flight paths $\gamma_i, i = 1, \dots, N$, are defined on the same time interval $[0, 1]$ to Ω a domain of $\mathbb{R}^3$, one can compute an entropy associated with the system of curves using the approach presented in [16]. Let a system of curves $\gamma_1, \dots, \gamma_N$ be given, its entropy is defined to be:

$$E(\gamma_1, \dots, \gamma_N) = -\int_\Omega \tilde{d}(x) \log\left(\tilde{d}(x)\right) dx,$$

where the spatial density $\tilde{d}$ is computed according to:

$$\tilde{d}\colon x \mapsto \frac{\sum_{i=1}^N \int_0^1 K\left(\|x - \gamma_i(t)\|\right) \|\gamma_i'(t)\| dt}{\sum_{i=1}^N l_i}. \tag{1}$$

In the last expression, l_i is the length of the curve γ_i and K is a kernel function similar to those used in nonparametric estimation. A standard choice is the Epanechnikov kernel:

$$K\colon x \mapsto C\left(1 - x^2\right) 1_{[-1,1]}(x),$$

with a normalizing constant C chosen so as to have a unit integral of K on Ω. In multivariate density estimation, a common practice is to build a multivariate kernel function by means of an univariate kernel K composed with a norm, denoted by $\|.\|$. The resulting mapping, $x \mapsto K(\|x\|)$ enjoys some important properties:

- Translation invariance.
- Rotational symmetry.

In Section V, the translation invariance will be used to cut the computational cost of kernel evaluation.

Since the entropy is minimal for concentrated distributions, it is quite intuitive to figure out that seeking for a curve system $(\gamma_1, \dots, \gamma_N)$ giving a minimum value for $E(\gamma_1, \dots, \gamma_N)$ will induce the following properties:

- The images of the curves tend to get close one to another.

- The individual lengths will be minimized: it is a direct consequence of the fact that the density has a term in γ' within the integral that will favor short trajectories.

Using a standard gradient descent algorithm on the entropy produces an optimally concentrated curve system, suitable for use as a basis for a route network. In Section V, this algorithm is applied on a curve system produced by an automated trajectory planner.

The displacement field for trajectory j is oriented at each point along the normal vector to the trajectory, with norm given by:

$$\int_\Omega \left. \frac{\gamma_j(t)-x}{\|\gamma_j(t)-x\|}\right|_{\mathcal{N}} K'\left(\|\gamma_j(t)-x\|\right)\log\left(\tilde{d}(x)\right)dx\|\gamma_j'(t)\| \tag{2}$$

$$-\left(\int_\Omega K\left(\|\gamma_j(t)-x\|\right)\log\left(\tilde{d}(x)\right)dx\right)\left.\frac{\gamma_j''(t)}{\|\gamma_j'(t)\|}\right|_{\mathcal{N}} \tag{3}$$

$$+\left(\int_\Omega \tilde{d}(x)\log(\tilde{d}(x))dx\right)\left.\frac{\gamma_j''(t)}{\|\gamma_j'(t)\|}\right|_{\mathcal{N}}, \tag{4}$$

where the notation $v_{|\mathcal{N}}$ stands for the projection of the vector v onto the normal vector to the trajectory. An overall scaling constant of:

$$\frac{1}{\sum_{i=1}^N l_i},$$

where l_i is the length of trajectory i, has to be put in front of the expression to get the true gradient of the entropy. In practice, it is not needed since algorithms will adjust the size of the step taken in the gradient direction. Another formulation using the scaled arclength in the entropy can be found in [2]. While being equivalent to the one presented above, since it relies on a reparametrization, only the term related to the kernel gradient remains in the final expression. As a consequence, there is no need to project moves onto the normal to the curves. However, it introduces a constraint that must be taken into account in numerical implementations. So far, the principle retained is to resample the curves after the update so as to ensure that the defining property (constant velocity) of the arclength is preserved.

B. A Lie group modeling

While satisfactory in terms of traffic flows, the previous approach suffers from a severe flaw when one considers flight paths that are very similar in shape but are oriented in opposite directions. Since the density is insensitive to direction reversal, flight paths will tend to aggregate while the correct behavior will be to ensure a sufficient separation in order to prevent hazardous encounters. Taking aircraft headings into account in the clustering process is then mandatory when such situations have to be considered.

This issue can be addressed by adding a penalty term to neighboring trajectories with different headings but the important theoretical property of entropy minimization will be lost in the process. A more satisfactory approach will be to take heading information directly into account and to introduce a notion of density based on position and velocity.

Since the aircraft dynamics is governed by a second order equation of motion of the form:

$$\begin{pmatrix}\gamma'(t)\\ \gamma''(t)\end{pmatrix} = F\left(t;\begin{matrix}\gamma(t)\\ \gamma'(t)\end{matrix}\right),$$

it is natural to take as state vector:

$$\begin{pmatrix}\gamma(t)\\ \gamma'(t)\end{pmatrix}.$$

The initial state is chosen here to be:

$$\left(\frac{0_d}{e_1}\right),$$

with e_1 the first basis vector, and 0_d the origin in $\mathbb{R}^d$. It is equivalent to model the state as a linear transformation:

$$0_d \otimes e_1 \mapsto T(t)\otimes A(t)(0_d\otimes e_1) = \gamma(t)\otimes\gamma'(t),$$

where $T(t)$ is the translation mapping 0_d to $\gamma(t)$ and $A(t)$ is the composite of a scaling and a rotation mapping e_1 to $\gamma'(t)$. Considering the vector $(\gamma(t),1)$ instead of $\gamma(t)$ allows a matrix representation of the translation $T(t)$:

$$\left(\frac{\gamma(t)}{1}\right) = \left(\begin{array}{c|c} Id & \gamma(t)\\ \hline 0 & 1\end{array}\right)\left(\frac{0_d}{1}\right).$$

From now, all points will be implicitly considered as having an extra last coordinate with value 1, so that translations are expressed using matrices. The origin 0_d will thus stand for the vector $(0,\dots,0,1)$ in $\mathbb{R}^{d+1}$. Gathering things yields:

$$\left(\frac{\gamma(t)}{\gamma'(t)}\right) = \left(\begin{array}{c|c} T(t) & 0\\ \hline 0 & A(t)\end{array}\right)\left(\frac{0_d}{e_1}\right). \tag{5}$$

The previous expression makes it possible to represent a trajectory as a mapping from a time interval to the matrix Lie group $\mathcal{G}=\mathbb{R}^d\times\Sigma\times S\mathbb{O}(d)$, where Σ is the group of multiples of the identity, $S\mathbb{O}(d)$ the group of rotations and $\mathbb{R}^d$ the group of translations. Please note that all the products are direct. The $A(t)$ term in the expression (5) can be written as an element of $\Sigma\otimes S\mathbb{O}(d)$. Starting with the defining property $A(t)e_1=\gamma'(t)$, one can write $A(t)=\|\gamma'(t)\|U(t)$ with $U(t)$ a rotation mapping $e_1\in\mathbb{S}^{d-1}$ to the unit vector $\gamma'(t)/\|\gamma'(t)\|\in\mathbb{S}^{d-1}$. For arbitrary dimension d, $U(t)$ is not uniquely defined, as it can be written as a rotation in the plane $\mathcal{P}=\text{span}(e_1,\gamma'(t))$ and a rotation in its orthogonal complement $\mathcal{P}^\perp$. A common choice is to let $U(t)$ be the identity in $\mathcal{P}^\perp$ which corresponds in fact to a move along a geodesic (great circle) in $\mathbb{S}^{d-1}$. This will be assumed implicitly in the sequel, so that the representation $A(t)=\Lambda(t)U(t)$ with $\Lambda(t)=\|\gamma'(t)\|\text{Id}$ becomes unique.

The Lie algebra $\mathfrak{g}$ of $\mathcal{G}$ is easily seen to be $\mathbb{R}^d\times\mathbb{R}\times$ **Asym**(d) with **Asym**(d) is the space of skew-symmetric $d\times d$ matrices. An element from $\mathfrak{g}$ is a triple (u,λ,A) with an associated matrix form:

$$M(u,\lambda,A) = \left(\begin{array}{cc|c} 0 & u & \\ \hline 0 & 0 & 0\\ \hline 0 & & \lambda Id + A\end{array}\right). \tag{6}$$

The exponential mapping from $\mathfrak{g}$ to $\mathcal{G}$ can be obtained in a straightforward manner using the usual matrix exponential:

$$\exp((u,\lambda,A)) = \exp(M(u,\lambda,A)).$$

The matrix representation of $\mathfrak{g}$ may be used to derive a metric:

$$\langle (u,\lambda,A),(v,\mu,B)\rangle_{\mathfrak{g}} = \mathbf{Tr}\left(M(u,\lambda,A)^t M(v,\mu,B)\right).$$

Using routine matrix computations and the fact that A, B being skew-symetric have vanishing trace, it can be expressed as:

$$\langle (u,\lambda,A),(v,\mu,B)\rangle_{\mathfrak{g}} = n\lambda\mu + \langle u,v\rangle + \mathbf{Tr}\left(A^t B\right). \quad (7)$$

A left invariant metric on the tangent space $T_g\mathcal{G}$ at $g \in \mathcal{G}$ is derived from (7) as:

$$\langle\!\langle X, Y, \rangle\!\rangle_g = \langle g^{-1}X, g^{-1}Y\rangle_{\mathfrak{g}},$$

with $X, Y \in T_g\mathcal{G}$. Please note that $\mathcal{G}$ is a matrix group acting linearly so that the mapping g^{-1} is well defined from $T_g\mathcal{G}$ to $\mathfrak{g}$. Using the fact that the metric (7) splits, one can check that geodesics in the group are given by straight segments in $\mathfrak{g}$: if g_1, g_2 are two elements from $\mathcal{G}$, then the geodesic connecting them is:

$$t \in [0,1] \mapsto g_1 \exp\left(t \log\left(g_1^{-1} g_2\right)\right),$$

where log is a determination of the matrix logarithm. Finally, the geodesic length is used to compute the distance $d(g_1, g_2)$ between two elements g_1, g_2 in $\mathcal{G}$. Assuming that the translation parts of g_1, g_2 are respectively u_1, u_2, the rotations U_1, U_2 and the scalings $\exp(\lambda_1), \exp(\lambda_2)$ then:

$$d(g_1,g_2)^2 = (\lambda_1 - \lambda_2)^2 + \quad (8)$$
$$\mathbf{Tr}\left(\log\left(U_1^t U_2\right)\log\left(U_1^t U_2\right)^t\right) + \|u_1 - u_2\|^2. \quad (9)$$

An important point to note is that the scaling part of an element $g \in \mathcal{G}$ will contribute to the distance by its logarithm.

Based on the above derivation, a flight path γ with state vector $(\gamma(t), \gamma'(t))$ will be modeled in the sequel as a curve with values in the Lie group $\mathcal{G}$:

$$\Gamma\colon t \in [0,1] \mapsto \Gamma(t) \in \mathcal{G},$$

with:

$$\Gamma(t).(0_d, e_1) = (\gamma(t), \gamma'(t)).$$

In order to make the Lie group representation amenable to statistical thinking, we need to define probability densities on the translation, scaling and rotation components that are invariant under the action of the corresponding factor of $\mathcal{G}$.

C. Nonparametric estimation on $\mathcal{G}$

Since the translation factor in $\mathcal{G}$ is the additive group $\mathbb{R}^d$, a standard nonparametric kernel estimator can be used. It turns out that it is equivalent to the spatial density estimate of (1), so that no extra work is needed for this component.

As for the rotation component, a standard parametrization is obtained recursively starting with the image of the canonical basis of $\mathbb{R}^d$ under the rotation. If R is an arbitrary rotation and $e_1, \ldots, e_d$ is the canonical basis, there is a unique rotation R_{e_1} mapping e_1 to Re_1 and fixing $e_2, \ldots, e_d$. It can be represented by the point $Re_1 = r_1$ on the sphere $\mathbb{S}^{d-1}$. Proceeding the same way for $Re_2, \ldots Re_d$, it is finally possible to completely parametrized R by a $(d-1)$-uple $(r_1, \ldots, r_{d-1})$ where $r_i \in \mathbb{S}^{i-1}$, $i = 1, \ldots, d$. Finding a rotation invariant distribution amounts thus to construct such a distribution on the sphere. In directional statistics, when we consider the spherical polar coordinates of a random unit vector $u \in \mathbb{S}^{d-1}$, we deal with spherical data (also called circular data or directional data) distributed on the unit sphere. For $d = 3$, a unit vector may be described by means of two random variables θ and φ which respectively represent the co-latitude (the zenith angle) and the longitude (the azimuth angle) of the points on the sphere. Nonparametric procedures, such as the kernel density estimation methods are sometimes convenient to estimate the probability distribution function (p.d.f.) of such kind of data but they require an appropriate choice of kernel functions.

Let $X_1, \ldots, X_n$ be a sequence of random vectors taking values in $\mathbb{R}^d$. The density function f of a random d-vector may be estimated by the kernel density estimator [17] as follows:

$$\widehat{f}(x) = \frac{1}{n}\sum_{i=1}^{n} \mathcal{K}_H\left(x - X_i\right),\ x \in \mathbb{R}^d,$$

where $\mathcal{K}_H(x) = \mid H \mid^{-1} \mathcal{K}(H^{-1}x)$, $\mathcal{K}$ denotes a multivariate kernel function and H represents a d-dimensional smoothing matrix, called bandwidth matrix. The kernel function $\mathcal{K}$ is a d-dimensional p.d.f. such as the standard multivariate Gaussian density $\mathcal{K}(x) = (2\pi)^{d/2}\exp\left(-\frac{1}{2}x^T x\right)$ or the multivariate Epanechnikov kernel. The resulting estimation will be the sum of "bumps" above each observation, the observations closed to x giving more important weights to the density estimate. The kernel function $\mathcal{K}$ determines the form of the bumps whereas the bandwidth matrix H determines their width and their orientation. Thereby, bandwidth matrices can be used to adjust for correlation between the components of the data. Usually, an equal bandwidth h in all dimensions is chosen, corresponding to $H = hId$ where Id denotes the $d \times d$ identity matrix. The kernel density estimator then becomes:

$$\widehat{f}(x) = \frac{1}{nh^d}\sum_{i=1}^{n} \mathcal{K}\left(h^{-1}(x - X_i)\right),\ x \in \mathbb{R}^d.$$

In certain cases when the spread of data is different in each coordinate direction, it may be more appropriate to use different bandwidths in each dimension. The bandwidth matrix H is given by the diagonal matrix in which the diagonal entries are the bandwidths $h_1, \ldots, h_d$.

In directional statistics, a kernel density estimate on $\mathbb{S}^{d-1}$ is given by adopting appropriate circular symmetric kernel functions such as von Mises-Fisher, wrapped Gaussian and wrapped Cauchy distributions. A commonly used choice is the von Mises-Fisher (vMF) distribution on $\mathbb{S}^{d-1}$ which is denoted $\mathcal{M}(m,\kappa)$ and given by the following density expression [18]:

$$K_{VMF}(x; m, \kappa) = c_d(\kappa)\, e^{\kappa m^T x},\ \kappa > 0,\ x \in \mathbb{S}^{d-1}, \quad (10)$$

where

$$c_d(\kappa) = \frac{\kappa^{d/2-1}}{(2\pi)^{d/2} I_{d/2-1}(\kappa)} \quad (11)$$

is a normalizing constant with $I_r(\kappa)$ denoting the modified Bessel function of the first kind at order r. The vMF kernel function is an unimodal p.d.f. parametrized by the unit mean-direction vector μ and the concentration parameter κ that controls the concentration of the distribution around the mean-direction vector. The vMF distribution may be expressed by means of the spherical polar coordinates of $x \in \mathbb{S}^{d-1}$ [19].

Given the random vectors X_i, $i = 1, \ldots, n$, in $\mathbb{S}^{d-1}$, the estimator of the spherical distribution is given by:

$$\widehat{f}(x) = \frac{1}{n}\sum_{i=1}^{n} K_{VMF}(x; X_i, \kappa) \tag{12}$$

$$= \frac{c_d(\kappa)}{n}\sum_{i=1}^{n} e^{\kappa X_i^T x},\ \kappa > 0,\ x \in \mathbb{S}^{d-1}. \tag{13}$$

The quantity $x - X_i$ which appears in the linear kernel density estimator is replaced by $X_i^T x$ which is the cosine of the angles between x and X_i, so that more important weights are given on observations close to x on the sphere. The concentration parameter κ is a smoothing parameter that plays the role of the inverse of the bandwidth parameter as defined in the linear kernel density estimation. Large values of κ imply greater concentration around the mean direction and lead to undersmoothed estimators whereas small values provide oversmoothed circular densities [20]. Indeed, if $\kappa = 0$, the vMF kernel function reduces to the uniform circular distribution on the hypersphere. Note that the vMF kernel function is convenient when the data is rotationally symmetric.

The vMF kernel function is a convenient choice for our problem because this p.d.f. is invariant under the action on the sphere of the rotation component of the Lie group $\mathcal{G}$. Moreover, this distribution has properties analogous to those of multivariate Gaussian distribution and is the limiting case of a limit central theorem for directional statistics. Other multidimensional distributions might be envisaged, such as the bivariate von Mises, the Bingham or the Kent distributions [18]. However, the bivariate von Mises distribution being a product kernel of two univariate von Mises kernels, it is more appropriate for modeling density distributions on the torus and not on the sphere. The Bingham distribution is bimodal and satisfies the antipodal symmetry property $K(x) = K(-x)$. This kernel function is used for estimating the density of axial data and is not appropriate for our clustering approach. Finally, the Kent distribution is a generalization of the vMF distribution, which is used when we want to take into account the spread of data. However, the rotation-invariance property of the vMF distribution is lost.

As for the scaling component of $\mathcal{G}$, the usual kernel functions such as the Gaussian and the Epanechnikov kernel functions are not suitable for estimating the radial distribution of a random vector in $\mathbb{R}^d$. When distributions are defined over a positive support (here in the case of non-negative data), these kernel functions cause a bias in the boundary regions because they give weights outside the support. An asymmetrical kernel function on $\mathbb{R}^+$ such as the log-normal kernel function is a more convenient choice. Moreover, this p.d.f. is invariant by change of scale. Let $R_1, \ldots, R_n$ be univariate random variables from a p.d.f. which has bounded support on $[0; +\infty[$. The radial density estimator may be defined by means of a sum of log-normal kernel functions as follows:

$$\widehat{g}(r) = \frac{1}{n}\sum_{i=1}^{n} K_{LN}(r; \ln R_i, h), r \geq 0, h > 0, \tag{14}$$

where

$$K_{LN}(x; \mu, \sigma) = \frac{1}{\sqrt{2\pi}\sigma x} e^{-\frac{(\ln x - \mu)^2}{2\sigma^2}} \tag{15}$$

is the log-normal kernel function and h is the bandwidth parameter. The resulting estimate is the sum of bumps defined by log-normal kernels with medians R_i and variances $(e^{h^2} - 1)e^{h^2} R_i^2$. Note that the log-normal (asymmetric) kernel density estimation is similar to the kernel density estimation based on a log-transformation of the data with the Gaussian kernel function. Although the scale-change component of $\mathcal{G}$ is the multiplicative group $\mathbb{R}^+$, we can use the standard Gaussian kernel estimator and the metric on $\mathbb{R}$.

IV. Unsupervised entropy clustering

The first thing to be considered is the extension of the entropy definition to curve systems with values in $\mathcal{G}$. Starting with expression from (1), the most important point is the choice of the kernel involved in the computation. As the group $\mathcal{G}$ is a direct product, choosing $K = K_t.K_s.K_o$ with K_t, K_s, K_o functions on respectively the translation, scaling and rotation part will yield a $\mathcal{G}$-invariant kernel provided the K_t, K_s, K_o are invariant on their respective components. Since the translation part of $\mathcal{G}$ is modeled after $\mathbb{R}^d$, the Epanechnikov kernel is a suitable choice. As for the scaling and rotation, the choice made follows the conclusion of Section III-C: a log-normal kernel and a von-Mises one will be used respectively. Finally, the term $\|\gamma'(t)\|$ in the original expression of the density, that is required to ensure invariance under reparametrization of the curve, has to be changed according to the metric in $\mathcal{G}$ and is replaced by $\langle\!\langle \gamma'(t), \gamma'(t) \rangle\!\rangle_{\gamma(t)}^{1/2}$. The density at $x \in \mathcal{G}$ is thus:

$$d_{\mathcal{G}}(x)) = \frac{\sum_{i=1}^{N} \int_0^1 K(x, \gamma_i(t)) \langle\!\langle \gamma_i'(t), \gamma_i'(t) \rangle\!\rangle_{\gamma_i(t)}^{1/2} dt}{\sum_{i=1}^{N} l_i} \tag{16}$$

where l_i is the length of the curve in $\mathcal{G}$, that is:

$$l_i = \int_0^1 \langle\!\langle \gamma_i'(t), \gamma_i'(t) \rangle\!\rangle_{\gamma_i(t)}^{1/2} dt. \tag{17}$$

The expression of the kernel evaluation $K(x, \gamma_i(t))$ is split into three terms. In order to ease the writing, a point x in $\mathcal{G}$ will be split into x^r, x^s, x^o components where the exponent r, s, t stands respectively for translation, scaling and rotation. Given the fact that K is a product of component-wise independent kernels it comes:

$$K(x, \gamma_i(t)) = K_t\left(x^t, \gamma_i^t(t)\right) K_s\left(x^s, \gamma_i^s(t)\right) K_o\left(x^o, \gamma_i^o(t)\right)$$

where:

$$K_t(x^t, \gamma_i^t(t)) = \frac{2}{\pi}\,\mathbf{ep}\left(\|\mathbf{x^t} - \boldsymbol{\gamma_i^t(t)}\|\right) \tag{18}$$

$$K_s(x^s, \gamma_i^s(t)) = \frac{1}{x^s \sigma\sqrt{2\pi}} \exp\left(-\frac{\left(\log x^s - \log \gamma_i^s(t)\right)^2}{2\sigma^2}\right) \tag{19}$$

$$K_o(x^o, \gamma_i^o(t)) = C(\kappa) \exp\left(\kappa \mathbf{Tr}\left(x^{oT} \gamma_i^o(t)\right)\right) \tag{20}$$

with $\mathbf{ep}$: $x \in \mathbb{R}^+ \mapsto (1 - x^2)1_{[0,1]}(x)$ and $C(\kappa)$ the normalizing constant making the kernel of unit integral. Please note that the expression given here is valid for arbitrary rotations, but for the application targeted by the work presented here, it boils down to a standard von-Mises distributions on $\mathbb{S}^{d-1}$:

$$K_o(x^o, \gamma_i^o(t)) = C(\kappa) \exp\left(\kappa x^{oT} \gamma_i^o(t)\right)$$

with normalizing constant as given in (11). In the general case, it is also possible, writing the rotation as a sequence of moves on spheres $\mathbb{S}^{d-1}, \mathbb{S}^{d-2}, \ldots$ and the distribution as a product of von-Mises on each of them, to have a vector of parameters κ: it is the approach taken in [21] and it may be applied verbatim here if needed.

The entropy of the system of curves is obtained from the density in $\mathcal{G}$:

$$E(d_{\mathcal{G}}) = -\int_{\mathcal{G}} d_{\mathcal{G}}(x) \log d_{\mathcal{G}}(x) d\mu_{\mathcal{G}}(x) \tag{21}$$

with $d\mu_{\mathcal{G}}$ the left Haar measure. Using again the fact that $\mathcal{G}$ is a direct product group, $d\mu$ is easily seen to be a product measure, with dx^t, the usual Lebesgue measure on the translation part, dx^s/x^s on the scaling part and dx^o on $\mathbb{S}^{d-1}$ for the rotation part. It turns out that the $1/x^s$ term in the expression of dx^s/x^s is already taken into account in the kernel definition, due to the fact that it is expressed in logarithmic coordinates. The same is true for the von-Mises kernel, so that in the sequel only the (product) Lebesgue measure will appear in the integrals.

Finding the system of curves with minimum entropy requires a displacement field computation as detailed in [16]. For each curve γ_i, such a field is a mapping $\eta_i \colon [0,1] \to T\mathcal{G}$ where at each $t \in [0,1]$, $\eta_i(t) \in T\mathcal{G}_{\gamma_i(t)}$. Compare to the original situation where only spatial density was considered, the computation must now be conducted in the tangent space to $\mathcal{G}$. Even for small problems, the effort needed becomes prohibitive. In Section V, we will present in detail an efficient implementation of this algorithm. First, note that the structure of the kernel involved in the density can help in cutting the overall computations needed. Since it is a product, and the translation part is compactly supported, being an Epanechnikov kernel, one can restrict the evaluation to points belonging to its support. Density computation will thus be made only in tubes around the trajectories. Second, for the target application that is to cluster the flight paths into a route network and is of pure spatial nature, there is no point in updating the rotation and scaling part when performing the moves: only the translation part must change, the other two being computed from the trajectory. The initial optimization problem in $\mathcal{G}$ may thus be greatly simplified. Finally, binning techniques [22] will be used to reduce the computational cost of the translation, rotation and scale components in the kernel K.

Let ϵ be an admissible variation of curve γ_i, that is a smooth mapping from $[0,1]$ to $T\mathcal{G}$ with $\epsilon(t) \in T_{\gamma_i(t)}\mathcal{G}$ and $\epsilon(0) = \epsilon(1) = 0$. We assume furthermore that ϵ has only a translation component. The derivative of the entropy $E(d_{\mathcal{G}})$ with respect to the curve γ_i is obtained from the first order term when γ_i is replaced by $\gamma_i + \epsilon$. First of all, it has to be noted that $d_{\mathcal{G}}$ is a density and thus has unit integral regardless of the curve system. When computing the derivative of $E(d_{\mathcal{G}})$, the term

$$-\int_{\mathcal{G}} d_{\mathcal{G}}(x) \frac{\partial_{\gamma_i} d_{\mathcal{G}}(x)}{d_{\mathcal{G}}(x)} d\mu_{\mathcal{G}}(x) = -\int_{\mathcal{G}} \partial_{\gamma_i} d_{\mathcal{G}}(x) d\mu_{\mathcal{G}}(x)$$

will thus vanish. It remains:

$$-\int_{\mathcal{G}} \partial_{\gamma_i} d_{\mathcal{G}}(x) \log d_{\mathcal{G}}(x) d\mu_{\mathcal{G}}(x).$$

The density $d_{\mathcal{G}}$ is a sum on the curves, and only the i-th term has to be considered. Starting with the expression from (16), one term in the derivative will come from the denominator. It computes the same way as in [16] to yield:

$$\left. \frac{\gamma_i^{t\prime\prime}(t)}{\langle\!\langle \gamma_i'(t), \gamma_i'(t) \rangle\!\rangle_{\mathcal{G}}} \right|_{\mathcal{N}} E(d_{\mathcal{G}}) \tag{22}$$

Please note that the second derivative of γ_i is considered only on its translation component, but the first derivative makes use of the complete expression. As before, the notation $|_{\mathcal{N}}$ stands for the projection onto the normal component to the curve.

The second term comes from the variation of the numerator. Using the fact that the kernel is a product $K_t K_s K_o$ and that all individual terms have a unit integral on their respective components, the expression becomes very similar to the case of spatial density only and is:

$$-\left(\int_{\mathcal{G}} K\left(x, \gamma_i(t)\right) \log d_{\mathcal{G}}(x) d\mu_{\mathcal{G}(x)} \right) \left. \frac{\gamma_i^{t\prime\prime}(t)}{\langle\!\langle \gamma_i'(t), \gamma_i'(t) \rangle\!\rangle_{\mathcal{G}}^{1/2}} \right|_{\mathcal{N}} \tag{23}$$

$$+ \int_{\mathbb{R}^d} e(t) K^{t\prime}\left(x^t, \gamma_i^t(t)\right) \log d_{\mathcal{G}}(x) \langle\!\langle \gamma_i'(t), \gamma_i'(t) \rangle\!\rangle_{\mathcal{G}}^{1/2} dx^t \tag{24}$$

with:

$$e(t) = \left. \frac{\gamma_i^t(t) - x^t}{\|\gamma_i^t(t) - x^t\|} \right|_{\mathcal{N}}.$$

V. IMPLEMENTATION

Two computational bottlenecks are associated with the implementation of the clustering algorithm. The first one is the computation of the curve system density and the second one is the entropy minimization, which relies on gradient iterations. These two aspects will be separately treated in the sequel. Please note that the algorithms introduced are mainly tailored for the application in air traffic and may not be adequate to problems with different state spaces.

A. Density evaluation

Assuming that the original trajectories are planar, the overall dimension of the Lie group $\mathcal{G}$ is 4. The method requires the evaluation of the integral

$$E(d_{\mathcal{G}}) = -\int_{\mathcal{G}} d_{\mathcal{G}}(x) \log d_{\mathcal{G}}(x) d\mu_{\mathcal{G}}(x) \tag{25}$$

that has potentially a very high computational cost. However, as mentioned in Section III-B, $\mathcal{G}$ is a direct product, so that the Haar measure $\mu_{\mathcal{G}}$ splits into three terms: one that is the usual Lebesgue measure on $\mathbb{R}^2$, the second one that is the Lebesgue measure on the unit circle and the last being of the form ds/s. Let a point x in $\mathcal{G}$ be represented as (x_1, x_2, θ, s) with (x_1, x_2) the spatial component in $\mathbb{R}^2$, θ be the angle giving the position on the unit circle (with the usual identification $2\pi = 0$) and s be the scale factor. The integral (25) becomes:

$$E(d_{\mathcal{G}}) = \tag{26}$$

$$-\int_{\mathbb{R}^2} \int_0^{2\pi} \int_{\mathbb{R}+} d_{\mathcal{G}}(x_1, x_2, \theta, s) \tag{27}$$

$$\log d_{\mathcal{G}}(x_1, x_2, \theta, s) dx_1 dx_2 d\theta \frac{ds}{s} \tag{28}$$

In computer implementation, multi-dimensional integrals can be evaluated either using polynomial approximations on a discrete grid [23] or Monte-Carlo methods when the dimensionality of the problem induces an intractable computational cost. In the present case, where the integration has to be conveyed in four dimensions, grid based approaches can still be applied. Extension to trajectories with values in $\mathbb{R}^3$ will increase the dimension to 6 which mandates the use of stochastic approximations. In any case, it must be noted that a high accuracy in the result is not needed, so that randomized algorithms may be used without impairing the convergence of the subsequent gradient iteration.

The computation of the density itself is more constraining as its original definition involves for each point where its value is needed a summation of integrals over all trajectories which may quickly become prohibitive. In a previous work [16] where the density was two-dimensional, a grid based approach was selected, which allows a very simple discrete convolution formulation. Here, due to the higher dimensionality, a crude extension of the method seems to yield an unacceptable increase of both the computational cost and memory footprint. However, it turns out that the problem is less complex than expected as a result of the product form of the kernel. Starting with the expression (16), the critical point in the evaluation of the density at a given point $x = (x_1, x_2, \theta, s)$ is the sum:

$$\sum_{i=1}^{N} \int_0^1 K\left(x, \gamma_i(t)\right) \langle\!\langle \gamma_i'(t), \gamma_i'(t) \rangle\!\rangle_{\gamma_i(t)}^{1/2} dt. \qquad (29)$$

Using any classical quadrature formula, the integral may be reduced to a finite sum, yielding a double sum:

$$\sum_{i=1}^{N} \sum_{j=1}^{M_i} w_{ij} K\left(x, \gamma_i(t_{ij})\right) \langle\!\langle \gamma_i'(t_{ij}), \gamma_i'(t_{ij}) \rangle\!\rangle_{\gamma_i(t_{ij})}^{1/2} \qquad (30)$$

where M_i is the number of sample points t_{ij} chosen on trajectory i and the w_{ij} are the quadrature weights. The expression (30) is fully general, but a simpler choice is made in practice: the sampling points t_{ij} are selected to be evenly spaced and the weights all equal to 1. It is nothing but the rectangle quadrature formula, whose accuracy is sufficient for the application in mind. Switching to a higher order formula is straightforward. In (30), the evaluation of the kernel has the highest cost since the norm $\langle\!\langle \gamma_i'(t_{ij}), \gamma_i'(t_{ij}) \rangle\!\rangle_{\gamma_i(t_{ij})}^{1/2}$ does not depend on x and can be computed once for all. To compute the density at a single point, the total number of kernel evaluations is $\sum_{i=1}^{N} M_i$, with typical values of $N = 100, M_i = 20$ for the analysis of a control sector to $N = 10000, M_i = 100$ in the case of a country sized airspace. While acceptable in the first case, a direct application of the formula is not efficient enough in the second.

Recalling that the kernel K is a product of three elementary kernels $K = K_t K_o K_s$, it is clear that K will vanish outside of the support of any of the three. As mentioned before, K_t is selected to be an Epanechnikov kernel which is compactly supported, so that K itself will vanish when the distance between the translation components of x and $\gamma_i(t_{ij})$ is large enough. The sum (30) will thus have almost all terms vanishing if the bandwidth of K_t is adequately selected. Finally, using the t superscript to denote the translation part of the points:

$$K_t(x^t, \gamma_i^t(t_{ij})) = \frac{2}{\pi} \mathbf{ep}\left(\|x^t - \gamma_i^t(t_{ij})\|\right)$$

with $\mathbf{ep}$: $x \in \mathbb{R}^+ \mapsto (1 - x^2) 1_{[0,1]}(x)$.

The final step towards efficient evaluation of the density is to reduce the computation to points located on a evenly spaced grid. This procedure is known in the non-parametric statistics community as binning [22]. First of all, the domain of interest in the translation component is assume to be of the form $[a_1, b_1] \times [a_2, b_2]$, which fits almost all possible cases in a real world application. For the air traffic clustering problem, it is a box covering the investigated airspace. Letting L_1, L_2 be the respective number of grid points desired in each direction, an evenly spaced grid is constructed by taking as vertices the points:

$$x_{k,l}^t = \left(a_1 + \frac{k(b_1 - a_1)}{L_1 - 1}, a_2 + \frac{l(b_2 - a_2)}{L_2 - 1}\right)$$

with $k \in \{0, \ldots L_1 - 1\}$, $l \in \{0, \ldots, L_2 - 1\}$ and $L_1 > 1, L_2 > 1$. Please note that the vertices $x_{k,l}$ define implicitly bins that are rectangular cells $[x_{k,l}, x_{k+1,l}] \times [x_{k,l}, x_{k,l+1}]$. The density will be evaluated at the vertices of the grid only, resulting in a final approximation made of $L_1 \times L_2$ discrete values. Furthermore, sample points $\gamma_i(t_{ij})$ will be considered equal to the grid vertex $x_{k,l}$ that is closest to it (the case of ties up to machine precision is unlikely to appear, but can be solved by either randomly drawing the vertex among those equally close or splitting the observation between ex-aequo vertices). Due to this approximation, the norm $\|x^t - \gamma_i^t(t_{ij})\|$ can only take a finite number of values, namely the distances between any pair of vertices and can thus be precomputed. Furthermore, since the kernel K_t is compactly supported, the number of non-zeros values is in practice much lower than the size of the grid.

Binning is used also for the rotation and scale components with respective kernels K_o and K_s. In both cases, the support of the kernel is identical to the domain of variation itself, so that cutting the computation cost using the previous trick is quite difficult. For the specific application to air traffic analysis, two remarks can be made:

- Within the frame of the current airspace organization, aircraft are bound to follow quite narrow paths. Even in the future, a complete free flight cannot be imagined unless humans are removed from the loop, which is not intended. As a consequence, one can assume a quite small bandwidth for the von-Mises kernel K_o.
- The main use of the rotation and scale components is to disambiguate between flows that are spatially closed, but with otherwise very different behaviors: opposite headings, different speed categories. In theses cases, a fine representation of the rotation and scale components is not needed, as the observed values are expected to be well separated.

Gathering things together, a coarse grid was selected for binning the rotation and scale components. In the experiments conducted so far, a 10×10 was enough to ensure the desired behavior. Since the translation component is discretized on a 100×100, the overall bins number is 1e6, which is well within acceptable limits for memory footprint (around 10MB with current implementation).

In the first of the complete density computation algorithm, the density grid is created as a block matrix $\mathcal{M}$ of size $m_1 \times m_2$, where m_1, m_2 are the respective number of bins desired in each component and each block is of size $p \times q$, with p (resp.

q) the number of bins in the rotation (resp. scale) component. The domain of variation for the translation component is a rectangle $[a_1, b_1] \times [a_2, b_2]$, the interval $[0, 2\pi]$ for the rotation and $[s_1, s_2]$ for the scale. An elementary cell in the grid where a given point (x_1, x_2, θ, s) lies can be determined using the following procedure:

- The block coordinates (i, j) is found from the couple (x_1, x_2) as:
$$i = (m_1 - 1)\frac{x_1 - a_1}{b_1 - a_1}, j = (m_2 - 1)\frac{x_2 - a_2}{b_2 - a_2}.$$
- Within the block $\mathcal{M}_{i,j}$, the respective rotation and scale indices (k, l) are obtained pretty much by the same way:
$$k = (p - 1)\frac{\theta}{2\pi}, \; l = (q - 1)\frac{s - s_1}{s_2 - s_1}.$$

Please note that all indices are zero-based, so that $\mathcal{M}_{0,0}$ is the first block in the matrix $\mathcal{M}$. Actual elements in $\mathcal{M}$ are referred to using quadruples (i, j, p, q), with the first two components designing the block and the remaining two locating the element in the block.

As mentioned above, a benefit of the binning procedure is the ability to pre-compute the kernel values, since the difference between any two grid points is known. As an example, for the translation component, the value for the kernel K_t can be stored as a $m_1 m_2 \times m_1 m_2$ matrix $\mathcal{K}^t$ with entries $\mathcal{K}^t_{(i,j),(k,l)} = K_t\left(d_{(i,j),(k,l)}\right)$ and:

$$d_{(i,j),(k,l)} = \sqrt{\left(\frac{k - i}{b_1 - a_1}\right)^2 + \left(\frac{l - j}{b_2 - a_2}\right)^2}.$$

The storage size is $m_1^2 \times m_2^2$ and seems prohibitive, but it turns out that most of the element values are redundant. It is assumed that the matrix $\mathcal{K}^t$ is stored in a lexicographic order, that is couples (i, j) are stored in increasing i then increasing j order. $\mathcal{K}^t$ is clearly symmetric, and all the elements on the diagonal have the same value $K_t(0)$. Furthermore, since the distance $d_{(i,j),(k,l)}$ is based only on the differences $k - i$ and $l - j$, it is invariant if the same shift (p, q) is applied to both couples. It implies that the matrix $\mathcal{K}^t$ has a block structure that is represented as:

$$\begin{pmatrix} A_0 & A_1 & \dots & \dots & A_{m_2} \\ A_1 & A_0 & \dots & \dots & A_{m_2 - 1} \\ \vdots & \vdots & \vdots & \vdots & \vdots \\ A_{m_2} & \dots & \dots & A_1 & A_0 \end{pmatrix}.$$

Each block A_i is symmetric and within a given block, all the diagonals are equal, thanks again to the integer shift invariance property. Therefore, the storage really required is just $m_1 \times m_2$ that is no more than the number of grid points. Please note that it is due entirely to the shift invariance property, that comes from the translation invariance of the distance: using more general kernels that do not exhibit invariance properties will require storing the full $\mathcal{K}^t$ matrix: in practical implementations, it is thus highly desirable to stick to distance based kernels.

A further reduction of complexity comes from the fact that K_t is compactly supported: for distance greater than a given threshold, K_t will be identically 0. It means that only a subset of the blocks A_i will not vanish. Within the blocks themselves, when the bandwidth parameter is low enough, only a subset of the diagonals will be non zero. As a consequence, the real needed storage is only a fraction of the original one and is well below $m_1 \times m_2$. In practice, the most convenient way is to store data in a $u \times v$ matrix $\mathbf{K}^t$ with entries:

$$\mathbf{K}^t_{ij} = K_t\left(\sqrt{\left(\frac{i}{b_1 - a_1}\right)^2 + \left(\frac{j}{b_2 - a_2}\right)^2}\right).$$

The size of $\mathbf{K}^t$ is of course depending on the kernel bandwidth, but is generally in the order of one tenth to one fifth of the size of $\mathcal{M}$ in each coordinates.

On the rotation and scale components, there is no particular vanishing property that can be used. Except when dealing with very small bandwidths, there is no interest in having less kernel values stored that possible distances. In the sequel, the corresponding vectors will be denoted as $\mathbf{K}^o$ (resp. $\mathbf{K}^s$) with size p (resp. q).

The density computation can then be performed using the Algorithm 1. On completion, the block matrix $\mathcal{M}$ contains as entries the density up to a scalar. Normalizing it so that all its elements sum to 1 yields the final density estimate. In practical implementations, the matrix $\mathcal{M}$ will have all its elements stored contiguously.

Algorithm 1 Density computation

$\mathcal{M} \leftarrow 0$
for $i = 0 \dots N - 1$ **do**
  for $j = 0 \dots M_i - 1$ **do**
    $x \leftarrow \gamma^t_i(t_j)$
    $(k, l, m, n) \leftarrow$ coordinate of cell containing x
    UPDATE(k,l,m,n)
  end for
end for
procedure UPDATE(k,l,m,n)
  for $i = -u \dots u$ **do**
    if $k + i \geq 0 | k + i < N$ **then**
      for $j = -v \dots u$ **do**
        if $l + j \geq 0 | l + j < M_i$ **then**
          $kt \leftarrow \mathbf{K}^t_{|i||j|}$
          UPDATEINNERBLOCK(kt, k+i,l+j,m,n)
        end if
      end for
    end if
  end for
end procedure
procedure UPDATEINNERBLOCK(kt, k,l,m,n)
  for $i = 0 \dots p$ **do**
    $ir \leftarrow (m + i) \bmod p$
    $k\theta \leftarrow \mathbf{K}^\theta_{ir}$
    for $j = 0 \dots q$ **do**
      $js \leftarrow n + j$
      if $js < q$ **then**
        $ks \leftarrow \mathbf{K}^s_{js}$
        $\mathcal{M}_{k,l,ir,js} \leftarrow \mathcal{M}_{k,l,ir,js} + kt * k\theta * ks$
      end if
    end for
  end for
end procedure

B. Moving density computation to GPUs

There is an increasing interest in the numerical analysis community for GPU computation. These massively parallel processors, first intended to perform tasks related to 3D scenes display, have proved themselves very efficient in problems where it is possible to formulate the solution has a set of asynchronous and independent tasks. Due to the high number of processing units available, GPUs excel in many algorithms coming from the field of linear algebra, simulation, PDE solving. In the clustering application described here, GPU computing can leverage the efficiency of density computation that leads naturally to parallel processing. Some care must be taken however as simultaneous accesses to common memory locations may impair the overall performance.

First of all, one can note that computation within a $\mathcal{M}$ block, that is updating the rotation and scale part of the density requires only the knowledge of the samples with translation coordinates falling within the corresponding grid cell and is independent of the computation made on another block. This gives access to the first level of parallelism. On most GPU architectures, the computation may be organized in thread blocks. It is the case within the CUDA programming model of NVIDIA, and a thread block size of 16×16 was selected. The size of the kernel grids in rotation and scale components were chosen accordingly. To maximize the performance, the corresponding block in the matrix $\mathcal{M}$ is first copied to local memory (designed as "shared memory" in CUDA), then all computation are performed on it within the given thread block. At the end of the updating phase, the local memory is transferred back to the global one. The storage needed for the local block is 256 times the size of a float, which yields a total of 1Ko, well below the 48Ko limit of the CUDA architecture.

At the beginning of the density computation, a global memory block representing the whole of matrix $\mathcal{M}$ is allocated on the device and set to 0. One thread block (256 threads) is dedicated to a single block in $\mathcal{M}$, for a total of $m_1 \times m_2 \times 256$ threads. Depending on the hardware and the choice made on m_1, m_2, this value can exceed the maximum number of threads allowed on a particular GPU. In such a case, the update is performed on submatrices of the original matrix $\mathcal{M}$. With the typical values given previously, the maximal number of threads of the GTX980 used for the development is not reached.

Using the GPU to affect the sample points $\gamma_i(t_{ij})$ to the right block in $\mathcal{M}$ will not improve the performance. A better choice is to use the CPU to perform the task, then to send the processed array of samples to the GPU device.

A second level of parallelism will be to consider updates of submatrices of blocks in $\mathcal{M}$ instead of single blocks. The expected gain is small, except when more that one GPU are present in the system. The implementation details are not given here, trying to improve the overall algorithm being still a work in progress.

C. Implementing the gradient descent algorithm

Once the density grid $\mathcal{M}$ has been computed, the implementation of the gradient move is quite straightforward and requires only the ability to estimate the first and second derivative on each trajectory. A very classical finite differences scheme gives a sufficient accuracy to obtain convergence on most situations. It takes the form of the product of a matrix D_i with the$N_i \times 4$ matrix of samples $(\gamma_i(t_{i1}), \dots, \gamma_i(t_{iN_i}))$ to yield the matrix of derivative estimates $(\gamma_i'(t_{i1}), \dots, \gamma_i'(t_{iN_i}))$. Please note that the coordinates are put in columns, while the samples are in row. Iterating the product with D_i will give rise to the second derivative. Generally speaking, D_i is obtained from the Lagrange interpolation polynomial and can be constructed using the algorithm 2 (in the sequel d is the degree of the interpolating polynomial).

Algorithm 2 Computation of the derivation matrix D_i

```
D_i ← 0
for k = 0 ... N_i do
    offset = GETOFFSET(k)
    for j = 0 ... N_1 do
        D_i[k, j + offset] = LAGRANGE(j,k,offset)
    end for
end for
function GETOFFSET(i)
    if i < d/2 then
        o ← 0
    else if i > N_i − d/2 − 1 then
        o ← N_i − d
    else
        o ← i − d/2
    end if
    return o
end function
function LAGRANGE(k,j,offset)
    w ← 1.0
    for a = 0 ... d do
        if a ≠ k then
            w ← w ∗ (t_{i,k+offset} − t_{i,a+offset})
        end if
    end for
    s ← 0.0
    for a = 0 ... d do
        if a ≠ k then
            p ← 1.0
            for b = 0 ... d do
                if b ≠ k ∧ b ≠ a then
                    p ← p ∗ (t_{i,j} − t_{i,b+offset})
                end if
            end for
            s ← s + p
        end if
    end for
    return s/w
end function
```

As mentioned before, integrals are computed using a quadrature formula, that was chosen to the simplest one, with all weights equal.

D. Results

In Figures 1 and 2, the problem of automatic conflict solving is addressed. From an initial flight plan, we have generated a conflicting set of trajectories that are converging to a single unsafe point. The median of the initial flows correspond to the flight plan showed in Figure 1. Next, an automated planner has proposed a solution by generating a set of safe trajectories that are relatively complex and may fail to be manageable by air traffic controllers. In Figure 2, the minimization entropy criterion has deformed the proposed flight paths and produced straighten trajectories with route-like behavior. The median of the initial and the final flows are represented in Figures 1 and 2.

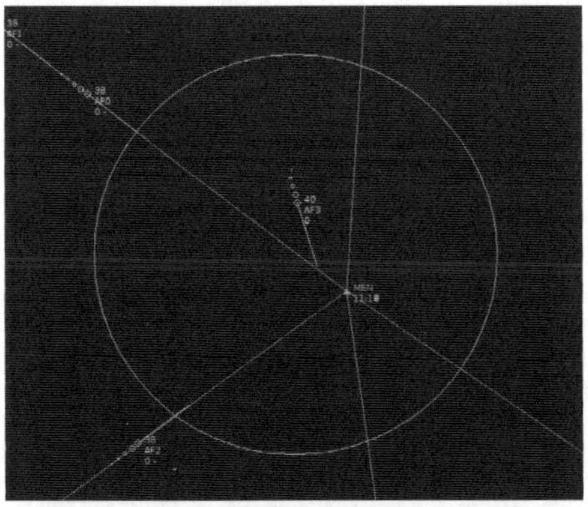

Figure 1. Initial flight plan.

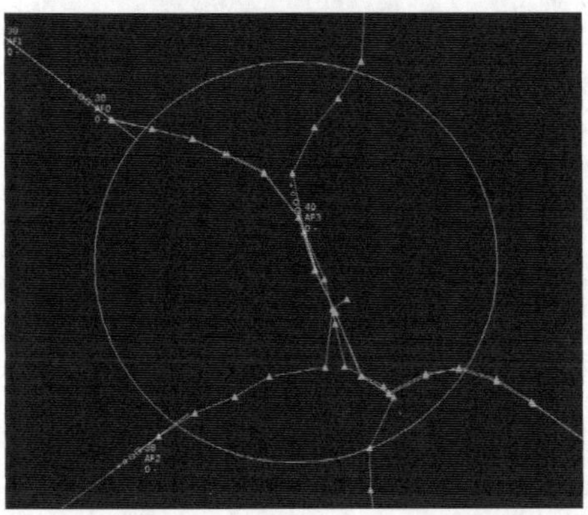

Figure 2. Entropy minimal curve system from the initial flight plan.

However, because the spatial density is not sensitive to the directional information, the entropy based procedure will tend to aggregate flight paths that should be sufficiently separated such that trajectories with opposite directions. The Lie group modeling will take into account the direction and the position of the curves and the algorithm works as expected, avoiding going too close to trajectories with opposite directions as indicated on Figure 3. Note that using the Lie approach properly separates the two left flight paths that have similar shape but opposite directions.

In a more realistic setting, arrivals and departures at Toulouse Blagnac airport were analyzed. The dataset used was a a record of approximately 1700 trajectories between Paris Orly and Toulouse Blagnac. The projection used focuses on Blagnac and exaggerates the lateral deviation to enlighten the fluxes separation. The algorithm performs well as indicated on Figure 4. Four clusters are identified, with mean lines represented through a spline smoothing between landmarks. It is quite remarkable that all density-based algorithms were unable to separate the two clusters located at the right side of the picture, while the present one clearly show a standard

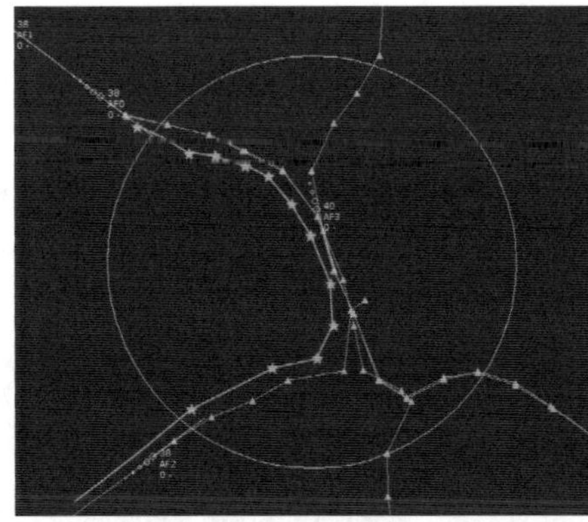

Figure 3. Clustering using the Lie approach.

approach procedure and a short one.

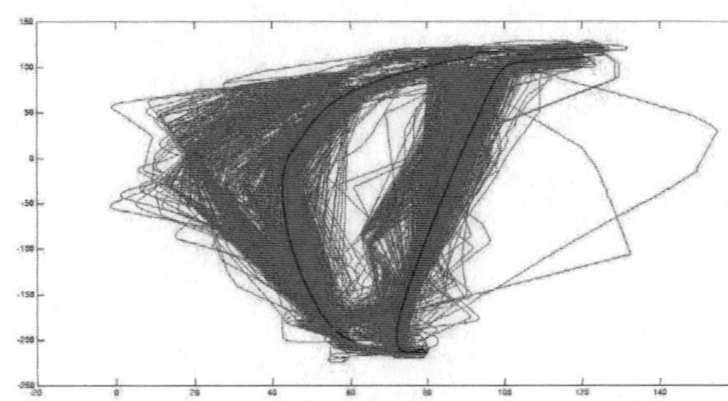

Figure 4. Mean cluster trajectories at Toulouse airport (nautical miles). Red arrivals and grey departures.

An important issue still to be addressed with the extended algorithm is the increase in computation time that reaches 20 times compared to the approach using only spatial density entropy. In the current implementation, the time needed to cluster the traffic presented in Figure 3 is in the order of 0.01s on a XEON 3Ghz machine and with a pure java implementation. For the case of Figure 4, 5 minutes are needed on the same machine for dealing with the set of 1784 trajectories.

Finally, a similar procedure was used to obtain the so-called bundled traffic. Here the purpose of the algorithm is not to cluster flight paths, but instead simplify the picture so that an operator is able to extract quickly the interesting features. The heading information was not used in the experiments, since the main goal was to extract the major flows followed by the aircraft so as to dimension the airspace sectoring. One picture represents one day of recorded traffic over France, with all low altitude flights removed: they correspond to general aviation and are not to be considered in the design of the airspace. Roughly 8000 trajectories are processed for one day. Since there is no heading information, the execution time is greatly reduced. Furthermore, the software was implemented here in C++, resulting in a total processing time of 5 seconds on the same machine as above.

Figure 5. Recorded trajectories for one day traffic over France.

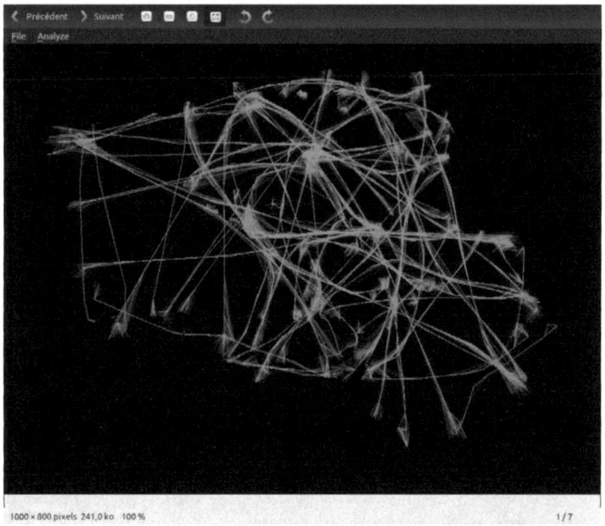

Figure 6. Bundled trajectories.

VI. Conclusion and Future Work

The entropy associated with a system of curves has proved itself efficient in unsupervised clustering application where shape constraints must be taken into account. For using it in aircraft route design, heading and velocity information must be added to the state vector, inducing an extra level of complexity. In our algorithm, we cannot enforce the regulatory separation norms, just construct clusters with low interactions. Please note that we can consider the current algorithm as a preprocessing phase. In a second step, we could imagine running an algorithm based on, for instance, optimal control in order to keep in line with the minimum separation norms. The present work relies on a Lie group modeling as an unifying approach to state representation. It has successfully extended the notion of curve system entropy to this setting, allowing the heading/velocity to be added in a intrinsic way. The method seems promising, as indicated by the results obtained on simple synthetic situations, but extra work needs to be dedicated to algorithmic efficiency in order to deal with the operational traffic datasets, in the order of tens of thousand of trajectories.

Moreover, the choice of the kernel bandwidth parameters should be explored in the next step of this work. Indeed, as it is noted in [2], kernel bandwidth values will influence the effect of the minimization entropy procedure on the curve straightening: straightening is preeminent for low values, while gathering dominates at high bandwidths. An automatic procedure in the choice of bandwidth parameter is then desirable and an adaptive bandwidth procedure may be of some interest.

Generally speaking, introducing a Lie group approach to data description paves the way to new algorithms dedicated to data with a high level of internal structuring. Studies are initiated to address several issues in high dimensional data analysis using this framework.

References

[1] F. Nicol and S. Puechmorel, "Unsupervised aircraft trajectories clustering: a minimum entropy approach," in ALLDATA 2016, The Second International Conference on Big Data, Small Data, Linked Data and Open Data. Lisbon, Portugal: IARIA, 2016.

[2] S. Puechmorel and F. Nicol, "Entropy minimizing curves with application to flight path design and clustering," Entropy, vol. 18, no. 9, 2016, p. 337. [Online]. Available: http://www.mdpi.com/1099-4300/18/9/337

[3] M. Enriquez, "Identifying temporally persistent flows in the terminal airspace via spectral clustering," in ATM Seminar 10, FAA-Eurocontrol, Ed., 06 2013.

[4] M. El Mahrsi and F. Rossi, "Graph-based approaches to clustering network-constrained trajectory data," in New Frontiers in Mining Complex Patterns, ser. Lecture Notes in Computer Science, A. Appice, M. Ceci, C. Loglisci, G. Manco, E. Masciari, and Z. Ras, Eds. Springer Berlin Heidelberg, 2013, vol. 7765, pp. 124–137.

[5] J. Kim and H. S. Mahmassani, "Spatial and temporal characterization of travel patterns in a traffic network using vehicle trajectories," Transportation Research Procedia, vol. 9, 2015, pp. 164 – 184, papers selected for Poster Sessions at The 21st International Symposium on Transportation and Traffic Theory Kobe, Japan, 5-7 August, 2015.

[6] M. Ester, H. P. Kriegel, J. Sander, and X. Xu, "A density-based algorithm for discovering clusters in large spatial databases with noise." AAAI Press, 1996, pp. 226–231.

[7] N. Ferreira, J. T. Klosowski, C. E. Scheidegger, and C. T. Silva, "Vector field k-means: Clustering trajectories by fitting multiple vector fields," in Computer Graphics Forum, vol. 32, no. 3pt2. Blackwell Publishing Ltd, 2013, pp. 201–210.

[8] T. W. Liao, "Clustering of time series data - a survey," Pattern Recognition, vol. 38, 2005, pp. 1857–1874.

[9] S. Rani and G. Sikka, "Recent techniques of clustering of time series data: A survey," International Journal of Computer Applications, vol. 52, no. 15, August 2012, pp. 1–9, full text available.

[10] F. Ferraty and P. Vieu, Nonparametric Functional Data Analysis: Theory and Practice, ser. Springer Series in Statistics. Springer, 2006.

[11] J. Ramsay and B. Silverman, Functional Data Analysis, ser. Springer Series in Statistics. Springer New York, 2006.

[12] W. Meesrikamolkul, V. Niennattrakul, and C. Ratanamahatana, "Shape-based clustering for time series data," in Advances in Knowledge Discovery and Data Mining, ser. Lecture Notes in Computer Science, P.-N. Tan, S. Chawla, C. Ho, and J. Bailey, Eds. Springer Berlin Heidelberg, 2012, vol. 7301, pp. 530–541.

[13] A. Delaigle and P. Hall, "Defining probability density for a distribution of random functions," The Annals of Statistics, vol. 38, no. 2, 2010, pp. 1171–1193.

[14] C. Bouveyron and J. Jacques, "Model-based clustering of time series in group-specific functional subspaces," Advances in Data Analysis and Classification, vol. 5, no. 4, 2011, pp. 281–300.

[15] S. Puechmorel, "Geometry of curves with application to aircraft trajectory analysis." Annales de la faculté des sciences de Toulouse, vol. 24, no. 3, 07 2015, pp. 483–504.

[16] S. Puechmorel and F. Nicol, "Entropy minimizing curves with application to automated flight path design," in GSI 2015, Second International Conference, Palaiseau, France, October 28-30, 2015. Springer, 2015.

[17] D. Scott, Multivariate Density Estimation: Theory, Practice, and Visualization, ser. A Wiley-interscience publication. Wiley, 1992.

[18] K. Mardia and P. Jupp, Directional Statistics, ser. Wiley Series in Probability and Statistics. Wiley, 2009.

[19] K. V. Mardia, "Statistics of directional data," Journal of the Royal Statistical Society. Series B (Methodological), vol. 37, no. 3, 1975, pp. 349–393.

[20] E. García-Portugués, R. M. Crujeiras, and W. González-Manteiga, "Kernel density estimation for directional–linear data," Journal of Multivariate Analysis, vol. 121, 2013, pp. 152–175.

[21] P. E. Jupp and K. V. Mardia, "Maximum likelihood estimators for the matrix von mises-fisher and bingham distributions," Ann. Statist., vol. 7, no. 3, 05 1979, pp. 599–606.

[22] M. P. Wand, "Fast computation of multivariate kernel estimators," Journal of Computational and Graphical Statistics, vol. 3, no. 4, 1994, pp. 433–445.

[23] G. Dahlquist and Å. Björck, Numerical Methods in Scientific Computing: Volume 1, ser. SIAM e-books. Society for Industrial and Applied Mathematics, 2008. [Online]. Available: https://books.google.fr/books?id=qy83gXoRps8C

An Approach to Automatic Adaptation of DAiSI Component Interfaces

Yong Wang and Andreas Rausch
Department of Informatics
Technical University Clausthal
Clausthal-Zellerfeld, Germany
e-mail: yong.wang, andreas.rausch@tu-clausthal.de

***Abstract*— The Dynamic Adaptive System Infrastructure (DAiSI) is a platform which supports dynamic adaptive system. DAiSI can change its behavior at runtime. Behavioral changes can be caused by user's needs, or based on context information if the system environment changes. It is a run-time infrastructure that operates on components that comply with a DAiSI-specific component model. The run-time infrastructure can integrate components into the system that were not known at design-time. Communication between components in DAiSI is supported by services. Services of components are described by domain interfaces, which have to be specified by the component developer. Components can use services of other components, if the respective required and provided domain interfaces of components are compatible. However, sometimes services that have been developed by different developers can do the same thing, e.g., provide the same data or operations, but they are represented by different syntactic. Therefore, in a previous article, we present an approach which enables the use of syntactically incompatible service by using an ontology-based adapter that connects services, which provide the same data in different format. In this paper we use an existing ontology to semantically describe interfaces of components and present an improved algorithm using SPARQL and reasoning to discover interfaces in triplestore. In addition, we propose to use the historical data to predict the best suitable interface.**

Keywords—component models; self-adaptation; dynamic adaptive systems; ontology.

I. Introduction

An increasing interest in dynamic adaptive systems could be observed in the last two decades. A platform for such systems has been developed in our research group for more than ten years. It is called Dynamic Adaptive System Infrastructure (DAiSI). DAiSI is a component based platform that can be used in self-managed systems. Components can be integrated into or removed from a dynamic adaptive system at run-time without causing a complete application to fail. To meet this requirement, each component can react to changes in its environment and adapt its behavior accordingly.

Components are developed with a specific use-case in mind. Thus, the domain interfaces describing the provided and required services tend to be customized to very specific requirements of an application. This effect limits the re-use of existing components in new applications. The re-use of existing components is one key aspect in software engineering for minimize re-developing existing components. One measure to aspect is to increase reusability. However, re-using components in other application contexts than they have been originally developed for is still a big challenge. This challenge gets even bigger, if such components should be integrated into dynamic adaptive systems at run-time.

A valid approach to tackle this challenge is adaptation. Because of the nature of DAiSI platform, in DAiSI applications, DAiSI components are considered as black boxes. Capabilities and behavior of DAiSI components are specified by interfaces that describe required and provided services. In this approach, we suggest a solution to couple provided and required services that are syntactically incompatible but semantically compatible. To be able to utilize specific provided services that offer the needed data or operations on a semantical level, we suggest constructing an adapter that enables interaction between services that are only compatible on some semantical level [1].

The goal of an adapter is to enable communication between two formerly incompatible components. In order to achieve a common understanding between components, a common knowledge-base is needed. In this work we use ontology as the common knowledge-base to represent services and the schema of data. Ontology and run-time information represented by an ontology language are stored in triplestore. Required interfaces can discover/map the representation of provided interfaces in the database by using a Query Engine. To illustrate that this approach is suitable for adaptive systems, we extend our DAiSI infrastructure by an ontology-based adapter engine for service adaptation.

To strengthen the dynamic adaptive nature of the DAiSI, we generate these adapters at run-time. We argue that these adapters cannot be generated at compile time, because the different components that should interact with each other are not known at compile time, but only at integration time, which is the same requirement just like dynamic adaptive systems.

In this work, we improve the algorithm for discovery of the provided interfaces with using semantic query language and reasoning. Programming interfaces with semantic notation are translated firstly into triplestore readable semantic format and then stored into the triplestore. Required interfaces can discover the required interfaces with help of their semantic description and relation of used ontologies. As opposed to by discovery one-to-one relation of entities of function, input- and output parameters between provided and required interfaces in OWL file, discovery of provide interfaces is supported by using SPARQL, which can represent the entire required interface based on the graph pattern including filter function. Especially, in this work, we use the historical data of output parameters of interface to predicate and filter for discovered provided interfaces.

To illustrate this approach, we use a parking space example to show how to create an adapter to enable interaction between semantical identical components that have been developed by different developers or for different applications.

The rest of this paper is structured as follows: In Section II, we describe the already sketched problem in more detail. Section III gives an overview of relevant related work. In Section IV, we give a short overview of the DAiSI component model and a few hints for further reading. Section V explains structure of the adapter engine and adaptation processes. In Section VI, we show Interface description with using ontology layer. Section VII explains the discovery process of provided services based on query engine and triplestore, before the paper is wrapped up by a short conclusion in Section VIII.

II. Problem Description

Specifications of interfaces between the components in a dynamic adaptive application are mostly the early stage of developing process. Specified interfaces could not be changed, whenever a dynamic adaptive application is developed. They are very domain specific and their definition is driven by the use cases of the future application in mind. To ensure many applications run in a shared context with other applications from different domains, all specified interfaces are centrally managed in a library that is so called interface pool.

It is a tedious task to harmonize one large interface pool among different developers from different vendors that operate in different domains. It often causes results in a slow standardization process. This slows the development process down and, especially in dynamic adaptive systems, diminishes the chances for the development of new applications. Developers will in those cases often start their own interface pool. This, on the other hand, reduces the chances to re-use existing components from other domains.

Additionally, the management of one central interface pool in a distributed system does not scale well. One way to mitigate this issue would be a de-centralization of management of interfaces. To tackle these challenges, we propose to keep the domain interfaces in de-centralization and allow the domain interfaces between different domains un-harmonized.

To be able to harmonize services across domains, every interface pool is required to use ontology. By either merging these ontologies later, or by using distributed ontologies we ensure that interfaces from different interface pools base on a common knowledge. Based on common knowledge, on-the-fly generated adapters enable to interaction syntactically incompatible services across domains.

Services of components can be provided by implementing domain interfaces, so called provided services. Desired services of components can be specified by other domain interfaces, so called required services. In this case, required and provided interfaces could not be the same domain interface. In order to build communication between provided and required services, they must stand in relation to each other, mapping between provided and required services are necessary. In the graphical notation of DAiSI components, provided services are marked as filled circles, required services are noted as semi-circles (similar to the UML lollipop notation [2]) and the relation between those two services are depicted by interfaces notations in domain area and across the DAiSI components linking interface for provided and required services (cf. Figure 1).

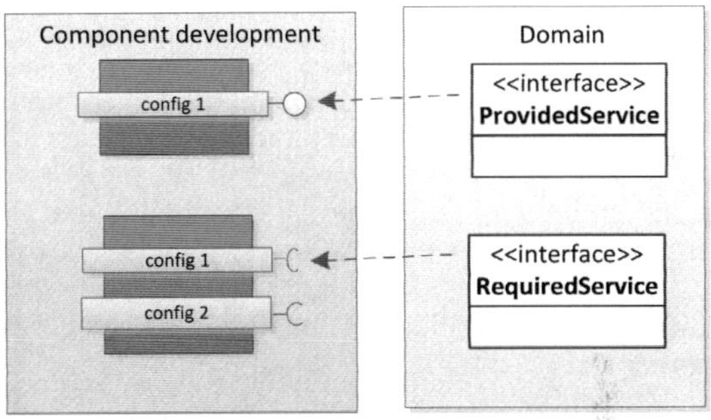

Figure 1. DAiSI components and domain specific interface definitions.

We propose that services that are semantically compatible, but lack compatibility on a syntactical level, should be usable. For example, an application wants to use parking spaces information, which is supported by different system providers. Each provider has its own service, they are mostly not compatible. The lack of compatibility can be covered by the following three types of incompatibility: Different Naming, Different Data Structure, and Different Control Structure. Adapters between the different services can be generated. We believe that we can connect all semantically compatible but syntactically incompatible services using adaptation based on these three types. We illustrate the three types of incompatibility below with parking use case.

A. *Different Naming*

By "Different Naming" we denote cases in which the names of interfaces describing services or names of functions do not match. While they are syntactically different, their names share the same semantics and could be used synonymous.

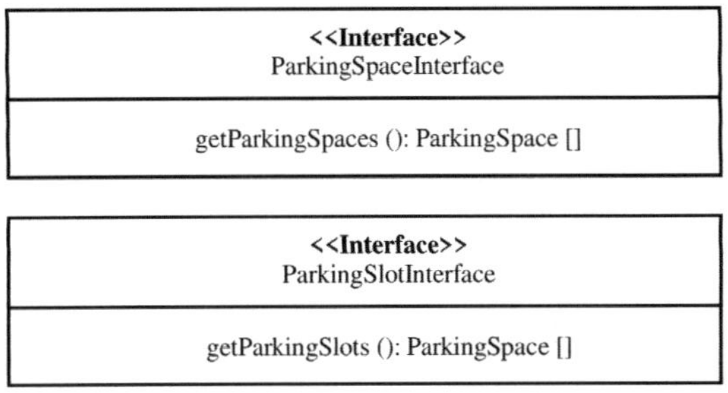

Figure 2. Example of two interfaces with Different Naming.

The first example, depicted in Figure 2, shows two interfaces: ParkingSlotInterface and ParkingSpaceInterface. Each of them defines one of the following methods: getParkingSlots, and getParkingSpaces respectively. The names of their input- and output parameter of the methods are identical. They are named differently, but offer the same service.

B. Different Data Structure

In this type of incompatibility, the names of the interfaces and their functions are the same. However, the parameters differ in their data types. Moreover, the encapsulated data is similar and the data structures can be mapped to each other. In Figure 3, in the Different Data Structure example an interface ParkingSpaceInterfacePV is depicted. It contains a function getParkingSlots which returns a parameter of the type ParkingSpace. In the interface ParkingSpaceInterfaceCS, there is a function getParkinSlots, with the same name but different output parameter ParkingSlot.

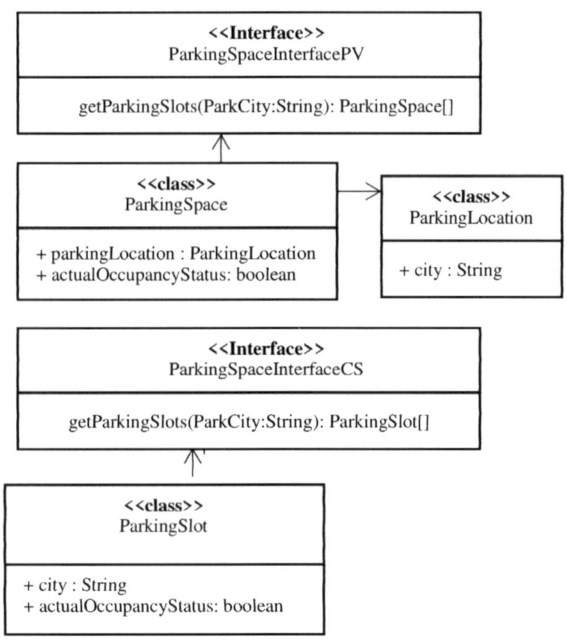

Figure 3. Example of two interfaces with a Different Data Structure.

C. Different Control Structure

In this case, the functions between provided interface and required interface have not one to one relation. One function could be mapped to many functions. To obtain valid results, the control structure has to be modified. In the example in Figure 4, two interfaces ParkingSpaceInterface and ParkingSpaceInterfaceTUC are given. By definition, an opening hour should be composed of the start– and the end time name of a parking space. As such, the two functions getParkingSpaceOpenHour and getParkingSpaceClosedHour from the ParkingSpaceInterfaceTUC interface in comparison provide the same information as getParkingSpaceOpeningHour from the ParkingSpaceInterface interface. Therefore, workflow of functions as a composite process is needed. A composite process specifies control structure of functions involved in the composition, in this example, a sequence control workflow is need for getParkingSpaceOpenHour and getParkingSpaceClosedHour to provide an integrated result to getParkingSpaceOpeningHour.

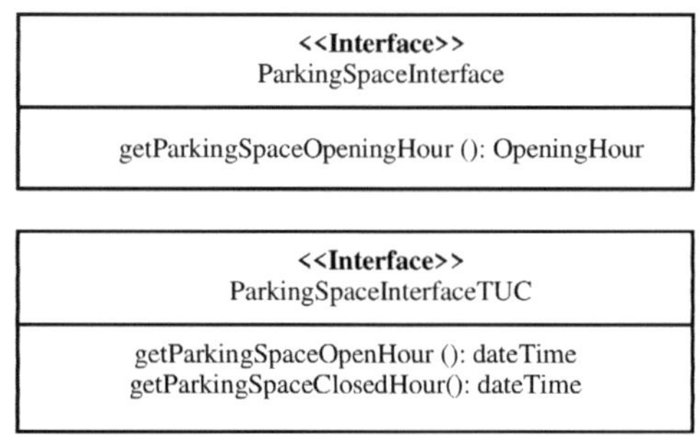

Figure 4. Example of two interface requiring Different Control Structures.

To enable the mapping between interfaces, a common knowledge-base is needed. Because of the issues stated earlier, it should not be mandatory that both sets of interface definitions are of the same domain. A common knowledge base defined by ontologies can be generated using merging or other integration mechanisms on classical ontology languages or by using a distributed ontology language. Both interfaces do not need to contain information on how to interpret the data of each other. That means that interfaces can be developed independently, without knowing anything about a possible re-use in another system.

III. Related Work

A dynamic adaptive system is a system that adjusts its structure and behavior according to the user's needs or to a change in its system context at run-time. The DAiSI is one example of an infrastructure for dynamic adaptive systems [3][4][5][6]. It has been developed over more than a decade by a number of researchers. This work is based on DAiSI and extends the current run-time infrastructure.

According to a publication of M. Yellin and R. Storm, challenges regarding behavioral differences of components have been tackled by many researchers [7]. The behavior of the interface of a component can be described by a protocol with the help of state-machines. The states of two involved components are stored and managed by an adapter. In further steps of this method, ontology is used as a language library to describe a component's behavior. To automate the adaptation of services, a semi-automated method has been developed to generate adapters with the analysis of a possible behavioral mismatch [8][9].

Another solution for the connection of semantically incompatible services is presented in [8]. They use buffers for the asynchronous communication between services and translate the contents of those buffers to match the syntactical representations of the involved services. The behavioral protocols of services can automatically be generated with a tool that is based on synthesis– and testing techniques [10]. Ontologies are used in their method to describe the behavior of components and to create a tool for automated adaptation [11]. Mapping-driven synthesis focuses on mapping of actions of the interfaces of services. Interfaces are identified by correspondence between actions of the interface of component based on the ontology and reasoning [12]. The data mapping is still not considered in this approach. All Approaches mentioned above are based on state-machine. However, some components require a very complex state-machine; the development of which can easily become very expensive. Thus, in this work, we present another way that does not rely on the consideration of dependencies within the behavior or the involved interfaces.

The method of transformation of an ontology into interfaces is already integrated into Corba Ontolingua [13]. With this tool an ontology can be transformed into the interface definition language (IDL). A. Kalyanpur [14] has developed a method which allows automatic mapping from Web Ontology Language (OWL) to Java. The Object Management Group (OMG) [15] has defined how to transform the Unified Markup Language (UML) into ontology. With their method, UML classes are first converted into a helper class and then transformed into ontology [16]. G. Söldner [17] has shown how to transform the UML itself into ontology. A downside of the above methods: The interface and the ontology have a strong relation. If a developer changes the ontology, all interfaces which are linked to this ontology have to be modified. In this work, we decouple this strong relation. Alternating a part of the ontology now only affects the interfaces directly linked to the specific part.

Another approach for semantically described Web service is pressed in [18][19]. Web Service Modeling Ontology (WSMO) is ontology that can be used to describe various aspect related to semantic Web Services. Web Ontology Language for Services (OWL-S) is an ontology for describing Web services. It consists of three elements, ServiceProfile, ServiceModel, and ServiceGrounding. Because of the similar structure of Web service and program interface, we consider OWL-S useful for semantic representation of programming interface of DAiSI components.

Matching and merging existing ontologies is still a big challenge regarding speed and accuracy. To simplify this, many application interfaces (APIs) have been developed, e.g., Agreement Maker [20] and Blooms [21]. Most of them follow a survey approach [22], or use data available on the Internet [23]. Many methods are used to match entities to determine an alignment, like testing, heuristics, etc. To improve accuracy, many of them use third-party vocabularies such as WordNet or Wikipedia. However, we simply use ontology merging in our approach and we did not conduct further research on the challenges mentioned.

IV. The DAiSI Component Model

The DAiSI component model can best be explained with a sketch of a DAiSI component. Figure 5 shows a DAiSI component. The blue rectangle in the background represents the component itself. The provided and required services are depicted with full– and semi circles, as stated earlier. The dependencies between these two kinds of services are depicted by the yellow bars. They are called component configurations. At run-time, only one component configuration can be active. Being active means that all connected, required services are present and consumed (the dependencies could be resolved), and the provided services are being produced. To avoid conflicts, the component configurations are sorted by quality with the best component configuration noted at the top (Conf1 in Figure 5) and the least favorable one noted at the bottom (Conf2 in our example). The following paragraphs explain the DAiSI component model, depicted in Figure 5.

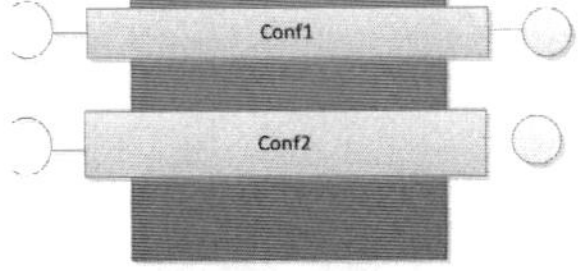

Figure 5. A DAiSI component.

The component model is the core of DAiSI and has been covered in much more detail in [24]. The component configurations (yellow bars) are represented by class with the same name. It is associated to a `RequiredServiceReferenceSet`, which is called a set to account for cardinalities in required services. The provided services are represented by the `ProvidedService` class. Interface roles, represented by `InterfaceRole`, allow the specification of additional constraints for the compatibility of interfaces that use run-time information, bound services and the internal state of a component, and are covered.

To be able to narrow the structure of a dynamic adaptive system down, blueprints of possible system configurations can be specified. The classes `Application`, `Template`, `RequiredTemplateInterface`, and `ProvidedTemplateInterface` are the building blocks in the component model that are used to realize application architecture conformance. One `Application` contains a number of `Templates`, each specifying a part of the possible application. A `Template` defines (needs and offers) `RequiredTemplateInterfaces` and `ProvidedTemplateInterfaces` which refer to `DomainInterfaces` and thus form a structure which can be filled with actual services and components by the infrastructure. More details about templates and application architecture conformance in the DAiSI can be found in [24].

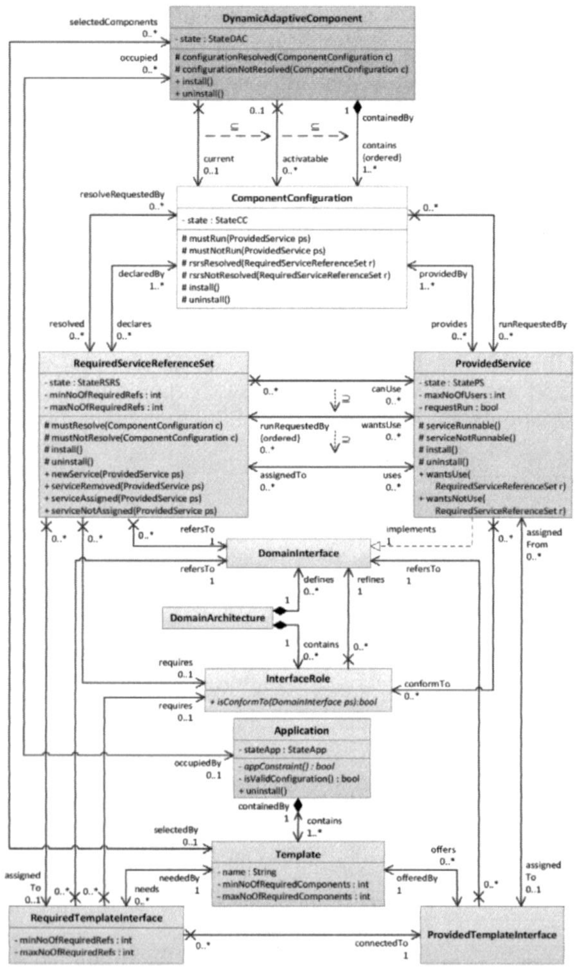

Figure 6. The DAiSI component model.

The DAiSI infrastructure is composed of the DAiSI component model, a registration service, which works like a directory for running DAiSI components, and a configuration service which manages how provided– and required services are connected to each other and what component configurations are marked as active. The configuration service constantly checks (either periodically, or event-driven), if the current system configuration (active component configurations, component bindings, etc.)) can be improved.

For the adaptation of syntactical incompatible services, we added a new infrastructure service: The adapter engine. The adapter engine keeps track of all provided and required services in the system. Whenever a new DAiSI component enters the system, the adapter engine analyzes its provided services and generates adapter components (which are DAiSI components themselves) to all syntactically incompatible, but semantically compatible services. We will describe this process in the following in more detail.

V. DAISI KOMPONENT FOR ADAPTATION

In this section, we show the basic concept of adapter generation based on Java programming language and structure of the adapter engine. In the end we present process for adaptation in DAiSI platform.

A. Basic principle of the adapter

```
//Interface of provided service
public interface ParkingSpaceInterfacePV {
 ArrayList<ParkingSpace> getParkingSpaces(String
parkCity);
}
//Implement of provider interface
public class ParkingSpacePV
        implements ParkingSpaceInterfacePV{
  public ArrayList<ParkingSpace>
             getParkingSlots(String parkCity) {
       }

//Interface of Required Service
public interface ParkingSpaceInterfaceCS {
  ArrayList<ParkingSlot> getParkingSlots(String park-
City);
}
```

Figure 7 Interfaces of service and their implement.

```
// generated adapter
public class generatedAdapter
                implements ParkingSpaceInterfaceCS {
public ArrayList<ParkingSlot>
        getParkingSlots(String parkCity)
    {
        ParkingSpaceInterfacePV ps;
        ArrayList<ParkingSpace> arrParkingSpace;
        ArrayList<ParkingSlot> arrParkingSlots;
                arrParkingSpace =
        ps.getParkingSlots(parkCity);
        arrParkingSlots =
        adapterEngine.mapping(arrParkingSpace);
        return arrParkingSlots;
    }
}
```

Figure 8. Basic principle of the adapter between two interfaces.

```
//Usage of generated adapter of required component
public class requiredComp {
        generatedAdapter adapter;
        ParkingSpaceInterfaceCS cs = adapter;
}
```

Figure 9. Provided interface and connection of adapter.

Adapter is a DAiSI component, which uses provided interface of provided component and implements required interface for required component to manage communications between provided interface and required interface. Required interface of required component uses provided interface of adapter to access provided interface of provided component. Figure 8 shows an example adapter component. The provided service of the adapter component class `generatedAdapter` implements the required interface `ParkingSpaceInterfaceCS` that is shown in Figure 7. The implementation of function `getParkingSlots` of provied interface in the adapter calls the function `getParkingSlots`, which provided by provided interface of provided component. The return of function `getParkingSlots` of required interface are mapped to function of required interface the through the function adapter Engine mapping. **Fehler! Verweisquelle konnte nicht gefunden werden.** shows connection of the adapter and the component with required interface.

B. Structure of the adapter engine

Figure 10 shows the structure of the adapter engine. The task of adapter engine is generating adapter based on semantic description of provided and required interfaces at runtime.

The information collector aggregates the information from provided– and required services (e.g., interface, methods, parameters, and return types) and then translates into knowledge representation language such as Resource Description Framework (RDF) and Web Ontology Language (OWL). In this approach, semantic descriptions of interfaces and related ontology are managed by a central triplestore which is a database for storage RDF triples.

The component Service Discovery discovers provided interfaces for a required interface in triplestore through SPARQL queries and screen out best candidates.

The component Mapper compares the discovered required and provided interface based on sematic descriptions of both interfaces and exports an assignment list, which maps the information from provided services to required services. Mapping of many-to-many relationship of functions is not supported by this work.

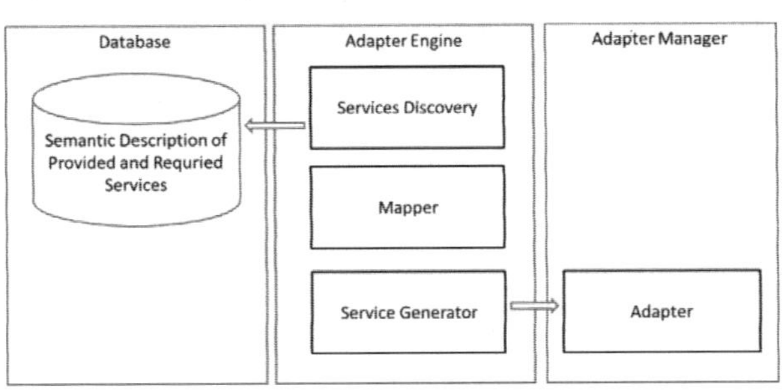

Figure 10. Structure of the adapter engine.

The Service Generator receives the assignment lists from the Mapper and generates a new DAiSI component, which can use the provided interface and implements the required interface. The Adapter Manager is a DAiSI component. It keeps track of the lifecycle of every DAiSI component adapter. Whenever a DAiSI component (provided or required) leaves the system, the adapter Manager destroys all generated adapters related to the DAiSI component and thereby removes them from the system.

C. Adaptation of DAiSi component

Figure 11 shows the process for involved DAiSI component. The component `comp.b` contains a configuration config1, which requires an interface A. The configuration `config1` of component `comp.b` runs at state NOT_RESOLVED as long as it cannot find an interface with same syntax or semantically compatible interface in the system. When the component `comp.a` enters the system, semantic descriptions of provided services are registered into the knowledge-base, this means, the description of service B can be found in the knowledge-base. After this, the service B is provided in the system. Adapter engine can now discover description of service B in triplestore. If service B and service A is syntactically and/or semantically compatible, the adapter engine could check another candidate, which wants to use service `B`, if number of components which service B can only serve are limit. As long as a free place is provided by service B, thus, it generates an adapter – a DAiSI component called adapter, which requires the service `B` and provides service `A`. The DAiSI configuration service connects `comp.b` to adapter and adapter to `comp.a`. The dependency of `comp.b` could be resolved.

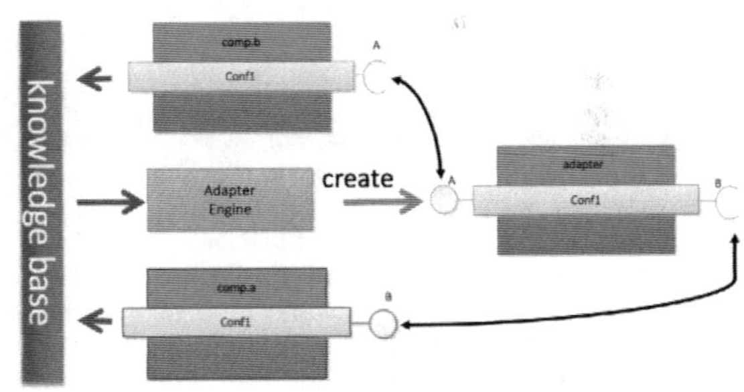

Figure 11. Adaptation process with adapter engine.

VI. SEMANTIC DESCRIPTION OF DAISI COMPONENTS INTERFACE

Description of a machine-readable interface with all relevant semantical information is a key aspect of our concept. In this section we show how to describe a interface semantically.

There are two abstract semantic levels in our system, software level, which contains programming code and instance of parameter (data), semantic level, which provides semantic representation of programming code and data. Required Interface can discover provided interface in triplestore based on his semantic representations. Figure 12 shows interface GetParkingSlot noted with Parking Ontology is represented by ParkingSpace Interface in T-Box. Instances of parameters of interface GetParkingSlot is descripted in A-Box with TUCParkSSE, which link to ParkingSpaceInterface in T-Box.

For our system, we use a four-layer ontolgy structure for the construction of the knowledge-base. The four layers are part of two groups A-Box and T-Box. T-Box describes the concepts of domain in terms of controlled vocabularies, e.g., classes, properties and relationship of classes. A-Box contains the knowledge of instance of domain concepts, e.g., instance of classes. The basic knowledge is defined in the T-Box group. Such knowledge can be divided in different upper ontologies. Corresponding of ontologies can be merged, if different dynamic adaptive systems are being associated. Merging ontologies is a different research area on which we do not focus, however, the available results are sufficient for our work.

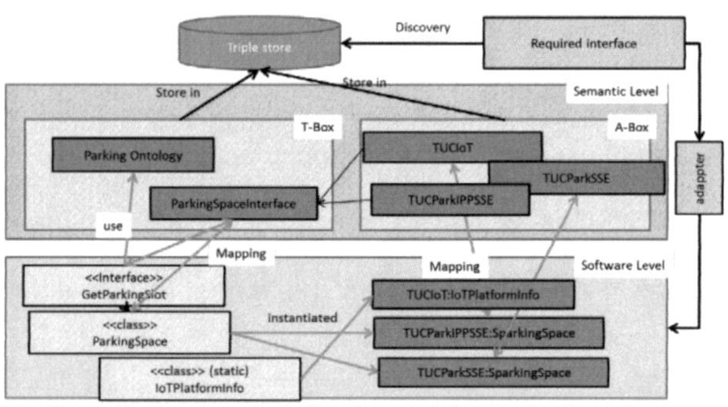

Figure 12. Overview of relation of semantic level and software level.

Figure 13 shows the four-layer ontology structure. The Basic Thing and Domain independent Ontologie, called Upperontolgoy layer, define the basic knowledge, which can be widely used in different domains and has already got agreement by many committees, such as OWL-S, schema.org, Dbpedia, etc. Domain ontology describes the domain related vocabularies. Every application or domain can define its own domain ontology. In the Domain Ontology, which is the second, or middle layer, all necessary definitions can be found that are relevant for an application. In our approach, we develop a parking ontolgoy for our application to extentent the vocabularies for the parking relevant services. The layer of the Application dependent ontology is the lowest level in T-Box. It represents the code of domain interfaces, more precisely their names, methods, parameters and return types. The domain dependent and independant ontology could be used in the application ontology in order to enriche the represention of services. This three-layer ontology in T-Box has the main advantage that every part can be developed separately. Every fragment of a layer can be merged with other fragments using ontolgy-merging and ontolgy-mapping. In addition, data, e.g., instance of java class or vaule of parameter, can be semantically represented in the A-Box.

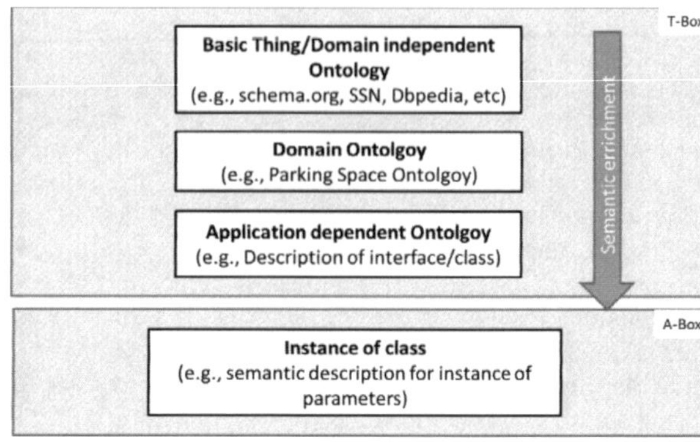

Figure 13. Layers ontology structure.

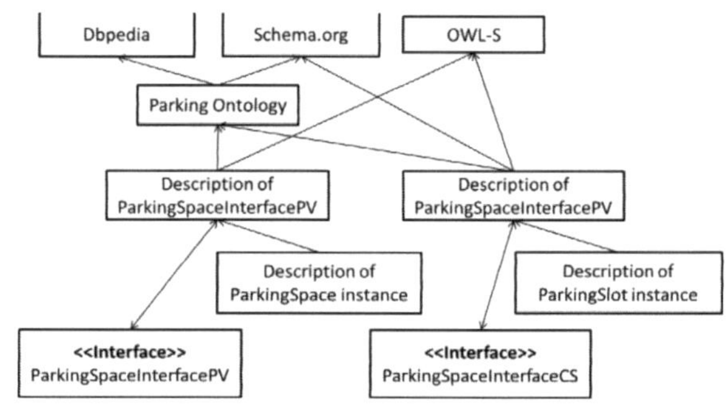

Figure 14. Data structure of the example.

Figure 14 shows the layout of the ontologies for the parking use case. We used upmost ontologies, OWL-S, Dbpedia and Schema.org. The Parking ontolgoy is delevoped based on the Dbpedia and schema.org. To describe interfaces, OWL-S is needed to define relations for representation of the interfaces, like methods, relation between parameters and methods. Paramter and return tpyes are created as new ontolgoy and directly mapped to the existing ontolgoy like Parking Ontolgoy, Dbpedia, etc. Represention of interface has no limit to usage of ontologies. Every information in any of the ontologies can be used in any interface. Semantic description of interface and java Interface can be bi-directional translated. Each description of interface could have an ontology item, in order to facilitate management of the ontology data in datastore such as updata, remove, modification. Run-time information such as instance of input and output parameters, so called datatyp object, could be descripted with owl instance of owl class, which can be found in T-Box. In our approach, we use historical datatyp objects to increase accuracy of services discovery. The following examples show how the Ontology is defined.

A. *Domain independent ontology*

Domain independent ontologies could be used for different domains. They are independent on domains and commonly are upper ontology to define basic vocabularies and data schema, e.g., schema.org, which is schemas for structured data on the Internet, Semantic Sensor Network Ontology (SSN), which can be used to describe sensor, observations and related concepts. In our approach, Domain independent ontology can be used to directly describe interface and to link to the domain dependent ontology. Especially, OWL-S is an important part for description of interfaces.

OWL-S is one ontology for describing Web services. The essence of semantic Web Servic description is to realize automatic web Service discovery, which shares the same goals of automatic adaptation of DAiSI components in our approach. Three elements of OWL-S, ServiceProfile, ProcessModel and ServiceGrounding, can be well mapped to DAiSI services. ServiceProfile uses for publishing and discovering services. ProcessModel describes in detail for the operation of a service. ServiceGrounding provides details of how the message service interoperability. In particular, because of similarity of ServiceProfile and interface, ServiceProfile can be used to describe programming interface.

Figure 15 shows relation of OWL-S and programming interface. Interface name can be descripted with Ontology Serviceprofile, which are depicted by anelliptical shape. Function name corresponds to process and input and output parameter corresponds to process:input and process:ouput.

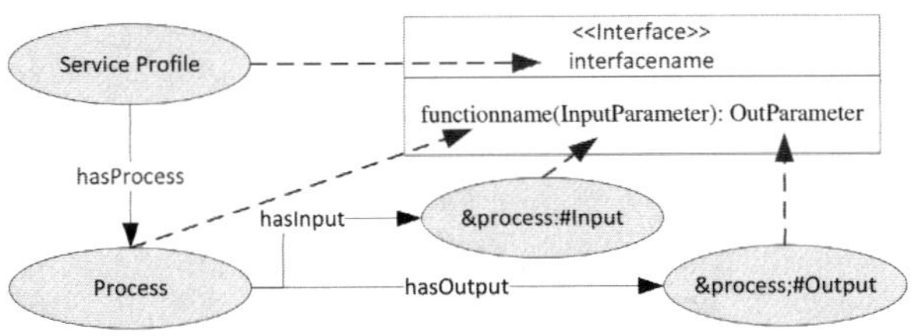

Figure 15. Relationship of programming interface and process in OWL-S.

B. *Application Ontology Parking Ontolgoy*

Unfortunately, domain independent ontology cannot cover requirements of vocabularies in every individual domain. We need to develop domain ontologies to meet the demand. Domain ontology can use the independent domain ontology to increase its reusability.

In our approach, we define a Parking Ontology. Parking Ontology is an ontology, which describes Parking space relevant issues, such as location, usage, ticket, opening hours, etc. Figure 16 shows a fragment of Parking Ontology, which contains relevant parts for the example in this paper. ParkingSpace is the main part, it relates to ParkingLocation with OWL objectproperty parkingLocation and StatusOfParkingSpot with statusOfParkingSport. ParkingLocation is static information.Static means, the information is not modified in run-time, mostly the value is stored in database or local in device. StatusOfParkingSpot is run-time information, which's value can be changed at run-time.

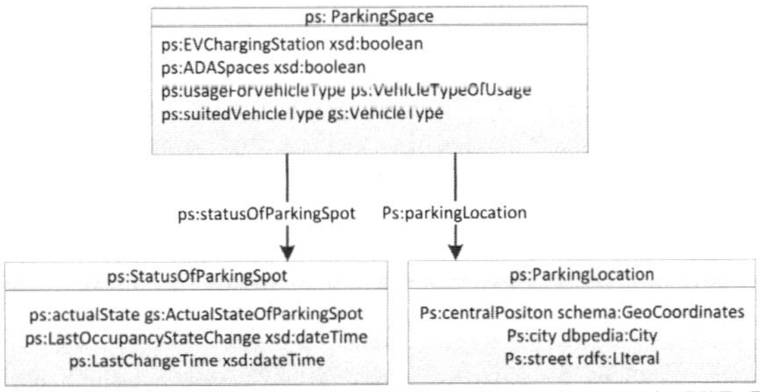

Figure 16. Relationship of programming interface and process in OWL-S.

C. *Descrption of Interface*

To semantically understand programming interfaces, they should be translated into semantic technology supported data format. In fact, the chosen sematic language has big influence for interface discovery. On the one hand, translation between semantic data formats is supported mostly only in one direction, e.g., JSON-LD can be translated into RDF/XML, but it is difficult to translate it back to its original format. On the other hand, format of results of the translations from different language of same programming interface are usually not identical. Therefore, in our approach, we use only semantic Language RDF/XML, so that the system is kept more harmonious.

In this work, we use OWL-S (implemented in RDF/XML) to descript an interface. The descriptions are separated into 3 parts, description interface, description function, description parameters.

1) *Interface description*

Figure 17 shows an interface description. An interface contains many methods, which are described by processes. In this example, an interface is described by the process `GetParkingProcess` with Service:describedBy.

```
<service:Service rdf:ID="ParkingSlotService">
    <service:presents
    rdf:resource="&Parking_profile;#Profile_Parkin
    gSlot_Service"/>
    <service:describedBy
    rdf:resource="&Parking_process;#GetParkingProc
    ess"/>
</service:Service>
```

Figure 17. interface description.

2) *Function description*

Figure 18 shows the structure of a method description. A method is described by AtomicProcess and constants of input and output parameters. The parameter can use existing ontology, e.g., for input `ParkingCity` use Ontology from Ddpeida `db;#City`, or use self-defining parameter `THIS;#ParkingSlot`, which we will show below.

```
<process:AtomicProcess rdf:ID=getParkingProcess">
   <process:hasInput>
       <process:Input rdf:ID="ParkingCity">
       <process:parameterType
       rdf:datatype="&xsd;#string">&db;#City</pro
       cess:parameterType>
       </process:Input>
   </process:hasInput>
   <process:hasOutput>
       <process:Output
       rdf:ID="ExpressParkingSpace">
       <process:parameterType
       rdf:datatype="&xsd;#anyURI">&THIS;#Parking
       Slot</process:parameterType>
       </process:Output>
   </process:hasOutput>
</process:AtomicProcess>
```

Figure 18. Function description.

3) Input and Output Parameter

Figure 19 shows the self-defining parameter description. Self-defining datatype is described by owl-class and relate to the developed Parking Ontology. Linking to existing Ontologies ensures the relations between the elements of different parameters can be also discovered. Each relations for this class should be described by owl:objectproperty or owl:dataproperty and relate to existing ontology on demand.

```
<owl:Class rdf:ID="ParkingSlot">
   <owl:equivalentClass
   rdf:resource="&ps;#ParkingSpace"/>
</owl:Class>

<owl:ObjectProperty rdf:about="parkingLocation">
   <owl:equivalentProperty
   rdf:resource="&ps;#parkingLocation"/>
   <rdfs:range rdf:resource="#ParkingLocation"/>
   <rdfs:domain rdf:resource="#ParkingSlot"/>
</owl:ObjectProperty>

<owl:ObjectProperty
rdf:about="actualOccupancyStatus">
   <owl:equivalentProperty
rdf:resource="&ps;#ActualState"/>
   <rdfs:range
rdf:resource="#ActualStatueOfParkingSpot"/>
   <rdfs:domain rdf:resource="#ParkingSlot"/>
</owl:ObjectProperty>
```

Figure 19. Two example interfaces with annotations.

D. Java-Annotations for the Interface and Class Description

Programming interface and semantic interface description should be bilateral transformable. In this approach, Java is used to implement DAiSI framework. We use an aspect oriented method – annotations in Java as a link between the ontology and the actual implementation.

In an interface, every element has at least one label that links it to the ontology. Every label has an attribute `hasName` to reference the ontology. Ontology names can be found in the application layer. Interface names, for example, need only one label: `@Interfacename`. Functions have three types of labels: `@Activity`, `@OutputParam` and `@InputParameter`. The label for input or output is used only if a function has input– or output parameters. With the help of annotations, the definition of elements of an interface is decoupled from the actual ontology. This measure was taken to ease the changes of either an interface or the ontology, without the necessity to alter both. The code-snippets in Figure 20 present two Java interfaces as examples.

```
@Interfacename(hasName = " ParkingSlotService")
public interface ParkingSpaceInterfacePV{
   @Activity(hasName = "GetParkingProcess")
   @OutputParam(hasName= "ParkingSpace")
   public ParkingSpace []getParkingSlots (
      @Inputparam(hasName = "&db;#City")
         ParkCity:String);
   }
```

Figure 20. Example interface with annotations.

VII. Discovery and Mapping

Discovery and Mapping play an important role in adapter. In this approach, discovery process bases on database, which stores semantic information of services. Mapper uses results from discovery process to create the alignment between required and provided DAiSI services. In this section, we present the details below.

A. Storage of Semantic Information.

Semantic descriptions of all interfaces should storage in dynamic adaptive systems. Management of huge information in memory is a big challenge for the device. Therefore, we store semantic information in permanent storage to tackle this issue. Triplestore is a kind of database for storing RDF triples. It can build on relational database or non-relational such as Graph-base databases. Querying of semantic information in these databases is partly supported by the SPARQL.

The ontology layers, which mentioned above, are not forced to be stored in one triplestore. They could be distributed in different databases and expose their ontology through a Web service end-point, typically urls in an ontology, so that increase the reusability of the ontology. SPARQL engine supports partly discovery in using such external urls. In order to reduce management difficulty, we save domain ontology, application ontology and corresponding instance of parameters in a database.

Input and output parameters contain two kinds of information, static value and dynamic value. Static value is value of parameter, which usually save in local database and do not change in the run-time. Accordingly, dynamic value changes at run-time. However, because of huge amount of data, it is difficout even impossible to store all historical datat in database. Therefore, in our appraoch, we store last few historical data.

B. Discovery

SPARQL is a set of specifications that define a query language for RDF data, concerning explicit object and prop erty relations, along with protocols for querying, and serialization formats for the results. Reasoner can infer new triples by applying rules on the data, e.g., RDFS reasoner, OWL reasoner, transitive reasoner and general purpose rule engine. By using reasoner more required information can be found, e.g., equivalent classes, classes with parents relation, etc. SPARQL engine can use reasoner in forward chaining, which proceed to add any inferred triples to data set in data store, and backward chaining, which reasoning between a SPARQL endpoint and the data store. Backward chaining is used when ontologies are constantly updated. DAiSI is an adaptive system, components frequently enter and discharge a system, this issue causes regularly addition of new ontologies for service of components in data store. Hereby, change backward chaining is most suitable for DAiSI.

Discovery has two steps, first step is discovery with definition of interface's information, that means only with interface name, input and output parameter name; second step is using static instance information of class to filter results. E.g., application wants to look for services, which could provide parking space in Clausthal in Germany. In the first step, all semantic compatible interfaces, which could provide parking spaces in different locations, are found. Locations of parking spaces are static information which saved mostly in database. Such location information can be used to filter the mount of discovered interfaces to find interfaces which can provide parking spaces in Clausthal. Using static information avoids accessing each interface, so that it avoids the side effect, -component state changed with calling function.

```
select ?interface
where {
?interface <process#hasInput> ?var
?var <process#paramterTyp> "dbpedia#City"

?interface <process#hasOutput> ?var2
?var2 <process#paramterTyp> "this#ParkingSlotApp"
}
```

Figure 21. Example SPARQL query.

Figure 21 shows the SPARQL query example. To find interface we need description required input and output parameters in query. Query could be created directly from semantic noted programming interface.

C. Mapping

Discovery result is the interface name of component. In order to create an adapter we need create details relation between required and provide interface. Mapping of each parameter in input and output parameter can be restructured with help of his sematic annotation. According to the results of mapping, an adapter (new DAiSI component) will be created.

VIII. Conclusion

This paper is an extended version of the work published in [1]. In first approach, we presented the enhancement to the DAiSI: A new infrastructure service. Syntactically incompatible services can be connected with the help of generated adapters, which are created by the adapter engine. The adapter engine is prototypically implemented with Java. Reuse of component across different domains is enabled with this approach. In this paper, we extend our previous work by detail of the layered structure of ontologies, an improved discovery process based on SPARQL and triplestore. The new layer structure supports description of instance of parameters and it increases the re-use of ontology. By using triplestore and SPARQL, it facilitates discovery service in a huge number of components. Semantic description hat still strength influence on discovery results. In further steps, we will reduce the closed related relation between semantic description and discovery.

IX. Acknowledgement

This work is supported by BIG IoT (Bridging the Interoperability Gap of the Internet of Things) project funded by the European Union's Horizon 2020 research and innovation programme under grant agreement No. 688038

References

[1] Y. Wang, D. Herrling, P. Stroganov, and A. Rausch, "Ontology-based Automatic Adaptation of Component Interfaces in Dynamic Adaptive Systems," in Proceeding of ADAPTIVE 2016, The Eighth International conference on Adaptive and Self-Adaptive Systems and Application, 2016, pp. 51-59.

[2] OMG, OMG Unified Modeling Language (OMG UML) Superstructure, Version 2.4.1, Object Management Group Std., August 2011, http://www.omg.org/spec/UML/2.4.1, [Online], retrieved: 06.2015.

[3] H. Klus and A. Rausch, "DAiSI–A Component Model and Decentralized Configuration Mechanism for Dynamic Adaptive Systems," in Proceedings of ADAPTIVE 2014, The Sixth International Conference on Adaptive and Self-Adaptive Systems and Applications,Venice, Italy, 2014, pp. 595–608.

[4] H. Klus, "Anwendungsarchitektur-konforme Konfiguration selbstorganisierender Softwaresysteme," (Application architecture conform configuration of self-organizing software-systems), Clausthal-Zellerfeld, Technische Universität Clausthal, Department of Informatics, Dissertation, 2013.

[5] D. Niebuhr, "Dependable Dynamic Adaptive Systems: Approach, Model, and Infrastructure," Clausthal-Zellerfeld, Technische Universität Clausthal, Department of Informatics, Dissertation, 2010.

[6] D. Niebuhr and A. Rausch, "Guaranteeing Correctness of Component Bindings in Dynamic Adaptive Systems based on Run-time Testing," in Proceedings of the 4th Workshop on Services Integration in Pervasive Environments (SIPE 09) at the International Conference on Pervasive Services 2009, (ICSP 2009), 2009, pp. 7–12.

[7] D. M. Yellin and R. E. Strom, "Protocol Specifications and Component Adaptors," ACM Transactions on Programming Languages and Systems, vol. 19, 1997, pp. 292–333.

[8] C. Canal and G. Salaün, "Adaptation of Asynchronously Communicating Software," in Lecture Notes in Computer Science, vol. 8831, 2014, pp. 437–444.

[9] J. Camara, C. Canal, J. Cubo, and J. Murillo, "An Aspect-Oriented Adaptation Framework for Dynamic Component Evolution," Electronic Notes in Theoretical Computer Science, vol. 189, 2007, pp. 21–34.

[10] A. Bertolino, P. Inverardi, P. Pelliccione, and M. Tivoli, "Automatic Synthesis of Behavior Protocols for Composable Web-Services," Proceedings of the the 7th Joint Meeting of the European Software Engineering Conference and the ACM SIGSOFT Symposium on The Foundations of Software Engineering, 2009, pp. 141–150.

[11] A. Bennaceur, C. Chilton, M. Isberner, and B. Jonsson, "Automated Mediator Synthesis: Combining Behavioural and Ontological Reasoning," Software Engineering and Formal Methods, SEFM – 11th International Conference on Software Engineering and Formal Methods, 2013, Madrid, Spain, pp. 274–288.

[12] A. Bennaceur, L. Cavallaro, P. Inverardi, V. Issarny, R. Spalazzese, D. Sykes and M. Tivoli, "Dynamic connector synthesis: revised prototype implementation,", 2012.

[13] OMG, "CORBA Middleware Specifications," Version 3.3, Object Management Group Std., November 2012, http://www.omg.org/spec/#MW, [Online], retrieved: 02.2016.

[14] A. Kalyanpur, D. Jimenez, S. Battle, and J. Padget, "Automatic Mapping of OWL Ontologies into Java," in F. Maurer and G. Ruhe, Proceedings of the 17th International Conference on Software Engineering and Knowledge Engineering, SEKE'2004, 2004, pp. 98–103.

[15] OMG, OMG Unified Modeling Language (OMG UML) Superstructure, Version 2.4.1, Object Management Group Std., August 2011, http://www.omg.org/spec/UML/2.4.1, [Online], retrieved: 06.2015.

[16] J. Camara, C. Canal, J. Cubo, and J. Murillo, "An Aspect-Oriented Adaptation Framework for Dynamic Component Evolution," Electronic Notes in Theoretical Computer Science, vol. 189, 2007, pp. 21–34.

[17] G. Söldner, "Semantische Adaption von Komponenten," (semantic adaption of components), Dissertation, Friedrich-Alexander-Universität Erlangen-Nürberg, 2012.

[18] D. Martin, M. Bursten, J.Hobbs, et al., "OWL-S: Semantic markup for web services," W3C member submission, 22, 2007-04.

[19] D. Martin, M. Bursten, J.Hobbs, et al., "OWL-S: Semantic markup for web services," W3C member submission, 22, 2007-04.

[20] D. Faria, C. Pesquita, E. Santos, M. Palmonari, F. Cruz, and M. F. Couto, The AgreementMakerLight ontology matching system, in On the Move to Meaningful Internet Systems: OTM 2013 Conferences, Springer Berlin Heidelberg, pp. 527–541.

[21] P. Jain, P. Z. Yeh, K. Verma, R. G. Vasquez, M. Damova, P. Hitzler, and A. P. Sheth, "Contextual ontology alignment of lod with an upper ontology: A case study with proton," in The Semantic Web: Research and Applications, Springer Berlin Heidelberg, 2011, pp. 80–92.

[22] P. Shvaiko and J. Euzenat, "Ontology matching: state of the art and future challenges," IEEE Transactions on Knowledge and Data Engineering, vol. 25(1), 2013, pp. 158–176.

[23] M. K. Bergmann, "50 Ontology Mapping and Alignment Tools," in Adaptive Information, Adaptive Innovation, Adaptive Infrastructure, http://www.mkbergman.com/1769/50-ontology-mapping-and-alignment-tools/, July 2014, [Online], retrieved: 02.2016.

[24] H. Klus, A. Rausch, and D. Herrling, "Component Templates and Service Applications Specifications to Control Dynamic Adaptive System Configuration," in Proceedings of AMBIENT 2015, The Fifth International Conference on Ambient Computing, Applications, Services and Technologies, Nice, France, 2015, pp. 42–51.

International Journal on Advances in Software, vol 9 no 3 & 4, year 2016, http://www.iariajournals.org/software/

Implementing a Typed Javascript and its IDE: a case-study with Xsemantics

Lorenzo Bettini

Dip. Statistica, Informatica, Applicazioni
Università di Firenze, Italy
Email: lorenzo.bettini@unifi.it

Jens von Pilgrim, Mark-Oliver Reiser

NumberFour AG,
Berlin, Germany
Email: {jens.von.pilgrim, mark-oliver.reiser}@numberfour.eu

Abstract—**Developing a compiler and an IDE for a programming language is time consuming and it poses several challenges, even when using language workbenches like Xtext that provides Eclipse integration. A complex type system with powerful type inference mechanisms needs to be implemented efficiently, otherwise its implementation will undermine the effective usability of the IDE: the editor must be responsive even when type inference takes place in the background, otherwise the programmer will experience too many lags. In this paper, we will present a real-world case study: N4JS, a JavaScript dialect with a full-featured Java-like static type system, including generics, and present some evaluation results. We will describe the implementation of its type system and we will focus on techniques to make the type system implementation of N4JS integrate efficiently with Eclipse. For the implementation of the type system of N4JS we use Xsemantics, a DSL for writing type systems, reduction rules and in general relation rules for languages implemented in Xtext. Xsemantics is intended for developers who are familiar with formal type systems and operational semantics since it uses a syntax that resembles rules in a formal setting. This way, the implementation of formally defined type rules can be implemented easier and more directly in Xsemantics than in Java.**

Keywords–DSL; Type System; Implementation; Eclipse.

I. INTRODUCTION

In this paper, we present N4JS, a JavaScript dialect implemented with Xtext, with powerful type inference mechanisms (including Java-like generics). In particular, we focus on the implementation of its type system. The type system of N4JS is implemented in Xsemantics, an Xtext DSL to implement type systems and reduction rules for DSLs implemented in Xtext.

The type system of N4JS drove the evolution of Xsemantics: N4JS' complex type inference system and the fact that it has to be used in production with large code bases forced us to enhance Xsemantics in many parts. The implementation of the type system of N4JS focuses both on the performance of the type system and on its integration in the Eclipse IDE.

This paper is the extended version of the conference paper [1]. With respect to the conference version, in this paper we describe more features of Xsemantics, we provide a full description of the main features of N4JS and we describe its type system implementation in more details. Motivations, related work and conclusions have been extended and enhanced accordingly.

The paper is structured as follows. In Section II we introduce the context of our work and we motivate it; we also discuss some related work. We provide a small introduction to Xtext in Section III and we show the main features of Xsemantics in Section IV. In Section V, we present N4JS and its main features. In Section VI, we describe the implementation of the type system of N4JS with Xsemantics, with some performance benchmarks related to the type system. Section VII concludes the paper.

II. MOTIVATIONS AND RELATED WORK

Integrated Development Environments (IDEs) help programmers a lot with features like syntax aware editor, compiler and debugger integration, build automation and code completion, just to mention a few. In an agile [2] and test-driven context [3] the features of an IDE like Eclipse become essential and they dramatically increase productivity.

Developing a compiler and an IDE for a language is usually time consuming, even when relying on a framework like Eclipse. Implementing the parser, the model for the Abstract Syntax Tree (AST), the validation of the model (e.g., type checking), and connecting all the language features to the IDE components require lot of manual programming. Xtext, `http://www.eclipse.org/Xtext`, [4], [5] is a popular Eclipse framework for the development of programming languages and Domain-Specific Languages (DSLs), which eases all these tasks.

A language with a static type system usually features better IDE support. Given an expression and its static type, the editor can provide all the completions that make sense in that program context. For example, in a Java-like method invocation expression, the editor should propose only the methods and fields that are part of the class hierarchy of the receiver expression, and thus, it needs to know the static type of the receiver expression. The same holds for other typical IDE features, like, for example, navigation to declaration and quickfixes.

The type system and the interpreter for a language implemented in Xtext are usually implemented in Java. While this works for languages with a simple type system, it becomes a problem for an advanced type system. Since the latter is often formalized, a DSL enabling the implementation of a type system similar to the formalization would be useful. This would reduce the gap between the formalization of a language and its actual implementation.

Besides functional aspects, implementing a complex type system with powerful type inference mechanisms poses several challenges due to performance issues. Modern IDEs and compilers have defined a high standard for performance of compilation and responsiveness of typical user interactions, such as content assist and immediate error reporting. At the same time, modern statically-typed languages tend to reduce the verbosity of the syntax with respect to types by implementing type inference systems that relieve the programmer from the burden of declaring types when these can be inferred from the context. In order to be able to cope with these high demands on both type inference and performance, efficiently implemented type systems are required.

In [6] Xsemantics, `http://xsemantics.sf.net`, was introduced. Xsemantics is a DSL for writing rules for languages implemented in Xtext, in particular, the *static semantics* (type system), the *dynamic semantics* (operational semantics) and relation rules (subtyping). Given the type system specification, Xsemantics generates Java code that can be used in the Xtext implementation. Xsemantics specifications have a declarative flavor that resembles formal systems (see, e.g., [7], [8]), while keeping the Java-like shape. This makes it usable both by formal theory people and by Java programmers.

Originally, Xsemantics was focused on easy implementation of prototype languages. While the basic principles of Xsemantics were not changed, Xsemantics has been improved a lot in order to make it usable for modern full-featured languages and real-world performance requirements [9]. In that respect, N4JS drove the evolution of Xsemantics. In fact, N4JS' complex type inference system and its usage in production with large code bases forced us to enhance Xsemantics in many parts. The most relevant enhanced parts in Xsemantics dictated by N4JS can be summarized as follows:

- Enhanced handling of the rule environment, simplifying implementation of type systems with generics.
- Fields and imports, simplifying the use of Java utility class libraries from within an Xsemantics system definition.
- The capability of extending an existing Xsemantics system definition, improving the modularization of large systems.
- Improved error reporting customization, in order to provide the user with more information about errors.
- Automatic caching of results of rule computations, increasing performance.

Xsemantics itself is implemented in Xtext, thus it is completely integrated with Eclipse and its tooling. From Xsemantics we can access any existing Java library, and we can even debug Xsemantics code. It is not mandatory to implement the whole type system in Xsemantics: we can still implement parts of the type system directly in Java, in case some tasks are easier to implement in Java. In an existing language implementation, this also allows for an easy incremental or partial transition to Xsemantics. All these features have been used in the implementation of the type system of N4JS.

A. *Related work*

In this section we discuss some related work concerning both language workbenches and frameworks for specifying type systems.

Xsemantics can be considered the successor of Xtypes [10]. With this respect, Xsemantics provides a much richer syntax for rules that can access any existing Java library. This implies that, while with Xtypes many type computations could not be expressed, this does not happen in Xsemantics. Moreover, Xtypes targets type systems only, while Xsemantics deals with any kind of rules.

XTS [11] (Xtext Type System) is a DSL for specifying type systems for DSLs built with Xtext. The main difference with respect to Xsemantics is that XTS aims at expression based languages, not at general purpose languages. Indeed, it is not straightforward to write the type system for a Java-like language in XTS. Type systems specifications are less verbose in XTS, since it targets type systems only, but XTS does not allow introducing new relations as Xsemantics, and it does not target reductions rules. Xsemantics aims at being similar to standard type inference and semantics rules so that anyone familiar with formalization of languages can easily read a type system specification in Xsemantics.

OCL (Object Constraint Language) [12], [13] allows the developer to specify constraints in metamodels. While OCL is an expression language, Xsemantics is based on rules. Although OCL is suitable for specifying constraints, it might be hard to use to implement type inference.

Neverlang [14] is based on the fact that programming language features can be plugged and unplugged, e.g., you can "plug" exceptions, switch statements or any other linguistic constructs into a language. It also supports composition of specific Java constructs [15]. Similarly, JastAdd [16] supports modular specifications of extensible compiler tools and languages. Eco [17], [18] is a language composition editor for defining composed languages and edit programs of such composed languages. The Spoofax [19] language workbench provides support for language extensions and embeddings. Polyglot [20] is a compiler front end for Java aiming at Java language extensions. However, it does not provide any IDE support for the implemented extension. Xtext only provides single inheritance mechanisms for grammars, so different grammars can be composed only linearly. In Xsemantics a system can extend an existing one (adding and overriding rules). These extensibility and compositionality features are not as powerful as the ones of the systems mentioned above, but we think they should be enough for implementing *pluggable type systems* [21].

There are other tools for implementing DSLs and IDE tooling (we refer to [22], [23], [24] for a wider comparison). Tools like IMP (The IDE Meta-Tooling Platform) [25] and DLTK (Dynamic Languages Toolkit), `http://www.eclipse.org/dltk`, only deal with IDE features. TCS (Textual Concrete Syntax) [26] aims at providing the same mechanisms as Xtext. However, with Xtext it is easier to describe the abstract and concrete syntax at once. Morever, Xtext is completely open to customization of every part of the generated IDE. EMFText [27] is similar to Xtext. Instead of deriving a metamodel from the grammar, the language to be implemented must be defined in an abstract way using an EMF metamodel.

The Spoofax [19], language workbench mentioned above, relies on Stratego [28] for defining rule-based specifications for the type system. In [29], Spoofax is extended with a collection of declarative meta-languages to support all the aspects of language implementation including verification infrastructure and interpreters. These meta-languages include NaBL [30] for name binding and scope rules, TS for the type system and DynSem [31] for the operational semantics. Xsemantics shares with these systems the goal of reducing the gap between the formalization and the implementation. An interesting future investigation is adding the possibility of specifying scoping rules in an Xsemantics specification as well. This way, also the Xtext scope provider could be easily generated automatically by Xsemantics.

EriLex [32] is a software tool for generating support code for embedded domain specific languages and it supports specifying syntax, type rules, and dynamic semantics of such languages but it does not generate any artifact for IDE tooling.

An Xsemantics specification can access any Java type, not only the ones representing the AST. Thus, Xsemantics might also be used to validate any model, independently from Xtext itself, and possibly be used also with other language frameworks like EMFText [27]. Other approaches, such as, e.g., [33], [34], [35], [36], [37], [32], [14], instead require the programmer to use the framework also for defining the syntax of the language.

The importance of targeting IDE tooling when implementing a language was recognized also in older frameworks, such as Synthesizer [38] and Centaur [33]. In both cases, the use of a DSL for the type system was also recognized (the latter was using several formalisms [39], [40], [41]). Thus, Xsemantics enhances the usability of Xtext for developing prototype implementations of languages during the study of the formalization of languages.

We just mention other tools for the implementation of DSLs that are different from Xtext and Xsemantics for the main goal and programming context, such as, e.g., [42], [43], [44], which are based on language specification preprocessors, and [45], [46], which target host language extensions and internal DSLs.

Xsemantics does not aim at providing mechanisms for formal proofs for the language and the type system and it does not produce (like other frameworks do, e.g., [47], [29]), versions of the type system for proof assistants, such as Coq [48], HOL [49] or Isabelle [50]. However, Xsemantics can still help when writing the meta-theory of the language. An example of such a use-case, using the traces of the applied rules, can be found in [9].

We chose Xtext since it is the de-facto standard framework for implementing DSLs in the Eclipse ecosystem, it is continuously supported, and it has a wide community, not to mention many applications in the industry. Xtext is continuously evolving, and the main new features introduced in recent versions include the integration in other IDEs (mainly, IntelliJ), and the support for programming on the Web (i.e., an Xtext DSL can be easily ported on a Web application).

Finally, Xtext provides complete support for typical Java build tools, like Maven and Gradle. Thus, Xtext DSLs also automatically support these build tools. In that respect, Xsemantics provides Maven artifacts so that Xsemantics files can be processed during the Maven build in a Continuous Integration system.

III. XTEXT

In this section we will give a brief introduction to Xtext. In Section III-A we will also briefly describe the main features of Xbase, which is the expression language used in Xsemantics' rules.

It is out of the scope of the paper to describe Xtext and Xbase in details. Here we will provide enough details to make the features of Xsemantics understandable.

Xtext [5] is a *language workbench* (such as MPS [51] and Spoofax [19]): Xtext deals not only with the compiler mechanisms but also with Eclipse-based tooling. Starting from a grammar definition, Xtext generates an ANTLR parser [52]. During parsing, the AST is automatically generated by Xtext as an EMF model (Eclipse Modeling Framework [53]). Besides, Xtext generates many other features for the Eclipse editor for the language that we are implementing: syntax highlighting, background parsing with error markers, outline view, code completion.

Most of the code generated by Xtext can already be used as it is, but other parts, like type checking, have to be customized. The customizations rely on Google-Guice, a *dependency injection* framework [54].

In the following we describe the two complementary mechanisms of Xtext that the programmer has to implement. Xsemantics aims at generating code for both mechanisms.

Scoping is the mechanism for binding the symbols (i.e., references). Xtext supports the customization of binding with the abstract concept of *scope*, i.e., all declarations that are available (visible) in the current context of a reference. The programmer provides a `ScopeProvider` to customize the scoping. In Java-like languages the scoping will have to deal with types and inheritance relations, thus, it is strictly connected with the type system. For example, the scope for methods in the context of a method invocation expression consists of all the members, including the inherited ones, of the class of the *receiver* expression. Thus, in order to compute the scope, we need the type of the receiver expression.

Using the scope, Xtext will automatically resolve cross references or issue an error in case a reference cannot be resolved. If Xtext succeeds in resolving a cross reference, it also takes care of implementing IDE mechanisms like navigating to the declaration of a symbol and content assist.

All the other checks that do not deal with symbol resolutions, have to be implemented through a *validator*. In a Java-like language most validation checks typically consist in checking that the program is correct with respect to types. The validation takes place in background while the user is writing in the editor, so that an immediate feedback is available.

Scoping and validation together implement the mechanism for checking the correctness of a program. This separation into two distinct mechanisms is typical of other approaches, such as [38], [47], [16], [30], [29], [55].

A. Xbase

Xbase [56] is a reusable expression language that integrates completely with Java and its type system. Xbase also implements UI mechanisms that mimic the ones of the Eclipse Java Development Tools (JDT).

The syntax of Xbase is similar to Java with less "syntactic noise" (e.g., the terminating semicolon ";" is optional) and some advanced linguistic constructs. Although its syntax is not the same as Java, Xbase should be easily understood by Java programmers.

In this section we briefly describe the main features of Xbase, in order to make Xsemantics rules shown in the paper easily understandable for the Java programmers.

Variable declarations in Xbase are defined using `val` or `var`, for final and non-final variables, respectively. The type is not mandatory if it can be inferred from the initialization expression.

A cast expression in Xbase is written using the infix keyword `as`, thus, instead of writing "`(C) e`" we write "`e as C`".

Xbase provides *extension methods*, a syntactic sugar mechanism: instead of passing the first argument inside the parentheses of a method invocation, the method can be called with the first argument as its receiver. It is as if the method was one of the argument type's members. For example, if `m(E)` is an extension method, and `e` is of type `E`, we can write `e.m()` instead of `m(e)`. With extension methods, calls can be chained instead of nested: e.g., `o.foo().bar()` rather than `bar(foo(o))`.

Xbase also provides *lambda expressions*, which have the shape `[param1, param2, ... | body]`. The types of the parameters can be omitted if they can be inferred from the context. Xbase automatically compiles lambda expressions into Java anonymous classes; if the runtime Java library is version 8, then Xbase automatically compiles its lambda expressions into Java 8 lambda expressions.

All these features of Xbase allow the developer to easily write statements and expressions that are much more readable than in Java, and that are also very close to formal specifications. For example, a formal statement of the shape

"$\exists x \in \mathtt{L} \,.\, x \neq 0$"

can be written in Xbase like

"`L.exists[ x | x != 0 ]`".

This helped us a lot in making Xsemantics close to formal systems.

IV. XSEMANTICS

Xsemantics is a DSL (written in Xtext) for writing type systems, reduction rules and in general relation rules for languages implemented in Xtext. Xsemantics is intended for developers who are familiar with formal type systems and operational semantics since it uses a syntax that resembles rules in a formal setting (e.g., [7], [57], [8]).

```
judgments {
  type |- Expression expression : output Type
    error "cannot type " + expression
  subtype |- Type left <: Type right
    error left + " is not a subtype of " + right
}
```

Figure 1. An example of judgment definitions in Xsemantics.

A system definition in Xsemantics is a set of *judgments*, that is, assertions about the properties of programs, and a set of *rules*. Rules can be seen as implications between judgments, i.e., they assert the validity of certain judgments, possibly on the basis of other judgments [7]. Rules have a conclusion and a set of premises. Typically, rules act on the EMF objects representing the AST, but in general they can refer to any Java class. Starting from the definitions of judgments and rules, Xsemantics generates Java code that can be used in a language implemented in Xtext for scoping and validation.

A. Judgments

An Xsemantics judgment consists of a name, a *judgment symbol* (which can be chosen from some predefined symbols) and the *parameters* of the judgment. Parameters are separated by *relation symbols* (which can be chosen from some predefined symbols).

Currently, Xsemantics only supports a predefined set of symbols, in order to avoid possible ambiguities with expression operators in the premises of rules.

Judgment symbols are

```
||-   |-   ||~   |~   ||=   |=   ||>   |>
```

Relation symbols are

```
<!   !>   <<!   !>>   <~!   !~>
 :   <:   :>    <<    >>    ~~
<|   |>   <~    ~>    \/    /\
```

All these symbols aim at mimicking the symbols that are typically used in formal systems.

Two judgments must differ for the judgment symbol or for at least one relation symbol. The parameters can be either input parameters (using the same syntax for parameter declarations as in Java) or output parameters (using the keyword `output` followed by the Java type). For example, the judgment definitions for an hypothetical Java-like language are shown in Figure 1: the judgment `type` takes an `Expression` as input parameter and provides a `Type` as output parameter. The judgment `subtype` does not have output parameters, thus its output result is implicitly boolean. Judgment definitions can include `error` specifications (described in Section IV-F), which are useful for generating informative error information.

B. Rules

Rules implement judgments. Each rule consists of a name, a *rule conclusion* and the *premises* of the rule. The conclusion consists of the name of the *environment* of the rule, a *judgment symbol* and the *parameters* of the rules, which are separated by *relation symbols*. To enable better IDE tooling and a more "programming"-like style, Xsemantics rules are written in the opposite direction of standard deduction rules, i.e., the conclusion comes before the premises (similar to other frameworks, like [29], [31]).

The elements that make a rule belong to a specific judgment are the judgment symbol and the relation symbols that separate the parameters. Moreover, the types of the parameters of a rule must be Java subtypes of the corresponding types of the judgment. Two rules belonging to the same judgment must differ for at least one input parameter's type. This is a sketched example of a rule, for a Java-like method invocation expression, of the judgment `type` shown in Figure 1:

```
rule MyRule
  G |- MethodSelection exp : Type type
from {
  // premises
  type = ... // assignment to output parameter
}
```

The rule *environment* (in formal systems it is usually denoted by Γ and, in the example it is named `G`) is useful for passing additional arguments to rules (e.g., contextual information, bindings for specific keywords, like `this` in a Java-like language). An empty environment can be passed using the keyword `empty`. The environment can be accessed with the predefined function `env`.

Xsemantics uses Xbase to provide a rich Java-like syntax for defining rules. The premises of a rule, which are specified in a `from` block, can be any Xbase expression (described in Section III-A), or a *rule invocation*. If one thinks of a rule declaration as a function declaration, then a rule invocation corresponds to a function invocation, thus one must specify the environment to pass to the rule, as well as the input and output arguments.

In a rule invocation, one can specify additional *environment mappings*, using the syntax `key <- value` (e.g., `'this' <- C`). When an environment is passed to a rule with additional mappings, actually a brand new environment is passed, thus the current rule environment will not be modified. If a mapping with the same key exists in the current environment, then in the brand new environment (and only there) the existing mapping will be overwritten. Thus, the rule environment passed to a rule acts in a stack manner.

The premises of an Xsemantics rule are considered to be in *logical and* relation and are verified in the same order they are specified in the block. If one needs premises in *logical or* relation, the operator `or` must be used to separate blocks of premises.

If a rule does not require any premise, we can use a special kind of rule, called *axiom*, which only has the conclusion.

In the premises, one can assign values to the output parameters, as shown in the previous rule example. When another rule is invoked, upon return, the output arguments will have the values assigned in the invoked rule. Alternatively, an expression can be directly specified instead of the output parameter in the rule conclusion.

If one of the premises fails, then the whole rule will fail, and in turn the stack of rule invocations will fail. In particular, if the premise is a boolean expression, it will fail if the expression evaluates to false. If the premise is a rule invocation, it will fail if the invoked rule fails. An explicit failure can be triggered using the keyword `fail`.

At runtime, upon rule invocation, the generated Java system will select the most appropriate rule according to the runtime types of the passed arguments (using the *polymorphic dispatch* mechanism provided by Xtext, which performs method dispatching according to the runtime type of arguments). Note that, besides this strategy for selecting a specific rule, Xsemantics itself does not implement, neither it defines, any other strategy. It is Xtext that decides when a part of a program has to be validated or a symbol has to be bound. This is consistent with the nature of frameworks, which dictate the overall program's flow of control.

C. Auxiliary Functions

Besides judgments and rules, one can write *auxiliary functions*. In type systems, such functions are typically used as a support for writing rules in a more compact form, delegating some tasks to such functions (for example, see [8]). *Predicates* can be seen as a special form of auxiliary functions.

D. Checkrules

In an Xsemantics system, we can specify some special rules, *checkrules*, which do not belong to any judgment. They are used by Xsemantics to generate a Java validator for the Xtext language. A checkrule has a name, a single parameter (which is the AST object to be validated) and the premises (but no rule environment). The syntax of the premises of a checkrule is the same as in the standard rules.

The Java validator generated by Xsemantics will automatically generate error markers for failed rules. Error markers will be automatically generated according to the error information found in the trace of a failure, which is computed and handled automatically by Xsemantics. When generating error markers the validator will use only the error information related to elements in the AST. The error marker will be generated in correspondence to the innermost failure, because this is usually the most informative error message. A custom error specification can be attached to a judgment or to a single rule, as described in Section IV-F.

E. Fields and Imports

Fields can be defined in an Xsemantics system. Such fields will be available to all the rules, checkrules and auxiliary functions, just like Java fields in a class are available to all methods of the class. This way, it is straightforward to reuse external Java utility classes from an Xsemantics system. This is useful when some mechanisms are easier to implement in Java than in Xsemantics.

Xsemantics also supports Java-like import statements, including Java static imports. This way, external Java classes' static methods can be used from within Xsemantics premises without the fully qualified name. In particular, the Xsemantics Eclipse editor supports automatic insertion of imports during code completion. This mimics what the Eclipse Java editor does. Both fields and static imports can be further decorated with the `extension` specification. This will enable the *extension methods* mechanism of Xbase (described in Section III-A) making Xsemantics code less verbose and more compact.

F. Error Information

Custom error information can be specified on judgments, rules and auxiliary functions. This can be used for providing error information that is useful in specific scenarios.

When specifying a custom error information, using the keyword `error` followed by a string describing the error, the developer can also specify the `source` element in the program that will be marked with error. Additional `data` can be attached to the error information that can be later reused in case of custom error handling.

Moreover, when using the explicit failure keyword `fail`, a custom error information can be specified as well. This use of `fail` is useful together with *or* blocks to provide more information about the error.

For example, consider the boolean premise

```
args.size() == params.size()
```

that checks that the number of arguments is equal to the number of parameters in a Java-like method invocation. If that premise fails, the default error message will show the original expression text, specifying that it failed. This would not be useful for the user (it would show an error with implementation details). To generate a better error message we can write

```
args.size() == params.size()
or
fail error "expected " + params.size() +
  " arguments, but was " + args.size()
```

There might be cases when we want to show errors containing more information about the cause that made a rule invocation fail, especially when the failure took place because of a rule invocation that is deep in the rule invocation stack. For such cases, the implicit variable `previousFailure` is available. This is automatically handled by Xsemantics at run-time: in case of a rule failure, it provides the developer with all the problems that took place when applying the rule. This allows us to build informative error messages as shown in Section VI-A.

G. Caching

In a language implemented with Xtext, types are used in many places by the framework, e.g., in the scope provider, in the validator and in the content assist. Besides that, some type computation rules, some subtyping checks and some auxiliary functions are also used more than once from the type system implementation itself. For example, the subtyping relation between the same two classes can be checked by many checkrules for the same sources.

For the above reasons, the results of type computations should be cached to improve the performance of the compiler and, most of all, the responsiveness of the Eclipse editor. However, caching usually introduces a few levels of complexity in implementations, and, in the context of an IDE that performs background parsing and checking, we also need to keep track of changes that should invalidate the cached values. Xsemantics provides automatic caching mechanisms that can be enabled in a system specification. These mechanisms internally use at run-time a cache that stores its values in the scope of a resource (a resource is an abstraction of a source file). The cached values will be automatically discarded as soon as the contents of the program changes. When caching is enabled in an Xsemantics system specification, then Xsemantics will generate Java code that automatically uses the cache, hiding the details from the programmer.

The programmer can enable caching, using the keyword `cached` on a per-judgment basis. The rationale behind this granularity is that caching should be enabled with care, otherwise it could decrease the performance. In fact, the caching is based on the Java hashing features, thus it makes sense only when used with actual object instances, not with references. In fact, in the AST of a program there might be many different references to the same object, and using such references as cache keys will only lead to many cache misses. Thus, it is responsibility of the programmer to be aware of which judgments and auxiliary functions to cache, depending on the nature of the involved input parameters.

The use of caching for the implementation of the N4JS' type system is described in Section VI-B.

H. Extensions

When defining a system in Xsemantics it is also possible to extend another Xsemantics system, using `extends`. Just like in Java class inheritance, an extended system implicitly inherits from the "super system" all judgments, rules, check rules and auxiliary functions. In the extended system one can override any such element; the overriding follows the same Java overriding rules (e.g., the types of input parameters must be the same and the types of output parameters can be subtypes). For example, an axiom in a super system can be turned into a rule in the extended system and vice versa. Similarly, we can override a judgment of the super system changing the names of parameters and error specifications. Since an Xtext grammar can inherit from another grammar, Xsemantics system extensions can be used when the language we inherit from already implements a type system using Xsemantics. Moreover, we used system extension to quickly test possible modifications/improvements to an existing type system, e.g., for testing that caching features do not break the type system implementation.

V. N4JS—A Typed JavaScript

We have used Xsemantics to implement the type system of a real-world programming language called N4JS. In this section, we give an overview of the syntax and semantics of N4JS, before presenting the Xsemantics-based implementation of the N4JS type system in Section VI.

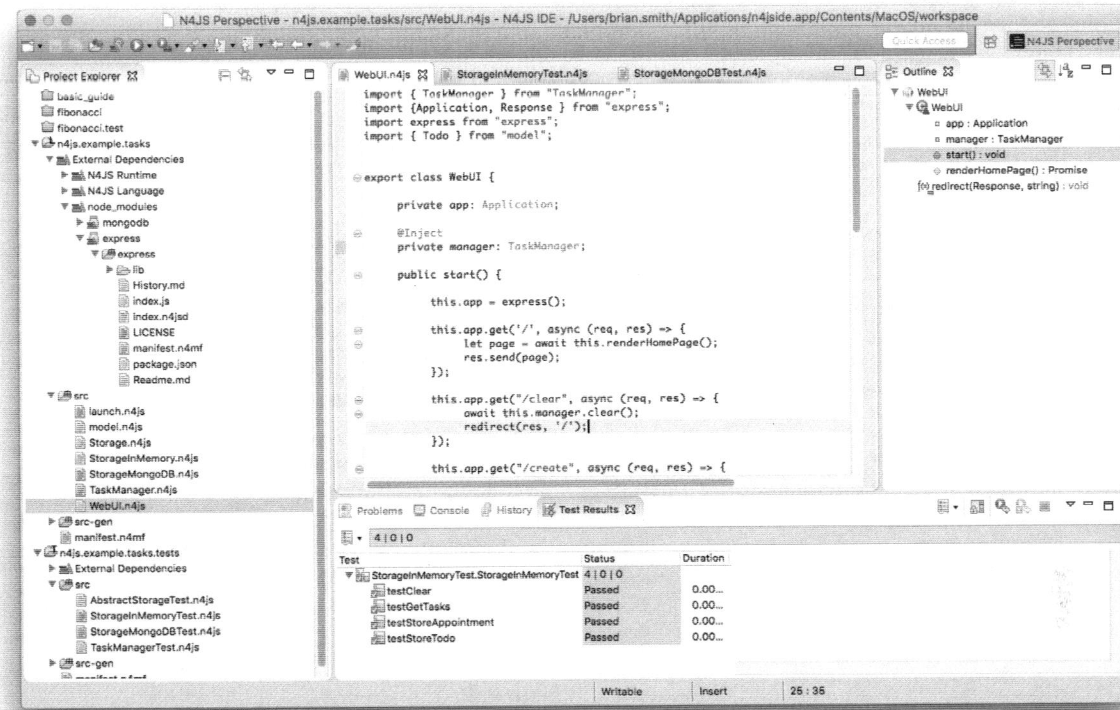

Figure 2. The N4JS IDE, showing the editor with syntax highlighting, the outline with type information, and the integrated test support.

A. Overview and Background

Before going into technical details of the language itself, let us provide some context. NumberFour AG is developing a platform for applications specifically tailored towards small businesses that will, on the client side, target JavaScript and the browser (among other targets such as iOS). Due to a large overall code base, high reliability requirements, interoperability with statically typed languages and their ecosystems, such as Scala or ObjectiveC, and for maintenance reasons, an explicit declaration of types together with static type checking was deemed a necessity across all targets, in particular JavaScript. This set of requirements led us to the development of the N4JS language.

N4JS is an extension of JavaScript, also referred to as ECMAScript, with modules and classes as specified in the ECMAScript 2015 standard [58]. Most importantly, N4JS adds a full-featured static type system on top of JavaScript, similar to TypeScript [59] or Dart [60]. N4JS compiles to plain JavaScript and provides seamless interoperability with JavaScript. In fact, most valid ECMAScript 2015 code is valid N4JS code (not considering type errors), but some recent features of ECMAScript 2015 are not supported yet. N4JS is still under development, but has been used internally at NumberFour AG for more than two years now, and was released as open source in March 2016, `https://numberfour.github.io/n4js/`.

Roughly speaking, N4JS' type system could be described as a combination of the type systems provided by Java, TypeScript and Dart. Besides primitive types, already present in ECMAScript, it provides declared types such as classes and interfaces, also supporting default methods (i.e., mixins), and combined types such as *union types* [61]. N4JS supports generics similar to Java, that is, it supports generic types and generic methods (which are supported by TypeScript but not by Dart) including wildcards, requiring the notion of existential types (see [62]).

Beyond its type-system-related features, the implementation of N4JS provides a transpiler that transforms N4JS code into ECMAScript 2015 code and a full featured IDE, shown in Figure 2. This IDE provides some advanced editing features such as

- live code validation, i.e., type errors and other code issues are shown and updated in the editor while the programmer is typing,
- a project explorer for managing large, multi-project code bases (left-hand side of the screenshot),
- convenience UI features such as an outline view showing the classes, interfaces, their fields and methods together with their signature and other elements defined in the currently active editor (right-hand side of the screenshot).

Since this IDE is based on the Eclipse framework, it inherits many features from Eclipse and readily available Eclipse plugins, without the need of any N4JS-specific implementation, for example, a seamless integration of the git version management system.

At NumberFour AG, N4JS and its IDE are being developed using agile development methodologies, in particular the Scrum process and test-driven development, aiming for a high test coverage with around 110.000 tests, at the moment, including a comprehensive test suite to ensure compatibility with ECMAScript 2015 syntax. Apache Maven is used as build tool and Jenkins for continuous integration.

The main frameworks being used are Xtext and Xsemantics, as introduced above. Most tests, especially those related to the type system, are written using the Xpect framework, `http://www.xpect-tests.org/`, which allows the developer to formulate test cases in the language being developed, i.e., N4JS in this case. For example, a test case for asserting that a number cannot be assigned to a variable of type `string` could be written as follows:

```
/* XPECT_SETUP N4JSSpecTest END_SETUP */

let x: string;
/* XPECT errors ---
   "int is not a subtype of string." at "123"
--- */
x = 123;
```

All information for testing is provided in ordinary N4JS comments, enclosed in `/* */`. The second to last line in the above code example shows an Xpect test expectation using a so-called *Xpect test method* called `errors` that asserts a particular error message at a particular location in the source (the integer literal `123` in this example) and fails if no error or a different error occurs. There are other test methods for checking for warnings or asserting the correct type of an element or expression.

In addition to N4JS, there exist other JavaScript dialects augmenting the language by static types with compile-time type checking, most notably TypeScript [59]. All these languages are facing the same, fundamental challenge: dynamic, untyped languages and statically typed languages follow two clearly distinct programming paradigms, leading in practice to different programming styles, idioms, and ecosystems of frameworks and libraries. Thus, when adding a static type system on top of an existing dynamic language there is a risk of breaking established programming idioms and conventions of the dynamic language. This is where an important difference between N4JS and, for example, TypeScript lies. While TypeScript aims for as much type safety as possible without sacrificing typical JavaScript idioms and convenience, N4JS would rather risk getting in the way of the typical JavaScript programmer from time to time than sacrificing type safety. N4JS aims at providing type soundness as its sole primary priority without compromises for the sake of programmer familiarity or convenience. In other words, TypeScript is designed primarily with existing JavaScript programmers in mind, whereas N4JS is more tailored to developers accustomed to statically typed languages, mainly Java and C# (though the needs of pure JavaScript developers and support for legacy JavaScript code bases have been considered as far as possible).

```
interface NamedEntity {
    get name(): string;
}
class Person implements NamedEntity { // class
    implementing an interface
    // three field declarations:
    public firstName: string;
    public lastName: string;
    protected age: number;
    // a method
    public marry(spouse: Person) {
        let familyName = this.lastName + '-' +
            spouse.lastName;
        this.lastName = familyName;
        spouse.lastName = familyName;
    }
    // a getter (required by interface)
    @Override get name(): string {
        return this.firstName + ' ' + this.lastName;
    }
}
class Employee extends Person { // a class extending
    another class
    private _salary: number;
    // a getter/setter pair:
    get salary(): number {
        return this._salary;
    }
    set salary(amount: number) {
        if(amount>=0) {
            this.salary = amount;
        }
    }
}
```

Figure 3. Defining classes, interfaces and their members in N4JS.

Language features where this difference in priorities can be observed include TypeScript's flexible yet unsafe default handling of built-in type `any` as well as TypeScript's use of bivariant function subtyping and method overriding, which has been identified by recent studies [63] as a form of unsoundness in the name of convenience and flexibility without clear usability benefits in practice (the latest TypeScript version has an optional compiler flag for activating a more rigid handling of `any`). In comparison, `any`, function subtyping and method overriding are handled in N4JS in a strictly type-safe manner according to how these concepts are commonly defined in the literature on object-oriented programming and type theory in general (e.g., strict observance of the Liskov substitution principle [64]). A more detailed comparison of N4JS with other typed JavaScript dialects is, however, beyond the scope of this article.

After this brief overview of why and how N4JS is being developed, we will now, for the remainder of Section V, focus on the syntax and semantics of the language itself.

B. Basic Language Features

N4JS provides the typical language features expected from an object-oriented language, such as declaration of classifiers (i.e., classes and interfaces), inheritance, polymorphism, etc. We do not aim for a full description of the language here, but Figure 3 is provided to give an impression of the syntax of the most common constructs.

In addition to fields and methods, classifiers may have so-called *getters* and *setters* members, which are similar to methods but are invoked as if the containing classifier had a field of that name. For example, the getter/setter pair `salary` of class `Employee` in Figure 3 would be invoked as follows:

```
let e = new Employee();
e.salary = 42;
console.log(e.salary);
```

Line 2 invokes setter `salary` with a value of 42 as argument and line 3 invokes the getter. Providing only either a getter or setter amounts to a read-only / write-only field from outside the type.

For the remainder of this section we focus on language features of N4JS that are less common and are most relevant from a type system perspective.

C. Union and Intersection Types

As a first advanced feature, N4JS allows the programmer to combine two or more existing types to form a new type that represents the union or intersection of the combined types. Given types $T_1, ..., T_n$, the union U of these types is a supertype of another type T' if and only if T' is a subtype of at least one of the combined types and is a subtype of T' if and only if T' is a subtype of all the combined types.

More formally, given types $T_1, ..., T_n$ and the union U of these types, for all types T' we have

$$T' <: U \iff T' <: T_1 \vee ... \vee T' <: T_n \quad (1)$$

$$U <: T' \iff T_1 <: T' \wedge ... \wedge T_n <: T' \quad (2)$$

In N4JS source code, the union of two types `A` and `B` is written as `A|B`. The following N4JS code snippet provides an example:

```
function foo(param: string | number) {
    let str: string;
    str = param; // ERROR
}
foo('hello'); // ok
foo(42); // ok
```

Function `foo` can be invoked with strings and with numbers as argument, because `string` is a subtype of the union `string|number` and also `number` is a subtype of this union. However, the assignment inside function `foo` fails, because union `string|number` is not a subtype of `string` (and also not a subtype of `number`).

Intersection types are defined accordingly: the intersection is a subtype of all its combined types. The notation for the intersection of two types `A` and `B` in N4JS source code is `A&B`.

Intersection types are actually more common in mainstream languages than union types. Java has support for intersection types, but they can only be used in very few places, for example, when declaring the upper bound of a type parameter:

```
public interface I {}
public interface J {}
public class G<T extends I & J> {
    /* ... */
}
```

Here, type parameter `T` has the intersection type `I & J` as its upper bound; Java developers often view this as parameter `T` having two upper bounds `I` and `J`.

From a practical point of view, union types are particularly important in N4JS, because N4JS—just as ECMAScript 2015—does not allow method overloading. So, union types are a means to provide methods than can handle different types of arguments in much the same way as done in Java using method overloading.

D. Nominal and Structural Typing

The fundamental notion for reasoning about types is the *subtype relation*. According to the Liskov substitution principle [64], given two types S, T we call S a subtype of T if and only if every property that can be observed from the outside for T, does also apply to S, and we can thus use instances of S wherever instances of T are expected.

One of the primary responsibilities of a type system is to decide whether a given type is, in the above sense, a subtype of another type. N4JS provides support for different strategies of checking whether two types are subtypes of one another, namely nominal and structural typing [8]. Additionally, it provides certain variations of structural typing to support typical use cases of ECMAScript.

In the context of a programming language, a type S is a subtype of type T if, roughly speaking, a value of type S may be used as if it were a value of type T. Therefore, if type S is a subtype of T, denoted as $S <: T$, a value that is known to be of type S may, for example, be assigned to a variable of type T or may be passed as an argument to a function expecting an argument of type T. There are two major classes of type systems that differ in how they decide on such type compatibility:

- *Nominal type systems*, as known from most object-oriented programming languages, e.g., Java, C#.
- *Structural type systems*, as more common in type theory and functional programming languages.

Since N4JS provides both forms of typing, we briefly introduce each approach in the following sections before we show how they are combined in N4JS.

1) Nominal Typing: In a *nominal*, or *nominative*, type system, two types are deemded to be the same if they have the *same name* and a type S is deemed to be an (immediate) subtype of a type T if and only if S is *explicitly declared* to be a subtype of T.

In the following example, `Employee` is a subtype of `Person` because it is declared as such using keyword `extends` within its class declaration. Conversely, `Product` is not a subtype of `Person` because it lacks such an "extends" declaration.

```
class Person {
    public name: string;
}

class Employee extends Person {
    public salary: number;
}
```

```
class Manager extends Employee { }

class Product {
    public name: string;
    public price: number;
}
```

The subtype relation is transitive and thus `Manager` is not only a subtype of `Employee` but also of `Person`. `Product` is not a subtype of `Person`, although it provides the same members.

Most mainstream object-oriented languages use nominal subtyping, for example, C++, C#, Java, Objective-C.

2) Structural Typing: In a *structural* type system, two types are deemed the same if they are of the same *structure*. In other words, if they have the same public fields and methods of compatible type/signature. Similarly, a type S is deemed a subtype of a type T if and only if S has all public members (of compatible type/signature) that T has (but may have more).

In the example from the previous section, we said `Product` is not a (nominal) subtype of `Person`. In a structural type system, however, `Product` would indeed be deemed a (structural) subtype of `Person` because it has all of `Person`'s public members of compatible type (the field `name` in this case). The opposite is, in fact, not true: `Person` is not a subtype of `Product` because it lacks `Product`'s field `price`.

3) Comparison: Both classes of type systems have their own advantages and proponents [65]. Nominal type systems are usually said to provide more type safety and better maintainability whereas structural typing is mostly believed to be more flexible. As a matter of fact, nominal typing *is* structural typing extended with an extra relation explicitly declaring one type a subtype of another, e.g., the `extends` clause in case of N4JS. So the real question is: What are the advantages and disadvantages of such an explicit relation?

Let us assume we want to provide a framework or library with a notion of indentifiable elements, i.e., elements that can be identified by name. We would define an interface as follows:

```
export public interface Identifiable {
    public get name(): string

    static checkNom(identifiable: Identifiable):
        boolean {
        return identifiable.name !== 'anonymous';
    }
    static checkStruct(identifiable: ~Identifiable):
         boolean {
        return identifiable.name !== 'anonymous';
    }
}
```

A nominal implementation of this interface could be defined as

```
import { Identifiable } from 'Identifiable';

class AN implements Identifiable {
    @Override
    public get name(): string { return 'John'; }
}
```

whereas here is a structural implementation of above interface:

```
class AS {
    public get name(): string { return 'John'; }
}
```

A client may use these classes as follows:

```
Identifiable.checkNom(new AN());
Identifiable.checkNom(new AS()); // ERROR "AS is not
    a (nominal) subtype of Identifiable"
Identifiable.checkStruct(new AN());
Identifiable.checkStruct(new AS());
```

Let us now investigate advantages and disadvantages of the two styles of subtyping based on this code; we will mainly focus on maintainability and flexibility.

Maintainability. As a refactoring, consider renaming `name` to `id` in order to highlight that the name is expected to be unique. Assume you have thousands of classes and interfaces. You start by renaming the getter in the interface:

```
export public interface Identifiable {
    public get id(): string
    // ...
}
```

With structural typing, you will not get any errors in your framework. You are satisfied with your code and ship the new version. However, client code outside your framework will no longer work as you have forgotten to accordingly rename the getter in class `AS` and so `AS` is no longer a (structural) subtype of `Identifiable`.

With nominal typing, you would have gotten errors in your framework code already at compile time: "Class AN must implement getter id." and "The getter name must implement a getter from an interface." Instead of breaking the code on the client side only, you find the problem in the framework code. In a large code base, this is a huge advantage. Without such a strict validation, you probably would not dare to refactor your framework. Of course, you may still break client code, but even then it is much easier to pinpoint the problem.

Flexibility. Given the same code as in the previous example, assume that some client code also uses another framework providing a class `Person` with the same public members as `AN`, `AS` in the above example. With structural typing, it is no problem to use `Person` with static method `checkStruct()` since `Person` provides a public data field `name` and is thus a structural subtype of `Identifiable`. So, the code inside the method would work as intended when called with an instance of `Person`.

This will not be possible with nominal typing though. Since `Person` does not *explicitly* implement `Identifiable`, there is no chance to call method `checkNom()`. This can be quite cumbersome, particularly if the client can change neither your framework nor the framework providing class `Person`.

4) Combination of Nominal and Structural Typing: Because both classes of type systems have their advantages and because structural typing is particularly useful in the context of a dynamic language ecosystem such as the one of JavaScript,

N4JS provides both kinds of typing and aims to combine them in a seamless way.

N4JS uses nominal typing by default, but allows the programmer to switch to structural typing by means of special type constructors using the tilde symbol. The switch can be done with either of the following:

- Globally when defining a type. This then applies to all uses of the type throughout the code, referred to as *definition-site structural typing*
- Locally when referring to an existing nominal type, referred to as *use-site structural typing*.

For the latter we have already seen an example in the signature of static method `checkStruct()`. For its parameter `elem` we used a (use-site) structural type by prefixing the type reference with a ∼ (tilde), which means we are allowed, when invoking `checkStruct()`, to pass in an instance of `AS` or `Person` even though they are not nominal subtypes of `Identifiable`.

This way, N4JS provides the advantages of nominal typing (which is the default form of typing) while granting many of the advantages of structural typing, if the programmer decides to use it. Additionally, if you rename `name` to `id`, the tilde will tell you that there may be client code calling the method with a structural type.

The full flexibility of a purely structurally typed language, however, cannot be achieved with this combination. For example, the client of an existing function or method that is declared to expect an argument of a nominal type N is confined to nominal typing. They cannot choose to invoke this function with an argument that is only a structural subtype of N (it would be a compile time error). This could possibly be exactly the intention of the framework's author in order to enable easier refactoring later.

5) Field Structural Typing: N4JS provides some variants of structural types. Usually two structural types are compatible, if they provide the same properties, or in case of classes, public members. In ECMAScript we often only need to access the fields. In N4JS, we can use ∼∼ to refer to the so-called *field structural type*. Two field structural types are compatible, if they provide the same `public` fields. Methods are ignored in these cases. Actually, N4JS provides even more options. There are several modifiers to further filter the properties or members to be considered:

- ∼`r`∼ only considers getters and data fields,
- ∼`w`∼ only considers setters and data fields,
- ∼`i`∼ is used for initializer parameters: for every setter or (non-optional) data field in the type, the ∼`i`∼-type needs to provide a getter or (readable) data field.

E. Parameterized Types

Generics in N4JS are a language feature that allows for generic programming. They enable a function, class, interface, or method to operate on the values of various (possibly unknown) types while preserving compile-time type safety. There are some differences with respect to Java generics, which we shall describe below.

1) Motivation: Several language elements may be declared in a generic form; we will start with focusing on classes, generic methods will be discussed after that.

The standard case, of course, is a non-generic class. Take the following class, for example, that aggregates a pair of two strings:

```
export public class PairOfString {
    first: string;
    second: string;
}
```

This implementation is fine as long as all we ever want to store are strings. If we wanted to store numbers, we would have to add another class:

```
export public class PairOfNumber {
    first: number;
    second: number;
}
```

Following this pattern of adding more classes for new types to be stored obviously has its limitations. We would soon end up with a multitude of classes that are basically serving the same purpose, leading to code duplication, bad maintainability and many other problems.

One solution could be having a class that stores two values of type `any` (in N4JS, `any` is the so-called *top type*, the common supertype of all other types).

```
export public class PairOfWhatEver {
    first: any;
    second: any;
}
```

Now the situation is worse off than before. We have lost the certainty that within a single pair, both values will always be of the same type. When reading a value from a pair, we have no clue what its type might be.

2) Generic Classes and Interfaces: The way to solve our previous conundrum using generics is to introduce a *type variable* for the class. We will then call such a class a *generic class*. A type variable can then be used within the class declaration just as any other ordinary type.

```
export public class Pair<T> {
    first: T;
    second: T;
}
```

The type variable `T`, declared after the class name in angle brackets, now represents the type of the values stored in the `Pair` and can be used as the type of the two fields.

Now, whenever we refer to the class `Pair`, we will provide a *type argument*, in other words a type that will be used wherever the type variable `T` is being used inside the class declaration.

```
import { Pair } from 'Pair';

let myPair = new Pair<string>();
myPair.first = '1st value';
myPair.second = '2nd value';
```

By using a type variable, we have not just allowed any given type to be used as value type, we have also stated that both values, first and second, must always be of the same type. We have also given the type system a chance to track the types of values stored in a Pair:

```
import { Pair } from 'Pair';

let myPair2 = new Pair<string>();
myPair2.first = '1st value';
myPair2.second = 42; // error: 'int is not a subtype
      of string.'

console.log(myPair2.first.charAt(2));
// type system will know myPair2.first is of type
     string
```

The error in line 3 shows that the type checker will make sure we will not put any value of incorrect type into the pair. The fact that we can access method charAt() (available on strings) in the last line indicates that when we read a value from the pair, the type system knows its type and we can use it accordingly.

Generic interfaces can be declared in exactly the same way.

3) Generic Functions and Methods: With the above, we can now avoid introducing a multitude of classes that are basically serving the same purpose. It is still not possible, however, to write code that manipulates such pairs regardless of the type of its values may have. For example, a function for swapping the two values of a pair and then return the new first value would look like this:

```
import { PairOfString } from 'PairOfString';

function swapStrings1(pair: PairOfString): string {
    let backup = pair.first; // inferred type of '
        backup' will be string
    pair.first = pair.second;
    pair.second = backup;
    return pair.first;
}
```

The above function would have to be copied for every value type to be supported. Using the generic class Pair<T> does not help much:

```
import { Pair } from 'Pair';

function swapStrings2(pair: Pair<string>): string {
    let backup = pair.first; // inferred type of '
        backup' will be string
    pair.first = pair.second;
    pair.second = backup;
    return pair.first;
}
```

The solution is not only to make the type being manipulated generic (as we have done with class Pair<T> above) but to make the code performing the manipulation generic:

```
import { Pair } from 'Pair';

function <T> swap(pair: Pair<T>): T {
    let backup = pair.first; // inferred type of '
        backup' will be T
    pair.first = pair.second;
    pair.second = backup;
    return pair.first;
}
```

We have introduced a type variable for function swap() in much the same way as we have done for class Pair in the previous section (we then call such a function a *generic function*). Similarly, we can use the type variable in this function's signature and body.

It is possible to state in the declaration of the function swap() above that it will return something of type T when having obtained a Pair<T> without even knowing what type that might be. This allows the type system to track the type of values passed between functions and methods or put into and taken out of containers, and so on.

Generic methods can be declared just as generic functions. There is one caveat, however: Only if a method introduces its own new type variables it is called a generic method. If it is merely using the type variables of its containing class or interface, it is an ordinary method. The following example illustrates the difference:

```
export public class Pair<T> {

    public foo(): T {      }
    public <S> bar(pair: Pair2<S>): void { /*...*/ }
}
```

The first method foo is a non generic method, while the second one bar is.

A very interesting application of generic methods is when using them in combination with function type arguments:

```
class Pair<T> {

    <R> merge(merger: {function(T,T): R}): R {
        return merger(this.first, this.second);
    }
}

var p = new Pair<string>();
/* ... */
var i = p.merge( (f,s)=> f.length+s.length )
```

You will notice that N4JS can infer the correct types for the arguments and the return type of the arrow expression. Also, the type for i will be automatically computed.

4) Differences to Java: Important differences between generics in Java and N4JS include:

- Primitive types can be used as type arguments in N4JS.
- There are no raw types in N4JS. Whenever a generic class or interface is referenced, a type argument has to be provided - possibly in the form of a wildcard. For generic functions and methods, an explicit definition of type arguments is optional if the type system can infer the type arguments from the context.

F. Use-site and Definition-Site Variance

In the context of generic types, the "variance of a generic type $G\langle T_1,\dots,T_n\rangle$ in T_i, $i\in\{1,\dots,n\}$," tells how G behaves with respect to subtyping when changing the type argument for type parameter T_i. In other words, knowing $X <: Y$, does this tell us anything about whether either $G\langle X\rangle <: G\langle Y\rangle$ or $G\langle Y\rangle <: G\langle X\rangle$ holds?

More formally, given a type $G\langle T_1,...,T_n\rangle$ and $i \in \{1,...,n\}$, we say

- G is *covariant* in T_i if and only if

$$\forall X,Y : X <: Y \Rightarrow G\langle X\rangle <: G\langle Y\rangle \quad (3)$$

- G is *contravariant* in T_i if and only if

$$\forall X,Y : X <: Y \Rightarrow G\langle Y\rangle <: G\langle X\rangle \quad (4)$$

If neither applies, we call G *invariant* in T_i. For the sake of conciseness, the case that both applies is not discussed, here.

In N4JS, the variance of a generic type G can be declared both on use-site, e.g., when referring to G as the type of a formal parameter in a function declaration, or on definition-site, i.e., in the class or interface declaration of G, and these two styles of declaring variance can be combined seamlessly.

For further investigating these two styles and for showing how they are integrated in N4JS, we first introduce an exemplary, single-element container class G as follows:

```
class G<T> {
    private elem: T;

    put(elem: T) { this.elem = elem; }
    take(): T { return this.elem; }
}
```

In addition, for illustration purposes, we need three helper classes $C <: B <: A$:

```
class A {}
class B extends A {}
class C extends B {}
```

1) Use-site Variance: N4JS provides support for *wildcards*, as known from Java [66]. In the source code, a wildcard is represented as ? and can be used wherever type arguments are provided for the type parameters of a generic type. Furthermore, wildcards can be supplied with upper or lower bounds, written as `? extends U` and `? super L`, with U, L being two types, here used as upper and lower bound, respectively.

Figure 4 shows three functions that all take an argument of type G, but using a different type argument for G's type parameter T.

The effect of the different type arguments becomes apparent when examining invocations of these functions. Using helper variables

```
let ga: G<A> = /* ... */ ;
let gb: G<B> = /* ... */ ;
let gc: G<C> = /* ... */ ;
```

we start with `fun1` by invoking it with each helper variable. We get:

```
fun1(ga); // ERROR: "G<A> is not a subtype of G<B>."
fun1(gb); // ok
fun1(gc); // ERROR: "G<C> is not a subtype of G<B>."
```

```
function fun1(p: G<B>) {
    let b: B = p.take(); // we know we get a B
    p.put(new B()); // we're allowed to put in a B
}
function fun2(p: G<? extends B>) {
    let b: B = p.take(); // we know we get a B
    p.put(new B()); // ERROR: "B is not a subtype of
          ? extends B."
}
function fun3(p: G<? super B>) {
    let b: B = p.take(); // ERROR: "? super B is not
          a subtype of B."
    p.put(new B()); // we're allowed to put in a B
}
```

Figure 4. Three functions illustrating the use of different wildcards.

In the first case, we get an error because the $G\langle A\rangle$ we pass in might contain an instance of A. The second invocation is accepted, of course. The third case, however, often leads to confusion: why are we not allowed to pass in a $G\langle C\rangle$, since all it may contain is an instance of C which is a subclass of B, so `fun1` would be ok with that argument? A glance at the body of `fun1` shows that this would be invalid, because `fun1` is, of course, allowed to invoke method `put()` of G to store an instance of B in G. If passing in an instance gc of $G\langle C\rangle$ were allowed, we would end up with a B being stored in gc after invoking `fun1(gc)`, breaking the contract of G.

Similarly, when invoking `fun2` and `fun3`, we notice that in each case one of the two errors we got in the previous listing will disappear:

```
fun2(ga); // ERROR: "G<A> is not a subtype of G<?
    extends B>."
fun2(gb); // ok
fun2(gc); // ok, G<C> is a subtype of G<? extends B>

fun3(ga); // ok, G<A> is a subtype of G<? super B>
fun3(gb); // ok
fun3(gc); // ERROR: "G<C> is not a subtype of G<?
    super B>."
```

By using a wildcard with an upper bound of B in the signature of `fun2`, we have effectively made G covariant in T, meaning

$$C <: B \Rightarrow G\langle C\rangle <: G\langle ?\ \texttt{extends}\ B\rangle \quad (5)$$

Checking the body of `fun2`, we see that due to the wildcard in its signature, `fun2` is no longer able to invoke method `put()` of G on its argument `p` and put in a B. Precisely speaking, `fun2` would be allowed to call this method, but only with a value that is a subtype of the unknown type `? extends B`, which is never the case except for values that are a subtype of *all* types. In N4JS this is only the case for the special values `undefined` and `null` (similar to Java's `null`); hence, `fun2` would be allowed to clear the element stored in `p` by calling `p.put(undefined)`.

Accordingly, the above three invocations of `fun3` show that by using a wildcard with a lower bound of B in the signature of `fun3`, we can effectively make G contravariant in T and can thus invoke `fun3` with an instance of $G\langle A\rangle$ (but no longer with an instance of $G\langle C\rangle$, as was the case with `fun2`). Consequently, while `fun3` is now allowed to put an instance of B into `p`, it can no longer assume getting back a B when calling method `take()` on `p`.

Using an unbounded wildcard in the signature of `fun1` would leave us, in its body, with a combination of both restrictions we faced in `fun2` and `fun3`, but would make all of the three invocations valid, i.e., both of the errors shown for the invocations of `fun1` would disappear.

2) Definition-Site Variance: Many more recent programming languages did not take up the concept of wildcards as introduced by Java, but instead opted for a technique of declaring variance on the definition-site, e.g., C#, Scala.

In N4JS this is also possible, using the keywords `out` and `in` when declaring the type parameter of a generic class or interface. As an example, let us create two variations of type G introduced above (beginning of Section V-F), first starting with a covariant type GR:

```
class GR<out T> {
    private elem: T;
// ERROR "Cannot use covariant (out) type variable
    at contravariant position."
//  put(elem: T) { this.elem = elem; }
    take(): T { return this.elem; }
}
```

We have prefixed the declaration of type parameter T with keyword `out`, thus declaring GR to be covariant in T. Trying to define the exact same members as in G, we get an error for method `put()`, disallowing the use of covariant T as the type of a method parameter. Without going into full detail, we can see that just those cases that had been disallowed in the body of function `fun2` (i.e., when using use-site covariance) are now disallowed already within the declaration of GR.

Given a modified version of `fun1`, using the above $GR\langle T\rangle$ as the type of its parameter, defined as

```
function funR(p: GR<B>) {
    let b: B = p.take(); // we know we get a B
//  p.put(new B()); // ERROR "No such member: put."
}
```

and helper variables

```
let gra: GR<A>;
let grb: GR<B>;
let grc: GR<C>;
```

we can invoke `funR` as follows:

```
funR(gra); // ERROR "GR<A> is not a subtype of GR<B
    >."
funR(grb);
funR(grc);
```

Note how having an error in the first and none in the last case corresponds exactly to what we saw above for use-site covariance through wildcards with upper bounds.

For completeness, let us see what a contravariant version of G would look like:

```
class GW<in T> {
    private elem: T;
    put(elem: T) { this.elem = elem; }
// ERROR "Cannot use contravariant (in) type
    variable at covariant position."
//  take(): T { return this.elem; }
}
```

Now, using T as the return type of a method is disallowed, meaning we cannot include method `take()`.

A comparison of GR and GW shows that in the first case methods with an information flow leading into the class are disallowed while methods reading information from the type are allowed, and vice versa in the second case. Therefore, read-only classes and interfaces are usually covariant, whereas write-only classes and interfaces are usually contravariant (hence the "R" and "W" in the names of types GR, GW).

3) Comparison: Use-site variance is more flexible, because with the concept of wildcards any type can be used in a covariant or contravariant way if some functionality (e.g., our example functions above) is using instances purely for purposes that do not conflict with the assumptions of co-/contravariance, for example, only reading from a mutable collection (covariance), or only computing its size or only reordering its elements (co- and contravariance). And this is possible even if the implementor of the type in question did not prepare this before-hand.

On the other hand, if a particular type can only ever be used in, for example, a covariant way, e.g., a read-only collection type, declaring this variance on definition-site has the benefit that implementors of functions and methods using this type do not have to take care of the extra declaration of wildcards.

G. Conclusion

We would like to conclude this section by highlighting that we here do not aim to make claims as to whether structural or nominal typing or their combination is ultimately preferable, nor as to whether use- or definition-site variance or its combination is preferable on a general level. This would require an extensive analysis and empirical study, which is outside the scope of this article. We provided the above brief discussions of advantages and disadvantages merely for the sake of understandability of the respective language features. Also, full introduction to N4JS, its syntax and semantics, is not intended.

Our main goal for this brief overview of N4JS and its main typing-related features is to illustrate that we have used Xsemantics to implement a fearure-rich, real-world programming language that requires a comprehensive, complex type system.

VI. Case Study

In this section we will describe our real-world case study: the Xsemantics implementation of the type system of N4JS, a JavaScript dialect with a full-featured static type system (described in Section V). We will also describe some performance benchmarks related to the type system and draw some evaluations.

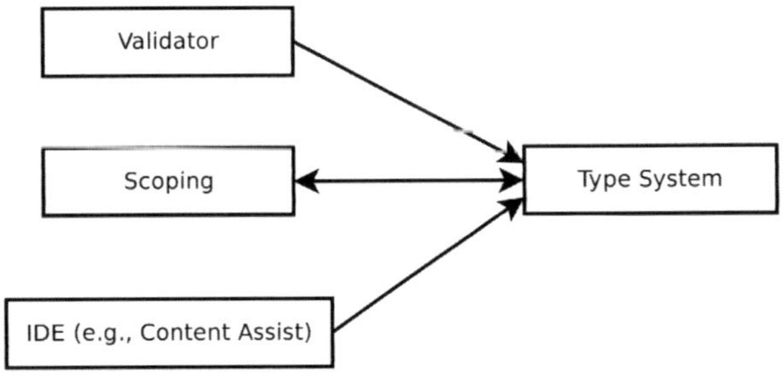

Figure 5. Interactions among the modules of the N4JS implementation.

A. Type System

The Xsemantics-based type system is not only used for validating the source code and detecting compile-time errors, but also for implementing scoping (see Section III), e.g., in order to find the actually referenced member in case of member access expressions:

```
class A {
    public method() {}
}
class B {
    public method() {}
}

let x: B;
x.method();
```

To know which method we are referring to in the last line, the one in class `A` or the one in class `B`, we need to first infer the type of `x`, which is a simple variable in this case, but, in general, it could be an arbitrary expression according to N4JS' syntax.

The relationship and interactions of the different modules of the N4JS implementation can be depicted as in Figure 5. Note that the interaction between scoping and the type system is bidirectional since, during the type inference some symbols may have to be resolved, and for symbol resolution, type inference is needed. Of course, the implementation of the type system takes care of avoiding possible cycles and loops.

The core parts of the N4JS type system are modeled by means of nine Xsemantics judgments, which are declared in Xsemantics as shown in Figure 6. The judgments have the following purpose:

- "type" is used to infer the type of any typable AST node.
- "subtype" tells if one given type is a subtype of another.
- "supertype" and "equaltype" are mostly delegating to "subtype" and are only required for convenience and improved error reporting.
- "expectedTypeIn" is used to infer a type expectation for an expression in a given context (the container).
- "upperBound" and "lowerBound" compute the lower and upper type bound, respectively. For example, given a wildcard `? extends C` (with C being a class) the "upperBound" judgment will return `C` and for wildcard `? super C` it will return the top type, i.e., `any`.
- "substTypeVariables" will replace all type variables referred to in a given type reference by a replacement type. The mapping from type variables to replacements (or bindings, substitutions) is defined in the rule environment.
- "thisTypeRef" is a special judgment for the so-called `this`-type of N4JS, which is not covered in detail, here.

This set of judgments does not only reflect the specific requirements of N4JS but arguably provides a good overview of what an Xsemantics-based type system implementation of any comprehensive Object-Oriented programming language would need.

These judgments are implemented by approximately 30 axioms and 80 rules. Since, with Xsemantics, type inference rules can often be implemented as a 1:1 correspondence to inference rules from a given formal specification, many rules are simple adaptations of rules given in the papers cited in Section V. For example, the subtype relation for union and intersection types is implemented with the rules shown in Figure 7. Note that we use many Xbase features, e.g., lambda expressions and extension methods (described in Section III-A).

In the implementation of the N4JS type system in Xsemantics we made heavy use of the rule environment. We are using it not only to pass contextual information and configuration to the rules, but also to store basic types that have to be globally available to all the rules of the type system (e.g., boolean, integer, etc.). This way, we can safely make the assumption that such type instances are singletons in our type system, and can be compared using the Java object identity. Another important use of the rule environment, as briefly mentioned above when introducing judgment "substTypeVariables", is to store type variable mappings and to pass this information from one rule to another. Finally, the rule environment is the key mechanism for guarding against infinite recursion in case of invalid source code such as cyclicly defined inheritance hierarchies.

To make the type system more readable, we implemented some static methods in a separate Java class `RuleEnvironmentExtensions`, and imported such methods as extension methods in the Xsemantics system:

```
import static extension RuleEnvironmentExtensions.*
```

These methods are used to easily access global type instances from the rule environment, as it is shown, for example, in the rule of Figure 8.

Other examples are shown in Figures 9 and 10. In particular, these examples also show how Xsemantics rules are close to the formal specifications. We believe they are also easy to read and thus to maintain.

Since the type system of N4JS is quite involved, creating useful and informative error messages is crucial to make the

```
judgments {

  type |- TypableElement element : output TypeRef
    error "cannot type " + element?.eClass?.name + " " + stringRep(element)
    source element

  subtype |- TypeArgument left <: TypeArgument right
    error stringRep(left) + " is not a subtype of " + stringRep(right)

  supertype |- TypeArgument left :> TypeArgument right
    error stringRep(left) + " is not a super type of " + stringRep(right)

  equaltype |- TypeArgument left ~~ TypeArgument right
    error stringRep(left) + " is not equal to " + stringRep(right)

  expectedTypeIn |- EObject container |> Expression expression : output TypeRef

  upperBound |~ TypeArgument typeArgument /\ output TypeRef

  lowerBound |~ TypeArgument typeArgument \/ output TypeRef

  substTypeVariables |- TypeArgument typeArg ~> output TypeArgument

  thisTypeRef |~ EObject location ~> output TypeRef
}
```

Figure 6. Declarations of Xsemantics judgments from the N4JS type system.

```
rule subtypeUnion_Left
  G |- UnionTypeExpression U <: TypeRef S
from {
  U.typeRefs.forall[T|
    G |- T <: S
  ]
}

rule subtypeUnion_Right
  G |- TypeRef S <: UnionTypeExpression U
from {
  U.typeRefs.exists[T|
    G |- S <: T
  ]
}

rule subtypeIntersection_Left
  G |- IntersectionTypeExpression I <: TypeRef S
from {
  I.typeRefs.exists[T|
    G |- T <: S
  ]
}

rule subtypeIntersection_Right
  G |- TypeRef S <: IntersectionTypeExpression I
from {
  I.typeRefs.forall[T|
    G |- S <: T
  ]
}
```

Figure 7. N4JS union and intersection types implemented with Xsemantics.

```
rule typeUnaryExpression
  G |- UnaryExpression e: TypeRef T
from {
  switch (e.op) {
    case UnaryOperator.DELETE: T= G.booleanTypeRef()
    case UnaryOperator.VOID: T= G.undefinedTypeRef()
    case UnaryOperator.TYPEOF: T= G.stringTypeRef()
    case UnaryOperator.NOT: T= G.booleanTypeRef()
    default: // INC, DEC, POS, NEG, INV
      T = G.numberTypeRef()
  }
}
```

Figure 8. Typing of unary expression.

```
rule typeConditionalExpression
  G |- ConditionalExpression expr : TypeRef T
from {
  G |- expr.trueExpression : var TypeRef left
  G |- expr.falseExpression : var TypeRef right
  T = G.createUnionType(left, right)
}
```

Figure 9. Typing of conditional expression.

language usable, especially in the IDE. We have 3 main levels of error messages in the implementation:

1) default error messages defined on judgment declaration,

```
rule typeArrayLiteral
  G |- ArrayLiteral al : TypeRef T
from {
  val elementTypes = al.elements.map[
    elem |
    G |- elem : var TypeRef elementType;
    elementType;
  ]

  T = G.arrayType.createTypeRef(
      G.createUnionType(elementTypes))
}
```

Figure 10. Typing of array literal expression.

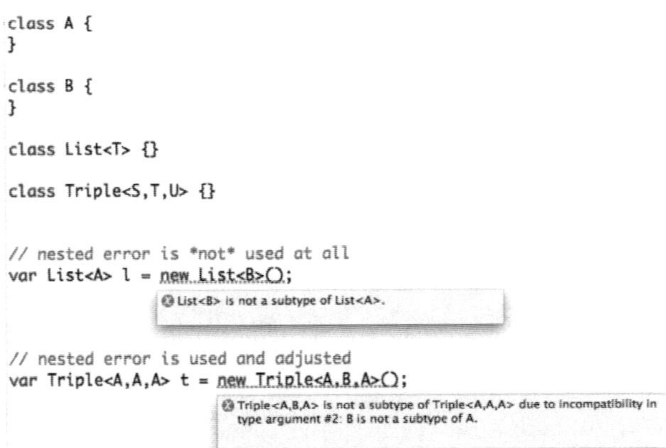

Figure 11. The N4JS IDE and error reporting.

2) custom error messages using `fail`,
3) customized error messages due to failed nested judgments using `previousFailure` (described in Section IV-F).

Custom error messages are important especially when checking subtyping relations. For example, consider checking something like A<string> <: A<number>. The declared types are identical (i.e., A), so the type arguments have to be checked. If we did not catch and change the error message produced by the nested subtype checks `string <: number` and `number <: string`, then the error message would be very confusing for the user, because it only refers to the type arguments. In cases where the type arguments are explicitly given, this might be rather obvious, but that is not the case when the type arguments are only defined through type variable bindings or can change due to considering the upper/lower bound. Some examples of error messages due to subtyping are shown in Figure 11.

Figure 12 shows an excerpt of the subtype rule for parameterized type references, in order to illustrate how such composed error messages can be implemented. The excerpt shows the part of the rule that checks the type arguments given on left and right side for compatibility. If one of these subtype checks fails, it creates an error message composed from the original error message of the failed nested subtype check (obtained via special property "previousFailure") and an additional explanation including the index of the incompatible type argument. Note that such a composed error message is only created in certain cases, in this example only if there are at least two type arguments. Otherwise the default error message of judgment "subtype" (Figure 6) is being issued automatically by using the keyword `fail`.

The Xsemantics code in Figure 12 also shows that whenever some more involved special handling is required and the special, declarative-style syntax provided by Xsemantics is not suitable, all ordinary, imperative programming language constructs provided by Xbase can be integrated seamlessly into an Xsemantics rule.

B. Performance

N4JS is used to develop large scale ECMAScript applications. For this purpose, N4JS comes with a compiler, performing all validations and eventually transpiling the code to plain ECMAScript. We have implemented a test suite in order to measure the performance of the type system. Since we want to be able to measure the effect on performance of specific constructs, we use synthetic tests with configured scenarios. In spite of being artifical, these scenarios mimic typical situations in Javascript programming. There are several constructs and features that are performance critical, as they require a lot of type inference (which means a lot of rules are to be called). We want to discuss three scenarios in detail, Figure 13 summarizes the important code snippets used in these scenarios.

Function Expression: Although it is possible to specify the types of the formal parameters and the return type of functions, this is very inconvenient for function expressions. The function definition `f` (Figure 13) is called in the lines below the definition. Function `f` takes a function as argument, which itself requires a parameter of type `C` and returns an `A` element. Both calls (below the definition) use function expressions. The first call uses a fully typed function expression, while the second one relies on type inference. *Generic Method Calls*: As in Java, it is possible to explicitly specify type arguments in a call of a generic function. Similar to type expressions, it is more convenient to let the type system infer the type arguments, which actually is a typical constraint resolution problem. The generic function `g` (Figure 13) is called one time with explicitly specified type argument, and one time without type arguments. *Variable Declarations*: The type of a variable can either be explicitly declared, or it is inferred from the type of the expression used in an assignment. This scenario demonstrates why caching is so important: without caching, the type of `x1` would be inferred three times. Of course, this is not the case if the type of the variable is declared explicitly.

Table I shows some performance measurements, using the described scenarios to set up larger tests. That is, test files are generated with 250 or more usages of function expressions, or with up to 200 variables initialized following the pattern described above. In all cases, we run the tests with and without caching enabled. Also, for all scenarios we used two variants: with and without declared types. We measure the time required to execute the JUnit tests.

There are several conclusions, which could be drawn from the measurement results. First of all, caching is only worth in

```
rule subtypeParameterizedTypeRef
  G |- ParameterizedTypeRef left <: ParameterizedTypeRef right
from {
  // ...
  or
  {
    left.declaredType == right.declaredType
    // so, we have a situation like A<X> <: B<Y> with A==B,
    // continue checking X, Y for compatibility ...

    val len = Math.min(Math.min(left.typeArgs.size, right.typeArgs.size), right.declaredType.typeVars.size);
    for(var i=0;i<len;i++) {

      val leftArg = left.typeArgs.get(i)
      val rightArg = right.typeArgs.get(i)
      val variance = right.declaredType.getVarianceOfTypeVar(i)

      G |~ leftArg /\ var TypeRef leftArgUpper
      G |~ leftArg \/ var TypeRef leftArgLower
      G |~ rightArg /\ var TypeRef rightArgUpper
      G |~ rightArg \/ var TypeRef rightArgLower

      {
        // require leftArg <: rightArg, except we have contravariance
        if(variance!==Variance.CONTRA) {
          G2 |- leftArgUpper <: rightArgUpper
        }
        // require rightArg <: leftArg, except we have covariance
        if(variance!==Variance.CO) {
          G2 |- rightArgLower <: leftArgLower
        }
      }
      or
      {
        if(len>1 && previousFailure.isOrCausedByPriorityError) {
          fail error stringRep(left) + " is not a subtype of " + stringRep(right)
              + " due to incompatibility in type argument #" + (i+1) + ": "
              + previousFailure.compileMessage
            data PRIORITY_ERROR
        } else {
          fail // with default message
        }
      }
    }
  }
  or
  // ...
}
```

Figure 12. Implementing advanced, composed error messages in Xsemantics.

some cases, but these cases can make all the difference. The first two scenarios do not gain much from caching, actually the overhead for managing the cache even slightly decreases performance in case of generic methods calls. In many cases, types are to be computed only once. In our example, the types of the type arguments in the method call are only used for that particular call. Thus, caching the arguments there does not make any sense. Things are different for variable declarations. As described above, caching the type of a variable, which is used many times, makes a lot of sense. Increasing the performance by the factor of more than 100 is not only about speeding up the system a little bit—it is about making it work at all for larger programs. Even if all types are declared, type inference is still required in order to ensure that the inferred type is compatible with the declared type. This is why in some cases the fully typed scenario is even slower than the scenario which uses only inferred types. While in some cases (scenario 1 and 3) the performance increases linearly with the size, this is not true for scenario 2, the generic method call. This demonstrates a general problem with interpreting absolute performance measurements: it is very hard to pinpoint the exact location in case of performance problems, as many parts, such as the parser, the scoping system and the type system are involved. Therefore, we concentrate on relative

```
// Scenario 1: function expression
function f ({function (C): A} func) { ... };
// typed
f( function (C p): A { return p.getA() || new A(); }
    )
// inferred
f( function (p) { return p.getA() || new A(); } )

// Scenario 2: generic method call
function <T> g (T p): T { ... }
// typed
var s1 = <string>g("");
// inferred
var s2 = g("");

// Scenario 3: variable declarations and references
// typed
var number y1 = 1;
var number y2 = y1; ...
// inferred
var x1 = 1;
var x2 = x1; var x3 = x2; ...
```

Figure 13. Scenario snippets used in performance tests

TABLE I. PERFORMANCE MEASUREMENTS (RUNTIME IN MS)

Scenario	**without caching**		**with caching**	
size	**typed**	**inferred**	**typed**	**inferred**
Function Expressions				
250	875	865	772	804
500	1,860	1,797	1,608	1,676
1000	4,046	3,993	3,106	3,222
2000	9,252	9,544	8,143	8,204
Generic Method Calls				
250	219	273	223	280
500	566	644	548	654
1000	1,570	1,751	1,935	1,703
2000	6,143	6,436	6,146	6,427
Variable Declarations				
50	19	580	18	39
100	27	3,848	26	102
200	44	31,143	36	252

performance between slightly modified versions of the type system implementation (while leaving all other subsystems unchanged).

We observe that it is not feasible to compare, on a more global level, the overall performance of N4JS to other languages implemented with more traditional approaches (without the use of Xsemantics), because there are too many factors that should be taken into consideration, starting from the complexity of the type system and its type inference up to the specific programming language and frameworks used for their compiler's implementation.

Summarizing, we learned that different scenarios must be taken into account when working on performance optimization, in order to make the right decision about whether using caching or not. Surely, when type information is reused in other parts of the program over and over again, like in the variable scenario, caching optimization is crucial. Combining the type system with control flow analysis, leading to effect systems, may make caching dispensable in many cases. Further investigation in this direction is ongoing work.

VII. CONCLUSION

In this paper, we presented the implementation in Xsemantics of the type system of N4JS, a statically typed JavaScript, with powerful type inference mechanisms, focusing both on the performance of the type system and on its integration in the Eclipse IDE. The N4JS case study proved that Xsemantics is mature and powerful enough to implement a complex type system of a real-world language, where types do not need to be declared, thus requiring involved type inference mechanisms.

Thanks to Xtext, Xsemantics offers a rich Eclipse tooling; in particular, thanks to Xbase, Xsemantics is also completely integrated with Java. For example, from the Xsemantics editor we can navigate to Java types and Java method definitions, see Java type hierarchies, and other features that are present in the Eclipse Java editor (see, e.g., Figure 14). This also holds the other way round: from Java code that uses code generated from a Xsemantics definition we can navigate directly to the original Xsemantics method definition.

Most importantly, the Xsemantics IDE allows the developer to debug the original Xsemantics system source code, besides the generated Java code. Figure 15 shows a debug session of the N4JS type system: we have set a break point in the Xsemantics file, and when the program hits Xsemantics generated Java code the debugger automatically switches to the original Xsemantics code (note the file names in the thread stack, the "Breakpoint" view and the "Variables" view).

With respect to manual implementations of type systems in Java, Xsemantics specifications are more compact and closer to formal systems. We also refer to [67] for a wider discussion about the importance of having a DSL for type systems in language frameworks. In particular, Xsemantics integration with Java allows the developers to incrementally migrate existing type systems implemented in Java to Xsemantics [68].

Xsemantics has been developed with *Test Driven Development* technologies, with almost 100% code coverage, using *Continuous Integration* systems and code quality tools, such as *SonarQube* (a report can be found at `http://www.lorenzobettini.it-/2014/09/dealing-with-technical-debt-with--sonarqube-a-case-study-with-xsemantics`).

ACKNOWLEDGMENT

We want to thank Sebastian Zarnekow, Jörg Reichert and the colleagues at NumberFour, in particular Jakub Siberski and Torsten Krämer, for feedback and for implementing N4JS with us.

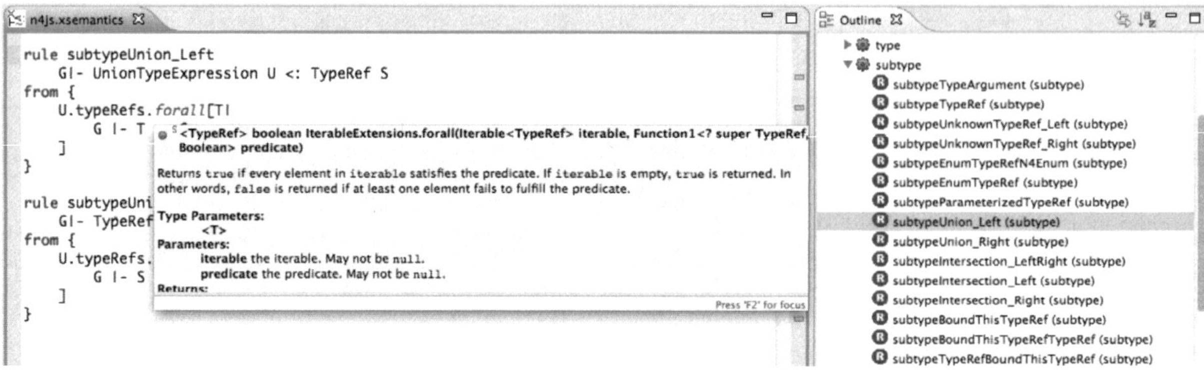

Figure 14. Accessing Java types from Xsemantics source code.

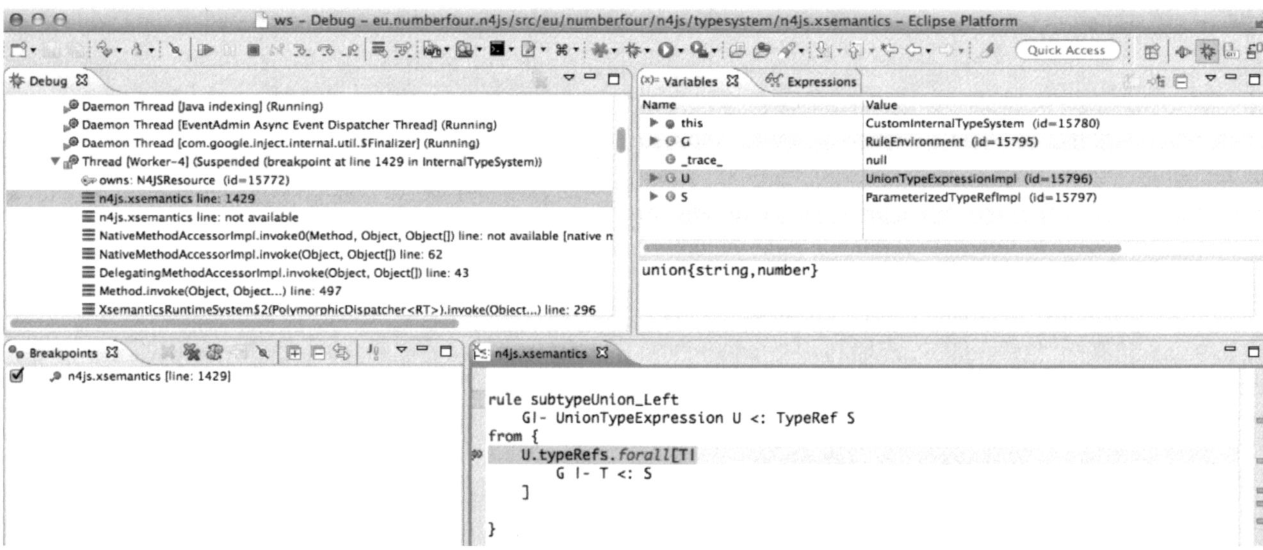

Figure 15. Debugging Xsemantics source code: a breakpoint was set in rule `subtypeUnion_Left` inside the Xsemantics editor (bottom right), stack trace and local variables are shown on the top left and right, respectively.

REFERENCES

[1] L. Bettini, J. von Pilgrim, and M.-O. Reiser, "Implementing the Type System for a Typed Javascript and its IDE," in COMPUTATION TOOLS. IARIA, 2016, pp. 6–11.

[2] R. C. Martin, Agile Software Development: Principles, Patterns, and Practices. Prentice Hall, 2003.

[3] K. Beck, Test Driven Development: By Example. Addison-Wesley, 2003.

[4] M. Eysholdt and H. Behrens, "Xtext: implement your language faster than the quick and dirty way," in SPLASH/OOPSLA Companion. ACM, 2010, pp. 307–309.

[5] L. Bettini, Implementing Domain-Specific Languages with Xtext and Xtend, 2nd ed. Packt Publishing, 2016.

[6] ——, "Implementing Java-like languages in Xtext with Xsemantics," in OOPS (SAC). ACM, 2013, pp. 1559–1564.

[7] L. Cardelli, "Type Systems," ACM Computing Surveys, vol. 28, no. 1, 1996, pp. 263–264.

[8] B. C. Pierce, Types and Programming Languages. Cambridge, MA: The MIT Press, 2002.

[9] L. Bettini, "Implementing Type Systems for the IDE with Xsemantics," Journal of Logical and Algebraic Methods in Programming, vol. 85, no. 5, Part 1, 2016, pp. 655 – 680.

[10] ——, "A DSL for Writing Type Systems for Xtext Languages," in PPPJ. ACM, 2011, pp. 31–40.

[11] M. Voelter, "Xtext/TS - A Typesystem Framework for Xtext," 2011.

[12] J. Warmer and A. Kleppe, The Object Constraint Language: Precise Modeling with UML. Addison Wesley, 1999.

[13] Object Management Group, "Object Constraint Language, Version 2.2," Omg document number: formal/2010-02-01 edition, 2010, `http://www.omg.org/spec/OCL/2.2`, Accessed: 2016-01-07.

[14] E. Vacchi and W. Cazzola, "Neverlang: A Framework for Feature-Oriented Language Development," Computer Languages, Systems & Structures, vol. 43, no. 3, 2015, pp. 1–40.

[15] W. Cazzola and E. Vacchi, "Neverlang 2: Componentised Language Development for the JVM," in Software Composition, ser. LNCS, vol. 8088. Springer, 2013, pp. 17–32.

[16] T. Ekman and G. Hedin, "The JastAdd system – modular extensible compiler construction," Science of Computer Programming, vol. 69, no. 1-3, 2007, pp. 14 – 26.

[17] L. Diekmann and L. Tratt, "Eco: A Language Composition Editor," in SLE, ser. LNCS, vol. 8706. Springer, 2014, pp. 82–101.

[18] E. Barrett, C. F. Bolz, L. Diekmann, and L. Tratt, "Fine-grained Language Composition: A Case Study," in ECOOP, ser. LIPIcs, vol. 56. Dagstuhl LIPIcs, 2016, pp. 3:1–3:27.

[19] L. C. L. Kats and E. Visser, "The Spoofax language workbench. Rules for declarative specification of languages and IDEs," in OOPSLA. ACM, 2010, pp. 444–463.

[20] N. Nystrom, M. R. Clarkson, and A. C. Myers, "Polyglot: An Extensible Compiler Framework for Java," in Compiler Construction, ser. LNCS, vol. 2622. Springer, 2003, pp. 138–152.

[21] G. Bracha, "Pluggable Type Systems," in Workshop on Revival of Dynamic Languages, 2004.

[22] M. Voelter et al, DSL Engineering - Designing, Implementing and Using Domain-Specific Languages, 2013.

[23] M. Pfeiffer and J. Pichler, "A comparison of tool support for textual domain-specific languages," in Proc. DSM, 2008, pp. 1–7.

[24] S. Erdweg, T. van der Storm, M. Völter, L. Tratt, R. Bosman, W. R. Cook, A. Gerritsen, A. Hulshout, S. Kelly, A. Loh, G. Konat, P. J. Molina, M. Palatnik, R. Pohjonen, E. Schindler, K. Schindler, R. Solmi, V. Vergu, E. Visser, K. van der Vlist, G. Wachsmuth, and J. van der Woning, "Evaluating and comparing language workbenches: Existing results and benchmarks for the future," Computer Languages, Systems & Structures, vol. 44, Part A, 2015, pp. 24–47.

[25] P. Charles, R. Fuhrer, S. Sutton Jr., E. Duesterwald, and J. Vinju, "Accelerating the creation of customized, language-Specific IDEs in Eclipse," in OOPSLA. ACM, 2009, pp. 191–206.

[26] F. Jouault, J. Bézivin, and I. Kurtev, "TCS: a DSL for the specification of textual concrete syntaxes in model engineering," in GPCE. ACM, 2006, pp. 249–254.

[27] F. Heidenreich, J. Johannes, S. Karol, M. Seifert, and C. Wende, "Derivation and Refinement of Textual Syntax for Models," in ECMDA-FA, ser. LNCS, vol. 5562. Springer, 2009, pp. 114–129.

[28] M. Bravenboer, K. T. Kalleberg, R. Vermaas, and E. Visser, "Stratego/XT 0.17. A language and toolset for program transformation," Science of Computer Programming, vol. 72, no. 1–2, 2008, pp. 52–70.

[29] E. Visser et al, "A Language Designer's Workbench: A One-Stop-Shop for Implementation and Verification of Language Designs," in Onward! ACM, 2014, pp. 95–111.

[30] G. Konat, L. Kats, G. Wachsmuth, and E. Visser, "Declarative Name Binding and Scope Rules," in SLE, ser. LNCS, vol. 7745. Springer, 2012, pp. 311–331.

[31] V. A. Vergu, P. Neron, and E. Visser, "DynSem: A DSL for Dynamic Semantics Specification," in RTA, ser. LIPIcs, vol. 36. Schloss Dagstuhl - Leibniz-Zentrum fuer Informatik, 2015, pp. 365–378.

[32] H. Xu, "EriLex: An Embedded Domain Specific Language Generator," in TOOLS, ser. LNCS, vol. 6141. Springer, 2010, pp. 192–212.

[33] P. Borras et al, "CENTAUR: the system," in Software Engineering Symposium on Practical Software Development Environments, ser. SIGPLAN. ACM, 1988, vol. 24, no. 2, pp. 14–24.

[34] M. Fowler, "A Language Workbench in Action - MPS," http://martinfowler.com/articles/mpsAgree.html, 2008, accessed: 2016-01-07.

[35] M. G. J. V. D. Brand, J. Heering, P. Klint, and P. A. Olivier, "Compiling language definitions: the ASF+SDF compiler," ACM TOPLAS, vol. 24, no. 4, 2002, pp. 334–368.

[36] A. Dijkstra and S. D. Swierstra, "Ruler: Programming Type Rules," in FLOPS, ser. LNCS, vol. 3945. Springer, 2006, pp. 30–46.

[37] M. Felleisen, R. B. Findler, and M. Flatt, Semantics Engineering with PLT Redex. The MIT Press, 2009.

[38] T. Reps and T. Teitelbaum, "The Synthesizer Generator," in Software Engineering Symposium on Practical Software Development Environments. ACM, 1984, pp. 42–48.

[39] G. Kahn, B. Lang, B. Melese, and E. Morcos, "Metal: A formalism to specify formalisms," Science of Computer Programming, vol. 3, no. 2, 1983, pp. 151–188.

[40] E. Morcos-Chounet and A. Conchon, "PPML: A general formalism to specify prettyprinting," in IFIP Congress, 1986, pp. 583–590.

[41] T. Despeyroux, "Typol: a formalism to implement natural semantics," INRIA, Tech. Rep. 94, Mar. 1988.

[42] D. Batory, B. Lofaso, and Y. Smaragdakis, "JTS: Tools for Implementing Domain-Specific Languages," in ICSR. IEEE, 1998, pp. 143–153.

[43] M. Bravenboer, R. de Groot, and E. Visser, "MetaBorg in Action: Examples of Domain-Specific Language Embedding and Assimilation Using Stratego/XT," in GTTSE, ser. LNCS, vol. 4143. Springer, 2006, pp. 297–311.

[44] H. Krahn, B. Rumpe, and S. Völkel, "Monticore: a framework for compositional development of domain specific languages," STTT, vol. 12, no. 5, 2010, pp. 353–372.

[45] T. Clark, P. Sammut, and J. Willans, Superlanguages, Developing Languages and Applications with XMF, 1st ed. Ceteva, 2008.

[46] L. Renggli, M. Denker, and O. Nierstrasz, "Language Boxes: Bending the Host Language with Modular Language Changes," in SLE, ser. LNCS, vol. 5969. Springer, 2009, pp. 274–293.

[47] P. Sewell, F. Z. Nardelli, S. Owens, G. Peskine, T. Ridge, S. Sarkar, and R. Strnisa, "Ott: Effective tool support for the working semanticist," J. Funct. Program, vol. 20, no. 1, 2010, pp. 71–122.

[48] Y. Bertot and P. P. Castéran, Interactive theorem proving and program development: Coq'Art: the calculus of inductive constructions, ser. Texts in theoretical computer science. Springer, 2004.

[49] M. Gordon, "From LCF to HOL: a short history," in Proof, Language, and Interaction: Essays in Honour of Robin Milner. The MIT Press, 2000, pp. 169–186.

[50] L. C. Paulson, Isabelle: A Generic Theorem Prover, ser. LNCS. Springer, 1994, vol. 828.

[51] M. Voelter, "Language and IDE Modularization and Composition with MPS," in GTTSE, ser. LNCS, vol. 7680. Springer, 2011, pp. 383–430.

[52] T. Parr, The Definitive ANTLR Reference: Building Domain-Specific Languages. Pragmatic Programmers, 2007.

[53] D. Steinberg, F. Budinsky, M. Paternostro, and E. Merks, EMF: Eclipse Modeling Framework, 2nd ed. Addison-Wesley, 2008.

[54] D. R. Prasanna, Dependency Injection: Design Patterns Using Spring and Guice, 1st ed. Manning, 2009.

[55] P. Neron, A. P. Tolmach, E. Visser, and G. Wachsmuth, "A Theory of Name Resolution," in ESOP, ser. LNCS, vol. 9032. Springer, 2015, pp. 205–231.

[56] S. Efftinge et al, "Xbase: Implementing Domain-Specific Languages for Java," in GPCE. ACM, 2012, pp. 112–121.

[57] J. R. Hindley, Basic Simple Type Theory. Cambridge University Press, 1987.

[58] ECMA, "ECMAScript 2015 Language Specification," ISO/IEC, International Standard ECMA-262, 6th Edition, Jun. 2015, accessed: 2016-01-07. [Online]. Available: http://www.ecma-international.org/publications/-files/ECMA-ST/Ecma-262.pdf

[59] A. Hejlsberg and S. Lucco, TypeScript Language Specification, 1st ed., Microsoft, Apr. 2014.

[60] Dart Team, Dart Programming Language Specification, 1st ed., Mar. 2014.

[61] A. Igarashi and H. Nagira, "Union types for object-oriented programming," Journal of Object Technology, vol. 6, no. 2, 2007, pp. 47–68.

[62] N. Cameron, E. Ernst, and S. Drossopoulou, "Towards an Existential Types Model for Java Wildcards," in Formal Techniques for Java-like Programs (FTfJP), July 2007, pp. 1–17.

[63] G. Mezzetti, A. Møller, and F. Strocco, "Type Unsoundness in Practice: An Empirical Study of Dart," in DLS. ACM, 2016, pp. 13–24.

[64] B. Liskov, "Keynote address – data abstraction and hierarchy," ACM SIGPLAN Notices, vol. 23, no. 5, 1987, pp. 17–34.

[65] D. Malayeri and J. Aldrich, "Integrating Nominal and Structural Subtyping," in ECOOP, ser. LNCS, vol. 5142. Springer, 2008, pp. 260–284.

[66] A. Igarashi and M. Viroli, "On Variance-Based Subtyping for Parametric Types," in ECOOP, ser. LNCS, vol. 2374. Springer, 2002, pp. 441–469.

[67] L. Bettini, D. Stoll, M. Völter, and S. Colameo, "Approaches and Tools for Implementing Type Systems in Xtext," in SLE, ser. LNCS, vol. 7745. Springer, 2012, pp. 392–412.

[68] A. Heiduk and S. Skatulla, "From Spaghetti to Xsemantics - Practical experiences migrating typesystems for 12 languages," XtextCon, 2015.

EMSoD — A Conceptual Social Framework that Delivers KM Values to Corporate Organizations

Christopher Adetunji, Leslie Carr
Web Science Institute
School of Electronics and Computer Science
University of Southampton
Southampton, England
Email: {ca6g14, lac}@soton.ac.uk

***Abstract*—As social software is becoming increasingly disruptive to organizational structures and processes, Knowledge Management (KM) initiatives that have hitherto taken the form of a 'knowledge repository' now need redefining. With the emergence of Social Media (SM) platforms like Twitter, the hierarchical boundaries within the organization are broken down and a lateral flow of information is created. This has created a peculiar kind of tension between KM and SM, in which one is perceived as threatening the continued relevance of the other. Particularly, with the advances of social media and social software, KM is more in need of delivering measurable value to corporate organizations, if it is to remain relevant in the strategic planning and positioning of organizations. In view of this, this paper presents *EMSoD* — *Enterprise Mobility and Social Data* — a conceptual social framework which mediates between KM and SM to deliver *actionable knowledge* and *employee engagement*. Meanwhile, given that the main objective of this research is in the delivery of KM value to corporate organizations, this paper devises some mechanisms for measuring *actionable knowledge* and *employee engagement*, both as parameters of KM value.**

Keywords*—*social-media; tacit-knowledge; actionable-knowledge; twitter; SMEs; employee-engagement; enterprise-mobility; social-network-analysis; folksonomy.

I. Introduction

Social media have become viable sources of data from which corporate organizations can discover knowledge and insights for their strategic competitive advantage. In [1], a case of a medium-sized enterprise that lacks a significant social media presence, is explored with regards to how public Twitter data is exploited to discover actionable knowledge that propels the enterprise's strategic competitive advantage. The work utilises text analysis techniques to make sense of the unstructured social media data harvested through Twitter's Streaming API.

The work in [1] is a cascading of our original research exploring the question of how social media platforms like Twitter can deliver Knowledge Management (KM) values to corporate organizations. As a form of social machinery that facilitates human interaction on the Web, social media enable people to create new knowledge by sharing and synthesizing knowledge from various sources [2]. Using this social infrastructure as leverage for corporate knowledge management is the main objective of the framework presented in this paper.

In this paper, we discuss our motivation for exploring the question of how social media platforms like Twitter can deliver KM values to corporate organizations. We present the *Enterprise Mobility and Social [media] Data (**EMSoD**)* framework, our proposed conceptual social framework, with KM value at its core. We provide an overview of our previous work that culminates in an important measure of KM value — *actionable knowledge* — upon which a significant business decision is made by a case study organization. This is underpinned by the fact that the real essence of knowledge is its actionability, especially when it contributes to the advancement of a proposed undertaking [3]. Measuring the value of such contributions has been one of the main issues of disagreement in Knowledge Management, which is why we devised a mechanism for measuring the KM value which our framework helps in delivering to corporate organizations.

Moreover, our framework identifies another important measure of KM values, which is *employee engagement*. Included in this paper therefore, is a report on a social network analysis of *@unisouthampton*, the Twitter handle for the University of Southampton, with the aim of examining the impact of the structure of the network on employee engagement.

The rest of this paper is organized as follows: Sections II and III provide some background to this study, with the aim of setting out the research motivation for our framework. Section IV presents the ***EMSoD*** social framework, describes its basic elements and discusses the central position of Knowledge Management Value (KMV) as the cynosure around which other basic components of the framework revolves, as well as its (KM value) measurement. In Section V we re-present our previous work on knowledge discovery that culminates in *actionable knowledge* as a measure of KM value. Also included in this section are further insights from recent data on the same subject. Sections VI and VII discuss *actionable knowledge* and *employee engagement* as a measures of KM value, respectively, with their measurement mechanisms. Section VIII concludes the paper with recommendation for corporate organizations and discusses indications for future work.

II. Background and Research Motivation

KM within organizations has traditionally been through a top-down, process approach [4, p.7][5] which precludes employees from collaborating and/or participating in the process of creating and sharing valuable knowledge that are relevant for the organizations competitive advantage. In making KM a part of everyone's job [6, p.107], the top-down approach to KM is being broken down by current and emerging Web technologies like microblogs (e.g., Twitter), social media/networking (e.g., YouTube/Facebook), and multimedia chat platforms (e.g.,

Skype) [7]. These are pervasive technologies, and are most profound in their capabilities to, in the words of Mark Weiser of Xerox Lab in [8], *weave themselves into the fabrics of everyday life until they are indistinguishable from it*, thanks to the ubiquity (and consumerization) of mobile devices like tablets and smartphones.

In recent times, these devices have woven themselves around us in so much so that employees are compulsively using them to keep in touch with friends and families even while at work. Many organizations have therefore, already subscribed to the theory and practice of enterprise mobility on the grounds that, allowing employees to access corporate systems and data over these devices (BYOD) enhances productivity while also helping to maintain work and life balances [9]. It also enhances knowledge sharing within the organization in its capacity for fostering discussions over documents and thereby enabling organizations to build social environment or communities of practice necessary for facilitating the sharing of tacit knowledge [10] [6, p.26].

Tacit knowledge is usually in the domain of subjective, cognitive and experiential learning; it is highly personal and difficult to formalise [11, p.478], which is why Polanyi [12] classifies it as one class of knowledge for which we cannot tell as much as we know. How then do we capture and/or engineer this tacit knowledge being inadvertently generated by employees in the enterprise mobility and social media space? This paper answers this question from a big social data perspective, drawing insights from the literature, using a conceptual social framework - EMSoD. Moreover, a vision of a knowledge social machine is encapsulated in this framework, which leverages the flow of tacit knowledge on existing social interactions within the boundary of the organization as defined by its enterprise mobility strategies. This social machine has the organizations workforce as its user base, using their own devices (BYOD) or using the company-owned devices that have been personally enabled for them (COPE). The social machine produces company-relevant insights and knowledge as output, taking its input from a combination of internal data (enterprise social media, transactional data, system/web logs, etc.) and open/public data, together with the active participation of the employees in the process of knowledge management, as illustrated in Figure 1.

Meanwhile, the traditional top-down approach to KM mentioned earlier has also resulted in KM becoming a lacklustre concept, considering the perceived lack of maturity and the general state of apathy in the field, as evidenced in a recent Knowledge Management Observatory survey referenced in [13] and the 2015 follow up of same report [14]. More so, there is hardly any sector in which organizations have not embarked on a Knowledge Management program or project to improve on their organization practice; research has shown that knowledge-oriented management has a significant influence on performance, in spite of the image problem suffered by KM due to its overselling by vendors and consultants in the 1990s [15].

To shake off this image problem and to douse the perceived tension between KM and social media [16], participants in a recent massive survey into the future of KM by the Global Knowledge Research Network (*GKRN - Network of Researchers sharing an interest in undertaking joint research on knowledge management*) published in [15], regard social software as an advancement of the KM field. The research suggestion in this regard, places clear emphasis on the economic, organizational and human context factors related to the use and implementation of this new social software technologies. This organizational and human context factor is what culminates in the concept of Enterprise Social Networking, fondly referred to as Enterprise 2.0 - another concept made possible by the advances in social media . Although, some of the proponents of Knowledge Management were initially hostile towards the new concept of Enterprise 2.0 as propagated by [17], describing it as a new wine in an old bottle, Davenport's [18] earlier comment in a HBR *(Harvard Business Review)* blog post is worth noting:

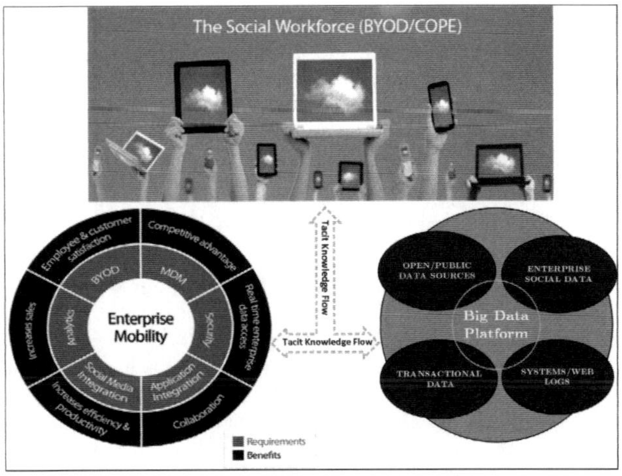

Figure 1: Tacit Knowledge Flow

> "If E2.0 can give KM a mid-life kicker, so much the better. If a new set of technologies can bring about a knowledge-sharing culture, more power to them. Knowledge Management was getting a little tired anyway."

These new sets of technologies that can bring about a knowledge sharing culture has been found in social media and their social networking capabilities, as enabled and popularised by the consumerization of mobile devices. KM can therefore, be repositioned within these innovative technological trends of enterprise mobility and social media analytics, which can be exploited for rejuvenating the concept and practice of KM, in consonance with Delic and Riley's [19] assertion that,

> "The field of knowledge management, having passed several hypes and disappointments, has yet another chance of reappearing in totally new technological and social circumstances."

The overarching issue recognised in the GKRN research mentioned above is the challenge for KM in being able to deliver measurable value for businesses. The conceptual social framework (see Figure 3) presented in this paper places the value proposition of KM at the centre of organizational knowledge management processes. To the best of our knowledge, this is the first framework of its kind that seeks to use the convergence of enterprise mobility and social (media) data as leverage for corporate knowledge management in such a way that corporate organizations can derive KM value from the synergy. Meanwhile, we did not arrive at this framework on the fly. The core elements of the framework have emanated from a rigorous review of relevant literature, the process of which is described in Section III.

III. The Making of the Social Framework

With regards to the image problem suffered by KM in the 1990s [15], there has been an increasing effort by KM consultants and academics, since the 2000s, to explore how the growing trends of enterprise mobility — as manifest in the surge in mobile devices and applications — can be exploited for corporate Knowledge Management. This is evident in Knowledge Management literature, which abounds with issues and concerns about Enterprise Mobility.

Figure 2: A Word Cloud for Mobilization from the Literature

For this research, about 160 KM literature materials published between 2004 and 2016 were examined. These include books, book sections, conference papers, journal articles, reports, thesis and web pages. The term, *'mobilization'* — with variants of mobile, mobility, mobilize — is topmost in the list of Top 50 most frequently used words in these KM literature (see Figure 2).

IV. EMSoD — The Conceptual Social Framework

***E**nterprise **M**obility and **So**cial [media] **D**ata (EMSoD)* is a conceptual social framework that exploits the convergence of enterprise mobility and social media data as leverage for corporate Knowledge Management. The proposed framework is presented cyclically in Figure 3 to emphasize the interdependence of its five core elements — Managed Platform, Social Media, Knowledge Discovery, Tacit Knowledge and, KM Values. The cyclical illustration of the framework also emphasizes that changing one element has an impact on other elements and on the capability for the framework to deliver the intended KM value at its core. Each of the five core elements are examined in this section.

A. Managed Platform

This framework supports the vision of a knowledge social machine, which serves as a leverage for the flow and conversion of tacit knowledge, on existing social interactions within the boundary of the organization, as defined by its enterprise mobility strategies. This social machine has the organizations workforce as its user base, using their own devices (BYOD - Bring Your Own Devices) or using the Company-Owned devices that have been Personally-Enabled for them (COPE). With BYOD for example, the choice of the brand, functionality and installed apps are entirely that of the employee and, when these devices are allowed to be used in accessing the corporate data from anywhere the employee may be located, it exposes the organization to the risk of compromise of the privacy and security of its corporate data. Also, because there are as many different devices as there are employees, the organization is faced with the challenge of how to integrate these disparate devices into a platform for ease of support and interoperability. To mitigate against these constraints of privacy, security and interoperability, there is need for the organization's enterprise mobility strategy and social media data to be contained within a managed platform.

Enterprise Mobility Strategies

> *"Given the plethora of devices, operating systems, solution providers and overall mobility commoditization, how will technology leaders meet their employees needs and offer mobile access to corporate system, data and information they crave, in order to maximise the potential for productivity and the competitive advantage that follows?"*

The above quote is from Mihaela Biti, the Programme Director of *Enterprise Mobility Exchange*, in her *Foreward* on the Global State of Enterprise Mobility [20] as reported by the company, following a global survey. The report shows that the bulk of the respondents are IT, Mobility and Technology workers, an industry where mobility is already widely embraced. Also, about 30.1% of the respondents have their operations globally, which presupposes they would have to mobilize anyway. Nonetheless, the mobility agenda for these enterprises are largely for automation aimed at operational performances and not for the facilitation of social interactions among employees. For example, when UPS successfully introduced the handheld Delivery Information Acquisition *mobile* Device (DIAD) for their drivers in 1991 [21], the question arose as to whether the next move was for customers to be able to quickly look and see real-time location of their driver and contact them directly. An answer to this question is FEDEX Mobile Solutions which allows customers to conveniently track their shipments, find the nearest FedEx station or drop-box, etc. An enterprise mobility strategy that is geared towards simple automation with mobile devices is good for enhancing operational efficiency of an enterprise. Of course, this is a source of competitive advantage, but only up to the point where they are unique to the company and as such, cannot easily be replicated (e.g., the Walmart Satelite investment [22]).

However, the consumerization of mobile devices has meant that the competitive advantage that a company derives, if any, from automation or implementation of mobile solutions will soon erode when competitors have adopted the same or similar solutions. In essence, a true competitive advantage is attainable when businesses and organizations proceed to the second - and third - order of organizational change, which are to *informate* and *transform* as highlighted in [23].

Therefore, the focus of this research is on mobile applications and devices that facilitate social interaction among

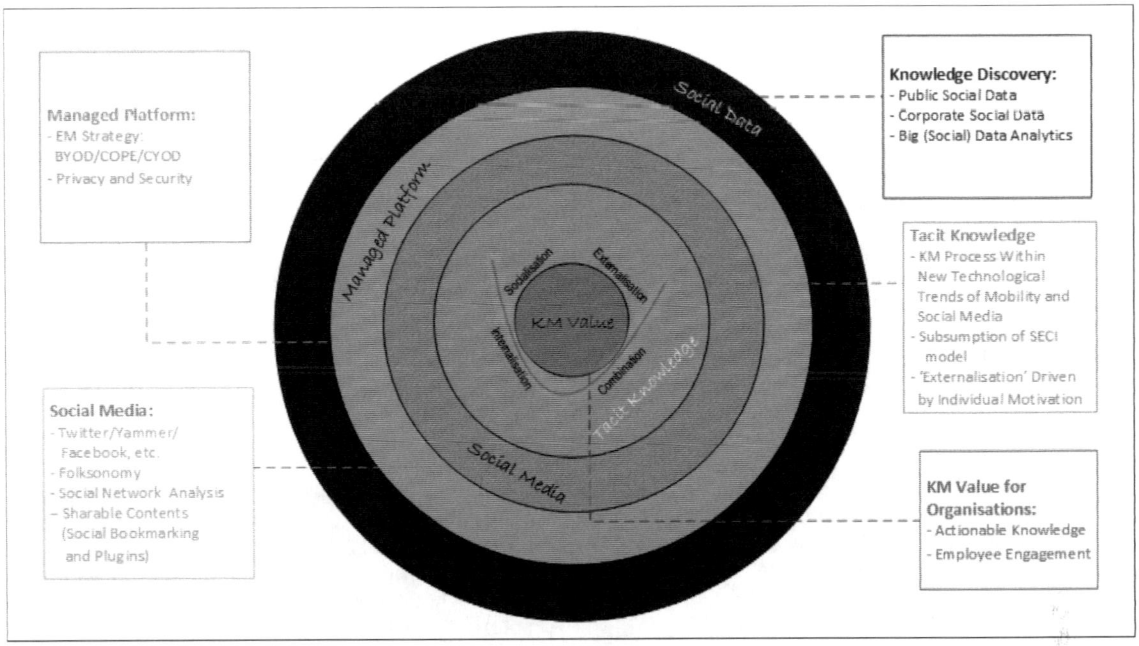

Figure 3: EMSoD - A Conceptual Social Framework for Corporate Knowledge Management

employees from which organizational knowledge could be gained. Such mobile devices as smart phones and tablets as well as the mobile applications like social media that they enable, which are in turn, enablers of social interaction within the organization.

KM based on the management and facilitation of these social interactions is potentially able to propel organization to strategic competitive advantage, especially in this era of knowledge economy where social media is playing a crucial role.

Technically, custom-made mobile devices for single applications like those used in the FEDEX and UPS examples can not be integrated with social interaction as the limitation of their design and capabilities precludes this. Therefore, employees cannot be expected to bring their own (BYOD), neither could they be expected to choose (CYOD) or personally enable (COPE) their own devices. Nonetheless, the newer technological trends of smart phones are already been used for the same functions, which means, delivery drivers can track and manage their delivery on their smart phones while also using the smart phones to interact with their colleagues on social media. They can, for example, tweet their locations or ask for direction and get immediate response from colleagues. On the same smart phone, they could make/receive calls to/from friends, family or colleagues or even interact with friends and family through social media on the smart phones. These are healthy for work life balances which results in a satisfied work force that is motivated to engage in social interaction and as such, knowledge sharing. This is altogether a function of the flexibility of the enterprise mobility management strategy adopted by the organization. If the organization's mobility strategy is aimed only at operational efficiency without the facilitation of social interaction, then the organization may not be able to reap the benefits in employee insights and knowledge for its strategic competitive advantage.

B. Tacit Knowledge

Inherent in humans is a *tacit power* by which all knowledge is discovered, and this propels an *active shaping of experience performed in the pursuit of knowledge* [12]. Our framework places more emphasis on the externalization of tacit knowledge, which, we believe, has become the dominant element of the widely known Nonaka's model of knowledge conversion (see Figure 4). This is due to the impact of the current trends of mobile devices and social media which allow an uninhibited externalization of thoughts even at the spur of the moment [10] except where the inhibiting factor is the individual motivation.

1) 'Externalization' Driven by Individual Motivation

The distinction between data and information is a given, from Computer Science and Information Systems perspectives. However, Information is often used interchangeably with Knowledge, albeit erroneously. [24] have gone a step further in attempting to create an understanding of data and information as necessary tools [or resources] for knowledge, discarding the notion that knowledge is data or information. [25, pp. 170-172], [26] and [27] all agree on a DIKW pyramid, which describes the configuration of data, information, knowledge and wisdom while [28] attempts to highlight the important differences between Knowledge Management and Information Management. It is because of the explicit nature of information that it has often been used interchangeably with knowledge whereas, explicit knowledge is only one side of the coin to knowledge. The other side of the coin is tacit knowledge, which people have in their minds and are not represented in an explicit way [29] because it is highly personal and difficult to formalise [5, 478]. One distinguishing factor between Knowledge and Information is in the disposition of tacit knowledge through its conversion to explicit knowledge (externalization) on the one hand, and the exchange of explicitly codified Knowledge on the other.

However, unlike the spiralling movement of tacit knowledge as described by the SECI model of [30] (see Figure 4), this framework considers the horizontal flow of tacit knowledge between individuals within an organization. This flow consists in each individuals 'externalizing' their views, opinions, sentiments and know-hows, at the spur of the moment [10], as enabled by the affordances of social media and mobile devices like smart phones and are supported by the current social interactions that exist within the organization. Having established engagement as a measurable value for organizations, the measurement of engagement is hinged upon the analysis of the social network that serves as the platform for the social interactions that exist within the organization. The thesis in this work is in the potential for a vast amount of data being generated by this social interaction, and from which actionable knowledge of value for the organization can be discovered.

2) Subsumption of SECI Model

[31] categorises KM processes into knowledge learning and developing phases. The main task in the knowledge learning phase is to learn new knowledge and increase employees' tacit knowledge from other tacit knowledge *(socialization)* or explicit knowledge *(internalization)*. The main task in the knowledge developing phase is to develop new knowledge by transforming tacit knowledge into explicit knowledge *(externalization)* or by combining explicit knowledge with other explicit knowledge *(Combination)*. In as much as tacit knowledge remains the conduit that connects both phases, the main thrust of this framework is to determine how the KM process can add value to organizations by enhancing tacit to explicit knowledge conversion within the construct of new technological trends of social media and enterprise mobility. This implies that this study is mostly concerned with the impact of the new technological trends of social media and enterprise mobility in supporting the "externalization" pane of SECI model. We believe that this is the first framework that subsumes an aspect of the SECI model into current technological circumstances. By the same token, this is the very first attempt at positioning an engaged workforce as the nucleus of an organizational knowledge creation process.

Moreover, [32] argues that socialization results in what he calls organization defensive routines with which most individual employees behave consistently even as the individuals move in and out of the organization. He concludes therefore that *because the actions used to create or to trigger organizational defensive routines are used by most people, their use cannot be attributed primarily to individual psychological anxiety*. In as much as knowledge conversion occurs when individual employees cooperate voluntarily in the process based on their own intrinsic motivation [33], the organizational culture would determine how this cooperation would engender positive knowledge sharing experience [34]. In supporting the externalization and combination

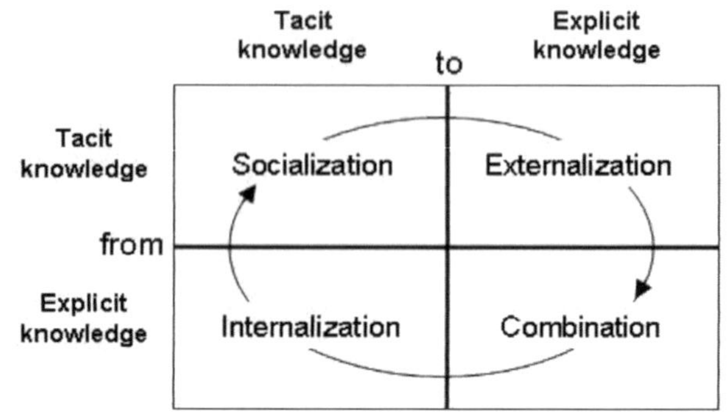

Figure 4: Nonaka's Model of Knowledge Conversion [30]

stages of SECI model, [29] observes the availability of knowledge acquisition methodologies for expert systems, discussion support systems or groupware in stimulating people's interaction. "However, these methods do not support the people's real-time discussion for knowledge acquisition", notes [29]. Mobile devices and social media trends enhance real-time discussion and as such require a new methodology in enabling them to support knowledge acquisition.

3) KM Process within New Trends

The tacit knowledge that exists within the socialization pane of SECI model cannot be converted to explicit knowledge if it existed solely at this pane, and therefore would not be usable except in an apprenticeship or a mentoring situation [31]. As mentioned above, the main thrust of the *EMSoD* framework is in how social media and enterprise mobility support employees in externalizing their tacit knowledge in such a way that shared knowledge is created through a combination of the explicit knowledge thus created with other explicit knowledge.

This framework subsumes the entire SECI model into the externalization of individuals' tacit knowledge which is enhanced by the Enterprise Mobility strategies of the organization coupled with the freedom of spontaneous expression offered by social media [10]. Social media tools like blogs and wikis, in addition to platforms like Twitter and Facebook, constitute the new technological trends with which KM must contend and subsist if it were to remain relevant [16, 17, 35, 36], ditto the perceived tension between KM and Social Media [4].

It is worth noting that existing methodologies in Computer Science do not sufficiently support the SECI model of knowledge conversion [29], especially in this new era in which IT has revolutionized the world [34]. Therefore, this framework is all about repositioning KM in a way that it delivers measurable value to organizations within these new trends.

C. Social Media

Social media are the collection of adaptable, scalable Web-based tools and technologies that facilitate the creation and sharing of user-generated contents [37, 38]. [39] describe them as " *browser or mobile-based applications that allow users to easily create, edit, access and link to content and/or to other individuals.*". "*Perhaps the best definition of social media, though, is content that has been created by its audience*", posits [40]. They include blogs, wikis and other social networking platforms like Facebook and Twitter [7, 16, 17, 35, 36], collaborative platforms like Myspace,Wikipedia, Ushahidi and Galaxy Zoo [2, 41]. Although, their origin can be traced back to the era of "*weblog*" which coincided with the creation of "*Open Diary*" which brought together online diary writers into one community in the sixties, they have become a popular trend that should be of interest to any company today [41]. Wikis are good for preserving the organization's memory while social networks like Facebook and micro-blogs like Twitter are helpful in expertise identification and location within the organization [42]. When it comes to including customer insight in an organization's social media strategies as suggested by [10], forums and message boards are probably the most common platform for questions and answers about products and brands [43], and can as well be included as a constituent source of external (public) social media that serve as external data source to the social data within the organization's managed platform.

1) Social Interactions on Social Media

Despite the media richness and "lifelike immersive world" that some social media platforms like Second Life provides, interactions on social media still cannot be as effective as face-to-face interactions [16], which has traditionally been the means of knowledge creation and transfer [44, pp. 7]. In fact, there has been a number of criticism with regards to the authenticity of the interaction and communication exchange over social media. One example pit forward by [45] is the story of a daughter who attempted suicide while in an actual state of distress whereas, she was at the same time using smiling emoticons and positive expressions to communicate a state of happiness to her mother. Perhaps this is why [46] believes that social media allows "*individuals to put on masks and hold up shields*". Yet the common denominator between all the Web-based social media tools and platforms is their ability to facilitate social interactions and conversations between people [17, 37, 39, 47, 48]. Moreover, it is not unusual for this online social interactions to extend even to face-face interaction, as it is found in [37] where an *Informant* comments that:

> " ...A lot of these people I have engaged in an online fashion have become part of our offline social functions and I formed real relationships with many. Hundreds of people: my network exploded it grew exponentially and it's through Twitter. It's through connecting with people. They find me. They reach out to me or I find them. I reach out to them. And we engage in ongoing conversations online, meeting up sometimes offline. These are real relationships."

.

In understanding the nature of social interaction on social media, [48] have aptly and succinctly provided some operational definitions of the following terms, which are reproduced here, with kind permission from the publishers (Emerald Insights):

1) Sociability
   The ability to interact with others, or to socialize... Websites use features, design standards or technologies to encourage sociability. For example, an online dating website uses profiles to encourage users to interact with other users. Or, a blog with user comments allows readers to respond to a topic and socialize with both the author and other readers.

2) Social network theory
   An interdisciplinary theoretical lens that emphasizes the relationships between actors (or users) within the network. The structure of the network is understood to be more important than the individual users... Social network theory, also called social network analysis (SNA), examines how the structure of a network affects users within the network.

3) Social networking sites
   Websites that encourage social interaction through profile-based user accounts. Social networking sites are commonly defined as Web 2.0..., meaning they mimic desktop applications. Popular social networking sites include Facebook and MySpace.

4) Social websites
   Websites and web technologies that promote socialization online. This term encompasses social networking sites as well as more traditional social web technologies including bulletin boards, message boards or web-based chat rooms. This will be the primary term used in this paper to describe social networking websites.

2) Folksonomy

Folksonomy is a term coined [49] as a linguistic contraction of *folk*, which informally refers to "people in general"; and *taxonomy*, which, as a formal system of structured classification of things and concepts, arose as a solution to the paramount problem in information management and retrieval: lack of organization [50]. Folksonomy is a practice in which individual users save/define Web contents as bookmarks/keyword in a social environment by attaching annotations in form of tags [51].

While taxonomy is a structured, top-down tagging system which the organization or a content creator imposed on the content for ease of retrieval and organization, folksonomy is an informal bottom-up approach to tagging where the user assigns tags to contents depending on the system. These tags are often used to create aggregated informal classifications (or, folksonomy), and as a navigational/discovery method.

3) Social Network Analysis

"*A social network is a social structure comprised of types of interdependency between nodes. Nodes are most commonly individuals or organizations. The configuration of individual nodes into a larger web of interdependency creates a social network*", explained [48], who also identify the two major types of interaction that exists within the social Web as:

1) People focused, which emphasizes social interaction through user-driven personal content centred around

a personal individual profile (e.g., Facebook, Twitter).

2) Activity focused, which emphasizes social interaction through site-specific content centred around a thematic focus for a website with users providing their own contributions to that specific theme (e.g., Youtube and Flickr for video and photo themes, respectively).

According to the authors [48], this analysis of the social web examines people focused websites and their strategies to encourage sociability. It also entails studying the structure of the connections and relationships within a social network like Twitter with regards to the further depths and insights they provide towards the pieces of knowledge discovered from the network as suggested in [1].

D. Knowledge Discovery

Frawley et al. [52] describe *knowledge discovery* as a nontrivial extraction of implicit, previously unknown, and potentially useful information from data. The word, *'nontrivial'* in the definition implies that a significant organizational effort must come to bear on a knowledge discovery initiative. Knowledge discovery has been a cause of significant concern for corporate organizations since the 1980s when the total number of databases in the world was an estimated five million [52]. Nowadays, with the proliferation of mobile devices and the social interactions enabled by them, there has been an exponential increase in the amount of data being produced — an amount that dwarfs the figure mentioned above.

As a result, corporate organizations are increasingly exploring and exploiting insights from the big (social) data being generated, for their competitive advantage [1]. Not only is there a need for organizations to focus on knowledge discovery from their private/corporate data, there are potential knowledge and insights to be gained from public social data as this would help organizations know their industry trends, know their environments and know their customers better [10].

Therefore, knowledge discovery efforts must be geared towards exploring and exploiting both public and private/corporate data, using big (social) data analytics techniques

E. KM Value

A couple of decades ago, "*discounted cash flow value*" may have been the best measure of value creation available [53]. Recently however, organizations have not only been regarding value in terms of the Returns on Investments, but they have also been giving considerations to intangible assets like organizational knowledge, patent and trademarks as measure of an organization's true value [54]. These indirect assets, according to [54], include employee morale, customer satisfaction and innovation; and, they are poised to "*transform the nature of business transactions by establishing the real value of enterprises for all stakeholders*".

Knowledge Managers and/or CIOs have often struggled to justify IT expenditure, especially, since when IT has been viewed from a cost centre perspective. This has often resulted in intangible field of practice like KM taking the hits from budget cuts as a result of a lack of measurable value [55]. However, since each process of Nonaka's SECI model (from *socialization* through *internalization*), "is positively associated with perceived knowledge satisfaction", [56] argue that organizations should focus more on perceived knowledge satisfaction rather than an objective measure of knowledge effectiveness. This is corroborated by "the Microsoft and Netscapes of the world..." which, according to [54, p. 6], show that, "even without a common yardstick for measuring Intellectual Capital, the recognition of its presence by informed observers will establish a value for a firm that dwarfs its balance sheet".

Moreover, with regards to value being defined as outcomes relative to cost, cost reduction without regard to the outcome achieved is dangerous and self-defeating, according to [57], who concludes that, outcomes, which are the numerator of the value equation, are inherently condition-specific and multidimensional. This position is strengthened by the NAO's definition of Value for Money (VFM): "*Good value for money is the optimal use of resources to achieve the intended outcomes*" [58]. What are these intended outcomes by which KM value can be measured and how can social media (the resources) be optimally used to achieve them? These are some of the issues encapsulated in the motivation for this research and the question this paper attempts to answer.

Based on the above premises, this paper identifies two intended outcomes from which knowledge satisfaction can be perceived, and by which we assert our measure of KM value to organizations: (i) the generation of *actionable knowledge* and, (ii) the facilitation of *employee engagement*.

Although many organizations have turned to storytelling and anecdotal success stories to show the value of their KM investments, there is an increasing need for businesses to show the business value of KM in terms of normalised quantitative measures in developing a case for Return on Investments [59]. This is what business managers and accountants, whose perception of realities is largely in terms of numbers, are looking for when they criticise KM for a want of measurable values. The *EMSoD* social framework proposed in this paper does not only deliver the KM value but also proffers solution for the measurement.

Meanwhile, "*Metrics fulfil the fundamental activities of measuring (evaluating how we are doing), educating (since what we measure is what is important; what we measure indicates how we intend to deliver value to our customers), and directing (potential problems are flagged by the size of the gaps between the metrics and the standard)*" [60]. It is worth noting that the topic of metrics is viewed differently from both Management and Academics, as Melnyk and others [60] observe:

> "The academic is more concerned with the validity and generalisability beyond the original context, of the results from such measurements that are defined, adapted and validated in addressing specific research questions. The manager, on the other hand, is more than willing to use a befitting measure if it can quickly provide useful information."

In view of this, we devised a simple measurement mechanism which, we believe, satisfies both academic and management concerns. This is denoted by the formula:

$$KMV = AK \times EW \quad (1)$$

where

$$KMV = KM\ Value,$$
$$AK = Actionable\ Knowledge$$
$$EW = Engaged\ Workforce.$$

Having laid out the *EMSoD* Framework, the next section proceeds with an overview of our work on *Knowledge Discovery from Social Media Data...* [1], with some additional insights that strengthen the work. This, we hope, would help the reader in making the connection between the background and our strong cases for *actionable knowledge* and *employee engagement* as measures of KM value, and the practical application of the above Formula (1) in measuring the value derived from KM through the *EMSoD* framework.

V. Knowledge Discovery from Social Media Data

In [1], we demonstrate the discovery of actionable knowledge from social media data with a case of Twitter data for small and medium-sized enterprises (SMEs). This is not only because SMEs are drivers of sustainable economic development [61], but also because their role within an Economy is so crucial that even the World Bank commits hugely to the development of the sector as a significant part of its efforts in promoting employment and economic growth [62].

Liaise Loddon is a medium-sized enterprise with about 220 employees, providing residential social care for adults with autism and learning disabilities in Hampshire, United Kingdom. As typical in this sector, operational procedures result in an enormous amount of documentation arising from daily diaries, incident/activity reports and several other reporting in compliance with regulatory requirements, analytical purposes and decision making. Although the company has recently deployed an enterprise mobility suite of mobile devices and applications to replace the existing paper-based documentation system, the research experiment explores how this enterprise mobility agenda could be hardened with knowledge sharing and knowledge extraction from the mass of social data freely available on Twitter, for example, in such a way as it supports the organization at the second level of organizational change. This highlights the people dimension of a socio-technical system [23, p.35-38].

As such, a total of 149,501 tweets based on categorical keyword, *autism*, is harvested from Twitter streaming API. Using textual analysis technique, extraneous elements are filtered out in order to reduce the data, as it is in data mining where one solution to the challenges of handling vast volumes of data is to reduce the data for mining [63]. We narrowed the investigation down to only the tweets emanating from the United Kingdom and in English language, out of which we discovered 1473 tweets containing meaningful contents within our research context. The contents, as categorised in Table I, are outlined in Subsection V-A below.

A. An Outline of Knowledge Contents from the Case Data

Despite the data collection being based on domain-specific keywords of interest to the paper's case study, the research is an exploratory study in which there was not a preconceived idea of the insights/knowledge inherent in the data. Out of an enormous amount of data, only a handful may contain the valuable and actionable knowledge that propels an organization towards strategic competitive advantage [63, p.5]. As such, the bulk of the contents as seen in Table I, are largely re-tweets (RT) of the original messages and so, may be regarded as extraneous amplification of the original tweets. Therefore, this section describes the categories observed in the data and the next section follows with a discussion on the value and actionability of the knowledge so discovered:

Table I: CONTENT CLASSIFICATION OF TWEET DATA

Contents	*No. of Tweets (Including RTs)*
Impact of Technology on Disability	15
Information Gathering	10
Political Opinions (#votecameronout)	132
Social Welfare Benefits	327
Living with Autism	989
Total Tweets	**1473**

1) Impact of Technology on Disability

> *"RT @BILD_tweets: Helping to unlock the secrets of autism - a project using innovative technology aims to change how we address autism http:..."*

The above tweet provides an insight into a project using innovative technology to change how we address *autism*. As this paper's case study organization is in the business of autism support and also currently implementing mobile technologies to enhance its operational performance, it is worth exploring this piece of insight further.

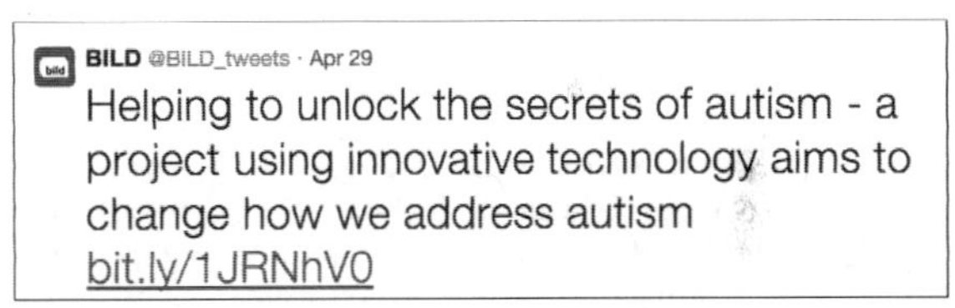

Figure 5: Original Tweet with Link to Project on Innovative Technology

Although the link to the actual URL of the story about the project is missing from the tweet, we can easily follow up with the original source of the tweet, as the above is a RT (Re-Tweet) of @BILD_tweets, which is the Twitter handle for BILD (British Institute of Learning Disabilities). BILD actually tweeted that piece of content on the 29th of April, which is a day before our data capture began, as can be seen in Figure 5. This explains why the original tweet was not captured in our twitter streaming data capture of 30th April to 6th May. From this original tweet, we have been able to extract the URL link (bit.ly/1JRNhV0) to the story about the project on innovative technology. This is about the National Autism Project, which "aims to create a more strategic approach to addressing the challenges of the condition". This project highlights the impact of iPads, picture dictionaries and interactive schedules on the improvements of communication and vocabulary of autistic people. Strategic competitive advantage requires an alignment/tagging along with this project. Below are samples of other tweets related to this content of Technology's impact

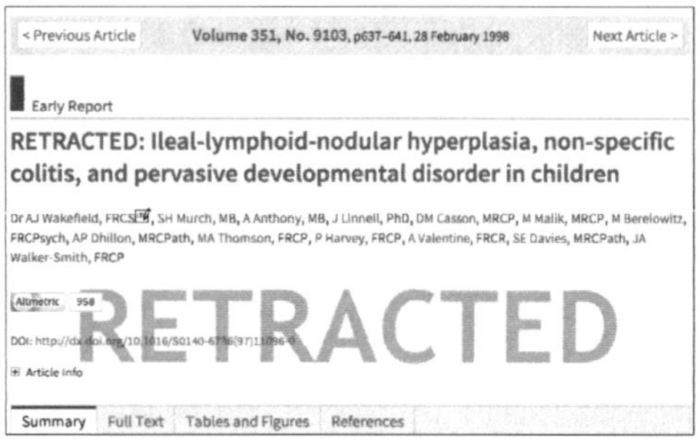
< Previous Article Volume 351, No. 9103, p637-641, 28 February 1998 Next Article >

Early Report

RETRACTED: Ileal-lymphoid-nodular hyperplasia, non-specific colitis, and pervasive developmental disorder in children

Dr AJ Wakefield, FRCS, SH Murch, MB, A Anthony, MB, J Linnell, PhD, DM Casson, MRCP, M Malik, MRCP, M Berelowitz, FRCPsych, AP Dhillon, MRCPath, MA Thomson, FRCP, P Harvey, FRCP, A Valentine, FRCR, SE Davies, MRCPath, JA Walker-Smith, FRCP

Altmetric 958

RETRACTED

DOI: http://dx.doi.org/10.1016/S0140-6736(97)11096-0

Article Info

Summary | Full Text | Tables and Figures | References

Figure 6: Retracted Study Linking Vaccine to Autism

on disability while its pertinence, as an actionable piece of knowledge, is discussed further in Section VI. Meanwhile, we have derived further insights from Twitter data, that helps in strengthening the position of this knowledge item (Impact of Technology on Disability). This is discussed in Section V-B

> *"tech reducing the impact of disability - or are the latest gadgets too pricey? Watch @SkyNewsSwipe at 2130 http://t.co/iHtX1spOqQ"*

> *"Technology limits impact of disability but is it affordable? @TwitterUser_GT http://t.co/Az3nJejO32"*

2) Information Gathering

Below is the first tweet about vaccines causing autism in this category, which is a request for information.

> *"@TwitterUser @BBCNewsUS @BBCWorld Please direct me to this research, the thing about vaccines causing autism was admitted to be a fraud."*

Just as an enterprise micro-blogging tool could be used within the organizational social network, public micro-blogging tools like Twitter provide the platform to quickly seek information, knowledge and/or ideas from a heterogeneous audience defying the constraints of space, time and location. Thus, the above tweet was almost instantly replied to by the one below:

> *"@TwitterUser Here's the original study that said that vaccines cause autism, from a respected, peer-reviewed journal: http://t.co/cmVVKpLQgh"*

Even though the original study is from a 'respected, peer-reviewed journal', as claimed by the sender of the above tweet, we know from the link provided that the publication of the research has been retracted as shown in Figure 6. The ability for anyone to search, gather and distribute information seamlessly in this manner provides an interesting dimension of social media as "relatively inexpensive and widely accessible electronic tools that enable anyone to publish and access information..."[64].

Meanwhile, the following two tweets provide link to further information that could help drive home the knowledge that the research study in question has actually been rebuffed:

> *"RT @TwitterUser: @SB277FF vaccines do not cause autism. They don't. But if they did, what would you prefer? Autism or incurable smallpox/po"*

> *"RT @BILD_tweets: There is 'no link between MMR and autism', major study concludes. http://t.co/Re9L8fPfGV via the @guardian #autism"*

In as much as Twitter allows for an almost spontaneous expression of opinions by anyone, it offers a good platform for healthy debate on topical issues from which knowledge could be mined, as exemplified by the question of preference between autism and incurable smallpox posed by one of the tweets above.

Moreover, the following tweet with a URL link to *Learning Disability Census* is an example in knowledge discovery (of an official census and regional data on Learning Disabilities), which when actioned in conjunction with the enterprise resource planning, could have an impact on the company's strategic planning:

> *"RT @dmarsden49: Learning disability census with regional stats is out. Check http://t.co/Ja3tk7ZRDZ"*

3) Political Opinions (#votecameronout)

The role of public opinion cannot be over-emphasized insofar as it shapes and is shaped by government policies. A recent and relevant example is the UK tax credits row [65], which has seen the planned tax credit cuts, at the time of writing this report, suspended by government because the scheme proved unpopular to the public and thus defeated in the House of Commons. Social media, especially Twitter, provides a means of capturing and measuring the sentiments and opinions of the electorate.

It is therefore, no coincidence that political opinions that have been expressed, are included in the Twitter data gathered over *autism* and *disability* keywords:

> *"#votecameronout Because he wants to get rid of Human Rights Act which will affect: Maternity Rights; Workers rights; Disability Rights"*

> *"For the harassment of people struggling on sick & disability benefits... #VoteCameronOut"*

> *"5 more years of the Tories we will lose Social Care, NHS, Human Rights, Workers Rights, Unions, Disability support. #VoteCameronOut"*

Using the hashtag #votecameronout in the run up to the UK General Elections of 2015, the above tweets represent an active campaign against the then incumbent Tory-led government in which David Cameron is Prime Minister. It is interesting to note that the bulk (129) of the political tweets in this experiment's Twitter data are a proliferated re-tweets (RT) of the above 3 original tweets. The correlation between public sentiments on social media and elections results and/or on government policies, is another growing area of interest in social media research. In politics meanwhile, it is not uncommon for opponents to whip up public sentiments by whatever means possible. Social Welfare issues are quintessentially core, and often politicised, concerns in the UK. A parallel category of tweets in this work is that of social welfare benefits, which is described in the next section. Although this research's data-set is based, as stated earlier, on categorical keywords that define

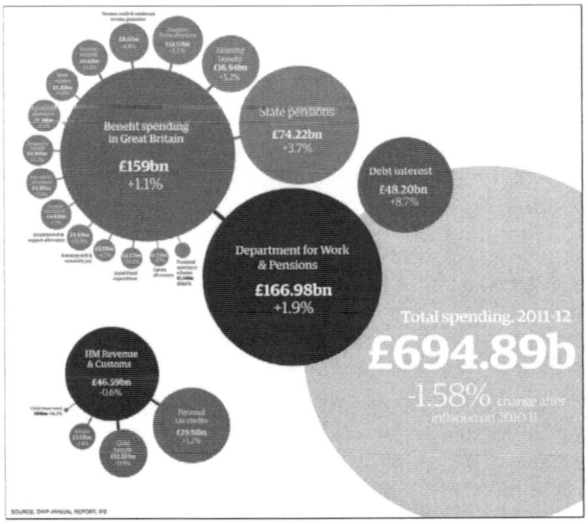

Figure 7: Public Spending on Benefits in the UK

the business of the case study organization, the infiltrated political opinions cannot be ignored in as much as these are public opinions that shape political trends which potentially impacts on businesses in terms of government policies. Akin to this is the category on social welfare benefits, described in the next section.

4) Social Welfare Benefits

Social Welfare simply implies the "Well being of the entire society" [66], which promotes inclusivity for the disabled, the sick, the elderly/pensioner, the unemployed and even the low income earners. As this is the hallmark of an egalitarian society, the UK government renders financial assistance to these categories of people in form of a range of Social Welfare Benefit payments. Figure 7 provides an insight into public spending on social welfare benefits in the UK [67]. As indicated in the preceding section, social welfare issues affect the fabrics of the society and any proposed significant cut in social welfare benefits is a natural invitation for public dissent. This category of tweets from this work represents genuine sentiments and opinion of those expressing them, without political motivations like the preceding category:

> "*Uproar at thought of @Conservatives cutting child benefits if elected - I wish there was same media outrage over disability cuts #GE2015*"

> "*@George_Osborne If only I could live until pensionable age. You've reduced my disability benefit well below living standards!*"

> "*39 yo woman killed herself after Department Work and Pensions threats to cut off disability benefits http://t.co/TkVQF2UYki...*"

Again, the above are a few samples of sentiments and opinions about *Child Benefits* and *Disability Benefits*, which provide an initial understanding to the unassuming, that social welfare benefits are not a one-size-fits-all affair but are multifarious (see Figure 7), with some being exclusively non-means tested (e.g, Child Benefit). These tweets provide some insights into public sentiments towards government policies. Since any of such social welfare benefit cuts would directly and/or indirectly impact the service users and providers of social care, it can be inferred that the case study organization would also share these public sentiments.

5) Living with Autism

Autism is defined as a *life-long neurodevelopmental condition interfering with the person's ability to communicate and relate to others* [68]. How can this definition be juxtaposed with one of the myths surrounding autism [69, item 8] that *autistic people do not interact*? This myth is however, dispelled by the tweet below, which is a re-tweet of an original tweet by an actual autistic blogger who attempts to use his blog posts to connect with the general public:

> "*@matt_diangelo RT? It would be truly amazing if u could view my blog about living with Autism&OCD. Would mean a lot- http://t.co/JCGBBZz8fJ*"

This category constitutes the bulk of the Twitter data for this work as it contains multiple unique re-tweet of the same tweet — over 900 times (see Table I). This is an indication of the public interest/curiosity and positive sentiment towards the subject of autism in general, and towards the autistic blogger in particular. Despite the National Health Service (NHS)'s attempts at educating the general public by diffusing some of the myth surrounding the subject of *Autism* [70], among several *Autism Awareness* initiatives, the story of autism as told by an autistic person appears to garner more public support and understanding. Measuring public opinion and sentiments through social media impact, reach and networks is another interesting research area in social media research towards which this work can potentially be extended.

B. *Further Insights from Twitter Data*

As it has been over one year since we gathered the data used for our previous study in [1] using the categorical keyword of *autism*, we decided to do a quick check on the current public conversation on the subject. We gathered 6118 tweets mentioning the categorical search keyword of *autism* for just one day on the 5th of August, 2016. Of this, 3,290 are original posts by Twitter users, 2828 are a Re-tweets of the original posts while the rest are *replies-to*. Although the day opens with a tweet containing a pleasant human story about the cure of autism (Figure 8), we found it pleasantly surprising that some top issues as discovered from our data of over a year ago, are still currently leading the conversations on the subject, as shown in Figure 9. Considering (A) and (B) from Figure 9, the following tweet content, as tweeted by the CNN, led the conversation at different times of the day, with 111 and 93 reactions, respectively:

> "How pokemon go helps kids with autism https://t.co/DZatqTX4sc #PokemonGo"

It is worth recalling that the theme of the *impact of technology on disability*, which was the most pertinent knowledge

Figure 8: Tweet about Cure for Autism

item from our previous data, did inform a significant corporate decision by the case study organization, as asserted in [1]. The above tweet on how the new *Pokemon Go* game helps autistic kids, is an indication of the fact that the theme of the impact of technology on disability, dominates the conversations on the subject of autism for the second year running. Although, not directly related to our *actionable knowledge* gains, another issue that gained prominence in our previous data was the debate over the causal relationship between vaccines and autism. The same debate still reappears prominently in the recent newer data on the subject of autism as shown in Figure 9 (C). The next section proceeds with a discussion on *actionable knowledge* and presents our proposed mechanism for placing a weighted measurement for KM value.

VI. Actionable Knowledge

Everyone agrees that Knowledge entails true belief [71], but this is not always the case. Using the man, the job and the coin analogy, Gettier [72] argues that it is possible for a person to be justified in believing a proposition that is in fact, false. This brings about the question of what actually counts as knowledge. In light of our data, we shall examine this question in our discussion on *actionable knowledge*, next.

A. Discussion on Actionable Knowledge

According to [73], propositions that are actionable are those that actors can use to implement effectively their intentions. A case in point is the enterprise mobility agenda of the case study organization as presented in Section V. The outcomes from an organization's KM efforts cannot adequately be measured from the report card perspective and indicator systems used in schools, for example. These systems, according to [74], contribute far less than they could to school improvement. Posner [74] highlights the following as the reasons for this assertion:

1) Their purposes and intended audiences are often diffuse or ill-defined.
2) They tend to focus too much on ranking and not enough on exemplary practices and models for action.
3) Many data sets are overly tied to consumer choice and not enough to citizen engagement.
4) Despite vast improvements, research remains inaccessible to many people, bringing knowledge online but not infusing it into capitols, classrooms and kitchen-table problem-solving

[74] therefore, suggests that information must be crafted around organising and action, citing [75], who says, "Actionable Knowledge is not only relevant to the world of practice, it is the knowledge that people use to create that world". The action triggered by knowledge is of the essence in determining the value that KM delivers to an organization. In fact, the real essence of knowledge is its actionability, especially when it contributes to the advancement of a proposed undertaking [3].

Each of the knowledge items discovered from the tweet data, as highlighted in Section V-A, is capable of providing significant insights that informs decision making, which impacts company's proposed undertakings at one point or another. However, as stated in [1], the first item, *Impact of Technology on Disability (No.1)*, is more pertinent to the enterprise mobility agenda by which the company deploys mobile application and devices to its operations. For example, one of the shortened URLs contained in one of the tweets (http://t.co/Az3nJejO32), leads to a Sky News supplement on *How Tech is Helping with Struggle of Disability*.

We assert therefore that, to aspire to a leadership position in the health and social care sector, the case study organization cannot afford to be oblivious to such reports as this, which could potentially shape the industry trends and direction. This knowledge, coupled with the insights gained from the use of iPads and pictorial dictionary mentioned in the *Project on Innovative Technology*, resulted in an official resolution by the company to extend the use of mobile devices to its service users as well, and not only to help staff in operational performances. It is worth noting that, although the piece of actionable knowledge regarding the impact of technology on disability was on the news prior to the extraction of data for that research, it was neither known nor acted upon by the company until the above decision was driven through a presentation made by the authors of this paper.

Meanwhile, we also discovered further insights from recent data, as discussed in Section V-B, which indicates that the theme of the *impact of technology on autism* is still leading the conversations on *autism* for the second year running. We had earlier alluded to the criticism of Knowledge Management as a field of practice, in spite of the gains — albeit intangible — from Knowledge Management and knowledge discovery efforts. This is due, in part, to the lack of a measurable value of those gains. With Equation (1) in Section IV-E, this paper proposes a measurement mechanism for KM Value delivered by our *EMSoD* framework, which is the main objective of this paper. The next section proceeds with a measurement mechanism for *actionable knowledge*.

B. Value Measurement Mechanism for Actionable Knowledge (AK)

The main objective of this paper is the delivery of KM value to corporate organizations which, we believe, our ***EMSoD*** framework helps to deliver. We had earlier identified *actionable knowledge* as a measure of KM value, in which actionable knowledge is denoted as AK for measurement purposes (see Equation 1 in Section IV-E).

To find the numerical value of (AK) in the equation $(KMV = AK \times EW)$, we devise a simple measurement mechanism as denoted in Equation (2):

$$\frac{\sum^{n} Weight_n}{n \times MaxWeight} \tag{2}$$

where

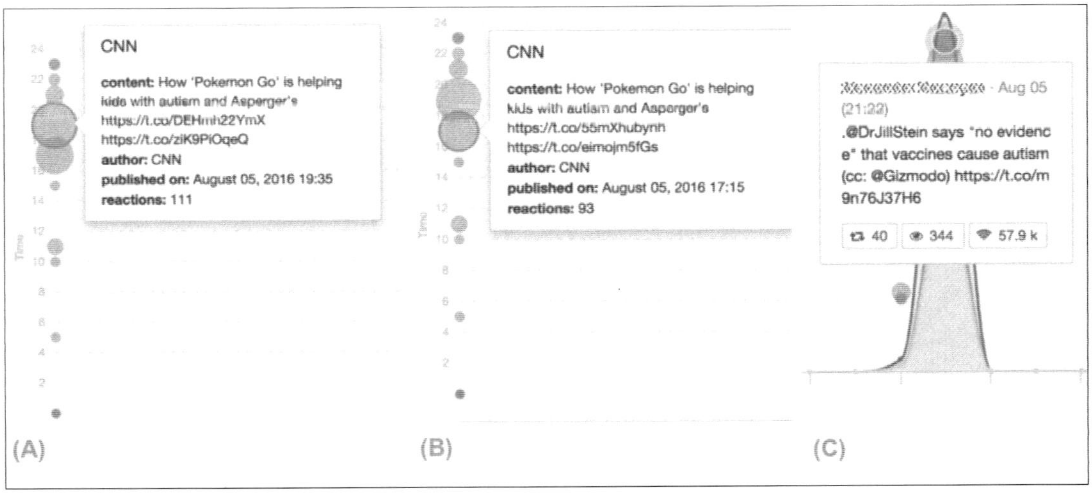

Figure 9: Top Issues from Newer Twitter Data

Table II: KNOWLEDGE CONTENTS AND THEIR WEIGHTS

Content	*Weight*
Impact of Technology on Disability	5
Information Gathering	2
Political Opinions (#votecameronout)	2
Social Welfare Benefits	3
Living with Autism	2

n = total content items
$MaxWeight$ = maximum assignable weight

As an example, we consider our knowledge content items from our previous work as outlined in Subsection V-A and displayed in Table I. The total content items (n) is 5 and each one of them is given a weight of 2, 3 or 5, which represent low, medium or high value, respectively. Please note that the weights have nothing to do with the *No. of Tweets* as displayed in the second column of Table I. However, the weights represent the pertinence of the knowledge item to the matter or issue at hand within the organization, where the maximum weight (MaxWeight) of 5 represents a high pertinence, 3 represents medium pertinence and the weight of 2 represents a low pertinence. High to low pertinence is directly mappable to high to low value, respectively. We acknowledge the probability and freedom for subjectivity in assigning these weights. However, in order to reduce the level of subjectivity, we recommend for this measurement activity to be carried out only after the KM activity/event in question has been concluded. In our example, the knowledge discovery from social media data has been completed and we know which of the knowledge items has had a high impact on management's decision making for us to assign a high weight of 5; and, medium weight of 3 and low weight of 2 to items we consider of medium and low values, respectively, as shown in Table II.

The item with the maximum weight (MaxWeight) of 5, *Impact of Technology on Disability*, is of a high pertinence to the enterprise mobility agenda by which the company deploys mobile application and devices to its operations.

Therefore, going by Equation (2), the maximum value is 25, being a product of the total number of content items (n, which in this case, is 5) and the maximum weight (5). The total number of content items (n) could be any whole number, which allows for AK to be representative of every knowledge content item or categories that is considered relevant for inclusion in the value measurement. Also, with the numerator being a sum of all the $Weights_n$, the value of AK from Equation (1) is given thus:

$$KMV = 0.56 \times EW \tag{3}$$

A Note on Weights and Values Assignment

One may ask why the *Impact of Technology on Disability* receives the maximum weight of 5? As stated earlier, it is because of being of more pertinence to the enterprise mobility agenda by which the company deploys mobile application and devices to its operations? For example, one of the shortened URLs from the tweets (http://t.co/Az3nJejO32) leads to a Sky News supplement on *'How Tech is Helping with Struggle of Disability'*. To aspire to a leadership position in the health and social care sector, the case study organization cannot afford to be oblivious to such reports as this, which could potentially shape the industry trends and direction. This knowledge, coupled with the insights gained from the use of iPads and pictorial dictionary mentioned in the *'Project on Innovative Technology'* resulted in an official resolution by the company to extend the use of mobile devices to its service users as well, and not only to help staff in operational performances. It is worth noting that, although the piece of actionable knowledge regarding the impact of technology on disability was on the news prior to the extraction of data for that research work, it was neither known nor acted upon by the company until the above decision was driven through a presentation made by the authors of this paper.

The *EMSoD* framework presented in this paper is predicated upon the capability of social media in delivering actionable knowledge to corporate organizations. We have thus, been able to place a measurable value on actionable knowledge (AK). This is ordinarily sufficient as a measure of KM value derived from such insights from social media data. However, our framework — and the KM value it delivers to corporate organizations — is further strengthened by an additional measure of the KM value, which is *employee engagement*, denoted as EW (Engaged Workforce) in Equation (1). The next section discusses *employee engagement* in the light of the social network that exists within the organization, the impact of the structure of the network on employee engagement and knowledge sharing as well as a measurement mechanism for the KM value of *employee engagement*.

VII. Employee Engagement

It is worth reiterating our assertion of *employee engagement* as a measure of KM value for business, given that "the level of employee engagement is one of the most important indicators of the likelihood of an organization succeeding financially and delivering to its vision and mission statements" [76]. Also, research has shown that, having a highly engaged workforce not only maximises a companys investment in human capital and improves productivity, but it can also significantly reduce costs (such as turnover) that directly impacts the bottom line [77].

Thus, the organization's Enterprise Mobility Management (see *Managed Platform* in Section IV-A) defines the organizational boundary within which employees' contributions are gathered as a measure of their engagement and as a reference point for the organizations Social Network Analysis, which can serve as knowledge input to the organizations Intellectual capital.

Based on the above premises, this work posits the prevalence of knowledge creation and knowledge sharing culture in an organization with a truly engaged workforce. How then, does the social network facilitate employee engagement? How does the structure of the connections and relationships within a social network provide further depth and insights to knowledge discovered from such networks [1]? We explore this question further, first in the light of the power of social networks and an anatomy of the social network of an engaged workforce.

A. Power to Know, Power to Tell

"*I shall reconsider human knowledge by starting from the fact that we can know more than we can tell*", writes Michael Polanyi [12], whose writings and philosophical thoughts provide an impetuous theoretical background for many scholars and practitioners of Knowledge Management. This lends credence to Turban and others [11, p.478]' idea of the difficulty in formalising tacit knowledge. Embroiled in information overload due to a deluge of data and exponential growth in information systems, technologies and infrastructures, the ability to know or tell as much as we know is limited by our human cognitive capabilities. However, the same information systems and technologies, which were not in existence during the times of Polanyi, allow us to offload our cognition on to them [78]. Such technologies (e.g., the Web) are enablers of online social networks, which does not only allow us to offload our cognition onto them but also allow us to benefit from the problem-solving and decision-making situations offered through the "wisdom of the crowd" [79] amazed through the cognition offloaded by several other individuals.

With several actors within a social network offloading their cognition onto the social network through explicit expression [10], a wealth of tacit knowledge is inadvertently built up, albeit explicitly converted. This wealth of knowledge is, of course, too massive for an individual to tell. It might even be impossible for one individual to be expected to know of the existence and/or extent of such knowledge, due in part, to the limitations in human cognitive capabilities, as mentioned earlier. It must be noted however, that this is only a limitation applicable to a single individual, but not to a corporate organization. With the affordances of social network analysis (SNA), a corporate organization is empowered to know more about, and exploit, the wealth of knowledge that is built up within its enterprise social network. The organization can tell, through visualisation and network analysis, the structure of the social network and its impact on *employee engagement* that propels externalization of tacit knowledge. In essence, we can assume that, if Polanyi [12] were to reconsider human knowledge within the context of social networking trends today, he would probably say that, *"we can tell as much as we can know."*

B. Social Network Analysis

Social Network Analysis (SNA) is described as a detailed examination of the structure of a network and its effect on users (actors) within the network, wherein the structure of the network is understood to be more important than the individual users [48]. A core component of our *EMSoD* framework is Social Media (see Section IV-C), which serve as platforms for social interactions on the Web. With peculiar example of Twitter, these social interactions are explained by the relationship types of *'mentions'*, *'replies to'* and just, *'tweets'*. A *mentions* relationship exist when a message on Twitter *tweet* mentions another user (@Username) while a *replies to* relationship exist when a *tweet* is in reply to another user's tweet by preceding the *tweet* with the other user's Twitter ID (@Username). When a tweet is neither a reply to - or contain a mention of - another Twitter user, the tweet creates a relationship type of *tweet*, which exist as a self loop and is indicated on a network visualisation as a node with an arrow that projects and returns unto itself. These relationships develop into a network of connections.

In SNA, the connections between people are considered as the units of analysis that reveal the flow of information and how these connections define the structure of the network, which also refers to the presence of regular patterns in relationship [80]. Gaining insights towards the understanding of the components and structure of a social network requires a vocabulary and techniques provided by Social Network Analysis (SNA) and Visualisation [81]. This vocabulary and techniques are described in our examination of two different kinds of networks identified by Rossi and Magnani [82] as, (i) the *topical network*, which is made up of relationships created through tweets/activities that are aggregated over a topic or the *#hashtag* and, (ii) the *Twitter network*, which is made up of all the relationships between the users (followers and friends). We believe that the relationship between the Twitter *[structural]* network and the topical network can be likened to that of the

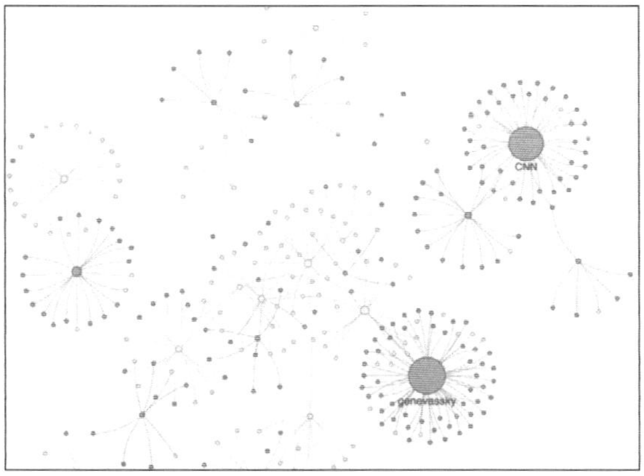

Figure 10: Influencers Engagement Network Graph

physical and logical topologies of a communications network infrastructure.

C. Understanding the Topical Network

A topical network is created when users are connected by common topical issues, where individuals save/define Web contents as bookmarks/keyword in a social environment by attaching annotations in form of tags [51], normally preceded by the hash symbol on most keyboards (#). The hashtag can be said to be the democratic manifestation of taxonomic principles in the social media era (see Section IV-C). Trant (2009) [83] highlights the description of such *tags* as publicly shared user generated keywords, which have been suggested for use as a trivial mechanism for further improving the description of online information resources and their access through broader indexing.

An example of the topical network is shown in the Influencers Engagement Network Graph presented in Figure 10. This network has been aggregated over the search keyword and hashtag of *#autism*, as found in our recent data on the subject (see Section V-B). Both this *topical network* study and the study that results in further insights on our previous study from recent data, were performed on the University's account on the Pulsal Platform — an audience intelligence analytic platform for social media.

D. Limitation of the Topical Network

The *EMSoD* social framework proposed in this research operates within a *managed platform* (Section IV-A), which defines the organizational boundary. Although the hashtag phenomenon has been successful in aggregating online topical discussions without boundaries, the relationships created over mutual hash-tagged conversation is ephemeral [82], and so is the network created. Unless the hashtag can be tamed, its use on a public Twitter account can be so widespread that it compromises the need, if there were, to keep the conversations within the organizational boundary. Even with the use of enterprise Twitter's alternative like *Yammer*, aggregating events and conversation over the hashtag cannot but include *Yammer-wide* conversations and events from outside the organizational boundary.

To illustrate, when one takes a look at the topical network created over our recent data on the subject of *autism* in Figure 10. The nodes are not defined within a single geographical boundary. The nodes in yellow colour represent those from the United Kingdom. The location information for the nodes in blue is unavailable. This means that users from various countries other than the UK are aggregated over this topic. In fact, the two most engaged influencers's networks (CNN and *genevassky*) are not from the UK. This may be good in that it provides further reach and depth around the topic but not for classified organizational conversation that needs to be kept within the boundary of the organization's network, assuming the UK was a corporate entity in the business sense.

Specifying network boundaries in terms of hashtag or keywords that connect people together in this manner is more akin to the *normalist approach* of specifying a network, which is based on the theoritical concerns of the researcher [80], whereas the actors may not even know one another. Contrarily, Wasserman and Faust [80] also describe a second way of specifying network boundaries, the *realist approach*, wherein the actors know one another, since membership of such network is as perceived and acknowledged by members themselves. In essence, employees would readily acknowledge and engage with fellow colleagues as members of the same network. The *realist approach* aligns with the *Twitter* network as identified by Rossi and Magnani [82]. The next section attempts to create an understanding of the *Twitter* network.

E. Understanding the Twitter Network

Considering its perceived ease of use and a broad coverage of SNA metrics and visualisation features [84], we used NodeXL — a network analysis and visualisation package designed for the analysis of online social media on Microsoft Excel [85] — to examine the egocentric network [86] of relationships that develop over a one month period from 26/07/2016 to 25/08/2016. As stated earlier, relationships emerge when a user (the source) *mentions* or *replies to* another user (the destination) in their tweet. For example, the following tweet of 29/07/2016, in which @unisouthampton *mentions* @nature — the Twitter handle for the International Weekly Journal of Science — creates a relationship (*mentions*) between the two entities:

> "Our #research places us top 50 globally and 4th in the UK, in @nature Index Rising Stars: https://t.co/XwXKR9N8Az https://t.co/VGQDxPE74y"

A relationship also emerges when a tweet is self sufficient without *mentioning* or *replying to* any other tweet by including or preceding with another Twitter @username, respectively. These are regarded as *self loop* and is indicated in Figure 11 by the red arrow proceeding and returning to the source (@unisouthampton). As can be expected that a user could tweet without having to mention or reply to any other user, there are 68 such self loops, 102 unique Edges and 129 Vertices (Nodes) within the network so generated (see Table III). The connections made through the *'replies to'* relationships are represented with Edges (connections lines) of 60% opacity than the connections made through the *mentions* relationship, which are represented by Edges of 20% opacity.

Figure 11: A Directed Network Graph of @unisouthampton

Meanwhile, the network graph in Figure 11 is a *directed graph*, or *digraph* for short, which represents directional relations comprised of a set of nodes representing the actors in the network and a set of arcs [lines] directed between pairs of nodes representing directed ties between nodes [80]. A social network graph is formally represented by a graph G = (V, E), where V is the set of nodes (vertices) and E is the set of edges (ties) [87]. However, a cursory look at the network graph in Figure 11 would reveal that the @unisouthampton account, represented with the large icon of the University of Southampton logo, has only an *Out-Degree* connection with up to the 129 nodes and 1 *In-Degree* connection, which is the self loop unto itself. The *directed* relations through In- and Out-Degree connections define the asymmetric relationship model of 'following' in Twitter, which allows one to keep up with the tweets of any other user without the need for the other user to reciprocate [88].

Table III: GRAPH METRICS FOR FIGURE 11

Vertices	129
Unique Edges	102
Edges With Duplicates	163
Total Edges	265
Self Loops	68

According to [80], "the concept of a network emphasizes the fact that each individual has ties to other individuals, each of whom in turn is tied to a few, some or many others. The phrase, "social network" refers to the set of actors and the ties among them. The network analyst would seek to model these relationships to depict the structure of a group. One could then study the impact of this structure on the functioning of the group and/or the influence of this structure on individuals within the group".

However, the network as it is presented in Figure 11 is not an ideal network that encourages knowledge sharing and engagement among the actors. The three relationships that develop were initiated by @unisouthampton's tweets in which other users were *mentioned* or *replied to* or in which the tweets were sent wholly to create a *tweet* relationship. Querying NodeXL with only the Twitter ID of a corporate or individual's Twitter account, as we did with @unisouthampton, would only result in a visualisation of the list of connections, as Figure 11 reveals. Moreover, with over 40,000 nodes, a meaningful visible visualisation of a network of such magnitude as the @unisouthampton's can be difficult because of the inherent complexity of the relationships and limited screen space [89]. According to Wasserman and Faust [80], "The restriction to a finite set or sets of actors is an analytic requirement."

Therefore, we identified 93 Twitter users (Vertices or Nodes) within the University of Southampton and examine the network of connections that evolves around them. Table IV presents the overall graph metrics.

Table IV: GRAPH METRICS FOR THE NETWORK GRAPH OF 93 VERTICES

Graph Metric	Value	Graph Metric	Value
Graph Type	Directed	Connected Components	9
Vertices	93	Single-Vertex Connected Components	8
Unique Edges	303	Maximum Vertices in a Connected Component	85
Edges with Duplicates	15925	Maximum Edges in a Connected Component	15758
Total Edges	16228	Maximum,Geodesic Distance (Diameter)	3
Self-Loops	13628	Average Geodesic Distance	1.962102
Reciprocated Vertex Pair Ratio	0.221206581	Graph,Density	0.078073866
Reciprocated Edge Ratio	0.362275449	NodeXL Version	1.0.1.355

1) Grouping the Network on the Basis of Node Importance

Various metrics (Degree centrality, eigenvector centrality, pagerank, etc) capture various ways in which each individual node (user) acts as a centre of attraction through which knowledge and information propagates within the network. Sorting by Betweenness Centrality for example, sorts people who have the quality of most broadly connecting across the network to the top while Clustering coefficient measures how closely connected each users connections connected to one another [90]. As this work is focused on measuring and seeking to facilitate employee engagement, we have used Betweeness Centrality (BC) as our measure of ranking for node importance based on the potential of such central points for binding the network together by coordinating the activities of other points, albeit, they may be viewed as structurally central to the extent that they stand between others and can therefore facilitate, impede or bias the transmission of messages [91]. Moreover, measuring proximities can help to characterise the global structure of a network by showing how closely coupled it is [92]

Table V: Groups of Vertices with Metrics

Group	Vertices	Unique Edges	Edges with Duplicates	Total Edges	Self Loops	MAX. Geodesic Distance	AVG. Geodesic Distance	Graph Density
G1	41	90	7415	7505	6972	4	2.083	0.115
G2	21	1	2112	2113	2113	0	0.000	0.000
G3	19	2	2759	2761	2751	1	0.240	0.012
G4	12	21	2151	2172	1792	2	1.194	0.462

Accordingly, the 93 nodes (users, also referred to as *vertices*) in the network are ranked and grouped on the basis of their Betweeness Centrality, with each group disc sized according to the number of nodes that make up the range of measures for the group, as visualised in Figure 12 and the group metrics in Table V.

2) Decomposing the Network Group of 93 Nodes

The smallest group in the network graph presented in Figure 12 (Light Green, G4:12) is a group of 12 nodes with the highest Betweeness Centrality ranging from 115.194 to 2494.640 (see Table VI), although the node with the highest Betweeness Centrality (2494.640) is @unisouthampton, and understandably with over 40,000 followers compared to only 558 followers of the next highest Betweeness Centrality node, @sotonwsi (at BC score of 522.543), and 2390 followers for @lescarr (with a betweeness centrality score of 425.512), in that order.

The largest group (Dark Blue, *G*1 : 41) is comprised of 41 nodes (vertices) with the second highest Betweeness Centrality ranging from 11.408 to 99.715, with the highest being @garethpbeeston (99.715), @lisaharris (94.079) and @mark_weal (93.573) in that order. Group 3 (Dark Green, G3:19) is composed of nodes with the third highest betweeness centrality ranging from 1.067 to 8.627.

Groups 4, 3 and 1 are subgroups of this directed graph, as demonstrated by the direction of the arrows on all sides, and as such, potentially represent an engaged network that could possibly facilitate knowledge sharing. Group 2 (Light Blue, G2:21) may be considered negligible as 16 out of the 21 nodes have not a single score for Betweeness Centrality, and thus, they would have little or no impact on the network. Expanding the graph to show the nodes in each group (see Figure 13 reveals some of the nodes in group 2 (light green dots) are actually outliers that have no tie with the network at all as they have not engaged in any relationship with any other member of the network, either by mentioning or replying to, other than themselves by way of tweeting (self loop), hence, they have each scored zero in the betweeness centrality measurement. We can even spot 2 of them that have never tweeted within the time-frame and as such, do not have the arrow-edged ring of self loop (tweet) but are standing aloof. The top 20 nodes are labelled 1 through 20 in order of their Betweeness Centrality while the top 12 are colour coded light green. Essentially, the groups are examples of subgroups in a one-mode network, in which measurement is based on just a single set of actors [80], albeit grouped according to their individual attributes of Betweeness Centrality.

Meanwhile, the chart in Figure 14 reveals that the Red, Dark Green and Green bars are in the top echelons of nodes with the highest Betweeness Centrality (a total of 23 nodes) while the bulk of the nodes in the entire graph - that is, a total of 70 nodes represented as Dark Blue bar on the chart - are with the lower range of Betweeness Centrality. With the highest Betweeness Centrality of 2,494.64 (Colour red on the far right), the node representing the egocentric network of @Unisouthampton, which is the official Twitter account of the University of Southampton, has over 40,000 followers. However, the measure of a node's Betweeness Centrality is not based on the number of followers but on the number of shortest paths from all nodes to all other nodes that pass through that node [91]. This explains why the node with only 558 followers (@sotonwsi) has the second highest betweeness centrality (522.543). Although it could be argued that both @unisouthampton and @sotonwsi are non-personal accounts, it must be noted that the node with the next highest betweeness centrality of 425.512 (@lescarr) has more follower count (2390) than the previous (@sotonwsi). The top 20 nodes by betweeness centrality can be visualised in the network graph in Figure 13 (with each node labelled 1 through 20) while Table VI presents the individual metrics for 12 of the top 20 nodes (users), according to betweeness centrality, within the network. The Individual Node Metrics in Table VI provides

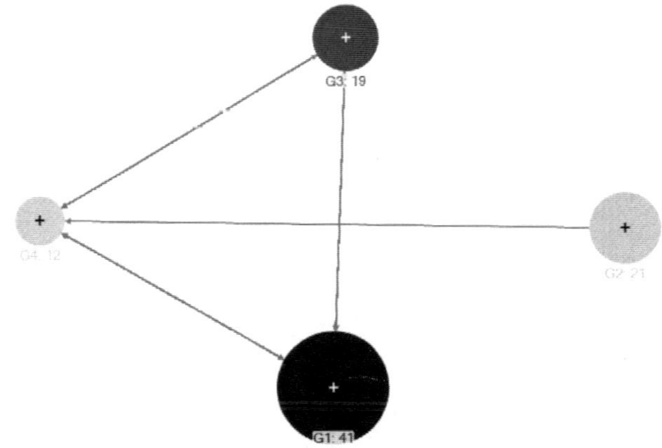

Figure 12: Network graph of 93 Vertices Grouped According to Betweenness Centrality

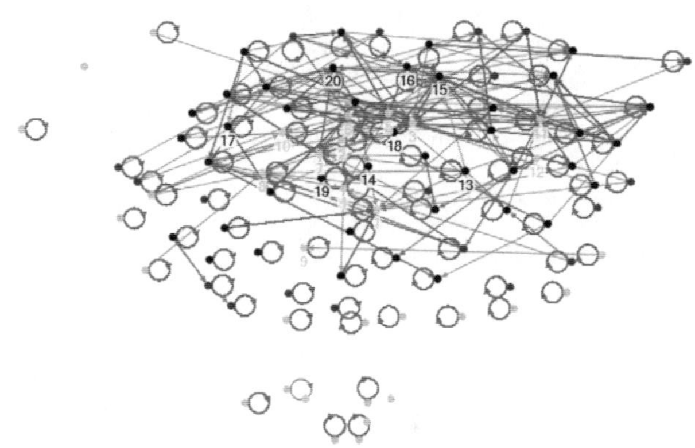

Figure 13: Expanded Group of Nodes According to Betweeness Centrality

Table VI: TOP 12 INDIVIDUAL NODE METRICS

No.	Node	Betweeness Centrality	Eigenvector Centrality	Page Rank	Clustering Coefficient
1	unisouthampton	2494.640	0.038	4.644	0.092
2	sotonwsi	522.543	0.037	2.764	0.198
3	lescarr	425.512	0.031	2.520	0.186
4	ecsuos	349.333	0.028	2.308	0.191
5	suukii	325.737	0.019	1.756	0.165
6	susanjhalford	206.940	0.029	2.065	0.227
7	damewendydbe	179.074	0.028	1.852	0.284
8	hughdavis	164.789	0.019	1.538	0.233
9	iliadsoton	150.258	0.015	1.646	0.174
10	webscidtc	146.866	0.026	1.784	0.268
11	richardgomer	134.370	0.14	1.321	0.180
12	sotonwais	115.194	0.015	1.176	0.233

another interesting aspect, which is that, another metric or a combination of metrics may be used depending on the intended purposes, although we have ranked these 12, out of 20 nodes, according to their scoring highest in Betweeness Centrality. For example, if the nodes were ranked in accordance with their Eigenvector Centrality, @susanjhalfod (No.6) would have ranked higher than @suukii (No.5). Eigenvector is a centrality measure that considers the value of a node, not in terms of its connections but in terms of the value of centrality of such connections [87]. In essence, the ranking of a node is based on the importance and/or ranking of the nodes it is connected to, which means @suukii may serve as bridge to propagate knowledge among a vast number of people than @susanjhalford; the connections in themselves are not as strong and vital within the network.

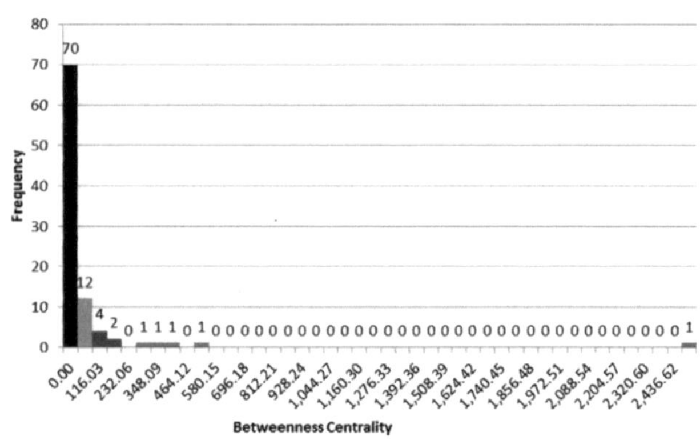

Figure 14: A Chart of Betweeness Centrality Spread among the 93 Vertices

F. Determination of an Engaged Workforce

With reference to our Knowledge Management Value measurement in Formula (1), where $KMV = AK \times EW$ (see KM Value in Section IV-E), we hereby devise a mechanism to determine the value of an engaged workforce (EW). We have established that the interactions that create the user network is based on users' activities in *tweeting* and/or *mentioning or replying-to* another user within their own tweets, thereby creating the relationships known as Edges in Table V. Each node in the network has been assigned to the groups in Table V based on individual node's measure of Betweenness Centrality. Table V also includes the graph density for each group. A sum of all the groups' graph densities equals 0.59, which indicates a sparse graph, owing that a dense graph is always equals to 1.

Graph density is an indicator of *connectedness* of a network, given as the number of connections in a graph divided by the maximum number of connections [93]. This *connectedness* is also a function of the interactions that create the relationships upon which the network is formed, as mentioned earlier. We therefore, measure *engagement* in terms of *graph density*. Whatever value we get for AK is either maintained or negated by the value of EW depending on whether the network is dense or sparse, respectively. This allows for the determination of Knowledge Management Value (KMV) to be inclusive of both values from AK and EW as indicated in Equation (4).

$$KMV = 0.56 \times 0.59 = 0.33 \tag{4}$$

This method can be used to compare Knowledge Management values derived from different KM activities/events or expressed in percentage to determine the return on investments on such activities/events.

VIII. Conclusion

This paper has presented *EMSoD*, a conceptual social framework that mediates between KM and SM, with the aim of delivering KM values to corporate organizations. The paper identifies *actionable knowledge* and *employee engagement* as parameters of KM values that the *EMSoD* framework helps in delivering. As KM has suffered an image problem due, in part, to the lack of measurable value, the paper devises a mechanism for measurement of the KM value delivered by the *EMSoD* social framework. Meanwhile, the paper has adopted very simple approaches, making it easy for any organization of any size to replicate the methods, not only for delivering KM value, but also for measuring and evaluating the KM values so delivered. Thus, the paper serves as basis and initial input for integration and operationalization of the *EMSoD* social framework within a corporate social software platform. To this end, it is important to, first, consider the interdependence and interactions between the core elements of the framework (as emphasized by the cyclical presentation of the *EMSoD* framework in Figure 3) as an iterative process that results in KM value for organizations, within the construct of social media. Then, the framework can further be modelled into entity relationship for database and software developers to operationalize by defining Entity classes that are independent of a database structure and then, map the core elements to the tables and associations of the database. This provides a suggestion for future direction to which this paper could be extended.

References

[1] C. Adetunji and L. Carr, "Knowledge Discovery from Social Media Data : A Case of Public Twitter Data for SMEs," in *8th International Conference on Information, Process and Knowledge Management (eKnow)*, no. c. Venice: IARIA XPS Press, 2016, pp. 119–125.

[2] P. R. Smart and N. R. Shadbolt, "Social Machines," in *Encyclopedia of Information Science and Technology*, M. Khosrow-Pour, Ed. Pennsylvania: IGI Global, Aug. 2014.

[3] R. Cross and L. Sproull, "More Than an Answer: Information Relationships for Actionable Knowledge," *Organization Science*, vol. 15, no. 4, Aug. 2004, pp. 446–462.
[4] D. P. Ford and R. M. Mason, "A Multilevel Perspective of Tensions Between Knowledge Management and Social Media," *Journal of Organizational Computing and Electronic Commerce*, vol. 23, no. 1-2, Jan. 2013, pp. 7–33.
[5] E. Turban, R. Sharda, and D. Delen, *Decision Support and Business Intelligence Systems*, 9th ed. Dorling Kindersly (India) Pvt, Ltd., 2011.
[6] T. H. Davenport and L. Prusak, *Working Knowledge: How Organizations Manage what They Know, Part 247*. Boston: Harvard Business Press, 1998.
[7] L. Razmerita, K. Kirchner, and T. Nabeth, "Social Media in Organizations: Leveraging Personal and Collective Knowledge Processes," *Journal of Organizational Computing and Electronic Commerce*, vol. 24, no. 1, Jan. 2014, pp. 74–93.
[8] C. Sorensen, "Enterprise Mobility," *Work and Globalization Series, Palgrave*, 2011.
[9] C. Sørensen, A. Al-Taitoon, J. Kietzmann, D. Pica, G. Wiredu, S. Elaluf-Calderwood, K. Boateng, M. Kakihara, and D. Gibson, "Exploring enterprise mobility: Lessons from the field - Information, Knowledge, Systems Management - Volume 7, Number 1-2 / 2008 - IOS Press," *Information, Knowledge, Systems Management*, vol. 7, no. 1-2, 2008, pp. 243–271.
[10] P. Zikopoulos, C. Eaton, D. DeRoos, T. Deutsch, and G. Lapis, *Understanding Big Data: Analytics for Enterprise Class Hadoop and Streaming Data*. New York: McGraw Hill, 2012.
[11] E. Turban, N. Bolloju, and T.-P. Liang, "Enterprise Social Networking: Opportunities, Adoption, and Risk Mitigation," *Journal of Organizational Computing and Electronic Commerce*, vol. 21, no. 3, Jul. 2011, pp. 202–220.
[12] M. Polanyi, *The Tacit Dimension*. University of Chicago Press, 2009.
[13] D. Griffiths and B. Moon, "The state of knowledge management A survey suggests ways to attain more satisfied users." 2011. [Online]. Available: http://goo.gl/2bqHLB [Last Accessed 17 November 2016].
[14] D. Griffiths, A. Jenkins, and Z. Kingston-Griffiths, "The 2015 Global Knowledge Management Observatory © Report," Juran Benchmarking, Tech. Rep., 2015.
[15] E. Bolisani and M. Handzic, Eds., *Advances in Knowledge Management - Celebrating Twenty Years of Research and Practice*. Springer International Publishing, 2015.
[16] D. P. Ford and R. M. Mason, "Knowledge Management and Social Media: The Challenges and Benefits," *Journal of Organizational Computing and Electronic Commerce*, vol. 23, no. 1-2, Jan. 2013, pp. 1–6.
[17] A. P. McAfee, "Enterprise 2 . 0 : The Dawn of Emergent Collaboration," *MIT Sloan Management Review*, vol. 47, no. 3, 2006, pp. 21–28.
[18] T. Davenport, "Enterprise 2.0: The New, New Knowledge Management?" 2008. [Online]. Available: https://hbr.org/2008/02/enterprise-20-the-new-new-know/ [Last Accessed: 17 November 2016].
[19] K. A. Delic and J. A. Riley, "Enterprise Knowledge Clouds: Next Generation KM Systems?" *2009 International Conference on Information, Process, and Knowledge Management*, Feb. 2009, pp. 49–53.
[20] "Global State of Enterprise Mobility 2016," Enterprise Mobility Exchange, London, Tech. Rep., 2016. [Online]. Available: http://eu.enterprisemobilityexchange.com/media/1001912/59471.pdf [Last Accessed 17 November 2016].
[21] L. Mallis, "Birth of the DIAD — upside Blog," 2009. [Online]. Available: http://blog.ups.com/2009/12/07/birth-of-the-diad/ [Last Accessed 15 March 2016].
[22] D. Dalmeyer and K. Tsipis, *Heaven and Earth:Vol. 16, USAS:Civilian Uses of Near-Earth Space*. Kluwer Law International, 1997.
[23] G. Piccoli, *Information Systems for Managers: Texts & Cases*. Hoboken: John Wiley & Sons, 2008.
[24] T. H. Davenport and L. Prusak, "Working knowledge: How organizations manage what they know," *Ubiquity*, vol. 2000, no. August, 2000.
[25] R. L. Ackoff, *Wiley: Ackoff's Best: His Classic Writings on Management - Russell L. Ackoff.* Wiley, 1999.
[26] R. Schumaker, "From Data to Wisdom: The Progression of Computational Learning in Text Mining." *Communications of the IIMA*, vol. 11, no. 1, 2011, pp. 1–14.
[27] G. Bellinger, D. Castro, and A. Mills, "Data, Information, Knowledge, & Wisdom," 2004. [Online]. Available: http://www.systems-thinking.org/dikw/dikw.htm [Last Accessed 15 March 2016].
[28] J. Terra and T. Angeloni, "Understanding the difference between information management and knowledge management," *KM Advantage*, 2003, pp. 1–9.
[29] Y. Hijikata, T. Takenaka, Y. Kusumura, and S. Nishida, "Interactive knowledge externalization and combination for SECI model," in *Proceedings of the 4th international conference on Knowledge capture - K-CAP '07*. New York, New York, USA: ACM Press, Oct. 2007, p. 151.
[30] I. Nonaka and H. Takeuchi, *The Knowledge-creating Company: How Japanese Companies Create the Dynamics of Innovation*. Oxford University Press, 1995.
[31] T.-C. Chou, "Internal learning climate, knowledge management process and perceived knowledge management satisfaction," *Journal of Information Science*, vol. 31, no. 4, 2005, pp. 283–296.
[32] C. Argyris, "Seeking truth and actionable knowledge: How the scientific method inhibits both," *Philosophica*, vol. 40, 1987, pp. 5–21.
[33] M. Böhringer and A. Richter, "Adopting social software to the intranet: a case study on enterprise microblogging," in *Proceedings Mensch und Computer 2009, Oldenbourg, Berlin*, 2009, pp. 1–10. [Online]. Available: http://citeseerx.ist.psu.edu/viewdoc/download?doi=10.1.1.520.9286&rep=rep1&type=pdf [Last Accessed 18 November 2016].
[34] N. Sousa, C. J. Costa, and M. Aparicio, "IO-SECI: A conceptual model for knowledge management," in *Proceedings of the Workshop on Open Source and Design of Communication - OSDOC '13*. New York, New York, USA: ACM Press, Jul. 2013, pp. 9–17. [Online]. Available: http://dl.acm.org/citation.cfm?id=2503848.2503850
[35] I. Guy, U. Avraham, D. Carmel, S. Ur, M. Jacovi, and I. Ronen, "Mining expertise and interests from social media," *Proceedings of the 22nd international conference on World Wide Web*, 2013, pp. 515–526.
[36] F. Sousa, M. Aparicio, and C. J. Costa, "Organizational wiki as a knowledge management tool," in *Proceedings of the 28th ACM International Conference on Design of Communication - SIGDOC '10*. New York, New York, USA: ACM Press, Sep. 2010, p. 33.
[37] E. Fischer and A. R. Reuber, "Social interaction via new social media: (How) can interactions on Twitter affect effectual thinking and behavior?" *Journal of Business Venturing*, vol. 26, no. 1, Jan. 2011, pp. 1–18.
[38] M. Kleek and K. O'Hara, "The Future of Social is Personal: The Potential of the Personal Data Store." [Online]. Available: http://eprints.soton.ac.uk/363518/1/pds.pdf [Last Accessed 19 November 2016].
[39] F. Cabiddu, M. D. Carlo, and G. Piccoli, "Social media affordances: Enabling customer engagement," *Annals of Tourism Research*, vol. 48, 2014, pp. 175–192.
[40] J. Comm, *Twitter Power 2.0: How to Dominate Your Market One Tweet at a Time*. Hoboken: John Wiley & Sons, Inc., 2010.
[41] A. M. Kaplan and M. Haenlein, "Users of the world, unite! The challenges and opportunities of Social Media," *Business Horizons*, vol. 53, no. 1, 2010, pp. 59–68.
[42] M. Miller, A. Marks, M. DeCoulode, J. Hagel, J. S. Brown, and D. Kulasooriya, "Social software for business performance The missing link in social software: Measurable business performance improvements," *Deloitte Center for the Edge*, 2011.
[43] J. Falls, "Why Forums May Be the Most Powerful Social Media Channel for Brands," 2012. [Online]. Available: http://www.entrepreneur.com/article/223493
[44] M. Alavi, "Knowledge Management Systems: Issues, Chanllenges and Benefits." *Communications of the Association for Information Systems*, vol. 1, no. 7, 1999, pp. 1–37.
[45] S. Tardanico, "Is Social Media Sabotaging Real Communication? - Forbes," 2012. [Online]. Available: http://www.forbes.com/sites/susantardanico/2012/04/30/is-social-media-sabotaging-real-communication/#366347a04fd8 [Last Accessed 19 November 2016].
[46] T. White, "Why Social Media Isn't Social," 2013. [Online]. Available: http://www.huffingtonpost.com/thomas-white/why-social-media-isnt-social_b_3858576.html [Last Accessed 19 November 2016].
[47] M. A. Zeng, "The Contribution of Different Online Communities in Open Innovation Projects," *Proceedings of The International Symposium on Open Collaboration - OpenSym '14*, 2014, pp. 1–9.
[48] A. Keenan and A. Shiri, "Sociability and social interaction on social networking websites," *Library Review*, vol. 58, no. 6, Jun. 2009, pp. 438–450.
[49] T. V. Wal, "Folksonomy Coinage and Definition," 2007. [Online].

Available: http://vanderwal.net/folksonomy.html [Last Accessed 19 November 2016].

[50] Delphi Group, "Information Intelligence: Content Classification and the Enterprise Taxonomy Practice," Boston, Tech. Rep., 2004. [Online]. Available: http://inei.org.br/inovateca/estudos-e-pesquisas-em-inovacao/InformationIntelligence-taxonomy-Delphi-2004.pdf [Last Accessed 19 November 2016].

[51] A. Zubiaga, ""Harnessing folksonomies for resource classification" by Arkaitz Zubiag with Danielle H. Lee as coordinator," *ACM SIGWEB Newsletter*, no. Summer, Jul. 2012, pp. 1–2.

[52] W. J. Frawley, G. Piatetsky-shapiro, and C. J. Matheus, "Knowledge Discovery in Databases : An Overview," *AI Magazine*, vol. 13, no. 3, 1992, pp. 57–70.

[53] T. Koller, "What is value-based management?" *The McKinsey Quarterly*, no. 3, Jun. 1994, pp. 87–102.

[54] L. Edvinsson and M. Malone, *Intellectual Capital: Realizing Your Company's True Value by Finding Its Hidden Brainpower*. Collins, 1997.

[55] G. Gruman, "IT Value Metrics: How to Communicate ROI to the Business — CIO," 2007. [Online]. Available: http://www.cio.com/article/2437929/it-organization/it-value-metrics--how-to-communicate-roi-to-the-business.html [Last Accessed 19 November 2016].

[56] I. Becerra-Fernandez and S. Rajiv, "Organizational Knowledge Management: A Contingency Perspective," *Journal of Management Information Systems*, vol. 18, no. June, 2001, pp. 23–55.

[57] M. E. Porter, "What Is Value in Health Care?" *New England Journal of Medicine*, 2010, pp. 2477–2481.

[58] National Audit Office, "Analytical framework for assessing Value for Money," National Audit Office, Tech. Rep. Step 6, 2010. [Online]. Available: http://www.bond.org.uk/data/files/National_Audit_Office__Analytical_framework_for_assessing_Value_for_Money.pdf [Last Accessed 25 November 2016].

[59] W. Vestal, "Measuring Knowledge Management," in *Symposium: A Quarterly Journal In Modern Foreign Literatures*. APQC, 2002, pp. 1–6.

[60] S. A. Melnyk, D. M. Stewart, and M. Swink, "Metrics and performance measurement in operations management: dealing with the metrics maze," *Journal of Operations Management*, vol. 22, no. 3, 2004, pp. 209–218.

[61] R. Blundel, "Is small still beautiful?: Exploring the role of SMEs in emerging visions of a green' economy," Middlesex University, London, Tech. Rep., 2016. [Online]. Available: http://oro.open.ac.uk/46768/ (Accessed 2 Aug., 2016).

[62] M. Ayyagari, T. Beck, and A. Demirguc-Kunt, "Small and Medium Enterprises Across the Globe," *Small Business Economics*, vol. 29, no. 4, 2007, pp. 415–434.

[63] T. W. Liao and E. Triantaphyllou, *Recent Advances in Data Mining of Enterprise Data: Algorithms and Applications*. World Scientific, 2008. [Online]. Available: http://www.worldscientific.com/worldscibooks/10.1142/6689 [Last Accessed 19 November 2016].

[64] D. Murthy, *Twitter: Social Communication in the Twitter Age*. Cambridge: Polity Press, 2013. [Online]. Available: http://www.lehmanns.de/shop/sozialwissenschaften/27894960-9780745665108-twitterhttp://wiley-vch.e-bookshelf.de/products/reading-epub/product-id/3973642/title/Twitter.html?lang=en

[65] "Tax Credits Row What Will Happen Now After Government Defeat?" 2015. [Online]. Available: https://uk.news.yahoo.com/tax-credits-row-happen-now-100031983.html [Last Accessed 29 February 2016].

[66] "What is social welfare? definition and meaning." [Online]. Available: http://www.businessdictionary.com/definition/social-welfare.html [Last Accessed 03 March 2016].

[67] S. Rogers, "UK welfare spending: how much does each benefit really cost?" 2013. [Online]. Available: http://www.theguardian.com/news/datablog/2013/jan/08/uk-benefit-welfare-spending [Last Accessed 30 April 2016].

[68] M. Elsabbagh, G. Divan, Y.-J. Koh, Y. S. Kim, S. Kauchali, C. Marcín, C. Montiel-Nava, V. Patel, C. S. Paula, C. Wang, M. T. Yasamy, and E. Fombonne, "Global prevalence of autism and other pervasive developmental disorders." *Autism research : official journal of the International Society for Autism Research*, vol. 5, no. 3, Jun. 2012, pp. 160–79.

[69] J. Baldock, "World Autism Awareness Day 2015: 16 autism myths debunked," Apr. 2015. [Online]. Available: http://metro.co.uk/2015/04/02/autism-sixteen-myths-debunked-5123051/ [Last Accessed 19 November 2016].

[70] NHS Choices, "Autism spectrum disorder - NHS Choices." [Online]. Available: http://www.nhs.uk/Conditions/Autistic-spectrum-disorder/Pages/Introduction.aspx

[71] D. Pritchard, "KNOWLEDGE," in *Central Issues of Philosophy*, J. Shand, Ed. Oxford: Wiley - Blackwell, 2009, pp. 1–16.

[72] E. Gettier, "Is Justified True Belief Knowledge?" *Analysis*, vol. 23, no. c, 1963, pp. 444–446.

[73] C. Argyris, *Actionable Knowledge*, C. Knudsen and H. Tsoukas, Eds. Oxford University Press, Mar. 2005. [Online]. Available: http://www.oxfordhandbooks.com/view/10.1093/oxfordhb/9780199275250.001.0001/oxfordhb-9780199275250-e-16 [Last Accessed 19 November 2016].

[74] L. Posner, "Actionable Knowledge: Putting Research to Work for School Community Action," 2009. [Online]. Available: http://www.idra.org/resource-center/actionable-knowledge/ [Last Accessed 19 November 2016].

[75] C. Argyris, *Knowledge for action: a guide to overcoming barriers to organizational change*. Jossey-Bass, 1993. [Online]. Available: http://eric.ed.gov/?id=ED357268 [Last Accessed 19 November 2016].

[76] B. Marr, "Employee Engagement Level," in *25 Need-to-Know Key Performance Indicators*, 1st ed. Harlow: Pearson Education Ltd., 2014, ch. 22, pp. 151 – 157.

[77] Harvard Business Review, "The Impact of Employee Engagement on Performance," Harvard Business Review, Tech. Rep., 2013. [Online]. Available: https://hbr.org/resources/pdfs/comm/achievers/hbr{_}achievers{_}report{_}sep13.pdf [Last Accessed 19 November 2016].

[78] L. Carr and S. Harnad, "Offloading cognition onto the Web," *IEEE Intelligent Systems*, Jan. 2011.

[79] S. K. M. Yi, M. Steyvers, M. D. Lee, and M. J. Dry, "The Wisdom of the Crowd in Combinatorial Problems," *Cognitive Science*, vol. 36, no. 3, Apr. 2012, pp. 452–470.

[80] S. Wasserman and K. Faust, *Social Network Analysis: Methods and Applications*. Cambridge University Press, 2012.

[81] A. Gruzd and C. Haythornthwaite, "Enabling Community Through Social Media," *Journal of Medical Internet Research*, vol. 15, no. 10, Oct. 2013.

[82] L. Rossi and M. Magnani, "Conversation practices and network structure in Twitter," *Proceedings of the Sixth International AAAI Conference on Weblogs and Social Media*, 2012, p. 4.

[83] J. Trant, "Studying social tagging and folksonomy: A review and framework," *Journal of Digital Information*, vol. 10, no. 1, 2009, pp. 1–44.

[84] D. L. Hansen, D. Rotman, E. Bonsignore, N. Milic-Frayling, E. M. Rodrigues, M. Smith, and B. Shneiderman, "Do you know the way to SNA': A process model for analyzing and visualizing social media network data," in *Proceedings of the 2012 ASE International Conference on Social Informatics, SocialInformatics 2012*. IEEE Explore Digital Library, 2013, pp. 304–313.

[85] D. Hansen, B. Shneiderman, and M. A. Smith, "Analyzing Social Media Networks with NodeXL: Insights from a Connected World," *Graduate Journal of Social Science*, vol. 8, no. 3, 2011, p. 284.

[86] J. Golbeck, *Introduction to Social Media Investigation - A Hands-On Approach*. Waltham: Elsevier Inc. (Syngress), 2015.

[87] B. Ruhnau, "Eigenvector-centrality a node-centrality?" *Social Networks*, vol. 22, 2000, pp. 357–365.

[88] M. A. Russell, *Mining the Social Web, 2nd Edition*. O'Reilly Media, 2013.

[89] C. Dunne and B. Shneiderman, "Motif Simplification: Improving Network Visualization Readability with Fan, Connector, and Clique Glyphs," *CHI '13: Proc. 2013 international conference on Human Factors in Computing Systems*, 2013, pp. 3247–3256.

[90] M. A. Smith, L. Raine, B. Shneiderman, and I. Himelboim, "How we analyzed Twitter social media networks with NodeXL," Pew Research Center, Tech. Rep., 2014. [Online]. Available: http://www.pewinternet.org/files/2014/02/How-we-analyzed-Twitter-social-media-networks.pdf [Last Accessed 19 November 2016].

[91] L. C. Freeman, "A Set of Measures of Centrality Based on Betweenness," *Sociometry*, vol. 40, no. 1, Mar. 1977, pp. 35–41.

[92] Y. Koren, S. C. North, and C. Volinsky, "Measuring and extracting proximity graphs in networks," *ACM Transactions on Knowledge Discovery from Data*, vol. 1, no. 3, Dec. 2007, pp. 12–es.

[93] D. G. Lorentzen, "Polarisation in political Twitter conversations," *Aslib Journal of Information Management*, vol. 66, no. 3, May. 2014, pp. 329–341.

An Integrated Semantic Approach to Content Management in the Urban Resilience Domain

Ilkka Niskanen, Mervi Murtonen
Technical Research Centre of Finland
Oulu/Tampere, Finland
Ilkka.Niskanen@vtt.fi, Mervi.Murtonen@vtt.fi

Francesco Pantisano
Smart System Infrastructures
Finmeccanica Company
Genova, Italy
francesco.pantisano@finmeccanica.com

Fiona Browne, Peadar Davis
School of Computing and Mathematics
Ulster University
Jordanstown, Northern Ireland, UK
f.browne@ulster.ac.uk, pt.davis@ulster.ac.uk

Ivan Palomares
School of Electronics, Electrical Engineering and Computer Science
Queen's University
Belfast, Northern Ireland, UK
i.palomares@qub.ac.uk

Abstract— **Content Management refers to the process of gaining control over the creation and distribution of information and functionality. Although there are several content management systems available they often fail in addressing the context specific needs of end-users. To enable more task specific and personalized support we present a content management solution developed for the domain of urban resilience. The introduced content management system is extended with a semantic layer that aims to support the management of heterogeneous and large content repository with domain specific annotation and categorization capabilities. In addition, the applied semantic intelligence allows better understanding of content items, linkages between unstructured information and tools, and provides more sophisticated answers to users' various needs.**

Keywords- content management; semantic technologies; heterogeneous data repository

I. INTRODUCTION

The field of Content Management (CM) refers to the process of gaining control over the creation and distribution of information and functionality. Concisely, an effective Content Management System (CMS) aims at getting the right information to the right people in the right way. Usually, CM is divided into three main phases namely collecting, managing, and publishing of content. The collection phase encompasses the creating or acquiring information from an existing source. This is then aggregated into a CMS by editing it, segmenting it into components, and adding appropriate metadata. The managing phase includes creating a repository that consists of database containing content components and administrative data (data on the system's users, for example). Finally, in the publishing stage the content is made available for the target audience by extracting components out of the repository and releasing the content for use in the most appropriate way [1] [2].

Currently, there are several commercial and open-source technologies available that are applied to address different content management needs across various industries including healthcare [3], and education [4], for example. However, the standard versions of the existing solutions are not always capable of supporting end-users in their specified context to reach their particular goals in an effective, efficient and satisfactory way [5]. For instance, the included content retrieval mechanisms are often implemented using traditional keyword based search engines that are not adapted to serve any task specific needs [6][7][8].

One of the main issues to be resolved is how to convert existing and new content that can be understood by humans into semantically-enriched content that can be understood by machines [9]. The human-readable and unstructured content is usually difficult to automatically process, relate and categorize, which hinders the ability to extract value from it [10]. Additionally, it results in the restriction of development of more intelligent search mechanisms [9]. To address some of the above described deficiencies, semantic technologies are being increasingly used in CM. In particular, the utilization of domain specific vocabularies and taxonomies in content analysis enables accurate extraction of meaningful information, and supports task-specific browsing and retrieval requirements compared to traditional approaches [9]. Furthermore, semantic technologies facilitate creating machine-readable content metadata descriptions, which allows, for example, software agents to automatically accomplish complex tasks using that data. Moreover, semantically enhanced metadata helps search engines to better understand what they are indexing and providing more accurate results to the users [11].

In this paper, we introduce the HARMONISE platform, developed in the FP7 EU HARMONISE [12] project. This paper is an extended version of work published in [1], where a semantic layer implemented on top of the HARMONISE platform was introduced. We extend our previous work by providing more details about the technical realizations of the platform and the semantic layer. Moreover, an evaluation process carried out for the platform and the semantic layer is depicted in this paper.

The HARMONISE platform is a domain specific CMS that provides information and tools for security-driven urban resilience in large-scale infrastructure offering a holistic view to urban resilience. A database contained by the system manages an extensive set of heterogeneous material that comes in different forms including tools, design guidance and specifications. The platform aims at serving as a 'one-stop-shop' for resilience information and guidance and it contains a wealth of information and tools specifically designed to aid built environment professionals. While the platform and the hosted toolkit are aimed to be used by a variety of potential end-users from planners and urban designers to construction teams, building security personnel and service managers, the specialized problem domain and heterogeneous content repository poses significant challenges for users to effectively retrieve information to accomplish their tasks and goals.

As earlier discussed, the HARMONISE platform is extended with a novel Semantic Layer for the HARMONISE (SLH) approach. The SLH is a semantic content management solution developed to address many of the above discussed challenges related to domain specific content management. It is implemented on top of the HARMONISE platform and it aims at offering more task specific and personalized content management support for end-users. Additionally, by utilizing domain specific annotation and categorization of content the SLH facilitates the management of heterogeneous and large content repository hosted by the HARMONISE platform.

The semantic information modelling allows better understanding of platform content, linkages between unstructured information and tools, and more sophisticated answers to users' various needs. Moreover, the semantic knowledge representations created by the layer help end-users to combine different data fragments and produce new implicit knowledge from existing data sets. Finally, by utilizing Linked Data [13] technologies the SLH fosters interoperability and improves shared understanding of key information elements. The utilization of interconnected and multidisciplinary knowledge bases of the Linked Data cloud also enables applying the solution in other problem areas such as health care or education.

The rest of paper is organized as follows. Section II provides a through description of the HARMONISE platform and its application area. In Section III the architecture and different components of the SLH are described. Section IV provides a Use Case example demonstrating the functionality of the SLH. Finally, Section V concludes the paper.

II. THE HARMONISE CONTENT MANAGEMENT PLATFORM

At present, there exist a number of content management systems that enable publishing, managing and organizing electronic documents. For example, Drupal [1] [14] and WordPress [2] [15] are well-known, general-purpose CM solutions providing such basic CM features such as user profile management, database administration, metadata management, and content search and navigation functionalities [5]. These tools provide functionality to create and edit a website's content often with easy-to-use templates for digital media content publishing.

The HARMONISE platform is a web platform that provides information and tools specifically designed to aid urban decision makers in enhancing the resilience of large scale urban built infrastructure. The platform includes an innovative search process designed to promote holistic decision making at each stage of the resilience cycle, an automatic content recommendation mechanism to suggest most relevant contents for a user, educational elements that provide content and self-assessment tools that help end-users to assess the general resilience and security level of an existing or proposed large scale infrastructure. Moreover, the semantic layer developed within the platform enables better understanding of data, linkages between unstructured information and tools, and more sophisticated answers to users' various needs.

The platform is mainly composed by two macro-components, the HARMONISE web site which represents the front-end of the platform to the user and the semantic layer that includes services for enhancing the overall functionality allowing more personalized user experience for stakeholders who utilize the platform their daily work. In Figure 1 the main elements of the HARMONISE platform are shown.

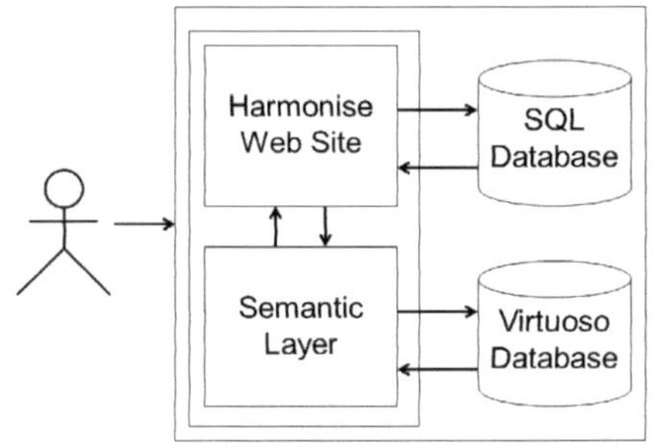

Figure 1. The key elements of the HARMONISE platform

As stated above, the HARMONISE platform is a CMS specifically tailored for the domain of urban resilience. The system provides information and tools for security-driven urban resilience in large-scale infrastructure and contains a variety of interactive elements allowing users to both import and export data to and from the platform and personalize the platform to their own needs. The core functionalities of the HARMONISE platform are implemented using ASP.NET

[1] www.drupal.org
[2] https://wordpress.org/

web application framework and it utilizes Microsoft SQL 2012 database to store content items.

The main features and functionalities are divided between three user profile categories defined for the HARMONISE platform. To begin with, a standard registered user can navigate through the different sections of the platform excluding the upload section, use the search functionalities and view all the platform contents. However, he cannot upload or edit any content. In contrast, an uploader who has been granted permission by the administrator can access the upload section and upload contents in addition to the functionalities available for the standard user. Moreover, the uploader can edit/delete the content he has uploaded. In order to become an uploader user has to insert a special password (i.e., uploader password) provided by the platform administrator. Finally, the administrator of the platform can edit/delete the content uploaded by an uploader. Moreover, he can manage the user assignment to a specific group and generate the uploader passwords. The main functionalities enabled for each user category are depicted in Figure 2.

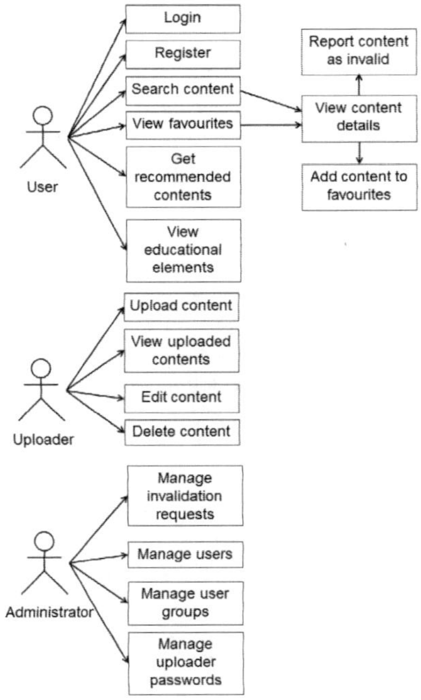

Figure 2. The user profiles and main features of the platform

An important part of the HARMONISE content management platform is the Thematic Framework [16] that was created to structure information within the platform and to guide end-users through an innovative step-by-step search process. The Thematic Framework is set out in Figure 3.

By unpacking resilience into a number of key layers the Thematic Framework provides the necessary taxonomy needed for realizing effective domain-specific content annotation and categorizing functionalities, as later discussed. The objective of the domain-specific annotation is to allow users to easily identify and access information and tools within the platform, and to search the platform according to their unique needs or interests.

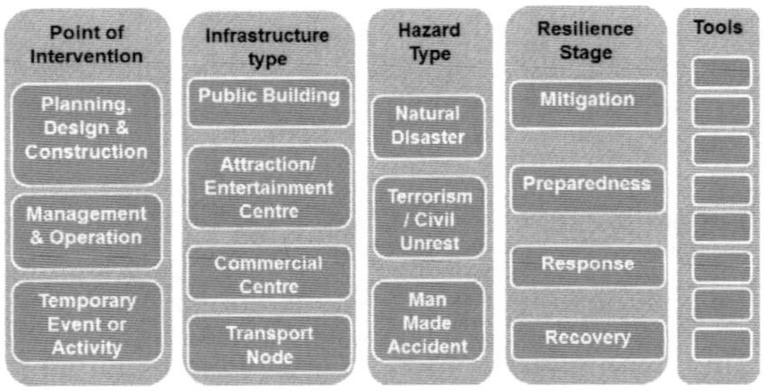

Figure 3. The Thematic Framework (adopted from [16])

III. THE SEMANTIC LAYER

The HARMONISE content management platform hosts a large portfolio of urban resilience related content. However, finding relevant information and tools from such a knowledge base with conventional information retrieval methods is usually both tedious and time consuming, and tends to become a challenge as the amount of content increases [9]. Often users have difficulties in grouping together related material or finding the content that best serve their information needs, especially when content is stored in multiple formats [17].

In general, the existing CMSs usually lack consistent and scalable content annotation mechanisms that allow them to deal with the highly heterogeneous domains that information architectures for the modern knowledge society demand [18]. The semantic layer described in this study aims at addressing the above mentioned challenges by integrating semantic data modelling and processing mechanisms to the core HARMONISE platform functionalities. For example, the application of semantic mark-up based tagging of web content enables expressively describing entities found in the content, and relations between them [9]. Moreover, by utilizing the Linked Data Cloud links can be set between different and heterogeneous content elements and therefore connect these elements into a single global data space, which further facilitates interoperability and machine-readable understanding of content [19].

The main features of the SLH are divided to four parts. First, the metadata enrichment part produces information-rich metadata descriptions of the content by enhancing content with relevant semantic metadata. Second, the semantic metadata repository implements the necessary means for storing and accessing the created metadata. The third component of the SLH realizes a semantic search feature. In more detail the search service aims at returning more meaningful search results to the user by utilizing both keyword-based semantic search and "Search by theme" filtering algorithm that restricts the searchable space by enabling users to select certain categories from the Thematic Framework. The final part, content recommendation, combines information about users' preferences and profile to find a target user neighborhood, and proactively recommends new urban resilience tools/resources that might be of potential interest to him/her. In Figure 4 the logical architecture of the SLH is represented.

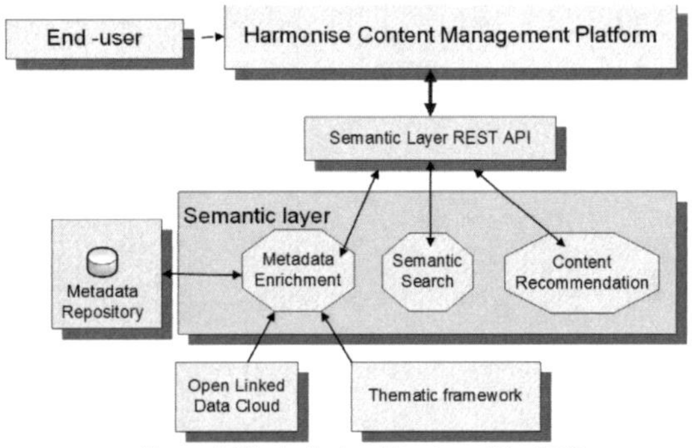

Figure 4. The logical architecture of the SLH

The following sections describe the logical architecture in more detail.

A. Semantic Layer REST API

The Semantic Layer REST API provides the necessary interface for the HARMONISE Platform to interact with the SLH. It enables, for example, to transmit query requests from the platform to the SLH or retrieve content recommendations personalized for a particular user.

B. Metadata Enrichment

The purpose of the Metadata Enrichment service is to produce information-rich metadata descriptions of the content that is uploaded to the HARMONISE platform. Enhancing content with relevant semantic metadata can be very useful for handling large content databases [2]. A key issue in this context is improving the "findability" of content elements (e.g., documents, tools).

The enrichment process is based on tagging. A tag associates semantics to a content item, usually helping the user searching or browsing through content. These tags can be used in order to identify the most important topics, entities, events and other information relevant to that content item. The tagging data is created by analyzing the uploaded content and the metadata manually entered by the user. This information consist e.g., title, keywords, Thematic Framework categories, topics, content types and phrases of natural language text.

In the metadata analysis the following three technologies that provide tagging services are utilized: ONKI [3] [20], DBPedia [4] [21] and OpenCalais [5] [22]. The ONKI and DBPedia knowledge bases provide enrichment of the human defined keywords by utilizing Linked Data reference vocabularies and datasets. The Metadata Enrichment service utilizes the APIs of the above mentioned technologies to search terms that are somehow associated to the entities defined by a user. The relationships between the enriched terms and the original entity are illustrated in Figure 5, in which examples of enriched concepts for the term 'Building' are represented.

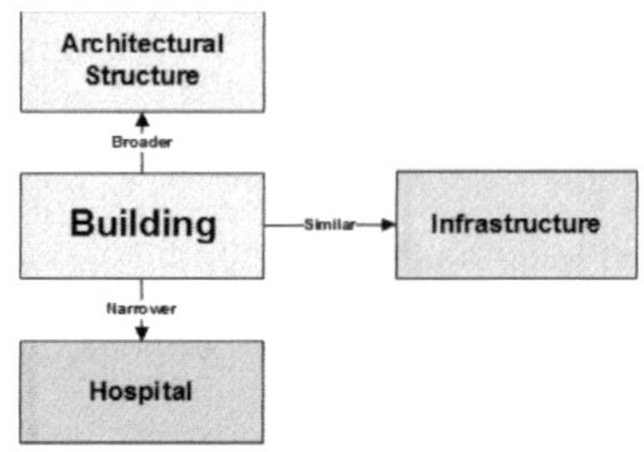

Figure 5. The enrichment of the human defined keywords

As shown in Figure 5, the enriched terms fall into three categories: similar, broader and narrower. The similar terms are synonyms to the original entities whereas broader terms can be considered as more general concepts. The narrower terms represent examples of more specific concepts compared to the original entity. Each of the acquired terms contains a Linked Data URI that can be accessed to get more extensive description of that term. By enriching the human defined keywords with additional concepts and Linked Data URIs more comprehensive and machine-readable information about uploaded content items can be generated.

The uploaded content items are also examined using the OpenCalais text analyzer tool. Using such mechanisms as natural language processing and machine learning the tool allows analyzing different text fragments contained by the uploaded content item. As a result, OpenCalais discovers entities (Company, Person etc.), events or facts that are related to the uploaded content element.

In the final part of the metadata enrichment process the metadata elements created by different tools are merged as a single RDF (Resource Description Framework) metadata description and stored to the metadata database.

C. Semantic Metadata Repository

The database technology used for storing the semantic metadata of content is OpenLink Virtuoso [23]. Virtuoso is a relational database solution that is optimized to store RDF data. It provides good performance and extensive query interfaces [24] and was thus selected as the metadata storage to be used in the SLH.

D. Semantic Search

The Semantic Search service aims at producing relevant search results for the user by effectively utilizing the machine-readable RDF metadata descriptions created by the Metadata Enrichment service. Unlike traditional search engines that return a large set of results that may or may not be relevant to the context of the search, the Semantic Search analyses the results and orders them based on their relevancy. Thus, users are emancipated from performing the time-consuming work of browsing through the retrieved results in order to find the content they are looking for.

[3] http://onki.fi/
[4] http://dbpedia.org/
[5] http://www.opencalais.com/

The Semantic Search service is implemented as a Java web application composed of three main components (see Figure 6):

- RESTful Web Service: based on Apache CXF framework, it represents the semantic search service front-end. It receives the search queries from the HARMONISE platform and returns the list of search results provided by the underlying components;
- Semantic Search Service Core (SSS Core): component based on Java/Maven project, customized to manage all the core processes (data indexing, content search, content retrieving, results formatting);
- Semantic Search Engine: component based on Apache Solr [25] enterprise search platform, in charge of the indexing and the search processes. When a new content is uploaded to the HARMONISE platform it reads from the Virtuoso database the data produced by the semantic content enrichment service in order to create the index to query on. When a user submits a query the semantic search engine queries the index in order to find the documents that best match the user request parameters.

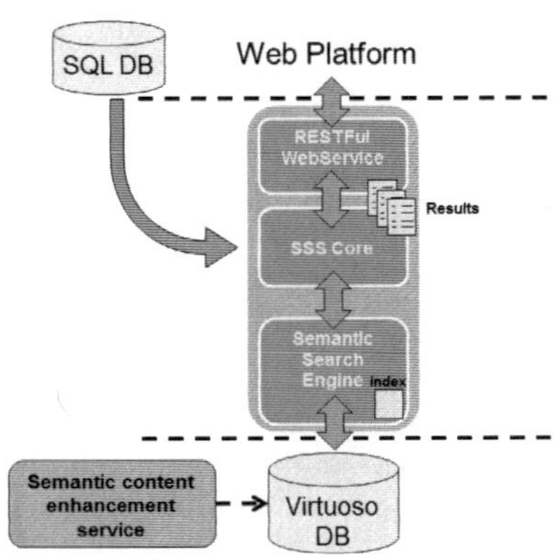

Figure 6. Logical architecture of the semantic search service

The Semantic Search service relies on the Solr search engine [26] in order to search across large amount of content metadata and pull back the most relevant results in the fastest way. The Solr component is a web application developed in Java and provided by the Solr open source enterprise search platform from the Apache Lucene project [25]. Solr is a document storage and retrieval engine and every piece of data submitted to it for processing is a document composed by one or more fields. Internally Solr uses Lucene's inverted index to implement its fast searching capabilities. Unlike a traditional database representation where multiple documents would contain a document ID mapped to some content fields containing all of the words in that document, an inverted index inverts this model and maps each word to all of the documents in which it appears. Solr stores information in its inverted index and queries that index to find matching documents.

According to the data structure of the contents uploaded to the Virtuoso database by the Metadata Enrichment service, the document fields shown in Table I have been defined for the construction of the Solr index.

TABLE I. SOLR INDEX FIELDS

Field	**Description**
Id	Content identifier on Virtuoso DB
Upload date	Date when the content has been uploaded
Topics	List of topics from the Thematic Framework
Resilience Tasks	List of Resilience Cycle tasks
Permissions	List of user groups allowed to view the document
Title	Title of the content
Description	Textual description of the content
Keywords	List of keywords (inserted by the uploader)
Tags	List of tags added by the metadata enhancement service.

The search results provided by the Semantic Search service are ranked according to the relevancy scores that measure the similarity between the user query and all of the documents in the index. The results with highest relevancy scores appear first in the search results list.

The scoring model is composed by the following scoring factors:

- Term Frequency: is a measure of how often a particular term appears in a matching document. Given a search query, the greater the term frequency value, the higher the document score.
- Inverse Document Frequency: is a measure of how "rare" a search term is. The rarer a term is across all documents in the index, the higher its contribution to the score.
- Coordination Factor: It is the frequency of the occurrence of query terms that match a document; the greater the occurrence, the higher is the score.
- Field length: the shorter the matching field, the greater the document score. This factor penalizes documents with longer field values.
- Boosting: is the mechanism that allows to assign different weights to those fields that are considered more (or less) important than others.

E. Content Recommendation

Similar to the Semantic Search, the Content Recommendation Service (CRS) is based on semantic modelling of content resources. The aim of the content recommendation service is to improve user experience in terms of the search functionality and the filtering of relevant information through the utilization of collaborative filtering. As the volume of content continues to increase, the development of recommendation systems (RS) have become essential to handle large volumes of data. They are widely used across diverse domains to predict, filter and extract content for users [27][28]. Examples of commercial applications of RS include Amazon, Twitter, Facebook and Ebay. A popular type of RS is collaborative filtering. This type of RS analyses information on users' preferences and predicts content to present to users based on their similarity to other users of the system [29]. Due to the information stored for users in their user profile, collaborative filtering was a natural selection to predict content to users based on similarities in their profiles. The developed CRS utilizes user profiles which are created and maintained by the HARMONISE platform

An overview of the CRS algorithm is provided in Figure 7. Figure 7 illustrates how user preference and user profile similarity are fused together along with a weighted sum to provide a ranked list of recommendation tailored to the user.

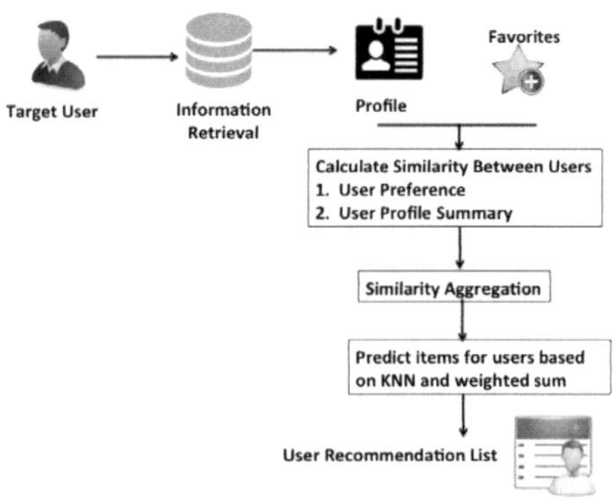

Figure 7. Overview of the CRS Algorithm

Figure 7 details the various stages of the recommendation process which includes the extraction of user details from the HARMONISE system through to the list of recommendations presented to the user at the end. A detailed overview of the CRS algorithm can be found in [30]. The user profiles contain information about user's preferences and favorite content. It also includes the content item IDs that have been already recommended for that particular user. This information is then utilized when content recommendations are created for different users. The CRS is triggered by the HARMONISE platform through the 'get recommendation' method provided by the Semantic Layer REST API. The ID of the user is transmitted as a method parameter. Once the recommendation service receives the ID, it retrieves the user profile of the user from the database and analyses the information it contains. Various pieces of information are stored in the profiles such as topics of interest, group membership, languages, lines of investigation. Furthermore, content that the user has marked as favorite is stored as user preferences. The CRS then combines all the information about users' preferences and profile information to find a target user neighborhood, and recommend new urban resilience tools/resources that might be of potential interest to him/her. To do this, firstly the ordered weighted average and uniform aggregation operators are applied to fuse user information and obtain global degrees of similarity between them using the formula below:

$sim_p^{i,j} = OWA_w(sim_I^{i,j}, sim_G^{i,j}, sim_L^{i,j})$ profile between users i and j, and sim_I, sim_G, sim_L are the profiles line of investigation, interests and groups respectively which are aggregated using ordered weighted sum.

The similarity between the preferences of users u_i and u_j as $sim_f^{i,j} \in [0,1]$ is also calculated using the Jaccard index $J_F^{i,j} = J(F_i, F_j)$ among the sets $F_i, F_j \subset I$ where I are the items marked favorite by u_i and u_j.This is schematically presented in Figure 8 from [30] below.

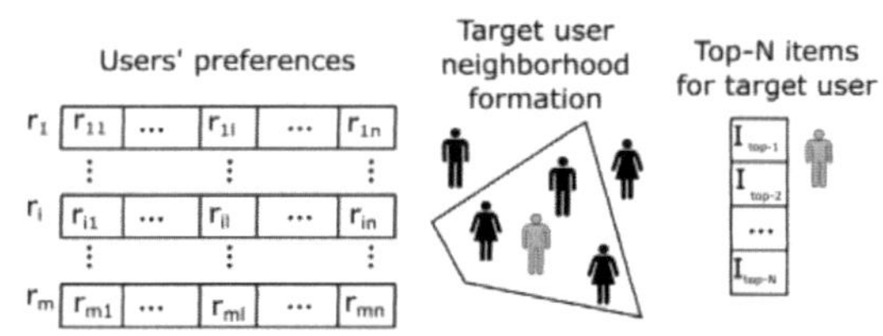

Figure 8. Schematic overview of User Preferences approach from [30]

When the profile similarity and preference similarity between users have been calculated, these are then fused together resulting in a global degree of similarity between the target user u_i and the rest of users in the system. We apply a uniform aggregation function to obtain the global similarity $sim^{i,j} \in [0,1]$ between u_i and u_j.

The actual recommendation generation process is carried out by comparing the user profile data with the semantic content metadata descriptions. Similarly as in the search algorithm described in the previous section, the content items whose metadata is associated with e.g., terms, topics or research areas as contained by the user profile are included to the initial recommendation results. Of course, the content items that have already been recommended for the user are excluded from the results list. Subsequently, the recommendation results are analyzed using the ranking model introduced by the Semantic Search. Using K-nearest neighbors, the content items that gets the highest score is returned to the platform as the most highly recommended content item. This involves the generation of a recommendation list $R_i = \{C_i, \ldots, C_n\}$ consisting of content C of size $h \in \mathbb{N}, h \ll n$ is presented to users on the HARMONISE interface as illustrated in Figure 9. This list contains items $C_k = i_l \in I$ with the highest values for $p(u_i, i_l)$. This results in the user receiving a list of content ordered by rating value.

IV. USE CASE EXAMPLE

The functionality of the SLH is demonstrated with a Use Case example in which a user uploads a document into the HARMONISE content management platform and tries to retrieve it with the search functionality. Additionally, the recommendation service is verified by creating a user profile that is interested in topics relevant to the uploaded content. The content item used in the Use Case example is an electronic manual that presents tools to help assess the performance of buildings and infrastructure against terrorist threats and to rank recommended protective measures. This kind of guidance document is a typical representative of a content item managed by the HARMONISE platform.

Once the user has provided necessary input in the upload form the content description is transmitted to the Metadata Enrichment component that processes the collected data and forms an RDF metadata description of the content. It was noted that the returned semantic content metadata contained five keywords that are enriched with 81 broader or narrower and 26 similar terms. Moreover, the content is annotated with several categories defined by the Thematic Framework.

Once the enriched metadata is stored to the Semantic Metadata Repository, and indexed by the Semantic Search service, it can be tried to be retrieved with the search functionality. The content retrieval is tested with the 'Resilience Search Wizard' feature provided by the SLH. The wizard allows to define keywords and to select those categories from the Thematic Framework that are considered as relevant to the uploaded content. The utilized search parameters are shown in the search wizard screenshot illustrated in Figure 9.

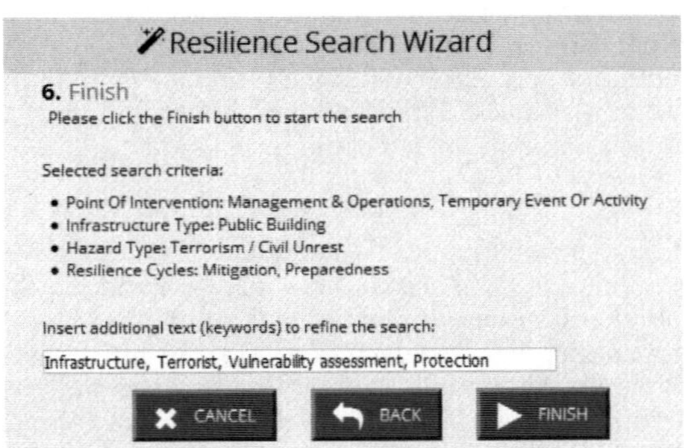

Figure 9. Search parameter definition

As earlier explained, the search functionality is able to sort the results based on their relevancy. Figure 10 represents the most highly ranked search results returned by the search service. As can be seen, the applied ranking algorithm identified the uploaded electronic manual document as the second relevant search result for the given search query. In total, the search functionality found 24 results with the defined search parameters.

In the final phase of the use case example, the Content Recommendation service is tested by creating a user profile and obtaining personalized recommendations. The user profile was created with 6 topics of interests of interest from a total of 13 topics namely: Point of Intervention, Management and Operation, Infrastructure type, Commercial Center, Hazard Type and Man Made Hazard. The user then marked 10 items of favorite content from a total of 156 items in the database.

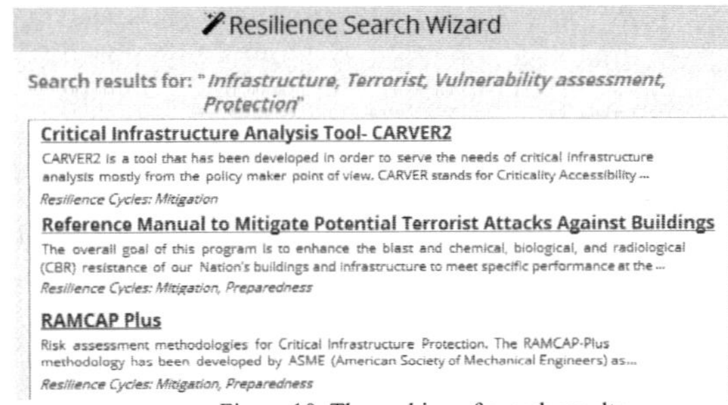

Figure 10. The ranking of search results

These included content such as "Tools of Regional Governance" and "Flood management in Linares Town". For the first step in the recommendation algorithm, Jaccard index is utilized to compute the degree of similarity between the favourite content and profile information of the user entered and all the users of the HARMONISE system. In the second step, a KNN algorithm is applied to identify the 5 most similar neighbors. Based on neighbor users, we compute for each item not marked as a favorite by the user, a predicted rating. This is used to construct an ordered recommendation list to the target user, which in this case study was a list of 5 recommendations including documents based on "Key issues of Urban Resilience", "Building urban resilience Details" and "Resilience: how to build resilience in your people and your organization".

V. A REVIEW OF EQUIVALENT TOOLS AND APPROACHES

As earlier discussed, at present there exist no similar content management tools that would address the special requirements set by the domain of urban resilience. However, over the past few years approaches that provide equivalent functionalities as the HARMONISE platform and the SLH have been delivered by research community. Although these tools are designed for different application areas, they have many similar end-user requirements and technological characteristics. In this chapter a selection of these tools are being reviewed and analyzed.

To start with, [31] introduces a platform for curation technologies that is intended to enable human experts to get a grasp and understand the contents of large and heterogeneous document collections in an efficient way so that they can curate, process and further analyze the collection according to their sector-specific needs. Furthermore, the platform aims at automating such tasks as looking for information related to and relevant for the domain, learning the key concepts, selecting the most relevant parts and preparing the information to be used. As in the HARMONISE project, the platform is extended with a semantic web-layer that provides linguistic analysis and discourse information on top of digital content.

The target audience of the platform for curation technologies is knowledge workers who conduct research in specific domains with the goal of, for example, preparing museum exhibitions or writing news articles. Currently, the focus in the platform is on written documents but in future the aim is to improve the platform by improving its abilities to convert non-textual data into text. Similarly as in HARMONISE platform, the semantic layer of the platform for curation technologies facilitates semantic annotation, enables connecting interlinked representation to external information sources, implements a semantic triple store and provides search functionalities.

As discussed above, the platform for curation technologies provides similar functionalities compared to the HARMONISE platform and the SLH. Moreover, the platform uses many of the same technologies. However, the platform for curation technologies is not as well optimized to address the needs of a special domain. For example, it does not provide an application area specific taxonomy that is often needed for realizing effective domain-specific content annotation and categorizing functionalities. Moreover, the HARMONISE platform and the semantic layer provide more comprehensive support for the management of heterogeneous content. However, the abilities of the platform for curation technologies to support natural language and multilingual text processing are more advanced compared to the HARMONISE platform and the SLH.

A second approach providing similar content management functionalities as the HARMONISE platform and the SLH is the Ondigita platform [32] that is developed for the management and delivery of digital documents to students enrolled in bachelor's courses within the field of engineering. The platform implements a cloud-based repository to allow educational organizations to create a digital collection of their educational materials and enable students to store and access these resources in their computers, tablets, or mobile phones. Moreover, the Ondigita platform supports the managing of heterogeneous learning material including books, audio and video, for example, and enables students to manually annotate content elements by highlighting important text passages and adding textual notes. The resulting annotations can be shared with others students.

The main components of the Ondigita platform include a course materials repository, an application server and a web application to access the content repository. The platform also offers adapters that enable integrating the infrastructure with such external file hosting services as Dropbox or Google Docs. Additionally, a mobile application available for Android OS is provided. When comparing to the HARMONISE platform and the SLH it can be concluded that the search services provided by the Ondigita platform are more constricted. Moreover, the Ondigita platform does utilize semantic technologies or include any domain specific taxonomies or ontologies. Also, the manual annotation of content items can be considered as relatively time-consuming and labour-intensive. However, the Ondigita platform offers better support for interoperability with widely used file hosting services and allows utilizing its services through a mobile application. Both of the aforementioned features are currently missing from the HARMONISE platform.

The final approach to be reviewed here is Sentic Album [33]. Sentic Album is a content-, concept-, and context-based online personal photo management system that exploits both data and metadata of online personal pictures to annotate, organize, and retrieve them. Sentic Album utilizes a multi-tier architecture that exploits semantic web techniques to process image data and metadata at content, concept, and context level, in order to grasp the salient features of online personal photos, and hence find intelligent ways of annotating, organizing, and retrieving them.

Similar to the HARMONISE platform and the SLH, Sentic Album includes semantic databases, automatic annotation features and a search and retrieval module. The search functionality provides users an UI that allows them to manage, search and retrieve their personal pictures online. Moreover, users are able to assign multiple categories to an image object, enabling classifications to be ordered in multiple ways. This makes it possible to perform searches combining a textual approach with a navigational one. The combination of key-word based search and content classification based search is similar to the search feature provided by the SLH. However, in HARMONISE platform the classifications are based on pre-defined domain knowledge which enables addressing more task specific needs and requirements. In general, the main difference between Sentic Album and the HARMONISE platform is their targeted group of end-users. The HARMONISE platform aims at serving a specific group of end-users including planners, urban designers and building security personnel, whereas Sentic Album is targeted to more heterogeneous group of end-users.

VI. System Evaluation

In order to test and demonstrate the viability and effectiveness of the HARMONISE Platform and the SLH, the developed system was applied in five different case study contexts under the project activities. The selected case study cities are Dublin, Ireland; London, United Kingdom; Genoa, Italy; Bilbao, Spain and Vantaa, Finland. Each of these case studies incorporates a large scale urban built infrastructure project, at different scales and contexts. Moreover, the case studies incorporate a combination of urban built infrastructure systems at various stages from completed, operational projects, to as yet unrealized proposals at design and planning stage.

The actual evaluation process was started by testing the platform and the SLH with a range of built environment professionals (including architects, urban designers and town planners) from the HARMONISE project consortium organisations. Subsequently, the developed system was demonstrated and assessed in case study specific workshops where the platform and the SLH were presented to the key stakeholders including various urban resilience professionals and policy makers. Moreover, the workshop participants were invited to experiment and criticize the system.

The evaluation process also included creating a set of standardised questionnaires. The questionnaires were to be used when interacting with the end-users in the case studies. The purpose of the questionnaires was to elicit feedback from users and associated stakeholders as to the performance (actual or intended) of the HARMONISE platform and the SLH being tested. Overall, this task aimed to discover '*what works'* on the ground in practice and learn about the user focussed process of implementation (what users want).

The survey was designed to focus on both the technical aspects of the platform as well as on the usability of the system. Importantly, the adopted approach incorporated a balance between quantitative and qualitative feedback. The results from this survey were to be used as feedback to designers so that improvements can be made to the platform.

The actual evaluation was divided into two phases: In phase 1 (between March and April 2015) a workshop was held in each case study area, led by the Case Study Leads (CSL's). The purpose of these workshops was to present the HARMONISE concept and the platform to key stakeholders and to gather feedback on the work-in-progress version of the platform. Furthermore, the phase 2 (between mid-October and early December 2015) a second workshop was held in each case study area. During these second workshops, an improved version of the platform was presented to stakeholders.

For the first testing phase, the created questionnaires were circulated to each CSL's in advance of the case study workshops as an online survey link. The survey was designed to be self-completed by the end user so each CSL then requested that all case study workshop participants complete this online questionnaire in their own time following the event. The survey was opened for responses for a period of one month following the workshop held in the case study location.

However, in some cases more emphasis was placed on gathering feedback within the context of the stakeholder workshops (rather than using the online questionnaire after the workshop). As such, feedback was gathered in two ways:

- During the stakeholder workshops only – In this case, some questions from the online questionnaire were used to stimulate discussion among the stakeholders. The discussion was then recorded by the HARMONISE facilitators in a manner which closely matched the format of the questionnaire (to ensure that feedback could be analyzed in a relatively consistent manner).
- During the stakeholder workshops and using the online questionnaire – In this case, stakeholders reported their 'first thoughts' during the workshops, with some also choosing to report more detailed feedback after the event through the use of the online questionnaire

Following the completion of phase 1 of the testing process, many CSL's reported that they had received the richest feedback during discussions as part of the workshops, with less feedback provided through the online survey. Indeed, many CSL's reported that some stakeholders felt that the online survey was too lengthy, a factor which discouraged them from inputting feedback in a detailed manner. As a result, the testing approach for the second phase of testing was adjusted in two minor ways – 1. The questionnaire survey was further edited (with stakeholders encouraged to focus on providing qualitative comments) 2. A soft copy version of the survey was circulated to each workshop participant during the various workshops – with a request for them to complete the survey during the workshop.

As discussed above, the evaluation was divided into two phases. In both parts questionnaires and end-user discussions were used to collect information about the abilities of the system to support urban resilience professionals and policy makers. The questionnaire included questions, for example, about perceived ease-of-use and perceived usefulness of the tool. Perceived usefulness that is defined as "the degree to which a person believes that using a particular system would enhance their job performance" and perceived ease-of-use that is defined as "the degree to which a person believes that using a particular system would be free from effort" were considered as important factors as they can determine whether people will accept or reject an emerging information technology [34].

The questionnaire used a five-level grading system where "Strongly agree" was the best and "Strongly disagree" the worst grade, with "Neither agree nor disagree" being average. Figure 11 summarizes the feedback on the platform, as gathered during evaluation phase 1.

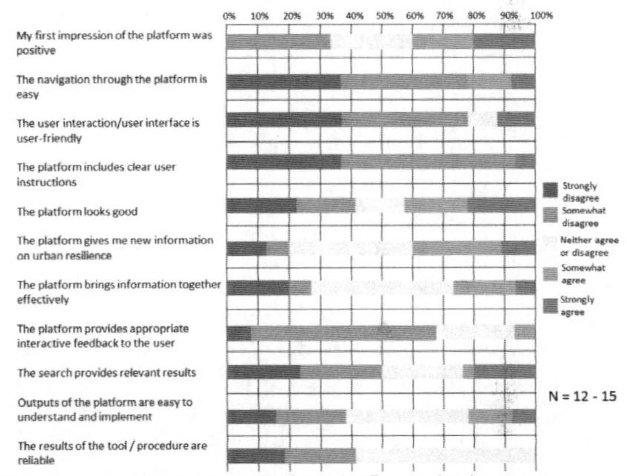

Figure 11. Questionnaire results from the first evaluation stage.

In general, the first evaluation was useful and revealed some extremely interesting points about the constructed system and enhanced the discovery of which features users find useful and easy to use, and which parts of the application still need to be improved. As depicted by the questionnaire results presented above, the usability and graphical user interface of the system was found to require improvements. Moreover, it was perceived as difficult to navigate through the platform. The search feature was also identified as deficient. In general, the first evaluation stage indicated that the platform and the SLH still require further development to reach its full potential.

The knowledge and experience gained from the first evaluation stage was utilized in the subsequent development of the HARMONISE platform and the SLH. The major improvements included, for example, re-designing the visual appearance, user interface and navigation of the platform. Moreover, the metadata management services of the SLH were completely redeveloped and optimized to better support the requirements set by the search feature. Finally, the utilized search algorithm was improved and integrated with the Thematic Framework based content classification mechanism.

The new versions of the HARMONISE platform and the SLH were tested in the second evaluation phase. Again, the actual testing was carried out in workshop sessions were end-users were allowed to test the system and fill in a questionnaire. Additionally, verbal feedback was collected from the workshop participants. Figure 12 summarizes the results from the second evaluation round.

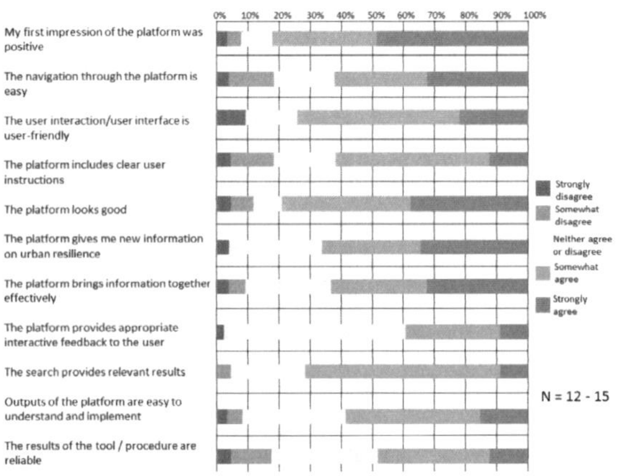

Figure 12. Questionnaire results from the second evaluation stage.

It should be noted that the chart for testing period 2 is not directly comparable with the results of testing period 1 as most of the test participants were already somewhat familiar with the system in test period 2. Nevertheless, the chart for test period 2 provide a useful indication of progress in meeting stakeholder expectations of the platform, and in addressing some of the stakeholder concerns raised during testing stage 1. In more detail, the stakeholder feedback from testing stage 2 illustrates far greater user satisfaction with the various elements of the platform than was recorded during testing stage 1 – shown by the far higher percentage of stakeholders who 'somewhat agreed' or 'strongly agreed' with some of the key stated aims for the platform functionality.

VII. CONCLUSION

In this work, we introduce a content management platform for the domain of urban resilience. The platform aims at serving as a 'one-stop-shop' for resilience information and guidance offering a holistic view to urban resilience. Furthermore, the platform contains information and tools specifically designed to aid decision makers in enhancing the resilience of large scale urban built infrastructure.

The developed content management platform is extended with an additional information processing layer that utilizes semantic technologies to manage an extensive set of heterogeneous material that comes in different forms including tools, design guidance documentation and specifications. Moreover, the developed semantic layer enables the creation of machine-understandable and machine-process able descriptions of content items. This has resulted in an improved shared understanding of information elements and interoperability.

With the effective utilization of Linked Data based analysis tools and domain specific content annotation mechanisms, the semantic layer offers task specific and personalized content management support for end-users. The enhanced intelligence has provided better understanding of urban resilience content, linkages between unstructured information and tools, and more sophisticated answers to users' various needs. Furthermore, the recommendation service provides the functionality to predict relevant content to the user of the system using our collaborative filtering approach. This approach is able to avail of the rich user data available in terms of profile information and also content preference information resulting in a set of recommendations tailored to individual users.

The developed HARMONISE platform and the SLH have been tested by HARMONISE project partners and other invited domain specialists. Additionally, several case study stakeholders have evaluated the system in terms of usability, perceived usefulness and the relevancy of received search and recommendation results. The performed evaluations have provided valuable information about the deficiencies and strengths of the HARMONISE platform and SLH.

The future work includes further refining the HARMONISE platform and the SLH on the basis of the feedback received from the evaluation process. Additionally, the graphical appearance of the platform's user interface as well as the usability of individual components will be improved.

REFERENCES

[1] I. Niskanen, M Murtonen, F Browne, P. Davis and F. Pantisano, "A Semantic Layer for Urban Resilience Content Management," 8th International Conference on Information, Process, and Knowledge Management (eKNOW 2016), Venice, Italy, April 24-28, 2016.

[2] B. Boiko, Content management bible, John Wiley & Sons, 2005.

[3] S. Das, L. Girard, T. Green, L. Weitzman, A. Lewis-Bowen, and T. Clark, "Building biomedical web communities using a semantically aware content management system," Briefings in bioinformatics, 10(2), pp. 129-138, 2009.

[4] N. W. Y Shao, S. J. H Yang, and A. Sue, "A content management system for adaptive learning environment," Multimedia Software Engineering, Proceedings. Fifth International Symposium on, IEEE, 2003.

[5] N. Mehta, Choosing an Open Source CMS: Beginner's Guide, Packt Publishing Ltd, 2009.

[6] D. Dicheva and D. Christo, "Leveraging Domain Specificity to Improve Findability in OER Repositories," Research and Advanced Technology for Digital Libraries. Springer Berlin Heidelberg, pp. 466-469, 2013.

[7] S. K. Patel, V. R. Rathod, and S. Parikh, "Joomla, Drupal and WordPress-a statistical comparison of open source CMS." Trendz in Information Sciences and Computing (TISC), 3rd International Conference on. IEEE, 2011.

[8] C. Dorai and S. Venkatesh, "Bridging the semantic gap in content management systems," Media Computing. Springer US, pp. 1-9, 2002.

[9] J. L. Navarro-Galindo and J. Samos, "The FLERSA tool: adding semantics to a web content management system," International Journal of Web Information Systems 8.1: pp. 73-126, 2012.

[10] A. Kohn, F. Bry, and A. Manta, "Semantic search on unstructured data: explicit knowledge through data recycling," Semantic-Enabled Advancements on the Web: Applications Across Industries, 194, 2012.

[11] D. R. Karger and D. Quan, "What would it mean to blog on the semantic web?," The Semantic Web–ISWC 2004. Springer Berlin Heidelberg, pp. 214-228, 2004.

[12] The HARMONISE project (Available online at: http://harmonise.eu/) [accessed: 13.4.2016]

[13] Linked Data (Available online at: http://linkeddata.org/) [accessed: 13.4.2016]

[14] Drupal (Available online at: https://www.drupal.org/) [accessed: 13.4.2016]

[15] WordPress (Available online at: https://wordpress.org/) [accessed: 13.4.2016]

[16] S. Purcell, W. Hynes, J. Coaffee, M. Murtonen, D. Davis, and F. Fiedrich, "The drive for holistic urban resilience," 9th Future Security, Security Research Conference, Berlin Sep. 16- 18, 2014.

[17] A Vailaya, M. A. Figueiredo, A. K. Jain, and H. J. Zhang, "Image classification for content-based indexing," Image Processing, IEEE Transactions on, 10(1), pp. 117-130, 2001.

[18] R. García, J. M. Gimeno, F. Perdrix, R. Gil, and M. Oliva, "The rhizomer semantic content management system," In Emerging Technologies and Information Systems for the Knowledge Society pp. 385-394, Springer Berlin Heidelberg, 2008.

[19] M. Hausenblas, "Exploiting linked data to build web applications," IEEE Internet Computing 4, pp. 68-73, 2009.

[20] ONKI - Finnish Ontology Library Service (Available online at: http://onki.fi/) [accessed: 13.4.2016]

[21] DBpedia (Available online at: http://dbpedia.org/) [accessed: 13.4.2016]

[22] OpenCalais (Available online at: http://www.opencalais.com/) [accessed: 13.4.2016]

[23] Virtuoso Universal Server (Available online at: http://semanticweb.org/wiki/Virtuoso) [accessed: 13.4.2016]

[24] O. Erling and I. Mikhailov. "RDF Support in the Virtuoso DBMS," Networked Knowledge-Networked Media. Springer Berlin Heidelberg, pp. 7-24, 2009.

[25] Solr (Available online at: http://lucene.apache.org/solr/) [accessed: 13.4.2016]

[26] Apache Lucene Core (Available online at: https://lucene.apache.org/core/) [accessed: 13.4.2016]

[27] F. Ricci, L. Rokach, and B. Shapira, Introduction to recommender systems handbook, Springer, 2011.

[28] G. Adomavicius and Y. Kwon, "New recommendation techniques formulticriteria rating systems," IEEE Intelligent Systems, vol. 22, no. 3, pp. 48–55, 2007.

[29] M. Ekstrand, J. Riedl, and J. Konstan, "Collaborative filtering recommender systems," Human-Computer Interaction, vol. 4, no. 2, pp. 81–173, 2010.

[30] I. Palomares, F. Browne, H. Wang, and P. Davis, "A collaborative filtering recommender system model using owa and uninorm aggregation operators," in Intelligent Systems and Knowledge Engineering (ISKE), 2015 10th International Conference on, 2015, pp. 382–388.

[31] F. Sasaki and A. Srivastava, "Towards a Platform for Curation Technologies: Enriching Text Collections with a Semantic-Web Layer," The Semantic Web: ESWC 2016 Satellite Events, Heraklion, Crete, Greece, May 29–June 2, 2016, Revised Selected Papers, 9989, 65.

[32] R. Mazza, A. Baldassari and R. Guidi, "Ondigita: A Platform for the Management and Delivery of Digital Documents," International Association for Development of the Information Society, 2013.

[33] E. Cambria and A. Hussain, "Sentic album: content-, concept, and context-based online personal photo management system," Cognitive Computation, vol. 4, no. 4, pp. 477-496, 2012.

[34] F.D. Davis, "Perceived usefulness, perceived ease of use, and user acceptance of information technology," MIS quarterly, 13 (3), pp. 319-340, 1989.

Four Public Self-Service Applications: A Study of the Development Process, User Involvement and Usability in Danish Public Self-Service Applications

Jane Billestrup, Jan Stage
Institute of Computer Science
Aalborg University
Aalborg, Denmark
{jane,jans}@cs.aau.dk

Marta Larusdottir
School of Computer Science
Reykjavik University
Reykjavik, Iceland
marta@ru.is

Abstract— **This paper presents a case study of four software companies in Denmark developing self-service applications for the same self-service area. This study outlines the process of how the four companies developed their self-service applications and a usability study of the completed software solutions. In this study, we have analysed the customer and end-user involvement and compared these results to the results of the usability evaluations. The main findings show that the usability varied in the four cases, and the ones who had the most customer involvement from case workers showed the highest number of usability problems in the self-service solutions for the citizens. We discuss the user-centred design approaches used, the drawbacks and benefits of customer and user involvement, and case workers acting as citizen representation during the development process of the software.**

Keywords-Case Study; Self-Service Applications; Usability; Development Process; User-Centred Design; Software Development

I. Introduction

This paper is an extended version of the paper "A case study of four IT companies developing usable public self-service solutions" [1].

European countries are currently developing digital self-service solutions for their citizens. These efforts are being launched to improve citizens' self-services and to reduce costs [2]. Though public self-services have been on the agenda in many countries for years, getting the end-users to use these applications is not easily achieved. For citizens to accept public digital services and websites, these sites need to have a high degree of usability for the citizens to accept the public digital services and websites [3]. Wangpipatwong et al. found that public digital websites in Thailand lack usability due to poor design and they recommend focusing more on the needs of the citizens to ensure that they will use these websites continuously [4].

The Digital Economy and Society Index (DESI) describes the level of digitalisation of the countries in EU [2]. The digitalisation level is measured in five areas, connectivity, human capital, use of the Internet, integration of digital technology, and digital public services, respectively [2]. The level of digitalisation varies in the countries in EU, from Romania, Bulgaria and Greece at the bottom to Sweden, Finland, and Denmark at the top [2]. Denmark is one of the top 3 countries in regards to all digitalisation areas in EU and is one of the leading countries in the world in regards to the level of digitalisation [2].

Denmark has a population of 5.6 million people and is divided into 98 municipalities as a single point of contact for citizens in regards to the public sector [5]. In 2012, a digitalisation process was launched with the goal that by the end of 2015, 80% of all communication between citizens and the municipalities should be conducted digitally. This digitalisation also included digital public self-service applications [6].

Until 2012, a contract based approach was used for developing digital public services, where the software companies competed by bidding. As of 2012, the software companies no longer had to put in a bid. Instead, they have to compete with other companies about selling their self-service applications to the municipalities. For the individual municipalities, it means that they can choose between competing designs for each digitalisation area for the citizen self-service applications.

To support the Danish initiative, the joint IT organisation of the municipalities in Denmark developed two set of user centred guidance materials in 2012, to help the self-service providers in developing user-friendly self-service applications for the citizens [7]. Similar initiatives have been taken in other countries like the United States, United Kingdom, and South Africa [8] [9] [10].

Development of self-service applications for all citizens involves a broad array of different stakeholders, including citizens, public institutions such as municipalities, support organisations like the joint IT organisation of the municipalities, IT companies that produce the applications and third party purveyors that the public institutions use to provide services to the citizens. In Denmark, the joint IT organisation of the municipalities has created guidelines to ensure that public digital self-service applications and websites are usable for all citizens [6].

From the self-service providers' point of view, focus on usability will increase the price of the product, making the developed solution harder to sell [11]. But studies show that the quality of the software and the cost are complementary, e.g., [12] [13]. To get public self-service providers to focus on usability, it has to be made a requirement. Both Jokela et al. [14] and Mastrangelo [15] describe the importance of usability being specified in the requirements specification document. Mastrangelo describes that public administration needs guidelines and guidance to get usability placed in the requirements to get the intended impact [15].

Jokela et al. found that to acquire usable digital self-service solutions the specified usability requirements have to be performance-based, as only these types of requirements would be verifiable, valid and comprehensive [11]. Additionally, the usability of digital self-service solutions should be validated before the solutions are sold to the municipalities [11].

According to Tarkkanen et al., formal and detailed criteria for validation will cause usability workarounds by the self-service providers as they will focus only on the verification of their applications in regards to what is stated in the usability requirements, instead of focusing on getting the usability of the digital self-service solutions optimised and, finding and fixing usability issues [16].

In this study, we have focused on analysing the development of public self-service applications, based on analysing each case based on the following four themes

- the development process used
- the customer involvement (case workers)
- the end-user focus (citizens)
- the characteristics of the products developed

These four themes were found by conducting a descriptive coding on all collected data as proposed by Saldana [17].

Additionally, we have analysed the number of usability problems found in each of the self-service solutions and compared it to the findings related to the four themes stated above.

In this paper, we have focused on analysing the customer and user involvement during the software development process. We discuss the user-centred design approaches used, the drawbacks and benefits of customer and user involvement found in these four cases, and describe the quality of each of the four self-service applications based on the analysis and the conducted usability evaluation.

Section II describes the background of this study. Section III presents the method of this case study. Section IV presents the results. Section V provides the discussion and finally, Section VI presents the conclusion.

II. Background

In opposition to the traditional development process based on a set of requirements and a fixed contract the joint IT organisation of the municipalities in Denmark decided on a new approach in 2012. According to the project manager at the joint IT organisation of the municipalities, the goal of conducting this change was to ensure that the developed self-service applications had a high degree of usability and that all relevant stakeholders were involved in the development process. The first wave was deployed in December 2012 and the last wave in 2015. Each wave released a new set of digital self-service applications. Table I shows the plan for the deployment of the four waves.

This study was conducted in 2013-14 mainly focusing on the development of one application for the second wave.

Since 2012 approximately 30 different public self-service application areas have been made mandatory for citizens to use. Across these self-service areas, around 100 different self-service applications have been sold to the municipalities from more than twenty self-service providers [18].

Table I. Plan for deployment of self-service applications [18]

	Public self-service applications area
Wave 1 2012	- Address change - National health service medical card - European health insurance card - Daycare - After school care - School registration
Wave 2 2013	- Aid for burial - Free day care - Assistive technologies for handicapped or elderly - Exit visa - Unlisted name or address - Reporting of rats - Loan for real estate tax - Letting out facilities - Changing medical practitioner - Marriage certificate - Passport - Drivers license
Wave 3 2014	- Garbage handling for citizens - Garbage handling for organisations - Construction work - Building permission - Loan for deposit - Registration in CPR - Services in roads and traffic areas - Notification of digging or work on pipelines - Certificates for Lodging - Parking permits
Wave 4 2015	- Personal supplement - Sickness benefits - Sickness supplement - Extended sickness supplement

The municipalities' joint IT organisation developed two sets of guidance materials supporting a user-centred approach in the development of public self-service applications [19] [21]. A User Journey and a set of 24 Usability Criteria, respectively.

The user journeys can be described as a person in a use situation described in a scenario [20] using graphical illustrations. An illustration showing six pictures from one user journey is presented in Figure 1. The usability criteria are a set of guidelines listing requirements for all developed self-service applications. An overview of the usability criteria for the development of public self-service applications can be seen in Table II.

Figure 1. Six pictures from one user journey [19]

Table II. 24 usability criteria [21]

	Language and text
1	Texts should be short and precise without containing legalised or technical terms
2	Text should be action-oriented and guide the citizens to fill out the form
3	Citizens should be informed of which information will be needed, before filling out the form
4	Citizens can access additional information if needed when filling out the form
5	If an error is made it should be made very clear to the citizens what they did wrong
6	Error messages should be in Danish
	Progress and flow
7	The form should be organised in logical steps
8	Before filling out the form, the extent of the form should be clear to the citizens
9	When filling out the form, the citizen knows the progress made and how many steps are left
10	A receipt should be made after finishing filling out the form
11	The receipt should also be sent by email to the citizens
12	After submitting the form, the next steps should be clear to the citizen
	Data and information
13	If login is required, NemLogin (National Danish Identity Service) should be used
14	Existing data should be reused as much as possible; citizens should not provide the same information more than once
15	A summary is shown before submitting the form
16	Submitting a form should only be possible if all required information is provided
17	The solution should validate the information provided by the citizens when possible
18	The solution should adapt questions to prior answers given, when possible
	Design and accessibility
19	It should be made clear to the citizens when are beginning to fill out a form
20	There should be a clear distinction between buttons like yes/no, forward/backwards, and the positioning should be continuous through the form
21	The authority behind the form should be clear
22	Navigating in the form should be possible both using mouse and keyboard
23	The form should be filled out by citizens who does not possess a high degree of IT skills
24	The solution meet relevant accessibility criteria for self-service solutions

The overall purpose of these materials was to provide the IT self-service providers with tools to keep a focus on the citizens and their needs to ensure that the developed self-service applications were usable for all citizens. The joint IT organisation of the municipalities functioned in a supporting role during the development process. All interested IT companies could decide which specific services they wanted to develop. The services were developed and made available for all of the 98 municipalities in Denmark. The municipalities buy individual solutions and are not bound by one self-service provider but can choose freely between all developed solutions in each area.

III. METHOD

We have conducted an empirical study of four competing IT development companies implementing usable digital self-service solutions for the same application area. Next, the four cases are presented, and the data collection and analysis are described in more detail.

A. *The Cases*

Below, the four companies are described. The companies have developed similar solutions and are competitors regarding the 98 municipalities in Denmark who are the potential customers. The SME scale (small and medium scale enterprise) [22] has been used to categorise the size of the four companies involved in this case study, in regards to the number of employees and turnover. The SME scale is shown in Table III.

Table III. SME Scale [22]

Company category	Employees	Turnover	or	Balance sheet total
Medium-sized	<250	≤ € 50 m		≤ € 43 m
Small	<50	≤ € 10 m		≤ € 10 m
Micro	<10	≤ € 2 m		≤ € 2 m

The four companies were chosen because they were the only companies developing applications for this particular self-service area, and the companies and their developed self-service solutions were different in terms of maturity of the company and if the company was developing a new solution or was optimising an existing solution. The applications for this self-service area had some degree of complexity, and the self-service area would be relevant to all types of citizens, though mainly older citizens. Next, the four companies are categorised.

Case A is a micro/small company in regards to the SME scale and the turnover and number of employees. The company has not previously developed other public digital self-service solutions, so it is categorised as immature. Their digital self-service solution is categorised as new for the same reason. This company is an independent consulting and software company.

Case B is a large company in regards to the SME scale. The company is categorised as mature in regards to digital self-service solutions in general as they have developed several public digital self-service solutions previously. This self-service solution is categorised as new, though they already have an existing solution, as they redid both the analysis and design phase, before developing this solution. This company has departments all over Scandinavia and creates and sells software solutions to several different markets.

Case C is a large company on the SME scale. The company is described as both immature and mature in regards to digital self-service solutions, as they are experienced in regards to developing self-service applications. This area of application is relatively new to them, though having an existing solution in this self-service area. This company has departments all over Scandinavia and creates and sells software solutions to different markets. Case D is a large company on the SME scale. The company is described as mature in regards to digital self-service solutions and has developed digital self-service applications for years. For this self-service area, their self-service solution is an optimisation of an existing self-service application. This company is an independent consulting and software company. Table IV shows the placement of the four cases in regards to maturity and if the digital self-service solution was new or an optimisation of an existing solution.

Table IV. Categorisation of the four companies and self-solutions in regards to maturity of the company and if the self-service solution is new or an optimisation

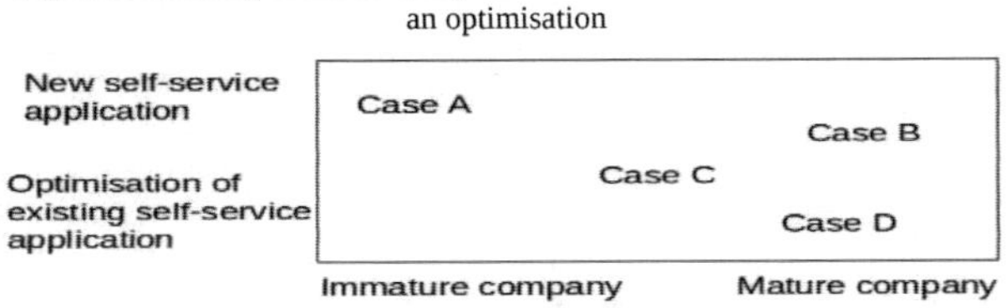

We have defined the organisation's maturity according to their experience developing self-service applications in general. We defined the self-service application as new if the organisation had no existing self-service solution in this area or had an existing solution, but the problem area was re-analysed before redesigning the system. Otherwise, the self-service solution was defined as an optimisation of an existing self-service application.

The data used for this categorisation was collected from each of the companies by the conducted interviews described in the following section.

B. *Data Collection*

This section describes the process of the data collection. The first sub-section describes how we collected the data that was analysed to determine the scope of this study in regards to which self-service area to focus on, and which companies it would be relevant to include in the study. The second sub-section describes the data collection for this study, which is the results documented in this paper.

1) *Exploratory Preparation*

All data was gathered over a period of one year. Qualitative interviews were conducted by phone with project managers from 11 of 12 identified digital self-service providers for all self-service providers identified for the second wave at this time. The primary objective was to learn how self-service providers were accepting and using the user-centred materials and learn about each company and their development approach [23]. Additional data was gathered on how the user-centred requirements were used, and how existing requirements were redesigned [24]. All interviews were transcribed and analysed by coding, using Dedoose [25].

This analysis leads to narrowing the focus on one public self-service area with four identified self-service providers.

2) *Gathering the Data*

For this case study, we had one half-day meeting with each of the four companies. The people present at the first meeting had the following job titles; for case A; CEO, Project Manager, and Usability Expert. For case B; Product Owner. For case C, Business Developer and, Senior Manager. For case D; Chief Consultant and, Chief Product Owner. The agenda for these meetings was an introduction to this study including a discussion of their gain of participating, as we offered inputs on their self-service solution and conducting a usability evaluation at the end of the process. The results of these activities would be usable to improve the four companies self-service applications.

Before the meetings, we had identified the roles of the people we would like to interview, as these functions were named differently in each company and some people would have more than one of these roles. The identified roles were the following; project manager, developer, interface designer, and the person responsible for the user experience and usability of the public self-service application. These roles were chosen to ensure to get different views of the development process and end-product, in relation to the user focus and involvement.

After the introduction the interviewee presented his/her company overall and, more specifically, how the practitioners were developing this chosen self-service application, including describing the development process and method, collaboration with stakeholders and end-user involvement. The product owner or project manager also gave a demonstration of the self-service application in its current state and handed over relevant internal documents describing their development process and showing design documents. Lastly, it was discussed which people they suggested for further interviews in the next part of our study to ensure we would cover all perspectives. At the meetings, we conducted a list of people covering the following roles previously described. We interviewed 14 people distributed across the four companies.

The purpose of the interviews was to determine current practice at each of the four companies in regards to customer and citizen involvement, and how the end-users were taken into consideration during the design and development process. We found that interviewing people with different roles and responsibilities would provide us with more data on different perspectives and areas of expertise inside each company. All interviews were conducted as semi-structured qualitative interviews as described by Kvale [26]. The interviews were conducted by phone and transcribed afterwards.

Table V shows the number of people involved in this study, from each of the four companies.

Table V. Number of participants from each company in each phase

	Preperation Meeting	Interviews	Workshop	Total amount of participants from each company
Case A	3	3	1	**3**
Case B	1	3 (2)	2	**3**
Case C	2	3 (1)	2	**3**
Case D	2	5 (3)	2 (1)	**6**
Total (in all)	**8**	**14**	**7**	**15**

The number of participants from each company is shown for all phases of this study. The number in () represents new people, who were not part of the previous step, e.g., case D had two people present at the preparation meeting, and five employees were interviewed. Of these five people, three were not present at the preparation meeting. At the workshop with case D, two people were present, of these two, one had not been present at the preparation meeting and was not interviewed.

Table VI. Shows the data collection process of the exploratory preparation and for this study

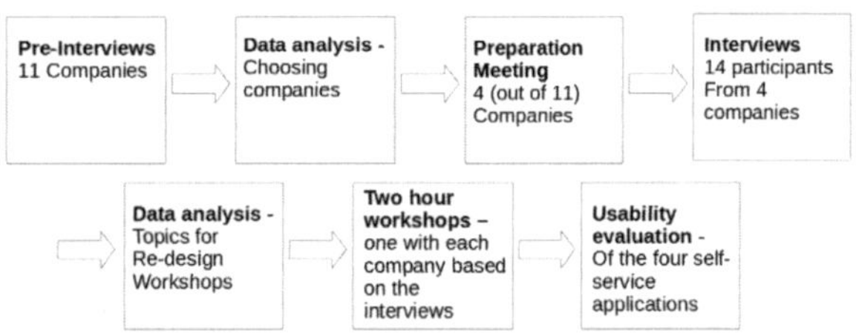

The workshops were used to discuss the results from the interviews in regards to their user-centred approach and how the user-centred materials developed materials from the joint IT organisation of the municipalities were used during the development process, and to clarify our results from the interviews and preparation meetings.

3) *Usability Evaluation of Products*

To evaluate if the development process had resulted in usable self-service applications for the citizens, a usability evaluation of these four self-service solutions was conducted. This evaluation was conducted as a think-aloud usability evaluation in a usability laboratory, with eight test persons. For the evaluations, all test persons received the same instructions explaining what they were meant to do during the evaluation, e.g., conduct a set of tasks and think aloud during the evaluation. All participants received the same tasks, and evaluated all four systems, but evaluated them in a different order to even out any bias.

The test persons were chosen to represent a user segment as large as possible. Our test persons ranged in age and had different educational backgrounds. The test persons varied in skill level and experience with computers, though all use the Internet on a regular basis. Most test persons had experience with other public digital self-service areas but not this specific area. An overview of the test persons can be found in Table VII.

All test persons received a small gift after participating in the evaluation. After conducting the evaluations, the data was analysed using the method Instant Data Analysis, as this method is also used på practitioners (IDA) [27]. The usability problems were categorised after the criteria described in Table 8. The problems were categorised in regards to levels of confusion and frustration of the participants, and whether they were able to fill out the forms correctly. These criteria and categorisations were described further by Skov and Stage [28].

Table VII. Overview of the demography of the test persons

Test person	Gender	Age	Education	Experience with public services
TP1	F	44	High school degree (early retirement because of health issues)	Yes, also for this application type, and done digitally
TP2	F	31	PhD-student in Social science	Yes, for other service areas, and done digitally
TP3	M	52	Accountant	Yes, for other service areas, and done digitally
TP4	F	64	Retired school teacher	Yes, for other service areas, but not digitally
TP5	F	66	Technical Assistant	Yes, also for this service area, and done digitally
TP6	M	30	Msc. Engineering	Yes, for other service areas, and done digitally
TP7	M	65	Retired computer assistant	Yes, for other service areas, and done digitally
TP8	M	22	Bachelor student in computer science	No experience

Table VIII. Defining the Severity of the Usability Problems in the Digital Self-Service Solutions [28]

	Slowed down	Understanding	Frustration or confusion	Test monitor
Critical	Hindered in solving the task	Does not understand how the information in the system can be used for solving the task	Extensive level of frustration or confusion – can lead to a full stop	Receives substantial assistance, could not have solved the task without it
Serious	Delayed in solving the task	Does not understand how a specific functionality operates or is activated	Is clearly annoyed by something that cannot be done or remembered or something illogical that one must do	Receives a hint, and can solve the task afterwards
Cosmetic	Delayed slightly in solving the task	Do actions without being able to explain why (you just have to do it)	Only small signs of frustration or confusion	Is asked a question that makes him come up with the solution

C. Data Analysis

The data was analysed with regard to the different perspectives of each interviewee and their job function to get an idea of what each company did during the development process.

The aim of these activities was to study the development process of the four companies developing the digital self-service solutions in this specific self-service area, into more detail. The cases were analysed exploratively.

We completed a content analysis of relevant documents from the companies. Both, interviews and documents were analysed using descriptive coding [17], and Dedoose [25] as a tool. All coding was conducted by one researcher and categories were discussed and verified by another researcher.

IV. RESULTS

In this section, we present our results. Our findings are divided into four subsections for each case, focusing on the development process, customer involvement, end-user focus and the final product, then the results are compared between the four cases for each focus area. All results are reported from the perspectives of the companies and their interviewed employees and the documents we got from them.

A. Case A

1) Development Process

Company A uses an agile development method and primarily in accordance with Scrum [29]. They describe their development process as flexible. "*Our development method is agile, primarily Scrum. We use a pragmatic approach and a flexible model, meaning we can add features quite late in the process.*" They describe choosing this approach as it makes the development process easier and more dynamic, also, needing fewer people working on each project, e.g., they primarily have a project manager involved in the development process, who is also the designer and the developer. This is doable because they can make changes quite late in the process and they feel that correcting errors are not a big deal. "*We are not afraid of making mistakes; we don't have a great need to get everything right the first time*". *One* municipality was involved giving the company a greater understanding of the entire field of application.

2) Customer Involvement

The company collaborated with one municipality as a customer and stakeholder. It was insisted that the involved personnel should be case workers who understood their own and the citizens' needs and not necessarily people with IT skills. From the case workers, they have learned about the field of application. "*We held a new workshop with the municipality every couple of weeks; here we created mock-ups that we used to design a new prototype, which was evaluated and redesigned at the next workshop, [...] until we were satisfied with the final prototype*". The Interviewees were confident that they had developed a solution that lives up to the wishes and needs of their on-site customer but is less confident that their solution is covering the needs of other municipalities. "*We have discussed if we should have created a standardised solution covering the needs of as many municipalities as possible.*" It was described as a problem as they were not aware of the fact that the interpretations of legislation are not the same in all municipalities.

3) End-User Focus

The citizens are not involved in the development process, but the company describes taking them into consideration by ensuring that the procedures for sending an application are as simple as possible. "*We have created the solution so it should be understandable for all types of people. We have a good feeling here and our self-service application have been verified several times (by case workers)*". They have built an application that in the simple cases can send a decision back to the applicant right away without a case worker having to go through the application first. One interviewee also described that their primary focus is on the customer and not the citizens. "*We have been focusing on the customers' needs and work procedures; it has been important for us to understand what they wanted the citizens to do*". This perspective was chosen because the municipalities are the paying customers and not the citizens.

4) Products

It was perceived as a strength that they have developed a "whole solution" covering both the necessities for the case workers and the citizens. "*Our solution has a good flow for the citizens with understandable screen displays. It is not heavy on wording, and we only ask for information that is relevant for the municipalities to keep things as simple as possible.*"

The company also identified some weaknesses in regards to their digital self-service application. They described that the fact that they only collaborated with one municipality might have been an issue, although they did not see it as a real option for them to have involved 3-5 municipalities in the development process. The company also recognises that there might be usability issues in the digital self-service application but argues that this is substantiated in what the municipalities are willing to pay for. "*Reality is just different than theory. If you want to pay for it, you can get the great solutions focused on usability, but that is not what the municipalities want to pay for*". One interviewee described that if the customers do not care about usability they will not focus on that either.

B. Case B

1) Development Process

Company B uses Scrum [29] as their development method, and they use an adjusted version of the project management method PRINCE2 [30].

One interviewee described that the company develops one solution to fit all municipalities. "*Our aim is to make one solution to fit all, [...] We only create products were we keep the property rights [...], so we can sell the same product to several customers*". All digital self-service applications are built in a module-based platform. This approach is chosen to give a certain amount of flexibility in regards to changing the design during the development process or when the system is tested by municipalities. Municipalities are involved early in the process.

2) Customer Involvement

The primary focus of the digital self-service application is on the back-end of the system, and to ease the workload of the case workers. "*Our primary focus is to simplify the working procedures for the case workers. Otherwise, this would never be a priority for the municipalities*". Before developing this solution, the company hosted workshops with five municipalities that are already customers, with the purpose of analysing the working procedures, used for creating a specification of requirements and a business case. "*On the first workshop we are not presenting anything, typically we say – we don't know anything, tell us about your work […] we use these workshops to learn how we digitally can support the digital workflow.*" This information is used in the development phase, where the first iteration is developed, and a prototype is created. The prototype was presented at the next workshop to case workers from the municipalities involved in the development process. The prototype shows the mapping when a citizen fills in a form and until it lands with the case worker. One interviewee also described sending emails to all municipalities that are existing customers, asking the case workers to answer questions in regards to their workflow.

3) End-User Focus

The company does not involve citizens in the development process, but two interviewees described involving the municipalities and case workers as a representation of the citizens' needs. "*The municipalities give us feedback in regards to what is not working for the citizens, e.g., parts of the application that citizens consistently fill out wrong*". Though the focus is not directly on the citizens, it was stated by one interviewee that an optimisation of the back-end also brings value to the citizens as this will give a better flow with the handling of their applications. It was stated that focusing on accessibility of the system is more important than focusing on usability for the citizens.

Two interviewees did describe testing the application with users before launching the digital self-service application. "*We have some pilot municipalities […] they are part of a test phase where we assemble data for statistics*". For the municipalities and case workers, the focus is on improving the efficiency of the workflows.

4) Products

The company perceives it as a strength of their digital self-service application that different kinds of professionals were involved in the development process. It was stated that the role of the product owner creates more value as he or she also has to ensure that the digital self-service application follows the legislations even if it changes. Two interviewees showed confidence in that they were ensuring to develop usable and intuitive digital self-service applications.

Late changes are described as being possible because the application is built in modules making changes less expensive. A perceived weakness is creating one solution to fit all needs. This approach was chosen as updating or testing would be too expensive if municipalities wanted something changed.

C. Case C

1) Development Process

Company C uses its own process, which is not a name given development method. "*We use our own method which is built on several different methods. It also varies if we work agile, it depends on the project and the customers and if they wish to be and have the skills to be involved in the development process. In regards to the public self-service solutions, we are not working agile*". The digital self-service applications are developed by the company without text and descriptions in the form the citizens are filling in. The municipalities have to write that information themselves. This approach was chosen to give the case workers at the municipalities the flexibility to get the information they think they need in a digital self-service application from their citizens and to be able to sell the same solution to all municipalities. The thought behind this is that all municipalities have different needs. "*There is a great difference between designing a solution for a large municipality or if it is a very small one. There is a great difference in usage and working procedures*". One interviewee described that providing each municipality with the flexibility for adjusting as a key element in regards to the digital self-service applications they are developing.

2) Customer Involvement

The focus of the company is creating a solution that all municipalities can use. "*It makes a very big difference if you are designing something for a large or small municipality. There is a very big difference in relation to how things are done or used.*" One interviewee described developing an application that fits all types of municipalities, by developing a blank form that the municipalities can set up as they wish to get the citizens' to provide the information that each municipality finds important. This also means that each municipality buying this solution has to write all the text going into this digital self-service application.

Case workers at the municipalities are involved in the development process by a forum for the exchange of experience that the company is hosting for the municipalities that are existing customers. These workshops are hosted several times a year. "*In regards to this specific solution we already have a solution that the citizens can access to fill out other applications or to get an overview of their own records, so this new application will be developed to be part of this existing system.*" Existing customers have been involved through these previously held workshops, but no customers are directly involved in the development of this digital self-service application.

3) End-User Focus

The company does not involve citizens in the development process. Two interviewees described creating a system that the municipalities can change to fit their needs. "*We have structured it so the municipalities can make adjustments where and if they see fit, e.g., in regards to rewriting phrasings or functions that can be added or removed*". The municipalities and case workers were involved before the design and development phase. The design and workflow were designed at workshops held before the redesign of this digital self-service application. The company focuses on usability by having usability specialists hired.

4) Products

It is perceived as a strength of their digital self-service application that they have developed a solution where the citizens can do everything in one place. *"The citizens never leave their medical file when they need to fill in the self-service application"*. Two interviewees also perceive it as a strength that they have tried to cover all aspects of the needs that both citizens and case workers have.

A perceived weakness is that an interviewee feels they might not have spent enough time on usability when developing the digital self-service application for the citizens. *"The self-service application might be kind of crude. People need to have prior knowledge to be able to use it."* The interviewees also raised a concern about if less IT skilled citizens would be able to fill out the application.

D. Case D

1) Development Process

Company D use a staged development method but have implemented some agile techniques in the past years. They described involving customers as much as possible in the development process. *"We use agile processes evolving around the customers. If we involve customers earlier in the process, we will learn earlier if there are processes we haven't understood"*. One interviewee did describe that this approach has been implemented in recent years and that the company earlier had the philosophy that they were the experts and not the customers.

The company have a department of User Experience Designers who are involved in designing and testing the front-end of the systems. Though they are isolated from the development teams and are mainly involved at the end of the development process by conducting summative usability evaluations.

The municipalities are involved several times during the development process, by conducting online meetings discussing prototypes. Two interviewees find this valuable as the company are developing one solution to fit all. The data collected from involving the municipalities are used for creating user-stories. "*We always start by creating user-stories. [...] The user-stories are primarily used when the system has been developed"*. The company described using the user-stories to check if the developed system lives up to the needs specified in the user-stories.

2) Customer Involvement

The primary focus of this company is on the back-end of the digital self-service application. The company has involved municipalities by conducting a workshop with people from municipalities who are already customers. Representatives from six municipalities participated as on-site customers. The company hosted a workshop to learn about the number of applications and generating of ideas. At the end of this workshop, a specification of requirements was generated.

The case workers from the municipalities were involved several times during the development process but mainly through online meetings or email. This approach was chosen as a consideration for the employees. "E*very time we have to pull the employees away from doing their regular job in the municipalities [...] Online meetings still gives them the ability to provide inputs. [...] Whenever we have a question we send an email asking if we are doing the right thing."* One interviewee described that involving the customers during the development process is a relatively new procedure and that they now see this as best practice as it means they can do changes during the development process as changes late in the process are expensive and complicated.

3) End-User Focus

For this digital self-service solution, two interviewees described focusing on the citizens' needs and their flow through the application. "*We know that this system is developed mainly for senior citizens, meaning that this system needs to be as simple as possible. This includes that all descriptions and wordings need to be easily understandable"*. One interviewee described that there had been a discussion about if they spent too much time on the citizen angle. *"The end-user is not the one buying our product, it is the municipalities, [...] what matters is if they think our self-service solution is good"*. The digital self-service application is described as being part of a larger health care system, where citizens will have access to, e.g., former applications and the municipality will have everything in regards to one citizen in one record. For this digital self-service application, senior citizens without much experience with computers, have been involved in filling out a digital self-service application. In regards to the case workers and municipalities, they described focusing on full automatic digital self-service applications when possible.

4) Products

It was described as a perceived strength that they had integrated this application in their general healthcare record solution. *"The citizens can see the full catalogue of the services the municipality offers and, after they have applied for something once, it is possible to make a reorder without starting over with the application."* One interviewee described that they have simplified processes that otherwise might be difficult for less IT skilled citizens. For the case workers the solution is perceived as a strength in regards to, when an application ends up with the case worker, the system has already validated that the citizens are entitled to what they have applied for.

It is perceived as both a strength and weakness that they always make applications that follow the legislation though some municipalities might have other requests. It is perceived as a weakness that they have been bound by an existing design on the general healthcare record solution. They feel this application might lack usability and that some written information might be too small for the application.

E. Summary of Results

1) Development Process

Case A and B describes using a module-based platform as this provides flexibility to make changes, also late in the development process. Case D tries to avoid late changes by involving the customers early in the process. The cases A, B, and D finds customer involvement to be a key element. Case C only work agile and involve customers if they find it relevant. Case B, C, and D describe making one solution to fit all municipalities, though case C describes developing a solution that is flexible so the municipalities can set it up as they wish, in regards to getting the information each municipality needs from the citizens.

2) Customer Involvement

Cases A, B and D asked on-site customers to participate during both design and development process. Cases A and B held continuously design workshops, where case D held one at the beginning and later primarily had remote access to the involved municipalities. Case C gathered information from workshops before the design phase but had no customer involvement besides that. Cases B and D stated that they mainly focused on the back-end of the system to be used by the case workers. Cases B, C, and D all stated that they were aware of that the municipalities have different needs as it depends on the size of the municipality and their interpretation of legislation. Case A described that they learned eventually that the municipalities have different needs, though learning this quite late in the process.

3) End-User Involvement

Neither of the companies has citizens directly involved in the design or development process, although cases B and D described testing their developed public self-service application on citizens after the development has been completed. Cases A and D implemented automatic decisions when possible, benefiting for both citizens and case workers. Cases A, B, C, and D all described that focusing on the needs of the citizens has not been made a priority, only the needs of the municipalities as customers. Case D described that they needed to focus less on the citizens and more on the municipalities as customers.

Cases A and D have mainly focused on the target user-group in regards to keeping the design simple for the citizens. Case B focused primarily on the flow of the end-users in their solution, and case C has used usability specialists to check if the design was usable for the citizens.

4) Products

Cases A and D highlight simplified processes as strengths in regards to their public self-service applications. Cases B and D find the fact that they focus on developing applications that follow the legislation as a strength. Cases C and D both describe it as a strength that the self-service application is integrated into one healthcare solution for all public healthcare applications. Cases A, C, and D believe that a weakness of the citizen-centred self-service applications is lacking usability. Usability has not been made a priority by the companies as it was not a priority for the municipalities.

The applications from Case C and to some extent Case D were significantly smaller and less complex than the applications developed by cases A and B, e.g., the application from case C was created as a paper application.

F. Usability of the self-service Solutions

In the previous sections, we have focused on how the four self-service applications have been developed and how it was ensured that these applications were usable for the citizens, and would save time for the caseworkers. In this section we look at the state of the finished self-service applications and whether these applications are usable for citizens.

Of the identified problems, 11 were found across all four digital public self-solutions. Among these general problems was a lack of understanding of the purpose and flow of the self-service solutions, problems with attaching files. Also, test persons getting annoyed or confused by not being able to understand helping texts and the descriptions of the rules and regulations of the application area, leading to test persons filling in the wrong information in the text fields. And, misunderstanding data fields, also leading to the test persons filling in the wrong information in the text fields. An overview of the usability problems is shown in Table IX.

Table IX. Usability Problems in Each Digital Self-Service Solution

	Company A	Company B	Company C	Company D
Critical	2	5	0	1
Serious	17	18	11	15
Cosmetic	17	14	6	13
Total	**36**	**37**	**17**	**29**

The self-service applications developed by case A and B were much more comprehensive than the applications develop by cases C and D. The self-service applications from cases C and D were both part of a larger healthcare system, meaning that less information had to be filled out manually by the participants. Especially the self-service application from case C was very simple compared to the self-service applications developed by cases A and B.

Two critical problems were found in the self-service application from case A. one was about test persons not understanding which information to put in where and ending up writing the wrong information at the wrong place. The other critical problem was about file attachment. The test persons experienced problems because the helping text was not optimised for the browser and when they tried following the written steps the test persons got confused and stopped as what they read did not match the options they had.

Five critical problems were found in the self-service application from case B. Examples of these problems could be in regards to file attachment, as the test persons do not realise when a file has been attached. Another problem is about test persons not understanding the search function and how to enter search parameters.

No critical problems were found in the self-service application from case C, and one critical problem was found in the public self-service application from case D. With this problem the test persons got into a full stop. They had to click a drop-down menu on the left side of the screen at all test persons experienced a lot of trouble trying to figure out what to do. Test persons mainly figured out what to do when they started clicking different menu options and then got the right one.

V. Discussion

In this section, the results are discussed. First, the results are discussed for each case, and then the user-centred approach is discussed.

A. Discussing the results for each case

For supporting the discussion of the results from each case, we have made an overview of the results from the four cases in Table X.

1) Case A

In case A, the company is micro/small in the SME classification and considered immature, since this is the first time they developed public self-service applications. The product is classified as new since the company does not have other existing products to base this product on. Their product is module based, so it is easy to make changes quite quickly to the product if needed. Their key features are that they frequently collaborated with one municipality through workshops and evaluating prototypes gathering information on the needs and getting feedback from case workers (the customer), but not the citizens (the end-users). The result of the usability evaluation showed 36 usability problems, but only two serious problems.

The high number of usability problems could be because the development team has not gained experience in developing products for this kind of customers. Another issue could be that they only involved one single municipality in their process, though having 98 municipalities as potential customers.

The company focused on easing the work process of the case workers and therefore involved the caseworkers as much as possible in the development process. This was done under the assumption that the caseworkers understood the citizens and their needs, but the high number of usability problems indicate that this is not the case, which means that citizens have to be involved in the development process to represent themselves and their own needs.

2) Case B

In contrast, to case A, case B is a large company and mature in developing public self-service applications, though this application is classified as new. Their product is module based on making it easy to conduct changes quite quickly to the product if needed. In case B, the developers collaborated with five municipalities through workshops, prototypes and emails, but did not collaborate with the citizens, although testing was done with citizens in pilot releases. The self-service application from case B had 37 usability problems, which was the highest amount of usability problems found in each of the four self-service applications. This self-service application also had the highest number of critical usability problems. This is surprising since it is a large, mature company and collaborated with several municipalities. Like in case A, case B also developed a solution focused on making the case workers activities more efficient. The fact that case B collaborated with five municipalities and experienced approximately the same amount of usability problems in their self-service application indicate that it is not the number of municipalities, and case workers involved that makes a difference.

Table X. An overview of the four companies in regards to the focus areas.

Theme	Sub-theme	Case A	Case B	Case C	Case D
The Cases	**Company size**	Micro/small	Large	Large	Large
	Maturity	Immature	Mature	Immature/mature	Mature
Development Process	**Method**	Agile, Scrum	In phases, SCRUM in development Phase Prince 2	In phases, own method	In phases, agile elements
	Team	Project Manager mainly, CEO part of analysis and sales process	Product Owner, allocating needed resources through the process	Project Manager, allocating needed resources through the process	Project Manager, allocating need resources through the process
	Platform	Module based, easy to make changes	Module based, easy to make small changes	Part of health care system, changes can be costly	Part of health care system, changes can be costly
Customer Involvement	**Focus area**	Case workers and their needs	Case workers and their work-load	System fits needs of municipalities	If System is needed customers' willingness to pay
	Involved municipalities	One	Around five	All existing customers	Six
	Involvement type	4-5 workshops, Prototypes, Customer involvement	Workshops, emails Prototypes, Customer involvement	Workshop	Workshop, emails Online meetings
End-users	**Citizen representation**	Primarily Case Workers	Primarily Case Workers	Primarily Case Workers	Primarily Case Workers
	Goal	Decisions at once	Optimizing work flows	Flexibility to fit each municipality	Decisions at once
	Usability	Verified by Case Workers	Testing on citizens in pilot releases	Hired specialists	Testing on citizens Hired specialists
Product	**Perceived strengths**	Applications verified right away	Follows legislation	Part of healthcare system	Part of healthcare system Applications verified right away Follows legislation
	Perceived weaknesses	Lacking usability	One solution fit all	Lacking usability	Lacking usability
Usability Problems	**Critical problems**	2	5	0	1
	Total number of problems	36	37	17	29

It also indicates that citizens should be involved in the development process, as stated in the previous section.

3) Case C

Case C is a large company developing a solution that is an optimisation of existing software. They are grouped as mature since they have been developing self-service applications, but also as immature since this area of application is new to them. They involved all existing customers while developing this solution but also hired specialists for gathering feedback on their solution. Their solution showed 17 usability problems, which was the lowest of the four evaluated self-service applications. None of the usability problems were critical problems. The reason could be the specialist's advice, and involvement made the solution usable. Another reason could be that the solution is more limited than the solution from case A and B as this application is part of a larger healthcare system, meaning that much less information has to be put in when filling in this application. Also, it was decided to make the solution from case C very simple, with actually little support for the caseworkers, so they still had to do some activities manually. Where case A and B are trying to optimise workflows and activities, which also makes the self-service applications more complex for the citizens and raises the risk of usability problems than transforming paper applications into digital self-service applications.

4) Case D

Case D is also a large company developing a solution that is an optimisation of existing software. It is grouped as mature since the company has been developing public self-service applications for years. They involved six municipalities in the development, did some testing with citizens and hired specialists to give advice. Still, there were 29 usability problems found, but only one critical problem. This might be the biggest surprise in the results since this company is using user-centred design processes and is experienced. This system is part of a larger healthcare system, meaning that much less information has to be filled in when filling in this application. So the solution is rather limited, but still, contains many usability problems. In case D usability professionals are a bit isolated from the development team and are mostly involved in a summative evaluation at the end of the development. This approach could have resulted in higher number of usability problems in the solution than if the usability professionals had been more integrated into the development process. But this also indicate that it is not a matter of how many municipalities, caseworkers or usability specialist's that is involved in the development process, but it might make a difference if citizens are involved in the development process.

B. Discussing the User-Centred Approaches used

The Danish digitalisation effort has been launched to support the development process and provide each municipality with more digital self-service solutions to choose from, and enhancing usability in these solutions. For this purpose, two sets of guidance materials were created, a user journey and a set of 24 usability criteria, respectively. The aim was that this approach would facilitate competition between the self-service providers, resulting in better and more user-centred self-service applications for the citizens. All four companies involved the municipalities in the design process both in regards to the back-end of the system meant for the case workers and in regards to the self-service applications meant for the citizens. Two of the companies described involving citizens quite late in the process for testing of the features, either by going live in a few "pilot-municipalities" or conducting a usability evaluation.

Though a user-centred approach has been taken, our results correspond with the findings of Wangpipatwong et al. who found that e-government websites are lacking usability due to poor design and non-employment of user-centred design methodologies [7]. The reason for this is that the municipalities according to the companies are only focusing on this to a small extent and are not willing to pay more than the bare minimum. This shows a mismatch between what the joint IT organisation of the municipalities and the municipalities are trying to achieve. The public self-service providers are focusing on what the municipalities are willing to pay for and want the citizens to do and not taking the user-centred approach with a citizens' perspective unless this is being requested by the municipalities. If the user-centred approach should be a success, it is important to involve the municipalities as well. They need to understand that quality and cost are complementary [12][13] and why usability needs to be a focus area and why a usable system will be a sound investment though it might be a bit more expensive to develop. Bruun and Stage have found that redesigning a digital self-service application focusing on usability, can reduce the amount of time the case worker has to spend on each application, with more than 50% [31].

Jokela et al. [11] and Mastrangelo [15] describe the importance of usability being specified in the requirements. It is questionable whether this approach will be successful unless the municipalities learn the values of these requirements and get the understanding that focusing on usability will reduce cost over time. The municipalities have some responsibility in this whole process also. If they are demanding that their solutions are assisting caseworkers in doing their job digitally in a fast and easy process, the software companies have more motivation for focusing on usability. The companies will not focus much on usability unless the municipalities are demanding usable products.

As described in Section IV.f we found 11 usability problems across self-service applications from different companies; this shows that self-service providers have problems understanding the end-users needs in general, though usability has been on the agenda for more than twenty years. If we compare the general problems we found with Nielsen's usability heuristics from 1995, we found that the self-service providers have violated three of these heuristics. Number 2, Match between the system and the real world. Number 6, Recognition rather than recall. And, number 10, Help and documentation [32]. This lack of understanding shows that the self-service providers have trouble understanding the basics of usability theory, and even more trouble understanding the needs of the end-users in general.

C. Benefits and Drawbacks of Customer and User Involvement

This paper documents the development process of four different self-service solutions and shows the use of three different approaches to digitalise self-service applications.

One approach used by case A and B was having case workers from the municipalities as onsite customers to represent both their own and the citizen's needs. This lead to self-service solutions that tried to simplify the caseworkers work processes and thereby ease their workload.

The second approach used by case C was not having an onsite customer but involving the caseworkers before starting the development process. This lead to a self-service solution less focused on easing the workload of the case workers, and this self-service application was closer to being a simple digitalised version of the paper applications used in the past.

The third approach used by case D was not having a direct onsite customer but involving caseworkers when it was felt to be needed. This approach leads to a self-service solution that was simple in some aspects but also trying to solve some tasks to ease the workload of the caseworkers.

From a citizen's point of view, the self-service solution from case C would be the most usable of these four, with 17 documented usability problems. Where the self-service solutions from case D had 29 documented usability problems, and the self-service solutions from case A and B had 36 and 37 usability problems, respectively. But looking at this from a caseworkers point of view, the self-service solution from case C would not be the optimal choice as this will not in any way ease their work processes or workload. Though it can be an argument that neither does the self-service solutions from case A, B or D at this time, as citizens experiencing problems filling out, self-service applications will mean that they are making mistakes. These mistakes will have to be corrected by the caseworkers later in the process, as documented by Bruun and Stage [31].

Both case A and B, and, partly case D all used caseworkers as onsite customers. Our results show that this approach is not sufficient when developing self-service solutions for the citizens, with the purpose of easing the workload of the caseworkers. The caseworkers simply do not understand the needs of the citizens to a degree where this approach would be sufficient. This means that to get an understanding of citizen's needs, citizen's have to be involved.

VI. Conclusion

In this study, we focused on analysing the customer and user involvement during the software development process, and the characteristics of the four products developed, and the results of usability evaluations thereof. We have discussed user-centred design approaches used, the drawbacks and benefits of customer and user involvement found in these four cases.

Our results show that citizens were not involved in the development process and that case workers were expected to represent and understand the citizen's interests. We conclude that this approach has not been successful as our usability evaluation of the four self-service application showed 17 – 37 usability problems experienced by the test persons. Several problems leading to a full stop or a high level of frustration for the test persons.

This lead us to conclude that case workers are not suitable for citizen's representation and if the goal is to ease the workload of the case workers, citizens have to be involved in the development process too.

We recognise that it is a limitation that four companies were involved, in regards to drawing conclusions in a broad term about the entire development process of self-service solutions. As future work, it would be interesting to learn the perspectives of the municipalities from themselves, and not only through the self-service providers. And if the focus was contrasted to more structured opinions coming from developers side. As future work, accessibility could also be a focus area.

Acknowledgement

We would like to thank the four companies who participated in this study and the joint IT organisation of the municipalities. We would also like to thank Infinit, for supporting this research, and the test persons participating in the usability evaluations.

References

[1] J. Billestrup, J. Stage, and M. Larusdottir, "A case study of four IT companies developing usable public self-service solutions," Proceedings of ACHI, 2016.

[2] DESI Index,https://ec.europa.eu/digital-agenda/en/scoreboard/ [retrieved: November, 2016]

[3] T. Clemmensen and D. Katre, "Adapting e-gov usability evaluation to cultural contexts," Usability of e-government systems, Boston: Morgan Kaufmann, 2012, pp. 331-344.

[4] S. Wangpipatwong, W. Chutimaskul, and, B. Papastratorn, "Understanding citizen's continuance intention to use e-government website: A composite view of technology acceptance model and computer self-efficiency," The Electronic Journal of e-Government, vol. 6, nr. 1 2008, pp. 55-64

[5] The Danish ministry of health. Reform of the municipalities. http://www.sum.dk/Aktuelt/Publikationer/Publikationer_IN/~/media/FilerPublikationerIN/Kommunalreformen/2005/Kommunalreformenkortfortalt/kommunalreformenkortforta lt.ashx [retrieved: November, 2016]

[6] Organisation of the Municipalities in Denmark, http://www.kl.dk/Administration-og-digitalisering/Lov-om-obligatorisk-digital-selvbetjening-og-digital-post-er-vedtaget-id105354/ [retrieved: November, 2016]

[7] Kombit, For self-service providers, http://www.kombit.dk/indhold/leverand%C3%B8rer [retrieved: November, 2016]

[8] M. Pretorius and A. Calitz, "The South African user experience maturity status for website design in provincial governments," Proceedings of the 12th European Conference on eGovernment, 2012 pp. 589-599,

[9] B. Soufi and M. Maguire, "Achieving usability within e-government websites illustrated by a case study evaluation," Proceedings of Human Interface, Springer-Verlag, 2007 part II, pp. 777-784.

[10] Z. Huang and M. Benyoucef, "Usability and credibility of e-government websites," Government Information Quarterly, 2014, pp. 584-595.

[11] T. Jokela, L. Juja, and M. Nieminen, "Usability in RFP's: The Current Practice and Outline for the Future," Proceedings of HCI International, 2013, pp. 101-106.

[12] P. B. Crosby, "Quality is free," Mcgraw-Hill, New York, 1979.

[13] D. E. Harter, M. S. Krishnan, and S. A. Slaughter, "Effects of process maturity on quality, cycle time, and effort in software product development," Management Science, vol. 46 nr. 4 2000, pp. 451-466.

[14] T. Jokela, "Determining Usability Requirements Into a Call-for-Tenders. A Case Study on the Development of a Healthcare System," Proceedings of NordiCHI 2010, 256-265.

[15] S. Mastrangelo, R. Lanzilotti, M. Boscarol, and C. Ardito, "Guidelines to Specify HCD Activities in the Call for Tender for Public Administration Websites," Proceedings of INTERACT 2015 pp. 497-513.

[16] K. Tarkkanen and V. Harkke, "From Usability Workarounds to Usability Around Work," Proceedings of INTERACT 2015. pp. 513-520

[17] Saldaña, J. The Coding Manual for Qualitative Researchers, Sage, 2015.

[18] Organisations of the Municipalities, http://www.kl.dk /ImageVaultFiles/id_76493/cf_202/Afslutning_af_Effektiv_digital_selvbetjening_1.PDF [retrieved: November, 2016]

[19] Kombit, User Journey for applying for a marriage certificate, December 2014 http://www.kl.dk/ImageVaultFiles/id_60480/cf_202/Illu.PDF [retrieved: November, 2016]

[20] L. Nielsen. "Engaging personas and narrative scenarios," Handelshøjskolen, 2004.

[21] The government agency for digitalisation in Denmark. Criteria for usability in self-service solutions. http://www.kl.dk/ImageVault/Images/id_56064/scope_0/ImageVault Handler.aspx [retrieved: November, 2016]

[22] SME definition. http://ec.europa.eu/enterprise/policies/sme/facts-figures-analysis/sme-definition/index_en.htm [retrieved: November, 2016]

[23] J. Billestrup and J. Stage, "E-government and the Digital Agenda for Europe," Proceedings of DUXU, Design, User Experience, and Usability. User Experience Design for Diverse Interaction Platforms and Environments. Springer International Publishing, 2014. pp. 71-80.

[24] J. Billestrup, A. Bruun, and J. Stage, "UX Requirements to Public Systems for All: Formalisation or Innovation," Workshop on Formalizing UX Requirements, Proceedings of Interact, 2015. pp. 407-427.

[25] Dedoose, www.dedoose.com [retrieved: November, 2016]

[26] S. Kvale, "Interview", København: Hans Reitzel, (1997)

[27] J. Kjeldskov, M. B. Skov, and J. Stage, "Instant Data Analysis: Conducting Usability Evaluations in a Day," Proceedings of NordiCHI, 2004 pp. 233-240.

[28] M. B. Skov and J. Stage, "Supporting Problem Identification in usability Evaluations," Proceedings of OzCHI, 2005, pp. 1-9.

[29] K. Schwaber and M. Beedle. "Agilè Software Development with Scrum," Prentice Hall, 2001.

[30] Colin Bentley, "Prince2: a Practical Handbook," Routledge, 2010.

[31] A. Bruun and J. Stage, "Supporting Diverse Users: Implementing Usability Improvements of an E-Government Data Entry Website," white paper, 2014.

[32] J. Nielsen, "10 Usability Heuristics for User Interface Design", (1995).

Using CASE Tools in MDA Transformation of Geographical Database Schemas

Thiago Bicalho Ferreira, Jugurta Lisboa-Filho
Departamento de Informática
Universidade Federal de Viçosa
Viçosa, Minas Gerais, Brazil
e-mail: thiagao.ti@gmail.com, jugurta@ufv.br

Sergio Murilo Stempliuc
Faculdade Governador Ozanan Coelho (FAGOC)
Ubá, Minas Gerais, Brazil
e-mail: smstempliuc@gmail.com

Abstract— **GeoProfile is a Unified Modeling Language (UML) profile proposed to standardize the conceptual modeling of geographic databases (GDB). GeoProfile can be used along with the Model Driven Architecture (MDA) added with integrity restrictions specified through the Object Constraint Language (OCL). Several Computer-Aided Software Engineering (CASE) tools provide support to those computational artifacts already consolidated by the UML infrastructure. Some CASE tools can be configured to automate the transformation of schemas at different levels of the MDA approach. The transformations in those tools occur from the Platform-Independent Model (PIM) abstraction level until to the generation of Structured Query Language (SQL) source codes. This study aimed to describe the evaluation process of a set of CASE tools with support to UML Profile technology based on specific requirements to use MDA approach, OCL restrictions, and other elements that aid in conceptual GDB modeling. This paper also describes an experience in using GeoProfile with one of the CASE tools evaluated, taking into account the tool's transformation language to allow for automated transformations among the different levels of the MDA approach.**

Keywords- CASE tools; Enterprise Architect; MDA transformations; OCL; Geographical Database.

I. INTRODUCTION

Based on the study developed in [1], this paper describes the assessment of CASE tools and the steps to reach vertical interoperability among schemas in the UML GeoProfile at the different levels of the Model Driven Architecture (MDA). GeoProfile is a Unified Modeling Language (UML) profile proposed by [2], employed in the conceptual modeling of Geographic Databases (GDB), which can use all of UML's infrastructure, which includes Object Constraint Language (OCL) to define integrity constraints and MDA for the transformation between its different abstraction levels [2][3]. Moreover, one of the advantages of using a UML profile is that it can be used in different CASE tools. However, not all tools offer the same features, making difficult to choose one. Examples of CASE tools with UML support include Enterprise Architect, Papyrus, StarUML, Visual Paradigm, and IBM Rational Software Architect.

In order to compare these tools and in the context of this study, some characteristics or features were prioritized such as the support to the UML Profile definition, validation of OCL constraints, and application of the MDA approach. The key aspect is that the tools need to allow models to be created using UML GeoProfile, the transformation among the different levels established by the MDA approach, the syntactic and semantic validation of spatial OCL constraints, and that the models should be implemented from scripts generated for a selected database management system.

This paper aims to describe the evaluation of a set of CASE tools considering important requirements from the conceptual project to the implementation of the geographical database. This paper also reports on an experience of using the CASE Enterprise Architect tool, which had the best result, and on the challenges of the development of a vertical transformation mechanism for geographic databases using UML GeoProfile.

The remaining of the paper is structured as follows. Section II briefly explains the representation of geographical data, the UML GeoProfile, the MDA approach and the syntax to specify OCL expressions and the Oracle Spatial Geographic Database Management System (GDBMS). Section III presents a description of each CASE tool analyzed according to the goal of this study. Section IV shows the requirements, the methodology and the result of the tool evaluations. Section V presents the MDA transformation applied to GeoProfile in the CASE Enterprise Architect tool. Section VI describes the SQL code generation step in the Enterprise Architect tool for the Oracle Spatial GDBMS. Section VII presents the conclusions and future works.

II. GEOGRAPHICAL DATABASE MODELING CONCEPTS

This section presents a literature review identifying the main concepts that contribute to the conceptual GDB modeling.

A. Representing Geographical Information in Computers

The representation of geographical space in computers is a challenge faced by researchers. According to Longley et al. [4], the world is infinitely complex and computing systems are finite, thus, it is up to the designer to limit the amount of details to be captured from the environment mapped. The two main approaches on computing are the continuous (fields) and discrete (objects) representations. Another representation also employed is in the form of networks, which takes into account graph theory.

Figure 1 shows part of a city with a sports center and represents part of this city focusing on the roads and the stadium. The GDB of Figure 1(b) must be conceptually modeled containing all structures of interest in the system while leaving aside other information such as the type of vegetation, vacant plots, terrain, and other characteristics that may be abstracted from Figure 1(a).

In order to design the conceptual data schema, first the vector structures used to represent the boundaries of each geographic entity must be understood, which is normally specified through basic geometric shapes: point, line and polygon (area) [5]. Figure 1(b) presents the use of these three types of vector structures. For instance, the stadium may be spatially represented as a point or as a polygon (multiple spatial representation); the main east road, as a line; and the sports center, as a polygon.

Additionally, presenting the structures, Figure 1(b) illustrates the relationship among the vector objects, which shows the stadium "is within" the sports center, the sports center "touches" the road to the stadium, the main west road "is near" the sports center, but does not "touch" it.

Such relationships are known as topological relationships and have been discussed by [6] and [7] and used by [8].

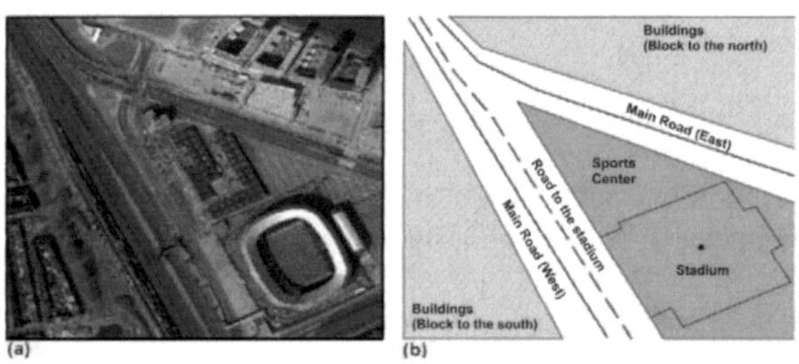

Figure 1. (a) Photograph of part of a city with a sports center between roads. (b) Spatial representation of this area. Source: Adapted from [9].

B. Model-Driven Architecture (MDA)

According to Kleppe et al. [10], MDA is a framework standardized by the [11] for the development of software employing a Model-Driven Development (MDD) view.

The MDA approach consists of three abstraction levels, namely, CIM, PIM and PSM. Computation-Independent Model (CIM) does not show details of the system's structure, but rather the environment in which the system will operate. Platform-Independent Model (PIM) is an independent model of any implementation technology containing the software requirements. Platform-Specific Model (PSM) specifies details about the platform in which it will be implemented. The artifacts produced by the MDA approach are formal models that can be processed by computers and, after undergoing transformations, will get to a final source-code step (top-down approach) or to high levels of abstraction (bottom-up approach). Figure 2 illustrates the action of transformation tools at MDA levels.

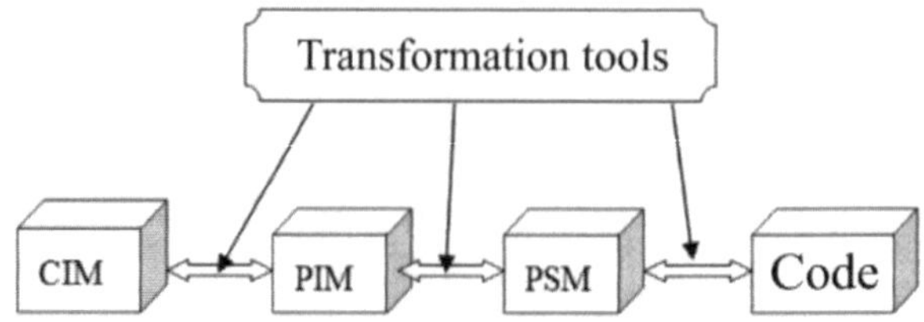

Figure 2. Use of transformation tools in the MDA approach. Source: Adapted from [10].

C. Object Constraint Language (OCL)

Conceptual modeling makes the problem easier to be understood through abstraction, thus enabling risk management and contributing to error correction early in the project, which minimizes the cost of maintenance [12]. However, Warmer and Kleppe [13] state that conceptual models may not be able to represent all requirements, resulting in problems to those who interpret them.

The OCL, adopted by OMG [14] since version 2.0, was defined as a formal language to complement the conceptual modeling using UML. Using OCL ambiguity-free integrity constraints can be created, which makes it possible to specify the data consistency wanted in the system at a high level of abstraction. Since it is a formal language, it can be processed by CASE tools until the source-code generation, which enables more powerful and satisfactory data consistency [13]. OCL is currently at version 2.4 [15].

The OCL expressions represent constraints that are needed in the system and not how they should be implemented. The evaluation of a constraint on the data always yields a Boolean value [13]. The syntax of a typical expression in OCL that represents a condition has the format presented by Code in Figure 3.

```
<context>
   inv:<expression>
```

Figure 3. Syntax of a typical expression in OCL.

Code in Figure 4 illustrates a hypothetical example of OCL constraint that specifies that a Brazilian municipality must be larger than 3,000 km² (note: The smallest Brazilian municipality, Santa Cruz de Minas, MG, is 3,565 km²). A detailed specification of the OCL can be found in [13] [15].

```
context Municipality
      inv:self.area > 3000
```

Figure 4. Hypothetical example of the use of OCL restrictions.

D. UML GeoProfile

In order to provide elements for specific domains without becoming excessively complex, UML has an extension mechanism called Profile. A UML Profile consists of: a metamodel; a set of stereotypes presented through texts in the form of <<text>> or through graphical icons called pictograms; tagged values; and constraints; all grouped in a stereotyped package called <<profile>>, thus formalizing the UML builder extension [16].

GeoProfile is a UML profile proposed for the geographical data modeling comprising the main characteristics of the existing models in the field [17]. GeoProfile is employed at the CIM and PIM levels of the MDA approach, using OCL constraints as a resource to validate the conceptual scheme generated by the designer [18].

The GeoProfile stereotypes are extensions of the Association and Class metaclasses. The stereotypes extended from the Class metaclass allow representing the geographic space in the discrete view (e.g., points, lined and polygons), in the continuous view (e.g., large cells and triangular networks), and through networks (nodes and arcs). The temporal aspects can also be represented with the stereotypes made up of tagged values that store instant and range values. The extended stereotypes of the Association metaclass allow representing topological relationships (e.g., touches and within) among the geographical stereotypes, and the temporal relationship (Temporal) among the temporal objects.

For the extended stereotypes of the Class metaclass, the abstracted stereotypes have been defined: <<Network>>, to group network stereotypes; <<GeoObject>>, to group the discrete view stereotypes; <<GeoField>>, to group the continuous view stereotypes; and <Arc>>, to group the <<UnidirectionalArc>> and <<BidirecionalArc>> stereotypes that represent the possible links between the nodes of a network.

E. Oracle Spatial

Oracle Spatial is a database management system by Oracle Corporation that supports geographic information through the Spatial module. According to [9], Oracle supports three primitive geometry types (point, line, and polygon) and a collection made up of other primitive geometries. Figure 5 presents an example of Structured Query Language (SQL) involving the creation of tables with support to spatial data.

```
CREATE TABLE <table name>
{
      attribute_1 NUMBER,
      attribute_2 VARCHAR (25),
      geom        SDO_GEOMETRY

};
```

Figure 5. Table creation with spatial data support.

Unlike a conventional table, the code shown in Figure 5 has a geom attribute with the SDO_GEOMETRY data type. According to [9], this data type is exclusive to Oracle GDBMS and is formed by five attributes that specify the geometry of the piece of data to be stored at the moment of its insertion, namely: SDO_GTYPE, SDO_SRID, SDO_POINT, SDO_ORDINATES, and SDO_ELEM_INFO. Further details on the use of each type of attribute can be obtained in [9].

III. CASE TOOLS ANALYZED

The tools analyzed in this study were chosen according to the ease of access to the software and documentation. These tools are open source and commercial with some support to the UML profile and are well known by the software development community. The sub-sections below describe the results of the analysis made on the following CASE tools, exploring the resources they offer compared to the GeoProfile: Enterprise Architect (EA) version 12.0, Papyrus UML2 Modeler (Papyrus) version 1.12.3, StarUML–UML/MDA Platform (StarUML) version 5.0.2.1570, Visual Paradigm for UML (VP) version 10.2 and IBM Rational Software Architect (RSA) version 9.0.

A. Enterprise Architect (EA)

Enterprise Architect (EA) [19] is a commercial CASE tool licensed by Sparx Systems that allows the visual creation of UML profiles and insertion with syntactic validation of OCL expressions. EA does not offer resources for semantic validation of OCL expressions.

Additionally, being a modeling tool, it acts as an MDA transformation tool, with its own language for transformation between the model levels. This language can be modified so that the users are able to reach the last MDA approach level, the source code [20]. Since the modeling in this paper refers to GDB, the last MDA step is the Data Definition Language (DDL) source code, which EA is able to generate.

The GeoProfile stereotypes in the EA tool can be represented graphically  or textually <<point>>. The tool also offers resources for multiple stereotype representation, e.g., depending on the scale, a city may be modeled as a point or a polygon <<point, polygon>>.

The advantage at using EA is that it makes possible to specify some constraints. For example, it does not allow the insertion of extended stereotypes of the Class metaclass in Association elements and vice versa. The problem is that it allows the use of abstract stereotypes in conceptual models, e.g. the abstract GeoProfile stereotypes: <<Arc>>, <<GeoField>>, <<GeoObject>>, <<Network>> and <<NetworkObj>>.

B. Papyrus UML2 Modeler

Papyrus UML2 Modeler [21] is an open-source tool based on the Eclipse environment and licensed by Eclipse (Eclipse Public License). It has a visual environment to insert UML profiles, thus providing support to insertion and syntactic validation of OCL constraints. However, it does not semantically validate these constraints.

Adding graphical icons to the stereotypes is possible. Thus, a class or association can be represented by stereotypes as follows: only text, only graphical icon, or graphical icon and text. The Papyrus tool allows multiple representation to be specified through stereotypes, but, in case the graphical representation is used, only the first stereotype used by the designer is presented.

Additionally, restricting the use of abstract GeoProfile stereotypes in conceptual models, in this CASE tool other GeoProfile stereotypes can only be used with correct UML elements, i.e., an extended stereotype of the Association metaclass cannot be used in a class defined by the Class metaclass.

The Papyrus tool does not support the MDA approach, the transformation language and DDL code generation.

C. StarUML

StarUML [22] is an open-source tool whose profile insertion is done through an Extensible Markup Language (XML) document. This tool does not support OCL and, despite being considered MDA, the features offered are incomplete. What it allows is transforming a model (PIM) into source code without going through the PSM. The source codes can be generated for the languages Java, C++ and C#. StarUML does not have a transformation language and the conceptual models produced from GeoProfile cannot be transformed into DDL source code.

Although multiple stereotype representation is not supported by the tool, the designer can choose between graphical and text representation, but only text is supported in associations. Therefore, the possible class stereotype representations are: textual, graphical, and textual and graphical. The tool can also restrict the use of abstract stereotypes at the same time that the others can be properly used with UML elements.

D. Visual Paradigm for UML (VP)

With an intuitive modeling environment, the commercial tool Visual Paradigm for UML [23] supports the visual creation of UML profiles. The stereotypes can be presented graphically or textually, with support for multiple representation with the graphical ones.

The tool does not allow the use of extended stereotypes of different metaclasses, as described in Section III.A, however, it does allow abstract GeoProfile stereotypes to be used during conceptual modeling.

The tool allows incomplete MDA approach, transforming PIM straight into source code. Nevertheless, it does not support DDL code generation from UML class diagrams, just only from those created through the ER model. Thus, the GeoProfile conceptual models cannot be transformed into DDL code.

Also, this tool does not support the syntactic and semantic validation of OCL constraints on conceptual models created from GeoProfile.

E. Rational Software Architect (RSA)

RSA [24] is a commercial CASE tool licensed by IBM that allows the visual creation of UML profiles. This tool supports the use of profiles and is designed to allow syntactic and semantic validation of OCL constraints applied to UML diagrams.

The representations by the stereotypes in an association or class may take place as follows: only textual stereotype, only graphical stereotype, and representation by the textual and graphical stereotypes. However, the multiple representation by the stereotypes can take place in two ways: All stereotypes applied to the class or association must be in textual format or the first stereotype applied takes on the graphical format and the others on textual format.

The tool does not allow inserting extended stereotypes of the Class metaclass in association elements and vice versa, and the stereotypes defined as abstract in GeoProfile cannot be used in the UML elements.

RSA has incomplete support to MDA since it does not natively allow DDL source-code generation. Although there is a transformation mechanism in which the origin, target, and some settings regarding the mapping in the transformation from model into source code can be determined, RSA does not have an MDA transformation language. Therefore, with RSA's native features and mechanisms, these transformations cannot be performed on models created from the GeoProfile.

IV. Results of the CASE Tools Comparison

This section initially presents a set of requirements the CASE tools must meet to support conceptual GDB modeling based on the GeoProfile. Next, it presents the method used in the evaluation, the results and the final classification of the CASE tools analyzed.

This method originally proposed by Rosario and Santos Neto [25] was used in exploratory research involving software project management tools. This method was also applied by Câmara et al. [26] on comparison of development environments for systems of Volunteered Geographic Information (VGI).

A. Requirements Survey

Based on the literature and on the descriptions of each CASE tool, this paper proposes requirements to evaluate which tool has the greatest number of features to support the GeoProfile use, aiming the transformation of data models at the different MDA levels and to specify integrity constraints at conceptual level using OCL. Table I lists these requirements.

B. Evaluation Method of CASE Tools

In the context of this study, the requirements were classified as follows:

- Requirements that are Essentials: Weight 3;
- Requirements that are Important: Weight 2;
- Requirements that are Desirable: Weight 1.

Additionally, to the weight attributed to requirements, a scale must be defined for how well the tools satisfy each one. They may not satisfy (NS), partially satisfy (PS), or satisfy (S) a requirement. Therefore, the following scales can be attributed:

- Does not satisfy the requirement: A scale with value 0 is attributed;

- Partially satisfies the requirement: A scale with value 1 is attributed;
- Satisfies the requirement. A scale with value 2 is attributed.

Based on this evaluation, the classification of each tool was calculated by adding up the products of the importance weight (W) and the satisfaction scale (S) for each requirement (n), represented in Figure 6. Access [25] for more details for this method.

$$X = \sum_{i=1}^{n} S_i . W_i$$

Figure 6. Formula used to calculate and sort CASE tools.

TABLE I. REQUIREMENTS TO EVALUATE CASE TOOLS

	Requirement description
Rq 01	Correct attribution of GeoProfile stereotypes in the UML elements
Rq 02	Restriction to the use of abstract stereotypes in elements of the model
Rq 03	Support to syntactic validation of OCL constraints
Rq 04	Support to semantic validation of OCL constraints
Rq 05	Support to MDA transformations
Rq 06	Support to transformation language
Rq 07	Support to graphical exhibition of profile stereotypes
Rq 08	Support to multiple representation through stereotypes
Rq09	Support to visual profile creation
Rq 10	Support to DDL code generation
Rq 11	Open-source tool

C. Evaluation of the CASE Tools

In order to evaluate each CASE tool and its practical capacity regarding the theoretical functionalities predicted for a UML profile, particularly GeoProfile, the requirements presented in Table I were classified according to the following criteria:

- The requirements considered essential are those that support MDA;
- Requirements that aid in transformations between MDA models are considered important;
- Requirements that care for quality of the GDB models are considered important;
- Requirements that facilitate understanding and contribute to the adoption of the tool are considered desirable.

Table II presents the classification of the requirements regarding their importance level, which are *Essential*, *Important* or *Desirable*. Table III presents the way each CASE tool satisfies the requirements of Table I. At the end, the summary of the evaluation based on Formula (4) is presented using the data from Tables II and III.

TABLE II. CLASSIFICATION OF THE REQUIREMENTS BASED ON THE IMPORTANCE LEVEL.

Importance	Requirements
Essential	Rq05
Important	Rq 01, Rq 03, Rq 04, Rq 06, Rq 08, Rq 10
Desirable	Rq 02, Rq 07, Rq 09, Rq 11

Table III shows the level of satisfaction for each of the CASE tools analyzed, considering each of the 11 requirements. A CASE tool may or may not support a requirement, or provide partial support. For example, EA offers full support for Rq 01. The assigned scale for this level of satisfaction is 2. Meanwhile, Rq 01 was classified as "important" in Table II, therefore receiving weight 2. So, when Formula (3) is applied, the sum of (scale x weight) is calculated for all requirements. Thus, the total sum for EA is 30. The same method was used for all the other tools.

An analysis of Table III shows that the Enterprise Architect tool was the one that best satisfied the requirements for the transformation of conceptual models so that the OCL constraints can be used in the tool. Since it has a customizable transformation language, the OCL constraints can be transformed into integrity constraints along with the SQL code generated in the last MDA level.

Another situation that can be observed in Table III is that the CASE tool RSA provides the best features to use the OCL constraints since it allows for both syntactic and semantic validations.

V. MDA TRANSFORMATION APPLIED TO GEOPROFILE IN THE CASE ENTERPRISE ARCHITECT TOOL

Based on the evaluation described in the previous section and using the Enterprise Architect (EA) CASE tool version 11.0.1106, this study sought to reproduce the different abstraction levels specified by the MDA approach.

Although GeoProfile, in its definition, works with the modeling of a CIM, the transformations from CIM into PIM were considered unnecessary for this research since, during the creation of the diagrams, abstract and specific concepts were found to mix in the EA tool. The diagram created with GeoProfile in that tool can be considered a CIM due to the abstraction and use of textual stereotypes, while it can be considered a PIM for allowing the specification of the types of data of the class attributes. By classifying its diagrams as PIM, in Figure 7, the classes City and Deposit are polygon spatial objects. The CoalMine class has multiple spatial representations as a point and polygon, however, only one stereotype can be represented graphically. The CoalCompany class is a class with no geographic representation.

TABLE III. CLASSIFICATION OF THE CASE TOOLS

CASE	Enterprise Architect			Rational Software Architect			Visual Paradigm			Papyrus			StarUML		
Requirement	S	PS	NS	S	PS	NS	S	PS	NS	S	PS	NS	S	PS	NS
Rq 01	X			X			X			X			X		
Rq 02			X	X					X	X			X		
Rq 03	X			X					X	X					X
Rq 04			X	X					X			X			X
Rq 05	X				X			X				X		X	
Rq 06	X					X			X			X			X
Rq 07	X			X			X			X			X		
Rq 08	X			X			X			X					X
Rq 09	X			X			X			X					X
Rq 10	X					X	X					X			X
Rq 11			X			X			X	X			X		
Total	30			25			19			20			12		

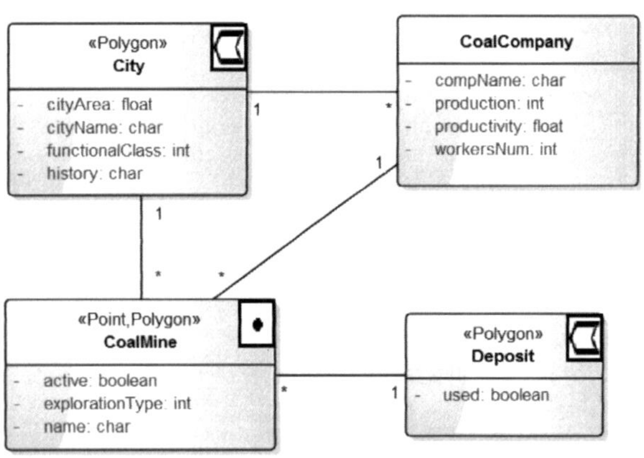

Figure 7. Diagram built in the Enterprise Architect tool based on UML GeoProfile, representing the PIM of the MDA approach.

After the PIM was obtained, the next step was to obtain the PSM. To that end, the tool provides transformation models in the Tools/Model Transformation (MDA) menu that spawn PSMs for C#, EJB, Java, DDL and other languages. However, since those are generic transformations, they only support data types common to those languages and not the specificities related to the use of stereotypes.

A transformation model into PSM closer to the generation of a database schema was the Data Definition Language (DDL) since it features transformation from class diagrams into table diagrams and allows for the transformation of data types according to the GDBMS selected. However, by default, DDL does not perform the transformation of class stereotypes, but the Settings/Transformations Templates menu features source codes in a stereotypes language for the transformation models that can be modified for specific transformation tasks of the GeoProfile diagrams.

In addition to modifying the codes of the templates, one may also create new transformation models. For a new MDA transformation model from PIM into GeoProfile PSM, codes from the DDL transformation model were reused for the transformation of classes into tables, transformation of the relationships, and creation of primary and foreign keys. The code referring to the creation of packages, common to all transformation models, was also reused and only the name of the package to be created was changed.

The code presented in Figure 8 illustrates the creation of the GeoProfile_PSM package and must be run whenever the GeoProfile transformation model is requested. The transformation of stereotypes was performed based on conditionals that assess the geographic type of a stereotype (point, line, polygon, etc.). Every geographic stereotype in a class diagram must become a column in its respective table. The code presented in Figure 9 illustrates the transformation of the stereotypes Point and Polygon and is similar to the transformation for the stereotype Line. For the Point stereotype, the column names are formed from the combination of the class name with the string Point, and the data type, which did not exist up until then (empty), converted into GM_Point. The same occurs for the type Polygon, which is formed by a combination with the string Polygon, and the data type GM_Polygon. Those are types of spatial data of Oracle GDBMS.

```
Package
{
        name = "GeoProfile_PSM" namespaceroot = "true"
        %list="Namespace" @separator="\n\n" @indent= " "%
}
```

Figure 8. Code to create the GeoProfile_PSM package.

```
%IF classStereotype == "Point"%
 COLUMN
 {
     name = %q%% CONVERT_NAME (className,"Pascal Case", "Camel Case")%Point%qt%
     typ= %qt%%CONVERT_TYPE(genOptDefaultDatabase,GM_Point")%%qt%
 }
 %endIf%

 %IF classStereotype == "Polygon"%
  COLUMN
  {
     name = %qt%%CONVERT_NAME(className, "Pascal Case", Camel Case)%Polygon%qt%
     typ= %qt%%CONVERT_TYPE(genOptDefaultDatabase,GM_Polygon")%%qt%

  }
  %endIf%
```

Figure 9. Code to transform classes with geographic stereotype.

Although the EA CASE tool allows the use of multiple stereotypes, they cannot all be processed during the transformation. It can be observed that, in Code 9, the first line has an *if* command to compare a variable classStereotype with a string (Point). That variable has only a string of the first stereotyped class and no solution has been found so far to capture the others. Figure 10 illustrates the CoalMine class, with multiple geographic representations, and the stereotype point separated by a comma from the stereotype Polygon. Figure 4 also presents the properties of that class, with special attention to the place where, despite being a combo box, it contains only the first stereotype (Point), also stored in the variable classStereotype.

Moreover, a code was developed for the transformation of the data types provided by the tool at the PIM level, e.g., Character and Integer, into data types recognized by the Oracle Spatial GDBMS. In case some type is different from those specified in the transformation, they are forwarded to the PSM as empty fields. The code presented in Figure 11 illustrates the transformation of the data type Character into Varchar.

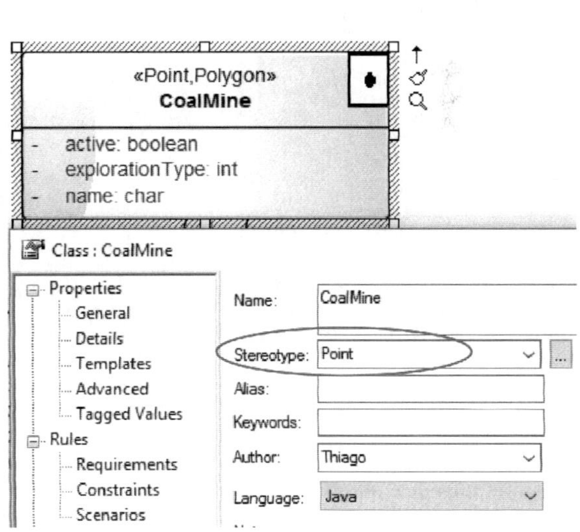

Figure 10. Issues in the geographic multirepresentation.

```
Column
{
   %TRANSFORM_CURRENT("type",stereotype"),"collection","constant","containment",
                     "ordered","static", "volatile")%
   $type1 = %attType%

   %if $type1 == "Character"
       %Type = %qt%%
       CONVERT_TYPE(genOptDefaultDatabase,"Varchar2")%%qt%
   %endIf%
}
```

Figure 11. Issues in the geographic multirepresentation.

However, there was no need to develop a code to attribute field sizes such as Varchar2(30) and Number(8,2) since the tool can be pre-configured to attribute values to those data types, as shown in Figure 12.

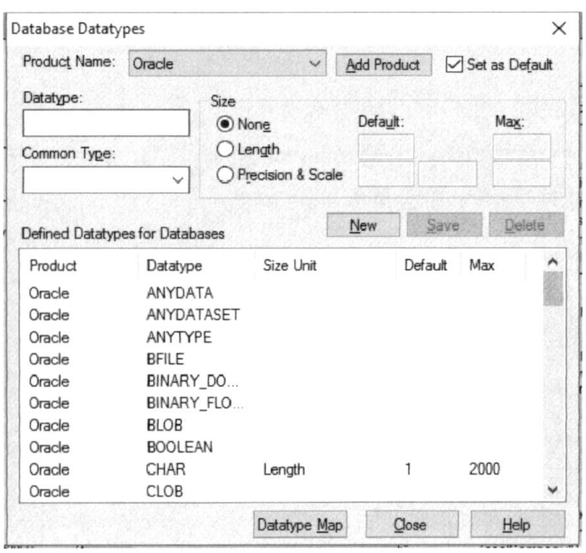

Figure 12. Customization of the data types of the attributes used during the transformation from PIM into PSM.

After following the steps (see the tutorial on the GeoProfile project's site <http://www.dpi.ufv.br/projetos/geoprofile>) for its incorporation into the EA tool and the concepts that have been presented so far, the Tools/Model Transformation (MDA) menu can be used and the GeoProfile_PSM transformation can be selected so that the PSM of Figure 13 can be generated from the PIM of Figure 7.

After following the steps described for PSM generation and comparing the diagram illustrated in Figure 7 (PIM) with the diagram in Figure 13 (PSM), it can be seen that, for semantic relationships, i.e., those that do not involve topological relationships among the geographic objects, the foreign keys are automatically created in the classes. For example, for the semantic relationship between the classes City and CoalMine, the foreign key cityID was created in the last class.

The relational model today no longer poses great challenges regarding the transformation between the PIM and PSM models. However, the spatial characteristics, which involve new data types and topological relationships, add difficulties during this transformation, which requires the investigation of an extension of the rule set for the relational model. Another difficulty is the lack of standardization concerning the implementation of those data types and relationships in the different GDBMSs.

Consequently, it is helpful that the new transformation rules can be specified in the CASE tools, which is available in the EA tool from the possibility of customizing or creating a new transformation language. Figure 12 shows that new data types can be created during the transformation into a particular GDBMS type, which helps specify spatial attributes. Nonetheless, some complications can occur when the types temporal, network, and field view are taken into account since the concept itself is different from the conventional types.

Furthermore, the transformation of topological relationships into PSM is also more complex since they specify integrity restrictions among the spatial types involved and such task cannot simply be performed by creating foreign keys.

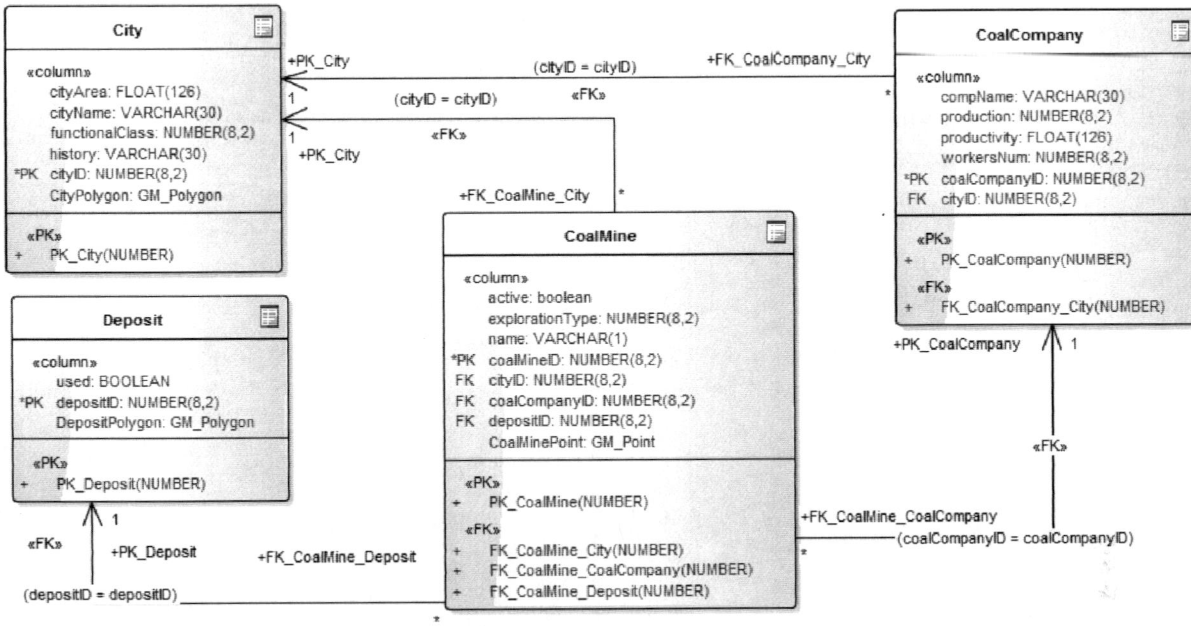

Figure 13. PSM generated from MDA transformations.

VI. SQL CODE GENERATION FOR ORACLE SPATIAL GDBMS

The SQL code with the table structure creation script, relationships, and integrity restrictions is the last step of the MDA so that the implementation of what was initially specified at high abstraction level (CIM) can be automated. The EA tool natively provides the generation of the SQL script for the classes with the stereotype Table present in the PSM. In order to perform this task, one must select the properties of the GeoProfile_PSM package and then use the transformation option Generate DDL so that the options for SQL code generation are provided. Figure 7 shows that, besides generating the table with the respective columns, the EA tool provides some options for SQL code generation. The steps are:

- In Figure 14, select the tables to be transformed into SQL codes;
- Indicate the place where the source code will be stored (in Single File);
- Select the options for SQL code generation, such as: Primary Key, Foreign Key, and Stored Procedures;
- Run the transformation of PSM into SQL code using the button Generate.

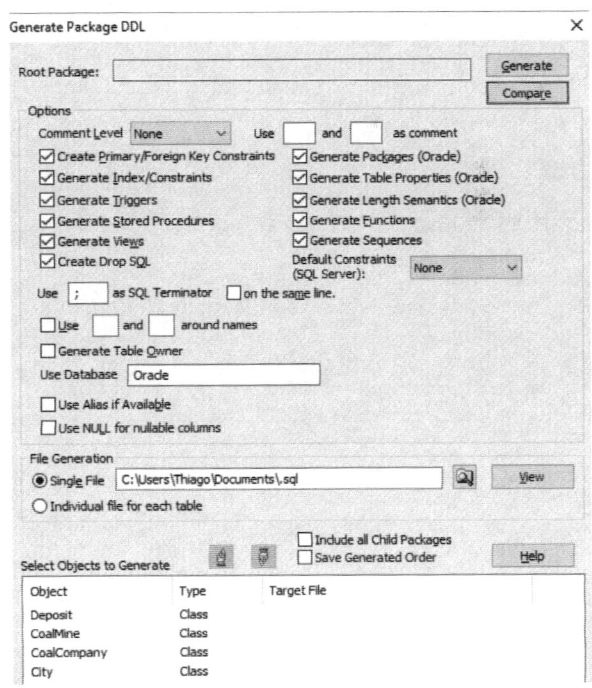

Figure 14. Window to generate SQL code in the GeoProfile_PSM package.

Figures 15 and 16 show the SQL codes generated in the EA tool as the last artifact of the MDA approach. Both the code presented in Figure 15 and the one presented in Figure 16 originate in the PSM presented in Figure 13, however, they have been separated for better understanding and adequacy to the present study.

Figure 15 presents the SQL script responsible for the creation of the database tables, in this case, Oracle Spatial.

```
USE DATABASE Oracle;
DROP TABLE Deposit CASCADE CONSTRAINTS;
DROP TABLE CoalMine CASCADE CONSTRAINTS;
DROPTABLE CoalCompany CASCADE CONSTRAINTS;
DROP TABLE City CASCADE CONSTRAINTS;

CREATE TABLE Deposit
(
   used             BOOLEAN,
   depositID       NUMBER(8,2) NOT NULL,
   DepositPolygon  GM_Polygon
);

CREATE TABLE CoalMine
(
   Active           BOOLEAN,
   explorationType NUMBER(8,2),
   name             VARCHAR(1),
   coalMineID      NUMBER(8,2) NOT NULL,
   cityID           NUMBER(8,2),
   coalCompanyID    NUMBER(8,2),
   depositID        NUMBER(8,2),
   CoalMinePoint    GM_Point
);

CREATE TABLE CoalCompany
(
   compName        VARCHAR(30),
   production      NUMBER(8,2),
   productivity    FLOAT(126),
   workersNum      NUMBER(8,2),
   coalCompanyID  NUMBER(8,2) NOT NULL,
   cityID          NUMBER(8,2)
);

CREATE TABLE City
(
   cityArea          FLOAT(126),
   cityName          VARCHAR(30),
   functionalClass   NUMBER(8,2),
   history           VARCHAR(30),
   cityID          NUMBER(8,2) NOT NULL,
   CityPolygon       GM_Polygon
);
```

Figure 15. DDL code for table creation.

The code presented in Figure 16 shows the changes made to the tables created for the inclusion of Primary Keys and Foreign Keys.

```
ALTER TABLE Deposit
      ADD CONSTRAINT PK_Deposit
      PRIMARY KEY (depositID)
      USING INDEX ;
ALTER TABLE CoalMine
      ADD CONSTRAINT PK_CoalMine
      PRIMARY KEY (coalMineID)
      USING INDEX;
ALTER TABLE CoalCompany
      ADD CONSTRAINT PK_CoalCompany
      PRIMARY KEY (coalCompanyID)
      USING INDEX;
ALTER TABLE City
      ADD CONSTRAINT PK_City
      PRIMARY KEY (cityID)
      USING INDEX;
ALTER TABLE CoalMine
      ADD CONSTRAINT FK_CoalMine_City
      FOREIGN KEY (cityID)
      REFERENCES   City (cityID);

ALTER TABLE CoalMine
      ADD CONSTRAINT
          FK_CoalMine_CoalCompany
      FOREIGN KEY
          (coalCompanyID)
      REFERENCES
          CoalCompany(coalCompanyID);

ALTER TABLE CoalMine
      ADD CONSTRAINT
          FK_CoalMine_Deposit
      FOREIGN KEY
         (depositID)
      REFERENCES Deposit (depositID);

ALTER TABLE CoalCompany
      ADD CONSTRAINT
          FK_CoalCompany_City
      FOREIGN KEY (cityID)
      REFERENCES City (cityID);
```

Figure 16. DDL code for table alteration.

As shown in Figure 7 (representing the PIM), Figure 13 (representing the PSM), and by codes 15 and 16 (representing the SQL source code), the MDA transformation can be performed in the PIM, PSM, and spatial SQL source code steps using GeoProfile in the EA tool. However, the tool enforces some restrictions; in the example at hand, the transformation of the multiple geographic representation of the CoalMine class. Since the SQL code is generated from the PSM model presented in Figure 6, the CoalMine table does not have the spatial features Polygon and Point initially specified in the PIM model. Despite this hurdle, the tool is able to generate an SQL code for implementation in the Oracle Spatial GDBMS.

The source code can be generated in the EA tool in several ways, however, the DDL model provides no customization option either for the PSM or SQL code generation. Customization for PSM generation was only achieved by using customizable templates, but, for now, SQL code generation used only direct transformation of the tool through the option Generate DDL.

It is evident that the option in the Settings/Code Generation Templates menu will also provide customizable languages and even the possibility of developing a new specific language to transform the PSM diagram of GeoProfile into a text file with the SQL source code for database creation.

VII. CONCLUSIONS AND FUTURE WORK

From this paper, it is possible to observe that the tools evaluated do not have features to meet all the theoretical needs of UML, mainly regarding the use of profiles, MDA and OCL. However, they all support conceptual GDB modeling using GeoProfile.

The results of the comparison show that at the time this paper was written the EA could be considered the best CASE tool regarding transformations at the different MDA levels of models created using the GeoProfile. The RSA can be considered the tool that best supports OCL constraints due to its semantic validation, which makes the conceptual models less prone to errors. Among the free-software tools, Papyrus stood out compared to StarUML for supporting the GeoProfile.

Based on the results in this paper, a designer intending to use GeoProfile can know which CASE tool currently best meets the needs of the GDB project. However, it is important to point out that all tools analyzed are being constantly improved, which can change the results of this comparison at any moment.

This study also showed that diagrams created based on GeoProfile in the CASE Enterprise Architect tool can be subjected to MDA transformations from the PIM up to the SQL source code using customizable transformation languages. Despite some momentary issues, such as a lack of resources for the transformation of multiple stereotypes into a class, the tool provides interesting resources to automate the generation of all models of the MDA approach, which ensures higher fidelity between what is specified at a high level and what is actually implemented in the GDBMS.

The method employed, originally proposed by Paranhos and Santos Neto [33], can be used for different comparisons so that designers can establish their own requirements and assign importance weights and satisfaction scales to each one.

Proposals for future works include enhancing the transformation language presented to enable the transformation of all GeoProfile stereotypes, which included the temporal, network, field view, and topological relationships aspects. In addition, it must be observed that, from the PSM model, the transformation must consider the data types used by the different GDBMSs both for the conventional attributes and geographic and temporal ones.

Other work to be developed involves studies which are being done and aim to reach interoperability of conceptual geographical data models created from different conceptual metamodels specific for geographical databases, whose transformation base is the GeoProfile metamodel.

ACKNOWLEDGEMENTS

Project partially funded by the Brazilians agencies FAPEMIG and CAPES. We also thank the support of Faculdade Governador Ozanan Coelho (FAGOC) and CEMIG.

REFERENCES

[1] T. B. Ferreira, J. Lisboa and S. M. Stempliuc, "Evaluation of CASE Tools with UML Profile Support for Geographical Database Design," Proc. of Geoprocessing, Venice, Italy, 2016, pp. 1-6.

[2] G. B. Sampaio, F. R. Nalon, and J. Lisboa-Filho, "GeoProfile-UML Profile for Conceptual Modeling of Geographic Databases," Proc. Int. Conf. on Enterprise Information Systems (ICEIS), Funchal-Madeira, Portugal, 2013, pp. 409-412.

[3] F. R. Nalon, J. Lisboa-Filho, K. A. V. Borges, J. L. Braga, and M. V. A. Andrade, "Using MDA and a UML Profile integrated with International Standards to Model Geographic Databases," Proc. Brazilian Symposium on Geoinformatics (GeoInfo), 2010, pp. 146-157.

[4] P. A. Longley, M. F. Goodchild, D. J. Maguire, and D. W. Rhind, Geographic Information Science and Systems, Danvers: Wiley, 2010.

[5] G. Câmara, "Computational representation of spatial data," In: M. A. Casanova, G. Câmara, C. A. Davis Jr., L. Vinhas, and G. R. Queiroz (Org.), "Bancos de Dados Geográficos". Curitiba: EspaçoGeo, cap. 1, 2005, pp. 1-44. (in Portuguese)

[6] E. Clementini, P. Di Felice, and P. Oosterom, "A Small Set of Formal Topological Relationships Suitable for End-User Interaction," Proc. Int. Symposium on Advances in Spatial Databases, 1993, p. 277-295.

[7] M. J. Egenhofer and R. D. Franzosa, "Point-set topological spatial relations," International Journal of Geographic Information Systems, vol. 5, no. 2, 1991, pp. 161-174.

[8] A. A. A. Ribeiro, S. M. Stempliuc, and J. Lisboa-Filho, J., "Extending OCL to specify and validate integrity constraints in UML-GeoFrame conceptual data model," Proc. Int. Conf. on Enterprise Information Systems (ICEIS), Angers Loire Valley, France, 2013, pp. 329-336.

[9] R. Kothuri, A. Godfrind, and E. Beinat, Pro Oracle Spatial for Oracle Database 11g, USA: Apress, 2007.

[10] A. Kleppe, J. Warmer, and W. Bast, MDA Explained: The Model Driven Architecture: Practice and Promise, Boston: Addison-Wesley, 2nd ed., 2003.

[11] OMG., MDA Guide, OMG Document formal/2003-06-01 edition, Needham, MA, USA, Version 1.0.1, 2003.

[12] G. Booch, J. Rumbaugh, and I. Jacobson, UML: user guide, Elsevier. Rio de Janeiro, 2nd ed., 2005.

[13] J. Warmer and A. Kleppe, The Object Constraint Language: Getting Your Models Ready for MDA, Boston: Addison Wesley, 2nd ed., 2003.

[14] OMG., Object Constraint Language, OMG Document formal/2006-05-01 edition, Needham, MA, USA. Version 2.0, 2006.

[15] OMG., Object Constraint Language, OMG Document formal/2014-02-03 edition, Needham, MA, USA. Version 2.4, 2014.

[16] H. Eriksson, et al., "UML 2 Toolkit", Wiley Publishing. Indianapolis. 552p, 2004.

[17] J. Lisboa Filho, G. B. Sampaio, F. R. Nalon, and K. A. V. Borges, "A UML profile for conceptual modeling," Proc. Int. Workshop on Domain Engineering (DE@CAISE), 2010, pp. 18-31.

[18] F. R. Nalon, J. Lisboa-Filho, J. L. Braga, K. A. V. Borges, and M V. A. Andrade, "Applying the model driven architecture approach for geographic database design using a UML Profile and ISO standards," Journal of Information and Data Management, vol. 2, no. 2, 2011, pp. 171-180.

[19] Sparx Systems, Enterprise Architect 12.1. [Online]. Available from: http://www.sparxsystems.com.au/ 2016.04.13

[20] T. B. Ferreira, S. M. Stempliuc, and J. Lisboa-Filho, "Data Modeling with UML Profile GeoProfile and Transformations in MDA tool Enterprise Architect," Actas. Conferencia Ibérica de Sistemas y Tecnologías de Informacion (CISTI), Barcelona, AISTI | ISEGI, 2014, pp. 603-608.

[21] Eclipse Foundation, Papyrus Modeling Environment. [Online]. Available from: http://www.eclipse.org/papyrus/ 2016.04.13

[22] Star UML, StarUML 2: A sophisticated software modeler. [Online]. Available from: http://staruml.io/ 2016.04.13

[23] Visual Paradigm International, Visual Paradigm, [Online]. Available from: https://www.visual-paradigm.com/ 2016.04.13

[24] IBM, Rational Software Modeler. Rational Software Architect Family. [Online]. Available from: http://www-03.ibm.com/software/products/en/rational-software-architect-family 2016.04.13

[25] R. D. D. Paranhos and I. Santos Neto, Comparative study of change control tools in the software development process, Salvador: Universidade Católica do Salvador, 2009.

[26] J. H. S. Câmara, T. Almeida, D. R. Carvalho, et al., "A comparative analysis of development environments for voluntary geographical information Web systems," Proc. of Brazilian Symposium Geoinformatics (GEOINFO), 2014, pp. 130-141

Semi-Supervised Ensemble Learning in the Framework of Data 1-D Representations with Label Boosting

Jianzhong Wang

College of Sciences and
Engineering Techonology
Sam Houston State University
Huntsville, TX 77341-2206, USA
Email: jzwang@shsu.edu

Huiwu Luo, Yuan Yan Tang

Faculty of Science and Technology
University of Macau, Macau, China
Email: luohuiwu@gmail.com
yytang@umac.mo

***Abstract*—The paper introduces a novel ensemble method for semi-supervised learning. The method integrates the regularized classifier based on data 1-D representation and label boosting in a serial ensemble. In each stage, the data set is first smoothly sorted and represented as a 1-D stack, which preserves the data local similarity. Then, based on these stacks, an ensemble labeler is constructed by several 1-D regularized weak classifiers. The 1-D ensemble labeler extracts a newborn labeled subset from the unlabeled set. United with this subset, the original labeled set is boosted and the enlarged labeled set is utilized into the next semi-supervised learning stage. The boosting process is not stopped until the enlarged labeled set reaches a certain size. Finally, a 1-D ensemble labeler is applied again to construct the final classifier, which labels all unlabeled samples in the data set. Taking the advantage of ensemble, the method avoids the kernel trick that is the core in many current popular semi-supervised learning methods such as Transductive Supported Vector Machine and Semi-Supervised Manifold Learning. Because the proposed algorithm only employs relatively simple semi-supervised 1-D classifiers, it is stable, effective, and applicable to data sets of various types. The validity and effectiveness of the method are confirmed by the experiments on data sets of different types, such as handwritten digits and hyperspectral images. Comparing to several other popular semi-supervised learning methods, the results of the proposed one are very promising and superior to others.**

Keywords–Data smooth sorting; one-dimensional embedding; regularization; label boosting; ensemble classification; semi-supervised learning.

I. Introduction

In this paper, we introduce a novel ensemble method for semi-supervised learning (SSL) based on *data 1-D representation* and *label boosting*, which is abbreviated to ESSL1dLB. A preliminary discussion of the topic has been present in the conference presentation [1]. The purpose of this paper is to provide an extension with some new developments.

A standard SSL problem can be briefly described as follows: Assume that the samples (or members, points) of a given data set $X = \{\vec{x}_i\}_{i=1}^{n} \subset \mathbf{R}^m$ belong to c classes and $\mathcal{B} = \{b_1, \cdots, b_c\}$ is the class-label set. Let the labels of the samples in X be $y_1, y_2, \cdots, y_n$, respectively. When X is observed, only the samples of a subset, say, $X_\ell = \{\vec{x}_1, \vec{x}_2, \cdots, \vec{x}_{n_0}\} \subset X$ have the known labels $Y_\ell = \{y_1, y_2, \cdots, y_{n_0}\} \subset \mathcal{B}$, while the labels of the samples in its complementary set $X_u = \{\vec{x}_{n_0+1}, \vec{x}_{n_0+2}, \cdots, \vec{x}_n\} = X \setminus X_\ell$ are unknown. A function $f : X \to \mathcal{B}$ is called a *classifier* (or *labeler*) if it predicts the labels for all samples in X_u. The *classification error* usually is measured by the number of the misclassified samples:

$$E(f) = |\{\vec{x}_i \in X|\ f(\vec{x}_i) \neq y_i,\ 1 \leq i \leq n\}|,$$

where $|S|$ denotes the cardinality of a set S. Then, the quality of a classifier is measured by the *classification error rate* (CErrRate) $E(f)/|X|$. The task of SSL is to find a classifier f with the CErrRate as small as possible.

In a SSL problem, if the samples of X only belong to two classes, say, Class A and Class B, it is called a *binary classification problem*. In this case, we may assign the sign-labels 1 and -1 to Classes A and B, respectively. In a binary classification problem, the error of a classifier f can be estimated by the ℓ_0 error:

$$E(f) = \sum_{k=1}^{n} \operatorname{sign}(|f(\vec{x}_i) - y_i|).$$

It is worth to point out that the binary classification is essential in SSL. When the samples of X belong to more than two classes, we can recursively apply binary classification technique to achieve multi-classification [2], [3]. In a binary classification model, the classifier f on X usually is designed to a continuous real-valued function. The sign $f(\vec{x})$ then gives the class label of $\vec{x}$ so that the decision boundary is determined by the level-curve $f(\vec{x}) = 0$

SSL models make use some assumptions. The main one is the *smoothness assumption*, which asserts that the samples in the same class are similar while those in different classes are dissimilar. It enables us to design classifiers in a smooth function space, say, Soblev space. Its special case is the *cluster assumption*, which asserts that the data tend to form discrete clusters, and points in the same cluster are most likely in the same class. Clustering models are based on this assumption. When the dimension of data is high, due to the curse of dimensionality [4], [5], most computations on the data become inaccurate and unstable. According to the *manifold assumption*, the high-dimensional data lie approximately on a manifold of much lower dimension. Therefore, the dimensionality reduction technique should be utilized in SSL models.

Many statistical and machine learning methods for SSL were proposed in the last two decades. The monograph [6] and the survey paper [7] gave a comprehensive review of various SSL methods. Geometrically, the main difficult in SSL is the nonlinearity of the decision boundary. In general, it is a combination of several disjoint surfaces in $\mathbf{R}^m$. To overcome the difficult, many popular methods, such as transductive support vector machines, manifold regularization, and various graph-based methods, utilize so-called *kernel trick* to linearize the decision boundary [8], [9]. That is, in such a model, with the help of a kernel function, one constructs a reproducing kernel Hilbert space (RKHS) [10], where the classifier is a linear function so that it can be constructed by a regularization method. The success of a kernel-based method strongly depends on the exploration of data structure by the kernel. However, it is often difficult to design suitable kernels, which precisely explore the data features. Therefore, recently researchers try to establish new SSL models, in which classifiers are constructed without kernel technique. These models include the data-tree based method [11], [12], SSL using Gaussian fields [13], and others.

In most of the models above, a single classifier is constructed for a given SSL task. However, when a data set has a complicate intrinsic structure, a single classifier usually cannot complete the task satisfactorily. The *multiple classifier systems* (MCSs) offer alternatives. The ensemble methodology in MCSs builds a single *strong classifier* by integrating several *weak classifiers*. Although each weak classifier is slightly correlated with the true classification, the strong classifier is well-correlated with the true one. MCSs perform information fusion at different levels to overcome the limitations of the traditional methods [14]–[16]. In MCSs two canonical topologies, parallel and serial ones, are employed in the ensemble (see Fig. 4 in [15]). In the parallel topology, all weak classifiers are built on the same data set and the strong classifier is made by a combination of their outputs. On the other hand, in the serial topology, the weak classifiers are applied in sequence, such that the output of the predecessor turns to be the input of the successor, and the final label prediction comes from the last weak classifier. Originally, ensemble algorithms are developed for supervised learning. A well-known parallel ensemble algorithm is bagging (bootstrap aggregating) [14], [17]. Boosting algorithms, such as AdaBoost [18], LPBoost, LSBoost, RobustBoost, and GentleBoost, apply serial ensemble. Due to the flexibility, MCSs open a wide door for developing various ensemble SSL algorithms.

The novelty of the introduced ensemble SSL method is the following: It adopts the framework of data 1-D representation, in which the data set is represented by several different 1-D sequences, then a labeler is constructed as an ensemble of several weak classifiers, which are built on these 1-D sequences. Here, we are partial to data 1-D models because 1-D decision boundary reduces to a set of points on a line, which has the simplest topological structure. As a result, the weak classifiers can be easily constructed by standard 1-D regularization methods without using kernel trick. Furthermore, the simplicity of 1-D models makes the algorithm more reliable and stable. Hence, the core of our method is an ensemble binary classification algorithm for SSL, whose architecture and technological process are described in the following.

1) **Making data 1-D (shortest path) representation.** The data set X first is smoothly sorted and mapped to several 1-D sets $\{T^i\}_{i=1}^k$, of which each preserves the local similarity of members in X. Correspondingly, the couple $\{X_\ell, X_u\}$ is mapped to $\{T_\ell^i, T_u^i\}$ such that $T_\ell^i \cup T_u^i = T^i$. The 1-D sets $\{T^i\}_{i=1}^k$ provide a framework of our method.
2) **Constructing ensemble labeler in the 1-D framework.** Based on T^i, a weak classifier g^i on X is constructed by a 1-D regularization method. Then an ensemble labeler is built from these weak classifiers. From the unlabeled set X_u, the labeler extracts a *feasibly confident subset* L, which contains the samples, whose predicted labels are accurate with high confidence.
3) **Developing label boosting algorithm.** A label selection function is constructed to select the *newborn labeled subset* S from the feasibly confident subset L to reduce the misclassification error. It computes *class weights* of the members of L for selection decision. Then, the initial labeled set X_ℓ is boosted to $X_\ell^{new} = X_\ell \cup S$. The process is repeated and not terminated until the boosted labeled set X_ℓ^{new} reaches a certain size.
4) **Building the final (strong) classifier.** Finally, several weak classifiers g^i are constructed based on the final updated labeled set X_ℓ^{new}. The final classifier f is defined as the mean of these weak classifiers.

Our strategy in the binary classification algorithm above adopts *Model-guided Instance Selection* approach to boosting [14]. But it is slightly different from the standard boosting algorithms [19] in the sense that they boost the misclassified weights on X_u, while our method boosts the labeled subset X_ℓ. The preliminary work of the proposed method can be found in [20]–[23].

In this paper, we employ the well-known *One-Against-All* strategy [2] to deal with multi-classification using a combination of binary classifications.

The paper is organized as follows: In Section II, we introduce our ensemble SSL method in details and present the corresponding ESSL1DLB algorithm. In Section III, we demonstrate the validity of our method in examples and give the comparison of our results with those obtained by several popular methods. The conclusion is given in Section IV.

II. Ensemble SSL Method in Framework of Data 1-D Representation with Label Boosting

In this section, we introduce the novel ensemble SSL method based on data 1-D representation and label boosting. The main steps of the method has been introduced in the previous section. We now introduce the method and corresponding algorithm in details.

A. Data 1-D representations by shortest path sorting

Assume that the data set X is initially arranged in a stack $\mathbf{x} = [\vec{x}_1, \cdots, \vec{x}_n]$. Let $w(\vec{x}, \vec{y})$ be a distance-type weight function on $X \times X$ that measures the dissimilarity between the samples $\vec{x}$ and $\vec{y}$. Let π be an index permutation of the index sequence $[1, 2, \cdots, n]$, which induces a permutation P_π on the initial stack $\mathbf{x}$, yielding a stack of X headed by $\vec{x}_{\pi(1)}$: $\mathbf{x}_\pi = P_\pi \mathbf{x} = [\vec{x}_{\pi(1)}, \cdots, \vec{x}_{\pi(n)}]$. We denote the set of all permutations of X with the head $\vec{x}_\ell$ by

$$\mathcal{P}_\ell = \{P_\pi; \quad \pi(1) = \ell\}.$$

According to [24], the *shortest-path sorting of X headed by $\vec{x}_\ell$* is the stack $\mathbf{x}_\pi$ that minimizes the path starting from $\vec{x}_\ell$ and though all points in X, i.e., $\mathbf{x}_\pi = P_\pi \mathbf{x} = [x_{\pi(1)}, x_{\pi(2)}, \cdots, \vec{x}_{\pi(n)}]$, where

$$P_\pi = \arg\min_{P \in \mathcal{P}_\ell} \sum_{j=1}^{n-1} w((P\mathbf{x})_j, (P\mathbf{x})_{j+1}). \quad (1)$$

Define the 1-D sequence $\mathbf{t} = [t_1, \cdots, t_n]$ by

$$t_1 = 0, \; t_{j+1} - t_j = \frac{w(\vec{x}_{\pi(j)}, \vec{x}_{\pi(j+1)})}{\sum_{k=1}^{n-1} w(\vec{x}_{\pi(k)}, \vec{x}_{\pi(k+1)})}. \quad (2)$$

Then, the 1-D stack $\mathbf{t}$ provides the *1-D (shortest-path) representation* of X headed by $\vec{x}_\ell$. We call the function $h_\ell : X \to [0,1], h_\ell(\vec{x}_{\pi(j)}) = t_j$ the (isometric) *1-D embedding* of X headed by $\vec{x}_\ell$. When the index ℓ is not stressed, we will simplify h_ℓ to h.

The sorting problem (1) essentially is a traveling salesman problem, which has NP computational complexity. To reduce the complexity, approximations of P_π in (1) are adopted. For instance, a greedy algorithm for the approximation was developed in [24] for sorting all patches in an image. In this paper, we slightly modify the algorithm in [24] so that it works for data sets that are represented by weighted data graphs. We first see how to construct weighted graphs for two popular types of data sets:

1) The data set forms a point cloud $X \subset \mathbf{R}^m$ equipped with a metric. To construct a weighted graph $[X, E, W]$ on X, we identify a point $\vec{x}$ with a node in the graph so that X can be considered as a set of nodes in the graph. By the metric on X, we derive a distance-type weight function $d(\vec{x}, \vec{y})$ on $X \times X$, which measures the dissimilarity between the samples in X. For any $\vec{x} \in X$, the k nearest neighbors (kNN) of the node $\vec{x}$ is denoted by $\mathcal{N}_{\vec{x}} \subset X$. Assume that $|X| = n$, and set $\mathcal{I} = \{1, 2, \cdots n\}$. Then the edge set in the graph is $E = \{(i,j) \in \mathcal{I} \times \mathcal{I};\ \vec{x}_j \in \mathcal{N}_{\vec{x}_i}\}$. Finally, we define the weight matrix $W = [w_{ij}]_{i,j=1}^n$, where $w_{i,j} = d(\vec{x}_i, \vec{x}_j)$.
2) The data set is a hyperspectral image (HSI) represented as an imaginary cube $X \in \mathbf{R}^{m \times n \times s}$. In the cube, the (i,j)-pixel, $X(i,j,:)$, is a spectral vector; and the spatial neighbors of $X(i,j,:)$ usually is defined as the pixel-square centered by $X(i,j,:)$: $\mathcal{N}_{(i,j)} = \{X(k,l,:);\ |k-i| \le q, |l-j| \le q\}$, where q is a preset positive integer. For a given HSI cube X, we construct the weighted graph $[X, E, W]$ as follows: We first map the double index (i,j) to the single one $k = i + (j-1)m$. Then we write $\vec{x}_k = X(i,j,:)$ and convert the 2-D neighborhood to the 1-D one: $\mathcal{N}_{\vec{x}_k} = \mathcal{N}_{(i,j)}$, which defines the edge set E. For a HSI data set, there are various ways to define the distance-type weights on edges. We propose the spectral-spatial weights introduced in the paper [22]. Similar to the first case, the node set $X = \{\vec{x}_k;\ 1 \le k \le nm\}$, the edge set E and the weight set W form a weight graph $[X, E, W]$ on the HSI cube X.enumerate

Note that the edge set E in the graph $[X, E, W]$ induces an index neighbor set from a node neighbor. For instance, the index set $\mathcal{N}_k = \{j;\ (k,j) \in E\}$ is corresponding to the neighbor set $\mathcal{N}_{\vec{x}_k}$. Using index neighbors to replace the node neighbors can simplify code writing. If the graph $[X, E, W]$ is complete, then the neighbor set of each node $\vec{x}$ is the set $X \backslash \{\vec{x}\}$, which leads to the global search scheme in the greedy algorithm.

Adopting weighted data graph $[X, E, W]$ as the input of the greedy sorting algorithm enables us to apply the algorithm to various data sets. For instance, it can be applied to the data set X, whose samples cannot be digitally represented by vectors, but the similarity between them can be measured. For this type of data, although X is not digitized, the algorithm works. Many data sets obtained by social survey are in this category.

The pseudocode of our data 1-D (shortest-path) representation (1dSPR) algorithm is presented at **Algorithm 1,** in which ϵ is called the *path selection parameter*. Since the algorithm is a slight modification of that one in [24], we omit the details of the explanation of the parameter settings here.

Algorithm 1 1dSPR Algorithm

Require: Data graph $[X, E, W]$; probability vector $\tilde{\mathbf{p}} = [\tilde{p}_1, \tilde{p}_2, \cdots, \tilde{p}_n]$, where $\tilde{p}_i \in (0,1)$, and $n = |X|$.
Initialization of **Output**: π: empty index stack; $\mathbf{t}$: n-dimensional zero vector.
Set $\pi(1) \leftarrow j$, j: random index; and set $t_1 = 0$.
Define $\mathcal{I} = \{1, 2, \cdots, n\}$.
for $k = 1, 2, \cdots, n-2$ **do**
  • set $\mathcal{N}^c_{\pi(k)} = \mathcal{N}_{\pi(k)} \backslash \pi$; $\mathcal{I}^c = \mathcal{I} \backslash \pi$
  • **if** $|\mathcal{N}^c_{\pi(k)}| = 1$
    — $\pi(k+1) \leftarrow j \in \mathcal{N}^c_{\pi(k)}$
  • **else**
    — **if** $|\mathcal{N}^c_{\pi(k)}| \ge 2$
      * Find $j_1 \in \mathcal{N}^c_{\pi(k)}$ such that $\vec{x}_{j_1}$ is the nearest neighbor to $\vec{x}_{\pi(k)}$ in $\mathcal{N}^c_{\vec{x}_{\pi(k)}}$
      * Find $j_2 \in \mathcal{N}^c_{\pi(k)}$ such that $\vec{x}_{j_2}$ is the second nearest neighbor to $\vec{x}_{\pi(k)}$ in $\mathcal{N}^c_{\vec{x}_{\pi(k)}}$
    — **elseif** $|\mathcal{N}^c_k| = 0$
      * Find $j_1 \in \mathcal{I} \backslash \pi$ such that, in all nodes with indices in $\mathcal{I} \backslash \pi$, $\vec{x}_{j_1}$ is the nearest node to $\vec{x}_{\pi(k)}$
      * Find $j_2 \in \mathcal{I} \backslash \pi$ such that, in all nodes with indices in $\mathcal{I} \backslash \pi$, $\vec{x}_{j_2}$ is the second nearest node to $\vec{x}_{\pi(k)}$
    — **endif**
  • **endif**
  Compute q_k:

$$q_k = \frac{1}{1 + \exp\left(\frac{w(\vec{x}_{\pi(k)}, \vec{x}_{j_1}) - w(\vec{x}_{\pi(k)}, \vec{x}_{j_2})}{\epsilon}\right)} \quad (3)$$

  Set $\pi(k+1) = \begin{cases} j_2 & \text{if } q_k < \tilde{p}_{\pi(k)} \\ j_1 & \text{otherwise.} \end{cases}$
  Set $t_{k+1} = t_k + w(\vec{x}_{\pi(k)}, \vec{x}_{\pi(k+1)})$.
end for
Set $\pi(n) \leftarrow j \in \mathcal{I} \backslash \pi$, $t_n = t_{n-1} + w(\vec{x}_{\pi(n-1)}, \vec{x}_{\pi(n)})$.
Normalize vector $\mathbf{t}$: $t_j \leftarrow t_j / t_n$
Ensure: $\mathbf{t}$; π.

Because sorting scheme is a serial process, it is a bias in the sense of smoothness. That is, in general the difference $\Delta t_j =$

$t_{j+1} - t_j$ is increasing with respect to j, i.e., earlier selected adjacent pairs are more similar than the later selected ones. This bias impacts cluster preserving when X is represented by T.

Enlightened by the spinning technique [25], we introduce multiple 1-D embedding of X to reduce the sorting dias. Let $\{\vec{x}_{j_1}, \vec{x}_{j_2}, \cdots, \vec{x}_{j_k}\}$ be a subset of X selected at random, and h_i be the 1-D embedding headed by $\vec{x}_{j_i}$. We call k the *spinning number* and the vector-valued function $\vec{h} = [h_1, h_2, \cdots, h_k]$ a k-ple 1-D embedding of X. Then $\vec{h}(X)$ gives a k-ple 1-D representation of X.

B. Construction of ensemble labeler from weak classifiers on data multiple 1-D representation

Let h be a (single) 1-D embedding of X (with $|X| = n$). We write $T_\ell = h(X_\ell)$ and $T_u = h(X_u)$. Then, T_ℓ is a labeled set and T_u is an unlabeled set, and a labeler on T induces a labeler on X. Since T is a 1-D set, its class decision boundary is reduced to a point set in the line segment $[0, 1]$. Therefore, no kernel trick is needed for constructing a labeler on T. Instead, a simple regularization scheme works.

As we mentioned above, a single 1-D representation may not truly preserve the data similarity because the sorting bias. In the proposed method, we create a multiple 1-D representation of X, and construct a weak labeler based on each of them. Then, from these weak labelers, we build an ensemble labeler (1dEL), which better predicts the labels of the samples in the unlabeled set X_u. The following is the details of **1dEL** Algorithm.

Let $\vec{h} = [h_1, \cdots, h_k]$ be a k-ple 1-D embedding of X with the head stack $[\vec{x}_{j_1}, \vec{x}_{j_2}, \cdots, \vec{x}_{j_k}]$. Let P_i be the permutation operator corresponding to h_i and $\mathbf{x}_{\pi_i} = P_i\mathbf{x}$. The embedding h_i produces a 1-D representation of X: $\mathbf{t}^i = h_i(\mathbf{x}_{\pi_i})$, and any function f on X through h_i derives a function $s^i = f \circ h_i^{-1}$ on $\mathbf{t}^i$. Equivalently, $f = s^i \circ h_i$, which given the relation of a labeler on $\mathbf{t}^i$ and a labeler on X. Since $\mathbf{t}^i$ is a discrete set, we can represent the function s^i on $\mathbf{t}^i$ in the vector form $\mathbf{s}^i = [s_1^i, \cdots, s_n^i]$, where $s_j^i = s(t_j^i)$.

To construct the labelers on $\mathbf{t}^i$, we define the first-order difference of s^i (at t_j^i) by $\Delta s_j^i = s(t_{j+1}^i) - s(t_j^i)$, and the first-order difference quotient by $Ds_j = (s(t_{j+1}^i) - s(t_j^i))/(t_{j+1}^i - t_j^i)$. Inductively, we define the kth-order difference of s^i (at t_j^i) by $\Delta^k s_j^i = \Delta^{k-1}s_{j+1}^i - \Delta^{k-1}s_j^i$ and the kth-order difference quotient by $D^k s_j^i = (D^{k-1}s_{j+1}^i - D^{k-1}s_j^i)/(t_{j+k}^i - t_j^i)$. They describe various smoothness of s^j. Let $T_\ell^i = h_i(X_\ell)$ and $T_u^i = h_i(X_u)$. As we have mentioned, a weak labeler g^i on X can be constructed as the composition $g^i = q^i \circ h_i$, where q^i is a labeler on $\mathbf{t}^i$. We construct q^i using one of the following 1-D regularization models:

1. Least-square regularization. Let q^i be the solution of the following unconstrained minimization problem:

$$q^i = \arg\min \frac{1}{n_0}\sum_{j=1}^{n_0}\left(s^i(h_i(\vec{x}_j)) - y_j\right)^2 + \frac{\lambda}{2}\sum_{j=1}^{n-1}(Ds_j^i)^2, \quad (4)$$

where λ is the standard *regularization parameter*. We denote by I_{n_0} the $n \times n$ diagonal matrix, in which only $(\pi^i(j), \pi^i(j))$-entries are 1, $1 \le j \le n_0$, but others are 0. Set $w_0 = w_n = 0$, $w_j = 1/(t_{j+1}^i - t_j^i)^2$, and denote by $D = [D_{i,j}]$ the $n \times n$ three-diagonal matrix, in which

$$\begin{cases} D_{j,j} = w_{j-1} + w_j & 1 \le j \le n, \\ D_{j,j+1} = D_{j+1,j} = -w_j & 1 \le j \le n-1, \end{cases}$$

Then, the vector representation of q^i on the stack $\mathbf{t}^i$ is

$$\mathbf{q}^i = (I_{n_0} + n_0\lambda D)^{-1}\,\vec{y}. \quad (5)$$

Assume that the class distribution on X_u is the same as on X_ℓ. Let $M = \frac{1}{n_0}\sum_{j=1}^{n_0} y_j$. Then we may add the constraint

$$\frac{1}{n}\sum_{j=1}^{n} s^i(t_j^i) = M$$

to the minimization problem (4). Correspondingly, the solution (5) is modified to

$$\mathbf{q}^i = (I_{n_0} + n_0\lambda D)^{-1}\,(\vec{y} + \mu\vec{1}) \quad (6)$$

with

$$\mu = \frac{M - \mathcal{E}\left((I_{n_0} + n_0\lambda D)^{-1}\vec{y}\right)}{\mathcal{E}\left((I_{n_0} + n_0\lambda D)^{-1}\vec{1}\right)},$$

where $\vec{1}$ denotes the vector whose all entries are 1 and $\mathcal{E}(\vec{v})$ the mean value of the vector $\vec{v}$.

Remark: In the Least-square regularization model (4), the difference quotient term $(Ds_j^i)^2$ may also be replaced by the difference term $(\Delta s_j^i)^2$. This replacement is equivalent to using the equal-distance sequence $\mathbf{t}^i$ in (4).

2. Regularization by interpolation. Let q^i be the solution of the following constrained minimization problem:

$$q^i = \arg\min \sum_{j=1}^{n-2}(D^2 s_j^i)^2 \quad (7)$$

subject to

$$s^i(h_i(\vec{x}_j)) = y_j, \quad 1 \le j \le n_0. \quad (8)$$

Write $\hat{t}_j = h_i(\vec{x}_j)$. Then q^i is the cubic spline that has the nodes at $\{\hat{t}_j\}_{j=1}^{n_0}$ and takes the values as in (8).

Let i run through 1 to k. Then we obtained k 1-D labelers $q^1, \cdots, q^k$. They further derive k weak labelers $g^i = q^i \circ h_i^{-1}, 1 \le i \le k$, on X. We will use $[g^1, \cdots, g^k]$ in two cases. Firstly, in the label boosting precess, they are used to construct the *feasibly confident subset*. Recall that each g^i predicts the label $\text{sign}(g^i(\vec{x}))$ for $\vec{x} \in X_u$. Let

$$g(\vec{x}) = \frac{1}{k}\sum_{i=1}^{k}\text{sign}(g^i(\vec{x})), \quad \vec{x} \in X_u, \quad (9)$$

and define

$$L^+ = \{\vec{x} \in X_u;\ g(\vec{x}) = 1\}, \quad L^- = \{\vec{x} \in X_u;\ g(\vec{x}) = -1\}.$$

Then we call L^+ the *feasibly confident subset of Class A*, L^- the *feasibly confident subset of Class B*, and $L = L^+ \cup L^-$ the *feasibly confident subset*. In a great chance, a sample in L^+ is in Class A, while a sample in L^- in Class B. For convenience, we denote the set operator that create the feasibly confident subset L from X_u by $\mathbf{G}: \mathbf{G}(X_u) = L$.

Secondly, we use $[g^1, \cdots, g^k]$ to construct the final classifier f in the last step of our algorithm as follows:

$$f(\vec{x}) = \frac{1}{k}\sum_{i=1}^{k} g^i(\vec{x}), \quad \vec{x} \in X_u. \tag{10}$$

C. Label boosting

To further eliminate the misclassification in L^+ and L^-, we will construct a subset $S^+ \subset L^+$ and a subset $S^- \subset L^-$ as follows: Let $X_\ell^+ \subset X_\ell$ be the subset that contains all Class-A members and $X_\ell^- \subset X_\ell$ the subset that contains all Class-B members. For each $\vec{x} \in L$, define

$$w^+(\vec{x}) = \frac{\sum_{\vec{y} \in X_\ell^+} w(\vec{x}, \vec{y})}{|X_\ell^+|}$$

and

$$w^-(\vec{x}) = \frac{\sum_{\vec{y} \in X_\ell^-} w(\vec{x}, \vec{y})}{|X_\ell^-|}.$$

We now create the *class weight* function by

$$w(\vec{x}) = \frac{w^+(\vec{x})}{w^+(\vec{x}) + w^-(\vec{x})}.$$

It is obvious that a greater value of $w(\vec{x})$ indicates that $\vec{x}$ is nearer the points in X_ℓ^-. Therefore, it is more likely in Class B. Let the set S^+ contain the half of members of L^+ with the smallest class weights and S^- contain the half of members in L^- with the greatest class weights. We call $S = S^+ \cup S^-$ the *newborn labeled subset*, call the operator $\mathbf{S} : \mathbf{S}(L) = S$ a *newborn labeled subset selector*, and call the composition $\mathbf{M} = \mathbf{S} \circ \mathbf{G}$ a *newborn labeled subset generater*. Therefore, we have the newborn labeled set $S = \mathbf{S}(L) = \mathbf{S}(\mathbf{G}(X_u)) = \mathbf{M}(X_u)$.

The *Label Boosting Algorithm* iteratively adds the newborn labeled subset to the original labeled set so that the labeled set is cumulatively boosted. In detail, let the initial labeled set x_ℓ and the unlabeled set $X - u$ be re-written as X_ℓ^0 and X_u^0, respectively. We apply the newborn labeled subset generater $\mathbf{M}_1$ on X_u^0 to create a newborn labeled set $S^1 = \mathbf{M}_1(X_u^0)$, which is united with X_ℓ^0 to produce $X_\ell^1 = X_\ell^0 \cup S^1$. Meanwhile, we set $X_u^1 = X_u^0 \setminus S_1$. Repeating the procedure for N times, the labeled set will be cumulatively boosted to a enlarged labeled set

$$X_\ell^N = X_\ell^0 \bigcup_{j=1}^{N} S_j, \quad S_j = \mathbf{M}_j(X_u^{j-1}). \tag{11}$$

We set a *boosting-stop parameter* $p, 0 < p < 1$. The process will not be terminated until the labeled set X_ℓ^N reaches the size $|X_\ell^N| \geq p|X|$. We call N the *label boosting times*.

D. Construction of the final classifier

Finally, we apply 1dEL algorithm on the couple $\{X_\ell^N, X_u^N\}$ to construct the final classifier f by (10). Then each $\vec{x} \in X$ is labeled by sign $f(\vec{x})$.

The whole algorithm that creates the final classifier f is called **ESSL1dLB**.

E. One-Against-All strategy for multi-classification

Many strategies are proposed in literature for handling multi-classification using binary ones [26]–[29]. We apply the well-known *One-Against-All* strategy for multi-classification tasks [2], [30], [31]. In the paper, we choose the simplest one, which is briefly described in the following:

Assume that X consists of c-classes ($c > 2$): Class 1 to Class c. Using **ESSL1dLB,** we create c binary classifier $\{f_1, f_2, \cdots, f_c\}$, where f_i classifies two classes: Class A is identical with Class i, and Class B contains all of other classes, as we described above. A simple one-vs-all classification strategy is the following: Let f be the multi-classifier. Then

$$f(\vec{x}) = \arg\max_{1 \leq i \leq c} f_i(\vec{x}).$$

III. Experiments on Hyperspectral Images

In this section, we evaluate our ensemble SSL method in the experiments on hyperspectral images. An earlier method in the ensemble SSL framework for the classification of hyperspectral images has been reported in [22], where we used the interpolation splines as 1-D weak labelers (see (7)) and adopted the following simpler label boosting method: Choosing the newborn labeled subset at random. The obtained results are still very promising and superior over many other popular methods. In this section, we apply **ESSL1dLB** algorithm for the multi-classification of hyperspectral images. There are two main differences between **ESSL1dLB** and the algorithm used in [22]: Firstly, the **ESSL1dLB** algorithm uses Least-square regularization for the construction of weak labelers (see (4)). Secondly, it uses the class-weight method for label boosting.

In this section, we first introduce the data formats and the metrics of the data sets used in our experiments. Then we tune the parameters in the **ESSL1dLB** algorithm. Finally, we report the results of the experiments and comparisons.

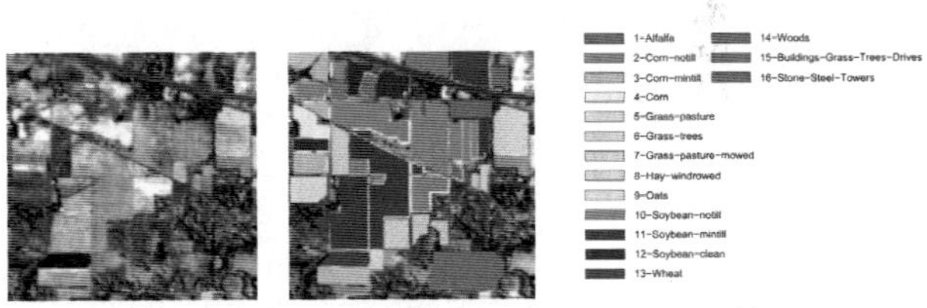

(a) (b) (c)

Figure 1. RGB composition and classification map for AVIRIS Indian Pines 1992 scenario. (a) Pseudocolor image. (b) Ground truth map. (c) Class labels.

A. Data Collection and Experiment Design

All of the data sets used in the experiments are published for research usage only. Three hyperspectral images are chosen for our experiments, which are particularly designed.

1) Data sets: The first data set used in our experiments is the *AVIRIS Indian Pines* 1992, which was gathered by the National Aeronautics and Space Administration's (NASA) Airborne Visible/Infrared Imaging Spectrometer (AVIRIS) sensor over the northwestern Indian Pines test site in 1992. The raw calibrated data are available on-line from [32] with the ground-truth class map. This data set consists of 145×145 pixels and 224 spectral reflectance bands in the wavelength range

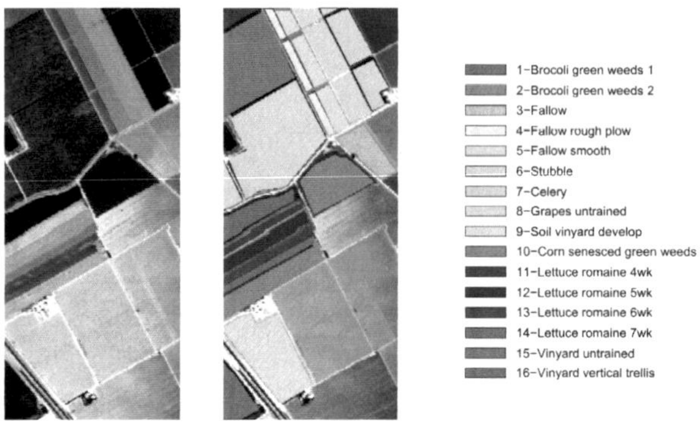

(a) (b) (c)

Figure 2. RGB composition and classification map for Salinas scenario. (a) Pseudocolor image. (b) Ground truth map. (c) Class labels.

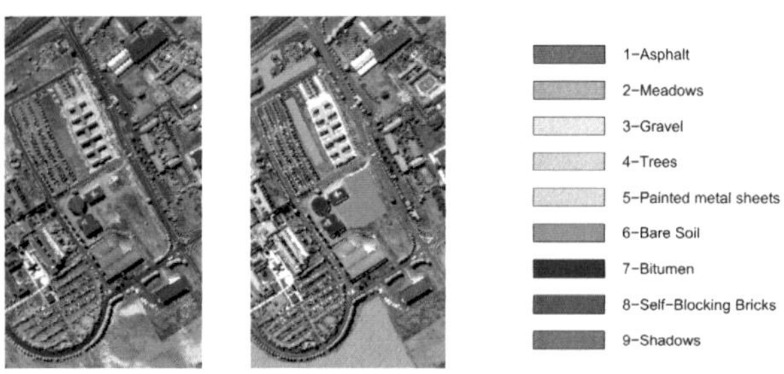

(a) (b) (c)

Figure 3. RGB composition and classification map for Pavia University scene scenario. (a) Pseudocolor image. (b) Ground truth map. (c) Class labels.

$0.4 \times 10^{-6} \sim 0.6 \times 10^{-6}$ meters, representing a vegetation-classification scenario. Among all pixels, two thirds are agriculture and one third is forest and other natural perennial vegetation. The image also contains two major dual lane highways, a rail line, some houses and other buildings with low density, and a few local roads. These objects are treated as background so that they will not be classified. When the image was captured, the main crops of soybean and corn are in their early stage of growing. We use the no-till, min-till, and clean-till denote the different growing status of the crops. The water absorption bands (104-108, 150-163, 220) are removed before experiment since they are useless bands for the classification. Hence, the exact 204 spectral bands are used. In the experiments, totally 10,249 (labeled) pixels are employed to form the data set X, in which about 10% are selected in the labeled set X_ℓ and the remains form the unlabeled set X_u in the test. The ground truth image contains 16 classes. Fig. 1 consists of three sub-images: (a) the pseudocolor image of Indian Pines; (b) the ground true map of the classifications; and (c) the color bar of 16 classes.

The second data set used in our experiments is the *AVIRIS Salinas* scenario, which was captured by the AVIRIS sensor over Salinas Valley, California, USA, with a spatial resolution of 3.7 meter per pixels. This data set has totally 224 bands of size 512×217. The 20 watered absorption bands (108-112, 154-167, 224) are excluded in experiment. Moreover, this scene was available only as at-sensor radiance data. It includes vegetables, bare soils, and vineyard fields. Totally 16 classes are included in this data set. Fig. 2 shows (a) the color composite of the Salinas image, (b) the ground truth map, and (c) the color bar of 16 classes.

The third data set *Pavia University* scene was captured by the Reflective Optics System Imaging Spectrometer (ROSIS-03) optical satellite sensor, which provides 115 bands HSI data during a flight campaign over the Pavia of the northern Italy. The size of Pavia University scene is 610×340 with 115 bands. In the experiment, 12 polluted bands are removed since they have no contribution for the classification. Likewise, some of the samples are treated as background since they are not in the classes we need to determine. The geometric resolution of the scenes is 1.3 meters per pixel, covering the wave ranges from 0.43 μm to 0.86 μm. The pixels of the HSI image cover 9 classes excluding the background. Fig. 3 shows the pixels used in the experiment in (a) pseudo-color image, (b) the ground truth map, and (c) the class bar of all classes, respectively.

2) Metrics on the data sets: It is a common sense that the performance of a classification scheme for HSI images is heavily relied on the quality of metric on HSI data [33]. Many experiences show that the standard Euclidean distance between the spectral vectors (pixels) of a HSI image may not represent the exact similarity. The main reason is that the spectral vectors in the HSI image are departed from their truthes by the noise. Note that a pixel in the spatial neighborhood of a pixel $\vec{x}$ is most likely in the same class as $\vec{x}$. Since the spatial positions of pixels are not impacted by noise, merging the spatial distance into the spectral one can correct the derivation caused by noise. In this paper, we adopt the following spectral-spatial affinity metric:

$$w_{ij}(\vec{x}_i, \vec{x}_j) = w_{ij}^r(\vec{x}_i, \vec{x}_j) + \mu w_{ij}^s(\vec{x}_i, \vec{x}_j), \tag{12}$$

where w_{ij}^r and w_{ij}^s are radian weight (or spectral distance) and spatial weight (a distance-type weight), respectively, and $0 \le \mu \le 1/2$ is the *weight balance parameter* that measures the strength of the spatial prior.(in the paper, we set $\mu = 1/2$).

The radian weight w_{ij}^r is defined by the following:

$$w_{ij}^r(\vec{x}_i, \vec{x}_j) = 1 - \exp\left(-\frac{\|\vec{x}_i - \vec{x}_j\|^2}{\rho_i \rho_j}\right) \tag{13}$$

where ρ_i denotes the local scaling parameter with respect to $\vec{x}_i$ defined by

$$\rho_i = \|\vec{x}_i - \vec{x}_i^s\|, \tag{14}$$

where $\|*\|$ denotes the l_2 norm, $\vec{x}_i^s$ is the s-th nearest neighbor of $\vec{x}_i$, and s is a preset positive odd integer (in our experiment, $s = 5$), called *spectral-weight parameter*. The distance in (13) is call a *diffusion distance*. It is more consistent of the manifold structure of data. More details on the spectral distance design are refer to [34].

The spatial weight in the paper is defined as follows: We first construct a spatial neighborhood system on HSI. Let $\vec{x}_i$ and $\vec{x}_j$ have the 2D index $i = (i_1, i_2)$ and $j = (j_1, j_2)$ in the HSI image X, respectively. Let $r > 0$ be the size of a spatial neighborhood system on X. (In this paper, we fix $r = 2$.) We define the spatial neighborhood of $\vec{x}_i$ by

$$\mathcal{N}_i = \{j;\ \max(|i_1 - j_1|, |i_2 - j_2|) \le r, \quad j \ne i\}$$

Aid with the neighborhood system, we formulate the spatial (distance-type) weight between two pixels $\vec{x}_i$ and $\vec{x}_j$ as the following:

$$w_{ij}^{s} = \begin{cases} -1, & \text{if } j \in \mathcal{N}_i \\ 0. & \text{otherwise} \end{cases} \quad (15)$$

Note that we use spatial weight -1 for the pixel in the neighborhood to shorten the spectral-spatial distance between neighbored pixels.

3) Optimization of parameters in the algorithm: The process for optimizing the free parameters in **ESSL1dLB** algorithm is very similar to that for the **SS1DME** one in [22]. For shortening the length of the paper, we only give a brief description of the process. The following parameters are tested and optimized: (a) regularization parameter λ in (4), (b) weight balance parameter μ in (12), (c) path selection parameter ϵ in (3), (d) the spinning number K in (9), and (e) the label boosting times N in (11).

The regularization parameter λ balances the fidelity term and smoothness one in the regularization algorithm. It can be learned in a standard way. The tuning process shows that it is insensitive in the range $[0.3, 5]$. We fix it to 0.5 in all experiments. The weight balance parameter μ impacts the definition of similarity between pixels. Its selection should not be dependent on an individual SSL method. The experiments show that it can be chosen in the range $[0.3, 0.7]$. The quantitative analysis for μ can bo found in Fig. 12-13 in [22].

The path selection parameter ϵ impacts the approximation quality of the greedy method presented in **Algorithm 1.** It is uniform for all SLL methods based on data 1-D representation, but possibly dependent on the data set. Fortunately, although differen data sets have different optimal ϵ, it is an insensitive parameter. The parameter tuning experiment results almost are similar when ϵ is selected in a very wide range, say in $[50, 500]$ (see Fig. 14 in [22]). Hence, the values used in [22] can also be applied to the proposed method in the paper. In our experiments, we choose $\epsilon = 100$.

To investigate how the spinning number K impacts the classification output. We use the HSI image "AVIRIS Indian Pines"in the parameter tuning experiments, where other parameters are fixed as following: $\lambda = 0.5, \mu = 0.5, \epsilon = 100$, and the boosting number $N = 5$; but the values of K are chosen in the integer range $[3, 10]$. The experiment is repeated 5 times for each value of K, and the average scores of OA, AA, and κ are reported. Their meanings are explained in the next subsection. The results are shown in Fig. 4 and Tab. I. We observe that the spinning parameter K in (9) is relatively insensitive too. In our experiments, we will set $K = 7$.

Finally, we test the effectiveness of the number of label boosting times N, which determines the enlargement of the labeled set. A greater number of the boosting times usually yields a larger size of the boosted set X_{ℓ}^{N} at the last step in the construction of the final classifier. Again, we use the HSI image "AVIRIS Indian Pines"as the train set, where other parameters are fixed as following: $\lambda = 0.5, \mu = 0.5, \epsilon = 100, K = 7$, but the number of label boosting times N is chosen in the integer range $[4, 10]$. The experiment is repeated 5 times for each value of N, and the average scores of OA, AA, and κ are reported in Fig. 5 and Tab. II. The experiment results indicate that the number of label boosting times can be chosen from the integer range $N \geq 4$.

All of the tests above indicate the stability and reliability of the **ESSL1dLB** algorithm: Although the algorithm is a multi-parametric one, all of parameters are relatively insensitive so that each of them can be chosen in a wide range without great deviation.

B. Measurements of performances of experiments

The maps of the thematic land covering, which are generated by different classification methods, are used in a variety of applications for data analysis. In this paper, each experiment contains five repeated tests at random using the same parameter settings. The quality of the output of the experiment is evaluated in the standard way commonly used in the classification of HSI images [35]. That is, the performance will be measured by *overall accuracy* (OA), *average accuracy* (AA), and *Kappa coefficient* (κ) of the five tests. As their names indicate, OA, one of the simplest and most popular accuracy, measures the accuracy of the classification weighted by the proportion of testing samples of each class in the total training set, AA measures the average accuracy of all classes, and Kappa measures the agreement of the tests, of which each classifies n samples into C mutually exclusive classes.

C. Experiment comparison settings

Similar to [22], three widely used hyperspectral data sets, the Indian Pines 1992 scene, the Salinas scene, and the University of Pavia scene are used in experiments to evaluate the classification performance. The pseudocolor images, the ground truth maps, and the class label bar of these HSI images are shown in Fig. 1–3, respectively. For comparison, we assess our proposed **ESSL1dLB** algorithm with several spectral-based and spectral-spatial extended methods, LDA [36], LDA with multi-logistic prior (LDA-MLL) [37], SVM [38], [39], Laplacian SVM (LapSVM) [40], SVM with component kernel (SVM_{CK}) [41], orthogonal matching pursuit (OMP) [42], simultaneous OMP (SOMP) [43], MLR*sub* [37], MLR*sub*-MLL [37], *semi*MLR-MLL [44], WT-EMP [45] for hyperspectral image classification. These methods are well established in the hypersepctral remotely sensing community. In the comparison, we also add SS1DME [22], which was an earlier work in the ensemble SSL framework developed by the author and his colleagues.

In all of the mentioned methods, the LapSVM and the *semi*MLR-MLL approaches are usually considered to be the reference benchmarks for semi-supervised learning in hyperspectral image classification, as summarized in [44], [46], [47].

For fair comparison, five experiments with different randomly sampled data are carried out for each data set to enhance the statistical significance. In the comparison, the experiment results of other methods are either directly obtained from the authors' papers, or obtained by running the code provided by the authors with the optimal parameters. In all of the following experiments, we use the unconstraint 1-D least-square regularization model, set $\lambda = \mu = 0.5, \epsilon = 100, N = 5$, and choose the spinning number $K = 7$ in the label boosting process and set $K = 10$ in the last spinning for producing the final classifier.

D. Experiment 1– AVIRIS Indian Pines Data Set

The first experiment is conducted on the AVIRIS Indian Pines data set, whose format and data structure information

TABLE I. THE RESULTS OF VARIOUS SPINNING NUMBERS USED IN THE EXPERIMENT FOR CLASSIFICATION OF AVIRIS INDIAN PINES. IN THE EXPERIMENT $\lambda = 0.5, \mu = 0.5, \epsilon = 100$ AND $N = 5$ ARE FIXED, BUT K ARE SELECTED IN THE INTEGER RANGE $[3, 10]$.

K	3	4	5	6	7	8	9	10
OA mean(%)	99.10	99.11	98.83	99.08	99.22	99.14	98.89	99.08
OA std	0.32	0.21	0.29	0.18	0.17	0.21	0.23	0.25
AA mean(%)	99.33	99.40	99.17	99.32	99.46	99.34	99.13	99.36
AA std	0.24	0.11	0.14	0.11	0.09	0.14	0.13	0.12
κ(%)	98.97	98.98	99.17	98.95	99.11	99.02	98.73	98.95
κ std	0.36	0.24	0.33	0.20	0.20	0.24	0.27	0.29

TABLE II. THE RESULTS OF VARIOUS SPINNING NUMBERS USED IN THE EXPERIMENT FOR CLASSIFICATION OF AVIRIS INDIAN PINES. IN THE EXPERIMENT, $\lambda = 0.5, \mu = 0.5, \epsilon = 100$, AND $K = 7$ ARE FIXED, BUT N ARE CHOSEN FROM THE INTEGER RANGE $[4, 10]$.

N	4	5	6	7	8	9	10
OA mean(%)	99.04	99.20	99.14	99.02	99.23	98.94	99.05
OA std	0.35	0.20	0.24	0.25	0.21	0.23	0.30
AA mean(%)	99.14	99.43	99.36	99.26	99.46	99.27	99.35
AA std	0.38	0.11	0.12	0.11	0.12	0.22	0.21
κ(%)	98.89	99.10	98.95	98.89	99.11	98.93	98.89
κ std	0.51	0.20	0.33	0.30	0.20	0.22	0.31

TABLE III. NUMBER OF TRAINING AND TEST SAMPLES FOR THREE HSIs.

ID	Indian Pines			Salinas			University of Pavia		
	Class Name	Train	Test	Class Name	Train	Test	Class Name	Train	Test
1	Alfalfa	20	26	Brocoli Green Weeds 1	144	1865	Asphalt	553	6078
2	Corn-notill	134	1294	Brocoli Green Weeds 2	200	3526	Meadows	1161	17488
3	Corn-mintill	75	755	Fallow	151	1825	Gravel	304	1795
4	Corn	44	193	Fallow Rough Plow	135	1259	Trees	328	2736
5	Grass-pasture	49	434	Fallow Smooth	159	2519	Painted metal sheets	261	1084
6	Grass-trees	56	674	Stubble	209	3750	Bare Soil	440	4589
7	Grass-pasture-mowed	17	11	Celery	192	3387	Bitumen	263	1067
8	Hay-windrowed	59	419	Grapes Untrained	404	10867	Self-Blocking Bricks	379	3303
9	Oats	11	9	Soil Vinyard Develop	282	5921	Shadows	232	715
10	Soybean-notill	95	877	Corn Senesced Green Weeds	179	3099			
11	Soybean-mintill	209	2246	Lettuce-Romaine-4wk	121	947			
12	Soybean-clean	65	528	Lettuce-Romaine-5wk	150	1777			
13	Wheat	29	176	Lettuce-Romaine-6wk	118	798			
14	Woods	104	1161	Lettuce-Romaine-7wk	129	941			
15	Buildings-Grass-Trees-Drives	37	349	Vinyard Untrained	289	6979			
16	Stone-Steel-Towers	20	73	Vinyard Vertical Trellis	138	1669			
	Total	1024	9225	Total	3000	51129	Total	3921	38855

TABLE IV. CLASSIFICATION ACCURACIES OBTAINED BY DIFFERENT METHODS FOR AVIRIS INDIAN PINE SCENE (%).

Class Name	LDA	LDA-MLL	SVM	LapSVM	SVM_{CK}	OMP	SOMP	MLR*sub*	MLR*sub*-MLL	*semi*MLR-MLL	WT-EMP	SS1DME	**ESSL1dLB**
Alfalfa	**100.00**	96.43	89.29	82.62	**100.00**	45.95	81.25	85.19	81.48	**100.00**	92.52	**100.00**	**100.00**
Corn-notill	61.21	92.61	69.92	78.70	92.07	56.13	92.09	65.09	89.15	86.20	90.30	99.30	**99.34**
Corn-mintill	56.80	77.97	57.78	66.69	97.30	56.33	89.20	47.56	**99.87**	76.05	93.15	98.68	99.12
Corn	71.72	**100.00**	71.43	76.91	**100.00**	44.74	96.65	72.78	99.40	82.13	79.76	99.48	98.92
Grass-pasture	91.76	94.85	90.39	91.54	97.88	84.46	92.65	87.85	93.69	91.41	94.79	96.31	**98.22**
Grass-trees	94.95	98.33	94.52	97.49	98.80	89.73	98.67	94.81	97.47	98.35	98.04	**100.00**	**100.00**
Grass-pasture-mowed	92.31	**100.00**	85.71	95.83	**100.00**	63.64	75.00	61.54	**100.00**	**100.00**	94.46	90.91	**100.00**
Hay-windrowed	96.80	**100.00**	96.98	98.56	98.33	95.81	**100.00**	99.29	**100.00**	99.53	96.83	**100.00**	**100.00**
Oats	**100.00**	**100.00**	88.89	98.89	**100.00**	50.00	44.44	77.78	**100.00**	**100.00**	97.78	**100.00**	**100.00**
Soybean-notill	59.07	82.08	75.17	77.61	91.72	69.15	87.53	65.32	95.96	83.72	87.68	99.54	98.16
Soybean-mintill	65.21	98.63	84.57	83.79	95.67	75.15	97.16	69.04	96.87	92.24	92.58	99.33	**99.46**
Soybean-clean	68.30	74.63	74.95	82.18	87.29	50.00	87.09	73.85	97.23	91.89	88.73	**98.30**	98.08
Wheat	98.87	99.44	97.16	99.45	99.44	95.12	**100.00**	99.31	100.00	99.42	98.25	**100.00**	**100.00**
Woods	91.47	92.47	96.62	94.70	99.22	91.50	99.74	93.05	98.03	96.43	98.01	**99.91**	99.72
Buildings-Grass-Trees-Drives	62.28	**100.00**	54.94	68.75	95.93	41.42	99.71	52.08	97.42	89.41	89.92	99.43	99.70
Stone-Steel-Towers	95.77	85.33	93.65	89.33	**100.00**	90.54	98.61	83.87	**100.00**	84.29	98.61	**100.00**	**100**
OA (mean)	71.54	91.98	80.74	84.11	94.94	71.38	94.42	73.64	94.95	89.32	92.80	99.05	**99.13**
OA (std)	0.25	0.15	0.62	0.37	0.66	0.32	0.18	0.37	0.50	0.95	0.19	0.13	0.24
AA (mean)	79.53	87.63	83.83	86.44	96.21	67.13	91.65	75.42	95.09	86.48	93.21	98.72	**99.36**
AA (std)	1.10	0.33	0.38	0.65	0.53	1.29	2.09	2.02	1.97	3.22	0.78	0.95	0.17
κ (mean)	67.62	90.76	78.03	81.81	94.22	67.32	93.62	69.78	94.18	93.77	91.78	98.92	**99.00**
κ (std)	0.38	0.17	0.70	0.43	0.75	0.38	0.20	0.42	0.58	2.76	0.21	0.15	0.28

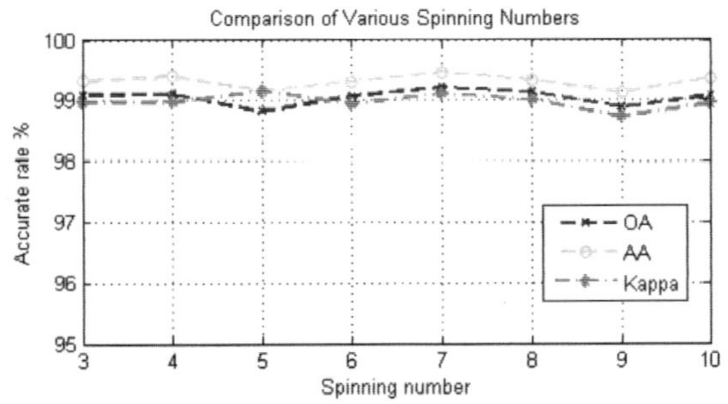

Figure 4. Sensitivity analysis of the spinning number K.

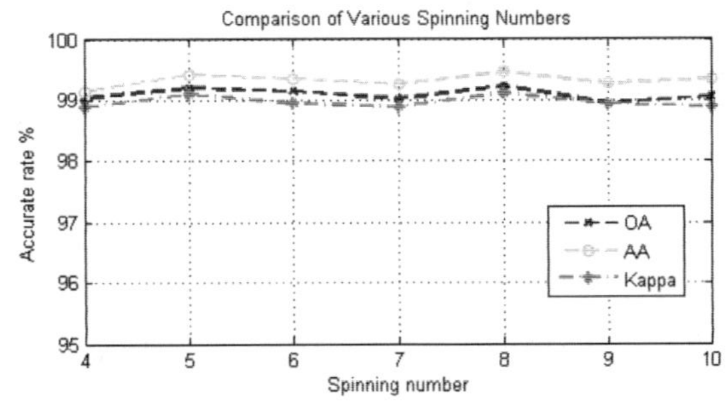

Figure 5. Sensitivity analysis of the label boosting times N.

are given in Subsection III-A. The number of training samples and test samples are given in Tab. III. Figure 6 shows the classification pseudo-color maps that are obtained by different methods along with the corresponding OA score. Among all of the methods, LDA-MLL, SVM_{CK}, SOMP, MLR*sub*MLL, *semi*MLR-MLL, WT-EMP, SS1DME, and **ESSL1dLB** yield high accuracy. Comparing with the all other methods method, the proposed **ESSL1dLB** method wins the best performance in all of OA, AA, and Kappa coefficient. We note that the classification accuracies of **ESSL1dLB** exceeds 98% for all of 16 classes.

Remark. In the Fig. 6, the OA score is slightly different from that in Tab. III. Because the OA score in Tab. III is the average of 5 experiments, while Fig. 6 is for one of the experiments selected at random. The same remark is also valid for the following two experiments.

E. Experiment 2—AVIRIS Salinas Data Set

The second experiment was performed on the AVIRIS Salinas hyperspectral image. The number of training and testing samples for the image are given in Tab. III, where the training set contains about 5.25% of all the labeled samples, chosen at random. Because the image size is too large to be treated on a Laptop, we divide the data set into 8 blocks in the experiment. A visual perspective of these methods are presented in Fig. 7. The quantitative results are presented in Tab. V. Similar to the AVIRIS Indian Pines image, it can be seen that the proposed **ESSL1dLB** beats the classification performances of other methods in terms of OA, AA and Kappa coefficient.

F. Experiment 3—ROSIS University of Pavia Data Set

The third experiment is conducted on the data set of *ROSIS University of Pavia scene*. In this experiment, we use the randomly chosen 3,921 labeled samples for training, which count about 8.4% of all labeled pixels, while the remains are used for testing. Detailed numbers for training and testing can be found in Tab. III. Because the data set has $512 \times 217 = 111104$ pixels, this size is too large to be treated on a Laptop too. Hence, we divide it into 8 disjoint blocks, then apply the proposed algorithm on each block. The classification maps obtained by different methods and the associated OA scores are presented in Fig. 8. Meanwhile, the quantitative results (means and standard deviations over the experiments on randomly selected five different training sets) are listed in Tab. VI. It can be observed that the proposed **ESS1DLB** algorithm again performs better than other methods significantly in both of quantitative results and visual qualities. For example, our algorithm obtains more than 99% accuracy for all classes. Particularly, for the *Gravel, Trees, Self-Blocking Bricks* classes, the classification accuracies obtained by most methods are not very satisfactory, but our method still produces a super result.

IV. EXPERIMENTS ON HANDWRITTEN DIGITS

In this section, we evaluate our ensemble SSL method in the experiments on handwritten digits. We use two benchmark databases of handwritten digits, MNIST [48] and USPS [49] in the experiments to present the validity and effectiveness of the proposed method. In the literature of machine learning, MNIST is often used to test the error rate of classifiers obtained by supervised learning. The best result for the error rate up to 2012 was 0.23%, reported in [50] by using the convolutional

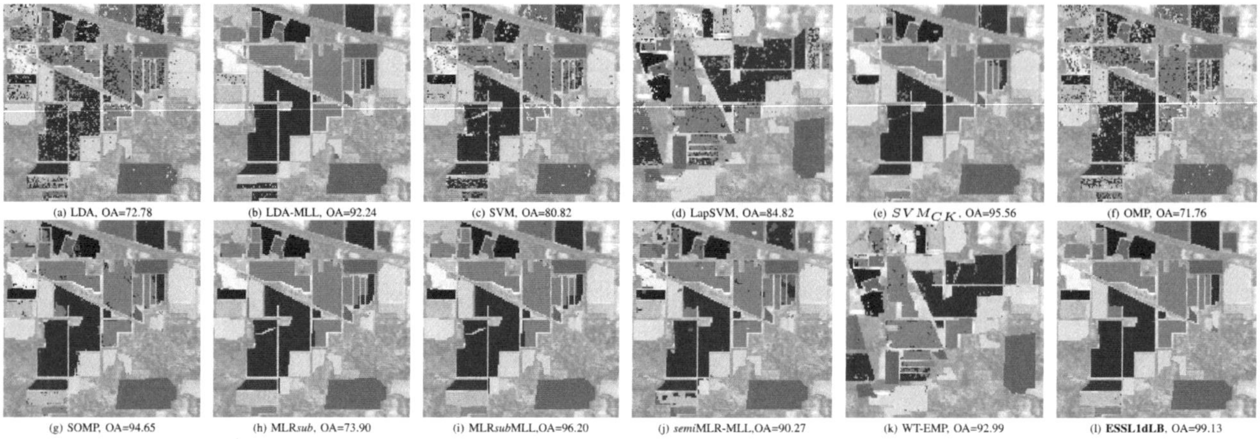

(a) LDA, OA=72.78 (b) LDA-MLL, OA=92.24 (c) SVM, OA=80.82 (d) LapSVM, OA=84.82 (e) SVM_{CK}, OA=95.56 (f) OMP, OA=71.76

(g) SOMP, OA=94.65 (h) MLR*sub*, OA=73.90 (i) MLR*sub*MLL,OA=96.20 (j) *semi*MLR-MLL,OA=90.27 (k) WT-EMP, OA=92.99 (l) **ESSL1dLB**, OA=99.13

Figure 6. Classification pseudocolor map obtained by different methods for the AVIRIS Indian Pines data set, where the value of OA is given in percent.

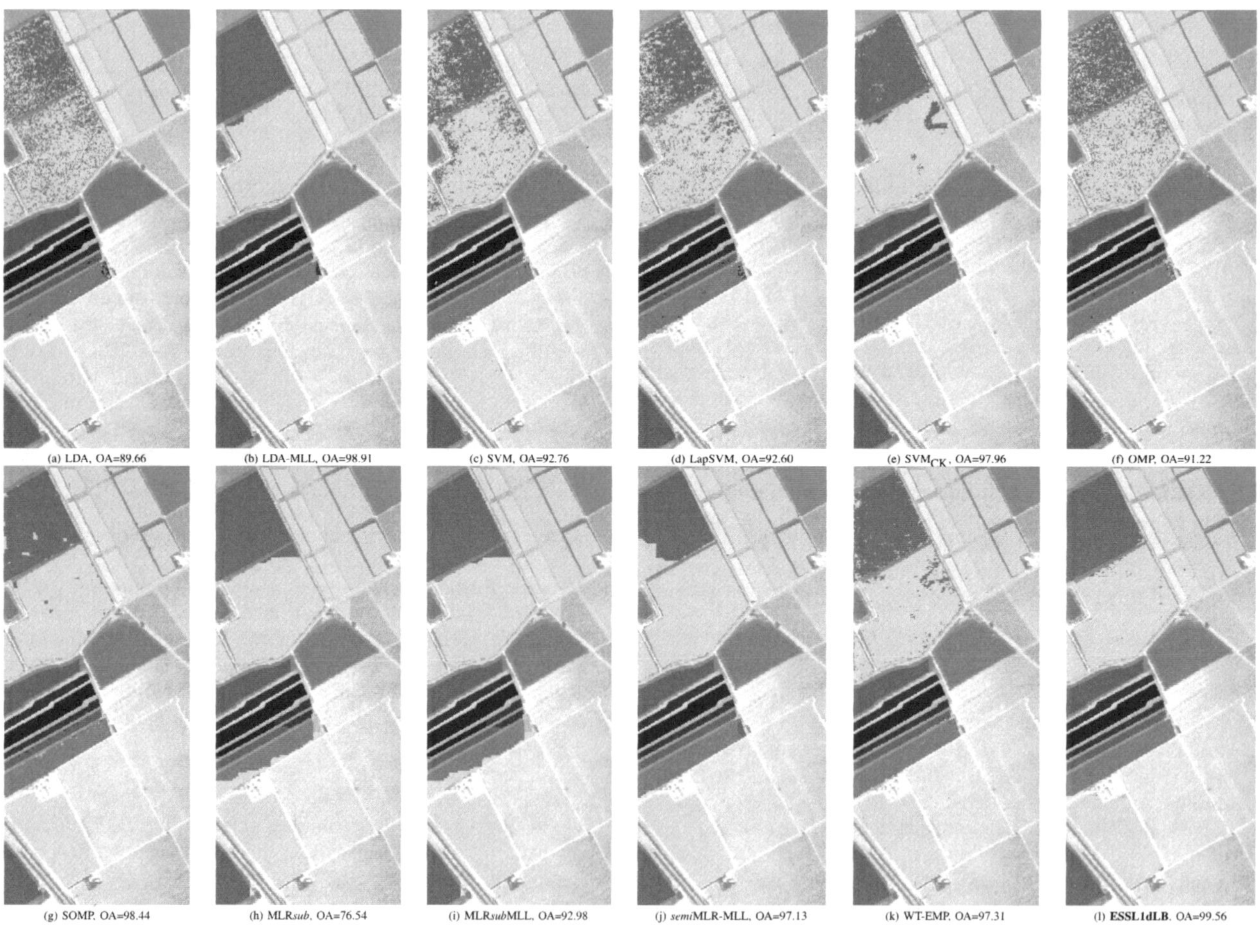

(a) LDA, OA=89.66 (b) LDA-MLL, OA=98.91 (c) SVM, OA=92.76 (d) LapSVM, OA=92.60 (e) SVM_{CK}, OA=97.96 (f) OMP, OA=91.22

(g) SOMP, OA=98.44 (h) MLR*sub*, OA=76.54 (i) MLR*sub*MLL, OA=92.98 (j) *semi*MLR-MLL, OA=97.13 (k) WT-EMP, OA=97.31 (l) **ESSL1dLB**, OA=99.56

Figure 7. Classification pseudocolor map obtained by different methods for the AVIRIS Salinas hyperspectral image, where the value of OA is given in percent.

TABLE V. CLASSIFICATION ACCURACIES OBTAINED BY DIFFERENT METHODS FOR AVIRIS SALINAS SCENE (%).

Class Name	LDA	LDA-MLL	SVM	LapSVM	SVM_{CK}	OMP	SOMP	MLR*sub*	MLR*sub*-MLL	*semi*MLR-MLL	WT-EMP	SSIDME	**ESSL1dLB**
Brocoli Green Weeds 1	99.78	**100.00**	99.57	99.84	99.84	99.13	**100.00**	99.78	**100.00**	**100.00**	99.59	99.95	**100.00**
Brocoli Green Weeds 2	99.94	**100.00**	99.83	99.76	**100.00**	99.43	**100.00**	88.44	**100.00**	**100.00**	99.79	99.89	99.98
Fallow	99.56	**100.00**	99.73	99.62	98.42	99.87	**100.00**	61.77	90.27	**100.00**	99.80	99.67	**100.00**
Fallow Rough Plow	99.60	99.44	99.44	99.41	99.92	99.64	97.94	10.85	**100.00**	99.20	99.43	99.60	99.60
Fallow Smooth	98.44	99.12	99.52	99.09	99.09	97.62	95.49	99.88	**100.00**	99.17	98.70	99.40	99.38
Stubble	99.89	99.89	99.89	99.89	99.97	99.94	99.89	99.66	99.97	**100.00**	99.85	99.97	99.92
Celery	99.62	99.91	99.74	99.58	99.82	99.76	98.91	99.85	99.94	**99.97**	99.57	99.88	99.91
Grapes Untrained	75.11	97.50	86.67	85.24	97.68	80.83	98.52	59.04	95.75	99.00	94.29	**99.05**	98.97
Soil Vinyard Develop	99.92	**100.00**	99.43	99.91	99.81	99.76	**100.00**	99.35	100.00	99.98	99.57	99.58	99.66
Corn Senesced Green Weeds	96.00	95.23	96.76	96.64	97.09	96.38	97.35	48.53	68.91	95.61	97.89	**98.84**	99.07
Lettuce-Romaine-4wk	99.26	94.60	99.25	99.00	99.89	99.77	99.37	93.87	99.43	99.68	98.89	**100.00**	99.82
Lettuce-Romaine-5wk	99.38	**100.00**	99.83	**100.00**	**100.00**	**100.00**	96.68	88.39	99.77	**100.00**	**100.00**	**100.00**	**100.00**
Lettuce-Romaine-6wk	99.24	99.37	98.73	98.94	99.87	98.23	95.11	99.04	39.64	99.49	99.72	**100.00**	99.81
Lettuce-Romaine-7wk	96.60	98.94	98.93	97.73	**99.79**	95.68	94.80	73.73	71.46	97.89	98.24	98.72	99.39
Vinyard Untrained	66.85	99.56	71.05	73.27	54.30	69.50	96.88	56.05	99.35	83.33	93.21	99.47	**99.54**
Vinyard Vertical Trellis	99.28	99.58	98.92	99.15	99.04	98.41	99.64	98.52	98.27	**100.00**	99.10	99.94	**100.00**
OA (mean)	89.59	97.48	92.67	92.78	97.24	90.96	97.93	76.37	91.79	96.55	97.44	99.45	**99.55**
OA (std)	0.26	0.88	0.09	0.06	0.61	0.18	0.47	0.09	1.27	0.38	0.26	0.04	0.05
AA (mean)	95.57	98.46	96.60	96.71	98.75	95.68	97.69	82.33	86.85	91.83	98.60	99.64	**99.69**
AA (std)	0.16	0.35	0.10	0.12	0.24	0.10	0.74	2.06	1.09	0.17	0.13	0.02	0.05
κ (mean)	87.95	97.18	91.81	91.93	96.92	89.93	97.68	73.75	90.83	96.36	97.15	99.39	**99.50**
κ (std)	0.30	0.99	0.10	0.06	0.68	0.20	0.53	0.09	1.40	0.47	0.29	0.04	0.05

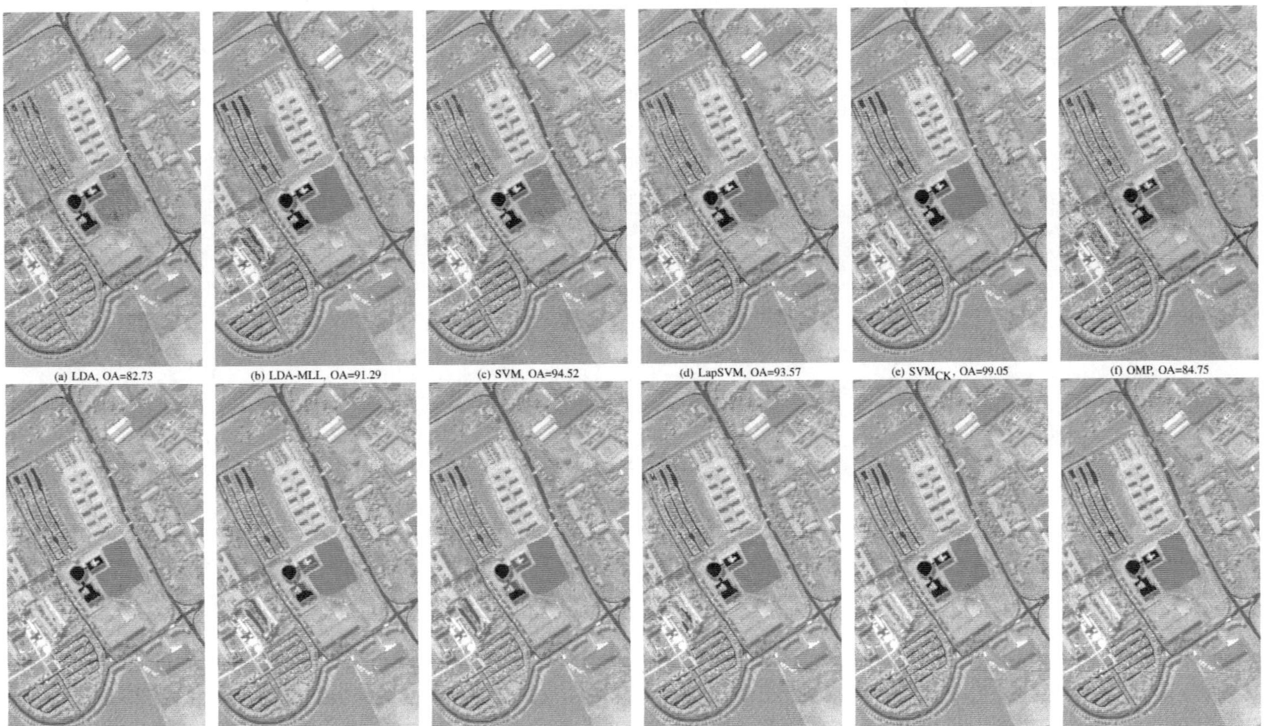

(a) LDA, OA=82.73 (b) LDA-MLL, OA=91.29 (c) SVM, OA=94.52 (d) LapSVM, OA=93.57 (e) SVM_{CK}, OA=99.05 (f) OMP, OA=84.75

(g) SOMP, OA=96.11 (h) MLR*sub*, OA=62.60 (i) MLR*sub*MLL, OA=89.31 (j) *semi*MLR-MLL, OA=96.49 (k) WT-EMPs, OA=98.72 (l) **ESSL1dLB**, OA=99.82

Figure 8. Classification pseudocolor map obtained by different methods for University of Pavia scene data set, where the value of OA is given in percent.

TABLE VI. CLASSIFICATION ACCURACIES OBTAINED BY DIFFERENT METHODS FOR ROSIS UNIVERSITY OF PAVIA SCENE(%).

Class Name	LDA	LDA-MLL	SVM	LapSVM	SVM_{CK}	OMP	SOMP	MLR*sub*	MLR*sub*-MLL	*semi*MLR-MLL	WT-EMP	SS1DME	**ESSL1dLB**
Asphalt	79.91	87.58	92.40	89.14	98.51	79.74	86.12	98.43	**99.87**	96.04	98.39	99.57	99.84
Meadows	90.48	92.53	97.83	97.44	**99.99**	95.64	99.44	98.78	98.96	98.65	99.49	99.98	**99.99**
Gravel	69.54	65.67	87.44	79.28	95.24	59.14	98.16	63.46	64.60	85.32	96.71	**99.94**	**99.94**
Trees	86.95	77.62	96.03	95.79	98.24	86.17	94.96	69.99	76.99	96.58	98.02	99.12	**99.48**
Painted metal sheets	99.91	99.82	99.72	99.30	**100.00**	99.54	**100.00**	99.89	**100.00**	99.53	99.86	**100.00**	**100.00**
Bare Soil	64.03	**100.00**	91.00	91.09	99.50	59.43	95.32	**100.00**	99.96	95.89	97.78	99.76	**100.00**
Bitumen	81.54	99.35	90.20	90.49	99.63	78.20	99.72	36.65	59.89	95.78	97.45	**100.00**	99.90
Self-Blocking Bricks	67.97	98.73	86.94	87.69	96.49	80.62	96.11	2.46	26.01	91.47	96.57	99.18	**99.81**
Shadows	99.29	93.90	99.86	99.63	**100.00**	96.17	92.72	98.05	99.80	99.30	99.95	99.86	99.69
OA (mean)	81.30	90.79	94.32	93.51	97.96	84.60	95.97	62.39	88.90	95.98	98.60	99.74	**99.91**
OA (std)	0.11	0.30	0.13	0.04	1.44	0.16	0.11	0.16	0.38	0.57	0.18	0.02	0.03
AA (mean)	83.02	90.15	93.59	92.21	96.98	81.80	95.89	75.48	82.84	83.90	98.25	99.70	**99.85**
AA (std)	0.22	0.49	0.11	0.21	2.53	0.20	0.11	0.87	3.45	0.41	0.30	0.02	0.04
κ (mean)	74.51	87.73	92.37	91.26	97.26	79.31	94.57	52.66	84.60	94.57	98.11	99.65	**99.87**
κ (std)	0.13	0.39	0.17	0.06	1.92	0.21	0.14	0.24	0.55	0.77	0.24	0.03	0.04

TABLE VII. ERROR RATE OF THE PROPOSED ESSL1DLB FOR 50 RANDOMLY SELECTED SUBSETS FROM MNIST WITH $|X| = 1000$.

$\|X_0\|$	10	20	30	40	50	60	70	80	90	100
Mean%	7.84	7.80	4.58	3.06	2.91	1.91	1.93	1.97	1.23	1.27
Min%	7.60	3.10	3.80	1.90	2.90	1.90	1.90	1.90	1.20	1.20
Max%	19.4	7.90	4.60	3.10	3.50	2.50	2.60	3.90	2.80	3.30
STD	1.65	0.67	0.11	0.19	0.08	0.08	0.14	0.35	0.22	0.37

TABLE VIII. ERROR RATE OF THE PROPOSED ESSL1DLB FOR 50 RANDOMLY SELECTED SUBSETS FROM USPS WITH $|X| = 1500$.

$\|X_0\|$	10	20	30	40	50	60	70	80	90	100
Mean%	3.07	1.933	1.55	1.49	1.28	1.38	1.37	1.39	1.34	1.20
Min%	3.00	1.27	1.53	1.07	1.27	1.20	1.07	1.33	0.80	1.20
Max%	3.73	2.87	1.67	1.53	1.40	1.40	1.40	1.40	1.40	1.20
STD	0.22	0.76	0.04	0.14	0.04	0.06	0.10	0.02	0.18	0.00

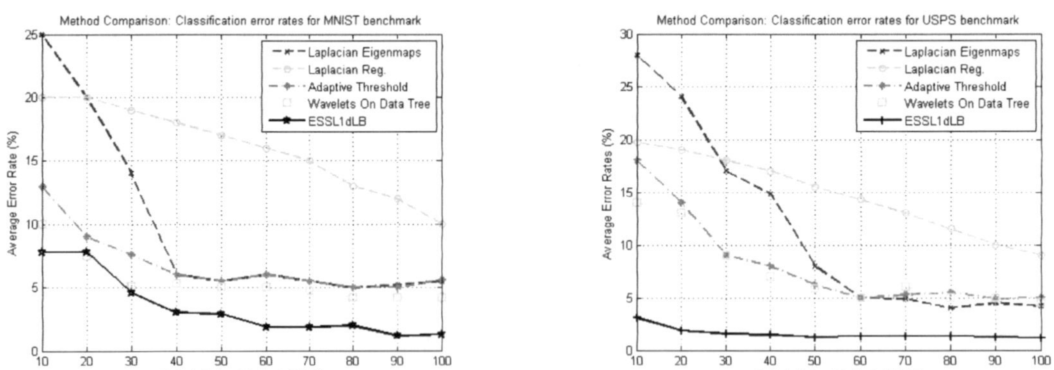

Figure 9. Result comparison with different SSL models.

neural network technique. In 2013, the authors of [51] claimed to achieve 0.21% error rate using **DropConnect** method, which is based on regularization of neural networks. Because in SSL no large training set is available for producing classifiers, the error rates obtained by SSL methods usually are much higher than the claimed error rates obtained by supervised learning. Besides, the error rates of SSL are strongly dependent the size of the initial label set X_ℓ. In general, the smaller the size of X_ℓ, the higher the error rate. Hence, it is unfair to compare the error rates obtained by SSL methods to the above recorded ones.

The parameters are tuned in the similar way as we have done above. Once again, the tuning experiments show the insensitivity of the parameters. Since the tuning process is very similar to that in Subsection III-A3, we omit the details here. In all of our experiments, the balance parameter in the least-square regularization is set to $\lambda = 0.5$. The spin number $K = 3$ is used for constructing 1DEL algorithm, while $K = 20$ is chosen for building the final classifier. The boosting-stop parameter p is set to 0.7, which yields 6 times of label boosting in most cases.

For comparison, we choose the same data setting as in [12]: In MINST, for each of the digits $\{3, 4, 5, 7, 8\}$, 200 samples are selected at random so that the cardinality of the data set is $|X| = 1000$, where the digit 8 is assigned to Class A, and others belong to Class B. In USPS, for each of the digits $0-9$, 150 samples are selected at random so that $|X| = 1500$, where the digits 2 and 5 are assigned to Class A, and others belong to Class B. In all experiments, the initial labeled set X_0 is preset to 10 various sizes of $10, 20, \cdots, 100$, respectively, and the labeled digits are distributed evenly on each chosen digit.

Note that a vector $\vec{x} \in X$ is originally represented by a $c \times c$ matrix $[x_{i,j}]_{i,j=1}^{c}$, where $c = 20$ for MNIST and $c = 16$ for USPS. To reduce the shift-variance, we define the *1-shift distance* between two digit images [1]:

$$d(\vec{x}, \vec{y}) = \min_{\substack{|i'-i|\leq 1 \\ |j'-j|\leq 1}} \sqrt{\sum_{i=2}^{c-1}\sum_{j=2}^{c-1} (x_{i,j} - y_{i',j'})^2}.$$

In the first experiment, we run our **ESSL1dLB** algorithm on 50 subsets, of which each has with 1000 members, randomly chosen from the MNIST database, where the regularization parameter λ in (4) is chosen to be 0.5. The experiment results are shown in Table VII, where the first row is the number of samples in X_ℓ, and the $2^{nd}-5^{th}$ rows are the mean, minimum, maximum, and standard deviation of the classification error rates of the 50 tests, respectively.

In the second experiment, we run our **ESSL1dLB** algorithm for USPS in a similar way: 50 subsets, of which each has 1500 members, are randomly chosen from USPS database. The test results are shown in Tab. VIII.

Tab. VII and Tab. VIII show that the standard deviations of the error rates are quite small. This indicates the high stability of the proposed algorithm.

In Fig. 9, we give the comparison of the average error rates (of 50 tests) of our 1-D based ensemble method **ESSL1dLB** to Laplacian Eigenmaps (Belkin & Niyogi, 2003 [8]), Laplacian Regularization (Zhu et al., 2003 [13]), Laplacian Regularization with Adaptive Threshold (Zhou and Belkin, 2011 [52]), and Haar-Like Multiscale Wavelets on Data Trees (Gavish et al., 2011 [12]) on the subsets randomly chosen from MNIST and USPS databases, respectively.

The results show that our method achieves competitive results comparing to others.

V. Conclusion

We propose a new ensemble SSL method (**ESSL1dLB**) based on data 1-D representations and label boosting, which enables us to construct ensemble classifiers assembled from several weak-classifiers for the same data set using classical 1-D regularization technique. Furthermore, a label boosting technique is applied for robustly enlarging the labeled set to a certain size so that the final classifier is built based on the boosted labeled set. The experiments show that the performance of the proposed method is superior to many popular SSL methods. The method also exhibits a clear advantage for learning the classifier when only a small labeled set is given. Because the method is independent of the data dimensionality, it can be applied to various types of data. Since the algorithm in the proposed method only employs 1-D regularization technique, avoiding the complicate kernel trick, they are simple and stable. The experiments also indicate that the parameters in the algorithm is relatively insensitive that makes the algorithm more controllable and reliable. The algorithm has been tested on various types of data sets, such as handwritten digits and hyperspectral images. The experimental results are very promising, showing that our method is superior to other existent methods. It can be expected that the created 1-D framework in this paper will be applied to the development of more machine learning methods for different purposes. In the algorithm, the most time-consuming step is data (shortest path) sorting. In the future work, we will study how to accelerate the sorting algorithm in 1-D embedding and consider to integrate the data-driven wavelets with the proposed method.

Acknowledgment

In this work, the first author was supported by SHSU-2015 ERG Grant-250711. The second and third authors were supported by the Research Grants of MYRG2015-00049-FST, MYRG2015-00050-FST, RDG009/FST-TYY/2012, 008-2014-AMJ from Macau; and the National Natural Science Foundation of China 61672114.

The authors would like to thank the anonymous reviewers for their highly insights and helpful suggestions.

References

[1] J. Wang, "Semi-supervised learning in the framework of data multiple 1-d representation," IMMM 2016, The Sixth International Conference on Advances in Information Mining and Management, 2016, pp. 1–5.

[2] R. K. Eichelberger and V. S. Sheng, "Does one-against-all or one-against-one improve the performance of multiclass classifications?" in Proceedings of the Twenty-Seventh AAAI Conference on Artificial Intelligence, Bellevue, Wash, USA, 2013.

[3] C. Yu, L. Jinxu, Z. Fudong, B. Ran, and L. Xia, "Comparative study on face recognition based on SVM of one-against-one and one-against-rest methods," in Future Generation Communication and Networking (FGCN), 2014 8th International Conference on, Dec 2014, pp. 104–107.

[4] R. Bellman, Adaptive Control Processes: A Guided Tour. Princeton: Princeton University Press, 1961.

[5] J. Wang, Geometric Structure of High-Dimensional Data and Dimensionality Reduction. Higher Education Press and Springer, 2012.

[6] O. Chapelle, B. Schölkopf, and A. Zien, Semi-supervised learning. MIT press Cambridge, 2006.

[7] X. Zhu, "Semi-supervised learning literature survey," University of Wisconsin-Madison, Computer Sciences TR-1530, July 2008.

[8] M. Belkin and P. Niyogi, "Using manifold structure for partially labeled classification," Advances in Neural Information Processing Systems, vol. 15, 2003, pp. 929–936.

[9] T. Joachims, "Transductive learning via spectral graph partitioning," in Proceedings of ICML-03, 20th International Conference on Machine Learning, 2003, pp. 290–297.

[10] V. Vapnik, Statistical Learning Theory. Wiley-Interscience, New York, 1998.

[11] R. Coifman and M. Gavish, "Harmonic analysis of digital data bases," Applied and Numerical Harmonic Analysis (Special issue on Wavelets and Multiscale Analysis), 2011, pp. 161–197.

[12] M. Gavish, B. Nadler, and R. R. Coifman, "Multiscale wavelets on trees, graphs and high dimensional data: Theory and applications to semi supervised learning," in Proceedings of the 27th International Conference on machine Learning, 2010.

[13] X. Zhu, Z. Ghahramani, and J. Lafferty, "Semi-supervised learning using Gaussian fields and harmonic functions," in Proceedings of the 20th International Conference on Machine Learning, 2003.

[14] L. Rokach, "Ensemble-based classifiers," Artif. Intell. Rev., vol. 33, 2010, pp. 1–39.

[15] M. Wozniak, M. Grana, and E. Corchado, "A survey of multiple classifier systems as hybrid systems," Information Fusion, vol. 16, 2014, pp. 3–17.

[16] Z.-H. Zhou, J. Wu, and W. Tang, "Ensembling neural networks: Many could be better than all," Artificial Intelligence, vol. 137, 2002, pp. 239–263.

[17] Breiman, "Bagging predictors," Machine Learning, vol. 24, no. 2, 1996, pp. 123–140.

[18] Y. Freund and R. E. Schapire, "A short introduction to boosting," Journal of Japanese Society for Artificial Intelligence, vol. 14, no. 5, 1999, pp. 771–780.

[19] D. Z. Li, W. Wang, and F. Ismail, "A selective boosting technique for pattern classification," Neurocomputing, vol. 156, 2015, pp. 186–192.

[20] J. Wang, "Semi-supervised learning using multiple one-dimensional embedding based adaptive interpolation," International Journal of Wavelets, Multiresolution and Information Processing (Special Issue on Semi-Supervised Learning and Data Processing in the Framework of Data Multiple One-Dimensional Representation), vol. 14, no. 2, February 2016, pp. 1 640 002: 1–11.

[21] ——, "Semi-supervised learning using ensembles of multiple 1d-embedding-based label boosting," International Journal of Wavelets, Multiresolution and Information Processing (Special Issue on Semi-Supervised Learning and Data Processing in the Framework of Data Multiple One-Dimensional Representation), vol. 14, no. 2, 2016, pp. 164 001: 1–33.

[22] H. Luo, Y. Y. Tang, Y. Wang, J. Wang, C. Li, and T. Hu, "Hyperspectral image classification based on spectral-spatial 1-dimensional manifold," submitted to IEEE Transaction of Geoscience and Remote Sensing.

[23] Y. Wang, Y. Y. Tang, L. Li, and J. Wang, "Face recognition via collaborative representation based multiple one-dimensional embedding," International Journal of Wavelets, Multiresolution and Information Processing (Special Issue on Semi-Supervised Learning and Data Processing in the Framework of Data Multiple One-Dimensional Representation), vol. 14, no. 2, 2016, pp. 1 640 003: 1–15.

[24] I. Ram, M. Elad, and I. Cohen, "Image processing using smooth ordering of its patches," IEEE Trans. on Image Processing, vol. 22, no. 7, July 2013, pp. 2764–2774.

[25] ——, "Image denoising using nl-means via smooth patch ordering," in Acoustics, Speech and Signal Processing (ICASSP), 2013 IEEE International Conference on, May 2013, pp. 1350–1354.

[26] T. Hastie and R. Tibshirani, "Classification by pairwise coupling," The Annals of Statistics, vol. 26, 1998, pp. 451–471.

[27] E. Allwein, R. Schapire, and Y. Singer, "Reducing multiclass to binary: A unifying approach for margin classifiers," Journal of Machine Learning Research, vol. 1, 2000, pp. 113–141.

[28] T. Hamamura, H. Mizutani, and B. Irie, "A multiclass classification method based on multiple pairwise classifiers," in International Conference on Document Analysis and Recognition, August 3-6 2003, pp. 809–813.

[29] D. Lu and Q. Weng, "A survey of image classification methods and techniques for improving classification performance," Int. J. Remote Sens., vol. 28, no. 5, 2007, pp. 823–870.

[30] J. Li, X. Huang, P. Gamba, J. Bioucas-Dias, L. Zhang, J. Atli Benediktsson, and A. Plaza, "Multiple feature learning for hyperspectral image classification," IEEE Trans. Geosci. Remote Sens., vol. 53, no. 3, March 2015, pp. 1592–1606.

[31] Z. Ye, H. Li, Y. Song, J. Wang, and Jon, "A novel semi-supervised learning framework for hyperspectral image classification," International Journal of Wavelets, Multiresolution, vol. 14, no. 2, February 2016, pp. 164 005–1–17.

[32] Aviras databases. Acceptable on November 17, 2016. [Online]. Available: https://engineering.purdue.edu/ biehl/MultiSpec/

[33] Y. Gu and K. Feng, "Optimized laplacian svm with distance metric learning for hyperspectral image classification," IEEE J. Sel. Topics Appl. Earth Observ., vol. 6, no. 3, June 2013, pp. 1109–1117.

[34] M. Sugiyama, "Dimensionality reduction of multimodal labeled data by local fisher discriminant analysis," J. Mach. Learn. Res., vol. 8, May 2007, pp. 1027–1061.

[35] C. Liu, P. Frazier, and L. Kumar, "Comparative assessment of the measures of thematic classification accuracy," Remote Sens. Environ., vol. 107, no. 4, 2007, pp. 606 – 616.

[36] T. Bandos, L. Bruzzone, and G. Camps-Valls, "Classification of hyperspectral images with regularized linear discriminant analysis," IEEE Trans. Geosci. Remote Sens., vol. 47, no. 3, March 2009, pp. 862–873.

[37] J. Li, J. Bioucas-Dias, and A. Plaza, "Spectral-spatial hyperspectral image segmentation using subspace multinomial logistic regression and Markov random fields," IEEE Trans. Geosci. Remote Sens., vol. 50, no. 3, March 2012, pp. 809–823.

[38] G. Mercier and M. Lennon, "Support vector machines for hyperspectral image classification with spectral-based kernels," in Geoscience and Remote Sensing Symposium, 2003. IGARSS '03. Proceedings. 2003 IEEE International, vol. 1, July 2003, pp. 288–290 vol.1.

[39] F. Melgani and L. Bruzzone, "Classification of hyperspectral remote sensing images with support vector machines," IEEE Trans. Geosci. Remote Sens., vol. 42, no. 8, Aug 2004, pp. 1778–1790.

[40] M. Belkin, P. Niyogi, and V. Sindhwani, "Manifold regularization: A geometric framework for learning from labeled and unlabeled examples." J. Mach. Learn. Res., vol. 7, 2006, pp. 2399–2434.

[41] G. Camps-Valls, L. Gomez-Chova, J. Munoz-Mari, J. Vila-Frances, and J. Calpe-Maravilla, "Composite kernels for hyperspectral image classification," IEEE Geosci. Remote Sens. Lett., vol. 3, no. 1, Jan 2006, pp. 93–97.

[42] Y. Chen, N. Nasrabadi, and T. Tran, "Sparsity-based classification of hyperspectral imagery," in Geoscience and Remote Sensing Symposium (IGARSS), 2010 IEEE International, July 2010, pp. 2796–2799.

[43] ——, "Hyperspectral image classification using dictionary-based sparse representation," IEEE Trans. Geosci. Remote Sens., vol. 49, no. 10, Oct 2011, pp. 3973–3985.

[44] J. Li, J. Bioucas-Dias, and A. Plaza, "Semisupervised hyperspectral image segmentation using multinomial logistic regression with active learning," IEEE Trans. Geosci. Remote Sens., vol. 48, no. 11, Nov 2010, pp. 4085–4098.

[45] P. Quesada-Barriuso, F. Arguello, and D. Heras, "Spectral-spatial classification of hyperspectral images using wavelets and extended morphological profiles," IEEE J. Sel. Topics Appl. Earth Observ., vol. 7, no. 4, April 2014, pp. 1177–1185.

[46] W. Kim and M. Crawford, "Adaptive classification for hyperspectral image data using manifold regularization kernel machines," IEEE Trans. Geosci. Remote Sens., vol. 48, no. 11, Nov 2010, pp. 4110–4121.

[47] H. Yang and M. Crawford, "Spectral and spatial proximity-based manifold alignment for multitemporal hyperspectral image classification," IEEE Trans. Geosci. Remote Sens., vol. 54, no. 1, Jan 2016, pp. 51–64.

[48] Y. LeCun, C. Cortes, and C. J. C. Burges. The mnist database of handwritten digits. Accepted November 17, 2016. [Online]. Available: http://yann.lecun.com/exdb/mnist/

[49] Usps handwritten digit data. Accepted November 17, 2016. [Online]. Available: http://www.gaussianprocess.org/gpml/data/ fide

[50] C. Dan, U. Meier, and J. Schmidhuber, "Multi-column deep neural network for image classification," 2012, pp. 3642–3649.

[51] W. Li, M. Zeiler, S. Zhang, Y. L. Cun, and R. Fergus, "Regularization of neural networks using dropconnect," Journal of Machine Learning Research, vol. 28, no. 3, 2013, pp. 1058–1066.

[52] X. Zhou and M. Belkin, "Semi-supervised learning by higher order regularization," in Proceedings of the 14th International Conference on Artificial Intelligence and Statistics (AISTATS). Fort Lauderdale, FL, USA: W&CP, 2011, pp. 892–900, volume 15 of JMLR.

International Academy, Research, and Industry Association (IARIA)
412 Derby Way
Wilmington, DE 19810

CURRAN ASSOCIATES INC.
proceedings.com

ISBN 978-1-5108-5634-9